FAR SECTOR

N.K. JEMISIN WRITER

JAMAL CAMPBELL ARTIST, COLORS, COVERS

DERON BENNETT LETTERER

FAR SECTOR

SPECIAL THANKS TO SHAWN MARTINBROUGH
DC'S YOUNG ANIMAL CURATED BY GERARD WAY

Andy Khouri, Jamie S. Rich Editors – Original Series • Maggie Howell Associate Editor – Original Series & Editor – Collected Edition • Steve Cook Design Director – Books

Marie Javins Editor-in-Chief, DC Comics

Daniel Cherry III Senior VP – General Manager • Jim Lee Publisher & Chief Creative Officer • Joen Choe VP – Global Brand & Creative Services • Amie Brockway-Metcalf Publication Design

Lawrence Ganem VP – Talent Services • Alison Gill Senior VP – Manufacturing & Operations • Nick J. Napolitano VP – Manufacturing Administration & Design • Don Fallett VP – Manufacturing Operations & Workflow Management • Nancy Spears VP – Revenue • Christy Sawyer Publication Production

FAR SECTOR

DC Comics, 2900 West Alameda Ave., Burbank, CA 91505
Printed by Solisco Printers, Scott, QC, Canada. 9/10/21. First Printing.
ISBN: 978-1-77951-205-5

Library of Congress Cataloging-in-Publication
Data is available.

A NEW GREEN LANTERN

When N.K. Jemisin asked for me to write this introduction I was incredibly moved. To receive the honor of introducing a story so important, not just to the imprint, not just to DC, or comics, but to the vast and eternal tapestry of the stories we share as people, was not something I took lightly.

So then, naturally, came the Fear.

The Fear, as I sometimes call it (along with other ominous designations), is something a creative person feels, especially when faced with the blank canvas, or the blank page in the case of the writer. This has been written about before—there are even whole books that deal with it, so I am sure I'm not telling you anything completely new. But I have had various artistic jobs over the years, and of all the art forms, exercises, and mediums, writing is the hardest and the scariest, and I think that's why I like it so much. But the Fear is a passenger, and that passenger can be difficult and rude, and can take up too much of the seat. You know the Fear and you've seen it before; you've felt it, so you know it exists—every time you stare into that empty void waiting to be filled with words and pictures.

But every once in a while, you will bear witness to such a fearless creative force that you find yourself not only in awe, but in the role of the student again. This writer, this teacher, this force, is N.K. Jemisin. Further adding to the admiration is the knowledge that Mr. Fear never leaves the train car, and so one can only naturally assume—this force, this being, this writer, plows right through that passenger. It's magical and inspiring to watch, and that is what it was like witnessing this book take shape—not only through Nora's words, but through the collaboration initiated when we found two other extraordinary creative forces to join her: Jamal Campbell, who so kinetically and gorgeously illustrated this world and all its heroes and villains, and Deron Bennett, whose masterful hi-fi lettering made this book so much fun to read. It was a true collaboration among the team, each of them embracing not only the story, but their creative role in the process.

Far Sector started as the seed of an idea. When I started DC's Young Animal, I leafed through DC Universe encyclopedias, but I also went further back into the *Who's Who* series from the 1980s, in which DC presented all of its characters—even the obscure ones. And it was through these old fact files that I found characters and inspiration for the imprint. But eventually, after Young Animal carved out its little piece of the DC Universe and things started to take shape, I started to think beyond the obscure and the unused—we had our own special place where we could try and tell the stories we wanted to, free from the daunting labyrinth of mainstream continuity. And to me, those were always the best stories—the ones that went beyond the sandboxes those before us had created. Freedom to explore, freedom to ask questions that had never been asked, and freedom to create something new. So it was with this very small seed of an idea—a Green Lantern, far beyond the jurisdiction of the Corps, alone and investigating the first murder a society has had in a very long time—that I sought a writer to take this minuscule seed and turn it into something far greater, something all their own, and with the freedom to tell the story they wanted to tell.

Conversing with another creative friend of mine named Ian, we would talk about this Green Lantern. Ian knew I needed a great writer but I didn't have any ideas beyond the fact that I felt it could be a novelist, someone outside of comics who might see this as an exciting challenge, someone who wrote fantasy and science fiction, my two favorite genres. Ian told me to immediately order the Inheritance Trilogy by an author named N.K. Jemisin. He told me of his experience reading the trilogy, excited because he thought it was so great, and knowing that this could in fact be the writer who writes this book, who shapes this world. The books showed up, very thick and intimidating, and I started to read. And as I read, very quickly the layers and complexities of the characters began to unfold, as well as an entire universe, a world, built from the ground up. Not only was it a vivid and tangible universe, it felt personal and at times intimate. And her characters had strength—so much of it. I was convinced we had found our writer—now it was a matter of reaching out and seeing if there was any interest in creating a new Green Lantern, in telling the amazing stories they tell in a whole new arena.

And then something amazing happened—this incredibly celebrated and accomplished novelist said yes, and we were so lucky for it. A phone call was had, a seed was handed over, and the real work began. Nora would go on to take that seed and come back with something new, changing, shaping, evolving, elevating, and doing one of the things she does so well—building worlds.

And it was vast. But it was also a personal and engaging setting. Complex but easy to understand, simple on the surface but with so much more, the City Enduring held many secrets, and its roots, corruptions, and machinations ran hidden and deep. The story needed a hero that could unmask this city, someone who needed to change, to overcome the past and make sense of the present, thereby changing the world she was assigned to protect. This character would become Lantern Sojourner "Jo" Mullein, in my opinion one of the greatest Lanterns of all time.

The incredible Shawn Martinbrough created some stunning early development art, which gave us a glimpse of what Jo could become—and when an editor suggested Jamal Campbell as our regular artist for the series, I was completely floored by his work. It was modern, technicolor, and beautiful, full of energy. It also transcended what I consider to be mainstream comics art— it was something all its own. Jo kept taking shape, and many new visions of the character were presented to us. In the end the creative team chose the perfect look for her—she wasn't like any kind of Lantern we had seen before. The scripts came in, the breakdowns began, and we were off to the races. Every step of this process was exciting to behold, and what would happen over the next year and a half or so was this incredible realization of a told story by an unforgettable team at the top of their game. Seeing the final files, and ultimately the printed issues, with Deron Bennett's lettering, brought it further together into completion. Every issue felt like a victory and was a true joy to witness—and I was in fact a witness. After my part, I existed as a reader and a believer—to fully support this creative team, always deferring to them in whatever decision there was to be made. I have felt over the years that the best thing you can do as a publisher is get out of the way of the people creating— the collective force and the engine behind it. And that is what you hold in your hands—an absolute realization by an amazing creative team.

Nothing I can say will come close to preparing you for or describing the vast universe of the City Enduring, its people, or its challenges. In fact, the best way to enjoy this book is to either ignore this introduction (probably should have told you that earlier) or leave me now and get started. But if you are sticking around I'll leave you with this—

Far Sector was a true honor to publish. Fearlessly crafted in all its glorious cosmic noir, it's an important story with important lessons. Like all great science fiction, it is a mirror—reflecting back at us all of our beauty and all of our ugliness. It's as much a story about our world as it is about a place many light-years away. And to me, those have always been the most enduring stories—the timeless and eternal, the prescient and profound.

Go read.

Long live Lantern Sojourner Mullein,

GERARD WAY
July 2021

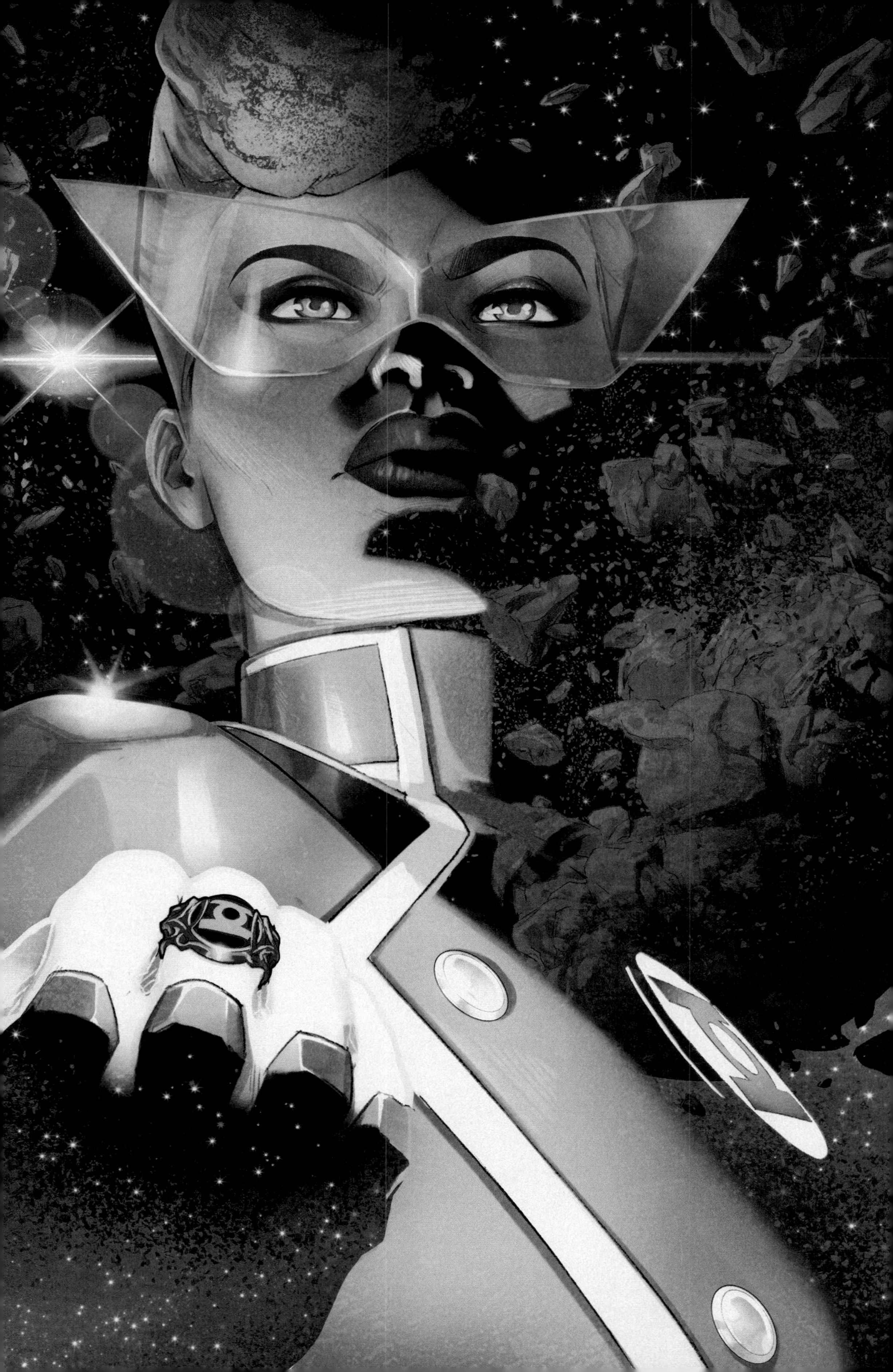

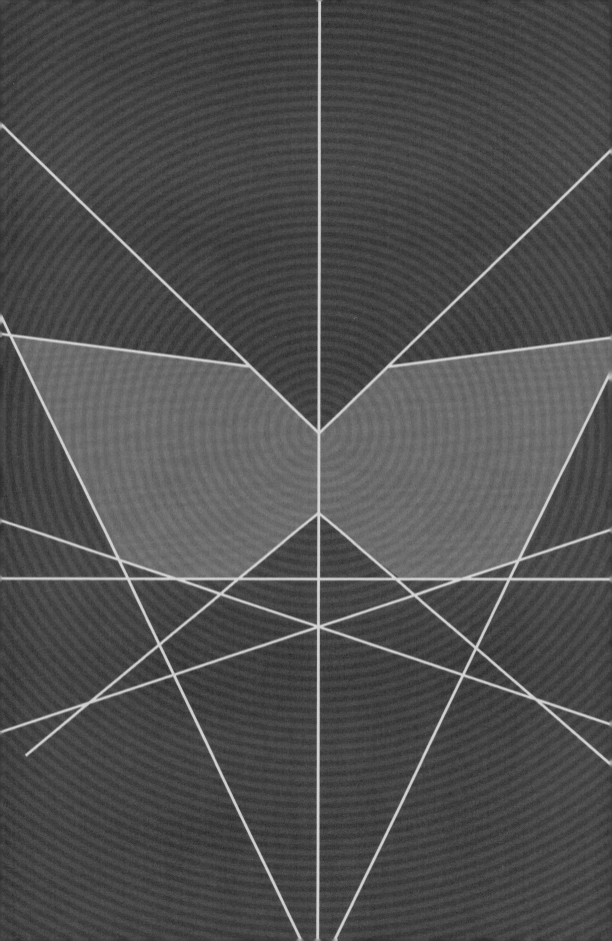

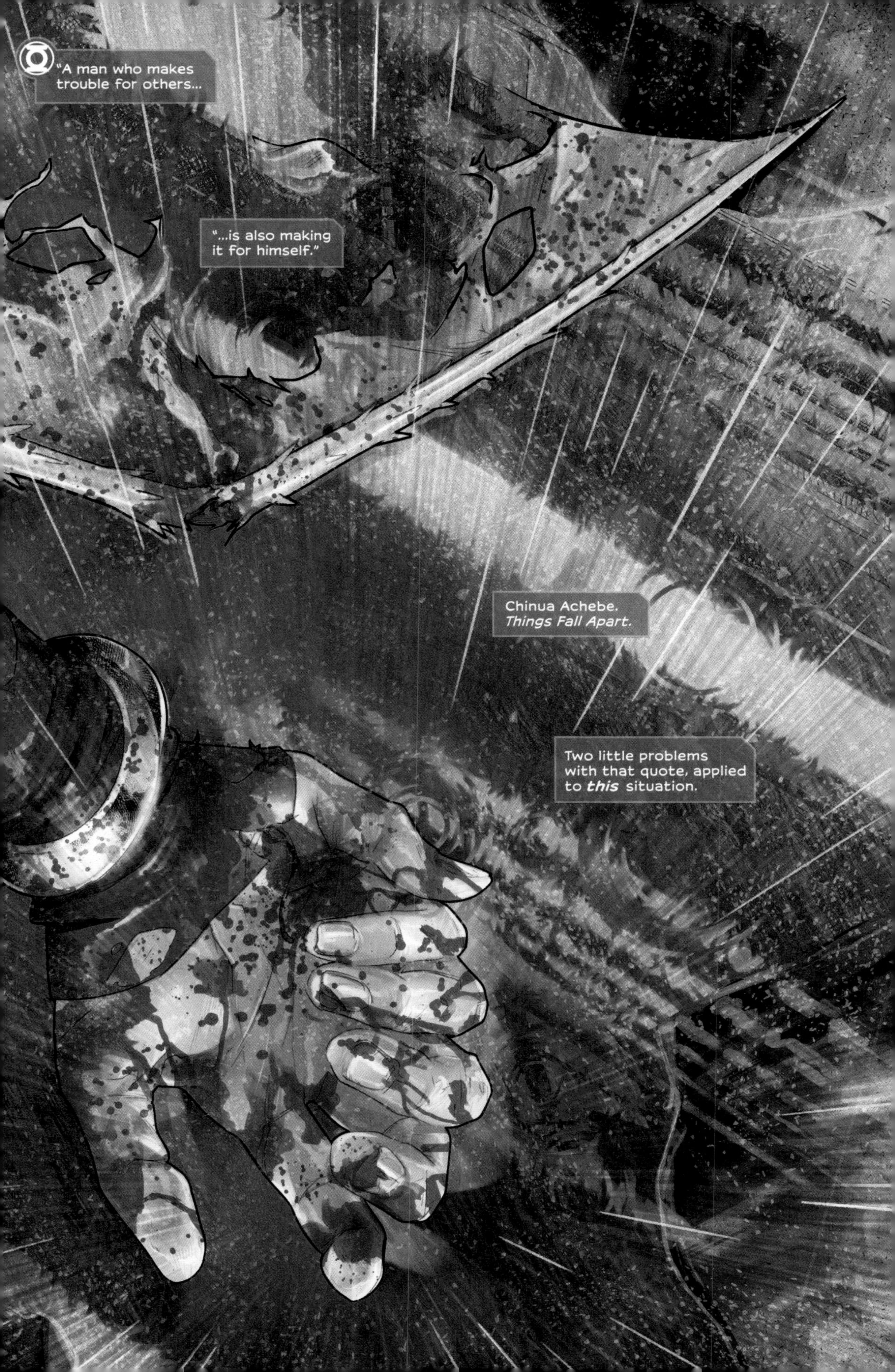
"A man who makes trouble for others...
"...is also making it for himself."
Chinua Achebe. *Things Fall Apart.*
Two little problems with that quote, applied to ***this*** situation.

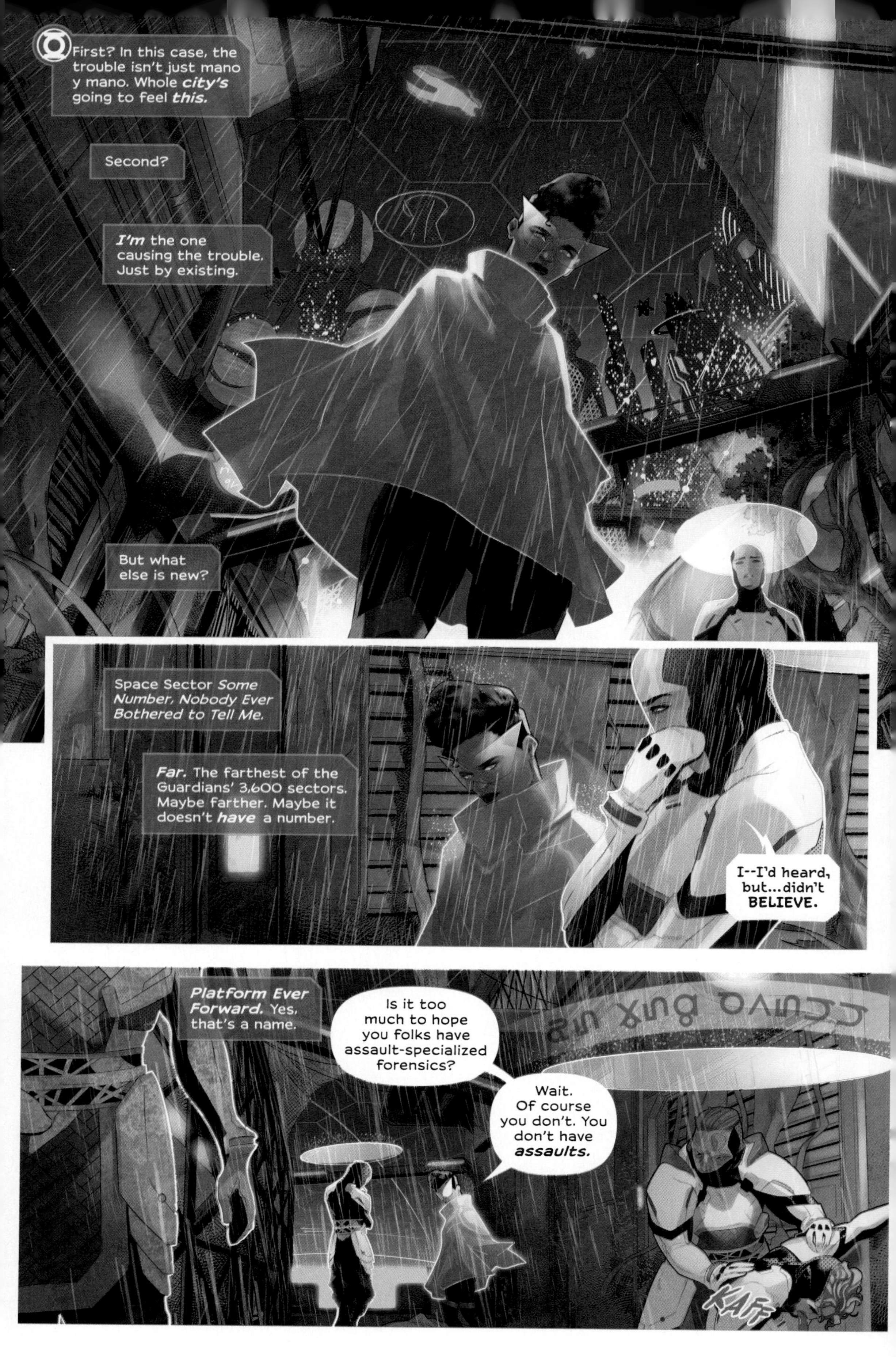
First? In this case, the trouble isn't just mano y mano. Whole *city's* going to feel ***this.***
Second?
I'm the one causing the trouble. Just by existing.
But what else is new?
Space Sector *Some Number, Nobody Ever Bothered to Tell Me.*
Far. The farthest of the Guardians' 3,600 sectors. Maybe farther. Maybe it doesn't ***have*** a number.
I--I'd heard, but...didn't **BELIEVE.**
Platform Ever Forward. Yes, that's a name.
Is it too much to hope you folks have assault-specialized forensics?
Wait. Of course you don't. You don't have ***assaults.***
KAFF

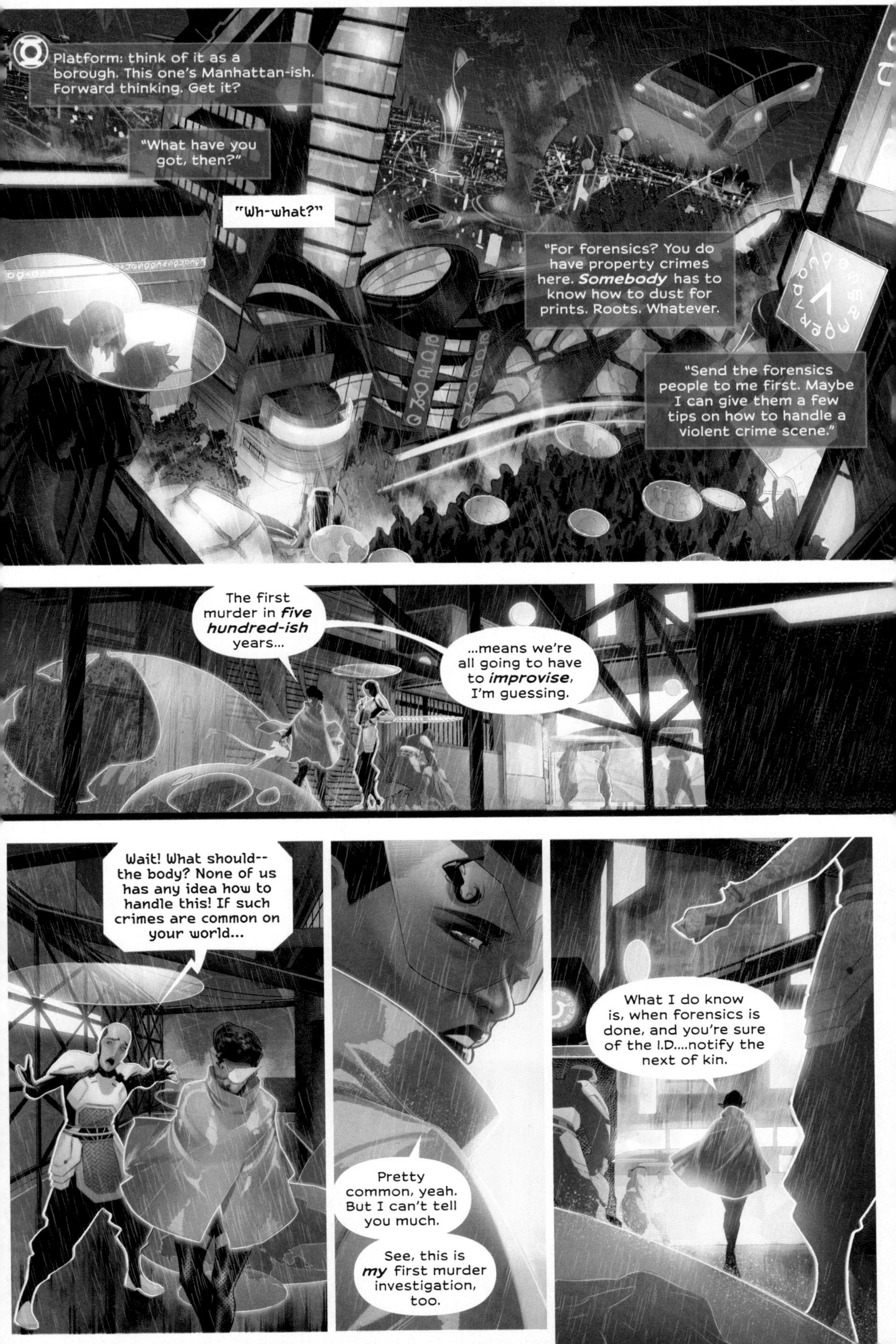
Platform: think of it as a borough. This one's Manhattan-ish. Forward thinking. Get it?
"What have you got, then?"
"Wh-what?"
"For forensics? You do have property crimes here. *Somebody* has to know how to dust for prints. Roots. Whatever.
"Send the forensics people to me first. Maybe I can give them a few tips on how to handle a violent crime scene."
The first murder in *five hundred-ish* years...
...means we're all going to have to *improvise*, I'm guessing.
Wait! What should-- the body? None of us has any idea how to handle this! If such crimes are common on your world...
Pretty common, yeah. But I can't tell you much.
See, this is *my* first murder investigation, too.
What I do know is, when forensics is done, and you're sure of the I.D....notify the next of kin.

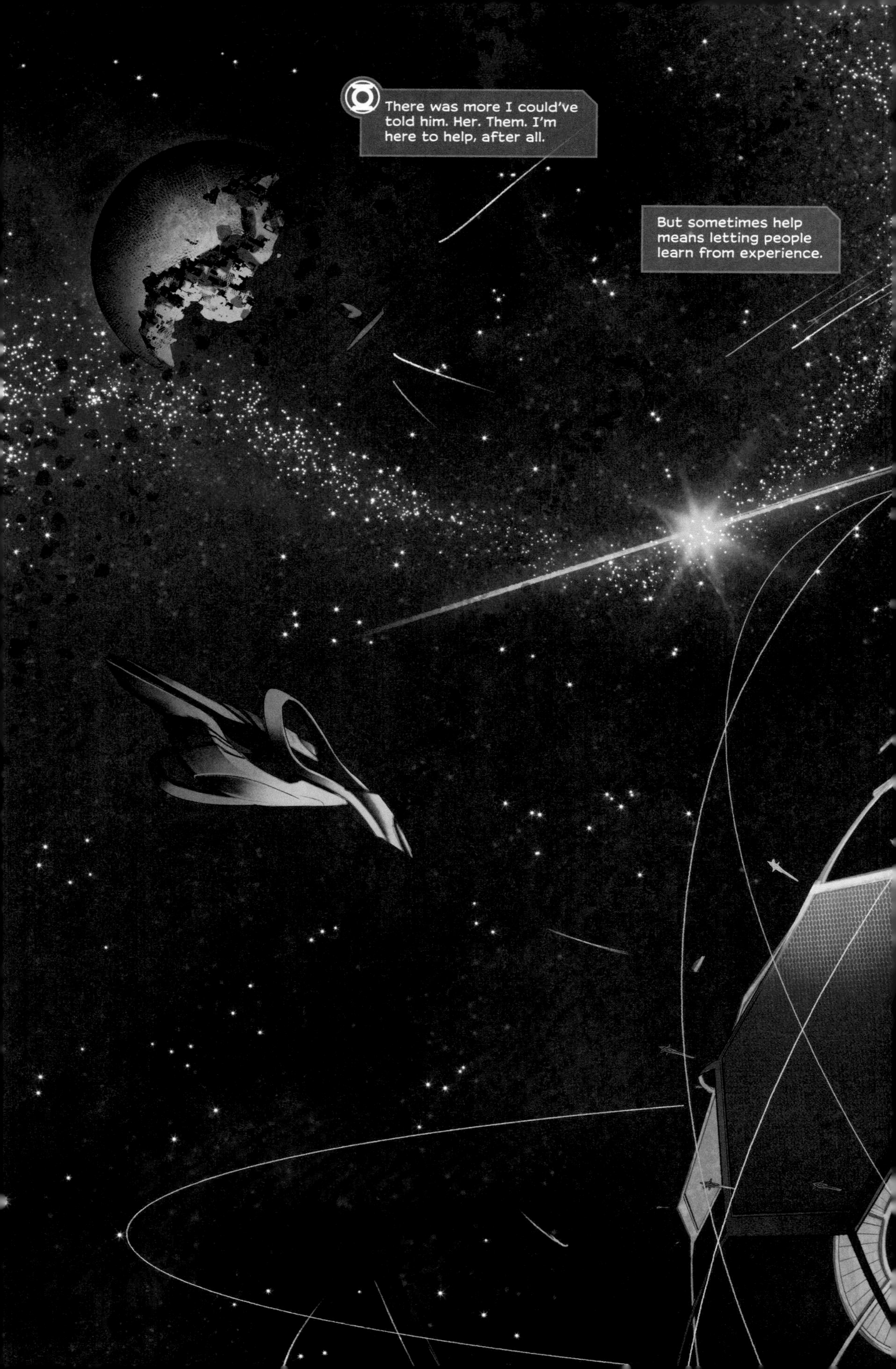
There was more I could've told him. Her. Them. I'm here to help, after all.
But sometimes help means letting people learn from experience.

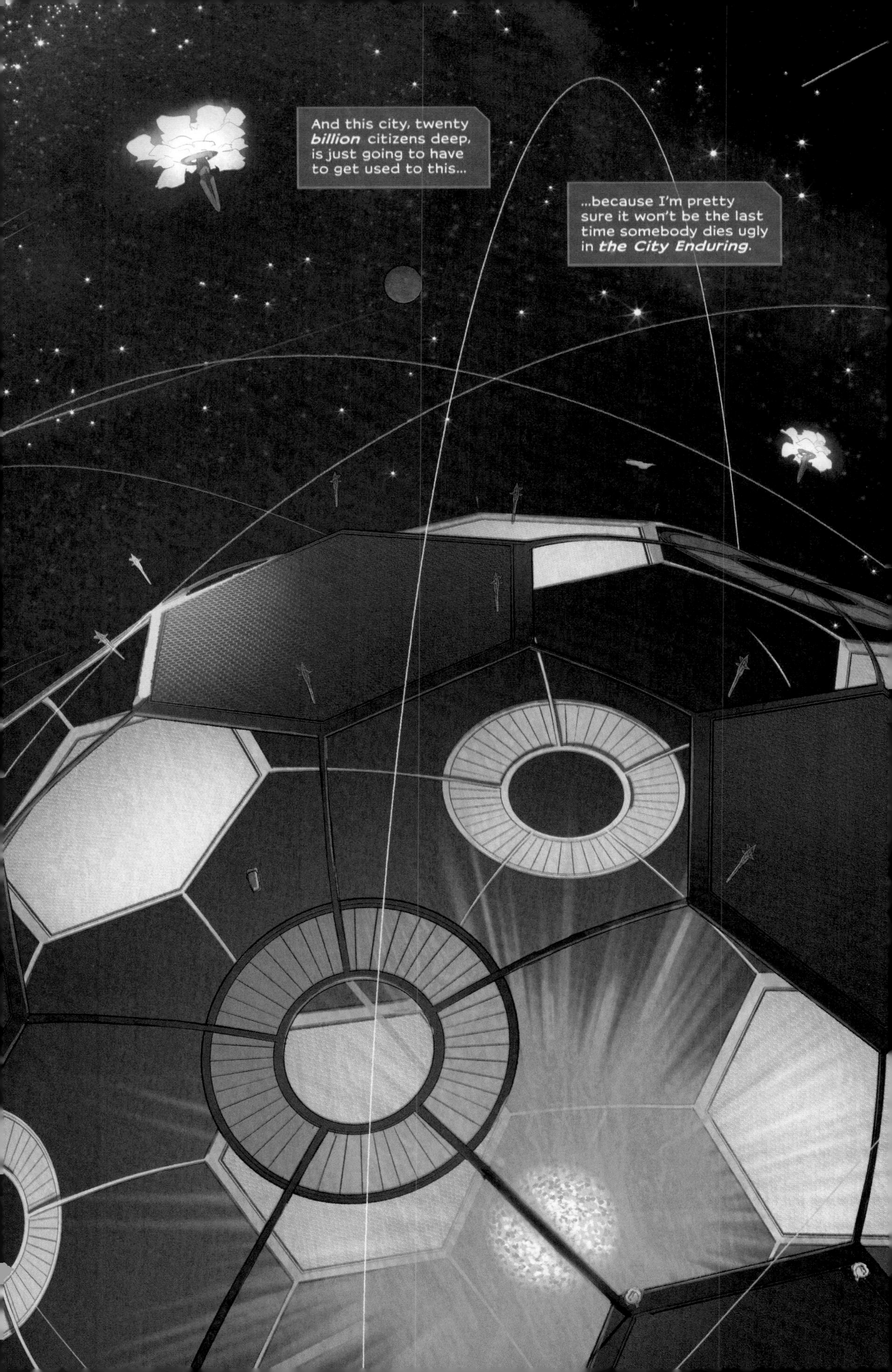
And this city, twenty *billion* citizens deep, is just going to have to get used to this...
...because I'm pretty sure it won't be the last time somebody dies ugly in ***the City Enduring***.

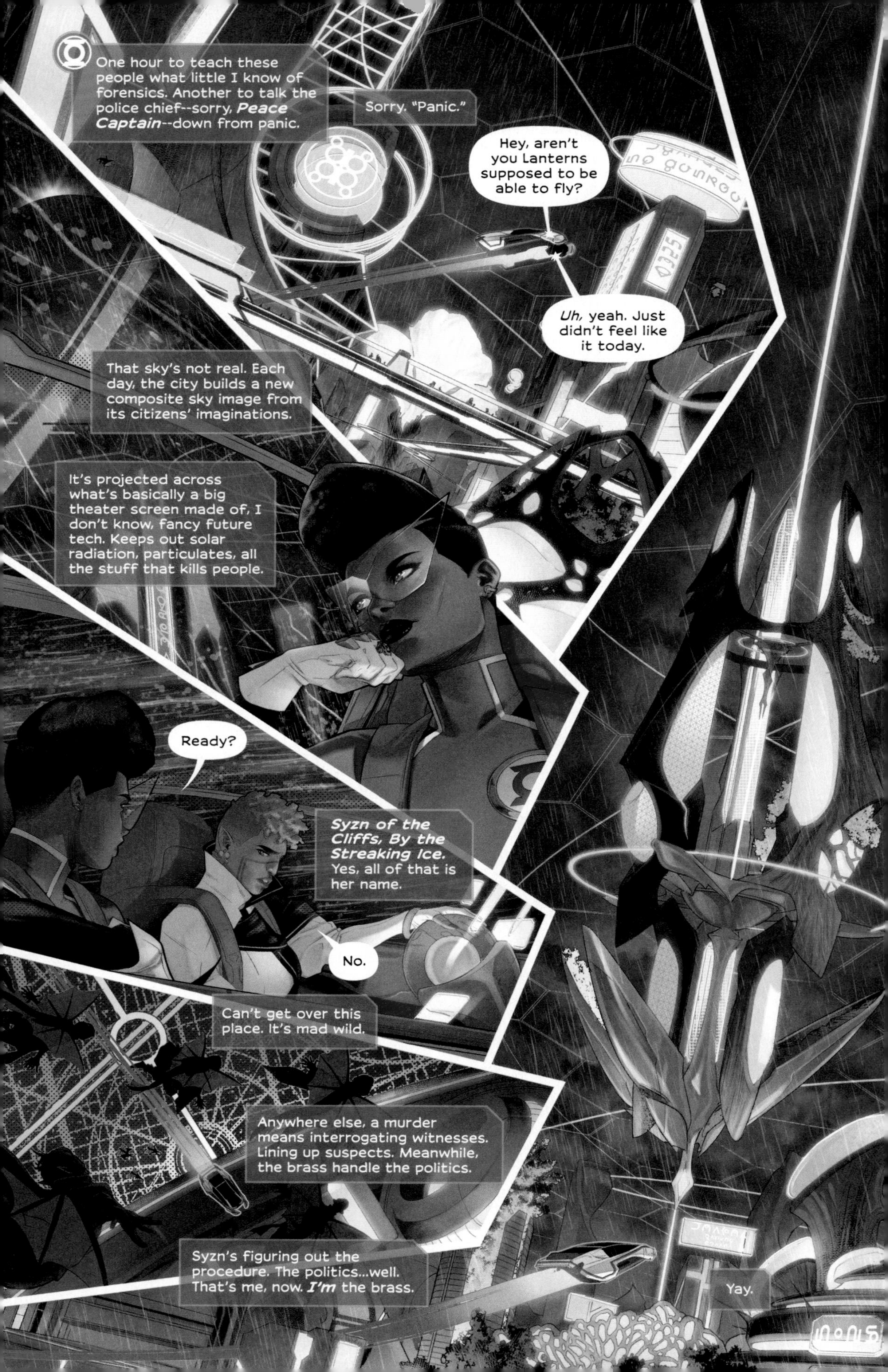

One hour to teach these people what little I know of forensics. Another to talk the police chief--sorry, *Peace Captain*--down from panic.
Sorry. "Panic."
Hey, aren't you Lanterns supposed to be able to fly?
Uh, yeah. Just didn't feel like it today.
That sky's not real. Each day, the city builds a new composite sky image from its citizens' imaginations.
It's projected across what's basically a big theater screen made of, I don't know, fancy future tech. Keeps out solar radiation, particulates, all the stuff that kills people.
Ready?
Syzn of the Cliffs, By the Streaking Ice. Yes, all of that is her name.
No.
Can't get over this place. It's mad wild.
Anywhere else, a murder means interrogating witnesses. Lining up suspects. Meanwhile, the brass handle the politics.
Syzn's figuring out the procedure. The politics...well. That's me, now. *I'm* the brass.
Yay.

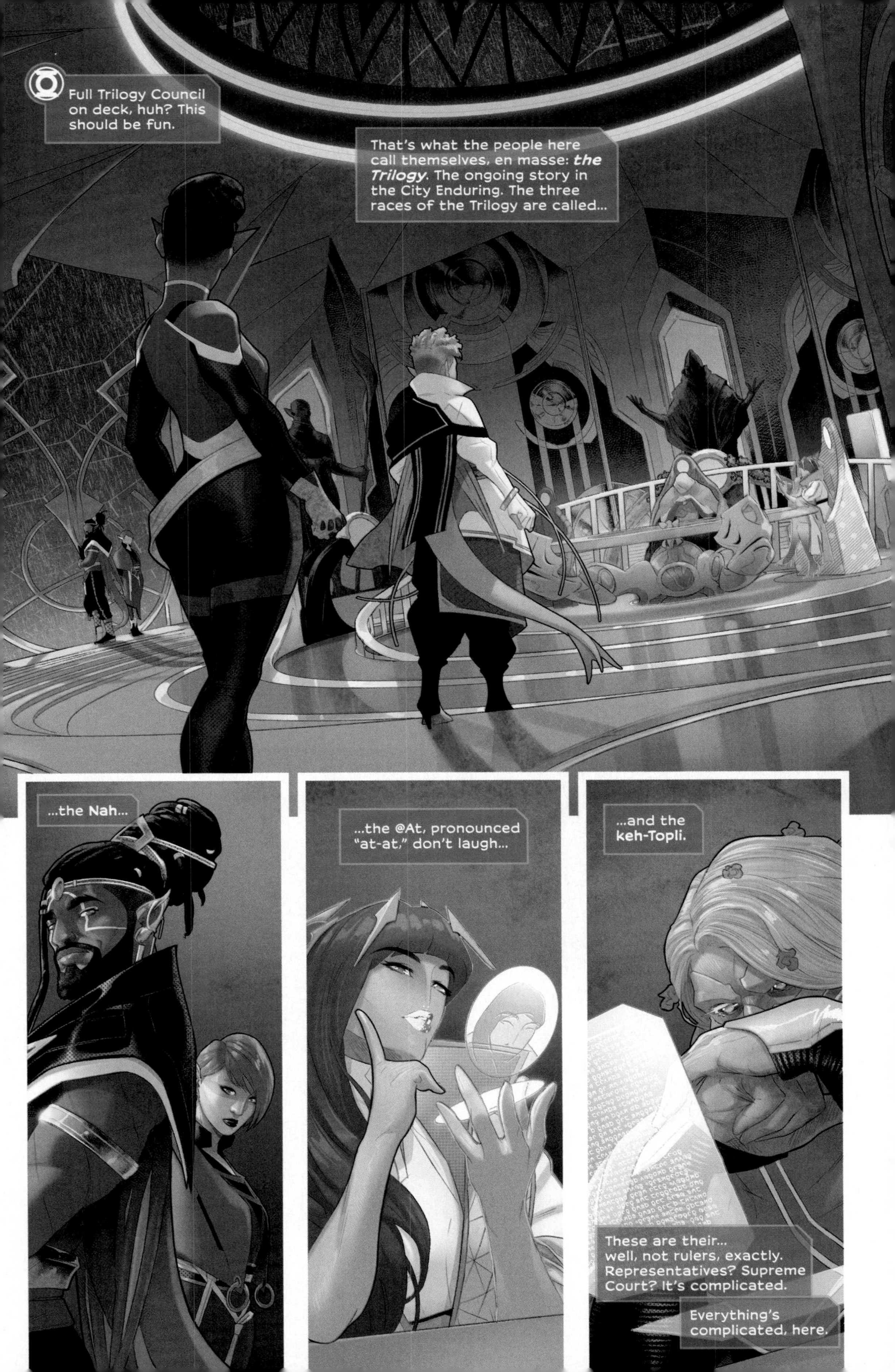
Full Trilogy Council on deck, huh? This should be fun.
That's what the people here call themselves, en masse: ***the Trilogy***. The ongoing story in the City Enduring. The three races of the Trilogy are called...
...the **Nah**...
...the @At, pronounced "at-at," don't laugh...
...and the **keh-Topli.**
These are their... well, not rulers, exactly. Representatives? Supreme Court? It's complicated.
Everything's complicated, here.

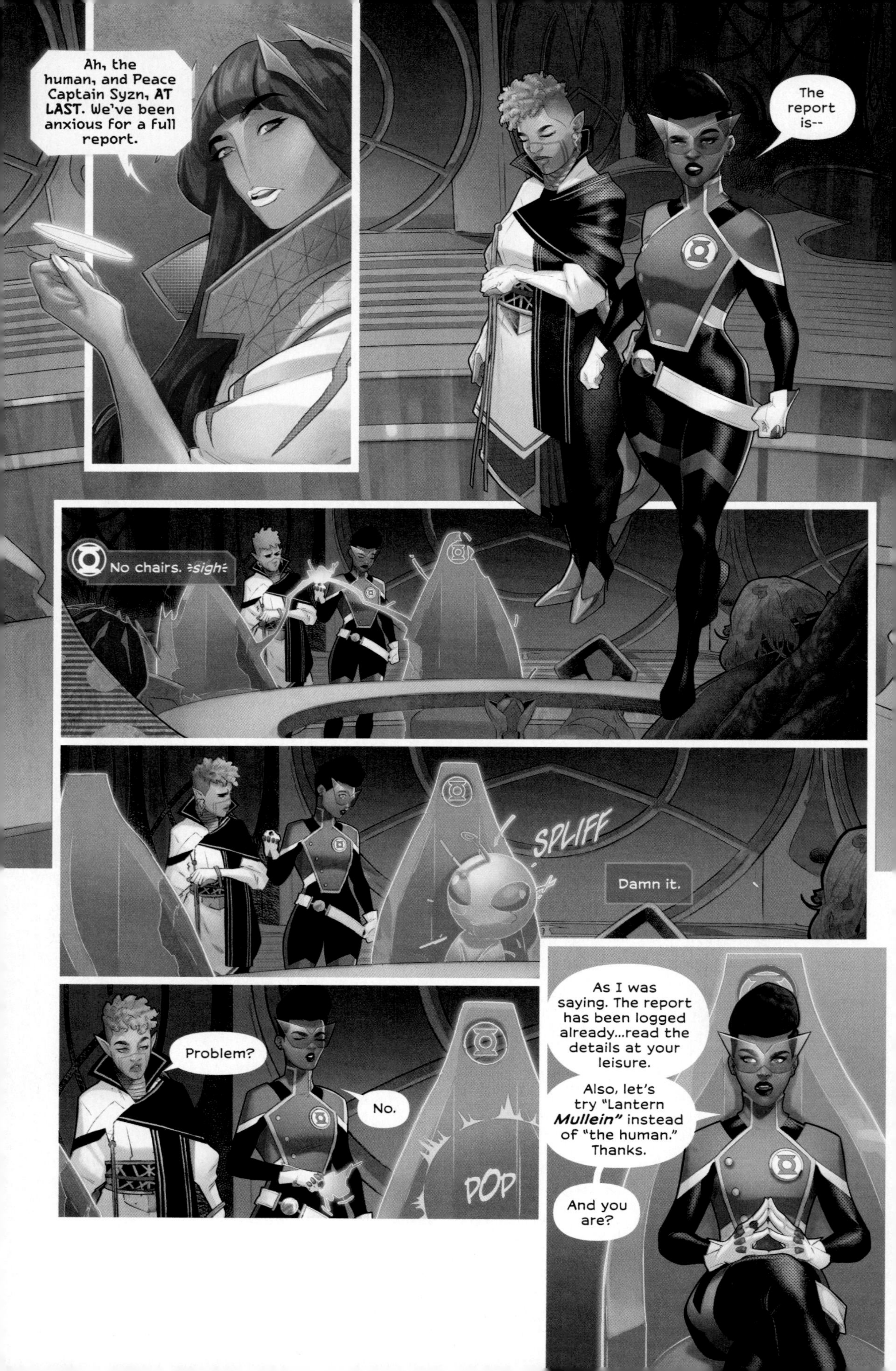
Ah, the human, and Peace Captain Syzn, AT LAST. We've been anxious for a full report.
The report is--
No chairs. sigh
SPLIFF
Damn it.
Problem?
No.
POP
As I was saying. The report has been logged already...read the details at your leisure.
Also, let's try "Lantern Mullein" instead of "the human." Thanks.
And you are?

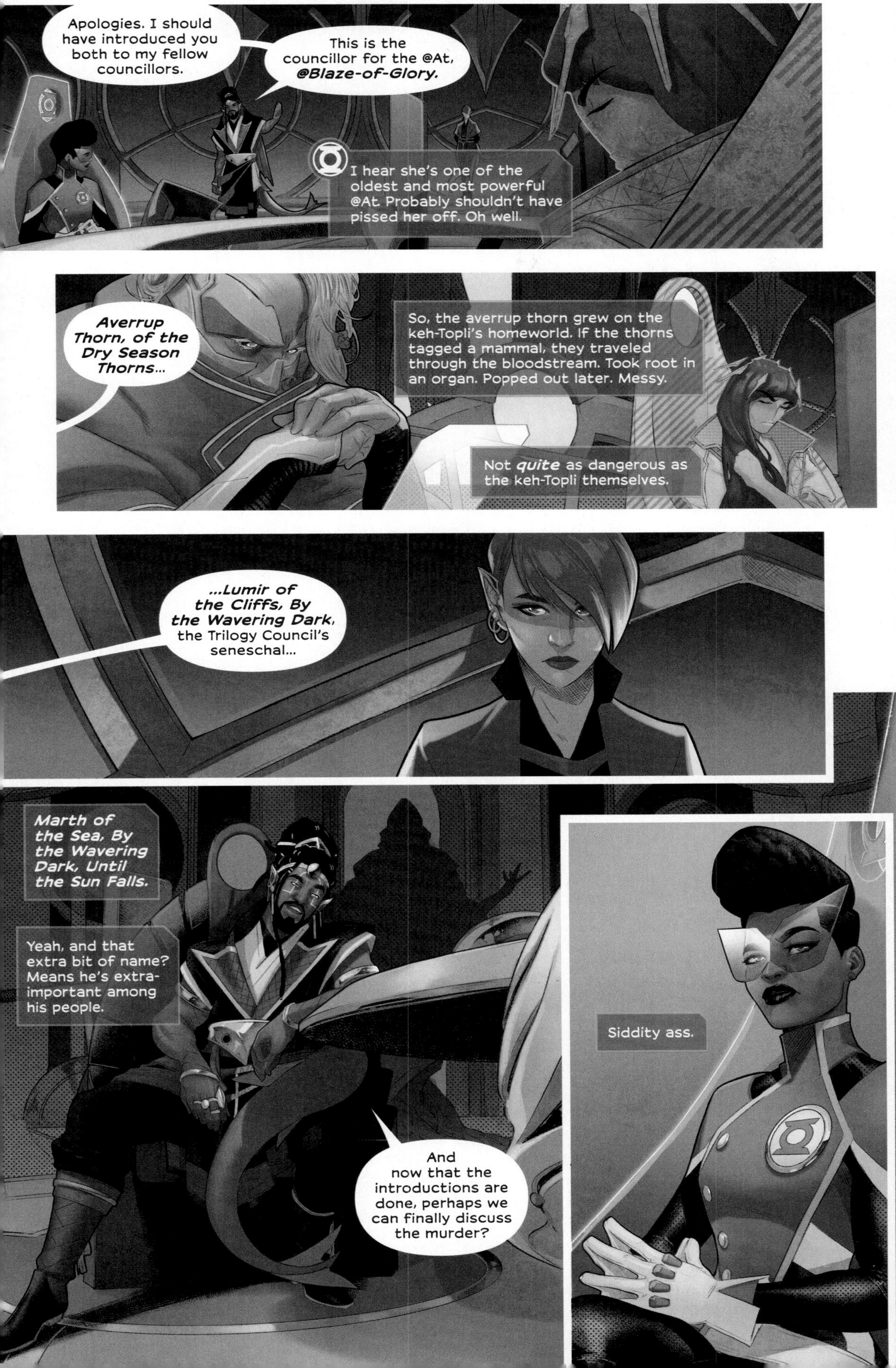
Apologies. I should have introduced you both to my fellow councillors.
This is the councillor for the @At, *@Blaze-of-Glory.*
I hear she's one of the oldest and most powerful @At. Probably shouldn't have pissed her off. Oh well.
Averrup Thorn, of the Dry Season Thorns...
So, the averrup thorn grew on the keh-Topli's homeworld. If the thorns tagged a mammal, they traveled through the bloodstream. Took root in an organ. Popped out later. Messy.
Not *quite* as dangerous as the keh-Topli themselves.
...Lumir of the Cliffs, By the Wavering Dark, the Trilogy Council's seneschal...
Marth of the Sea, By the Wavering Dark, Until the Sun Falls.
Yeah, and that extra bit of name? Means he's extra-important among his people.
Siddity ass.
And now that the introductions are done, perhaps we can finally discuss the murder?

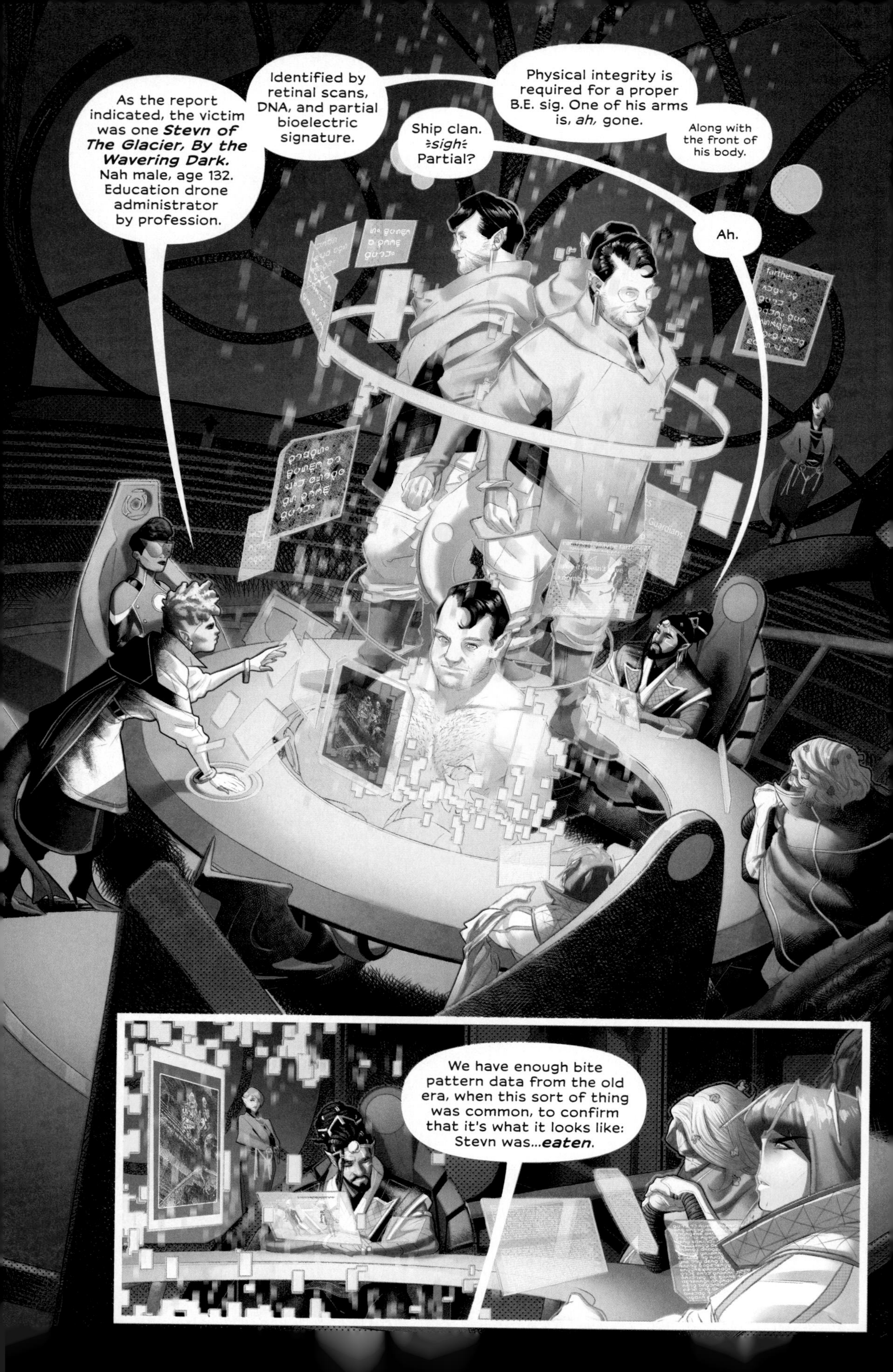
As the report indicated, the victim was one ***Stevn of The Glacier, By the Wavering Dark.*** Nah male, age 132. Education drone administrator by profession.
Identified by retinal scans, DNA, and partial bioelectric signature.
Ship clan. *sigh* Partial?
Physical integrity is required for a proper B.E. sig. One of his arms is, *ah,* gone.
Along with the front of his body.
Ah.
We have enough bite pattern data from the old era, when this sort of thing was common, to confirm that it's what it looks like: Stevn was...***eaten***.

So much...moisture. But could it have been an accident, Peace Captain? Something that just resembles INTENTIONAL violence?

We are considering all possibilities, Councillors.

Let's not dance around it, Peace Captain. I think it's clear that one of *my people* did this.

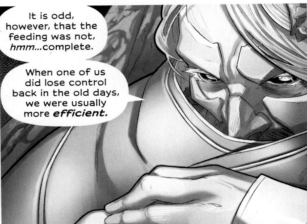

It is odd, however, that the feeding was not, *hmm...*complete.

When one of us did lose control back in the old days, we were usually more *efficient*.

All of that is irrelevant, council members.

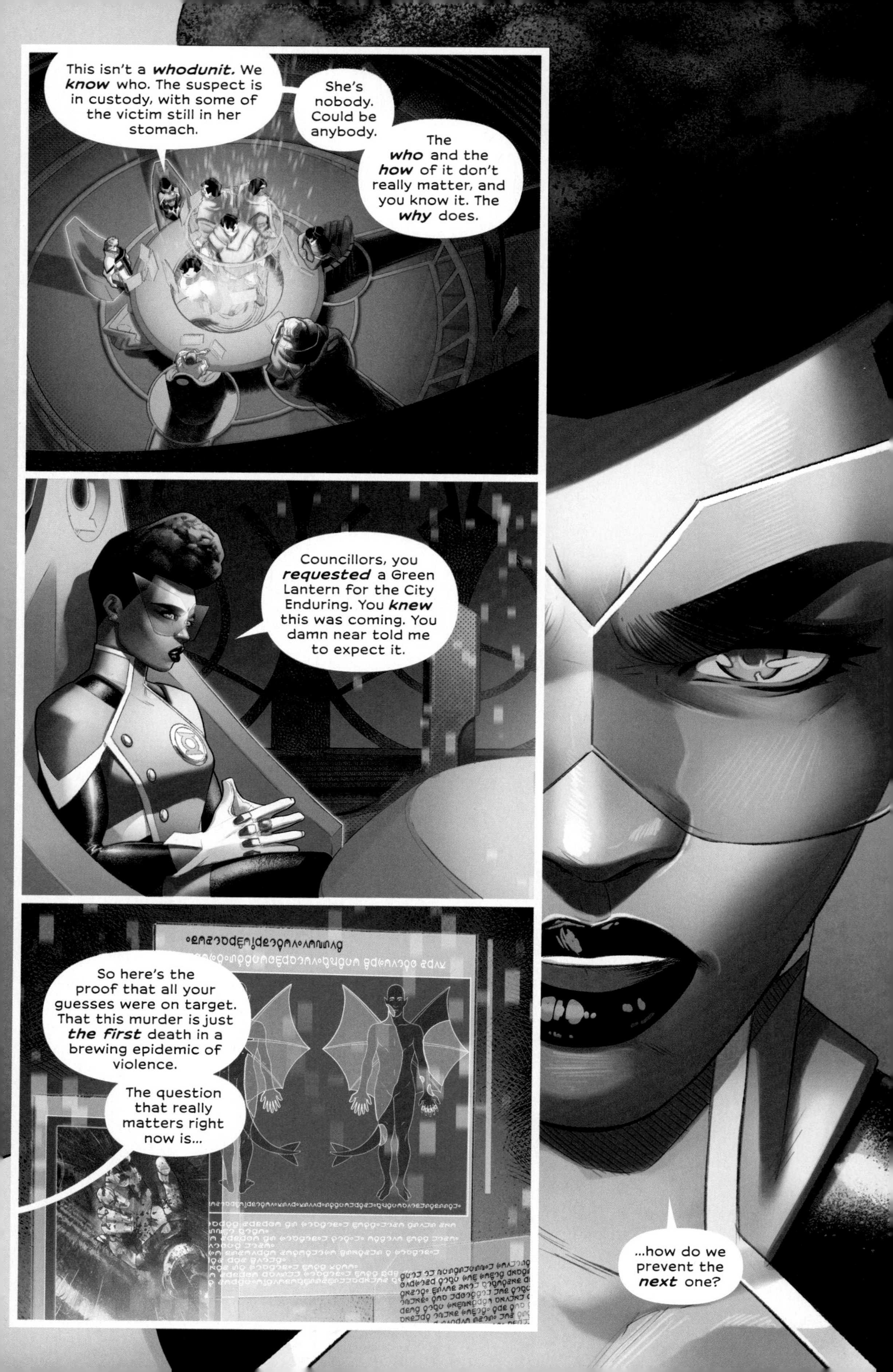
This isn't a ***whodunit.*** We ***know*** who. The suspect is in custody, with some of the victim still in her stomach.
She's nobody. Could be anybody.
The ***who*** and the ***how*** of it don't really matter, and you know it. The ***why*** does.
Councillors, you ***requested*** a Green Lantern for the City Enduring. You ***knew*** this was coming. You damn near told me to expect it.
So here's the proof that all your guesses were on target. That this murder is just ***the first*** death in a brewing epidemic of violence.
The question that really matters right now is...
...how do we prevent the ***next*** one?

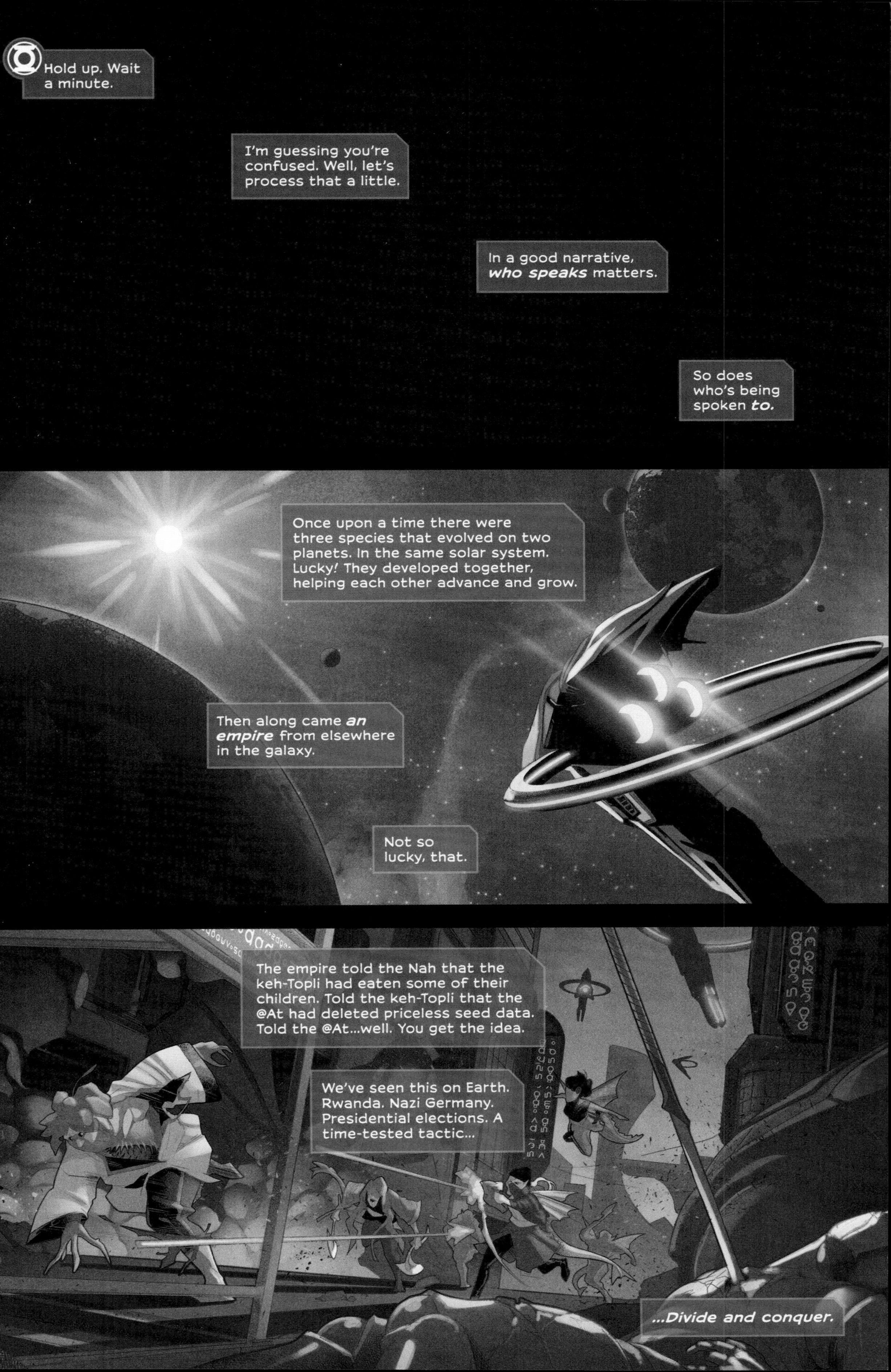
Hold up. Wait a minute.
I'm guessing you're confused. Well, let's process that a little.
In a good narrative, *who speaks* matters.
So does who's being spoken *to.*
Once upon a time there were three species that evolved on two planets. In the same solar system. Lucky! They developed together, helping each other advance and grow.
Then along came *an empire* from elsewhere in the galaxy.
Not so lucky, that.
The empire told the Nah that the keh-Topli had eaten some of their children. Told the keh-Topli that the @At had deleted priceless seed data. Told the @At...well. You get the idea.
We've seen this on Earth. Rwanda. Nazi Germany. Presidential elections. A time-tested tactic...
...Divide and conquer.

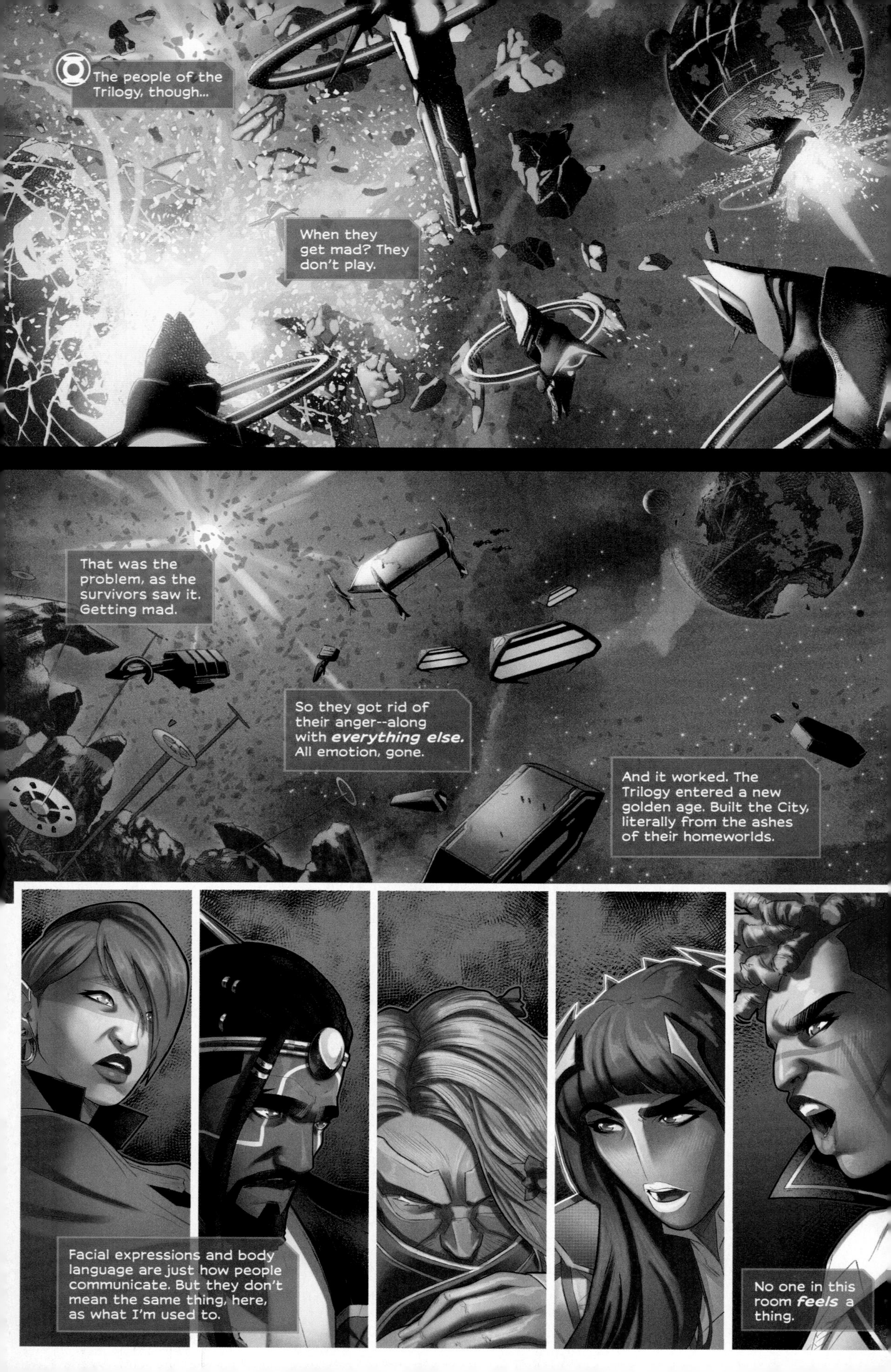

The people of the Trilogy, though...
When they get mad? They don't play.
That was the problem, as the survivors saw it. Getting mad.
So they got rid of their anger--along with ***everything else.*** All emotion, gone.
And it worked. The Trilogy entered a new golden age. Built the City, literally from the ashes of their homeworlds.
Facial expressions and body language are just how people communicate. But they don't mean the same thing, here, as what I'm used to.
No one in this room ***feels*** a thing.

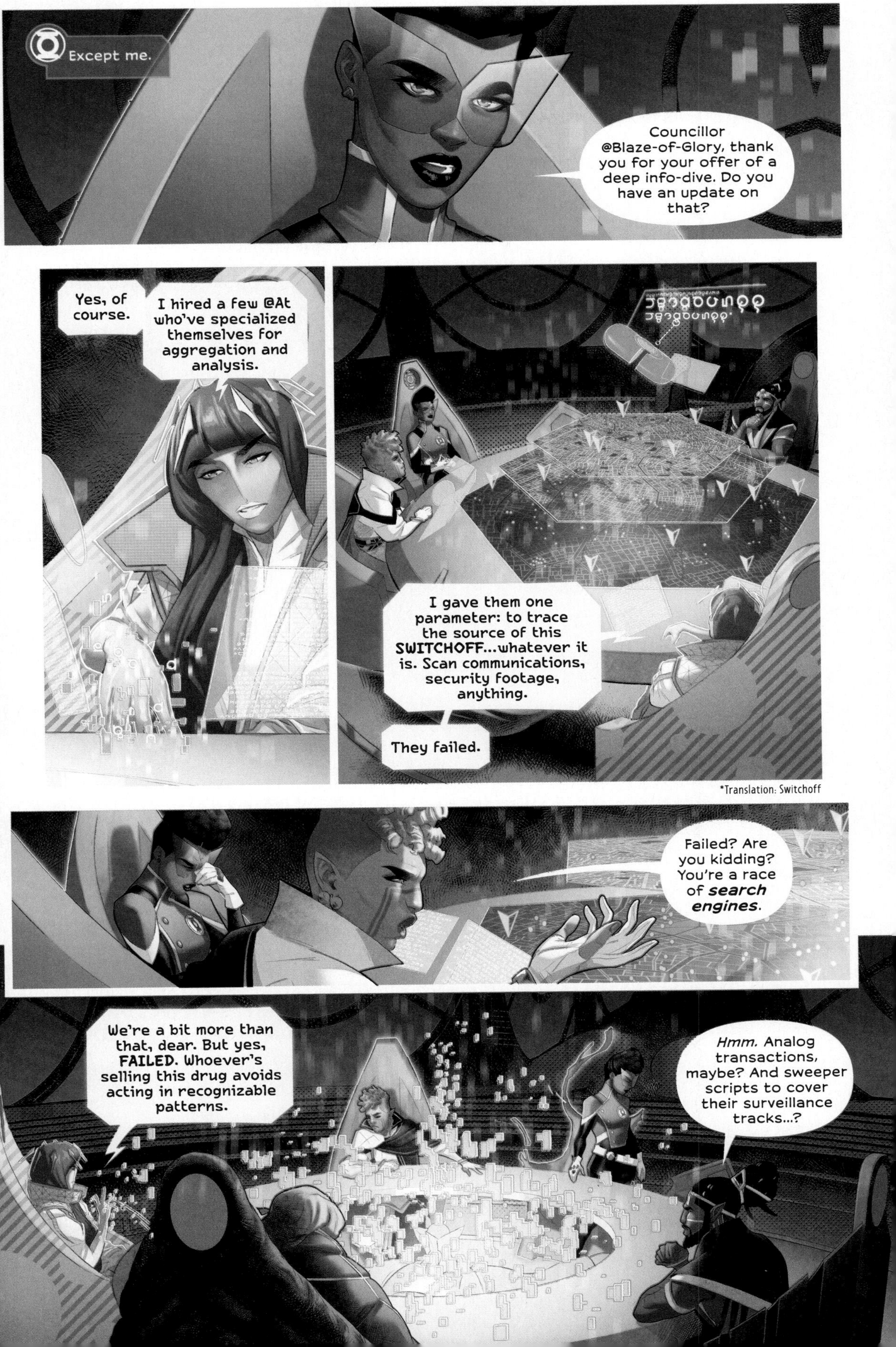
Except me.
Councillor @Blaze-of-Glory, thank you for your offer of a deep info-dive. Do you have an update on that?
Yes, of course.
I hired a few @At who've specialized themselves for aggregation and analysis.
I gave them one parameter: to trace the source of this SWITCHOFF...whatever it is. Scan communications, security footage, anything.
They failed.
Failed? Are you kidding? You're a race of ***search engines***.
We're a bit more than that, dear. But yes, **FAILED**. Whoever's selling this drug avoids acting in recognizable patterns.
Hmm. Analog transactions, maybe? And sweeper scripts to cover their surveillance tracks...?

*Translation: Switchoff

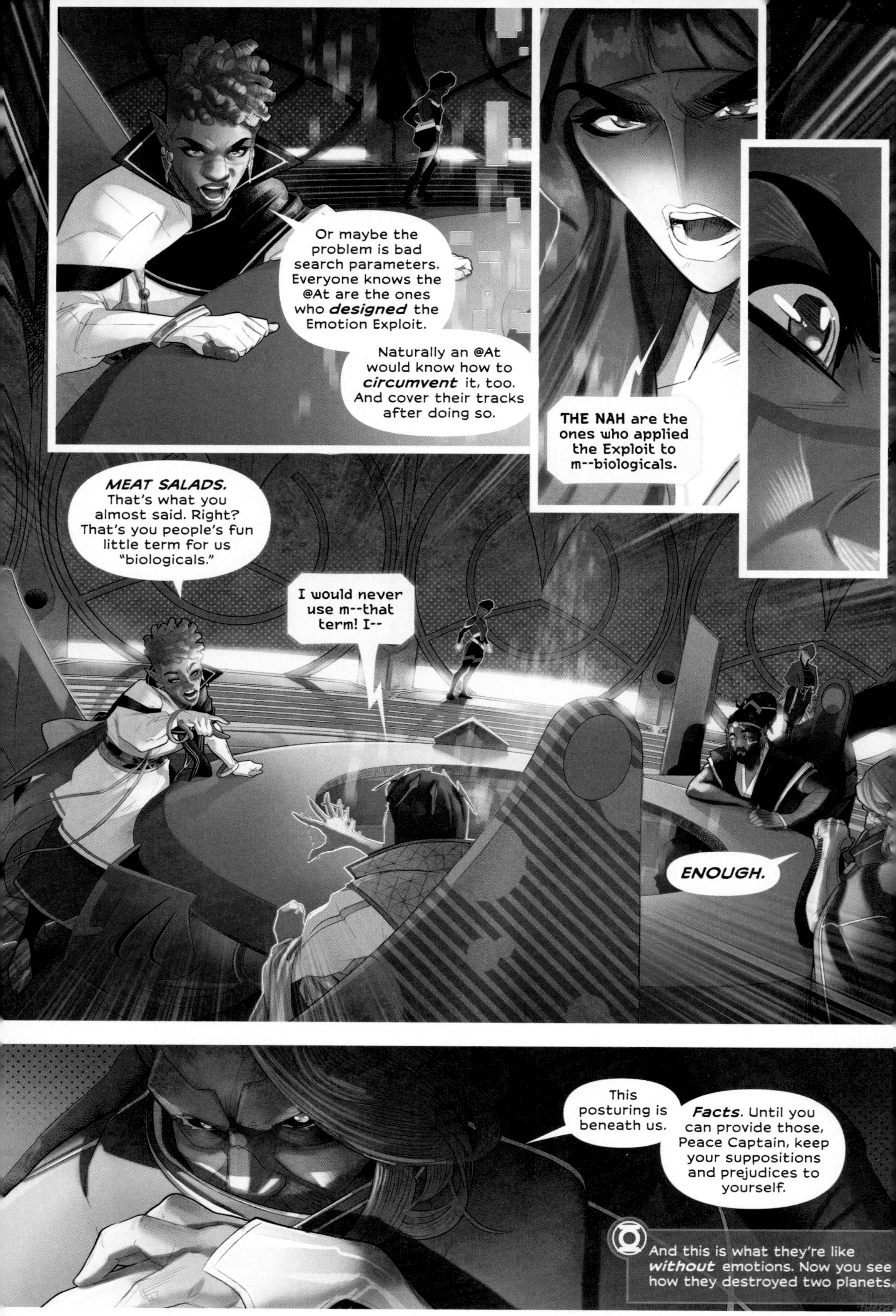
Or maybe the problem is bad search parameters. Everyone knows the @At are the ones who *designed* the Emotion Exploit.
Naturally an @At would know how to ***circumvent*** it, too. And cover their tracks after doing so.
THE NAH are the ones who applied the Exploit to m--biologicals.
MEAT SALADS. That's what you almost said. Right? That's you people's fun little term for us "biologicals."
I would never use m--that term! I--
ENOUGH.
This posturing is beneath us.
Facts. Until you can provide those, Peace Captain, keep your suppositions and prejudices to yourself.
And this is what they're like ***without*** emotions. Now you see how they destroyed two planets.

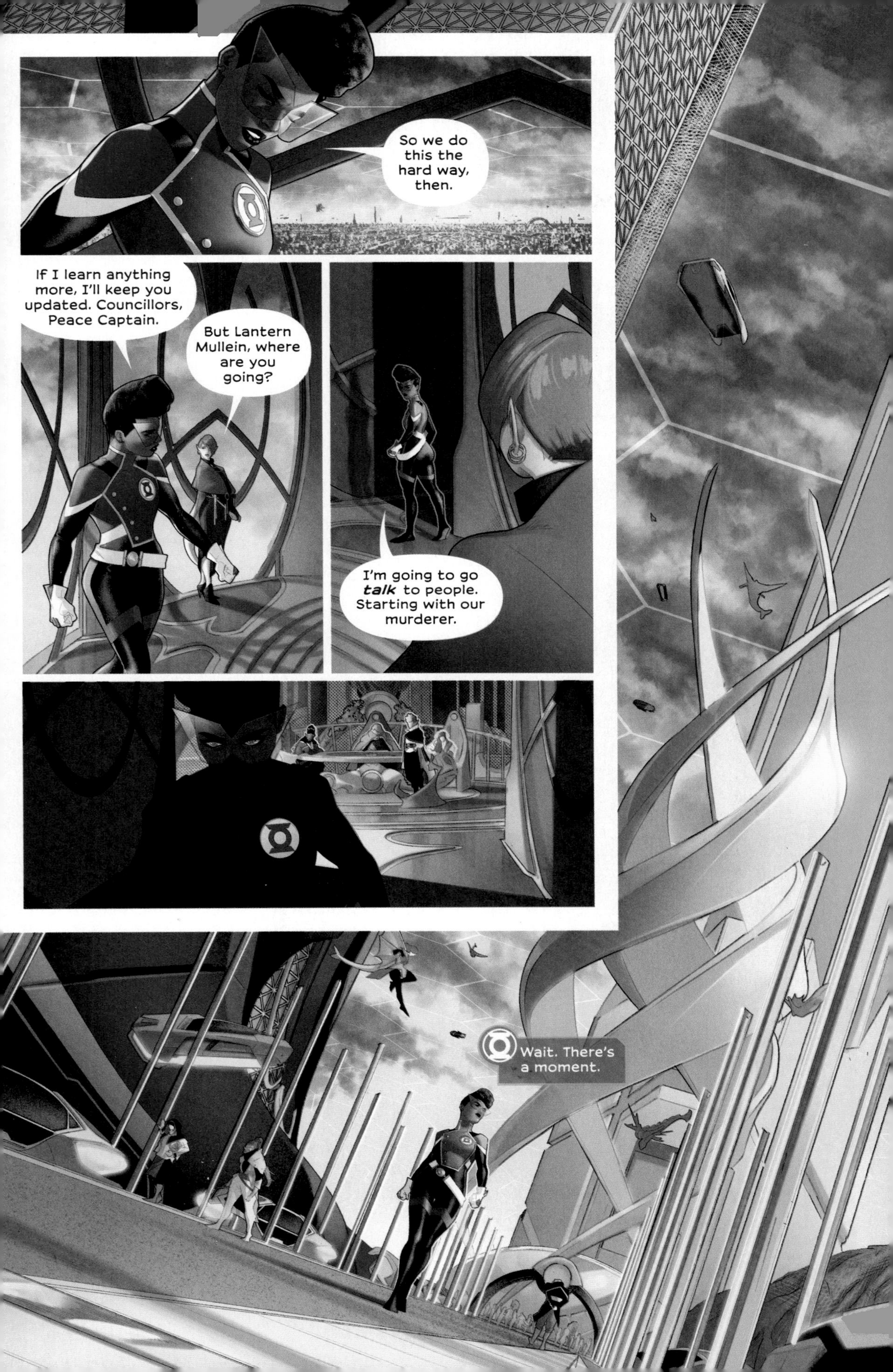
So we do this the hard way, then.
If I learn anything more, I'll keep you updated. Councillors, Peace Captain.
But Lantern Mullein, where are you going?
I'm going to go *talk* to people. Starting with our murderer.
Wait. There's a moment.

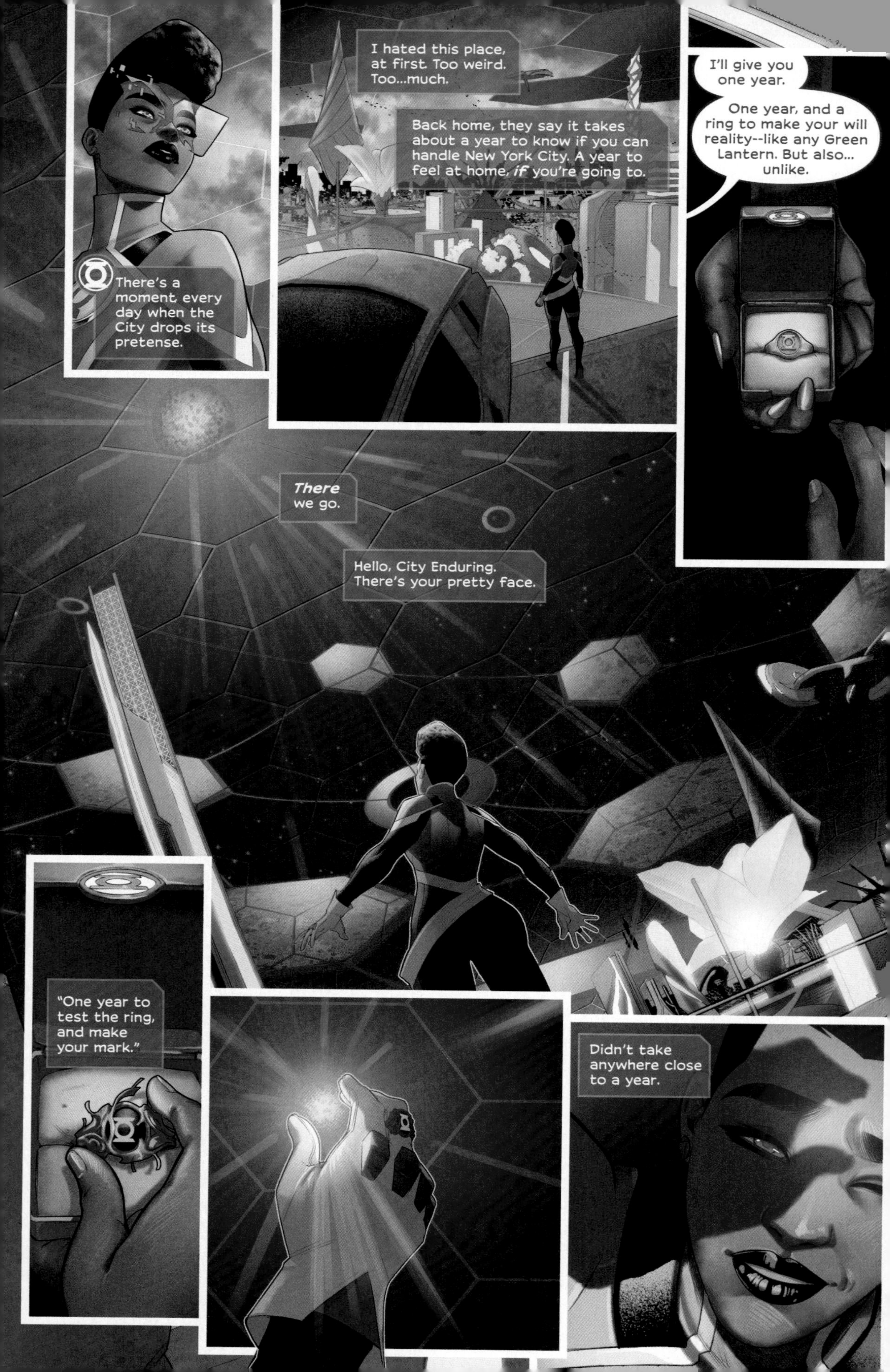

There's a moment every day when the City drops its pretense.
I hated this place, at first. Too weird. Too...much.
Back home, they say it takes about a year to know if you can handle New York City. A year to feel at home, *if* you're going to.
I'll give you one year.
One year, and a ring to make your will reality--like any Green Lantern. But also... unlike.
There we go.
Hello, City Enduring. There's your pretty face.
"One year to test the ring, and make your mark."
Didn't take anywhere close to a year.

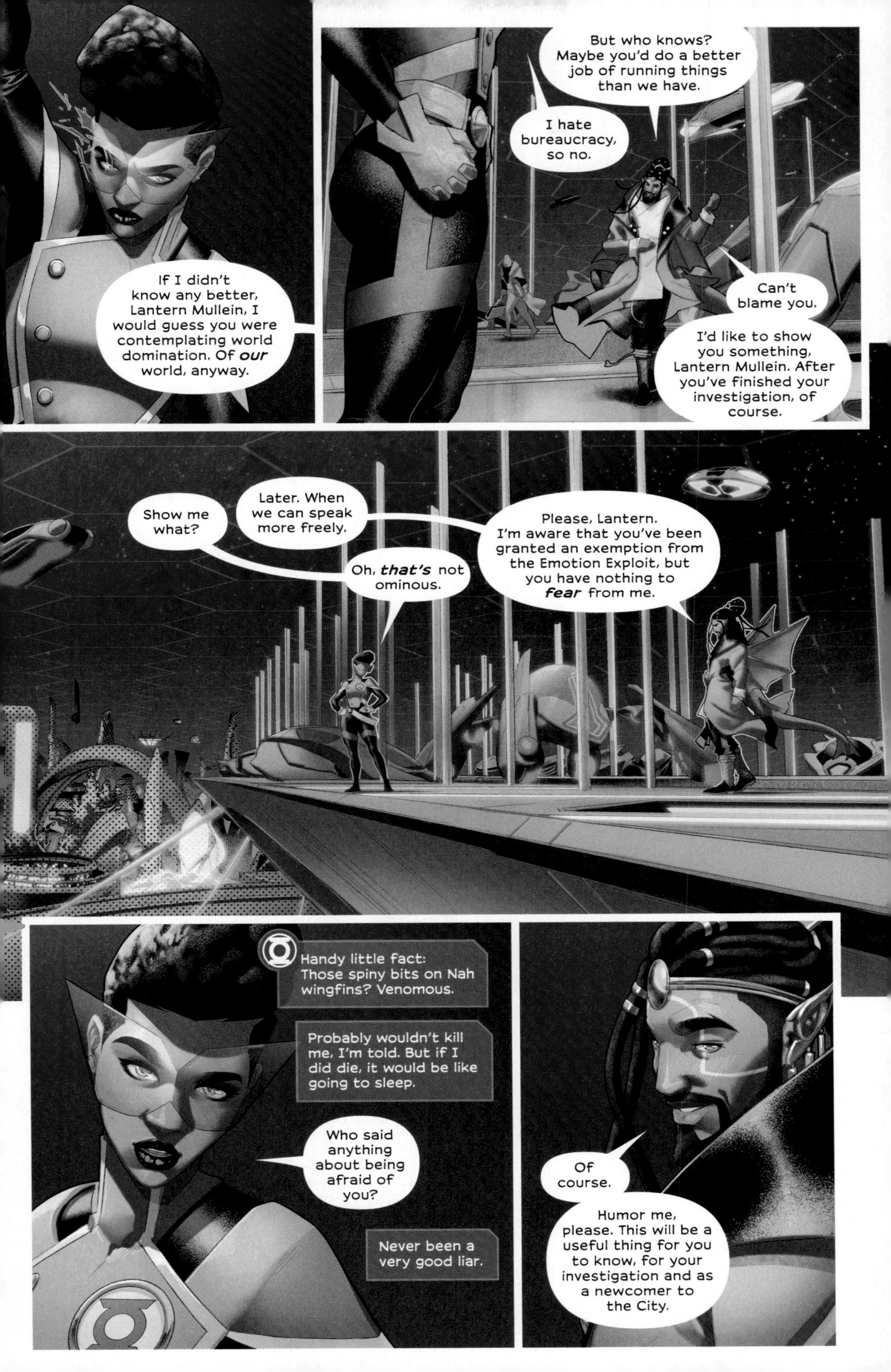
If I didn't know any better, Lantern Mullein, I would guess you were contemplating world domination. Of *our* world, anyway.
But who knows? Maybe you'd do a better job of running things than we have.
I hate bureaucracy, so no.
Can't blame you.
I'd like to show you something, Lantern Mullein. After you've finished your investigation, of course.
Show me what?
Later. When we can speak more freely.
Oh, ***that's*** not ominous.
Please, Lantern. I'm aware that you've been granted an exemption from the Emotion Exploit, but you have nothing to ***fear*** from me.
Handy little fact: Those spiny bits on Nah wingfins? Venomous.
Probably wouldn't kill me, I'm told. But if I did die, it would be like going to sleep.
Who said anything about being afraid of you?
Never been a very good liar.
Of course.
Humor me, please. This will be a useful thing for you to know, for your investigation and as a newcomer to the City.

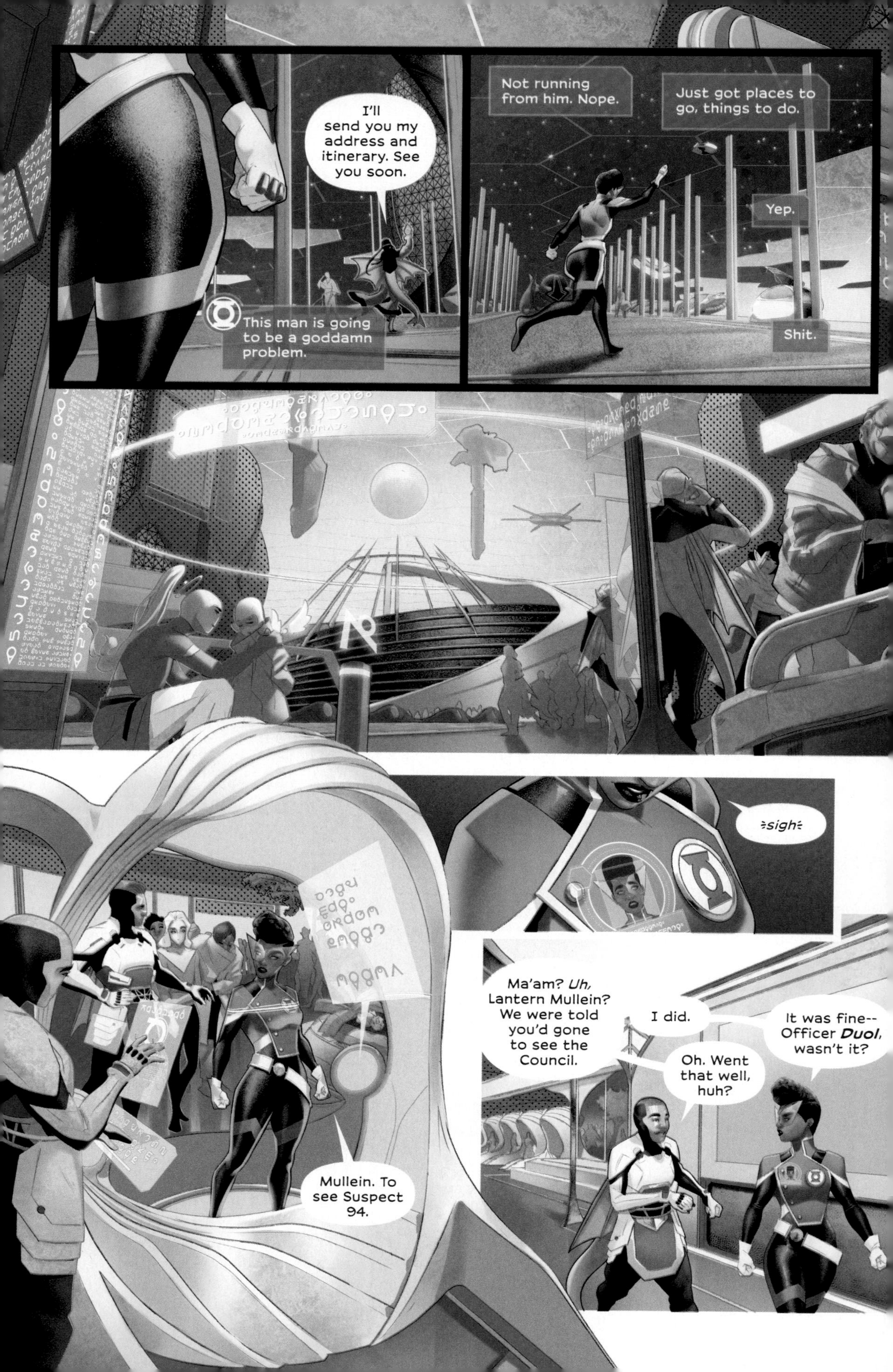

I'll send you my address and itinerary. See you soon.
This man is going to be a goddamn problem.
Not running from him. Nope.
Just got places to go, things to do.
Yep.
Shit.
=sigh=
Mullein. To see Suspect 94.
Ma'am? *Uh,* Lantern Mullein? We were told you'd gone to see the Council.
I did.
Oh. Went that well, huh?
It was fine-- Officer ***Duol***, wasn't it?

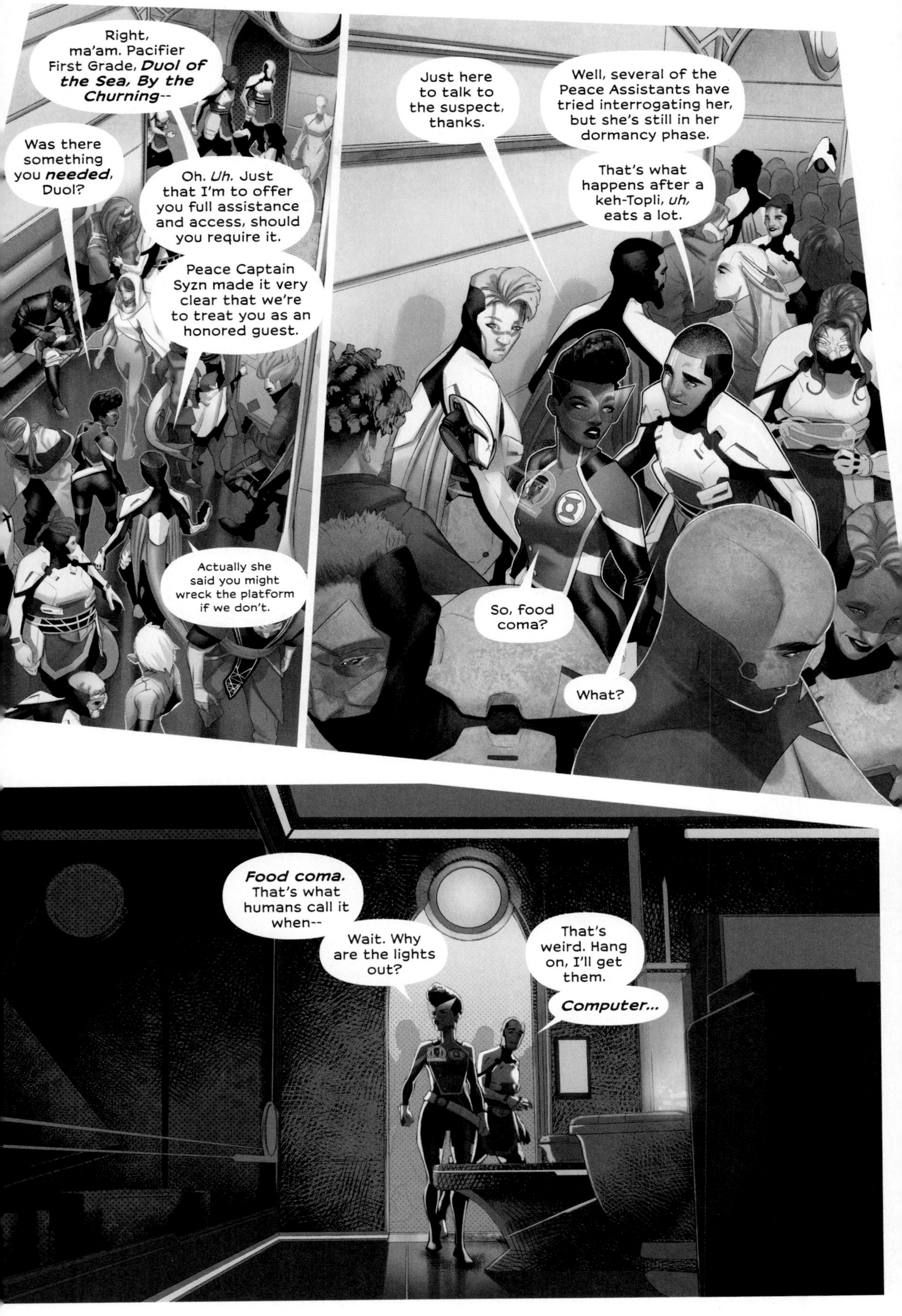
Right, ma'am. Pacifier First Grade, ***Duol of the Sea, By the Churning***--
Was there something you ***needed***, Duol?
Oh. *Uh.* Just that I'm to offer you full assistance and access, should you require it.
Peace Captain Syzn made it very clear that we're to treat you as an honored guest.
Actually she said you might wreck the platform if we don't.
Just here to talk to the suspect, thanks.
Well, several of the Peace Assistants have tried interrogating her, but she's still in her dormancy phase.
That's what happens after a keh-Topli, *uh*, eats a lot.
So, food coma?
What?
Food coma. That's what humans call it when--
Wait. Why are the lights out?
That's weird. Hang on, I'll get them.
Computer...

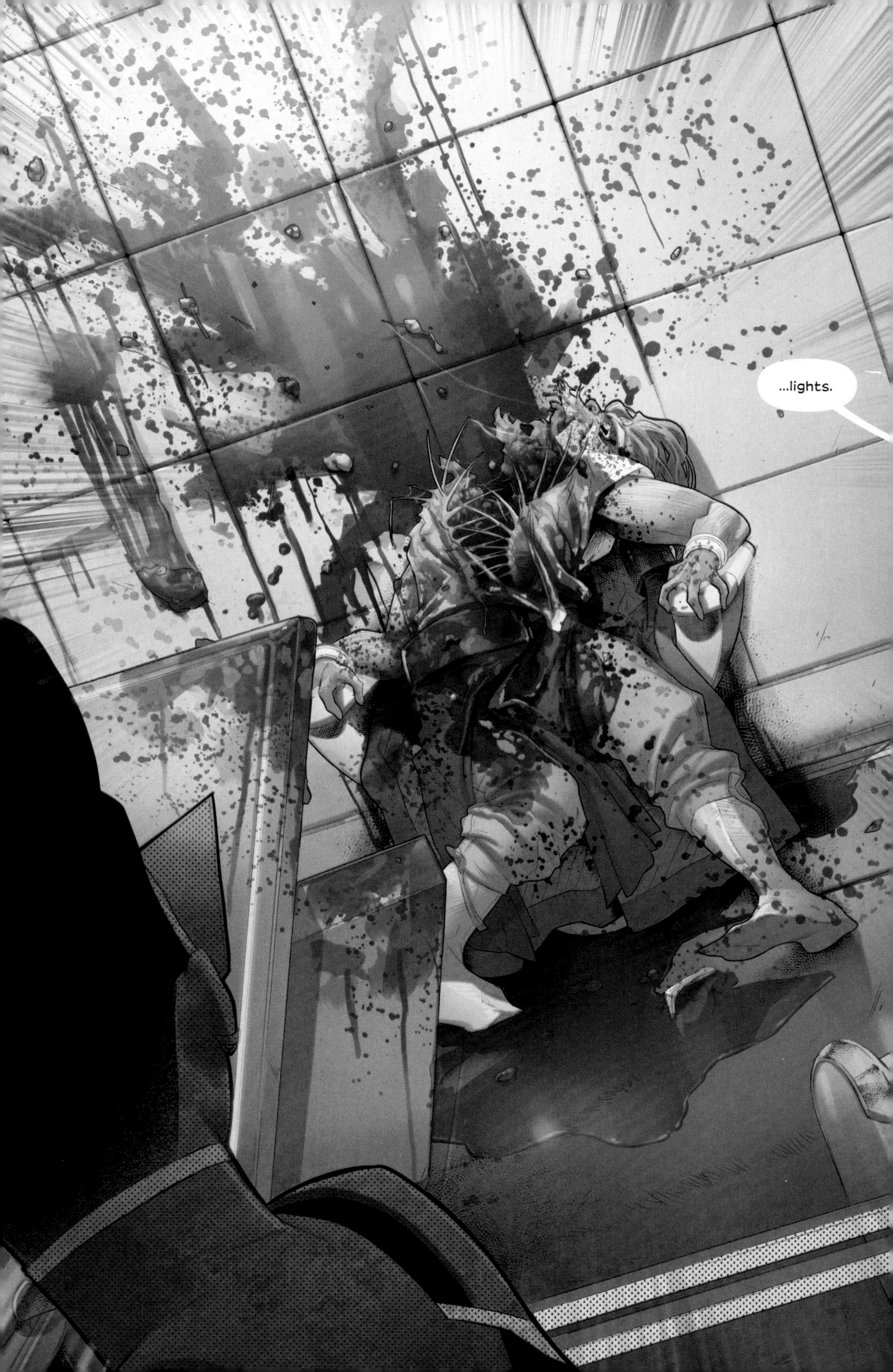
...lights.

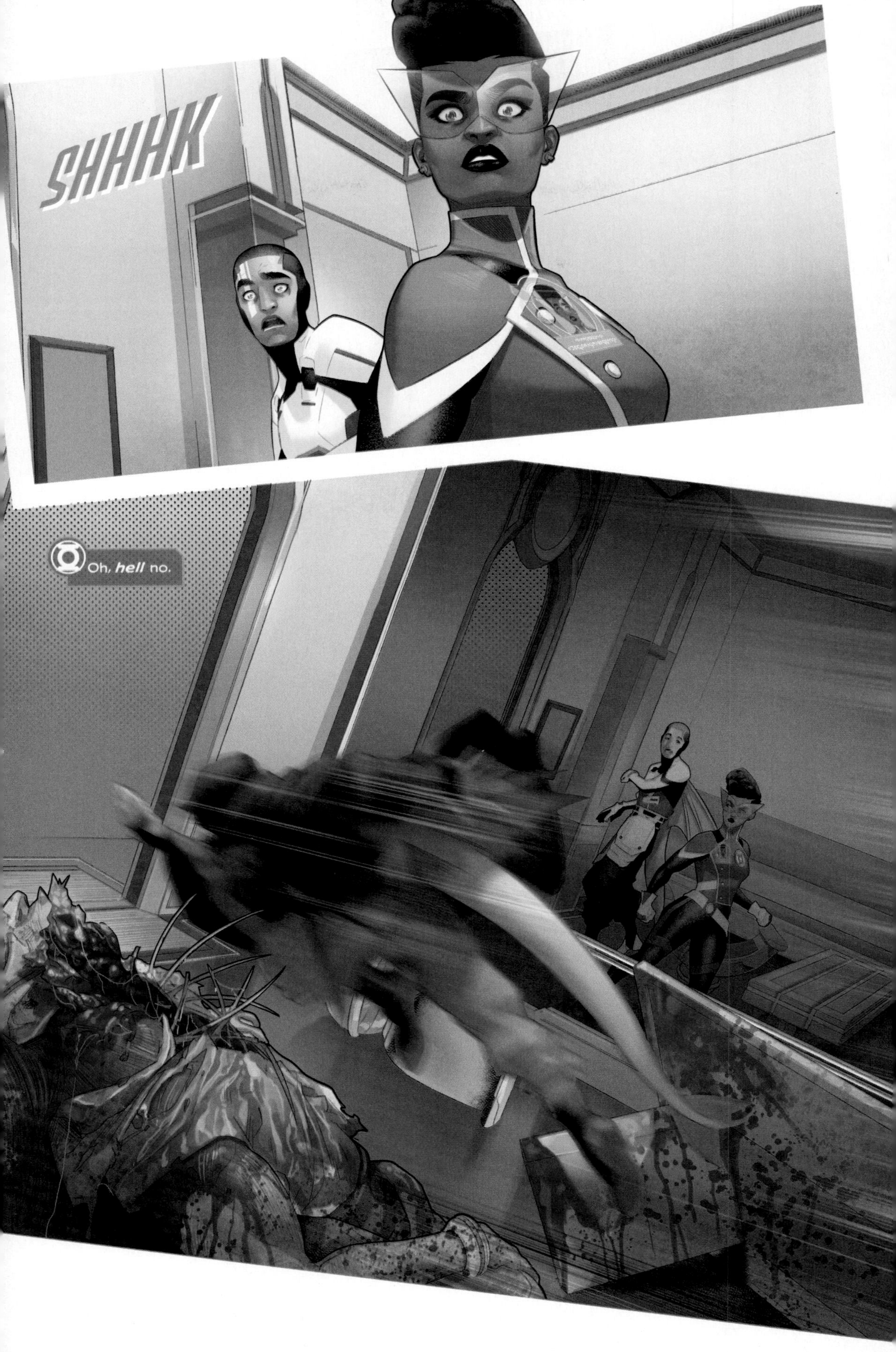
SHHHK
Oh, hell no.

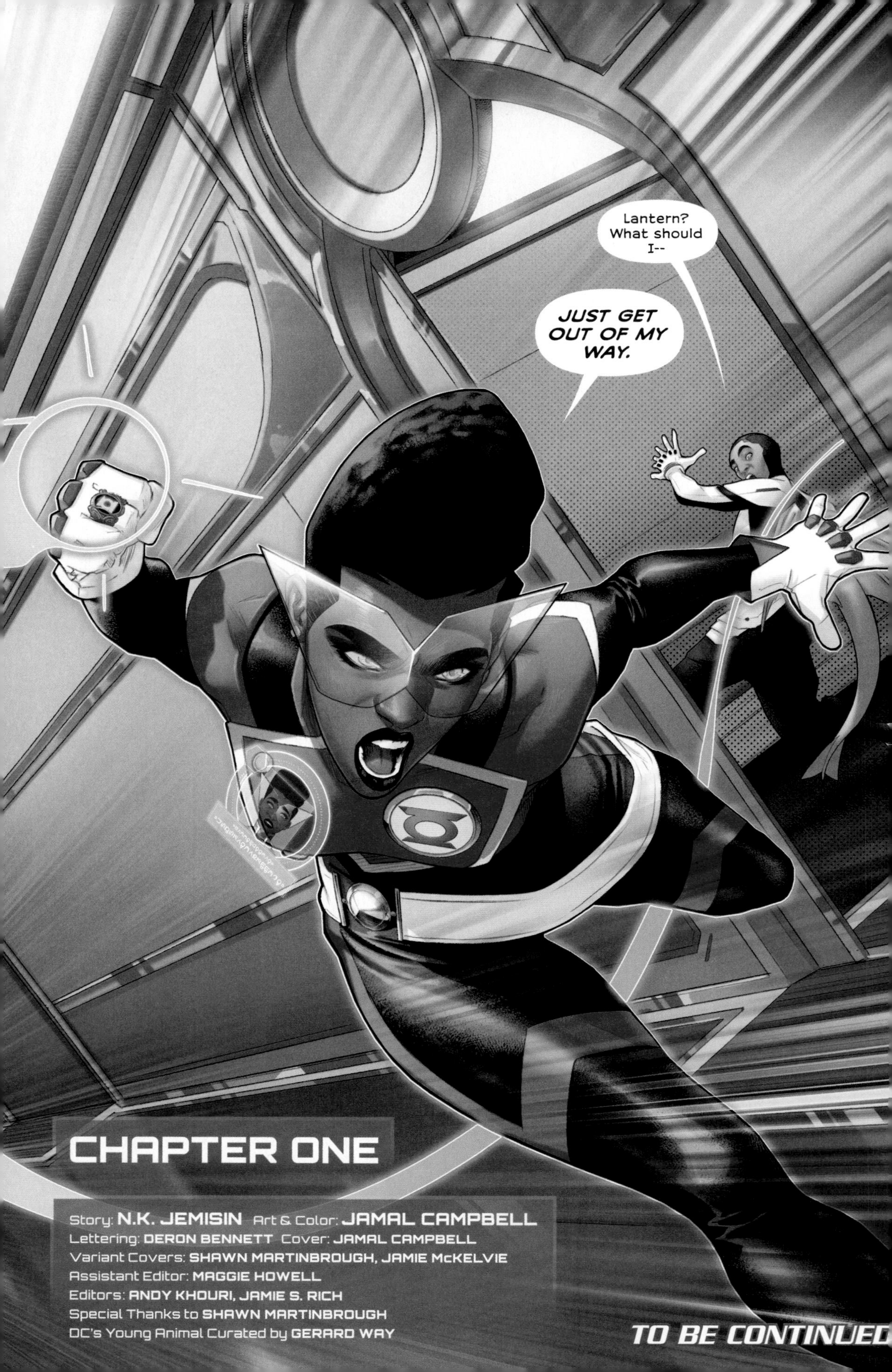
Lantern? What should I--
JUST GET OUT OF MY WAY.
CHAPTER ONE
Story: N.K. JEMISIN Art & Color: JAMAL CAMPBELL
Lettering: DERON BENNETT Cover: JAMAL CAMPBELL
Variant Covers: SHAWN MARTINBROUGH, JAMIE McKELVIE
Assistant Editor: MAGGIE HOWELL
Editors: ANDY KHOURI, JAMIE S. RICH
Special Thanks to SHAWN MARTINBROUGH
DC's Young Animal Curated by GERARD WAY
TO BE CONTINUED

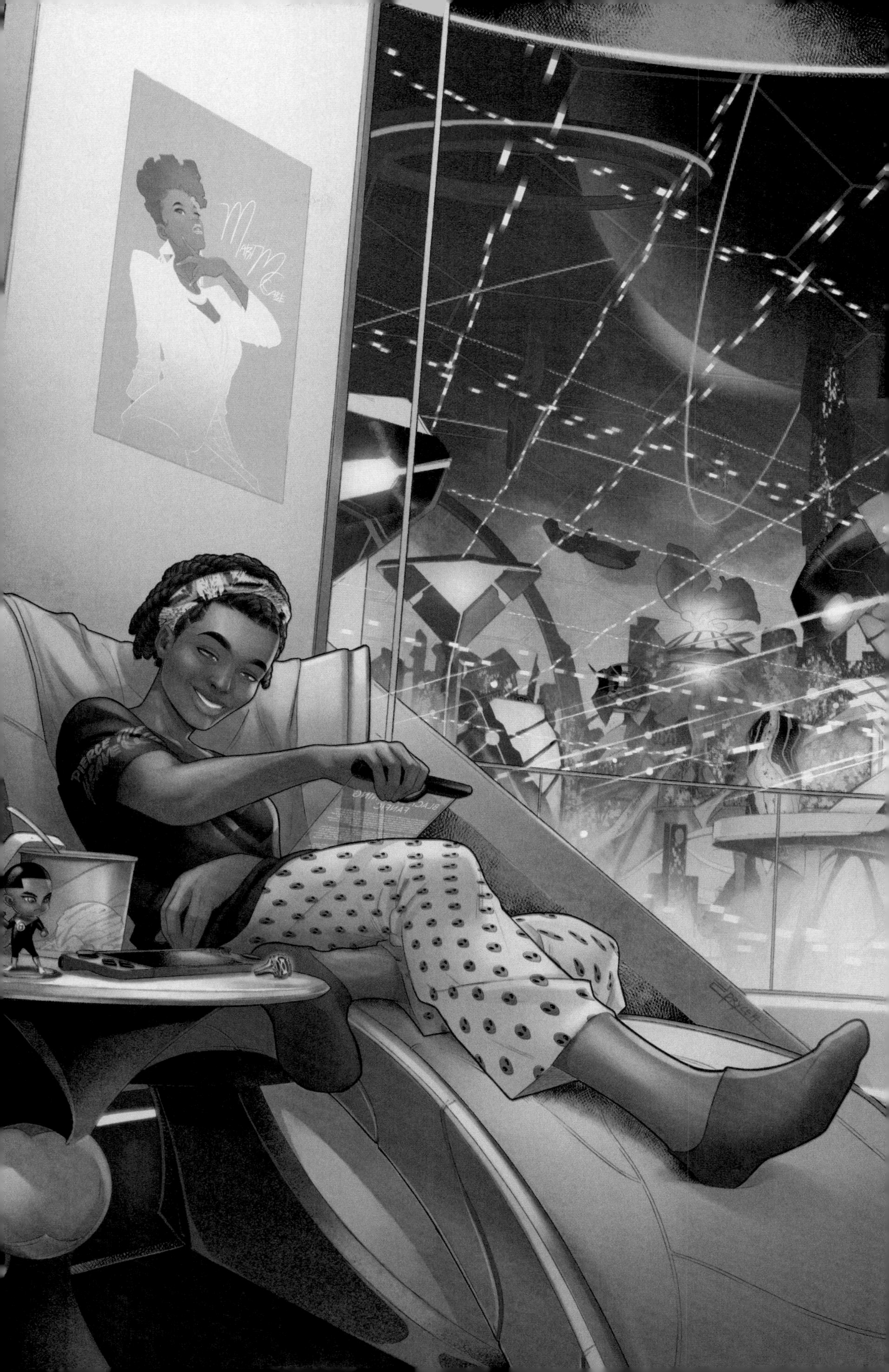

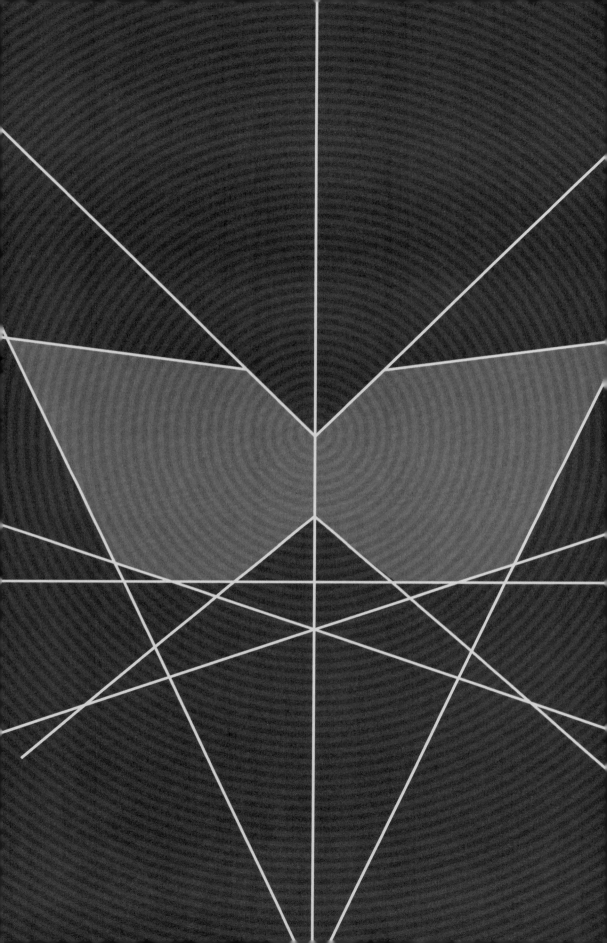

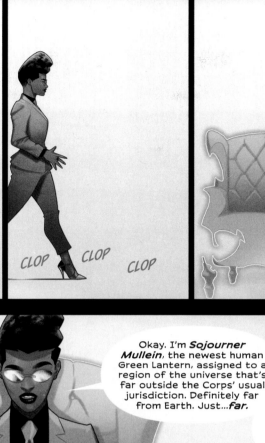

CLOP CLOP CLOP

CLOP CLOP CLOP

Okay. I'm *Sojourner Mullein*, the newest human Green Lantern, assigned to a region of the universe that's far outside the Corps' usual jurisdiction. Definitely far from Earth. Just...*far.*

It's just me out here. Lone sheriff on the frontier. I like it that way, so far.

This sector is home to the *City Enduring*, a metropolis of twenty billion citizens...

...which has just had its first *murder* in five centuries.

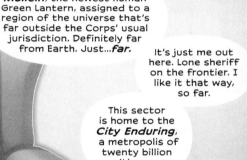

Code 187-- damn. Assault with a deadly weapon, possible homicide, suspect on foot, *GET OUT OF MY WAY!*

And my murderer? Just got murdered.

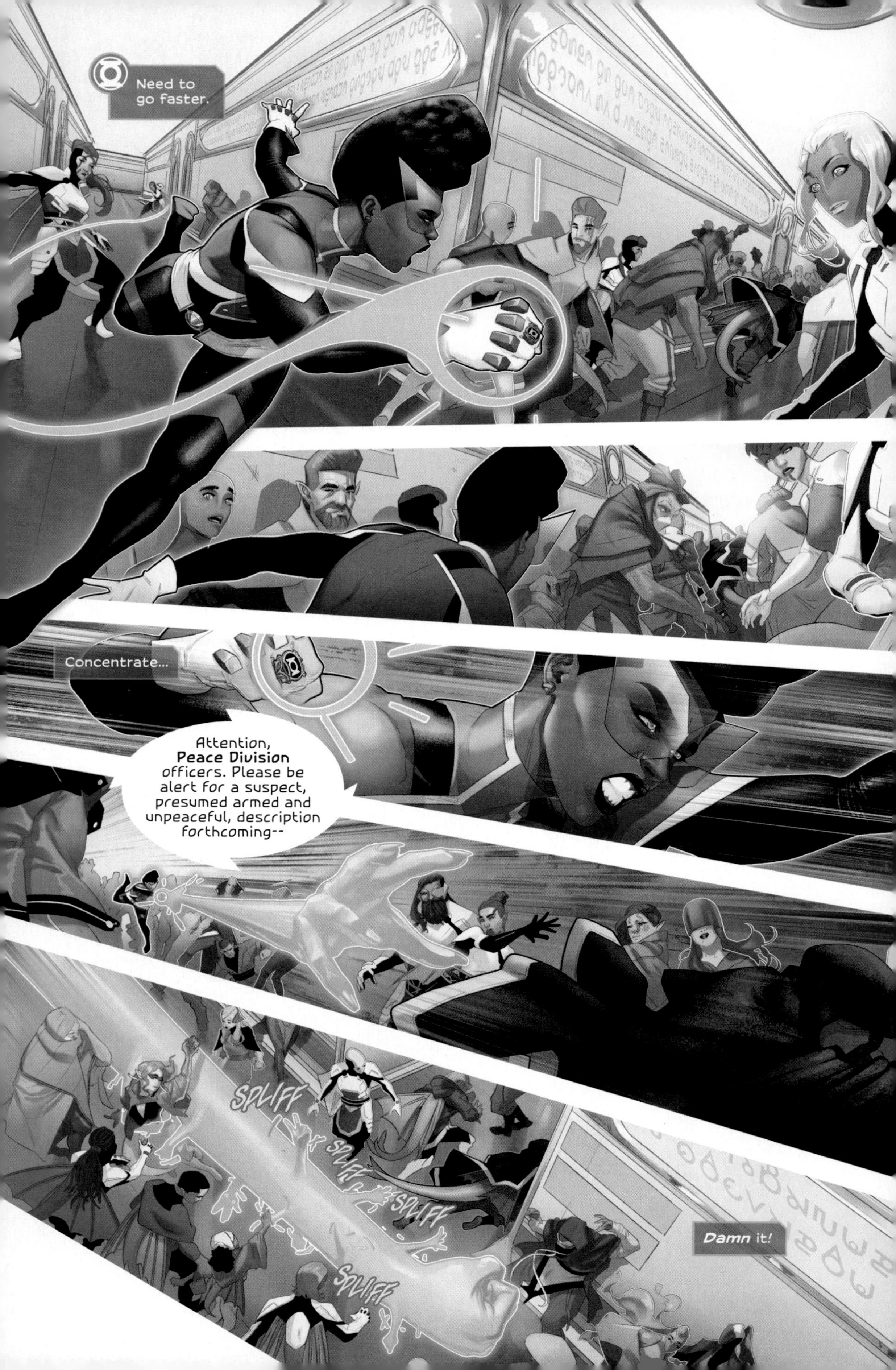
Need to go faster.
Concentrate...
Attention, **Peace Division** officers. Please be alert for a suspect, presumed armed and unpeaceful, description forthcoming--
SPLIFF
SPLIFF
SPLIFF
SPLIFF
SPLIFF
Damn it!

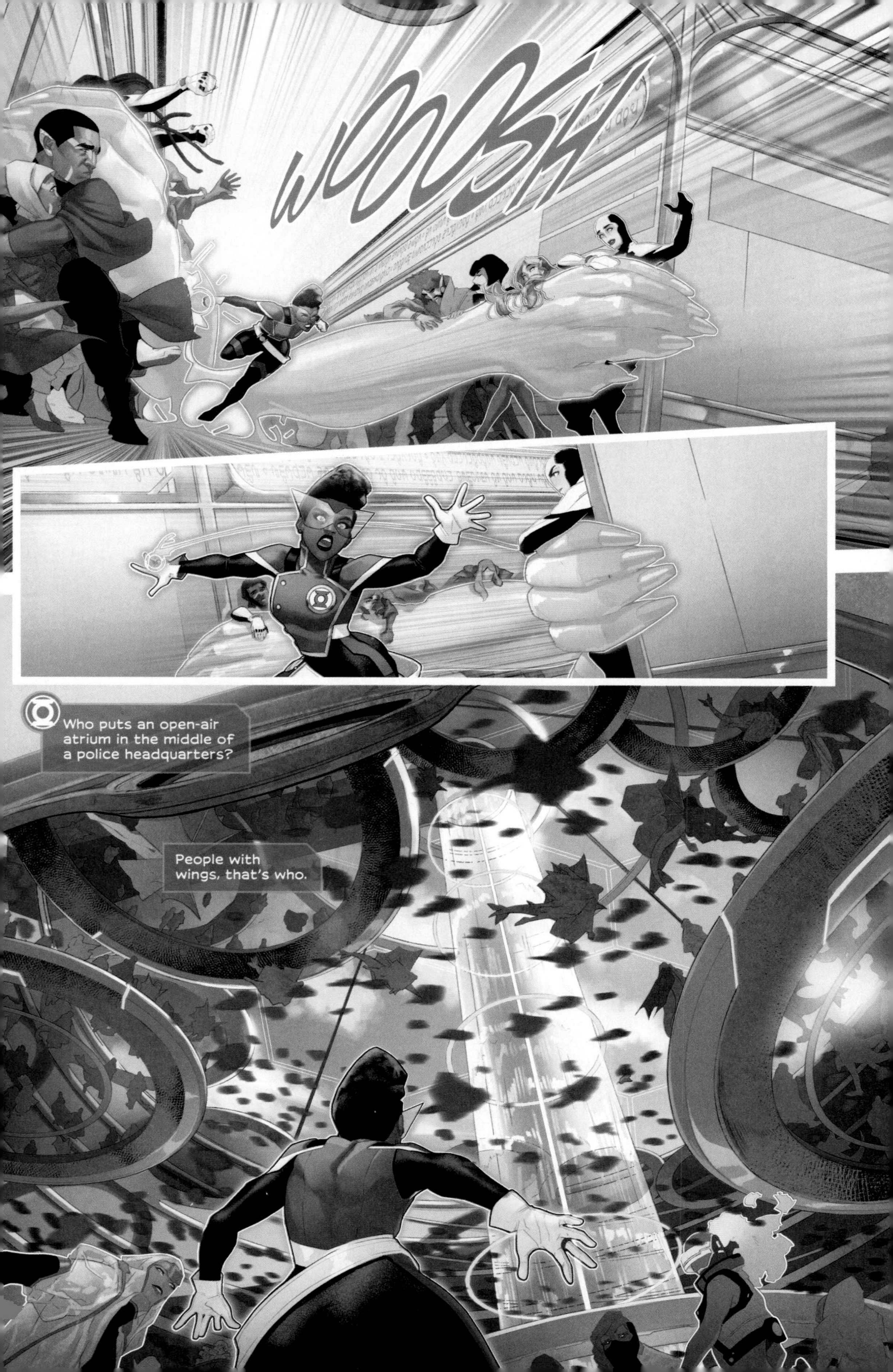
WOOOSH
Who puts an open-air atrium in the middle of a police headquarters?
People with wings, that's who.

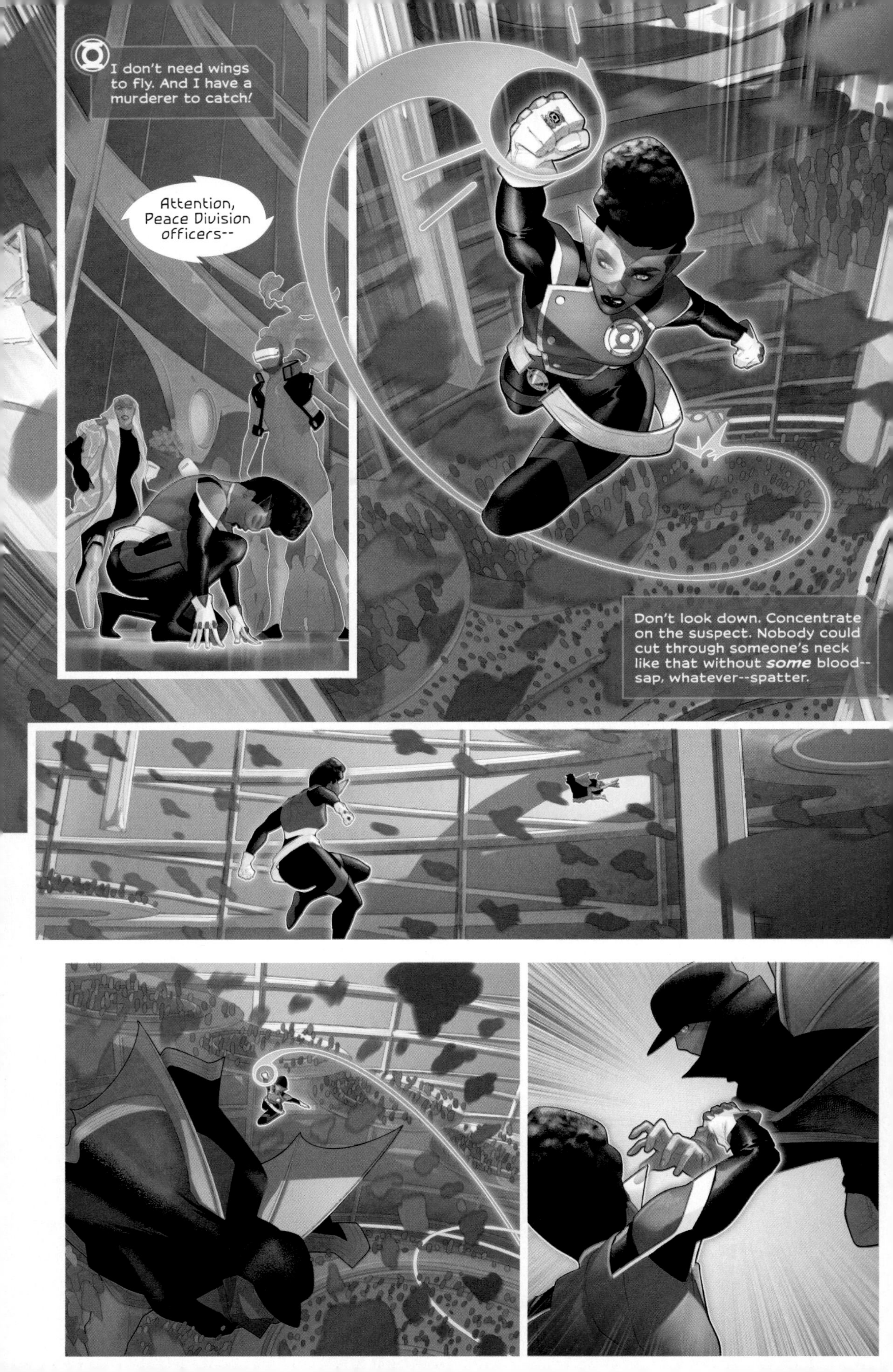
I don't need wings to fly. And I have a murderer to catch!
Attention, Peace Division officers--
Don't look down. Concentrate on the suspect. Nobody could cut through someone's neck like that without *some* blood--sap, whatever--spatter.

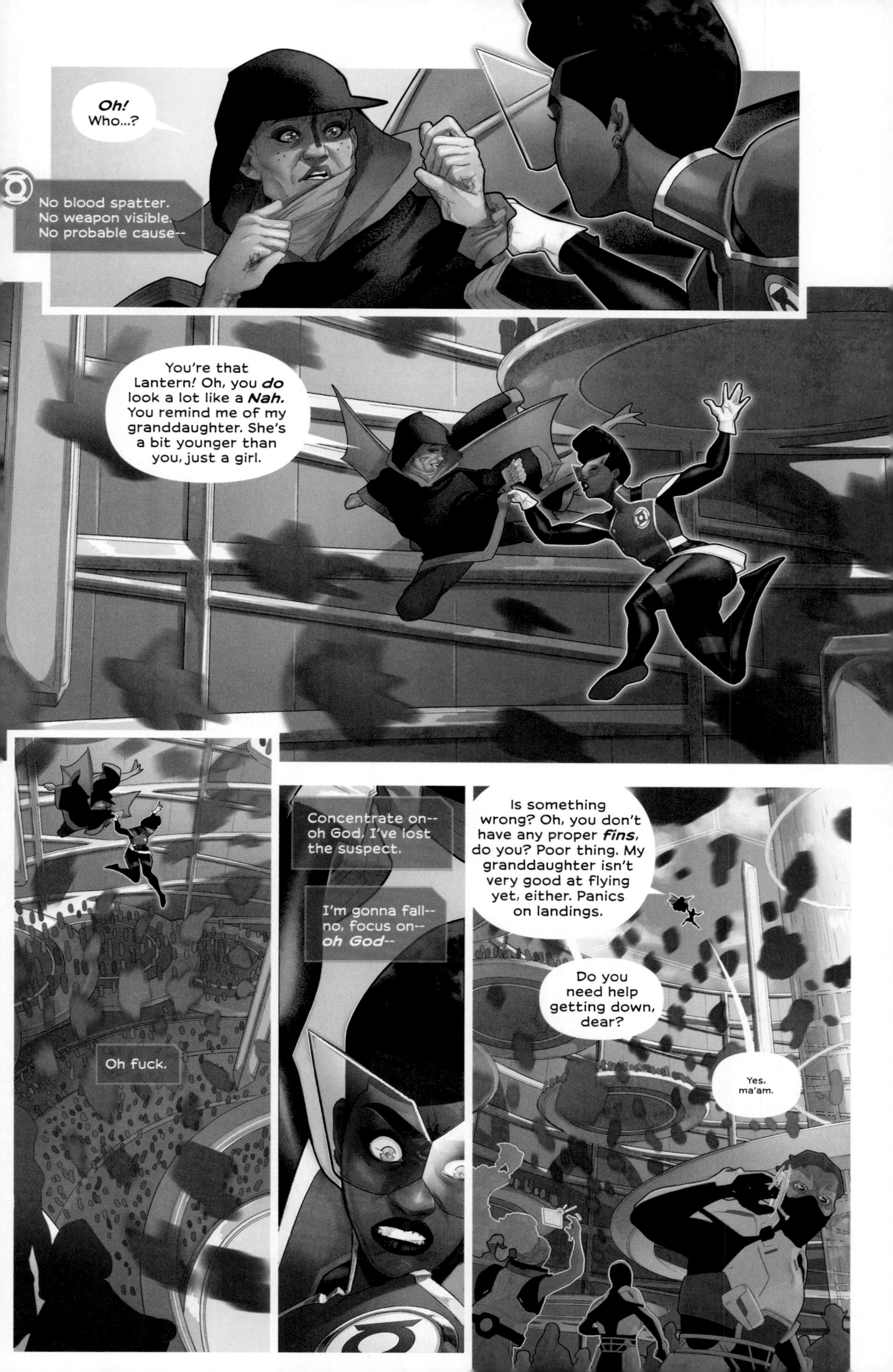

Oh! Who...?
No blood spatter. No weapon visible. No probable cause--
You're that Lantern! Oh, you *do* look a lot like a ***Nah.*** You remind me of my granddaughter. She's a bit younger than you, just a girl.
Oh fuck.
Concentrate on-- oh God, I've lost the suspect.
I'm gonna fall-- no, focus on-- *oh God*--
Is something wrong? Oh, you don't have any proper ***fins***, do you? Poor thing. My granddaughter isn't very good at flying yet, either. Panics on landings.
Do you need help getting down, dear?
Yes, ma'am.

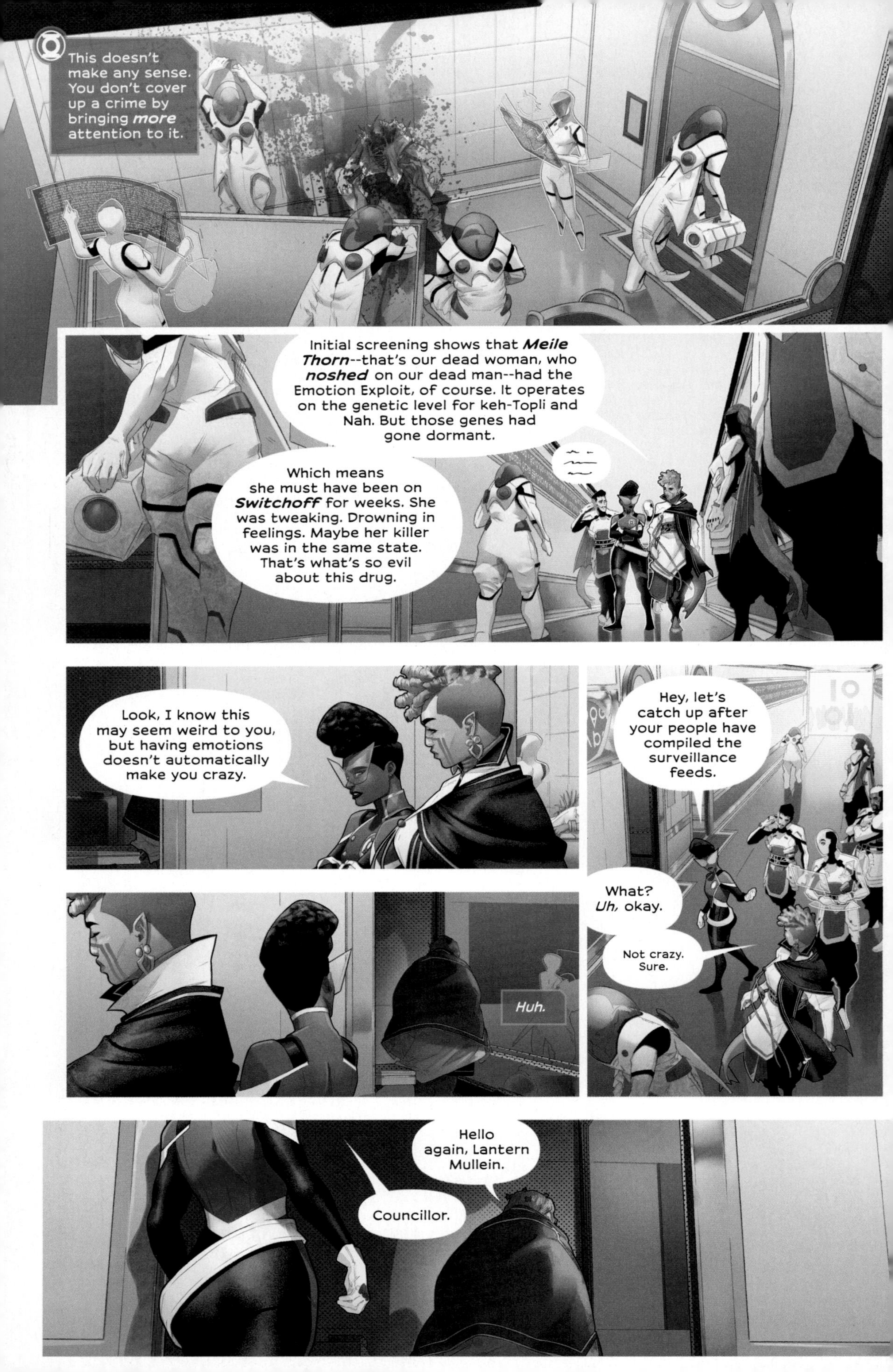
This doesn't make any sense. You don't cover up a crime by bringing *more* attention to it.
Initial screening shows that *Meile Thorn*--that's our dead woman, who *noshed* on our dead man--had the Emotion Exploit, of course. It operates on the genetic level for keh-Topli and Nah. But those genes had gone dormant.
Which means she must have been on *Switchoff* for weeks. She was tweaking. Drowning in feelings. Maybe her killer was in the same state. That's what's so evil about this drug.
Look, I know this may seem weird to you, but having emotions doesn't automatically make you crazy.
Huh.
Hey, let's catch up after your people have compiled the surveillance feeds.
What? *Uh,* okay.
Not crazy. Sure.
Hello again, Lantern Mullein.
Councillor.

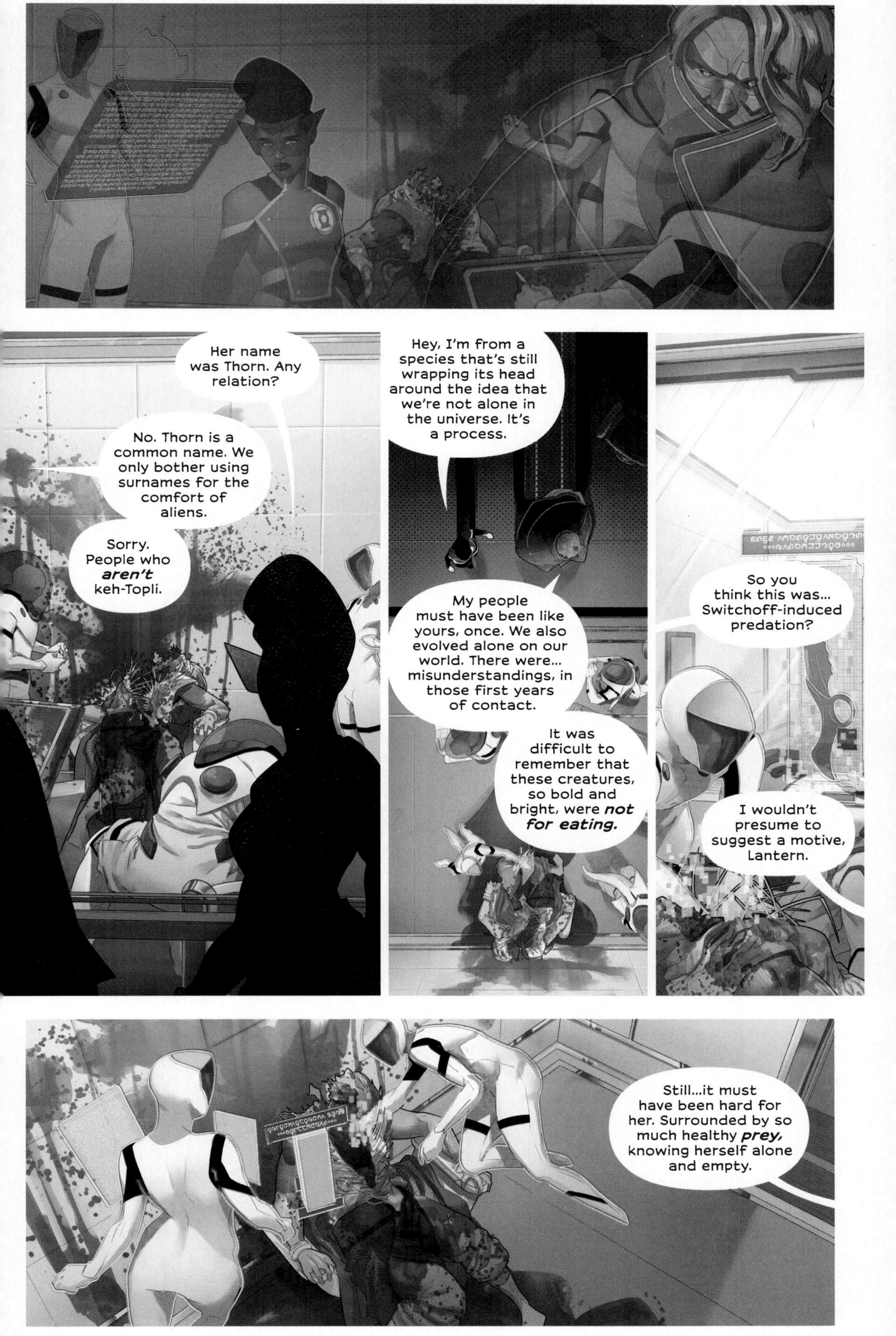

Her name was Thorn. Any relation?
No. Thorn is a common name. We only bother using surnames for the comfort of aliens.
Sorry. People who ***aren't*** keh-Topli.
Hey, I'm from a species that's still wrapping its head around the idea that we're not alone in the universe. It's a process.
My people must have been like yours, once. We also evolved alone on our world. There were... misunderstandings, in those first years of contact.
It was difficult to remember that these creatures, so bold and bright, were ***not for eating.***
So you think this was... Switchoff-induced predation?
I wouldn't presume to suggest a motive, Lantern.
Still...it must have been hard for her. Surrounded by so much healthy ***prey,*** knowing herself alone and empty.

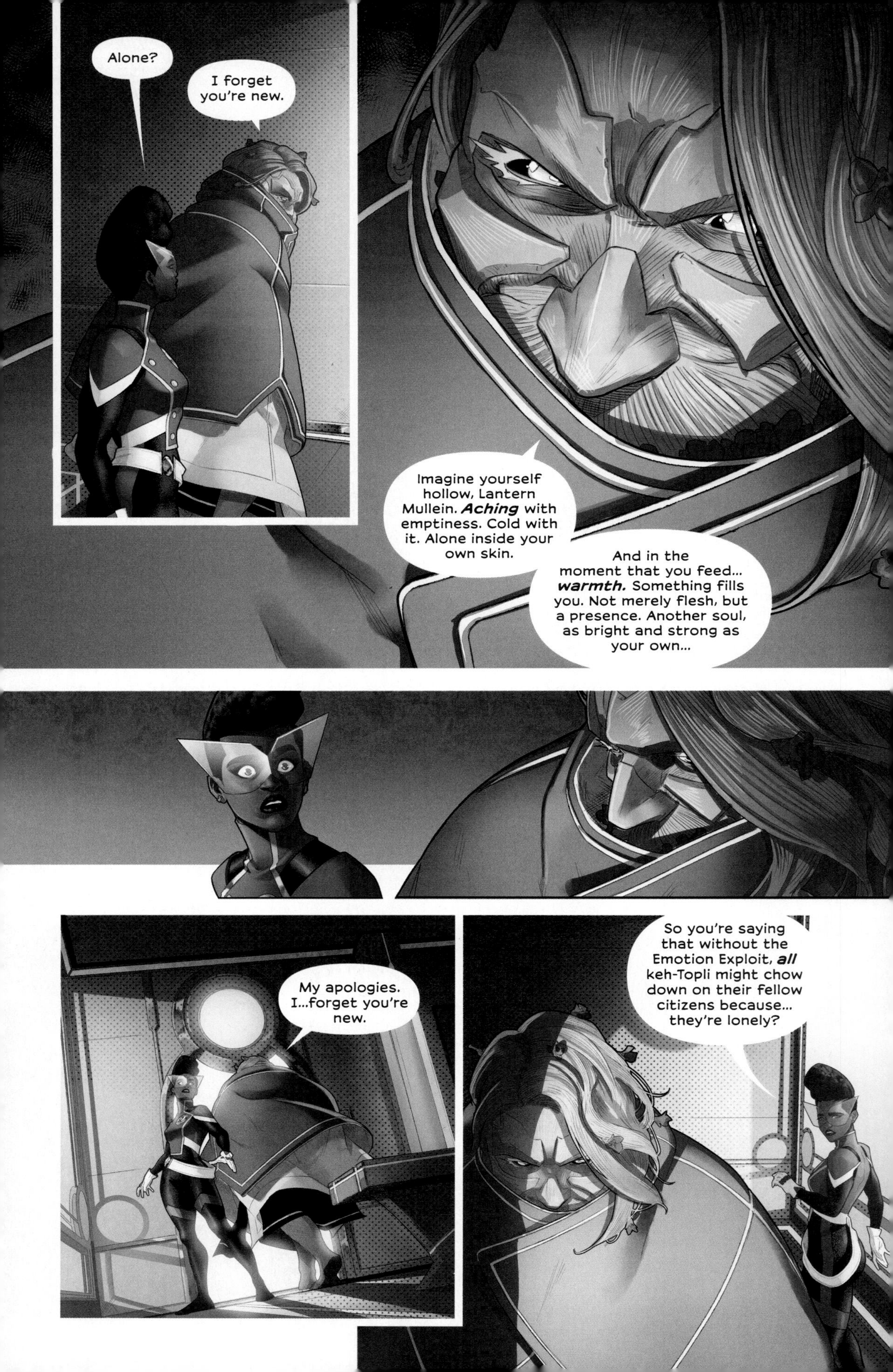
Alone?
I forget you're new.
Imagine yourself hollow, Lantern Mullein. ***Aching*** with emptiness. Cold with it. Alone inside your own skin.
And in the moment that you feed... ***warmth.*** Something fills you. Not merely flesh, but a presence. Another soul, as bright and strong as your own...
My apologies. I...forget you're new.
So you're saying that without the Emotion Exploit, ***all*** keh-Topli might chow down on their fellow citizens because... they're lonely?

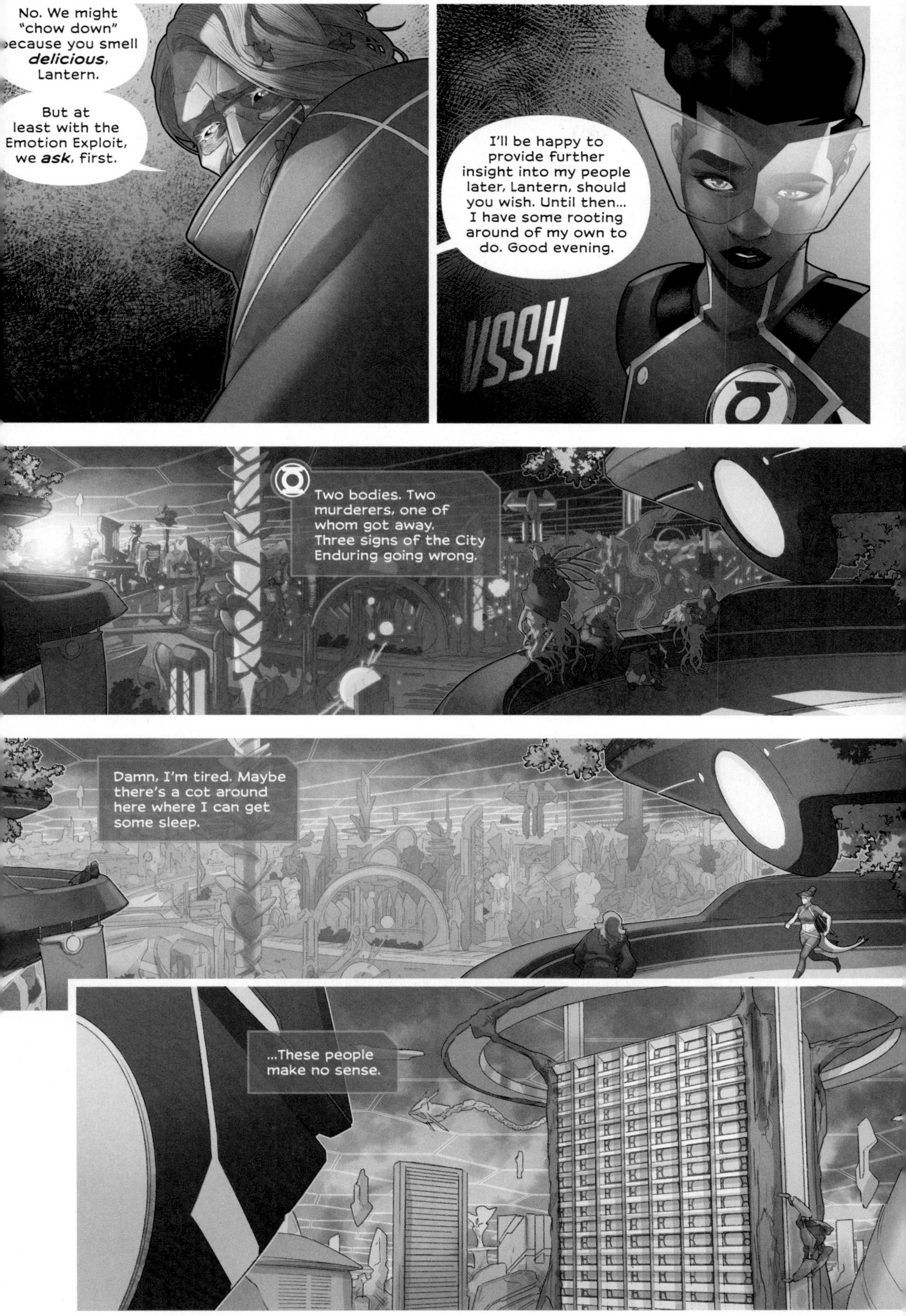
No. We might "chow down" because you smell *delicious*, Lantern.
But at least with the Emotion Exploit, we *ask*, first.
I'll be happy to provide further insight into my people later, Lantern, should you wish. Until then... I have some rooting around of my own to do. Good evening.
VSSH
Two bodies. Two murderers, one of whom got away. Three signs of the City Enduring going wrong.
Damn, I'm tired. Maybe there's a cot around here where I can get some sleep.
...These people make no sense.

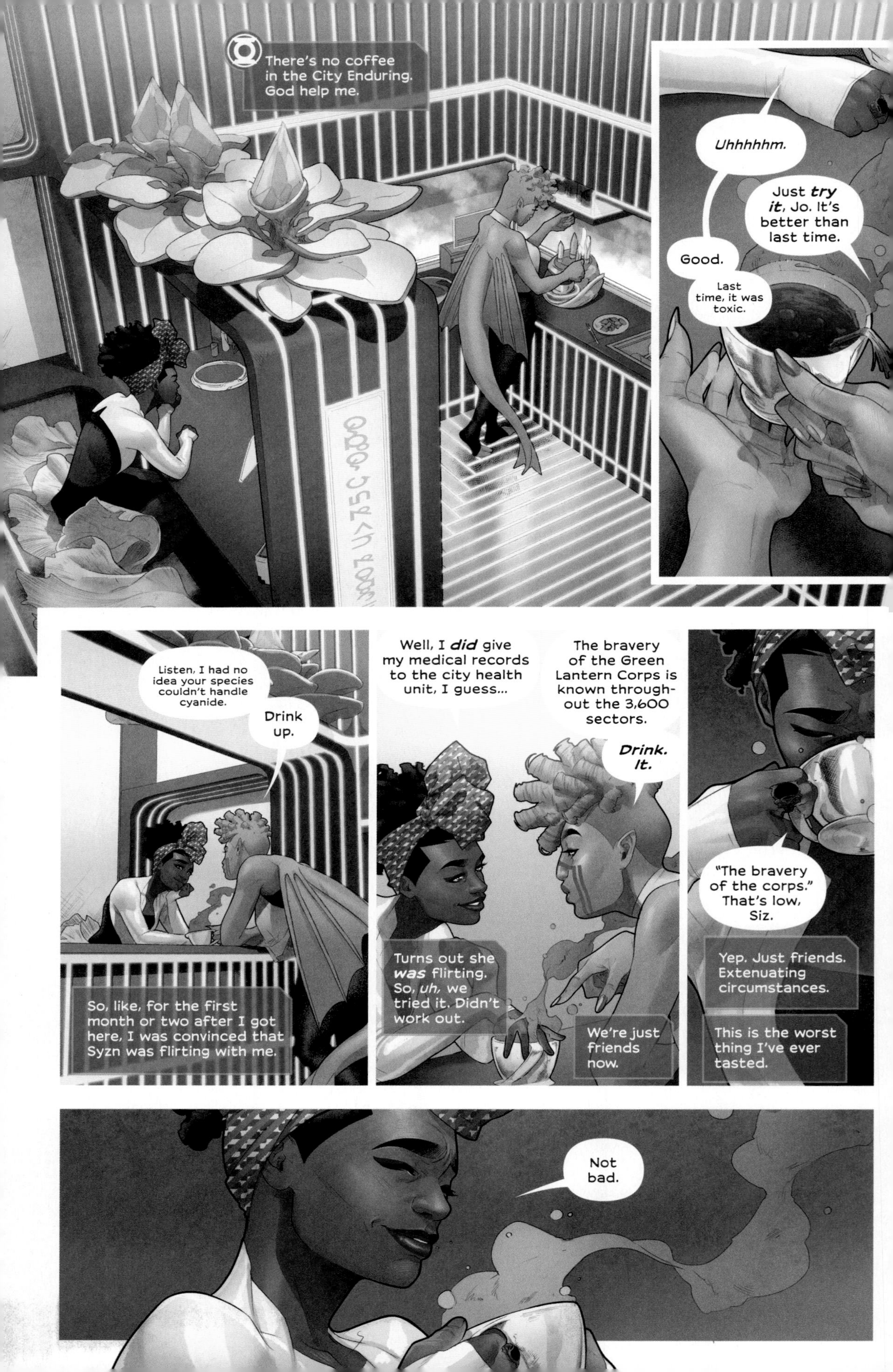
There's no coffee in the City Enduring. God help me.
Uhhhhhm.
Just *try it*, Jo. It's better than last time.
Good.
Last time, it was toxic.
Listen, I had no idea your species couldn't handle cyanide.
Drink up.
So, like, for the first month or two after I got here, I was convinced that Syzn was flirting with me.
Well, I *did* give my medical records to the city health unit, I guess...
The bravery of the Green Lantern Corps is known throughout the 3,600 sectors.
Drink. It.
Turns out she *was* flirting. So, *uh*, we tried it. Didn't work out.
We're just friends now.
"The bravery of the corps." That's low, Siz.
Yep. Just friends. Extenuating circumstances.
This is the worst thing I've ever tasted.
Not bad.

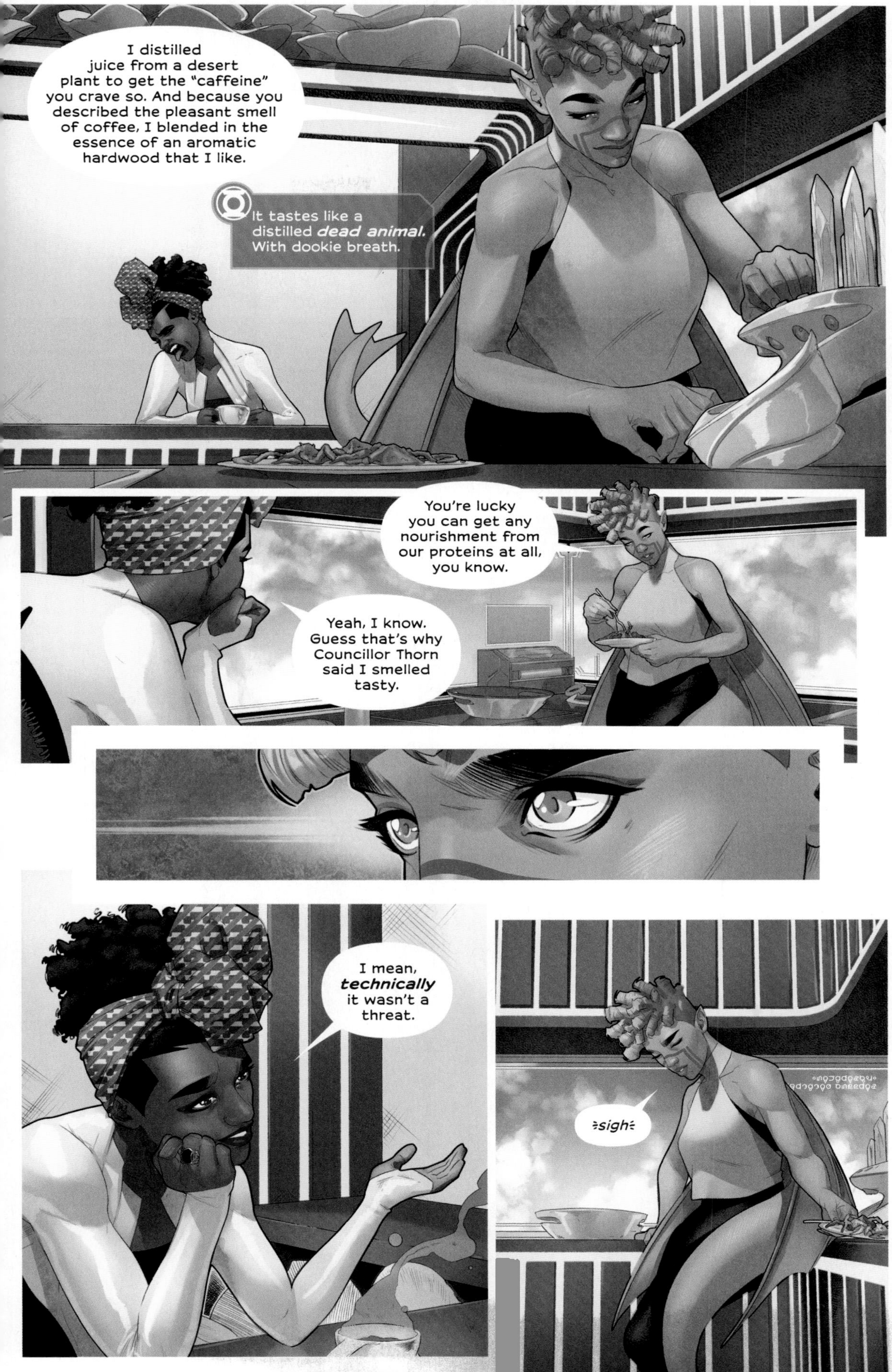
I distilled juice from a desert plant to get the "caffeine" you crave so. And because you described the pleasant smell of coffee, I blended in the essence of an aromatic hardwood that I like.
It tastes like a distilled *dead animal.* With dookie breath.
You're lucky you can get any nourishment from our proteins at all, you know.
Yeah, I know. Guess that's why Councillor Thorn said I smelled tasty.
I mean, ***technically*** it wasn't a threat.
sigh

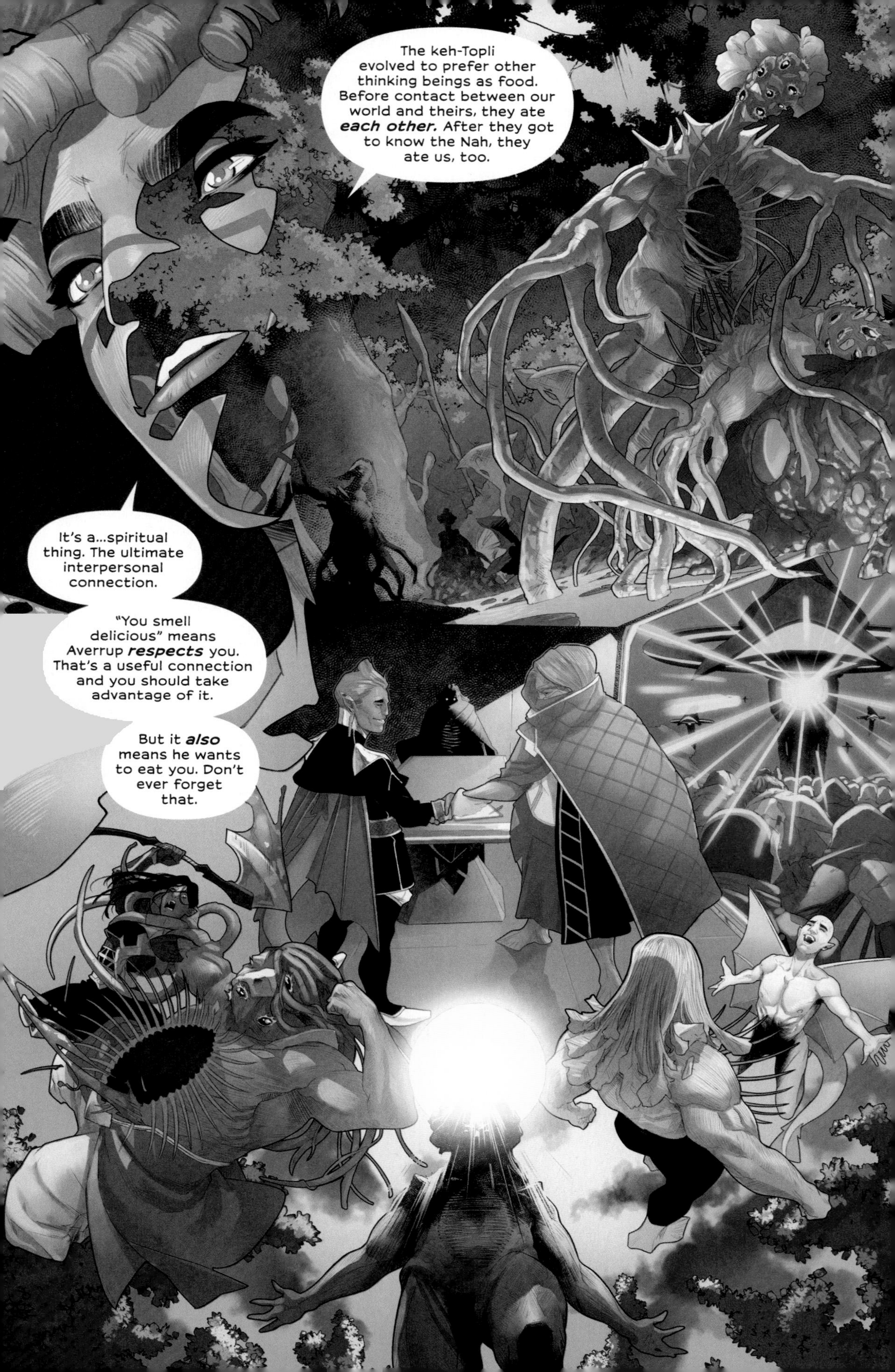
The keh-Topli evolved to prefer other thinking beings as food. Before contact between our world and theirs, they ate *each other.* After they got to know the Nah, they ate us, too.
It's a...spiritual thing. The ultimate interpersonal connection.
"You smell delicious" means Averrup *respects* you. That's a useful connection and you should take advantage of it.
But it *also* means he wants to eat you. Don't ever forget that.

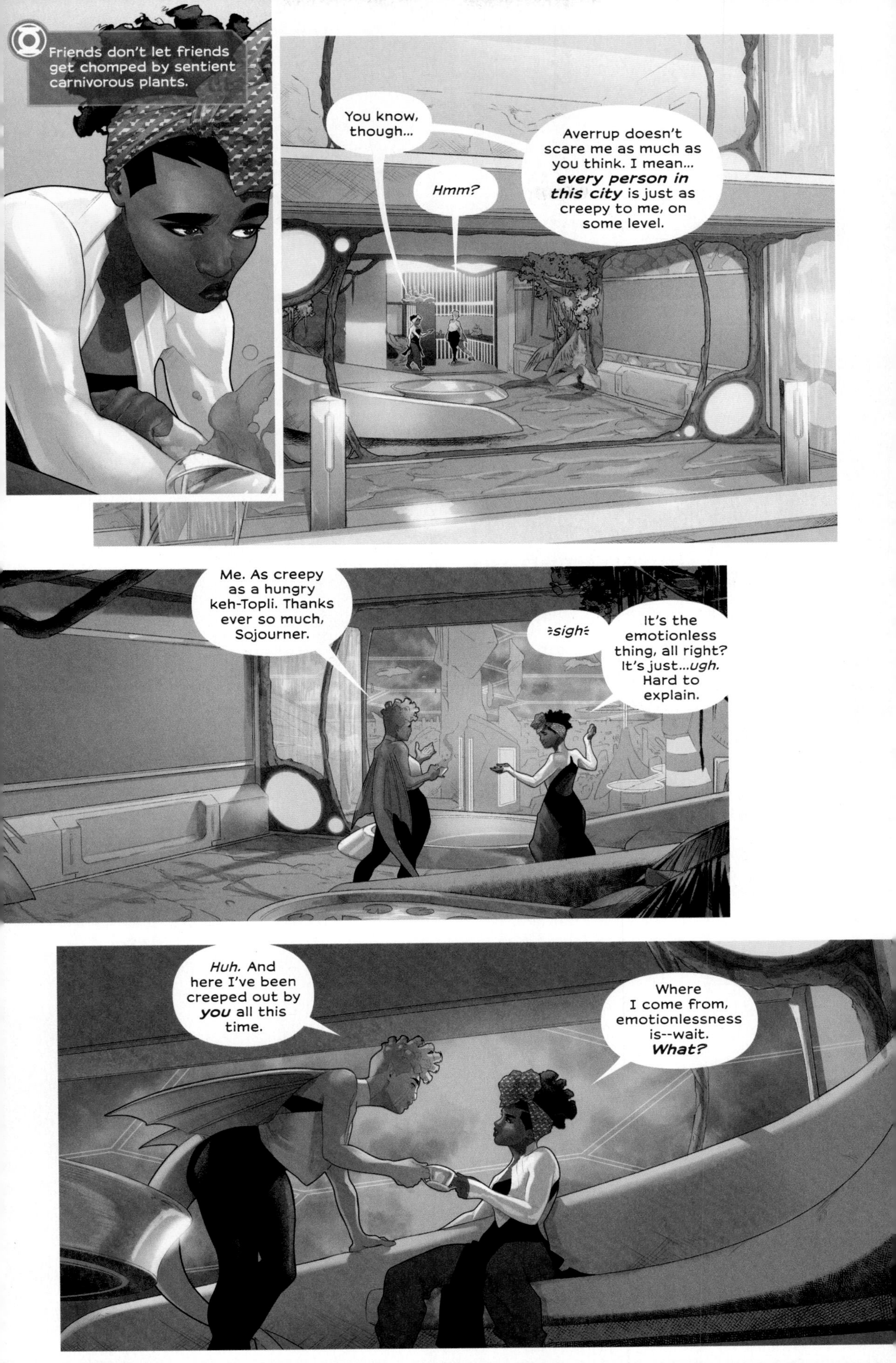

Friends don't let friends get chomped by sentient carnivorous plants.
You know, though...
Hmm?
Averrup doesn't scare me as much as you think. I mean... ***every person in this city*** is just as creepy to me, on some level.
Me. As creepy as a hungry keh-Topli. Thanks ever so much, Sojourner.
sigh
It's the emotionless thing, all right? It's just...*ugh.* Hard to explain.
Huh. And here I've been creeped out by ***you*** all this time.
Where I come from, emotionlessness is--wait. ***What?***

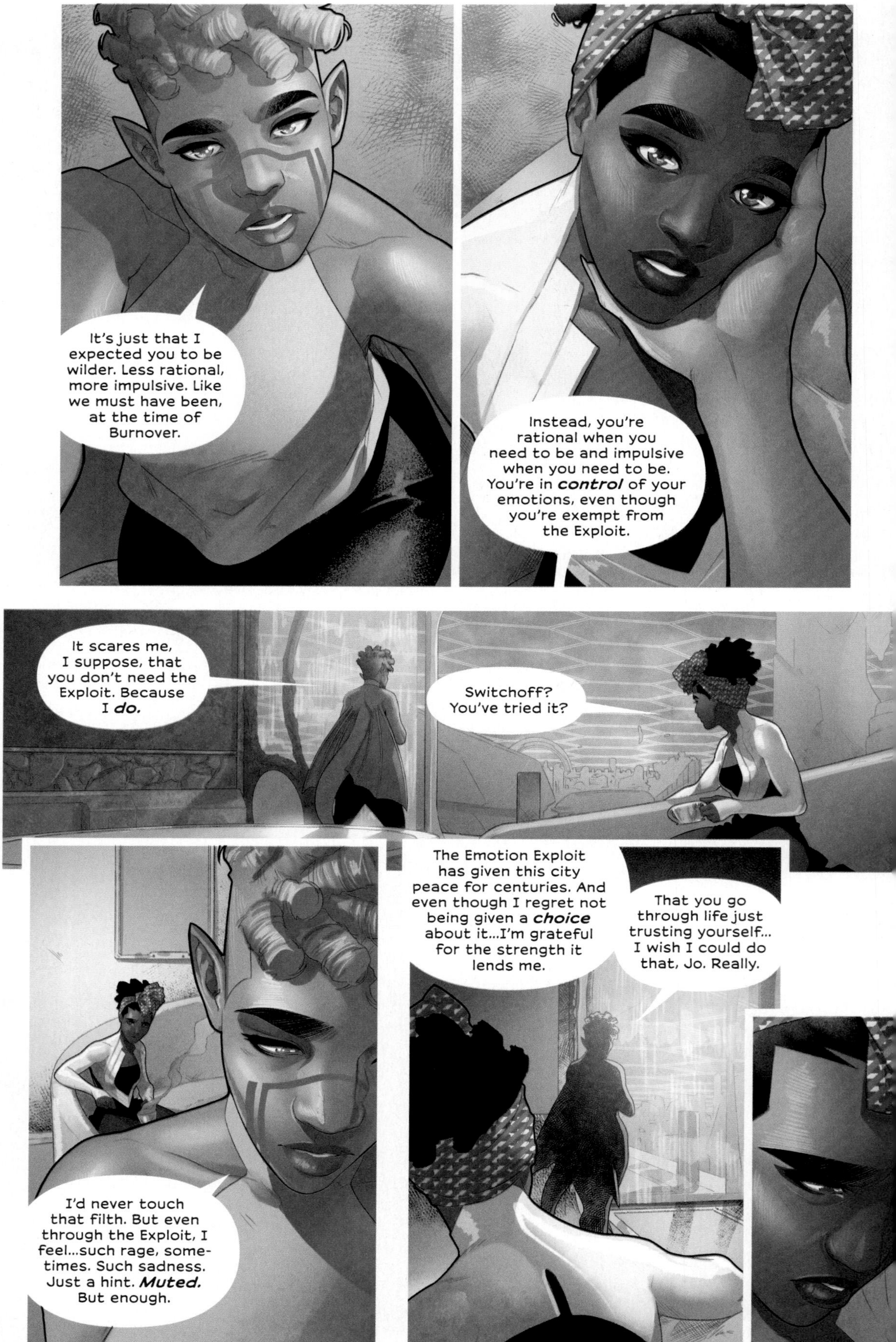
It's just that I expected you to be wilder. Less rational, more impulsive. Like we must have been, at the time of Burnover.
Instead, you're rational when you need to be and impulsive when you need to be. You're in *control* of your emotions, even though you're exempt from the Exploit.
It scares me, I suppose, that you don't need the Exploit. Because I *do.*
Switchoff? You've tried it?
I'd never touch that filth. But even through the Exploit, I feel...such rage, some-times. Such sadness. Just a hint. *Muted.* But enough.
The Emotion Exploit has given this city peace for centuries. And even though I regret not being given a *choice* about it...I'm grateful for the strength it lends me.
That you go through life just trusting yourself... I wish I could do that, Jo. Really.

I need a lead. Something I can pinch between my fingers and pull, to unravel this *mess.*

Sometimes it doesn't matter how advanced the technology is. Bad camera angles are still bad camera angles.

CEPD tells me you found the body.

ⴰⴹ ⴼⴰⴹⴻ ⵇⵄⴳ ⵊⵒⵎ ⴷⵇⵇⴰ ⵔ

What?

ⴷⵊ ⵔ ⵆⴷⵊ ⵊⴷⵡⵔⵆⴻ ⵔ ⴼⵒⵇⵄⴳ ⵌⵇⵒⴳ--why you're asking me, *alien.* I told them I didn't see anything.

*Some City denizens speak obscure or regional dialects. Jo's translator needs a moment to catch up.

Can't tell if he had time to scream. No one heard it, regardless. In space...*ugh.* Yeah.

Gotta switch this up somehow. There's something I'm not getting, here.

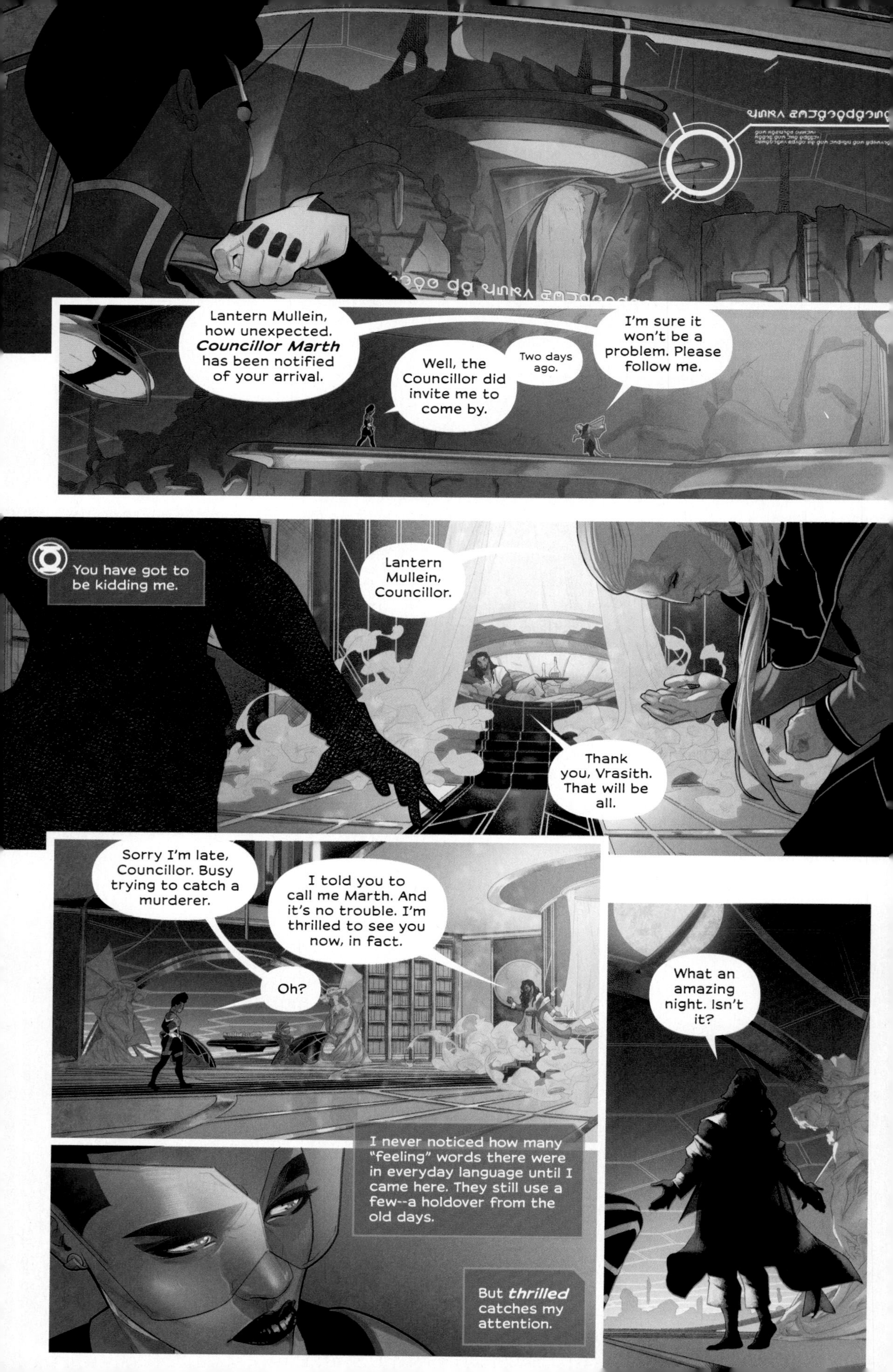
Lantern Mullein, how unexpected. **Councillor Marth** has been notified of your arrival.
Well, the Councillor did invite me to come by.
Two days ago.
I'm sure it won't be a problem. Please follow me.
You have got to be kidding me.
Lantern Mullein, Councillor.
Thank you, Vrasith. That will be all.
Sorry I'm late, Councillor. Busy trying to catch a murderer.
I told you to call me Marth. And it's no trouble. I'm thrilled to see you now, in fact.
Oh?
I never noticed how many "feeling" words there were in everyday language until I came here. They still use a few--a holdover from the old days.
But *thrilled* catches my attention.
What an amazing night. Isn't it?

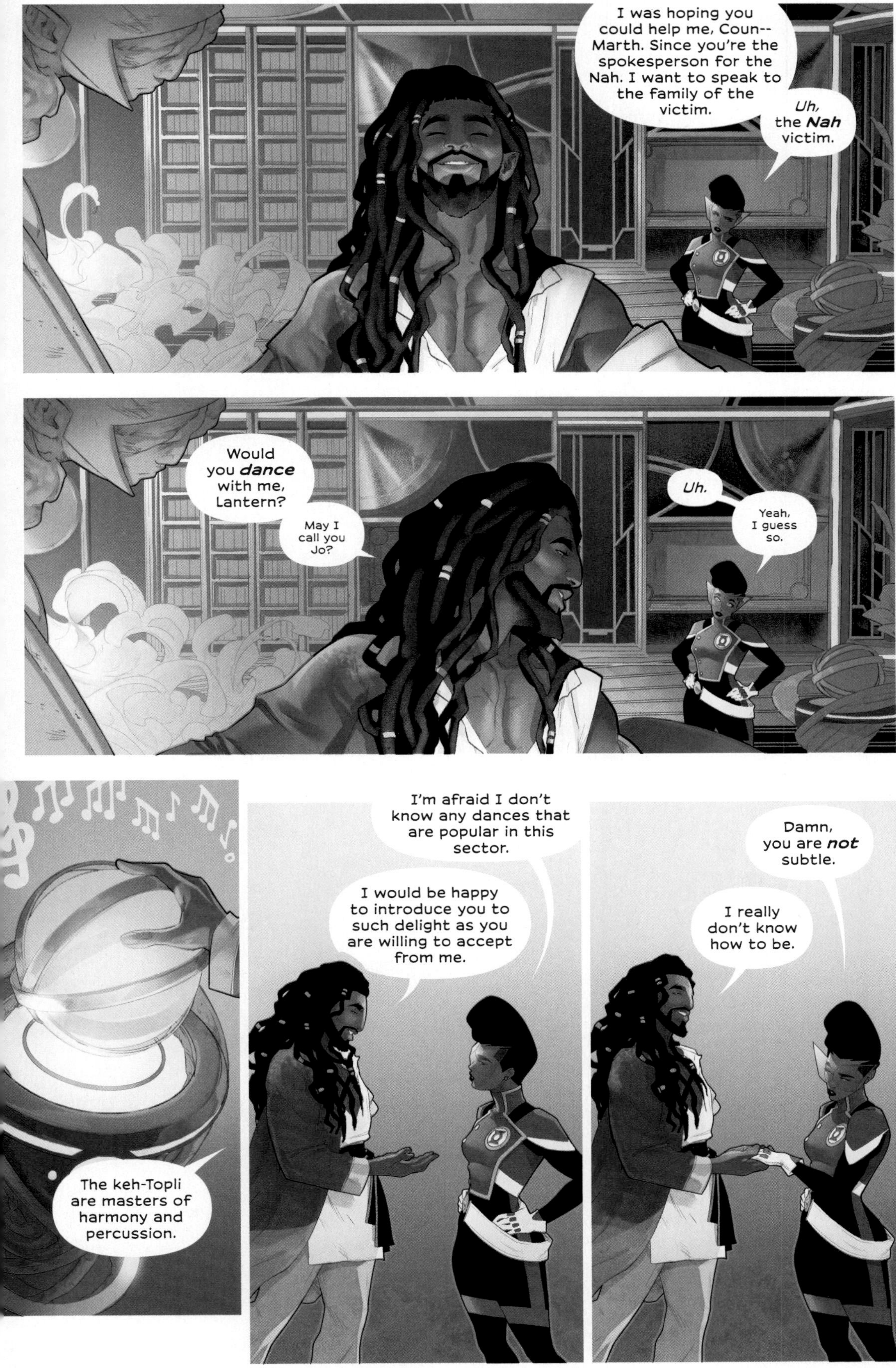
I was hoping you could help me, Coun-- Marth. Since you're the spokesperson for the Nah. I want to speak to the family of the victim.
Uh, the ***Nah*** *victim.*
Would you ***dance*** with me, Lantern?
May I call you Jo?
Uh.
Yeah, I guess so.
The keh-Topli are masters of harmony and percussion.
I'm afraid I don't know any dances that are popular in this sector.
I would be happy to introduce you to such delight as you are willing to accept from me.
Damn, you are ***not*** subtle.
I really don't know how to be.

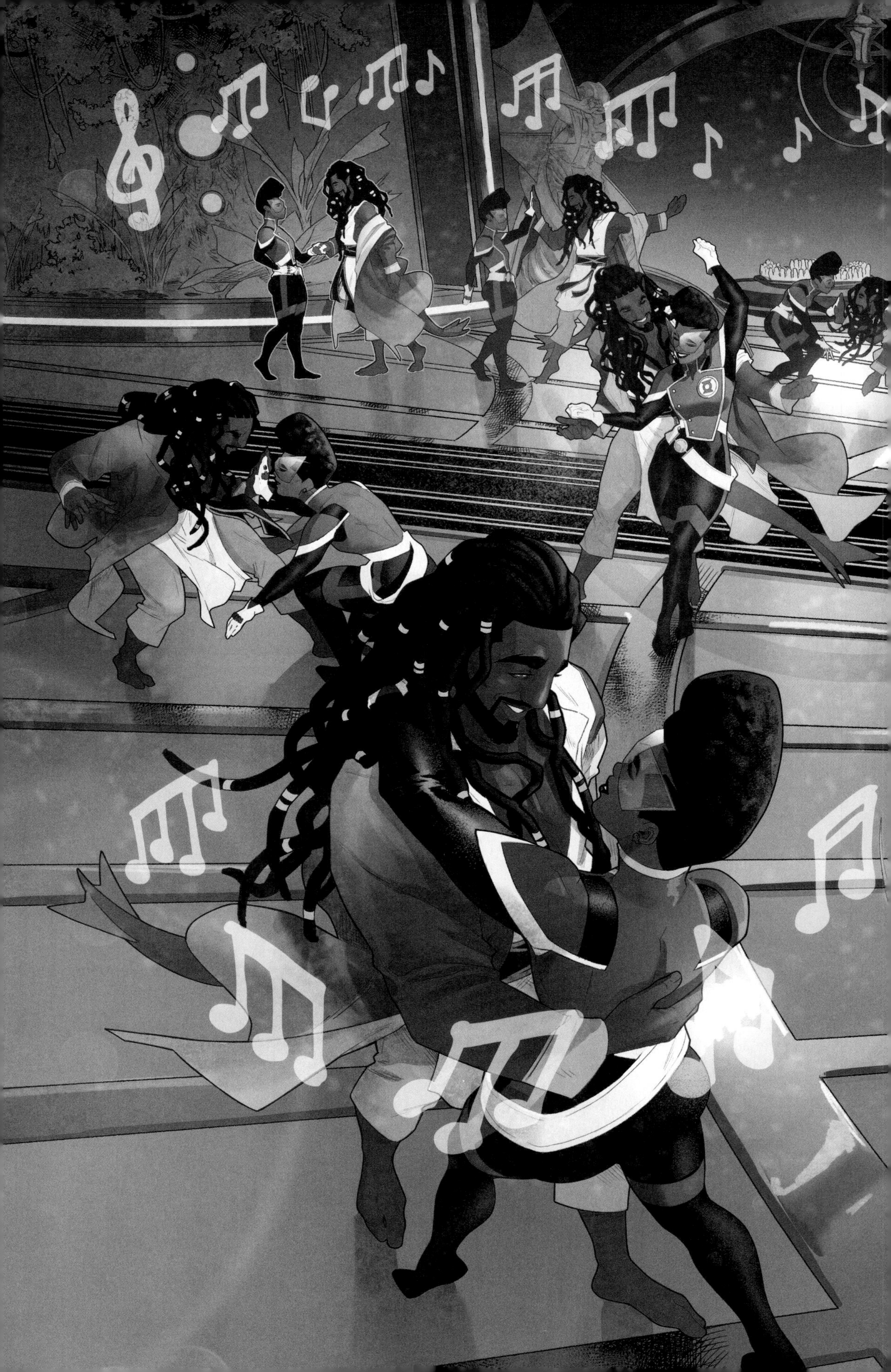

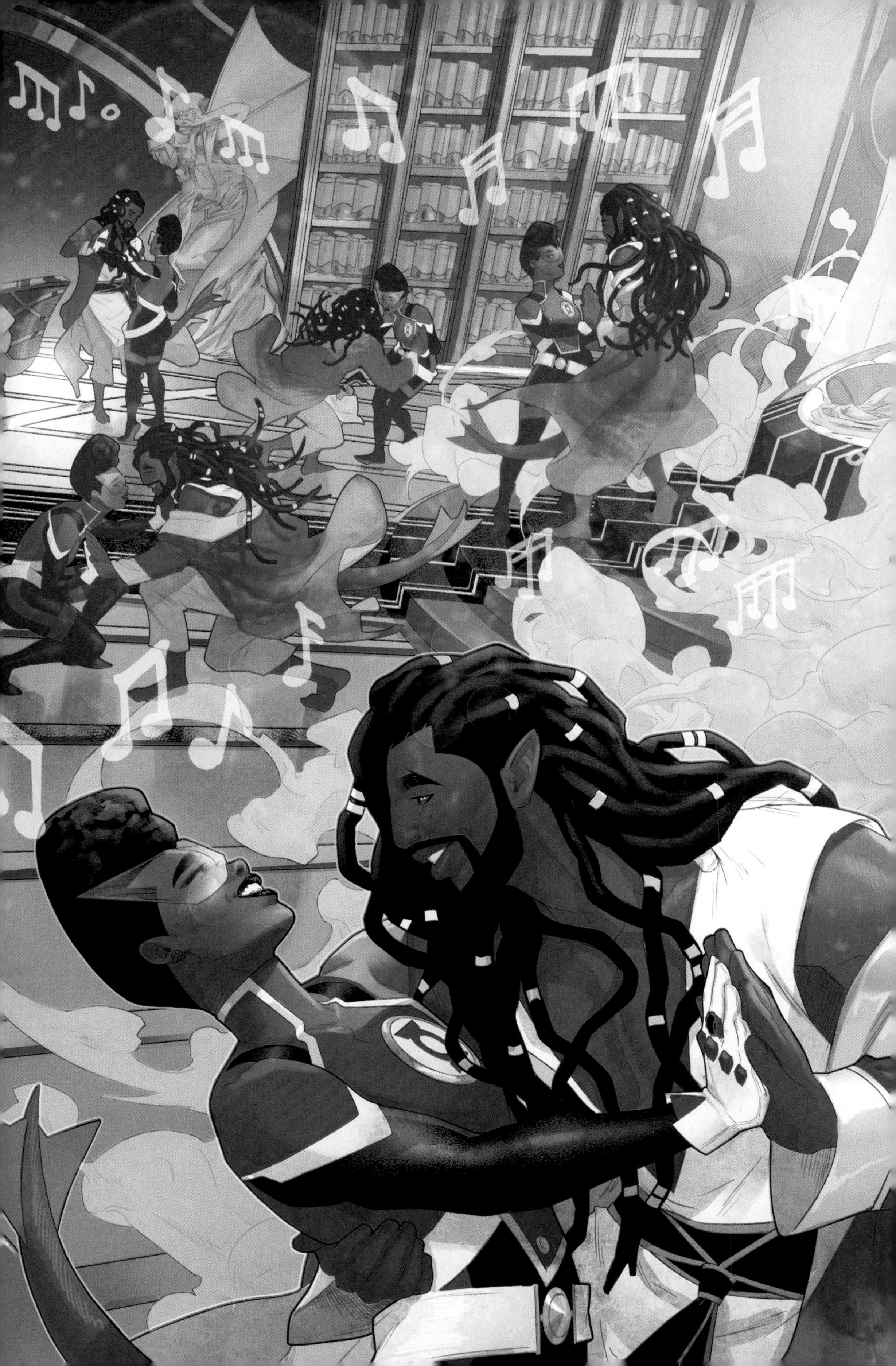

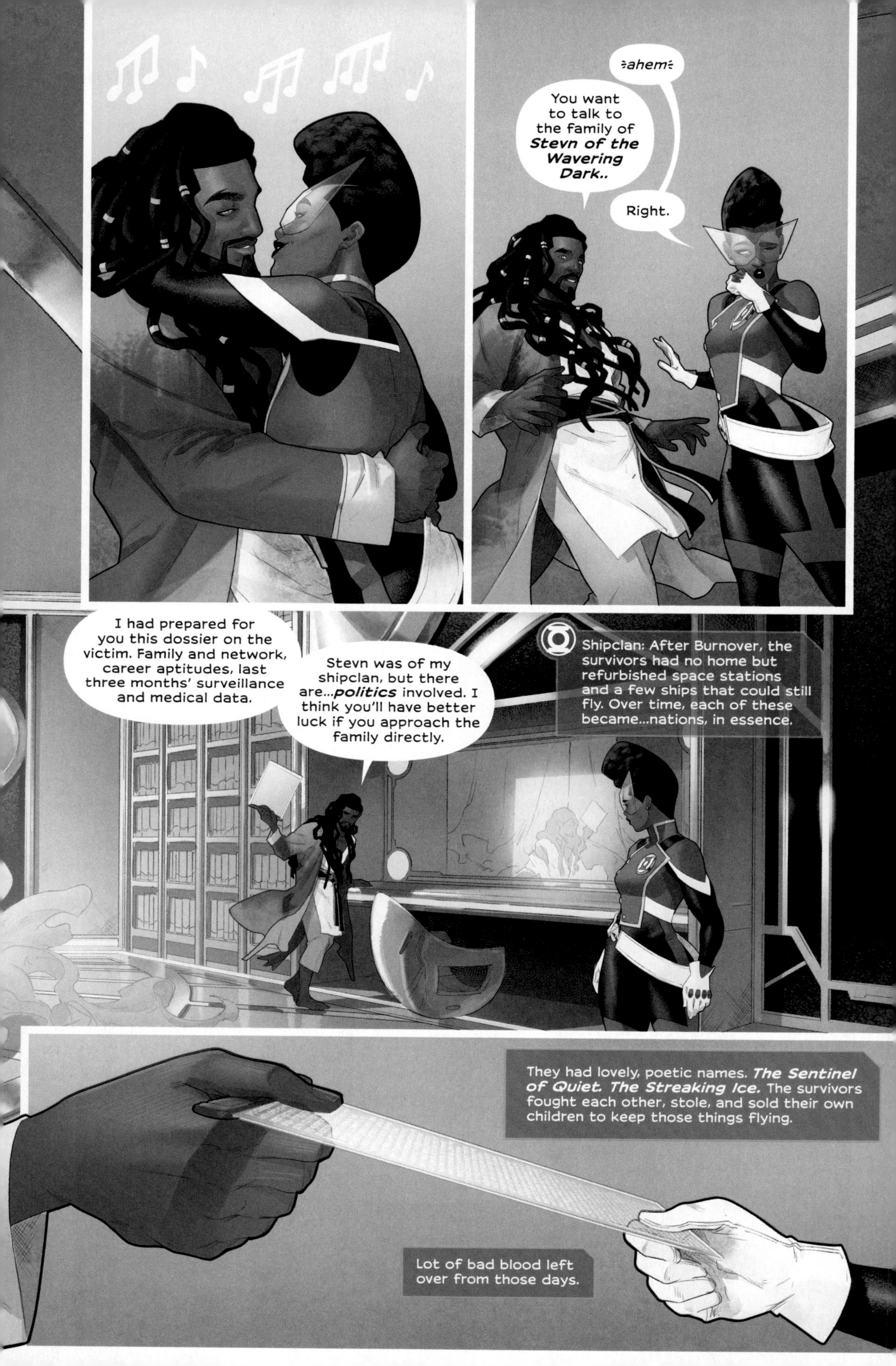

ahem
You want to talk to the family of Stevn of the Wavering Dark..
Right.
I had prepared for you this dossier on the victim. Family and network, career aptitudes, last three months' surveillance and medical data.
Stevn was of my shipclan, but there are...politics involved. I think you'll have better luck if you approach the family directly.
Shipclan: After Burnover, the survivors had no home but refurbished space stations and a few ships that could still fly. Over time, each of these became...nations, in essence.
They had lovely, poetic names. The Sentinel of Quiet. The Streaking Ice. The survivors fought each other, stole, and sold their own children to keep those things flying.
Lot of bad blood left over from those days.

Thanks. I'll reach out to them.

So, you seem... *different.*

Do I?

Perhaps the stress of being kept waiting so long has unhinged me.

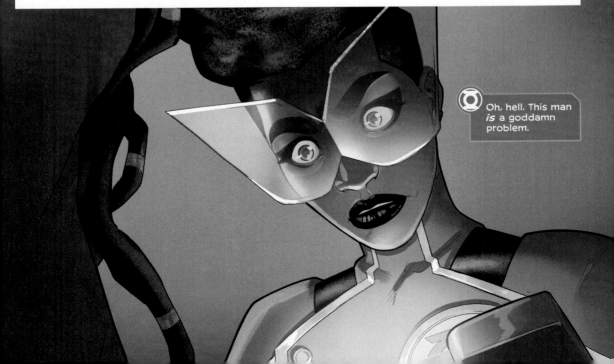

Oh, hell. This man *is* a goddamn problem.

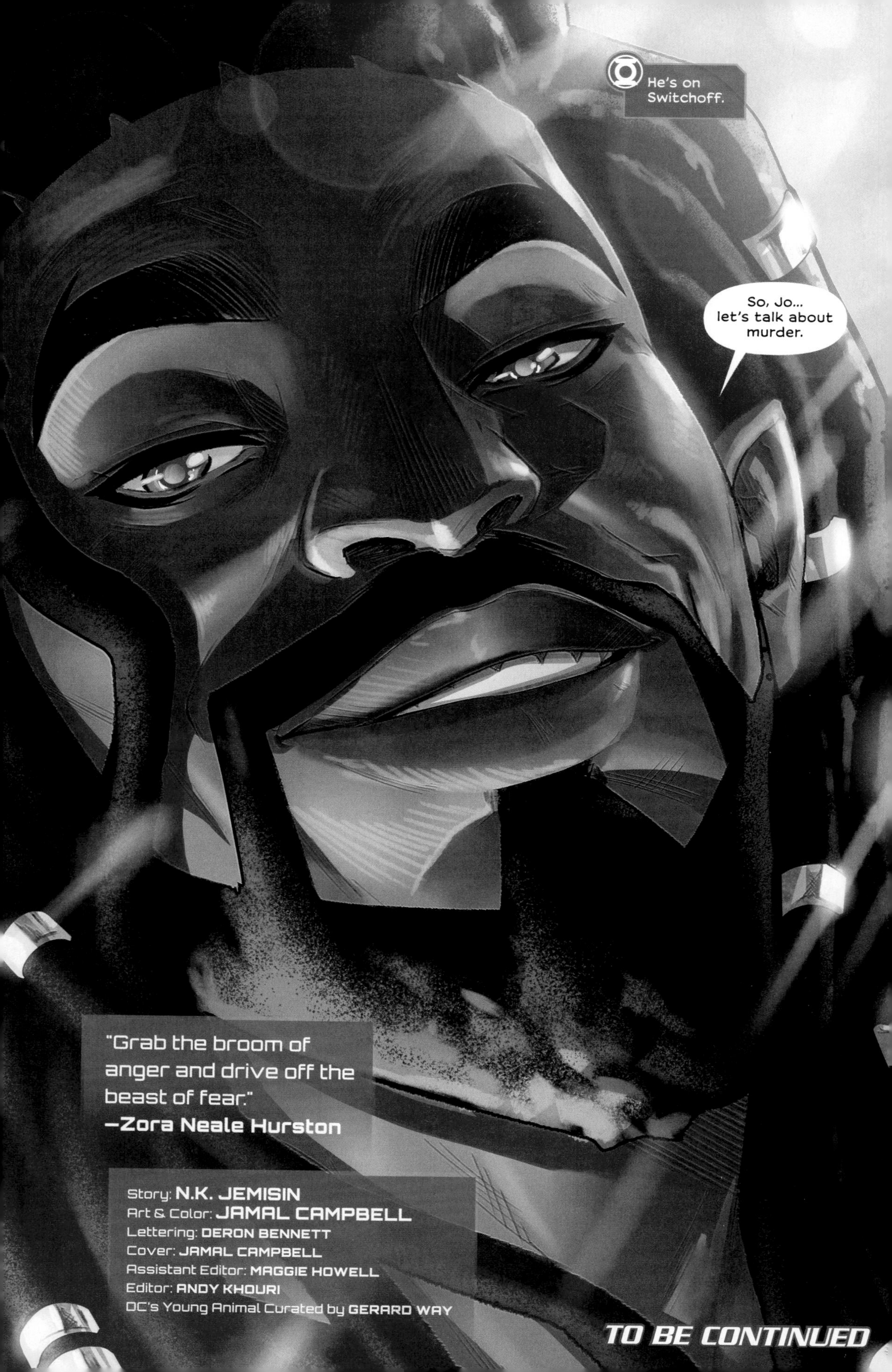
He's on Switchoff.
So, Jo... let's talk about murder.
"Grab the broom of anger and drive off the beast of fear."
—Zora Neale Hurston
Story: N.K. JEMISIN
Art & Color: JAMAL CAMPBELL
Lettering: DERON BENNETT
Cover: JAMAL CAMPBELL
Assistant Editor: MAGGIE HOWELL
Editor: ANDY KHOURI
DC's Young Animal Curated by GERARD WAY
TO BE CONTINUED

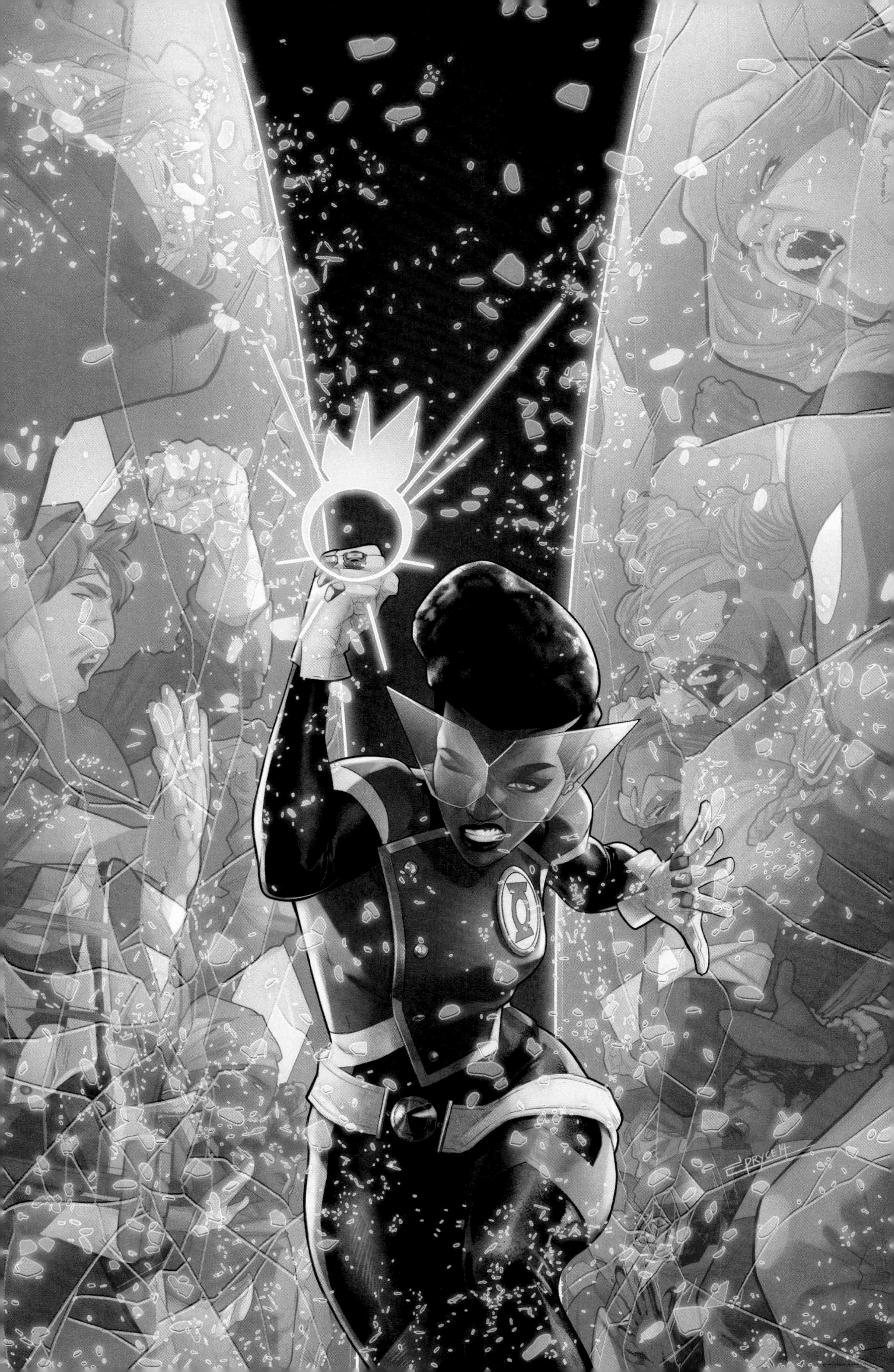
PRYCE14

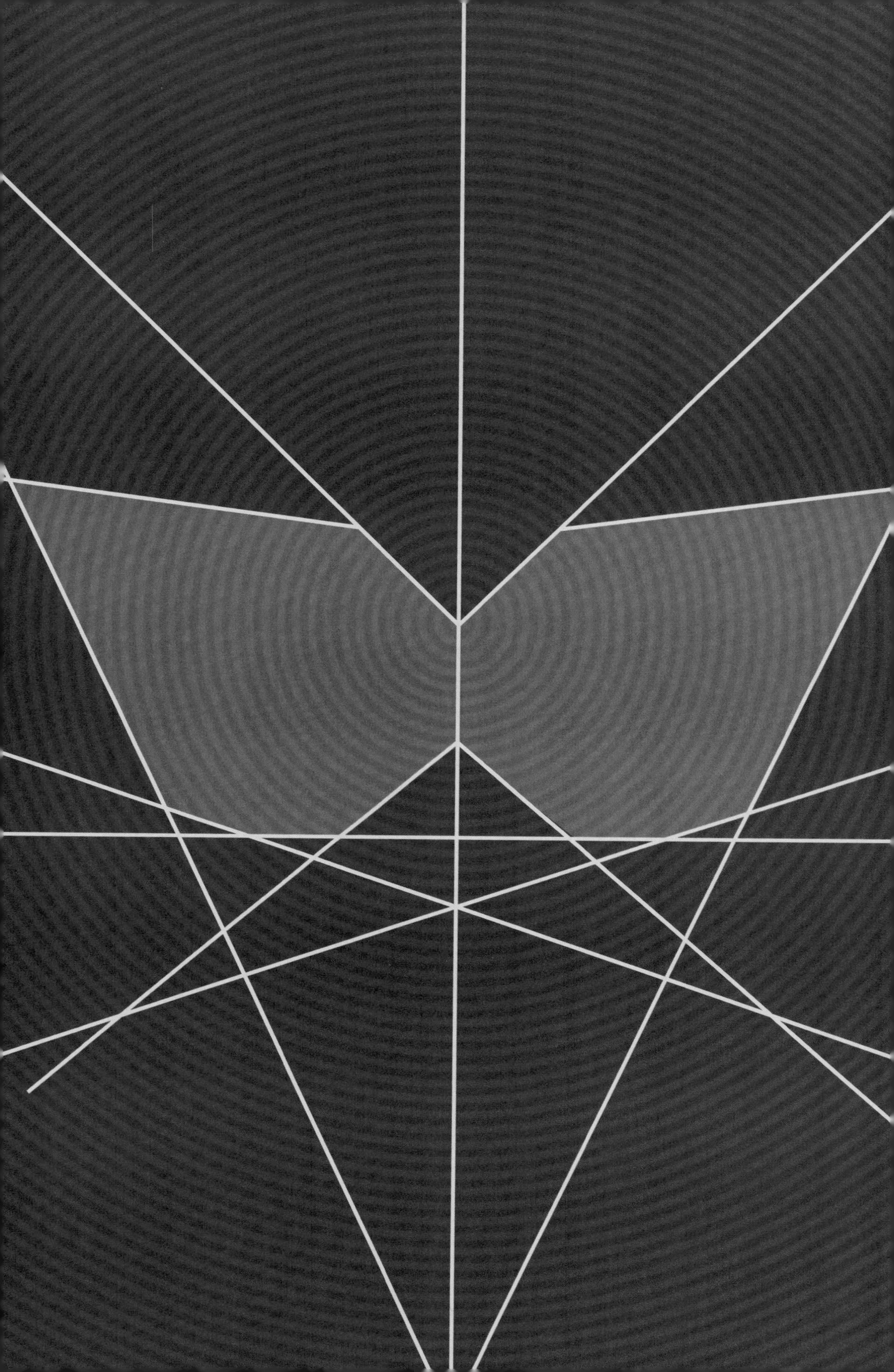

OAN INTELLIGENCE EXTRA-JURISDICTIONAL FILE ARCHIVE
THE CITY ENDURING: THREAT ASSESSMENT
TRANSLATION: ENGLISH
UPDATE: IN PROGRESS
STATUS: DIPLOMATIC RELATIONS ESTABLISHED WARNING: GREEN LANTERN PRESENCE PERMITTED BY REQUEST ONLY

THREE SPECIES IN MODIFIED POST-SCARCITY MICRODEMOCRACY. TERRITORY ENCOMPASSES HOME SYSTEM PLUS SEVERAL DOZEN ADJACENT SYSTEMS AND ROGUE PLANETS BEING ROBOTICALLY MINED. FTL-CAPABLE. RECENT HISTORY CHARACTERIZED BY RAPID PROGRESS TOWARD COMPLETE CONTROL OVER TIME, SPACE, MATTER, AND REALITY.

RECENT HISTORY ALSO CHARACTERIZED BY EXTREME AGGRESSION IN RESPONSE TO PRESUMED OR ANTICIPATED PROVOCATIONS. (SEE ALSO: GENOCIDES, BURNOVER.) SOCIOLOGICALLY UNSTABLE. SIGNIFICANT CAUTION RECOMMENDED DURING INTERACTIONS WITH LOCAL POPULATION.

Story: **N.K. JEMISIN** Art & Color: **JAMAL CAMPBELL**
Lettering: **DERON BENNETT** Cover: **JAMAL CAMPBELL**
Assistant Editor: **MAGGIE HOWELL** Editor: **ANDY KHOURI**
DC's Young Animal Curated by **GERARD WAY**

"Not everything that is faced can be changed, but nothing can be changed until it is faced."
—**James Baldwin**

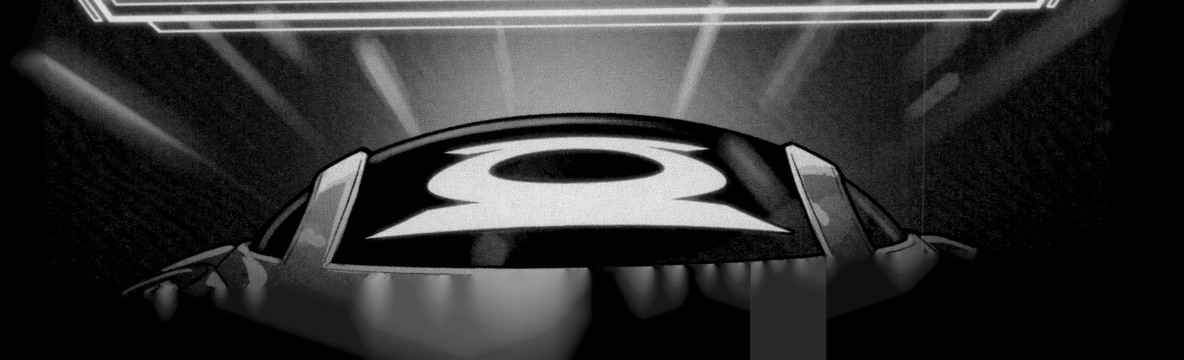

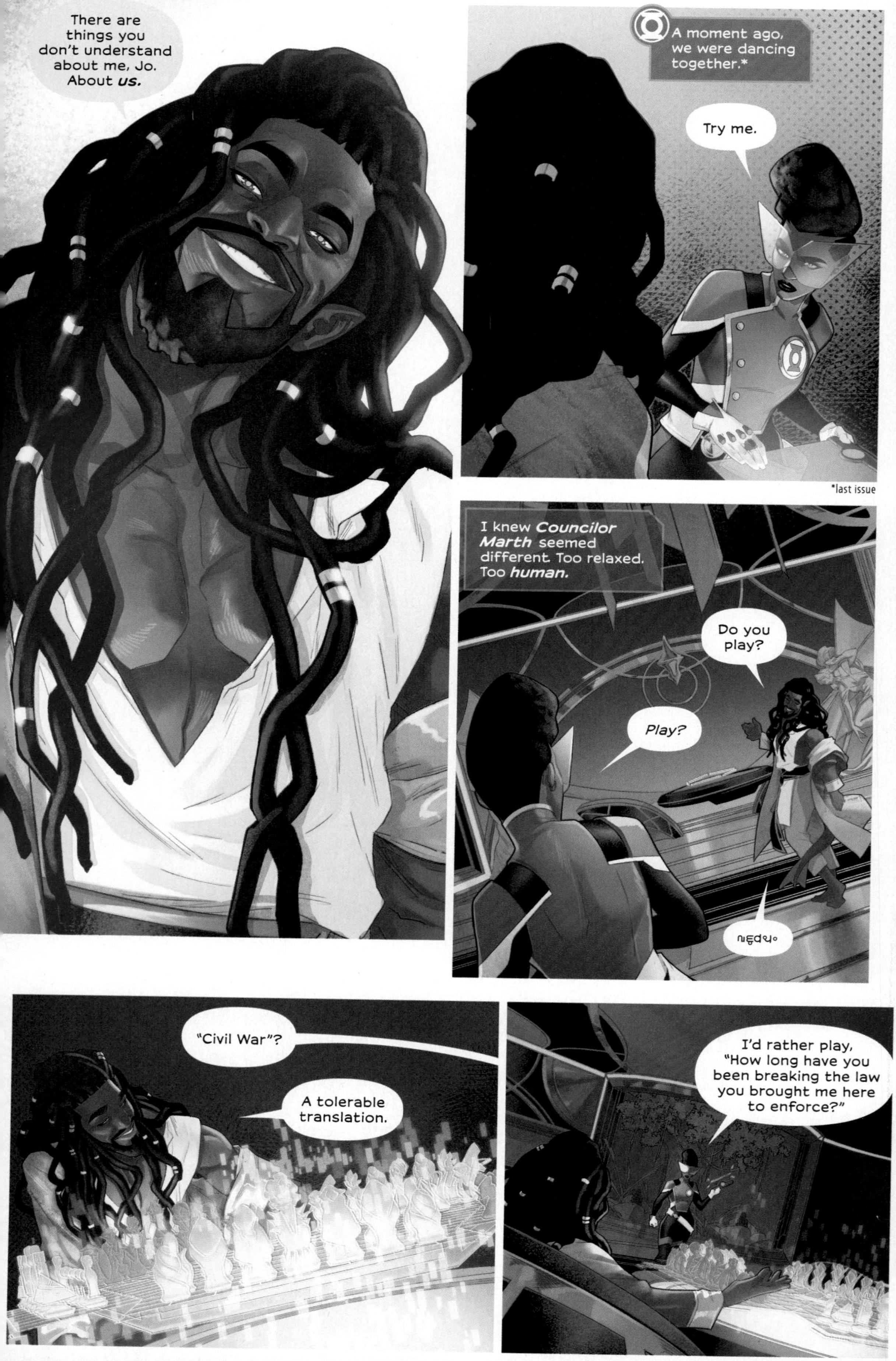
There are things you don't understand about me, Jo. About *us.*
A moment ago, we were dancing together.*
Try me.
*last issue
I knew *Councilor Marth* seemed different. Too relaxed. Too *human.*
Do you play?
Play?
"Civil War"?
A tolerable translation.
I'd rather play, "How long have you been breaking the law you brought me here to enforce?"

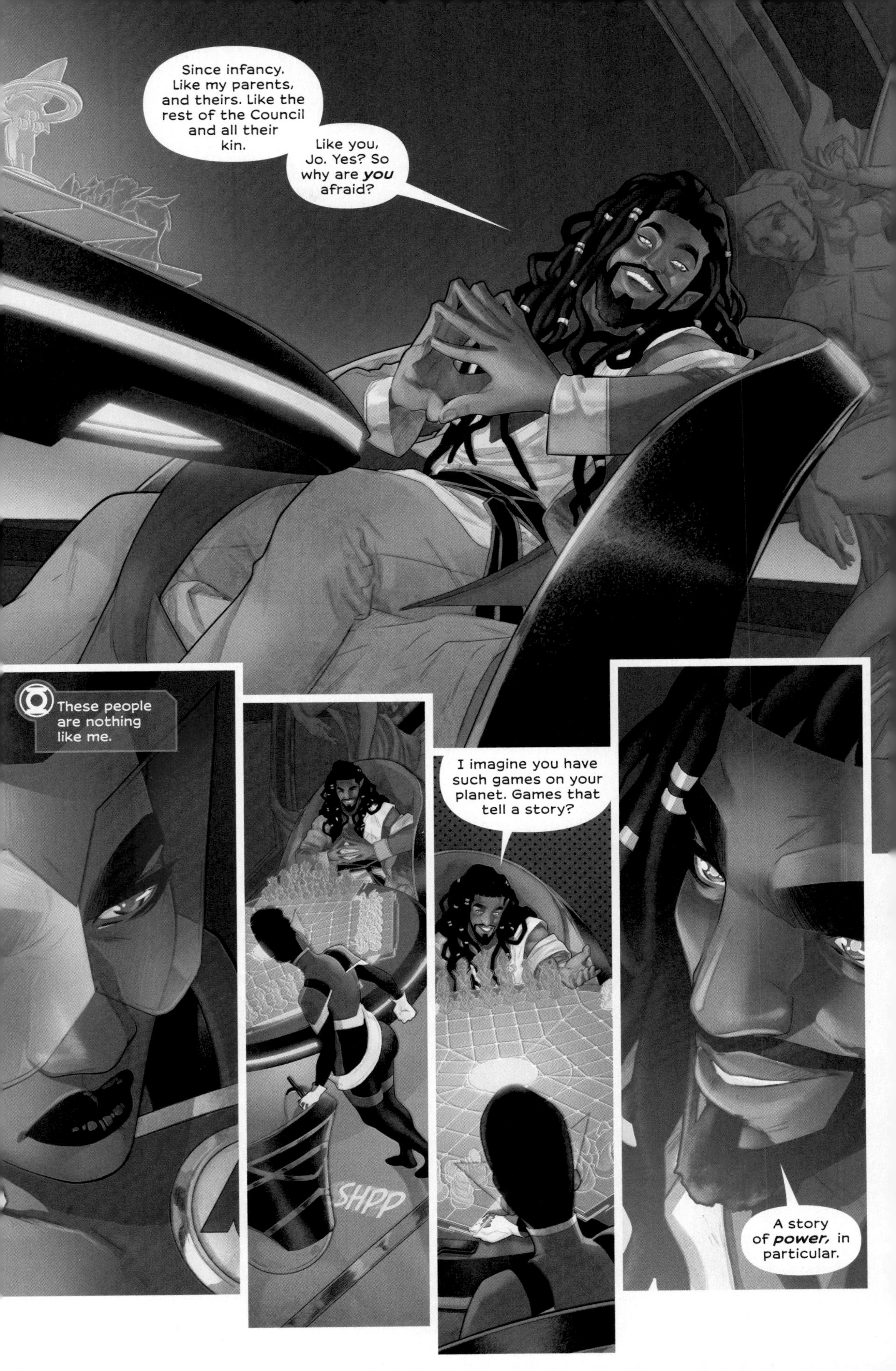
Since infancy. Like my parents, and theirs. Like the rest of the Council and all their kin.
Like you, Jo. Yes? So why are *you* afraid?
These people are nothing like me.
SHPP
I imagine you have such games on your planet. Games that tell a story?
A story of *power,* in particular.

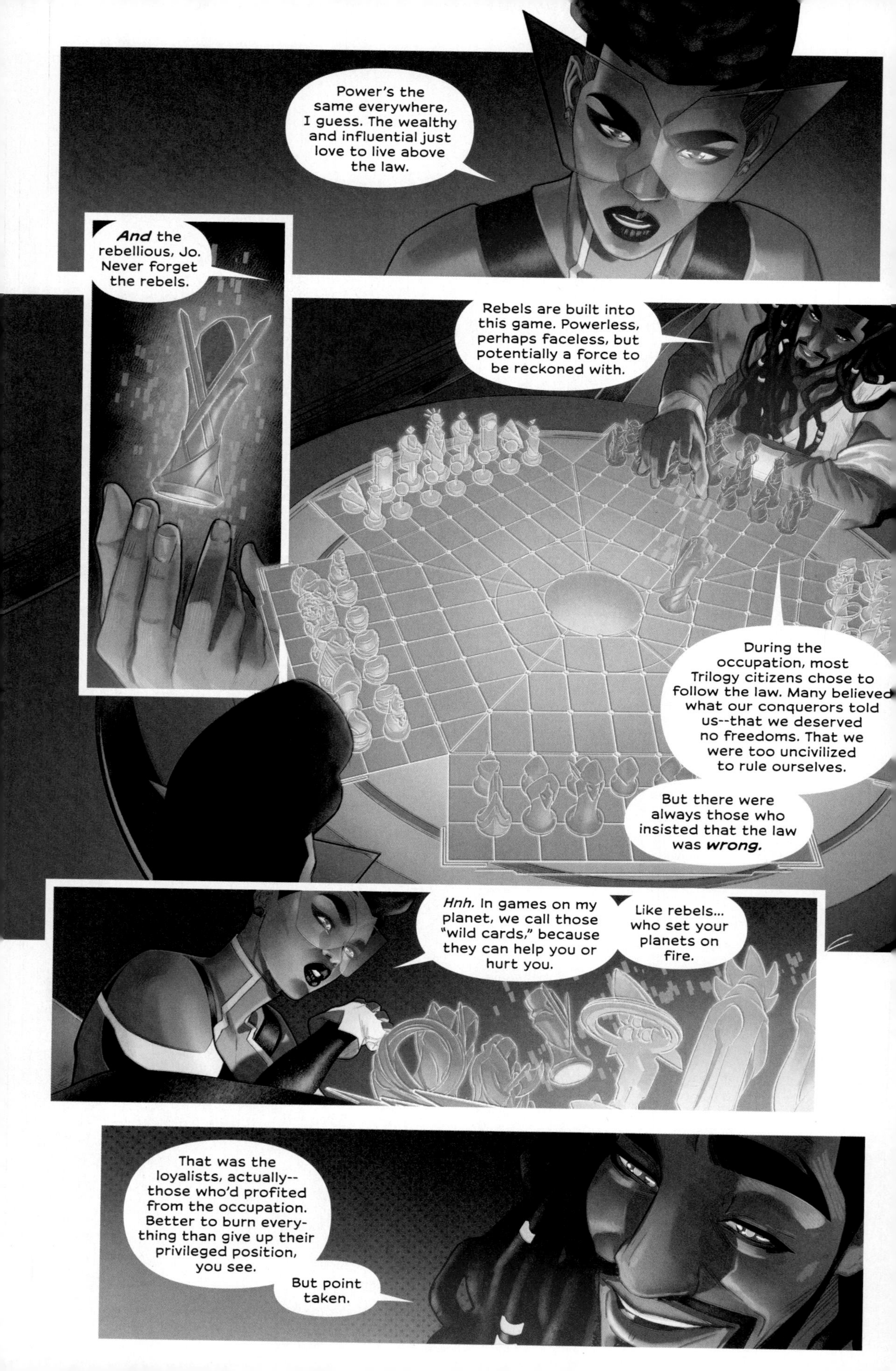
Power's the same everywhere, I guess. The wealthy and influential just love to live above the law.
And the rebellious, Jo. Never forget the rebels.
Rebels are built into this game. Powerless, perhaps faceless, but potentially a force to be reckoned with.
During the occupation, most Trilogy citizens chose to follow the law. Many believed what our conquerors told us--that we deserved no freedoms. That we were too uncivilized to rule ourselves.
But there were always those who insisted that the law was ***wrong.***
Hnh. In games on my planet, we call those "wild cards," because they can help you or hurt you.
Like rebels... who set your planets on fire.
That was the loyalists, actually--those who'd profited from the occupation. Better to burn everything than give up their privileged position, you see.
But point taken.

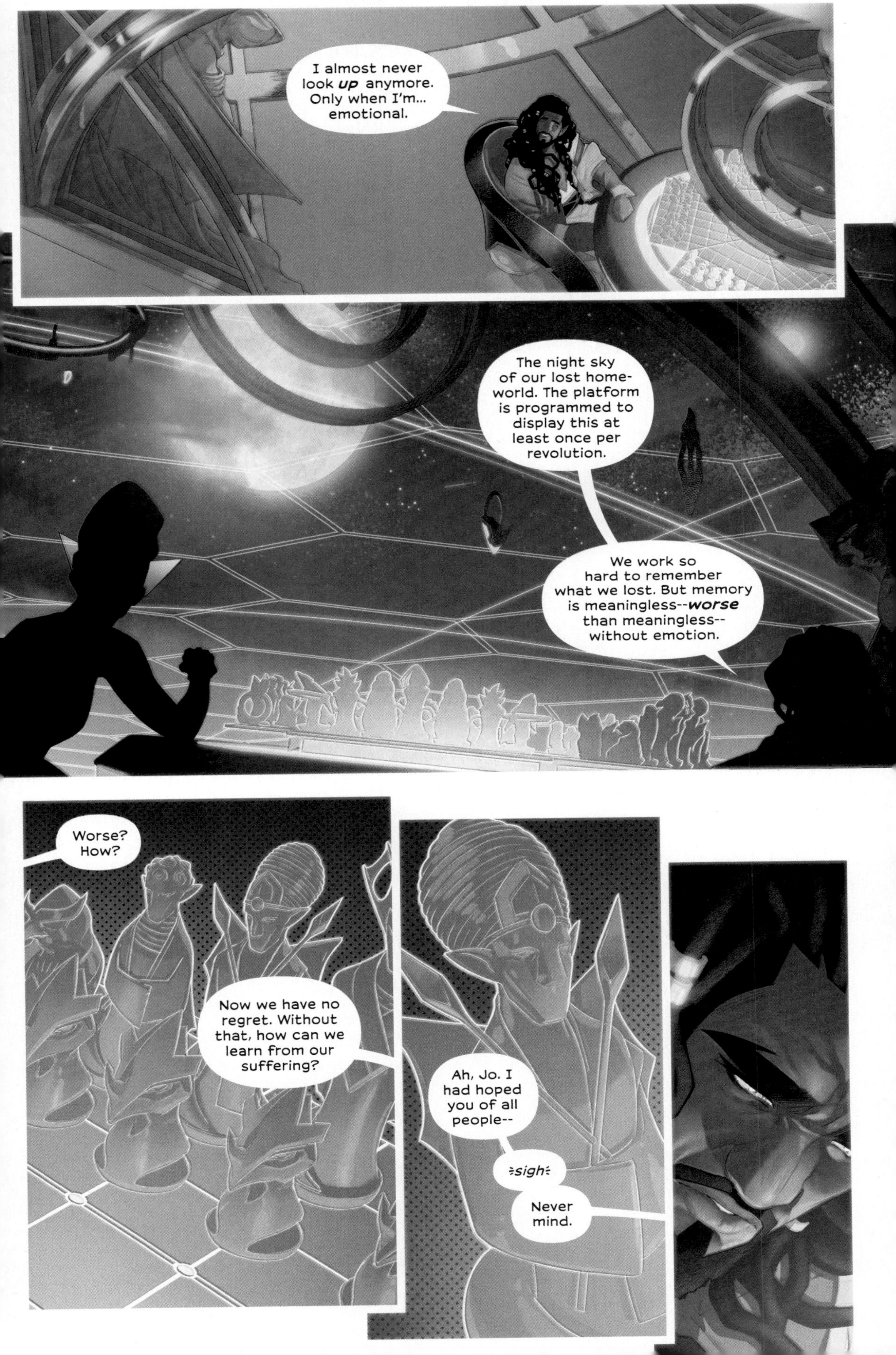
I almost never look *up* anymore. Only when I'm... emotional.
The night sky of our lost home-world. The platform is programmed to display this at least once per revolution.
We work so hard to remember what we lost. But memory is meaningless--*worse* than meaningless--without emotion.
Worse? How?
Now we have no regret. Without that, how can we learn from our suffering?
Ah, Jo. I had hoped you of all people--
sigh
Never mind.

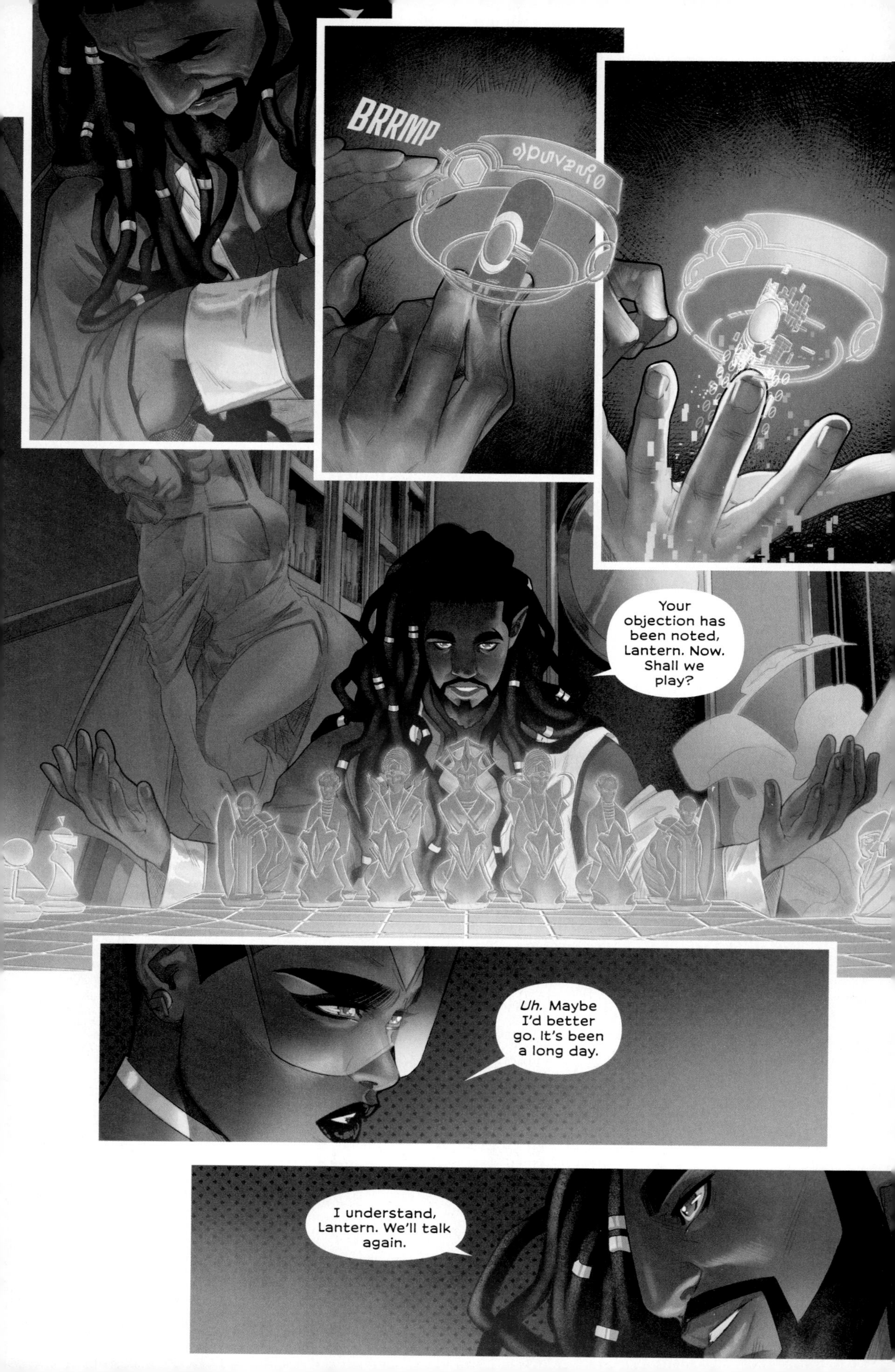
BRRMP
Your objection has been noted, Lantern. Now. Shall we play?
Uh. Maybe I'd better go. It's been a long day.
I understand, Lantern. We'll talk again.

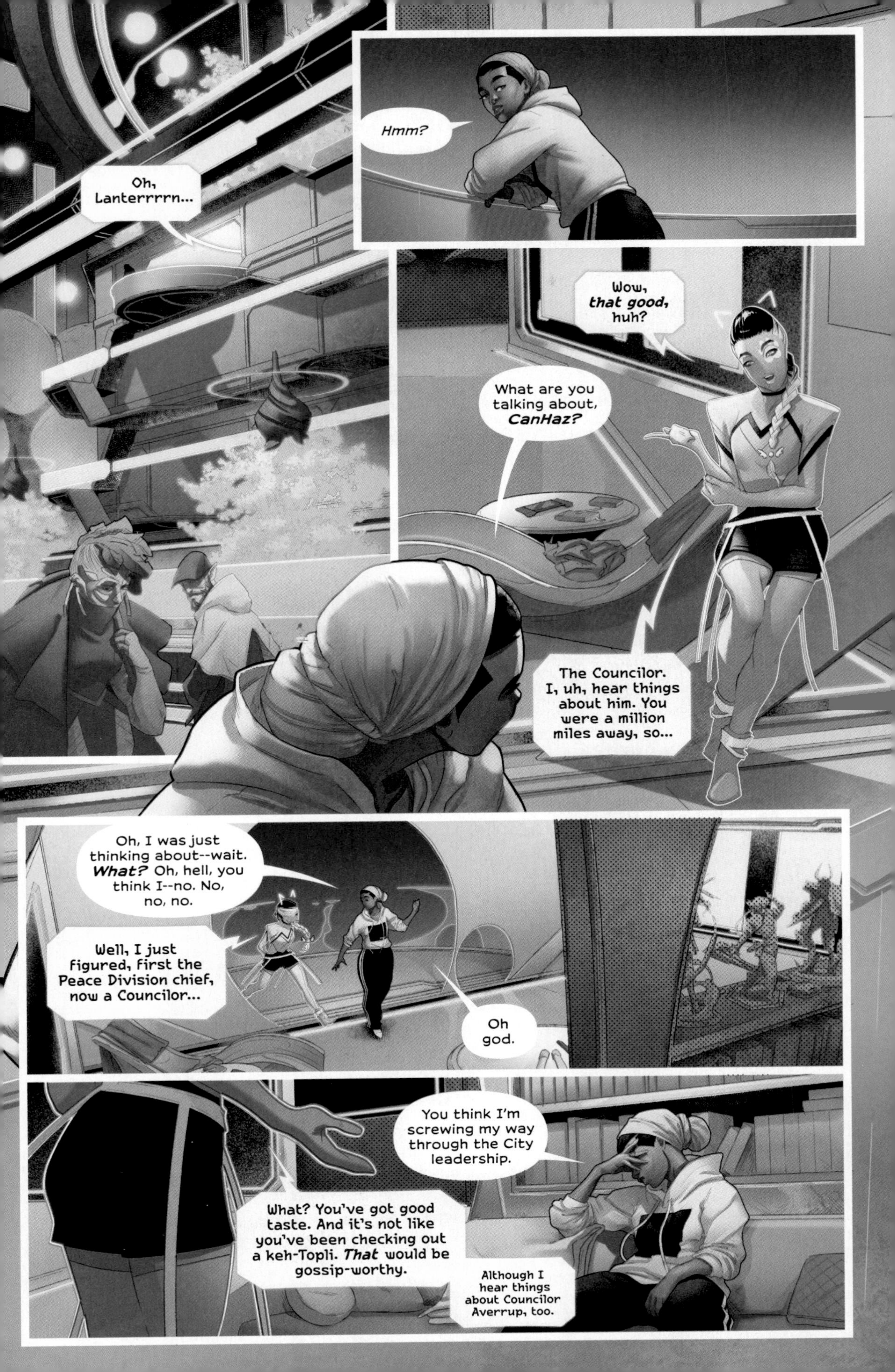
Oh, Lanterrrrn...
Hmm?
Wow, *that good,* huh?
What are you talking about, *CanHaz?*
The Councilor. I, uh, hear things about him. You were a million miles away, so...
Oh, I was just thinking about--wait. *What?* Oh, hell, you think I--no. No, no, no.
Well, I just figured, first the Peace Division chief, now a Councilor...
Oh god.
You think I'm screwing my way through the City leadership.
What? You've got good taste. And it's not like you've been checking out a keh-Topli. *That* would be gossip-worthy.
Although I hear things about Councilor Averrup, too.

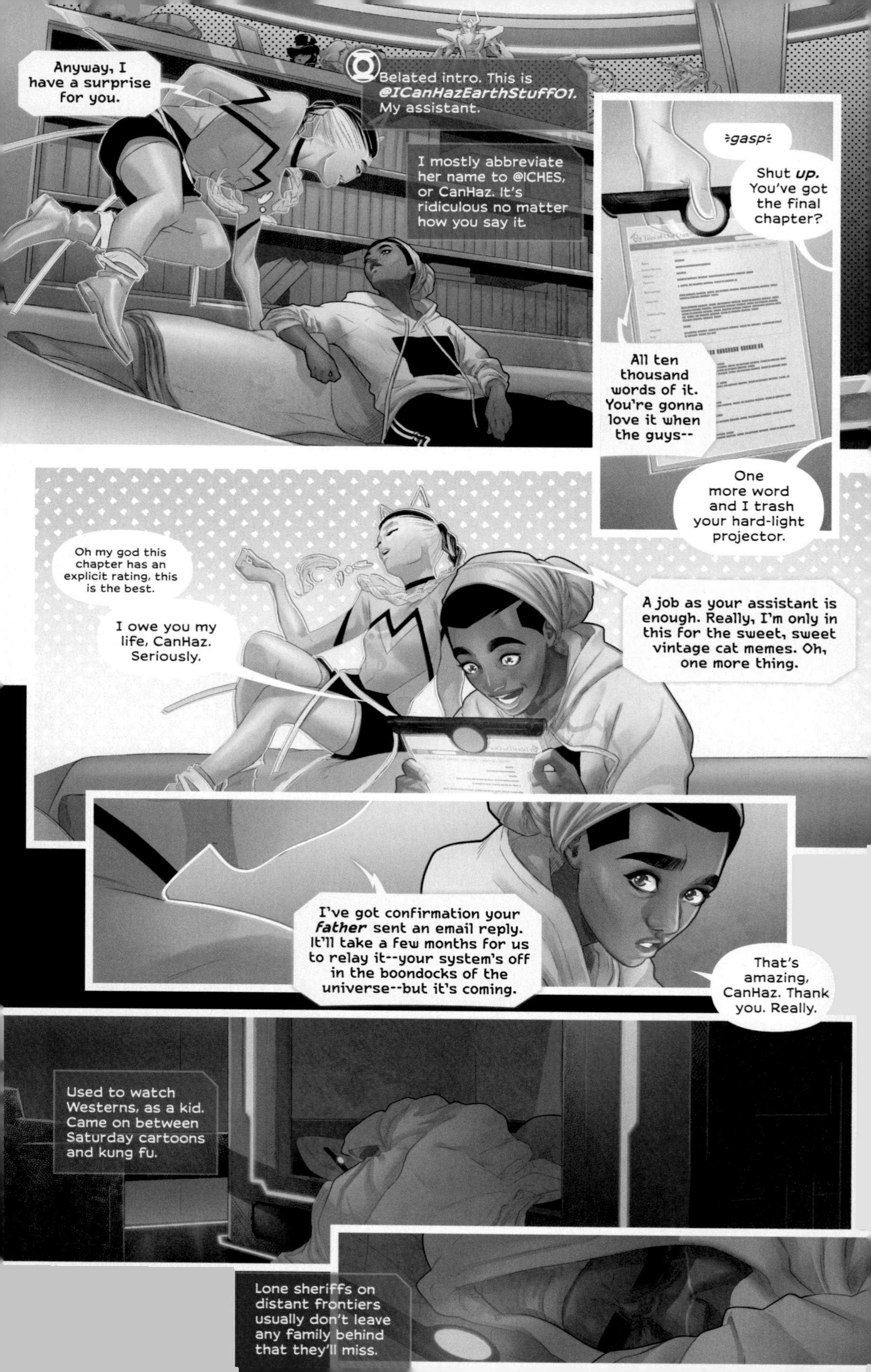
Anyway, I have a surprise for you.
Belated intro. This is @ICanHazEarthStuff01. My assistant.
I mostly abbreviate her name to @ICHES, or CanHaz. It's ridiculous no matter how you say it.
gasp
Shut up. You've got the final chapter?
All ten thousand words of it. You're gonna love it when the guys--
One more word and I trash your hard-light projector.
Oh my god this chapter has an explicit rating, this is the best.
I owe you my life, CanHaz. Seriously.
A job as your assistant is enough. Really, I'm only in this for the sweet, sweet vintage cat memes. Oh, one more thing.
I've got confirmation your father sent an email reply. It'll take a few months for us to relay it--your system's off in the boondocks of the universe--but it's coming.
That's amazing, CanHaz. Thank you. Really.
Used to watch Westerns, as a kid. Came on between Saturday cartoons and kung fu.
Lone sheriffs on distant frontiers usually don't leave any family behind that they'll miss.

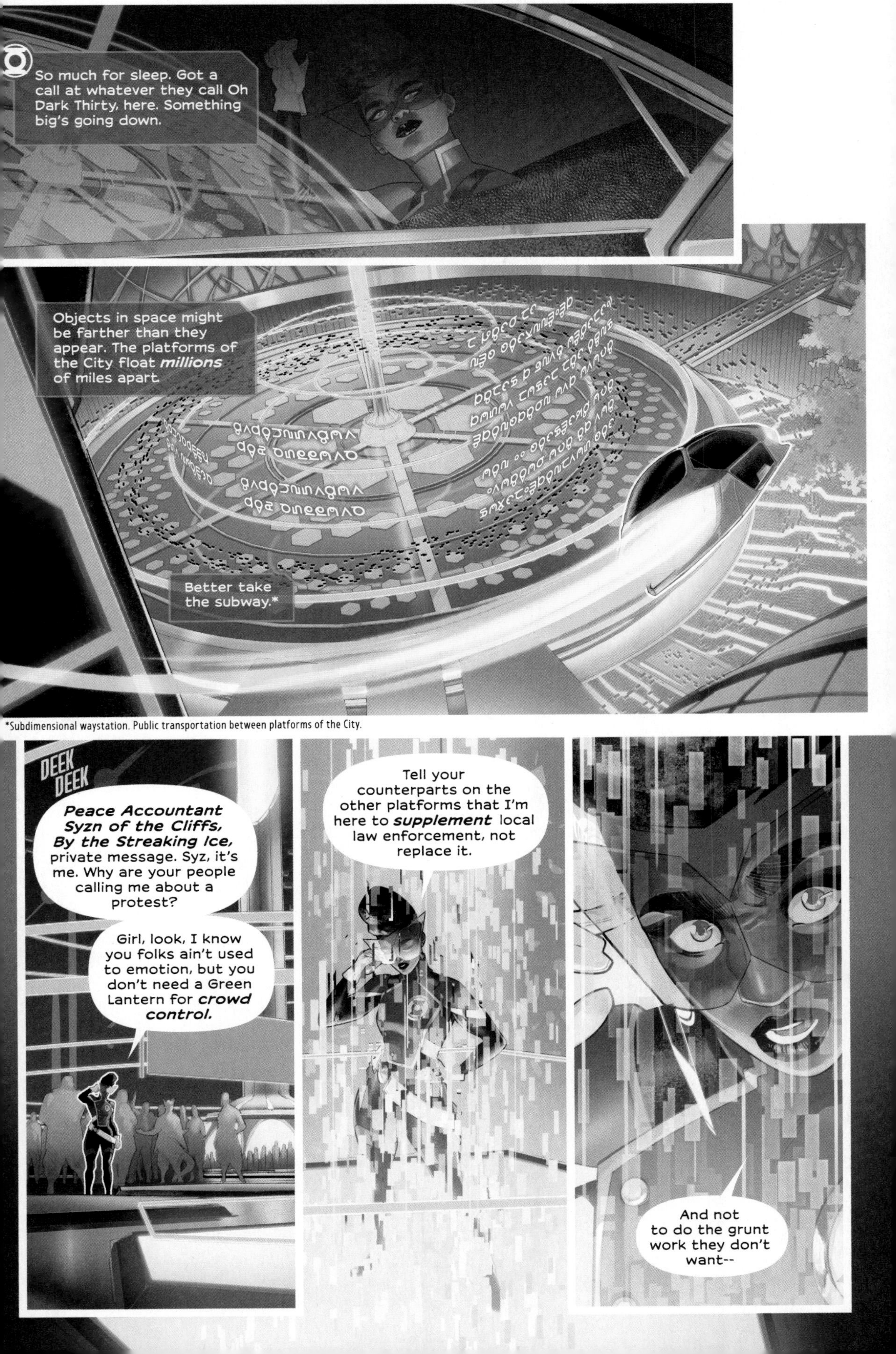

So much for sleep. Got a call at whatever they call Oh Dark Thirty, here. Something big's going down.
Objects in space might be farther than they appear. The platforms of the City float *millions* of miles apart.
Better take the subway.*
DEEK DEEK
Peace Accountant Syzn of the Cliffs, By the Streaking Ice, private message. Syz, it's me. Why are your people calling me about a protest?
Girl, look, I know you folks ain't used to emotion, but you don't need a Green Lantern for ***crowd control.***
Tell your counterparts on the other platforms that I'm here to ***supplement*** local law enforcement, not replace it.
And not to do the grunt work they don't want--

*Subdimensional waystation. Public transportation between platforms of the City.

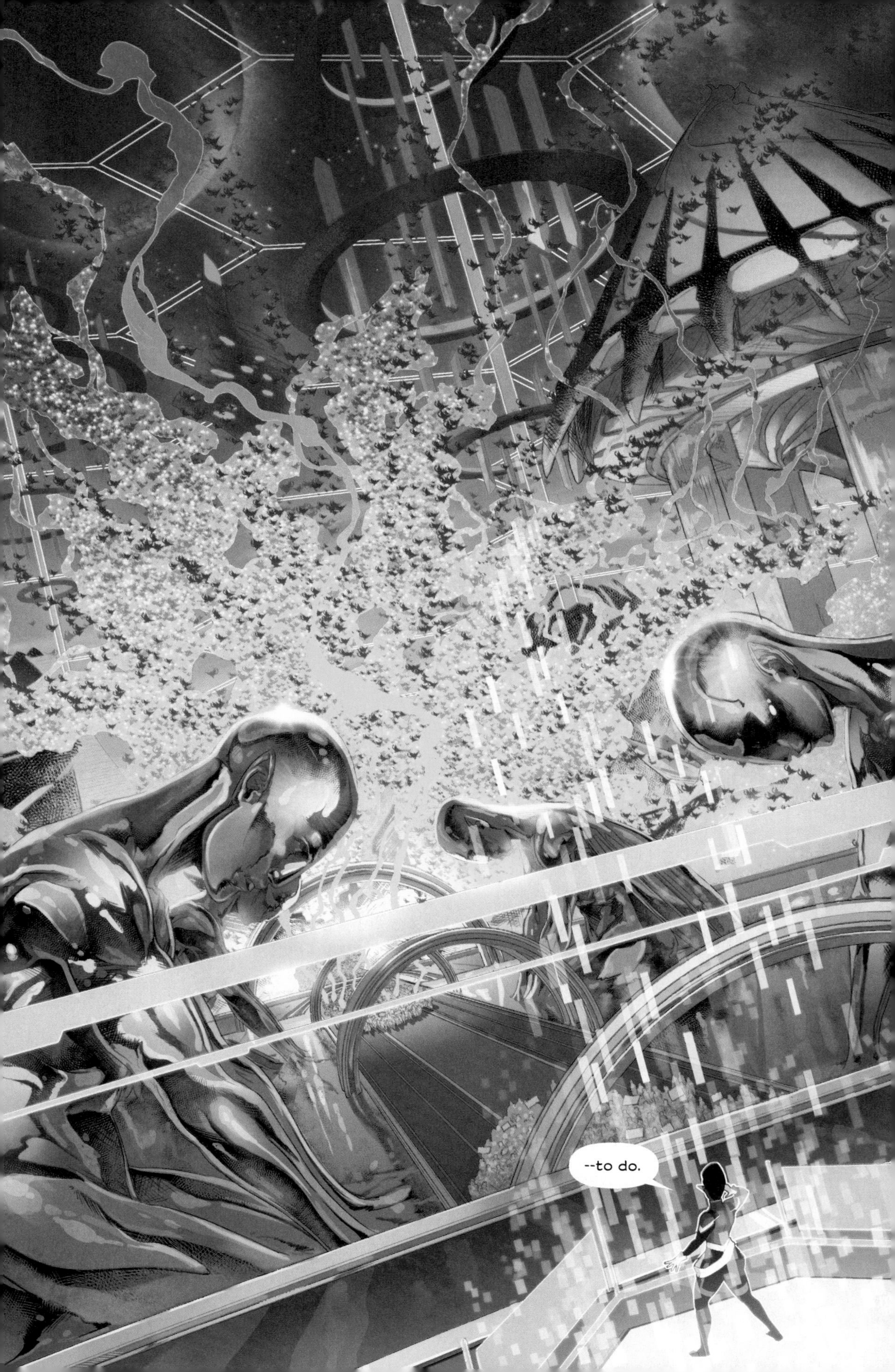
--to do.

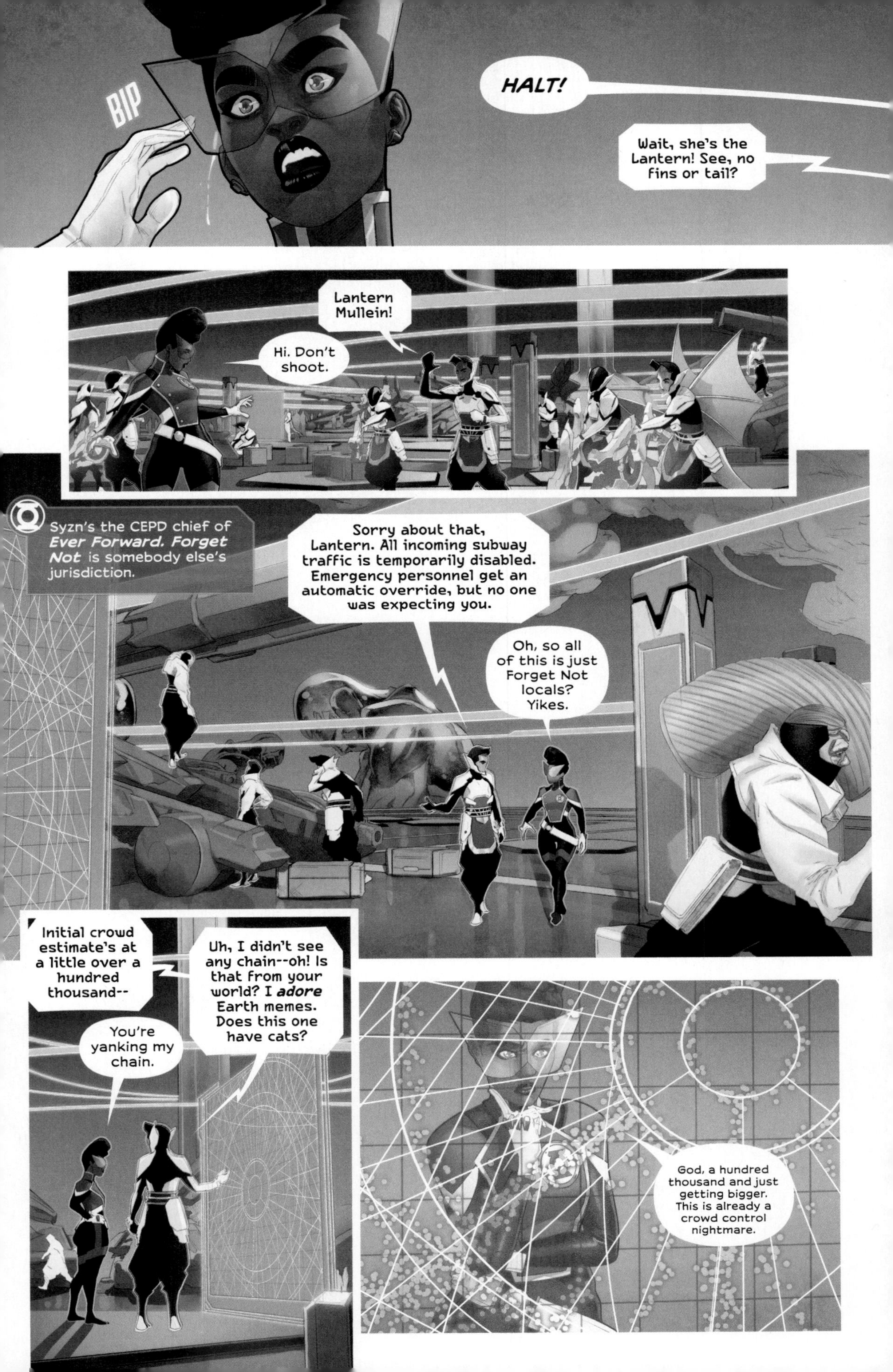
BIP
HALT!
Wait, she's the Lantern! See, no fins or tail?
Lantern Mullein!
Hi. Don't shoot.
Syzn's the CEPD chief of *Ever Forward. Forget Not* is somebody else's jurisdiction.
Sorry about that, Lantern. All incoming subway traffic is temporarily disabled. Emergency personnel get an automatic override, but no one was expecting you.
Oh, so all of this is just Forget Not locals? Yikes.
Initial crowd estimate's at a little over a hundred thousand--
You're yanking my chain.
Uh, I didn't see any chain--oh! Is that from your world? I *adore* Earth memes. Does this one have cats?
God, a hundred thousand and just getting bigger. This is already a crowd control nightmare.

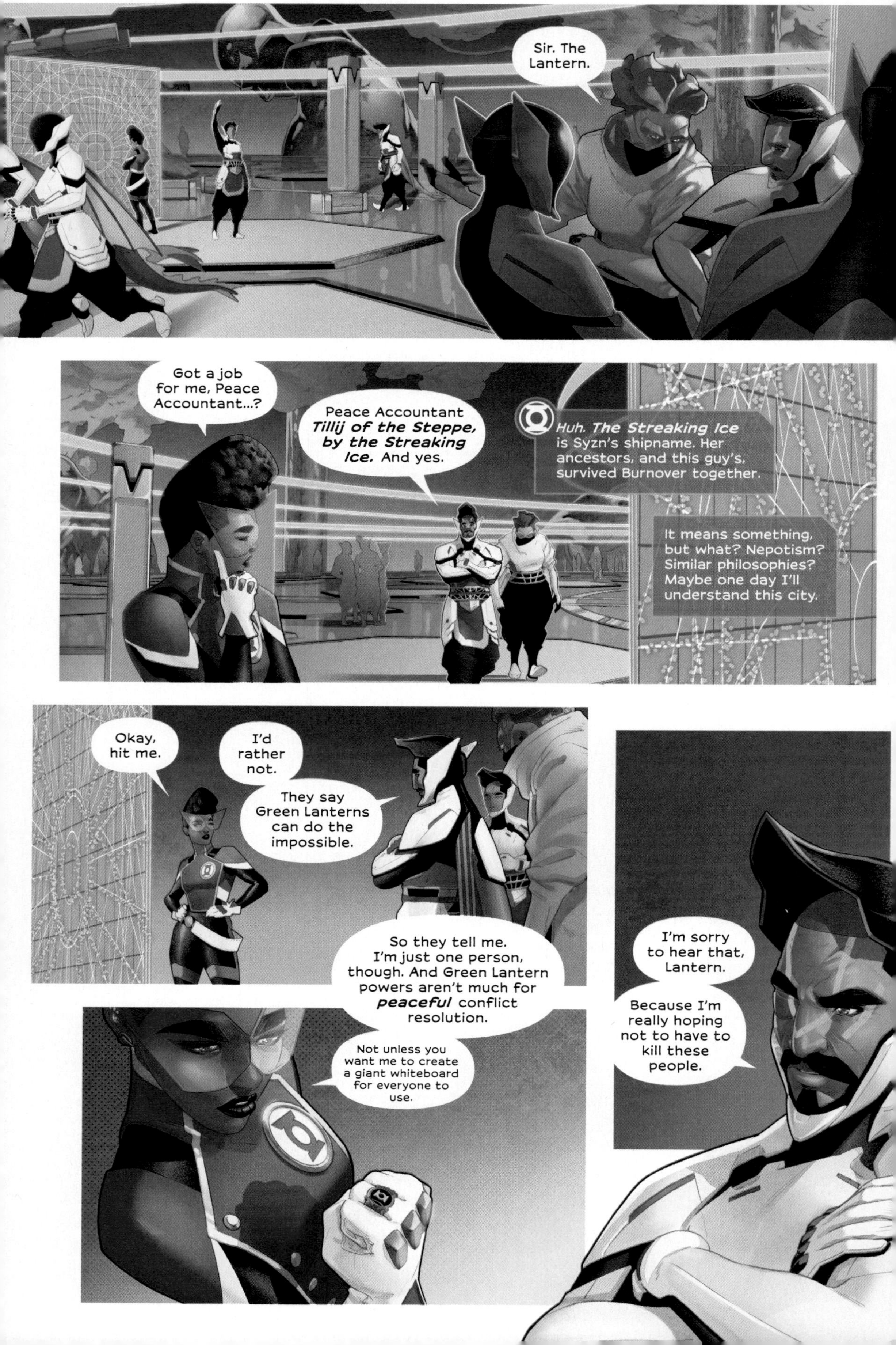
Sir. The Lantern.
Got a job for me, Peace Accountant...?
Peace Accountant *Tillij of the Steppe, by the Streaking Ice.* And yes.
Huh. The Streaking Ice is Syzn's shipname. Her ancestors, and this guy's, survived Burnover together.
It means something, but what? Nepotism? Similar philosophies? Maybe one day I'll understand this city.
Okay, hit me.
I'd rather not.
They say Green Lanterns can do the impossible.
So they tell me. I'm just one person, though. And Green Lantern powers aren't much for *peaceful* conflict resolution.
Not unless you want me to create a giant whiteboard for everyone to use.
I'm sorry to hear that, Lantern.
Because I'm really hoping not to have to kill these people.

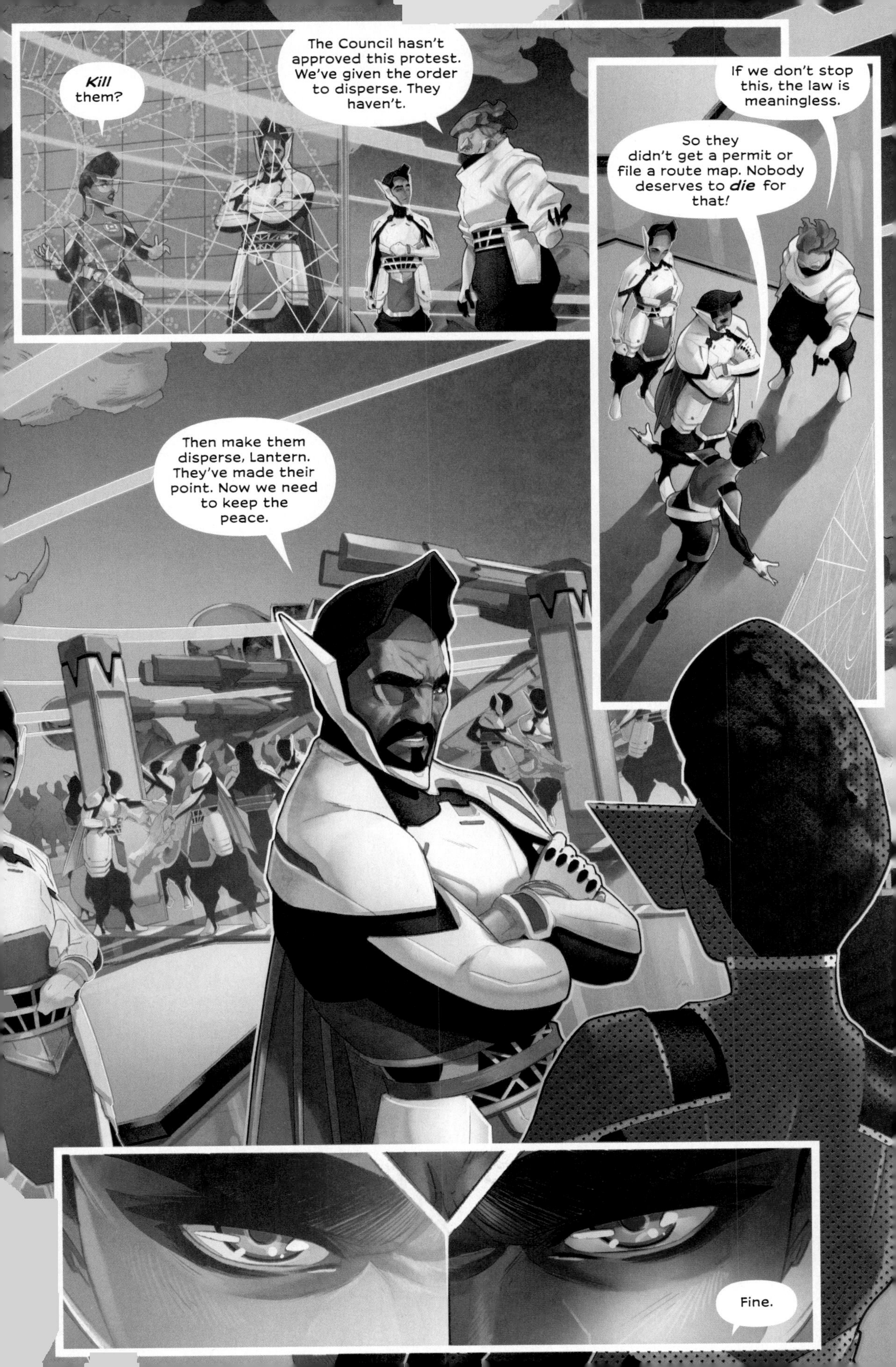

Kill them?
The Council hasn't approved this protest. We've given the order to disperse. They haven't.
If we don't stop this, the law is meaningless.
So they didn't get a permit or file a route map. Nobody deserves to *die* for that!
Then make them disperse, Lantern. They've made their point. Now we need to keep the peace.
Fine.

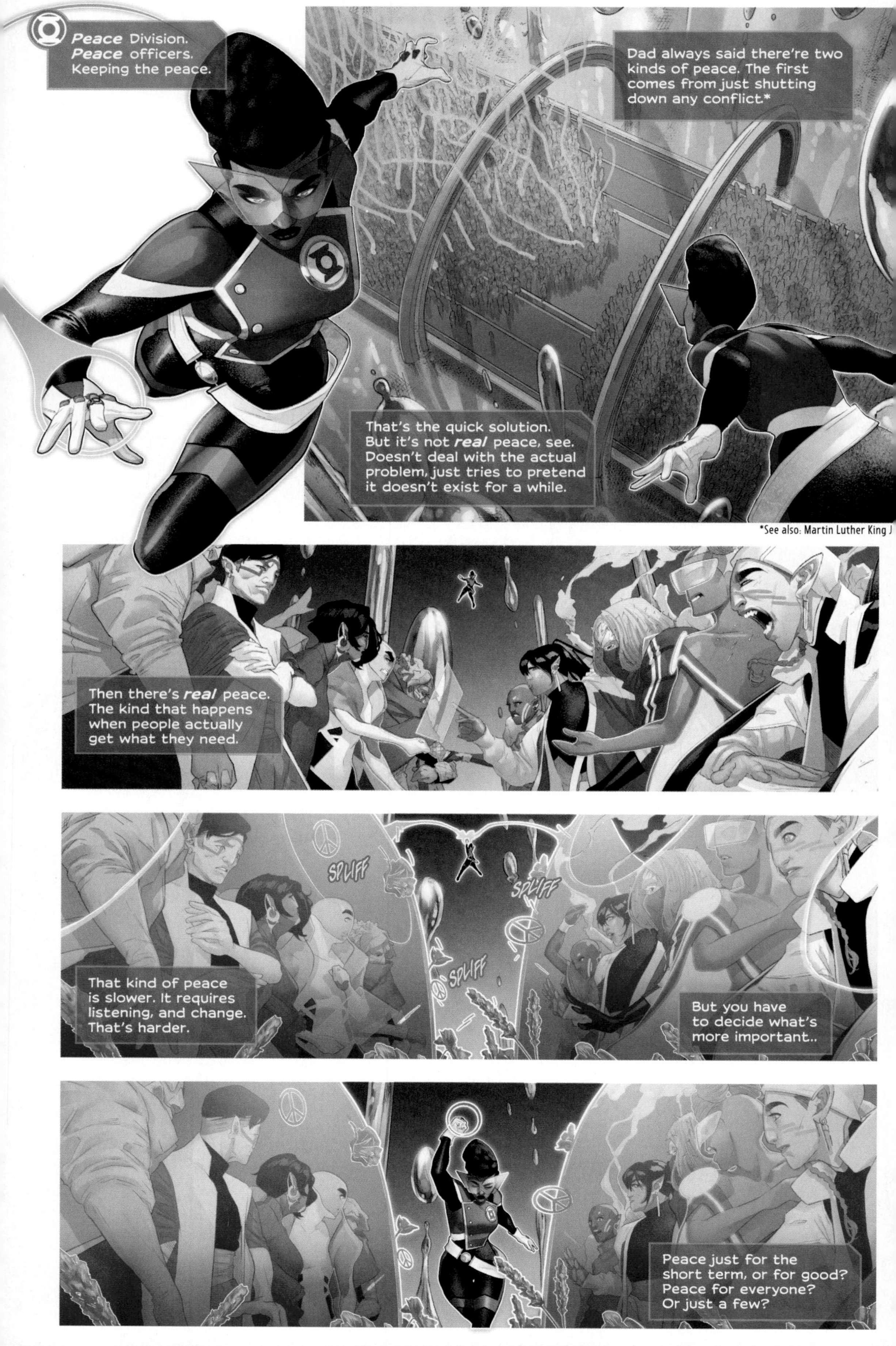

Peace Division. *Peace* officers. Keeping the peace.
Dad always said there're two kinds of peace. The first comes from just shutting down any conflict.*
That's the quick solution. But it's not *real* peace, see. Doesn't deal with the actual problem, just tries to pretend it doesn't exist for a while.
*See also: Martin Luther King J
Then there's *real* peace. The kind that happens when people actually get what they need.
SPLIFF
SPLIFF
SPLIFF
That kind of peace is slower. It requires listening, and change. That's harder.
But you have to decide what's more important..
Peace just for the short term, or for good? Peace for everyone? Or just a few?

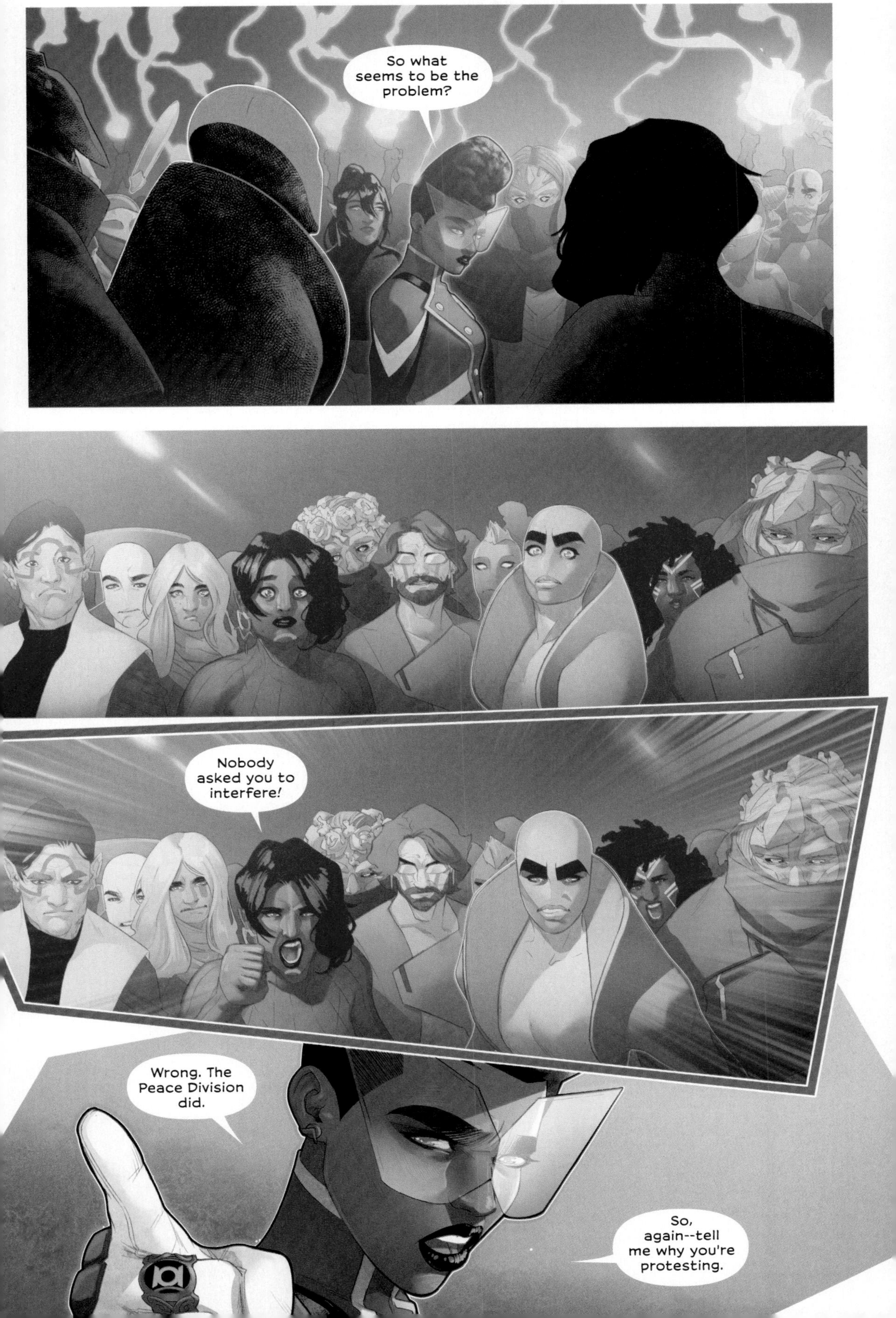
So what seems to be the problem?
Nobody asked you to interfere!
Wrong. The Peace Division did.
So, again--tell me why you're protesting.

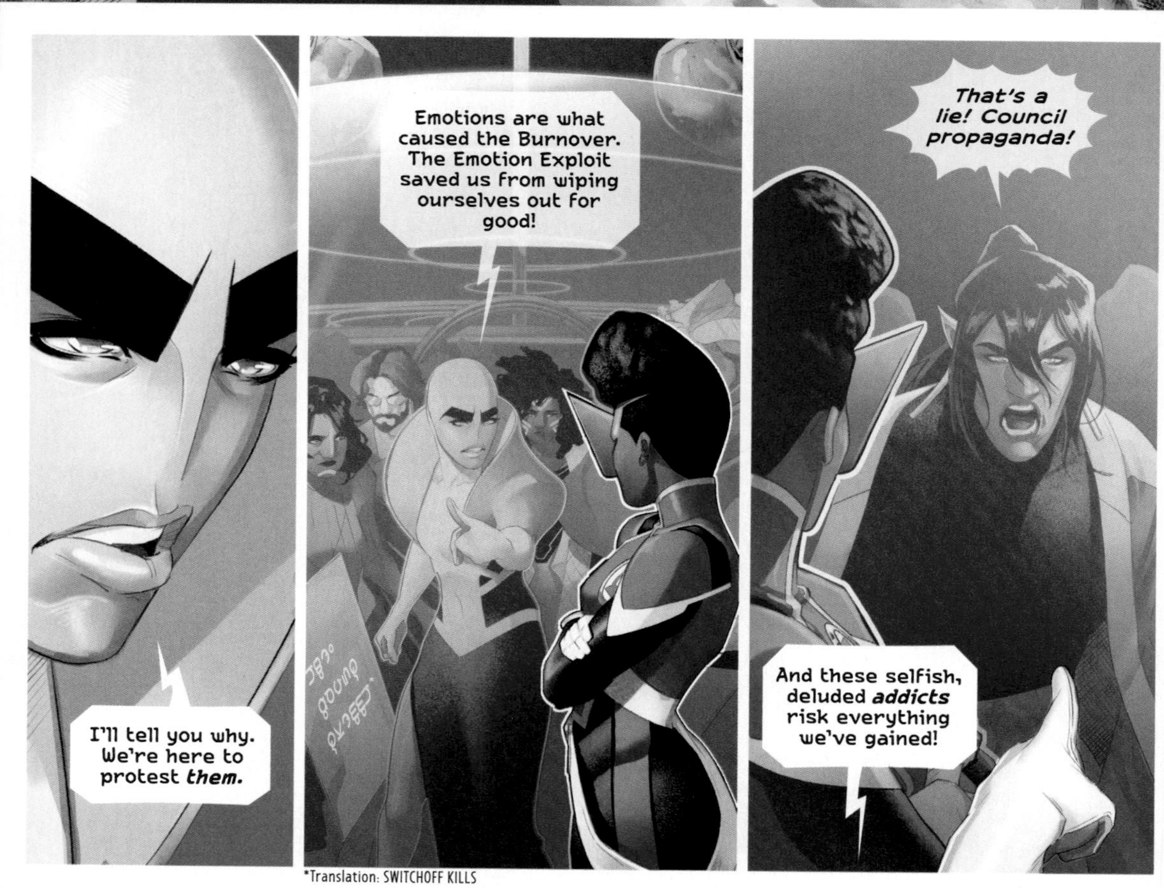
I'll tell you why. We're here to protest *them.*
Emotions are what caused the Burnover. The Emotion Exploit saved us from wiping ourselves out for good!
That's a lie! Council propaganda!
And these selfish, deluded *addicts* risk everything we've gained!

*Translation: SWITCHOFF KILLS

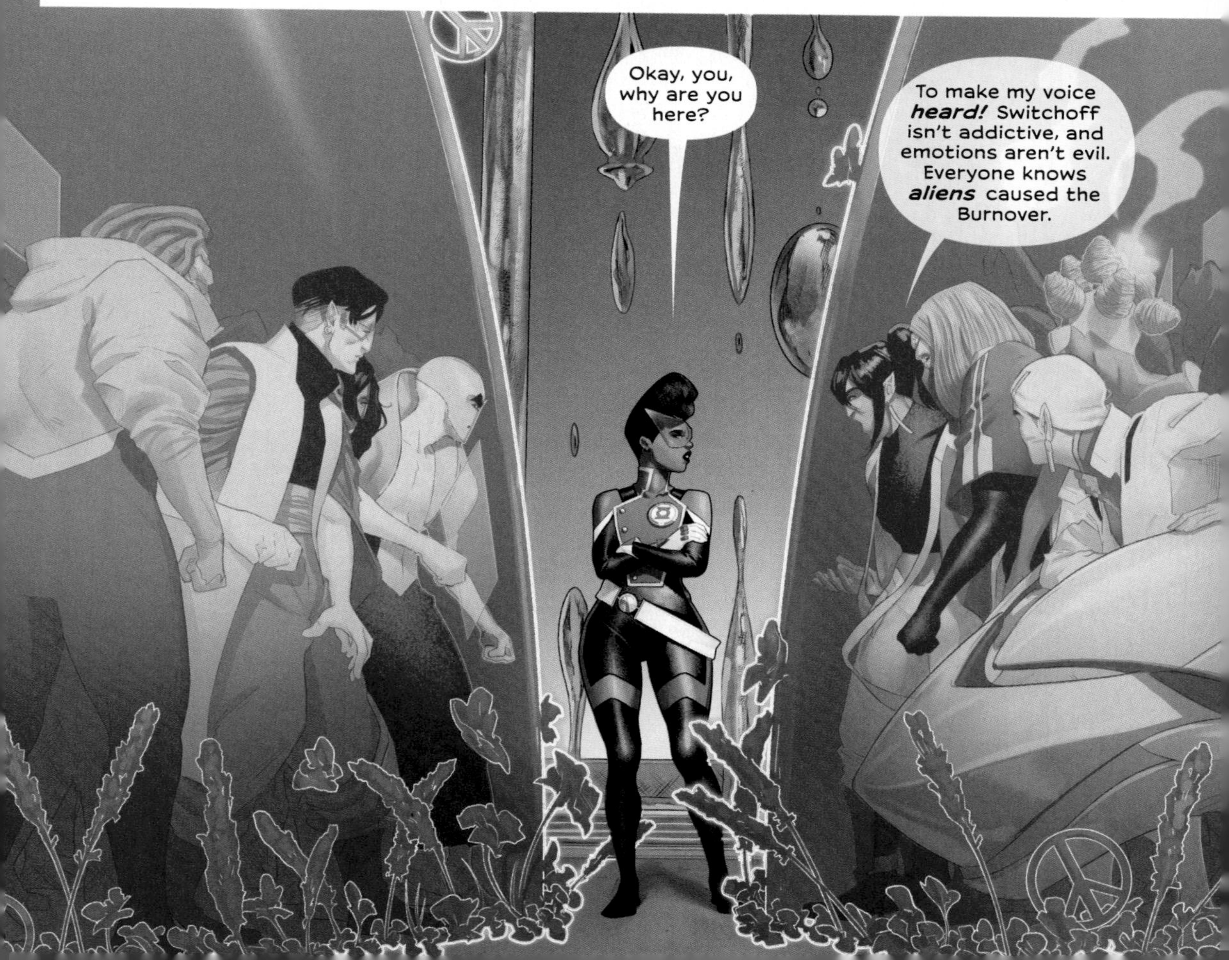
Okay, you, why are you here?
To make my voice *heard!* Switchoff isn't addictive, and emotions aren't evil. Everyone knows *aliens* caused the Burnover.

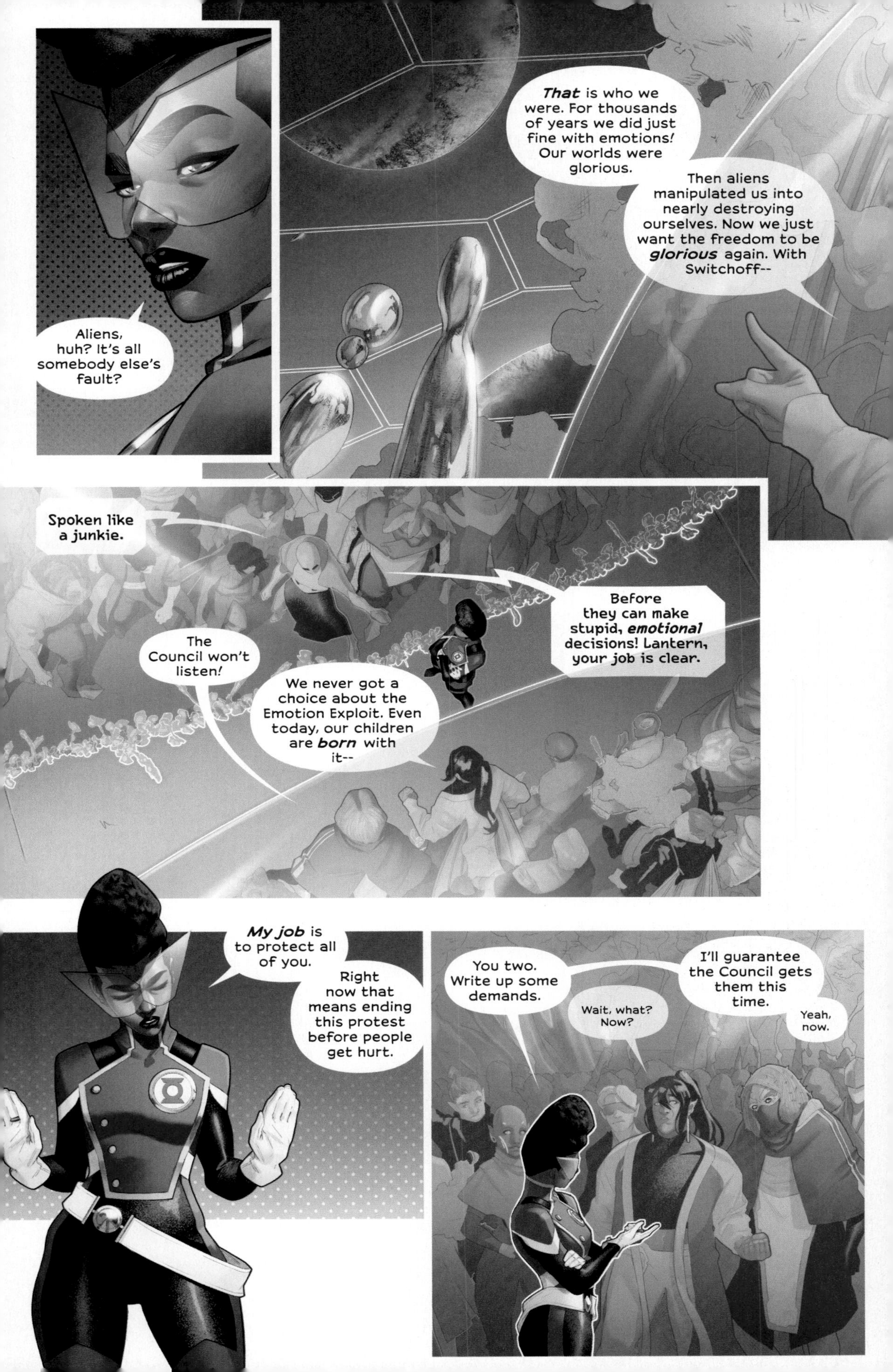
That is who we were. For thousands of years we did just fine with emotions! Our worlds were glorious.
Then aliens manipulated us into nearly destroying ourselves. Now we just want the freedom to be glorious again. With Switchoff--
Aliens, huh? It's all somebody else's fault?
Spoken like a junkie.
Before they can make stupid, emotional decisions! Lantern, your job is clear.
The Council won't listen!
We never got a choice about the Emotion Exploit. Even today, our children are born with it--
My job is to protect all of you.
Right now that means ending this protest before people get hurt.
You two. Write up some demands.
I'll guarantee the Council gets them this time.
Wait, what? Now?
Yeah, now.

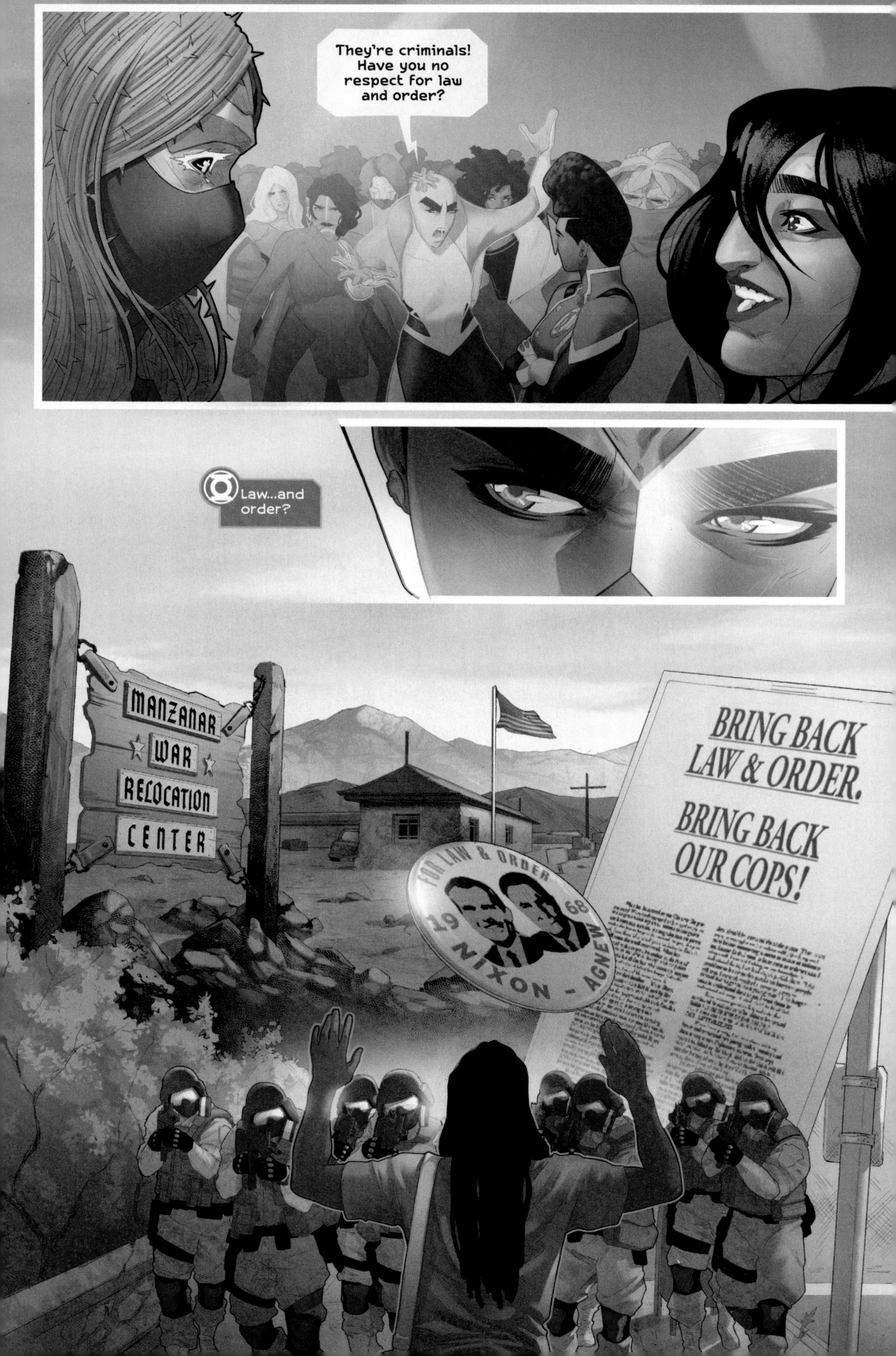
They're criminals! Have you no respect for law and order?
Law...and order?
MANZANAR WAR RELOCATION CENTER
FOR LAW & ORDER 1968 NIXON - AGNEW
BRING BACK LAW & ORDER.
BRING BACK OUR COPS!

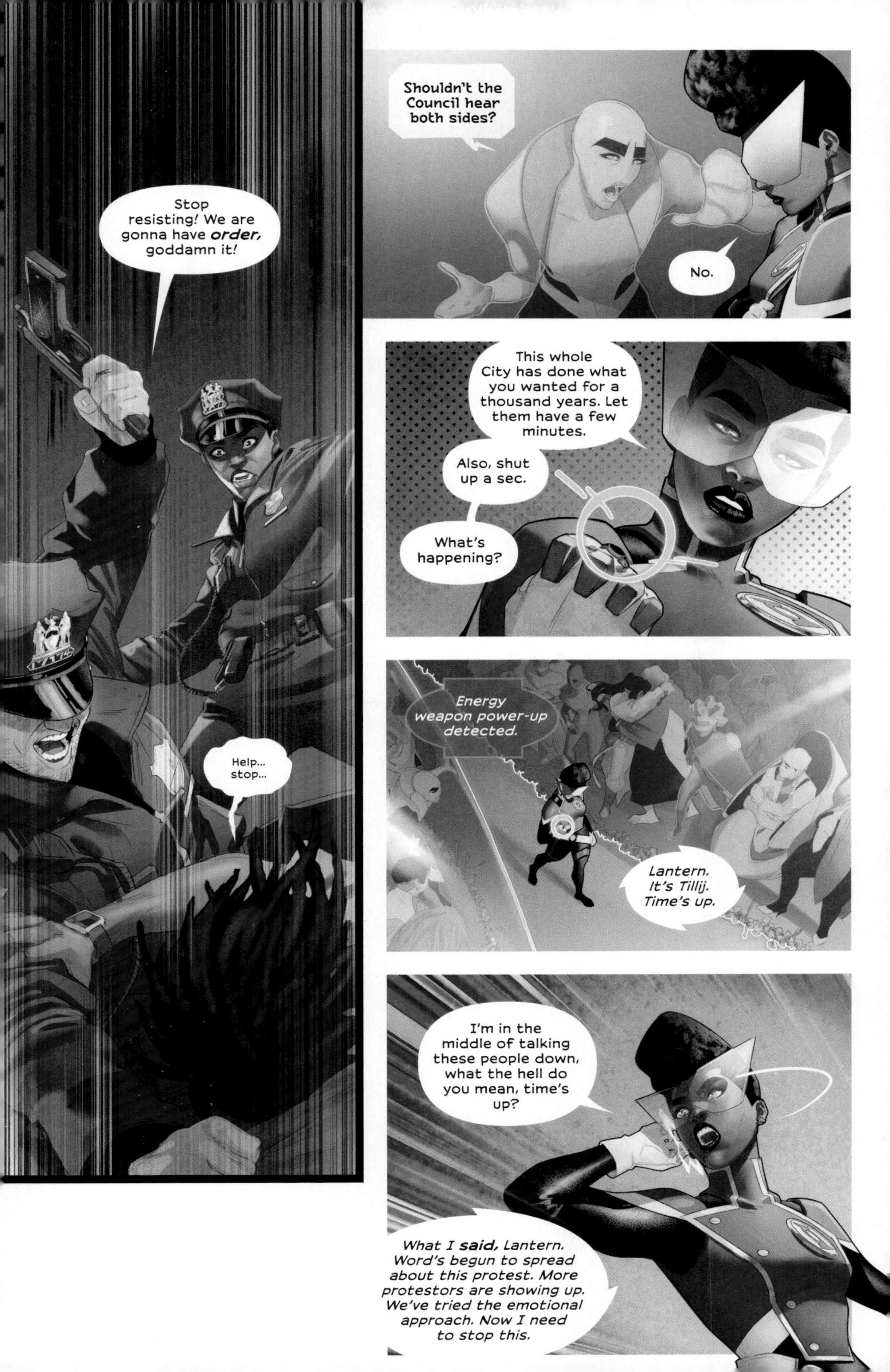
Stop resisting! We are gonna have *order,* goddamn it!
Help... stop...
Shouldn't the Council hear both sides?
No.
This whole City has done what you wanted for a thousand years. Let them have a few minutes.
Also, shut up a sec.
What's happening?
Energy weapon power-up detected.
Lantern. It's Tillij. Time's up.
I'm in the middle of talking these people down, what the hell do you mean, time's up?
*What I **said,** Lantern. Word's begun to spread about this protest. More protestors are showing up. We've tried the emotional approach. Now I need to stop this.*

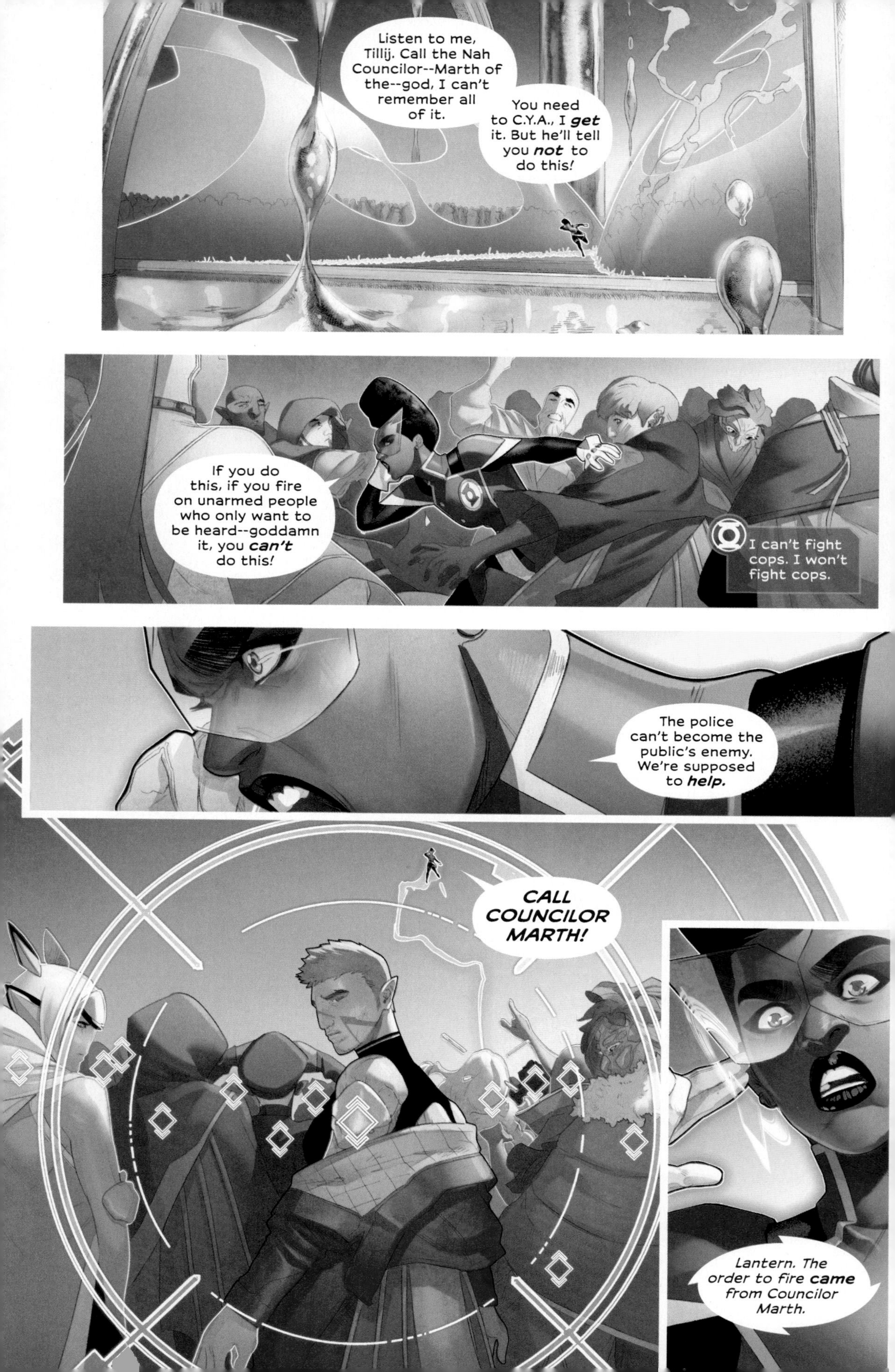

Listen to me, Tillij. Call the Nah Councilor--Marth of the--god, I can't remember all of it.
You need to C.Y.A., I *get* it. But he'll tell you *not* to do this!
If you do this, if you fire on unarmed people who only want to be heard--goddamn it, you *can't* do this!
I can't fight cops. I won't fight cops.
The police can't become the public's enemy. We're supposed to *help.*
CALL COUNCILOR MARTH!
Lantern. The order to fire **came** *from Councilor Marth.*

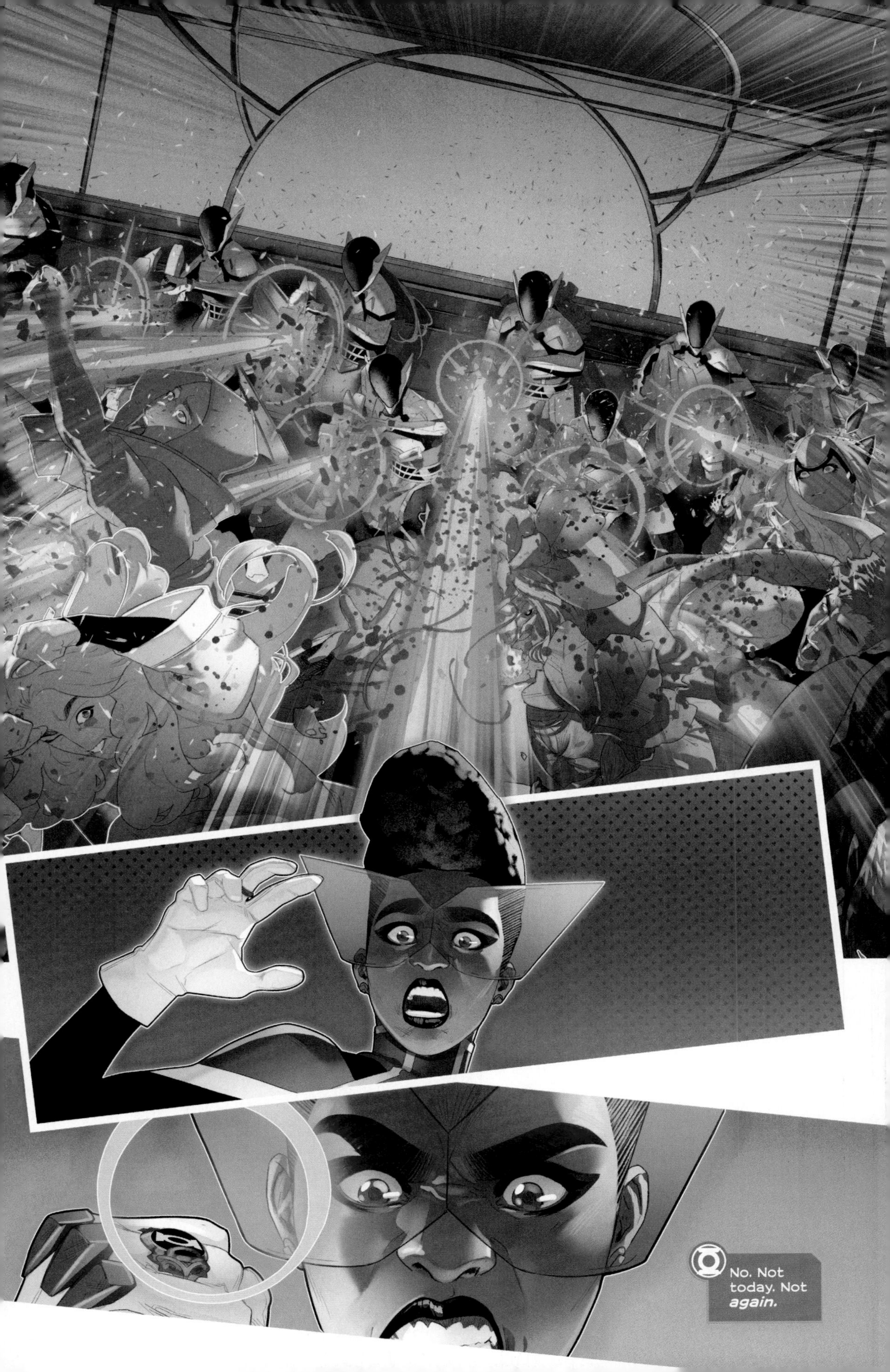
No. Not today. Not *again.*

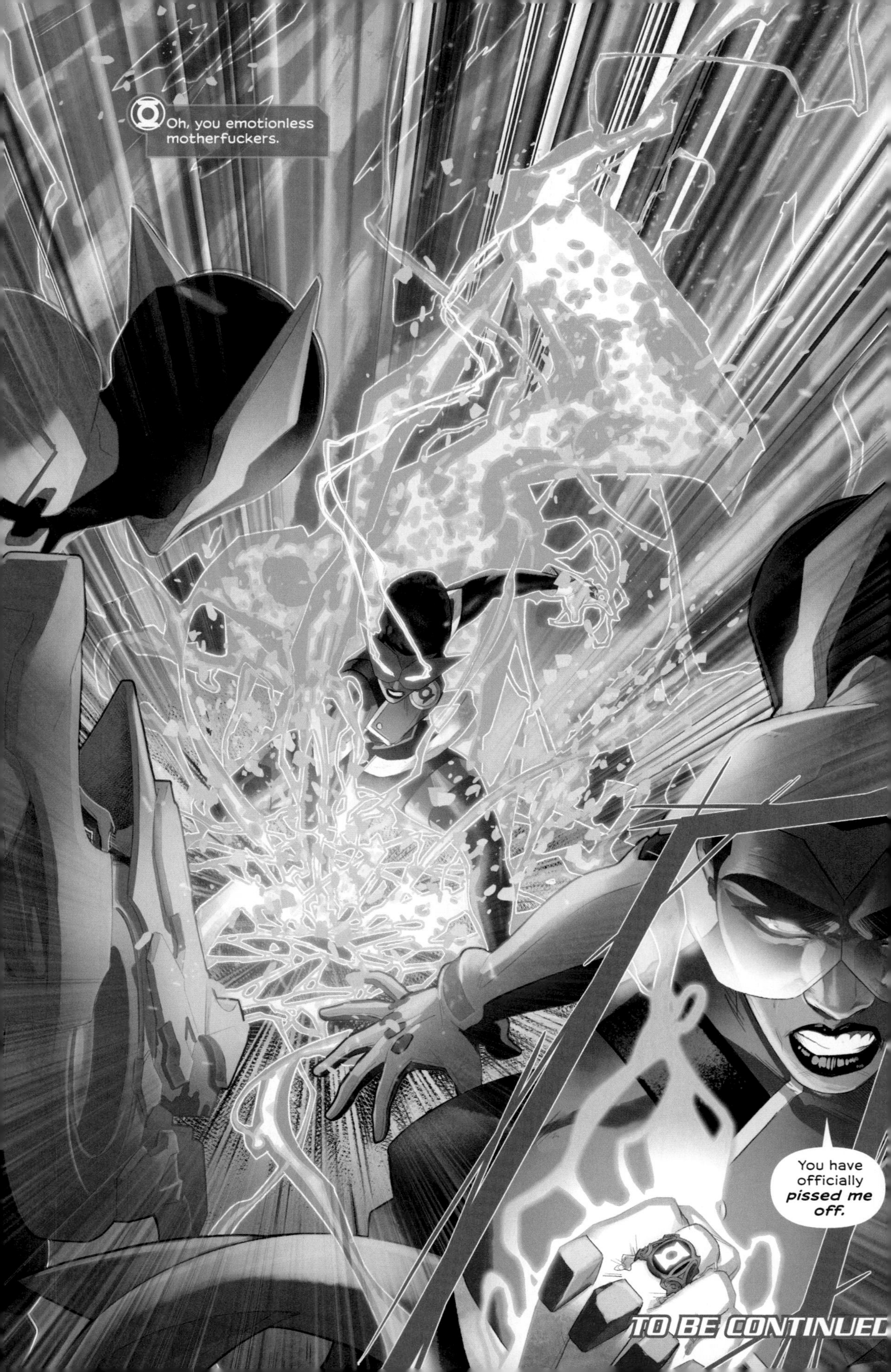
Oh, you emotionless motherfuckers.
You have officially *pissed me off.*
TO BE CONTINUED

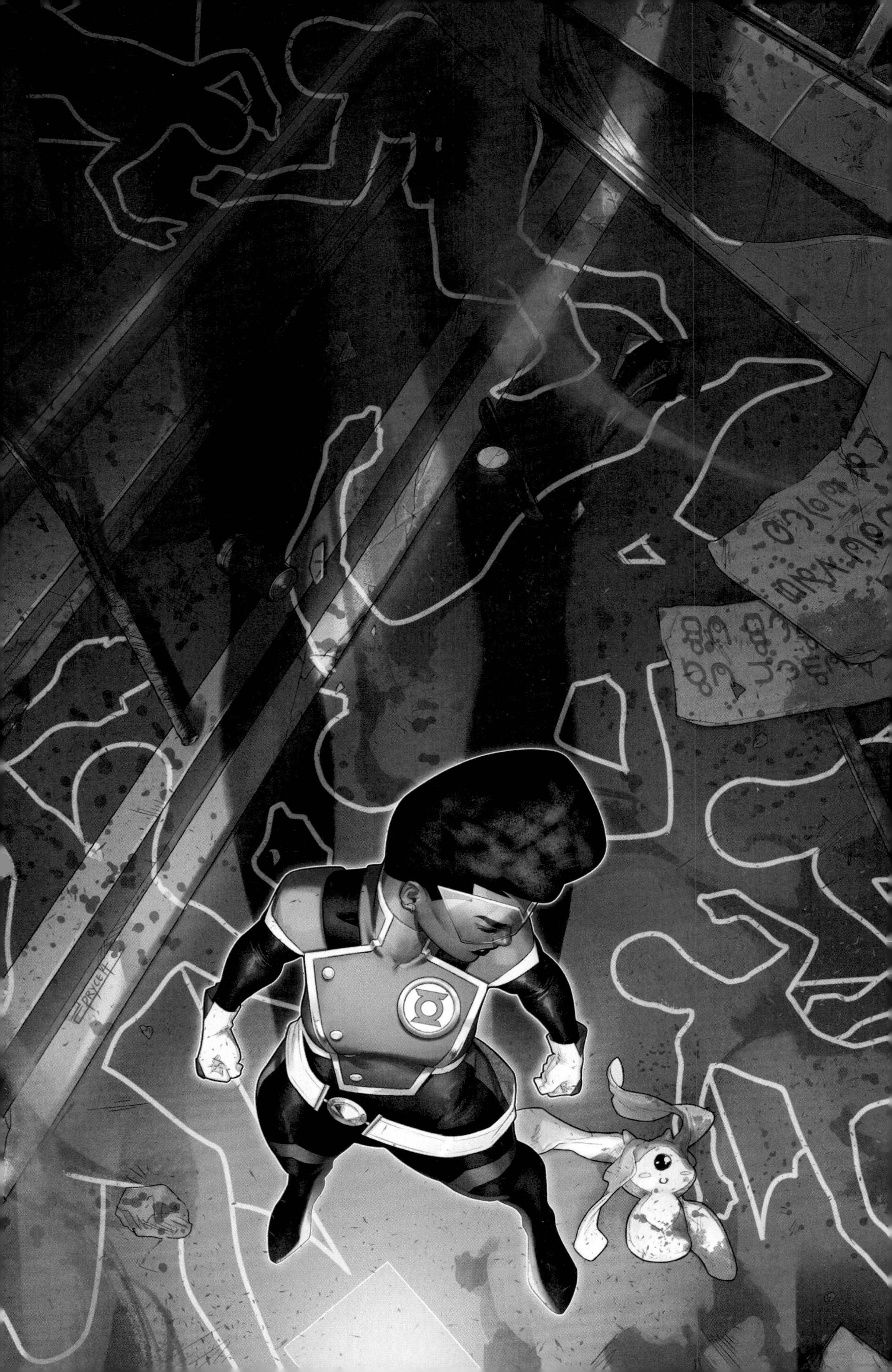

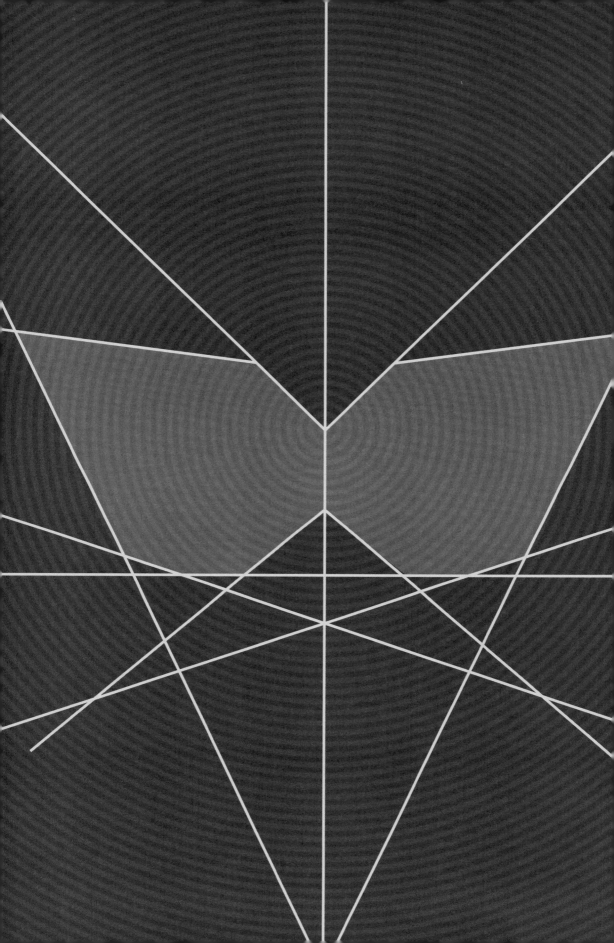

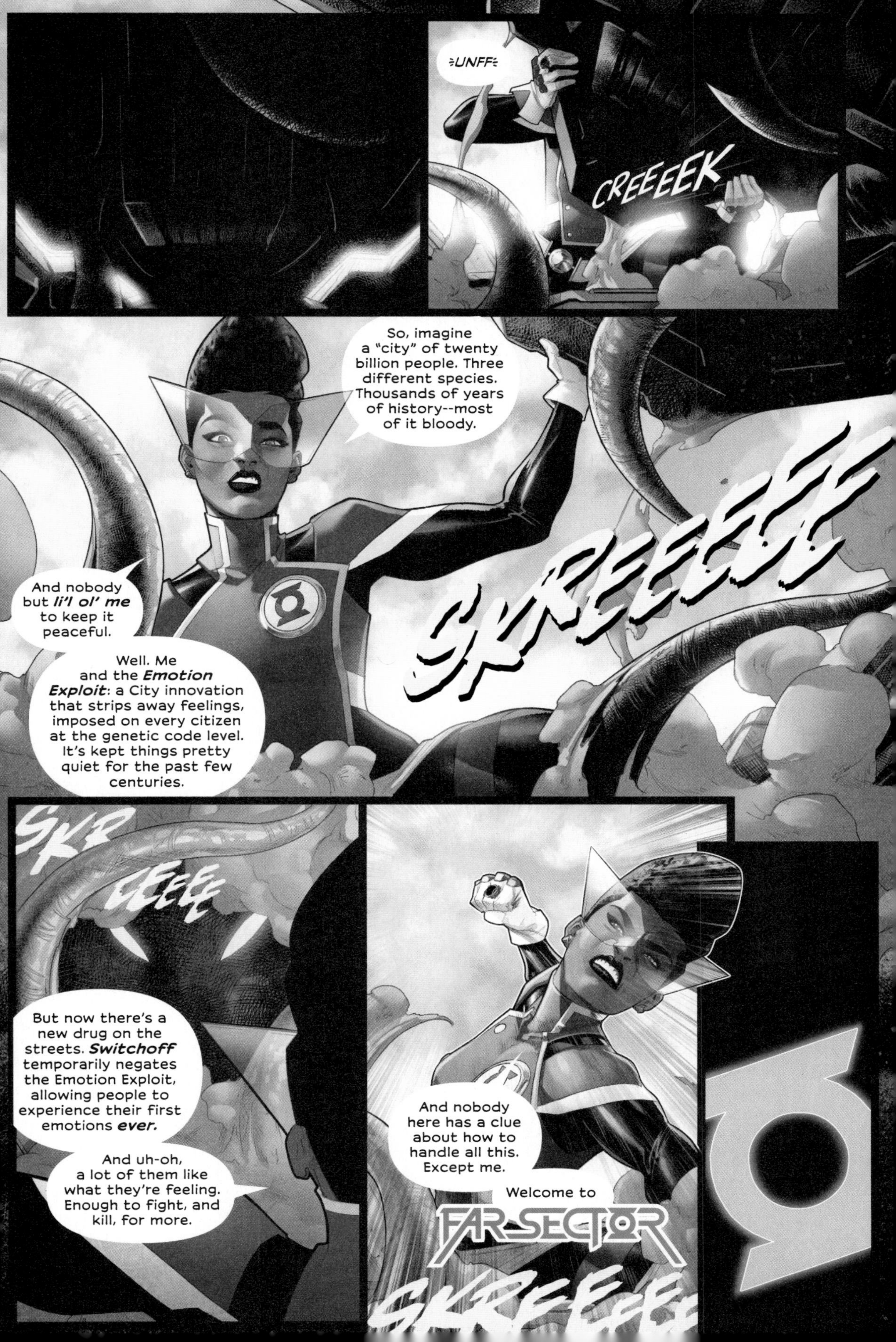

UNFF
CREEEEK
So, imagine a "city" of twenty billion people. Three different species. Thousands of years of history--most of it bloody.
SKREEEEEE
And nobody but li'l ol' me to keep it peaceful.
Well. Me and the Emotion Exploit: a City innovation that strips away feelings, imposed on every citizen at the genetic code level. It's kept things pretty quiet for the past few centuries.
SKR
EEEE
But now there's a new drug on the streets. Switchoff temporarily negates the Emotion Exploit, allowing people to experience their first emotions ever.
And uh-oh, a lot of them like what they're feeling. Enough to fight, and kill, for more.
And nobody here has a clue about how to handle all this. Except me.
Welcome to
FAR SECTOR
SKREEEEE

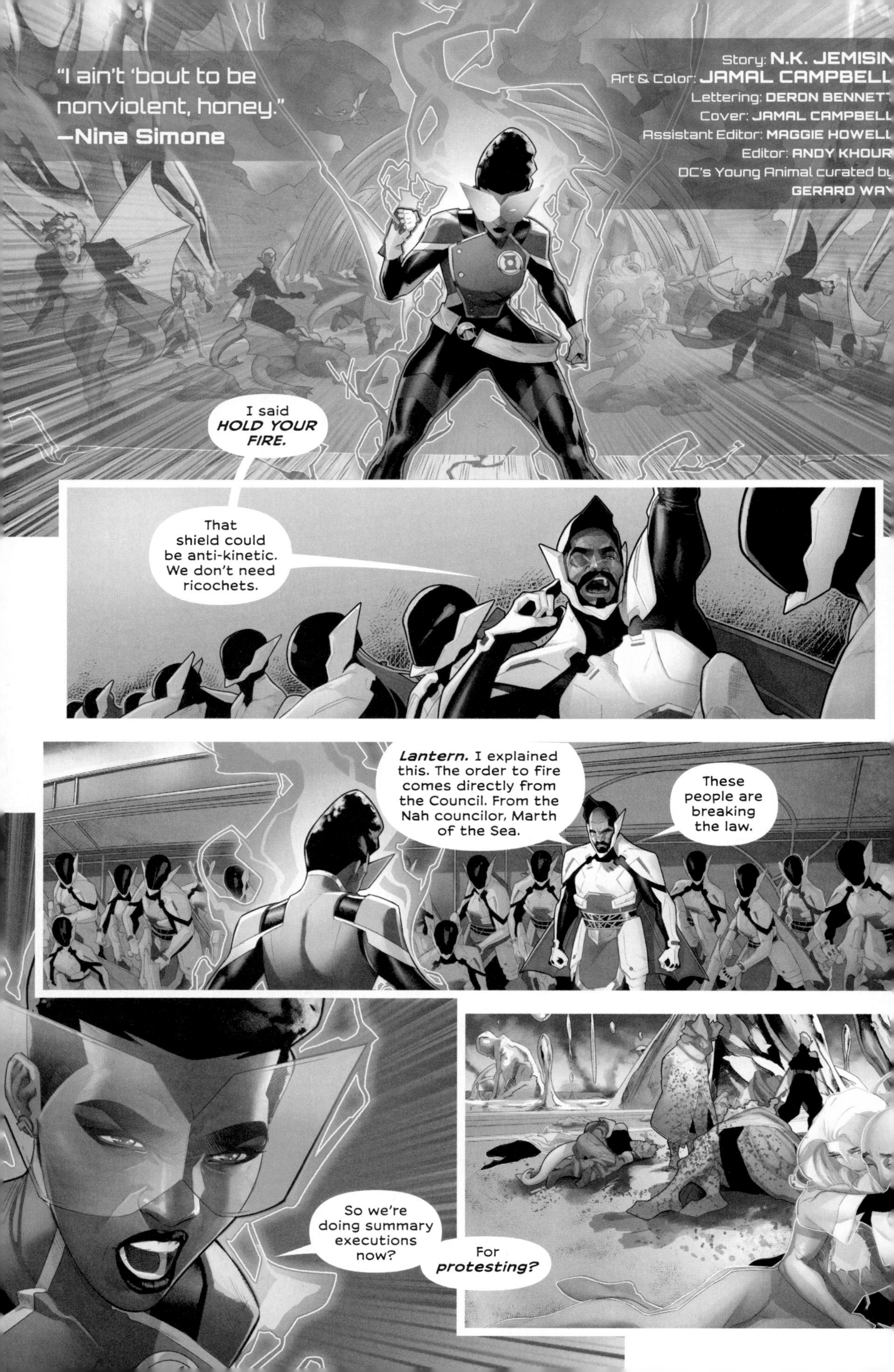
"I ain't 'bout to be nonviolent, honey."
—Nina Simone
Story: N.K. JEMISIN
Art & Color: JAMAL CAMPBELL
Lettering: DERON BENNET
Cover: JAMAL CAMPBELL
Assistant Editor: MAGGIE HOWELL
Editor: ANDY KHOUR
DC's Young Animal curated by
GERARD WAY
I said *HOLD YOUR FIRE.*
That shield could be anti-kinetic. We don't need ricochets.
Lantern. I explained this. The order to fire comes directly from the Council. From the Nah councilor, Marth of the Sea.
These people are breaking the law.
So we're doing summary executions now?
For *protesting?*

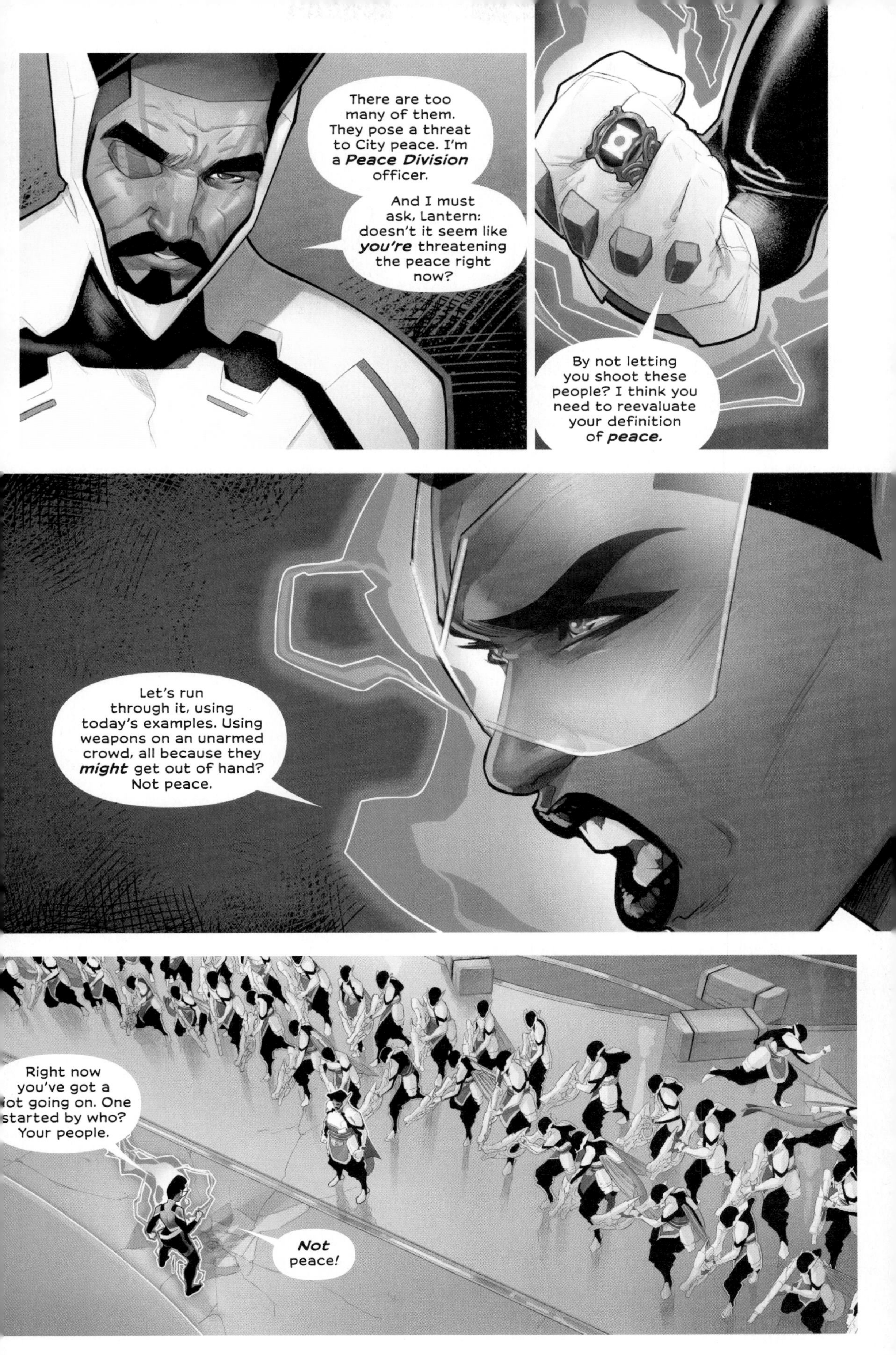
There are too many of them. They pose a threat to City peace. I'm a *Peace Division* officer.
And I must ask, Lantern: doesn't it seem like *you're* threatening the peace right now?
By not letting you shoot these people? I think you need to reevaluate your definition of *peace.*
Let's run through it, using today's examples. Using weapons on an unarmed crowd, all because they *might* get out of hand? Not peace.
Right now you've got a iot going on. One started by who? Your people.
Not peace!

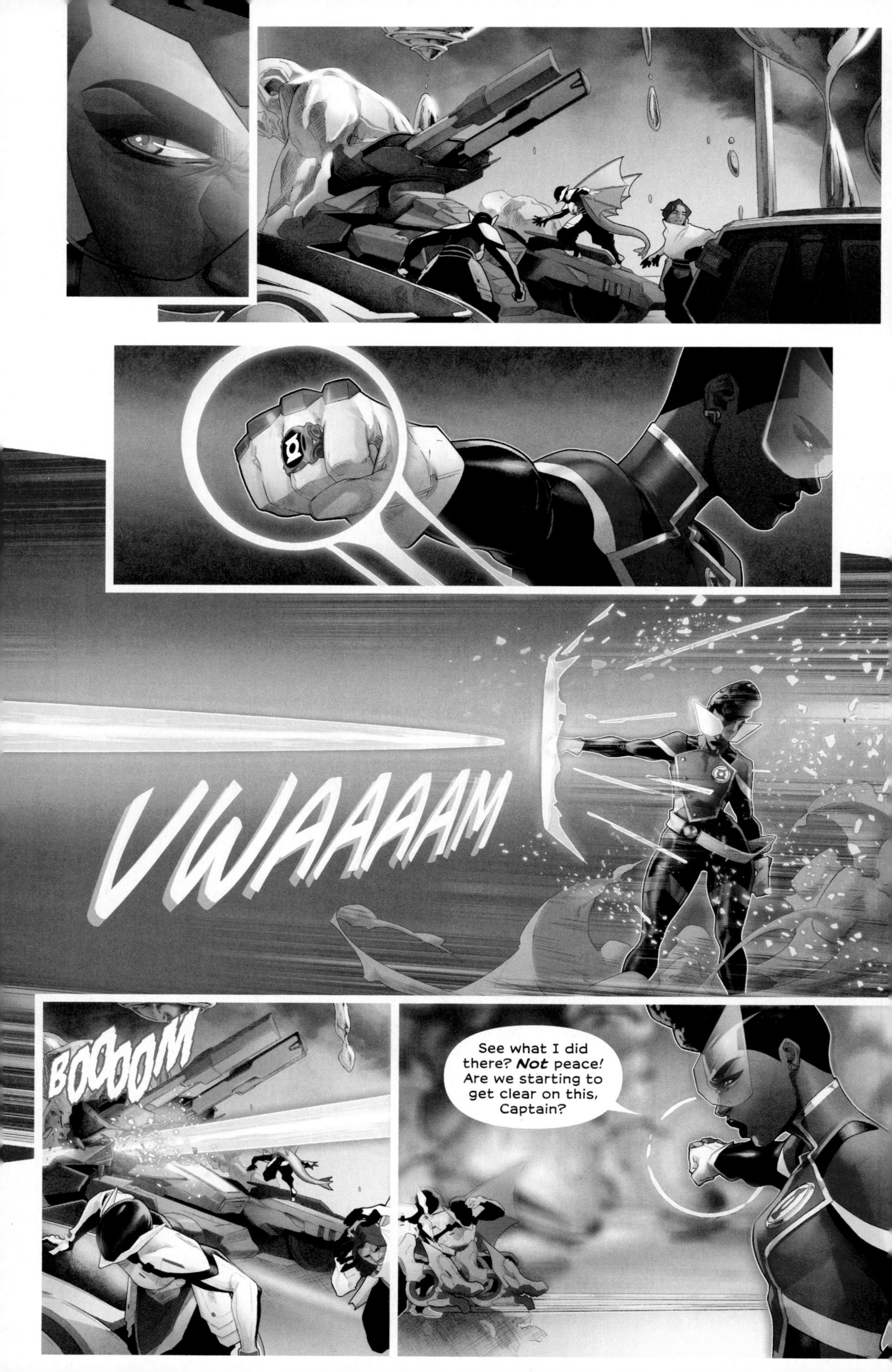
VWAAAAAM
BOOOOM
See what I did there? Not peace! Are we starting to get clear on this, Captain?

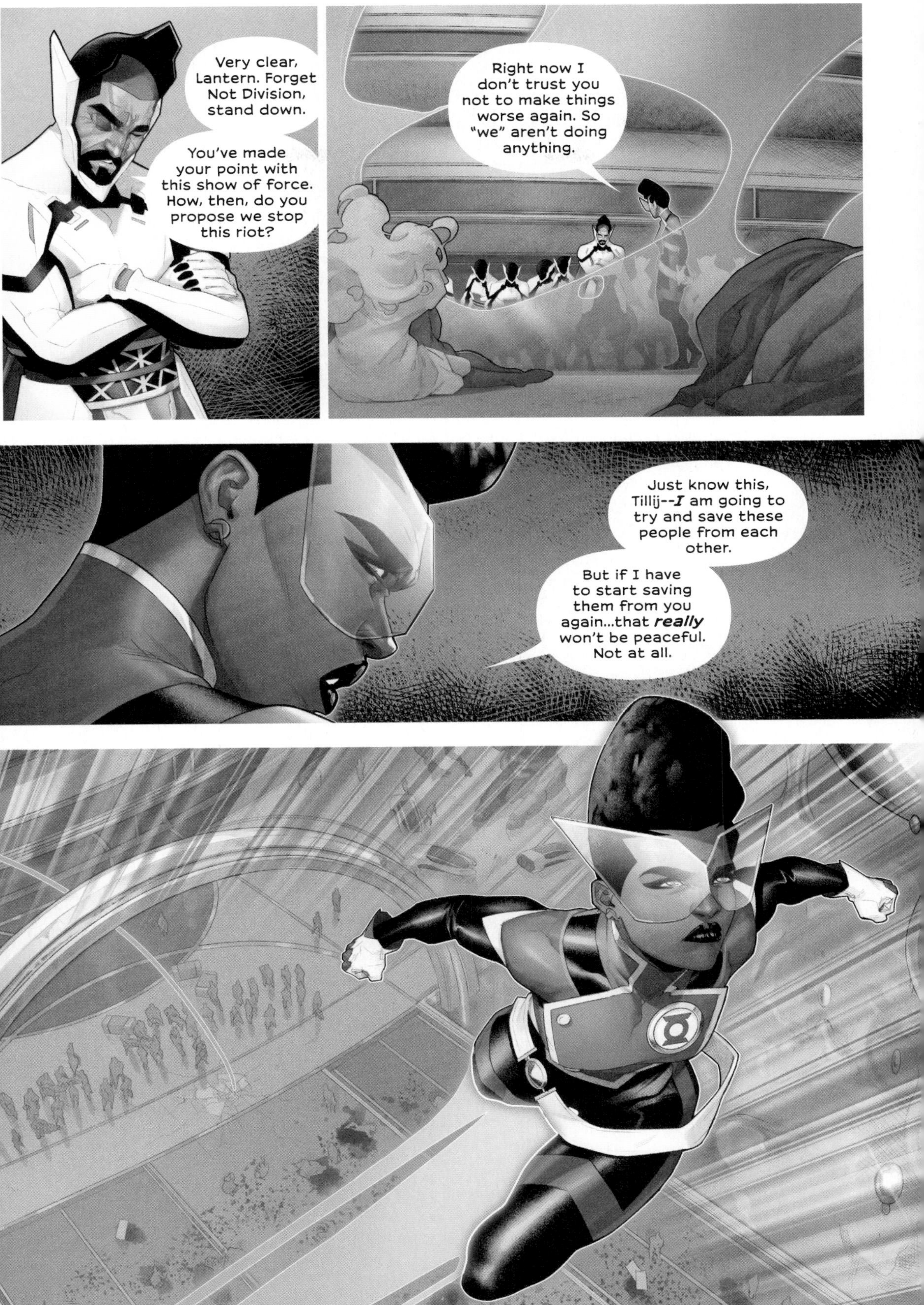
Very clear, Lantern. Forget Not Division, stand down.
You've made your point with this show of force. How, then, do you propose we stop this riot?
Right now I don't trust you not to make things worse again. So "we" aren't doing anything.
Just know this, Tillij--*I* am going to try and save these people from each other.
But if I have to start saving them from you again...that ***really*** won't be peaceful. Not at all.

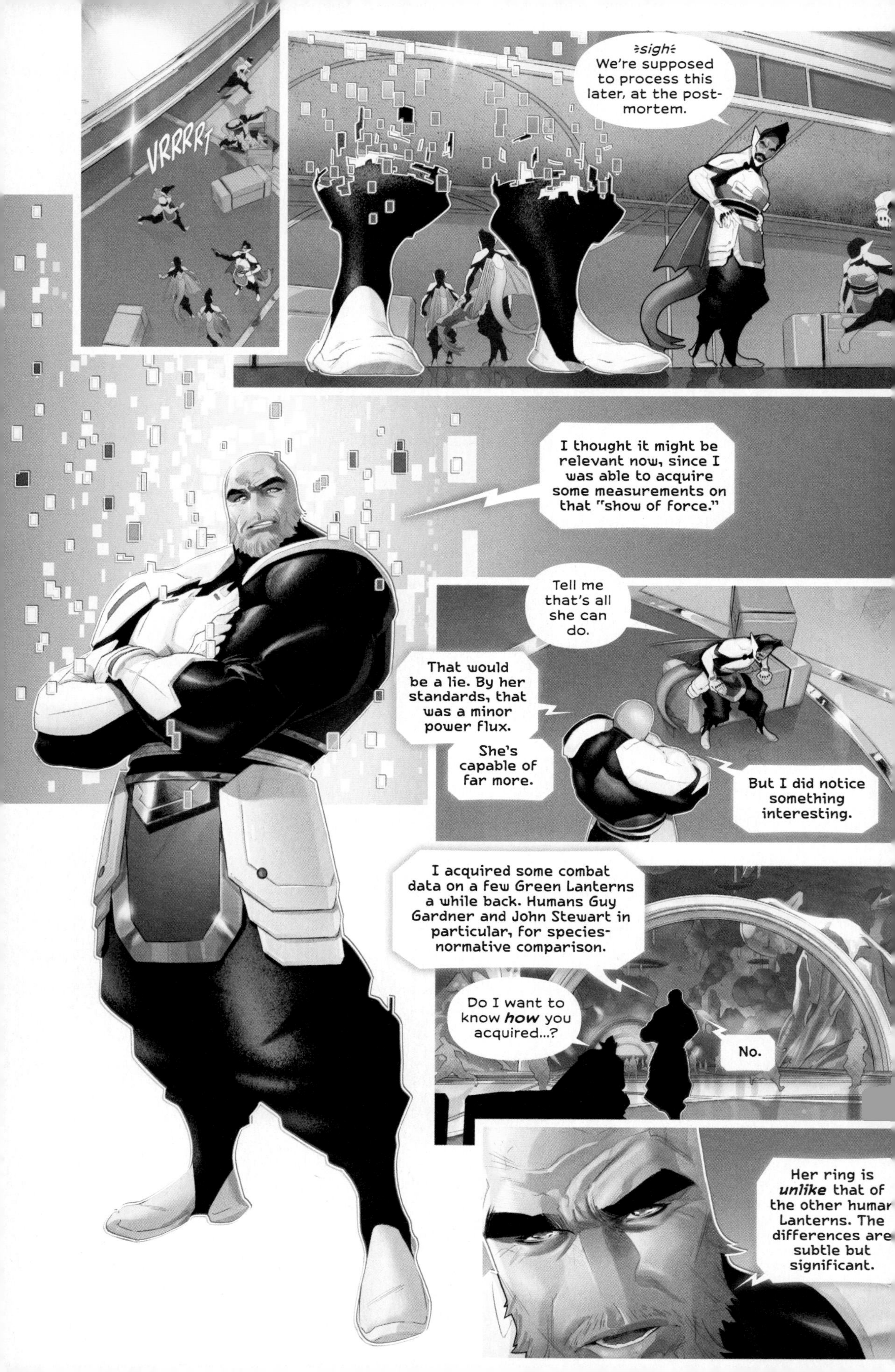
VRRRRT
sigh
We're supposed to process this later, at the post-mortem.
I thought it might be relevant now, since I was able to acquire some measurements on that "show of force."
Tell me that's all she can do.
That would be a lie. By her standards, that was a minor power flux.
She's capable of far more.
But I did notice something interesting.
I acquired some combat data on a few Green Lanterns a while back. Humans Guy Gardner and John Stewart in particular, for species-normative comparison.
Do I want to know *how* you acquired...?
No.
Her ring is *unlike* that of the other human Lanterns. The differences are subtle but significant.

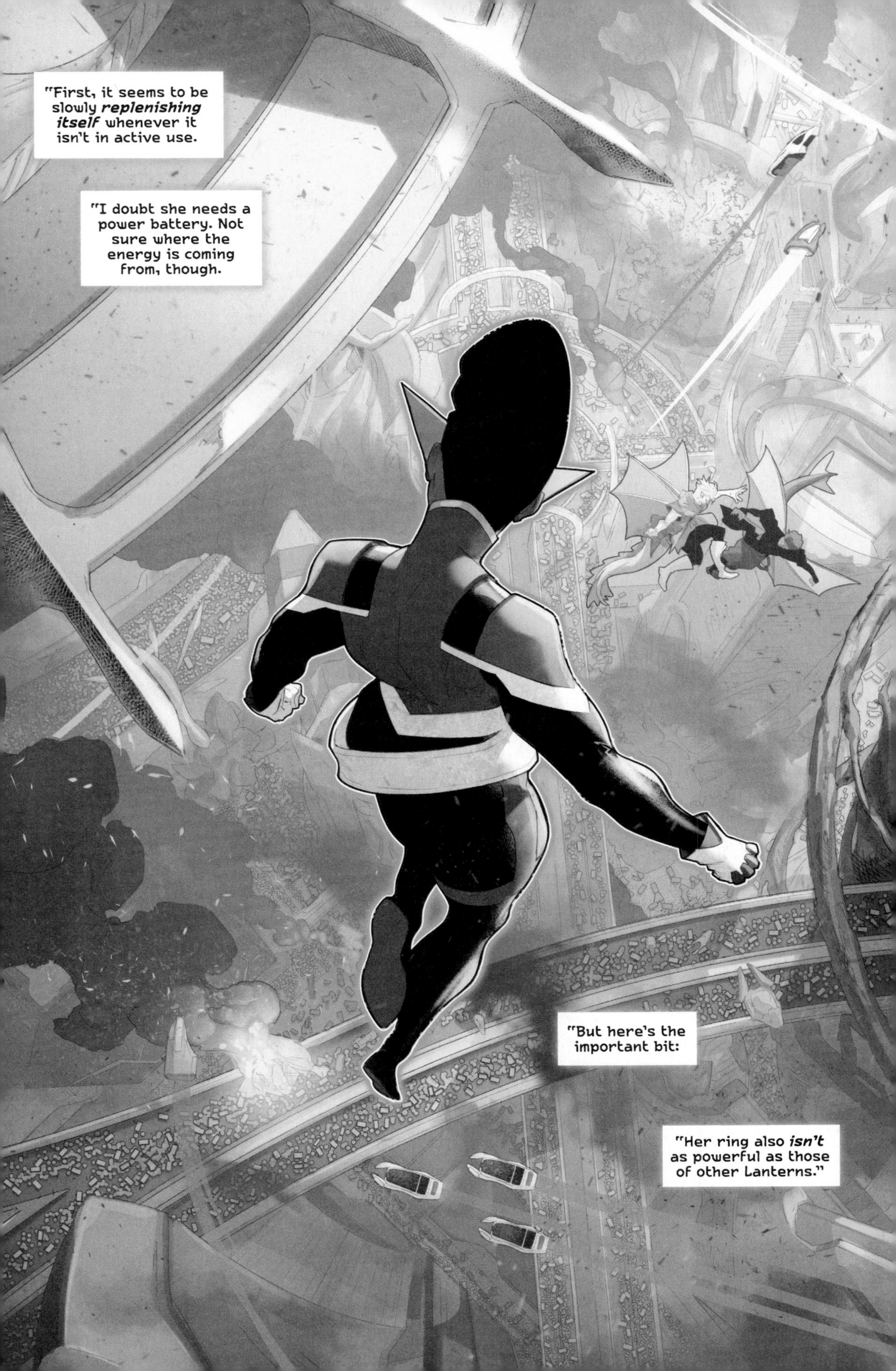
"First, it seems to be slowly *replenishing itself* whenever it isn't in active use.
"I doubt she needs a power battery. Not sure where the energy is coming from, though.
"But here's the important bit:
"Her ring also *isn't* as powerful as those of other Lanterns."

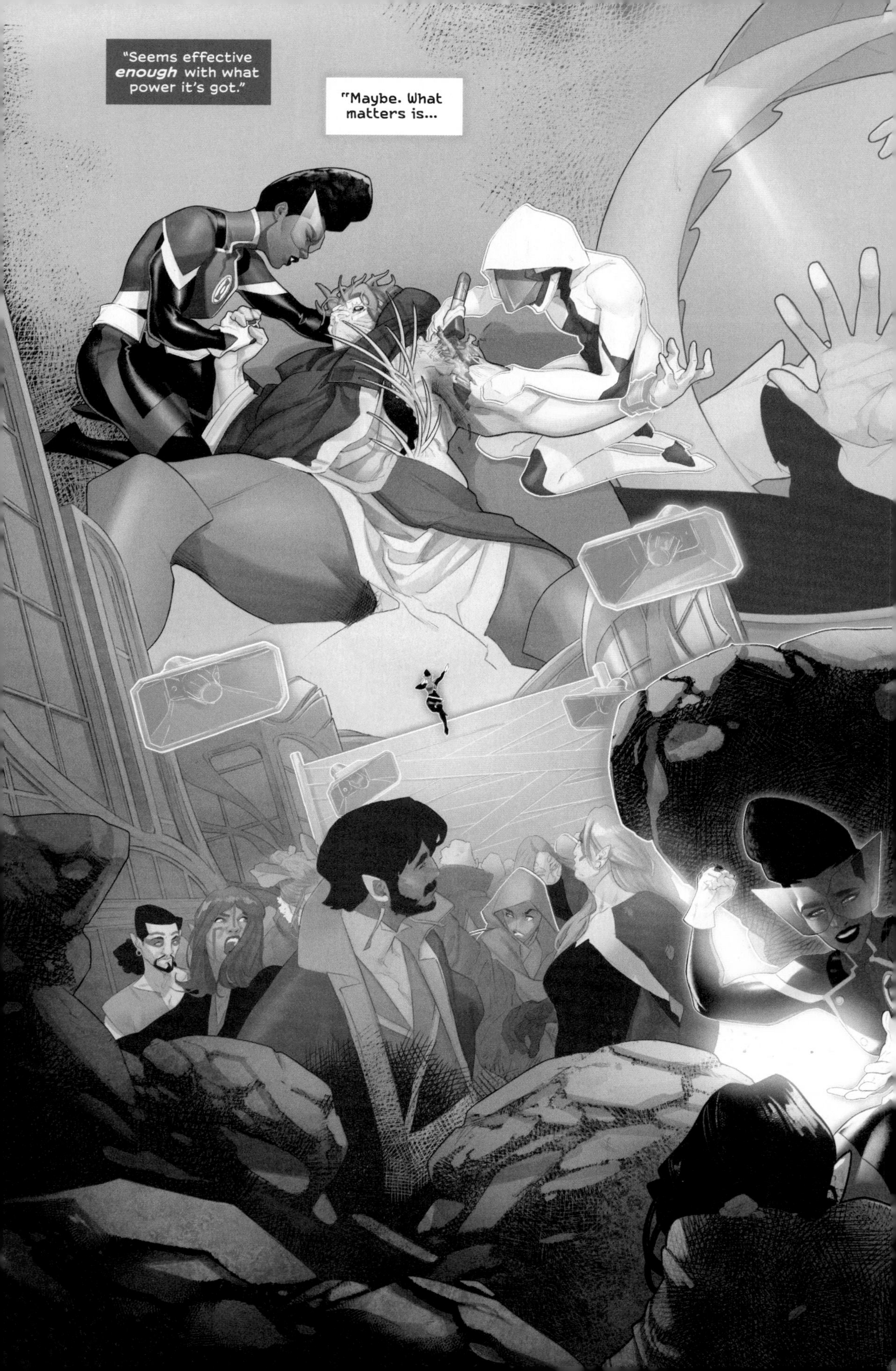
"Seems effective *enough* with what power it's got."
"Maybe. What matters is...

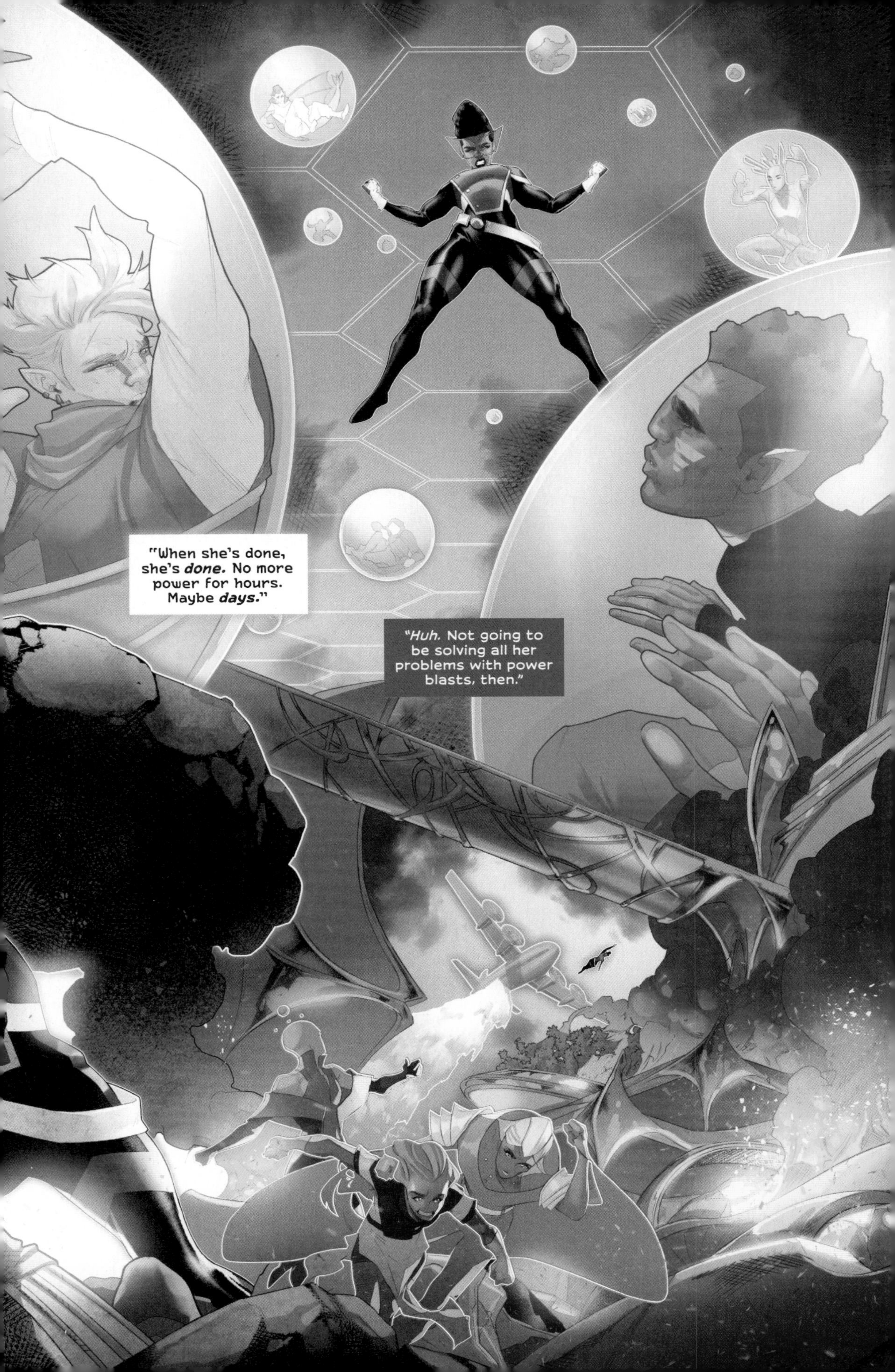
"When she's done, she's *done.* No more power for hours. Maybe *days.*"
"*Huh.* Not going to be solving all her problems with power blasts, then."

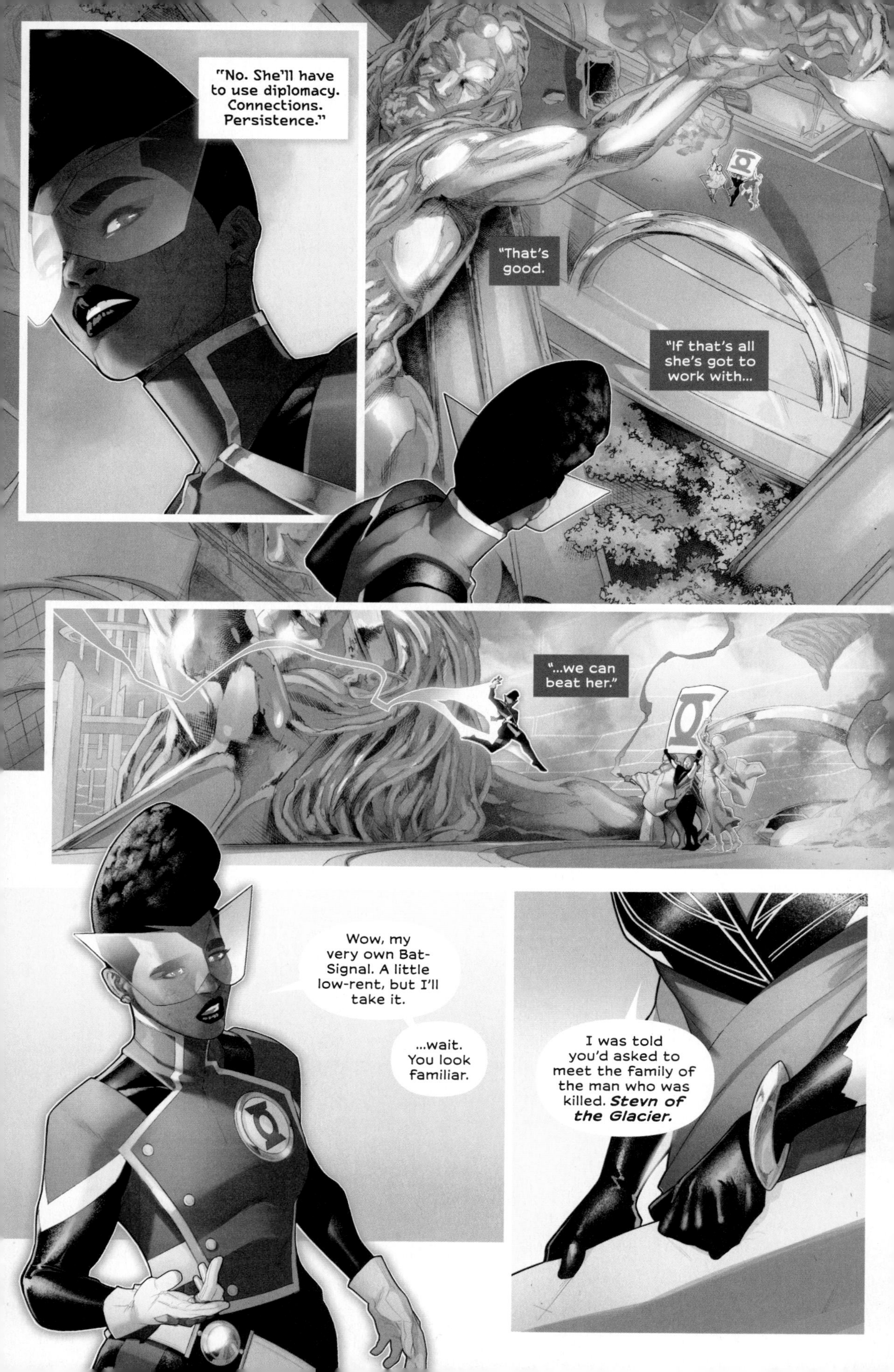
"No. She'll have to use diplomacy. Connections. Persistence."
"That's good.
"If that's all she's got to work with...
"...we can beat her."
Wow, my very own Bat-Signal. A little low-rent, but I'll take it.
...wait. You look familiar.
I was told you'd asked to meet the family of the man who was killed. *Stevn of the Glacier.*

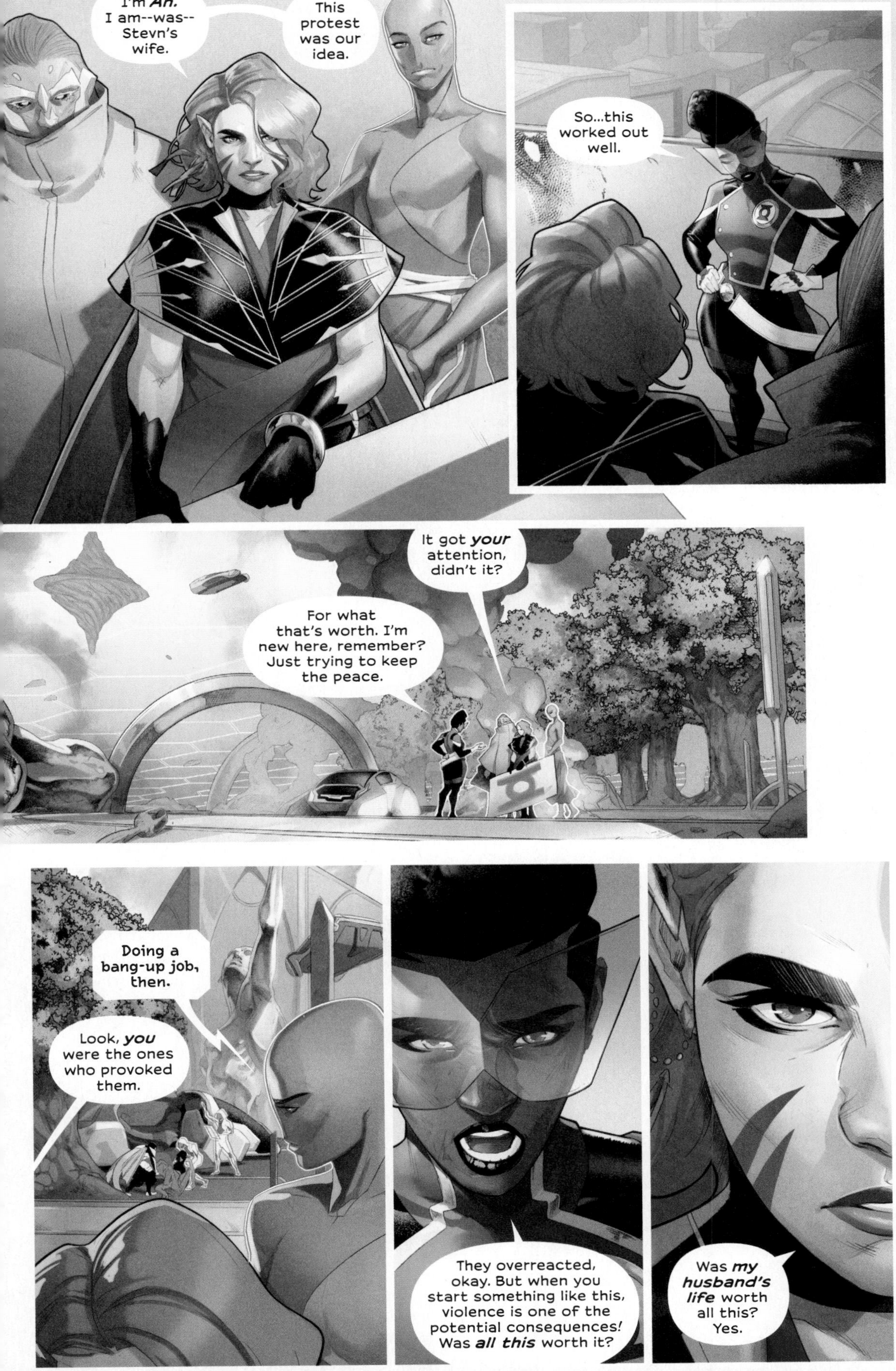

I'm *An.* I am--was-- Stevn's wife.
This protest was our idea.
So...this worked out well.
It got *your* attention, didn't it?
For what that's worth. I'm new here, remember? Just trying to keep the peace.
Doing a bang-up job, then.
Look, *you* were the ones who provoked them.
They overreacted, okay. But when you start something like this, violence is one of the potential consequences! Was *all this* worth it?
Was *my husband's life* worth all this? Yes.

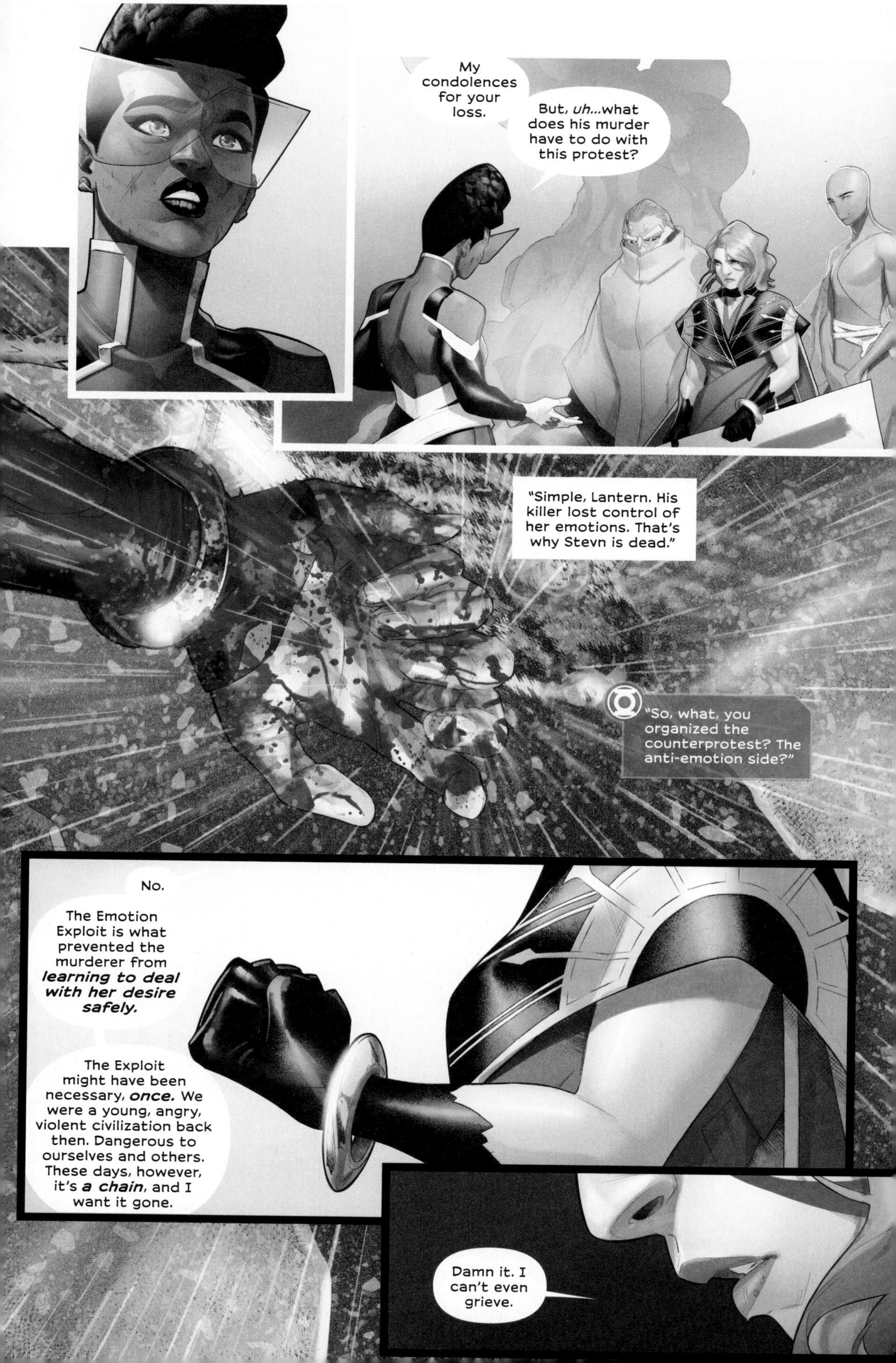
My condolences for your loss.
But, *uh*...what does his murder have to do with this protest?
"Simple, Lantern. His killer lost control of her emotions. That's why Stevn is dead."
"So, what, you organized the counterprotest? The anti-emotion side?"
No.
The Emotion Exploit is what prevented the murderer from ***learning to deal with her desire safely.***
The Exploit might have been necessary, ***once.*** We were a young, angry, violent civilization back then. Dangerous to ourselves and others. These days, however, it's ***a chain***, and I want it gone.
Damn it. I can't even grieve.

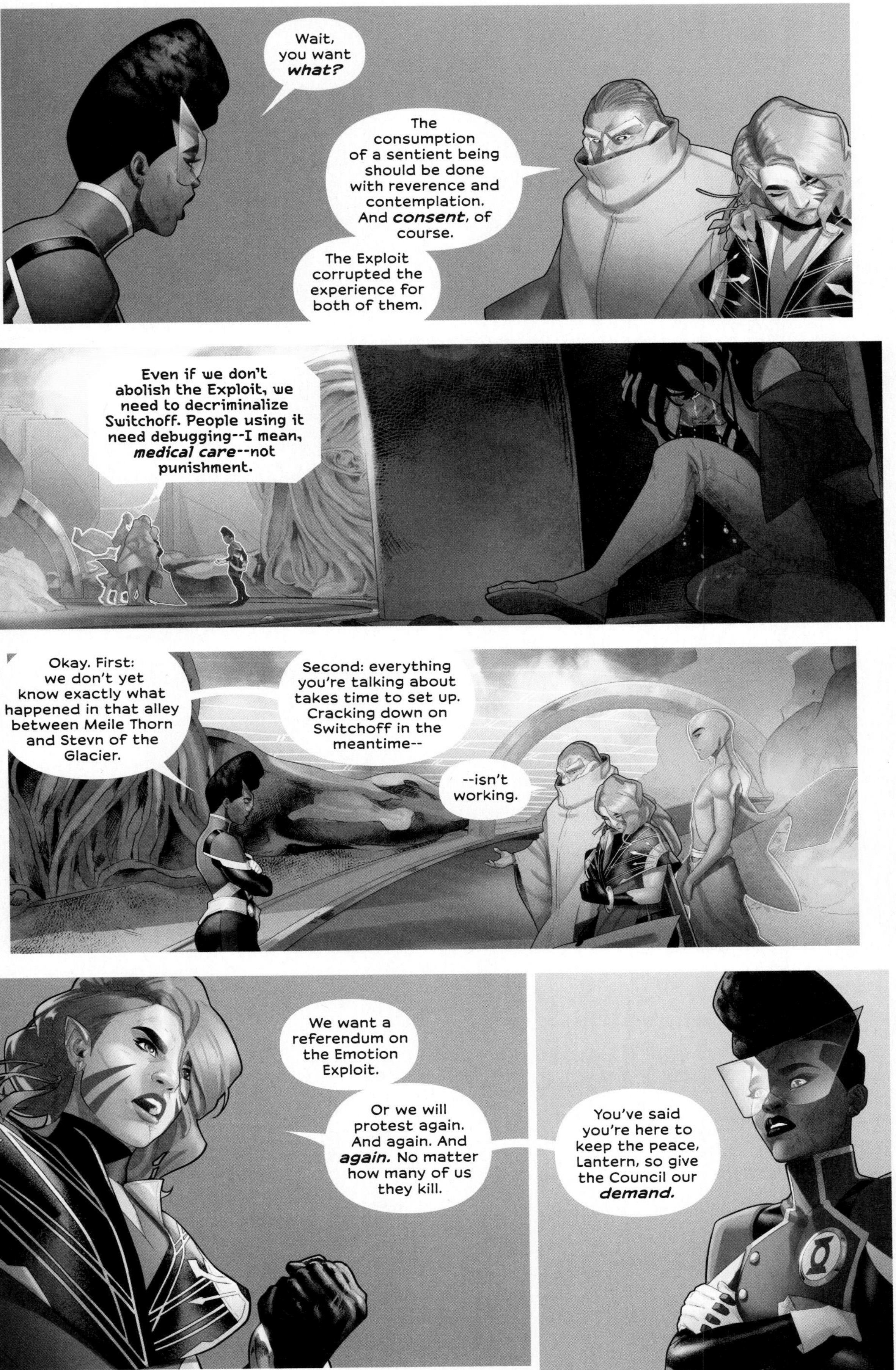

Wait, you want *what?*
The consumption of a sentient being should be done with reverence and contemplation. And *consent*, of course.
The Exploit corrupted the experience for both of them.
Even if we don't abolish the Exploit, we need to decriminalize Switchoff. People using it need debugging--I mean, *medical care*--not punishment.
Okay. First: we don't yet know exactly what happened in that alley between Meile Thorn and Stevn of the Glacier.
Second: everything you're talking about takes time to set up. Cracking down on Switchoff in the meantime--
--isn't working.
We want a referendum on the Emotion Exploit.
Or we will protest again. And again. And *again.* No matter how many of us they kill.
You've said you're here to keep the peace, Lantern, so give the Council our *demand.*

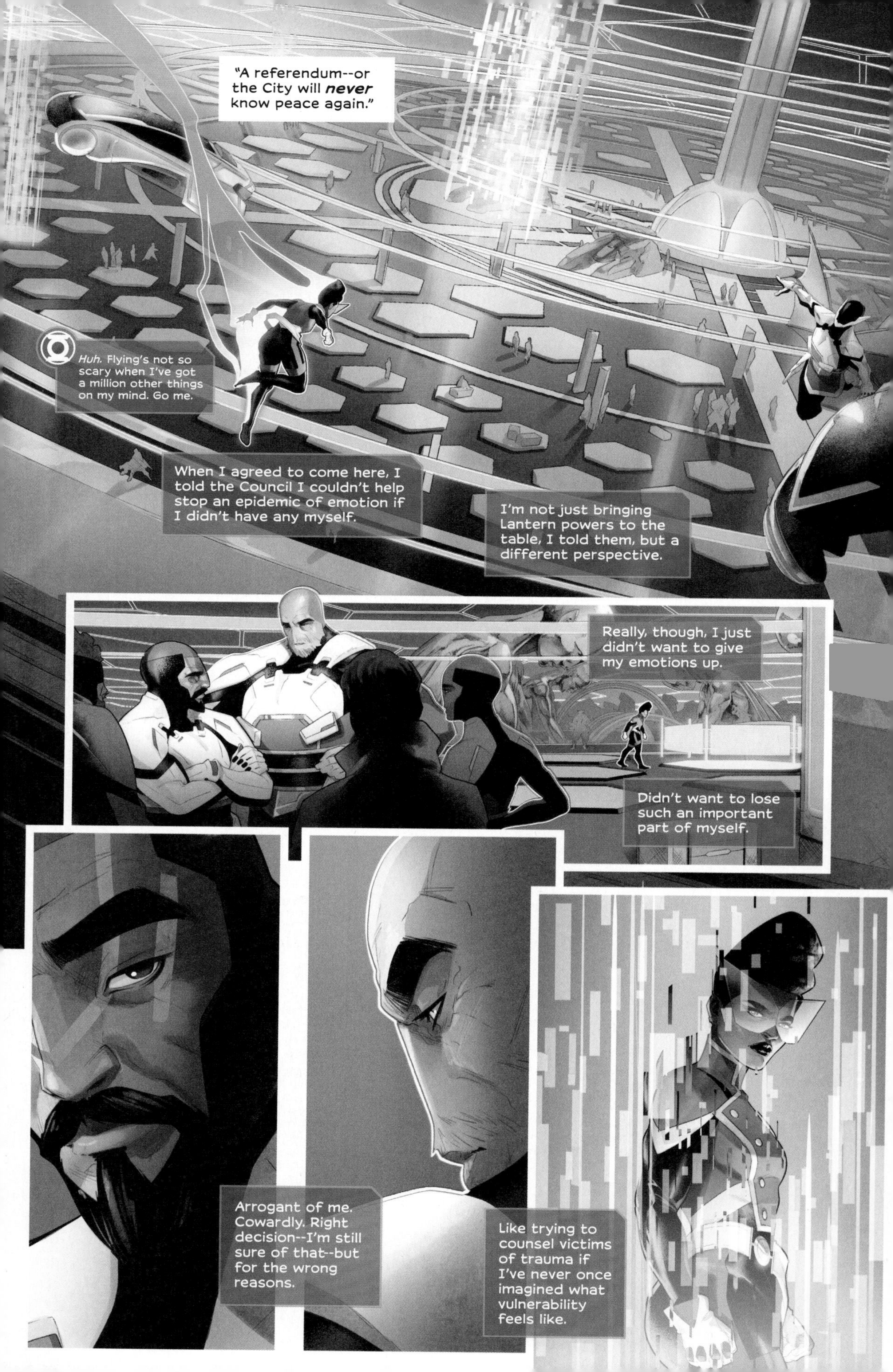
"A referendum--or the City will ***never*** know peace again."
Huh. Flying's not so scary when I've got a million other things on my mind. Go me.
When I agreed to come here, I told the Council I couldn't help stop an epidemic of emotion if I didn't have any myself.
I'm not just bringing Lantern powers to the table, I told them, but a different perspective.
Really, though, I just didn't want to give my emotions up.
Didn't want to lose such an important part of myself.
Arrogant of me. Cowardly. Right decision--I'm still sure of that--but for the wrong reasons.
Like trying to counsel victims of trauma if I've never once imagined what vulnerability feels like.

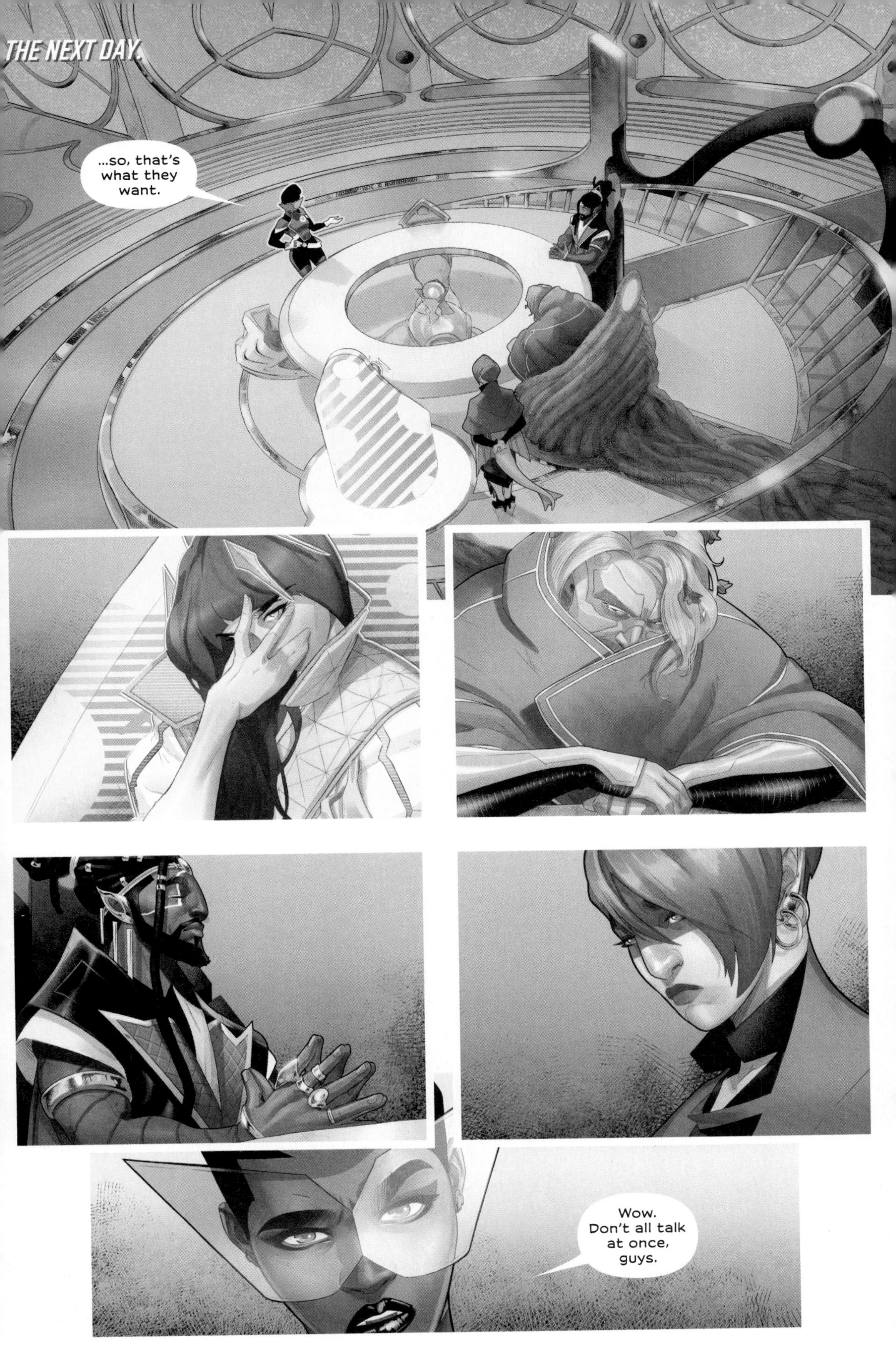
THE NEXT DAY.
...so, that's what they want.
Wow. Don't all talk at once, guys.

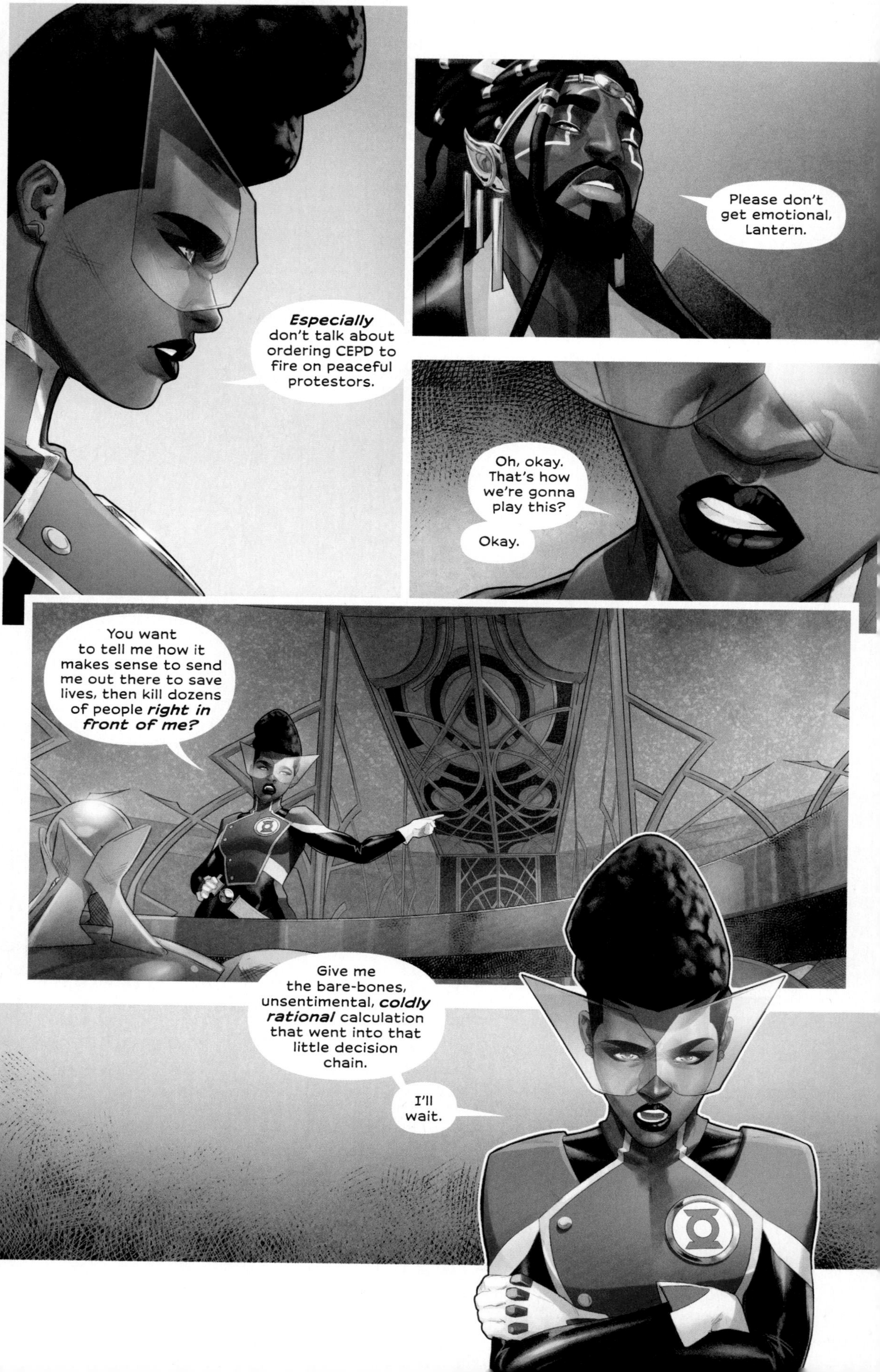
Please don't get emotional, Lantern.
Especially don't talk about ordering CEPD to fire on peaceful protestors.
Oh, okay. That's how we're gonna play this?
Okay.
You want to tell me how it makes sense to send me out there to save lives, then kill dozens of people *right in front of me?*
Give me the bare-bones, unsentimental, *coldly rational* calculation that went into that little decision chain.
I'll wait.

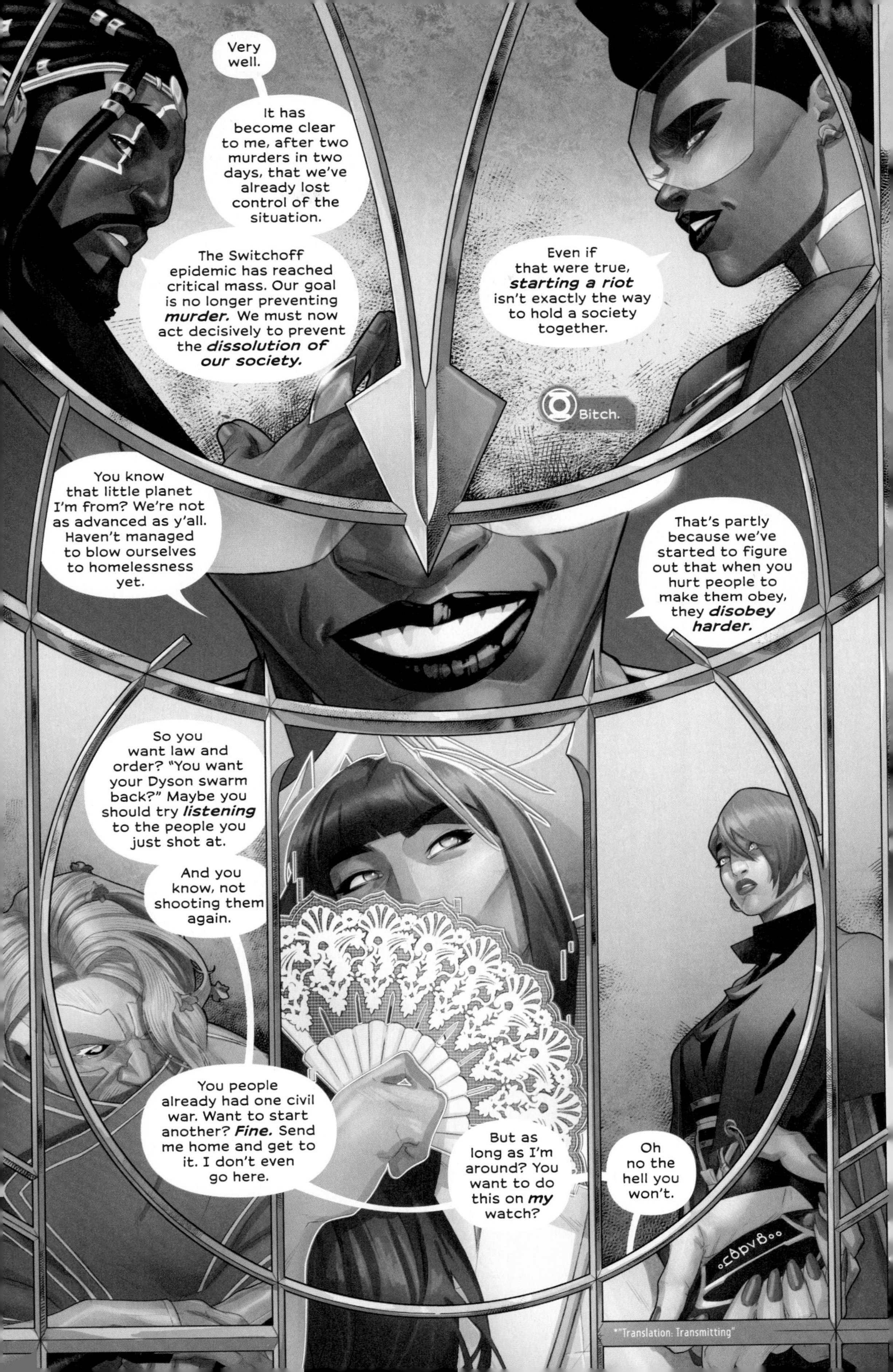
Very well.
It has become clear to me, after two murders in two days, that we've already lost control of the situation.
The Switchoff epidemic has reached critical mass. Our goal is no longer preventing *murder.* We must now act decisively to prevent the *dissolution of our society.*
Even if that were true, ***starting a riot*** isn't exactly the way to hold a society together.
Bitch.
You know that little planet I'm from? We're not as advanced as y'all. Haven't managed to blow ourselves to homelessness yet.
That's partly because we've started to figure out that when you hurt people to make them obey, they *disobey harder.*
So you want law and order? "You want your Dyson swarm back?" Maybe you should try *listening* to the people you just shot at.
And you know, not shooting them again.
You people already had one civil war. Want to start another? *Fine.* Send me home and get to it. I don't even go here.
But as long as I'm around? You want to do this on *my* watch?
Oh no the hell you won't.
*"Translation: Transmitting"

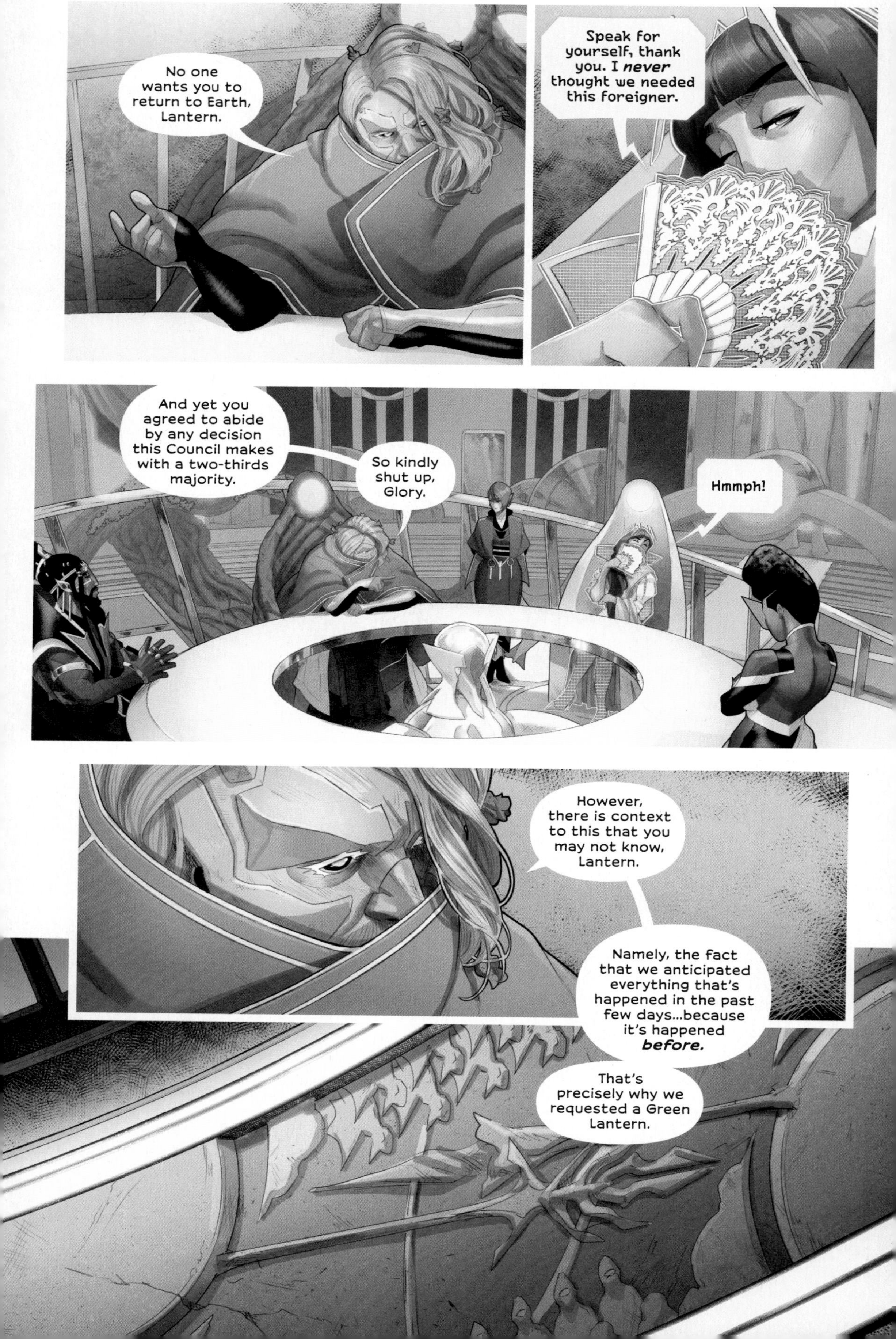
No one wants you to return to Earth, Lantern.
Speak for yourself, thank you. I *never* thought we needed this foreigner.
And yet you agreed to abide by any decision this Council makes with a two-thirds majority.
So kindly shut up, Glory.
Hmmph!
However, there is context to this that you may not know, Lantern.
Namely, the fact that we anticipated everything that's happened in the past few days...because it's happened *before.*
That's precisely why we requested a Green Lantern.

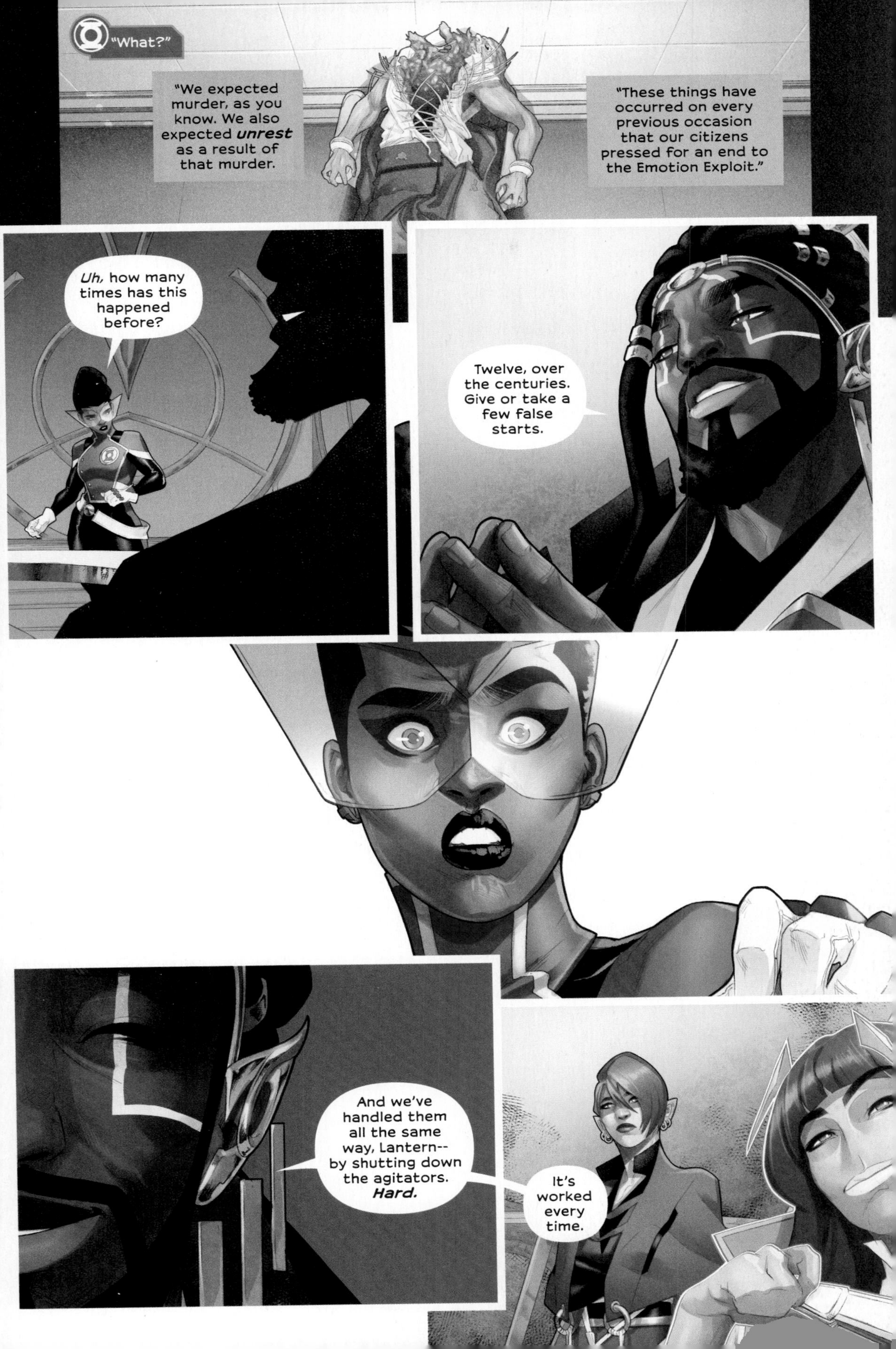
"What?"
"We expected murder, as you know. We also expected *unrest* as a result of that murder.
"These things have occurred on every previous occasion that our citizens pressed for an end to the Emotion Exploit."
Uh, how many times has this happened before?
Twelve, over the centuries. Give or take a few false starts.
And we've handled them all the same way, Lantern-- by shutting down the agitators. ***Hard.***
It's worked every time.

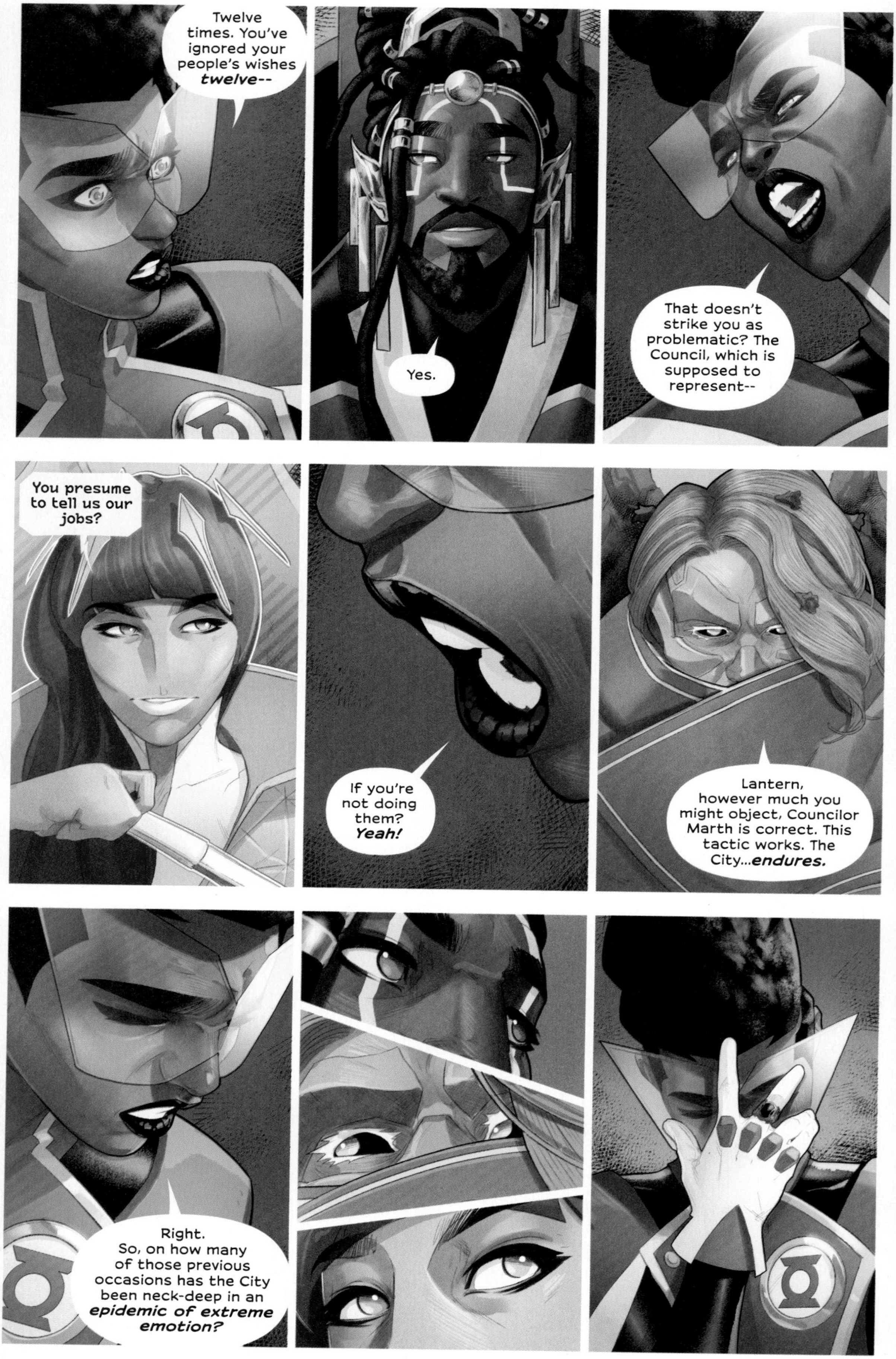
Twelve times. You've ignored your people's wishes *twelve--*
Yes.
That doesn't strike you as problematic? The Council, which is supposed to represent--
You presume to tell us our jobs?
If you're not doing them? *Yeah!*
Lantern, however much you might object, Councilor Marth is correct. This tactic works. The City...*endures.*
Right. So, on how many of those previous occasions has the City been neck-deep in an *epidemic of extreme emotion?*

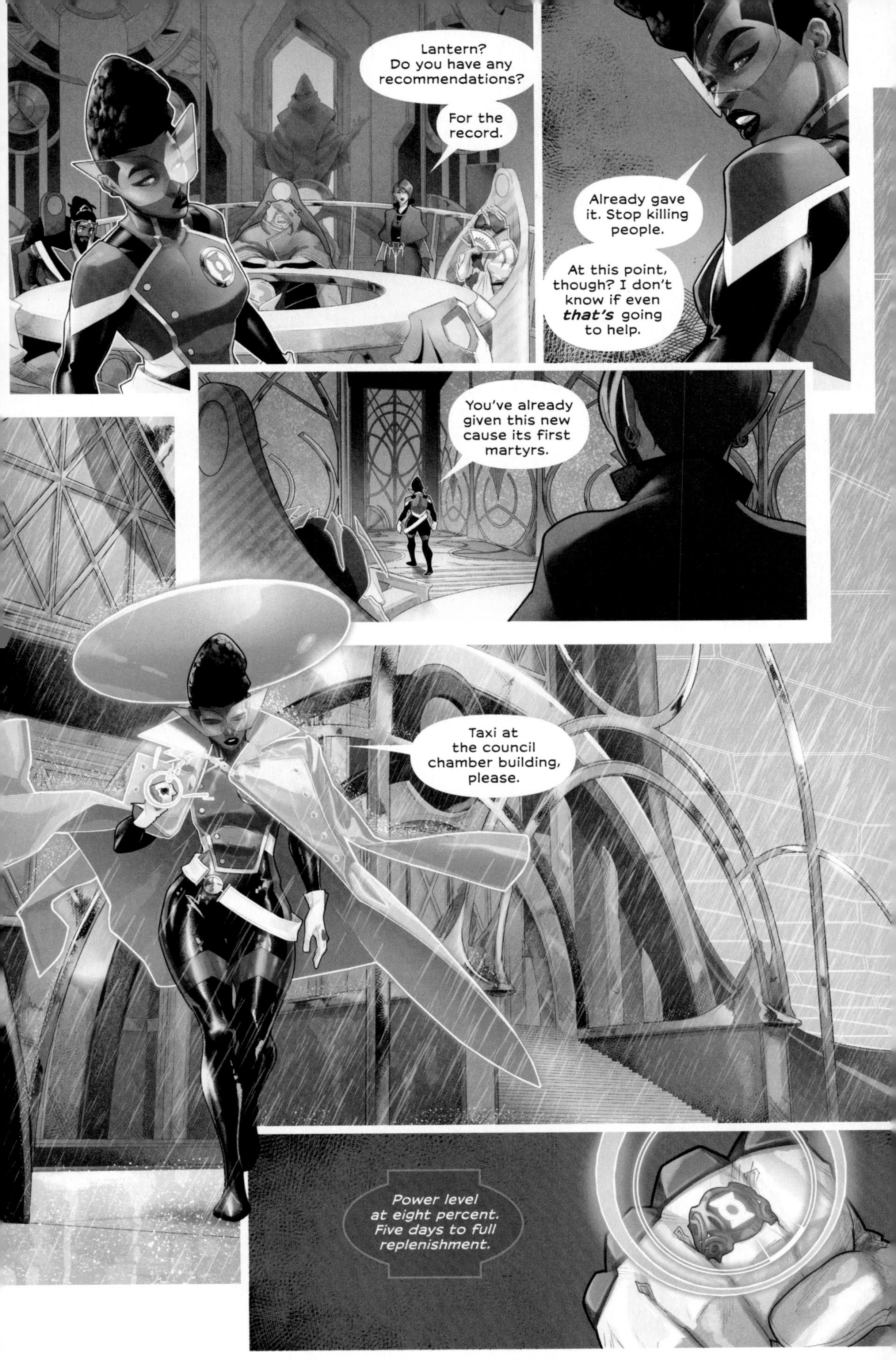
Lantern? Do you have any recommendations?
For the record.
Already gave it. Stop killing people.
At this point, though? I don't know if even *that's* going to help.
You've already given this new cause its first martyrs.
Taxi at the council chamber building, please.
Power level at eight percent. Five days to full replenishment.

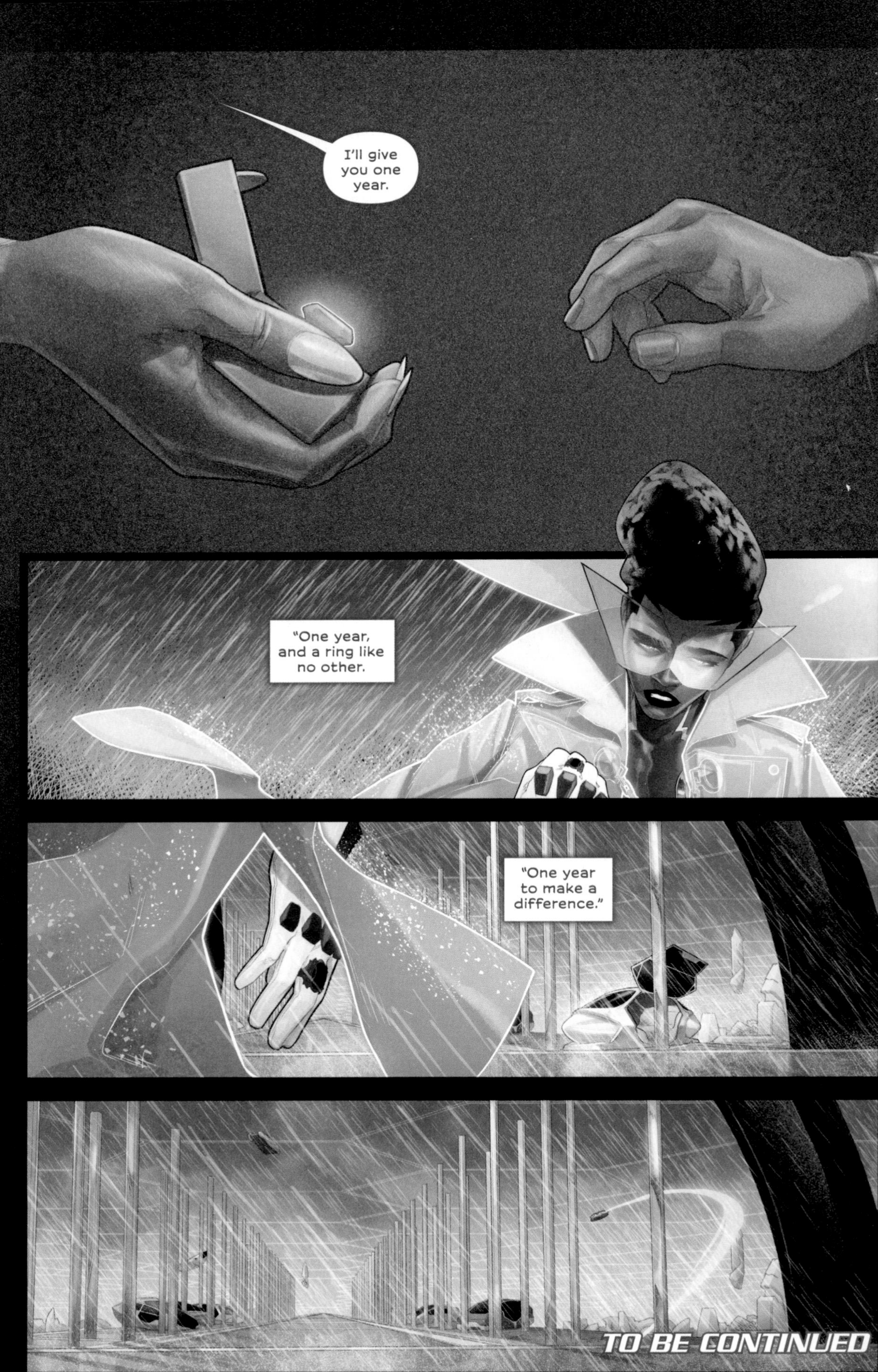
I'll give you one year.
"One year, and a ring like no other.
"One year to make a difference."
TO BE CONTINUED

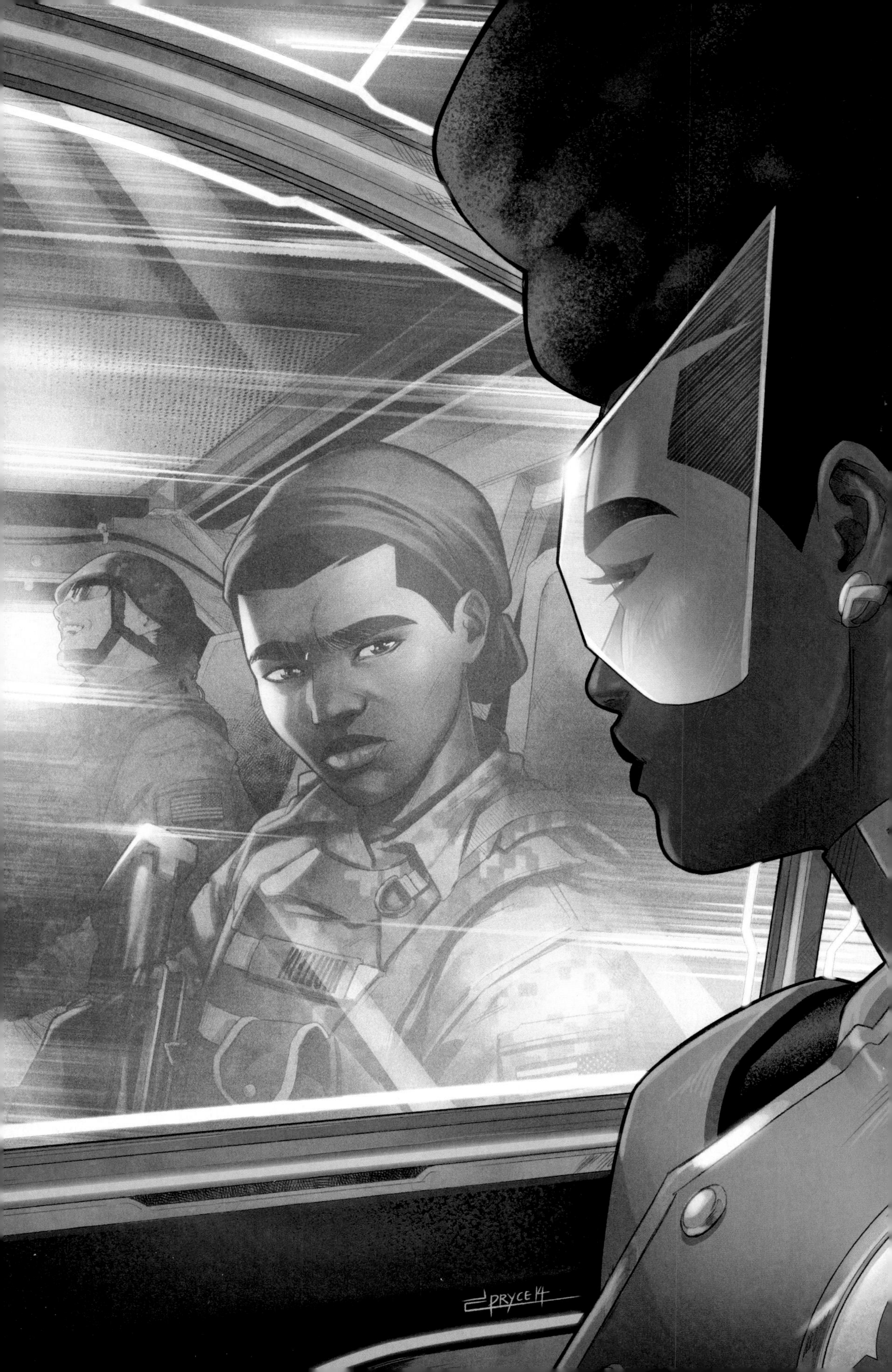

PRYCE 14

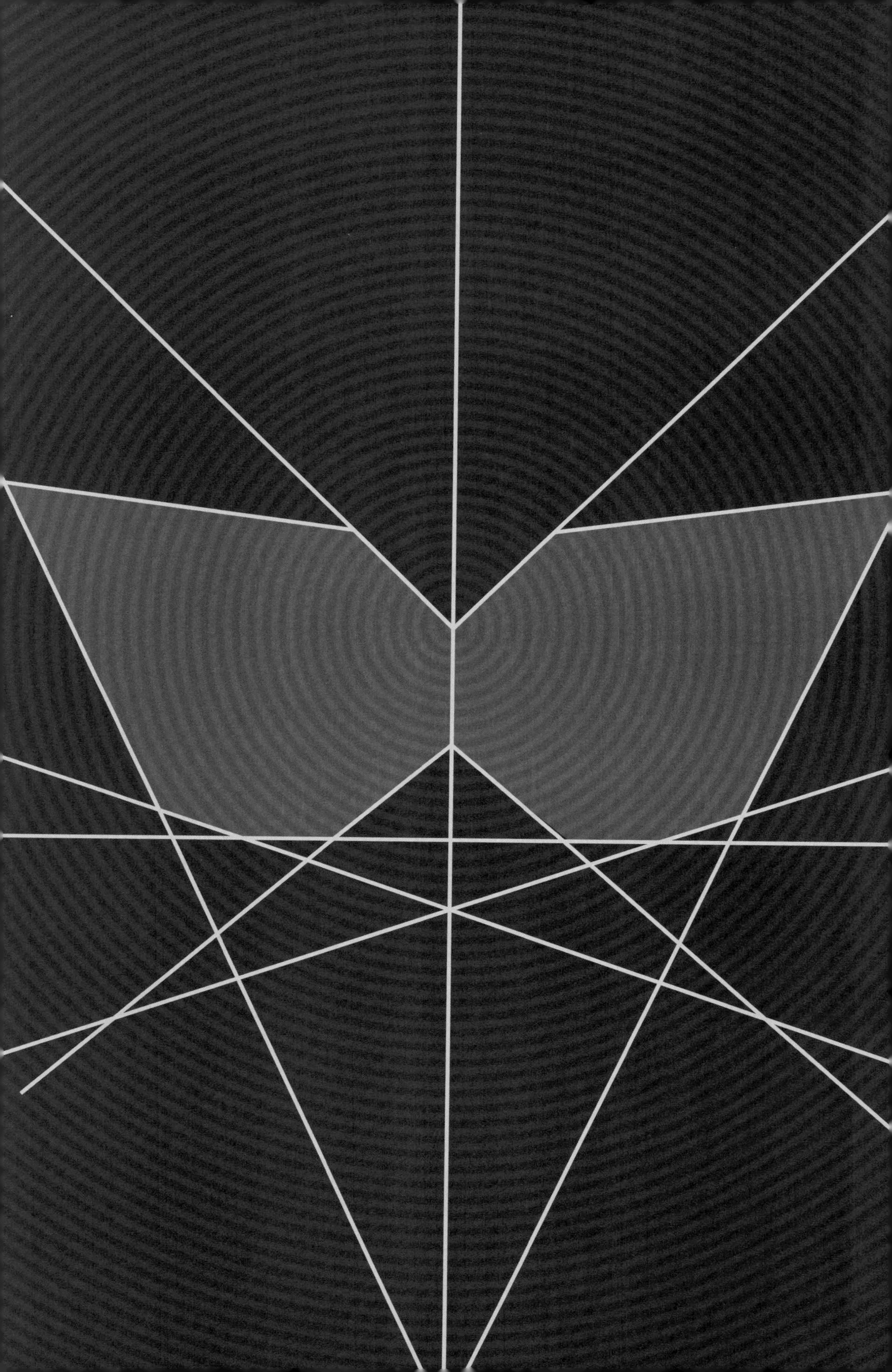

OAN INTELLIGENCE EXTRA-JURISDICTIONAL FILE ARCHIVE
THE CITY ENDURING: SOCIOLOGY
TRANSLATION: ENGLISH
UPDATE: IN PROGRESS

THE TRILOGY CONSISTS OF THREE SPECIES: TWO BIOLOGICALLY EVOLVED, ONE ARTIFICIALLY EVOLVED. THE NAH ARE ENDOGAMOUS AERIAL PURSUIT PREDATORS ANALOGOUS TO EARTH'S PRIMATES. THE @AT ARE OPTIONALLY-CORPOREAL CYBERNETIC SYMBIOTES. THE KEH-TOPLI ARE CARNIVOROUS AMBULATORY SOCIAL PLANTS. OFFICIAL STRIFE BETWEEN THESE THREE SPECIES ENDED WITH BURNOVER. SIGNIFICANT UNOFFICIAL RIVALRY CONTINUES.

Story: **N.K. JEMISIN** Art & Color: **JAMAL CAMPBELL**
Lettering: **DERON BENNETT** Cover: **JAMAL CAMPBELL**
Variant Cover: **WARREN LOUW**
Associate Editor: **MAGGIE HOWELL** Editor: **ANDY KHOURI**
DC's Young Animal Curated by **GERARD WAY**

"The master's tools will never dismantle
the master's house."
—Audre Lorde

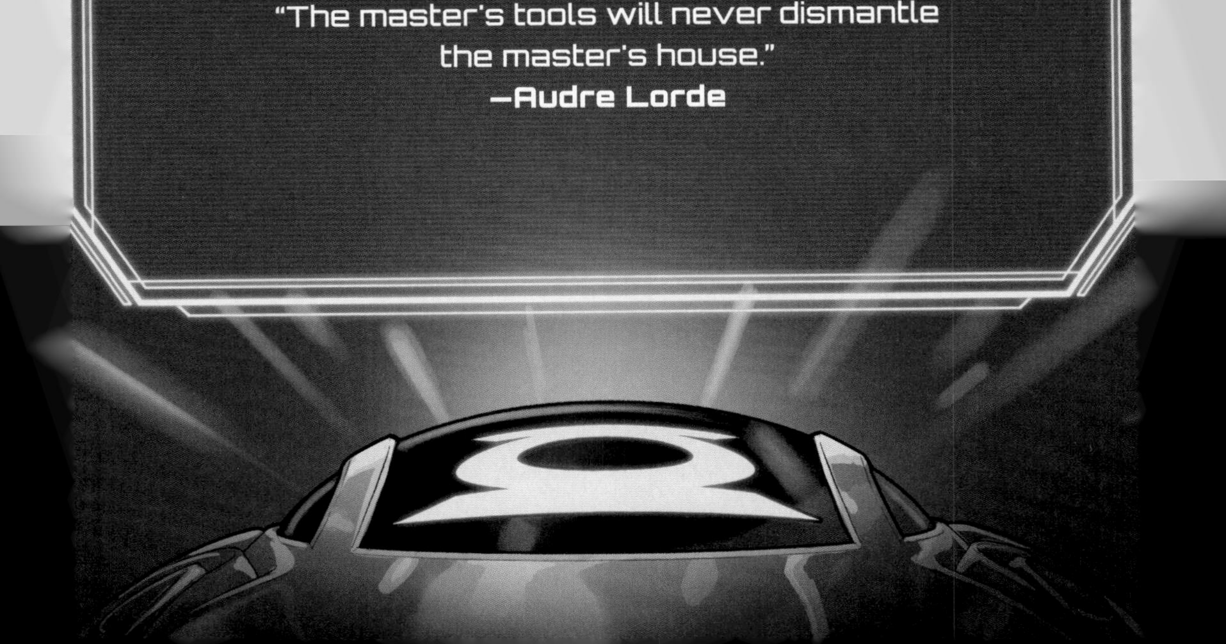

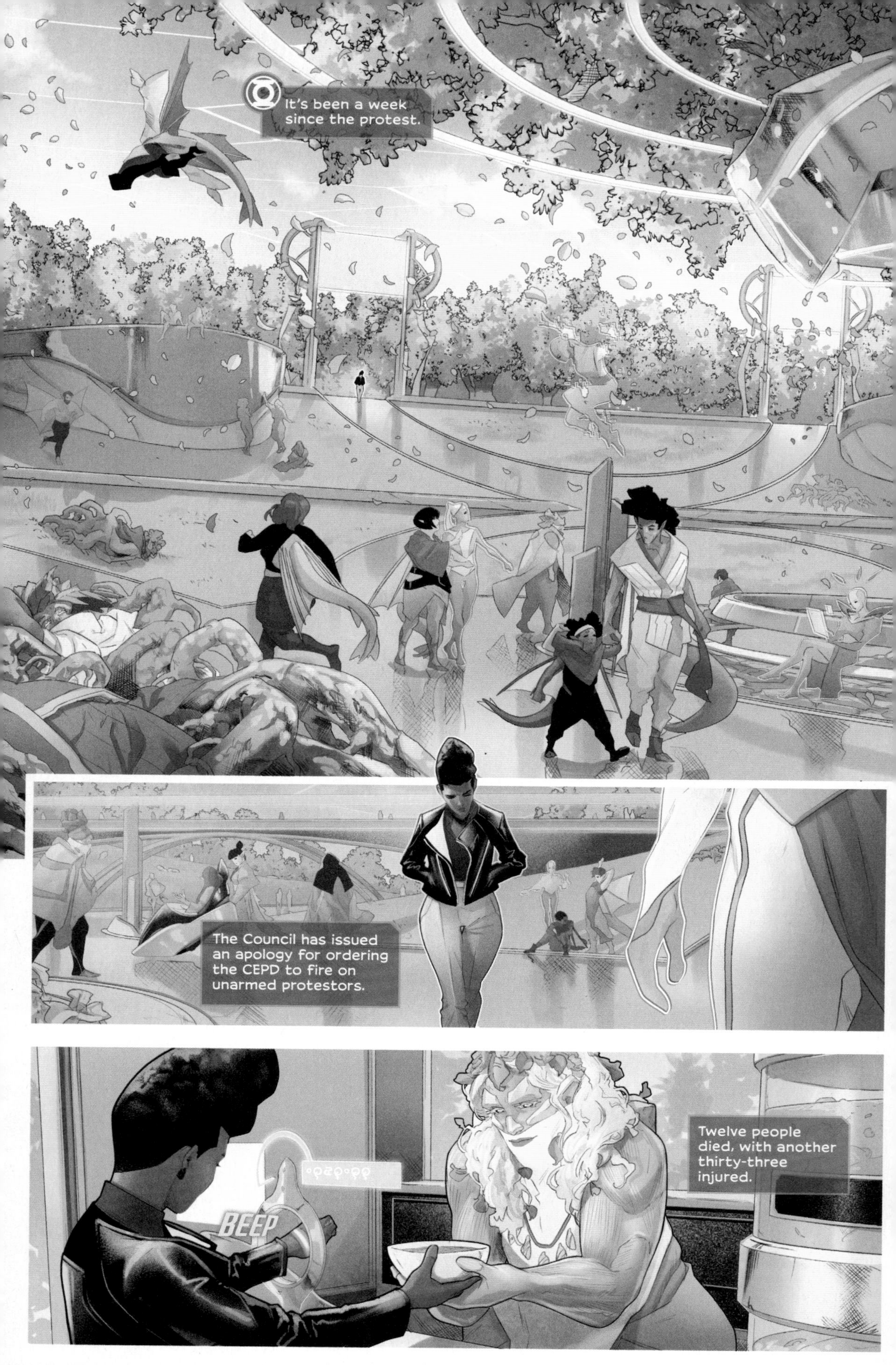
It's been a week since the protest.
The Council has issued an apology for ordering the CEPD to fire on unarmed protestors.
BEEP
Twelve people died, with another thirty-three injured.

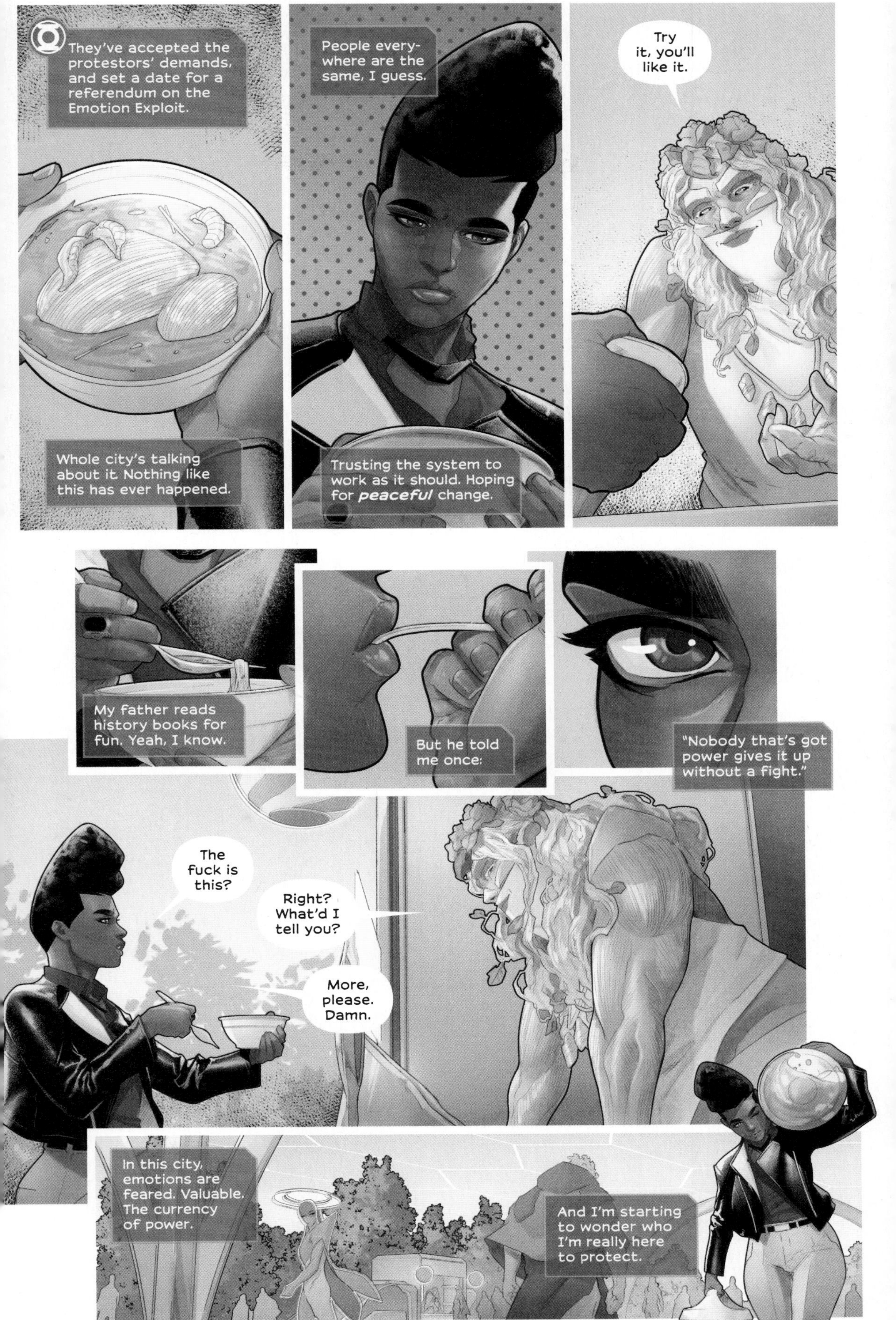
They've accepted the protestors' demands, and set a date for a referendum on the Emotion Exploit.
Whole city's talking about it Nothing like this has ever happened.
People every-where are the same, I guess.
Trusting the system to work as it should. Hoping for *peaceful* change.
Try it, you'll like it.
My father reads history books for fun. Yeah, I know.
But he told me once:
"Nobody that's got power gives it up without a fight."
The fuck is this?
Right? What'd I tell you?
More, please. Damn.
In this city, emotions are feared. Valuable. The currency of power.
And I'm starting to wonder who I'm really here to protect.

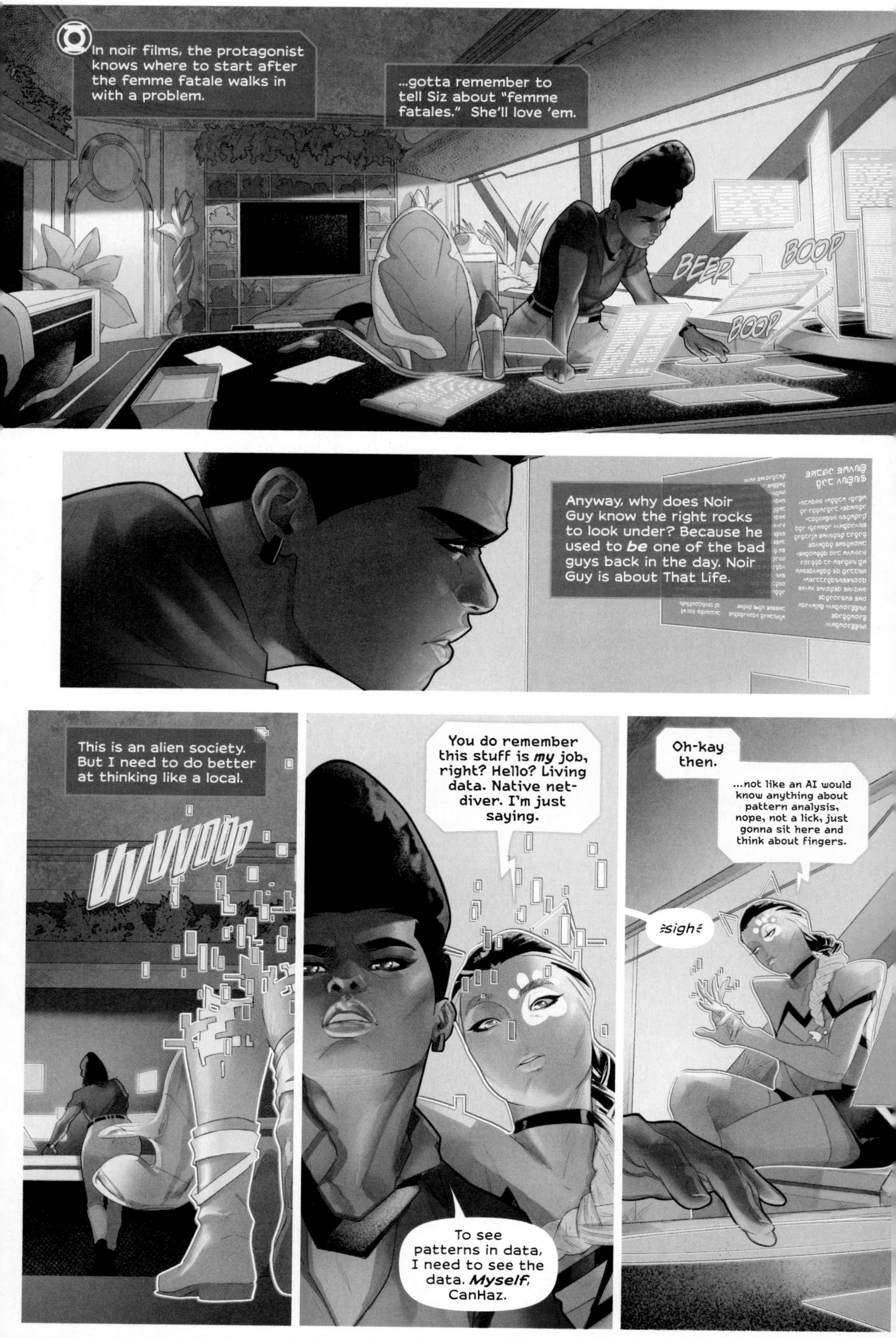
In noir films, the protagonist knows where to start after the femme fatale walks in with a problem.
...gotta remember to tell Siz about "femme fatales." She'll love 'em.
BEEP
BOOP
BOOP
Anyway, why does Noir Guy know the right rocks to look under? Because he used to *be* one of the bad guys back in the day. Noir Guy is about That Life.
This is an alien society. But I need to do better at thinking like a local.
VVVVOOP
You do remember this stuff is *my* job, right? Hello? Living data. Native net-diver. I'm just saying.
To see patterns in data, I need to see the data. *Myself*, CanHaz.
Oh-kay then.
...not like an AI would know anything about pattern analysis, nope, not a lick, just gonna sit here and think about fingers.
sigh

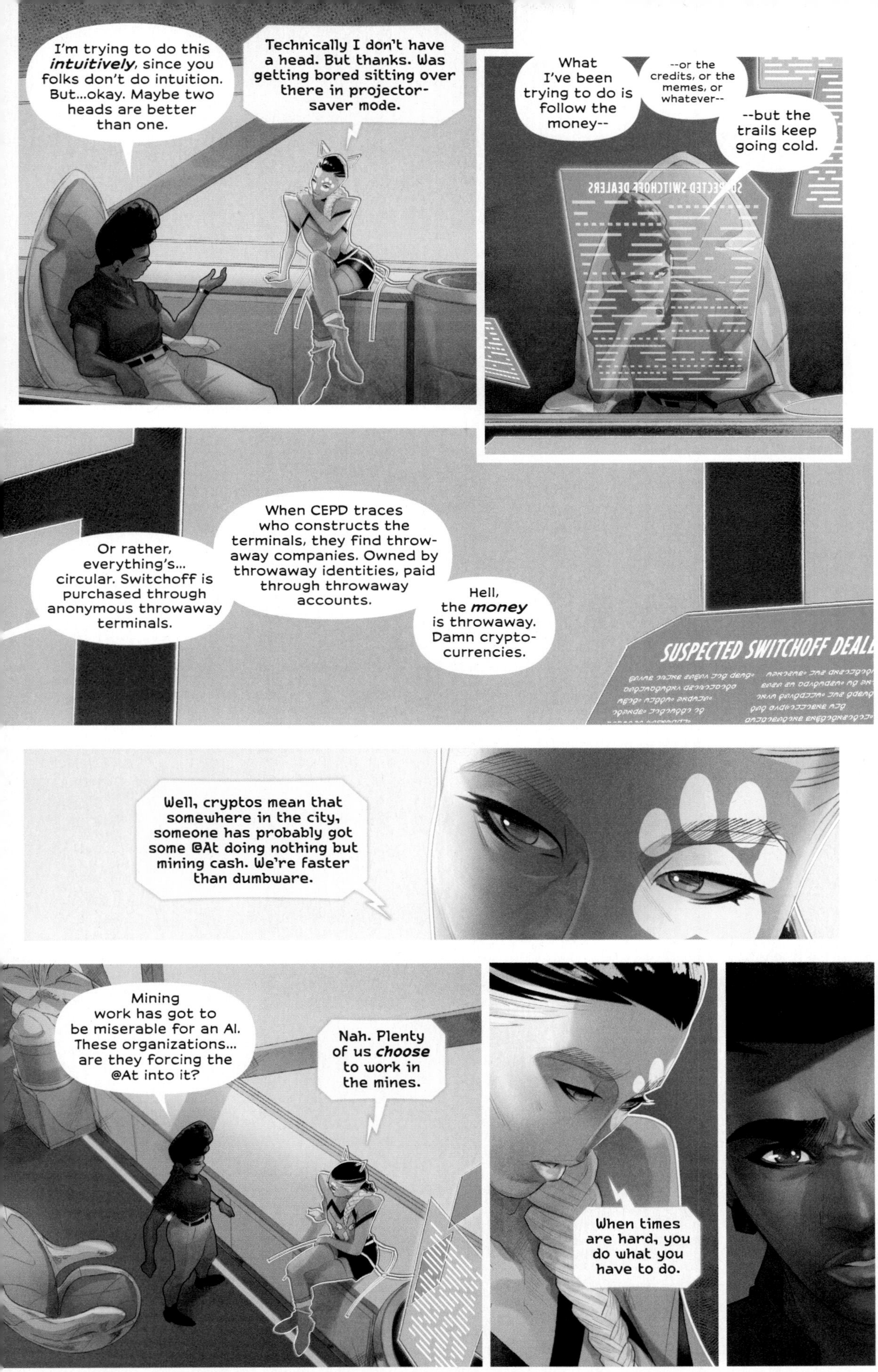
I'm trying to do this *intuitively*, since you folks don't do intuition. But...okay. Maybe two heads are better than one.
Technically I don't have a head. But thanks. Was getting bored sitting over there in projector-saver mode.
What I've been trying to do is follow the money--
--or the credits, or the memes, or whatever--
--but the trails keep going cold.
Or rather, everything's... circular. Switchoff is purchased through anonymous throwaway terminals.
When CEPD traces who constructs the terminals, they find throwaway companies. Owned by throwaway identities, paid through throwaway accounts.
Hell, the *money* is throwaway. Damn cryptocurrencies.
SUSPECTED SWITCHOFF DEAL
Well, cryptos mean that somewhere in the city, someone has probably got some @At doing nothing but mining cash. We're faster than dumbware.
Mining work has got to be miserable for an AI. These organizations... are they forcing the @At into it?
Nah. Plenty of us *choose* to work in the mines.
When times are hard, you do what you have to do.

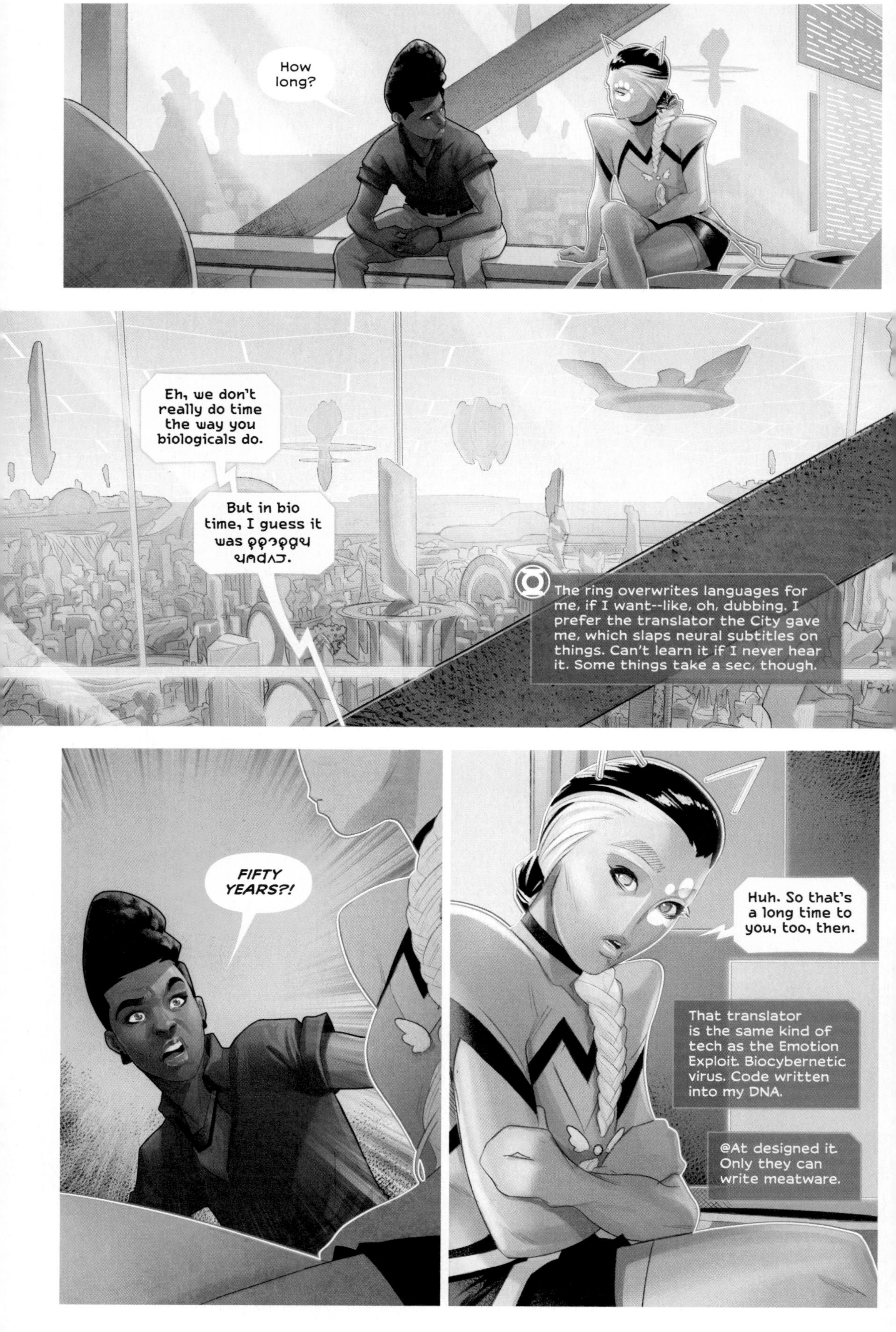
How long?
Eh, we don't really do time the way you biologicals do.
But in bio time, I guess it was
The ring overwrites languages for me, if I want--like, oh, dubbing. I prefer the translator the City gave me, which slaps neural subtitles on things. Can't learn it if I never hear it. Some things take a sec, though.
FIFTY YEARS?!
Huh. So that's a long time to you, too, then.
That translator is the same kind of tech as the Emotion Exploit. Biocybernetic virus. Code written into my DNA.
@At designed it. Only they can write meatware.

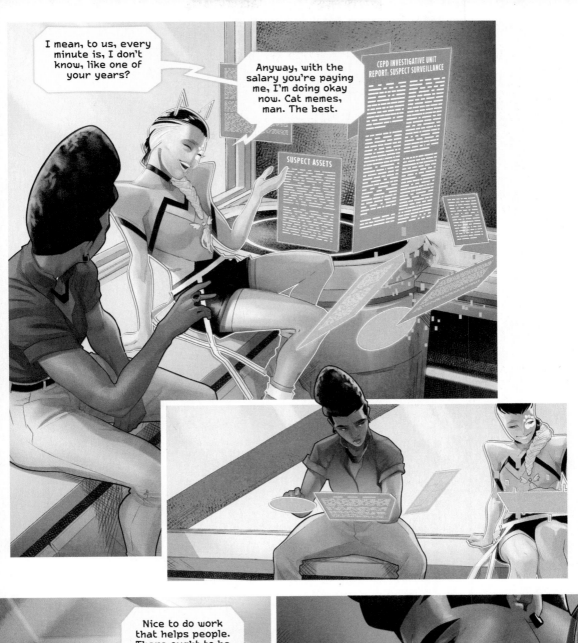

I mean, to us, every minute is, I don't know, like one of your years?

Anyway, with the salary you're paying me, I'm doing okay now. Cat memes, man. The best.

CEPD INVESTIGATIVE UNIT REPORT: SUSPECT SURVEILLANCE

SUSPECT ASSETS

Nice to do work that helps people. There ought to be more to life than just...getting by. Right?

Right.

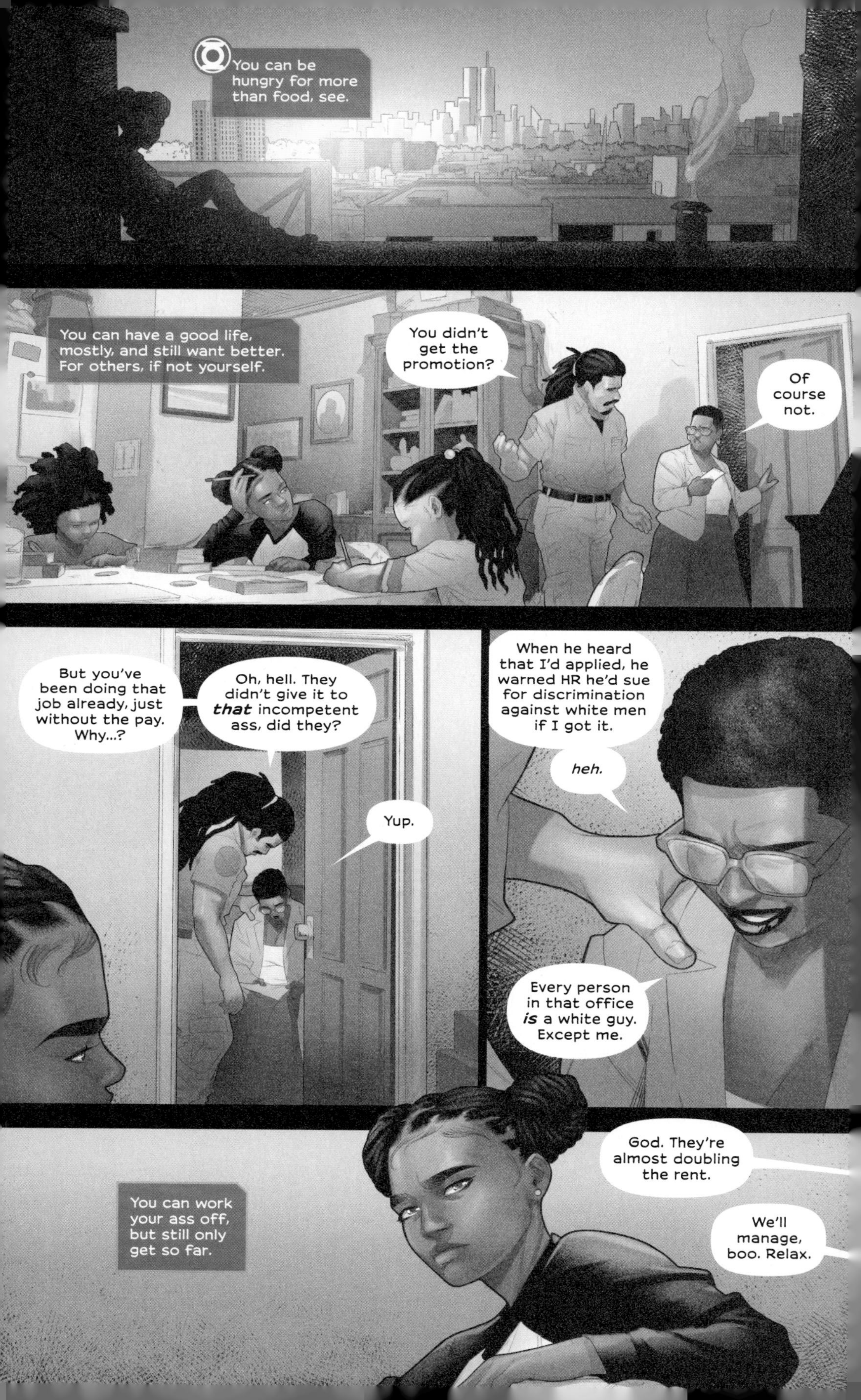

You can be hungry for more than food, see.
You can have a good life, mostly, and still want better. For others, if not yourself.
You didn't get the promotion?
Of course not.
But you've been doing that job already, just without the pay. Why...?
Oh, hell. They didn't give it to *that* incompetent ass, did they?
Yup.
When he heard that I'd applied, he warned HR he'd sue for discrimination against white men if I got it.
heh.
Every person in that office *is* a white guy. Except me.
You can work your ass off, but still only get so far.
God. They're almost doubling the rent.
We'll manage, boo. Relax.

The world isn't fair--but you can *want* it to be. That's a kind of hunger, too.

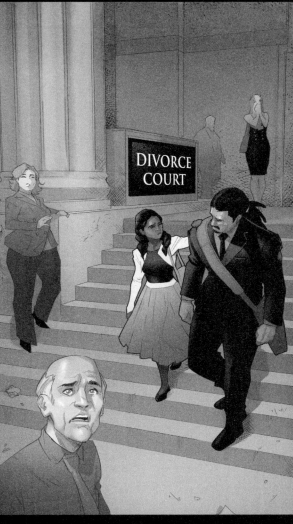

DIVORCE COURT

Then every-thing changes.

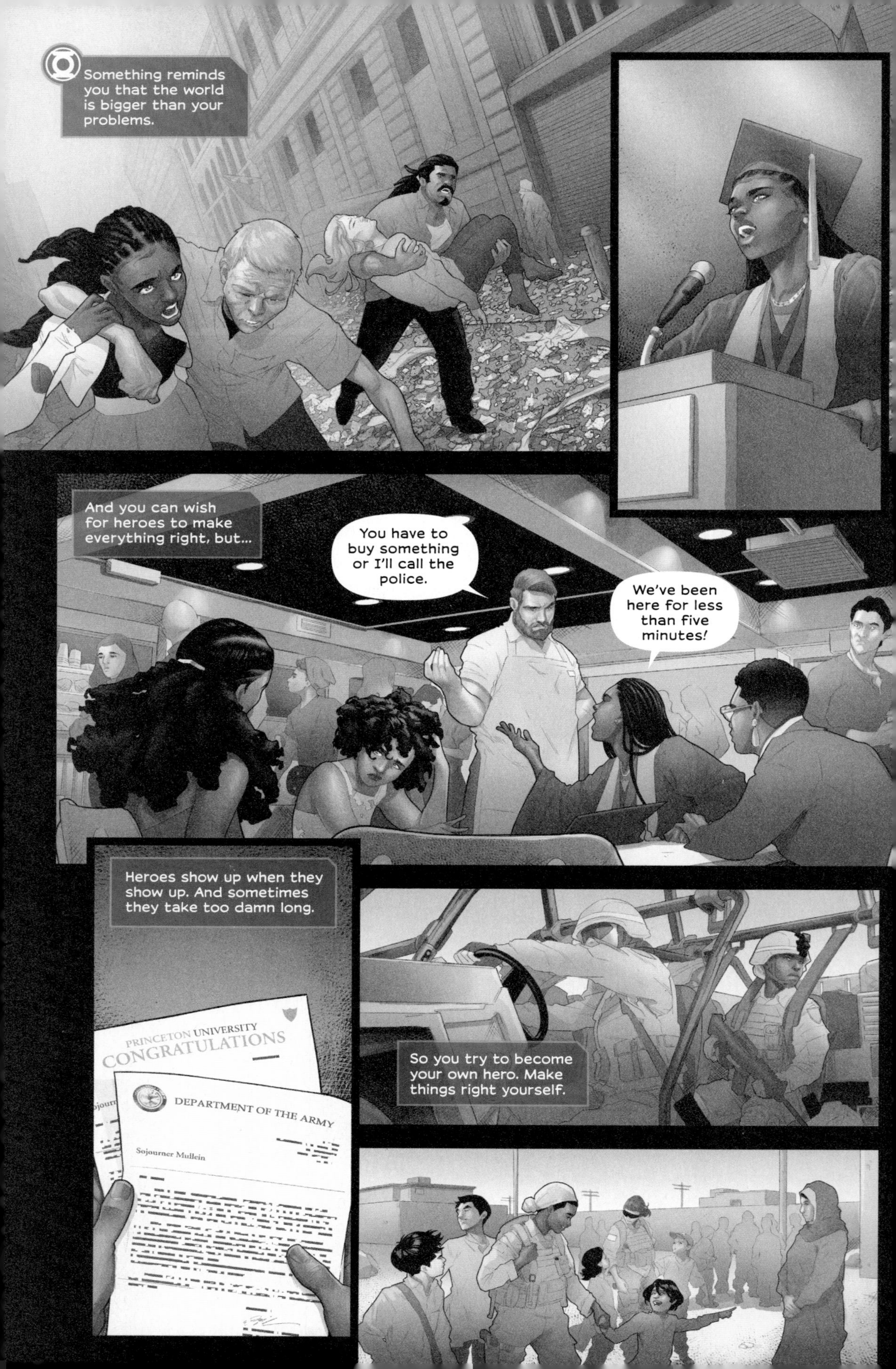
Something reminds you that the world is bigger than your problems.
And you can wish for heroes to make everything right, but...
You have to buy something or I'll call the police.
We've been here for less than five minutes!
Heroes show up when they show up. And sometimes they take too damn long.
PRINCETON UNIVERSITY
CONGRATULATIONS
DEPARTMENT OF THE ARMY
Sojourner Mullein
So you try to become your own hero. Make things right yourself.

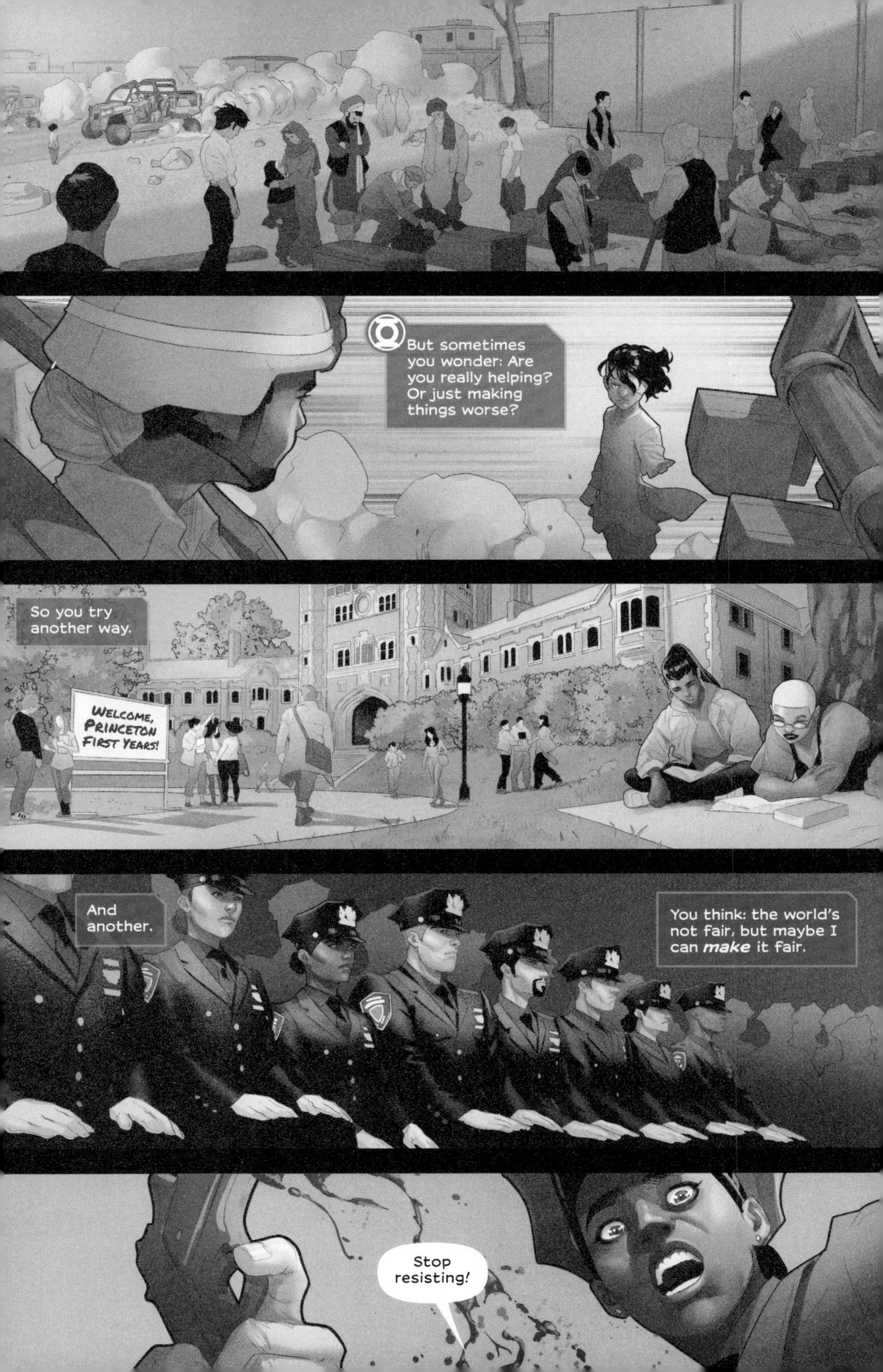

But sometimes you wonder: Are you really helping? Or just making things worse?
So you try another way.
Welcome, Princeton First Years!
And another.
You think: the world's not fair, but maybe I can *make* it fair.
Stop resisting!

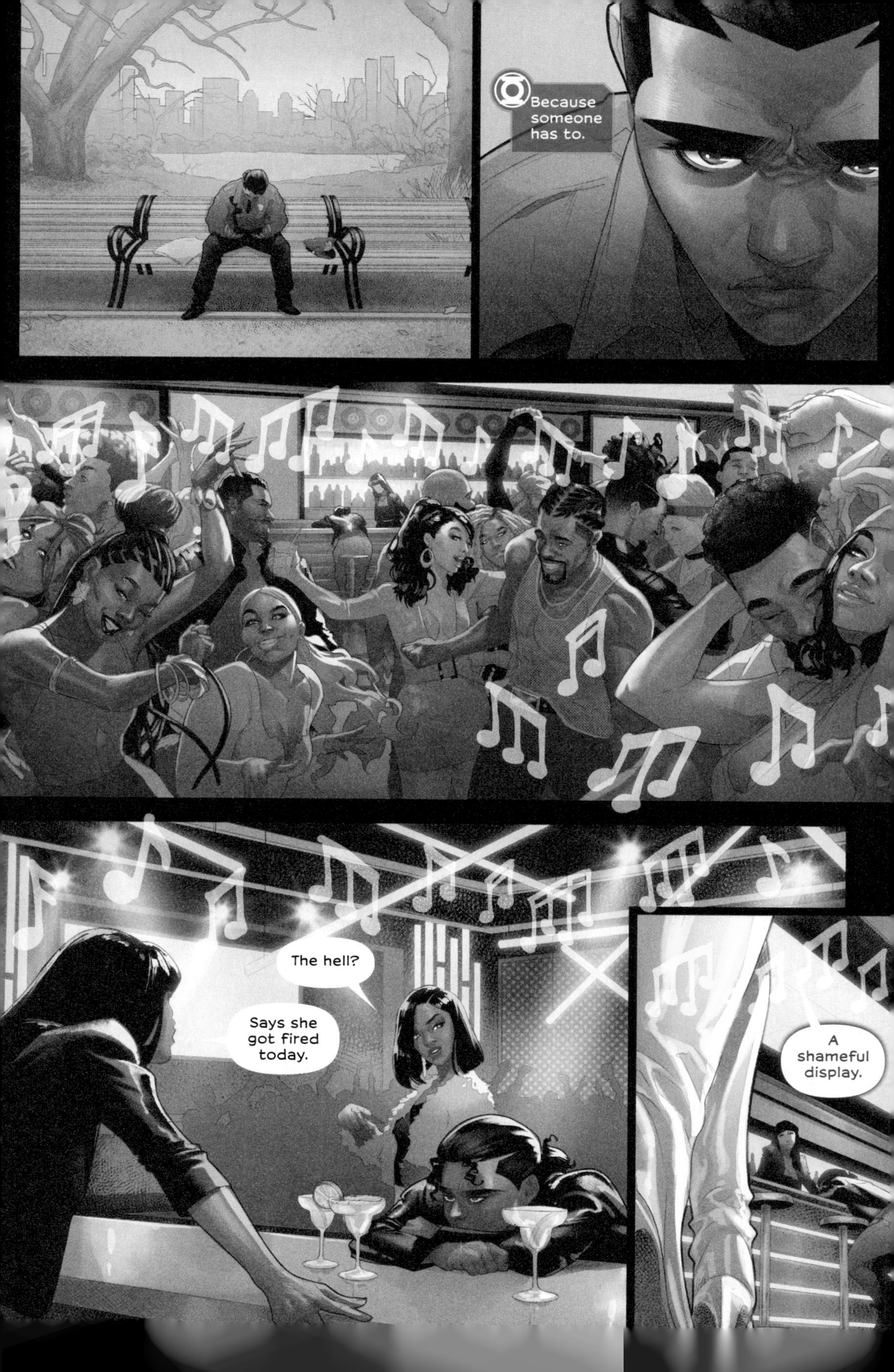
Because someone has to.
The hell?
Says she got fired today.
A shameful display.

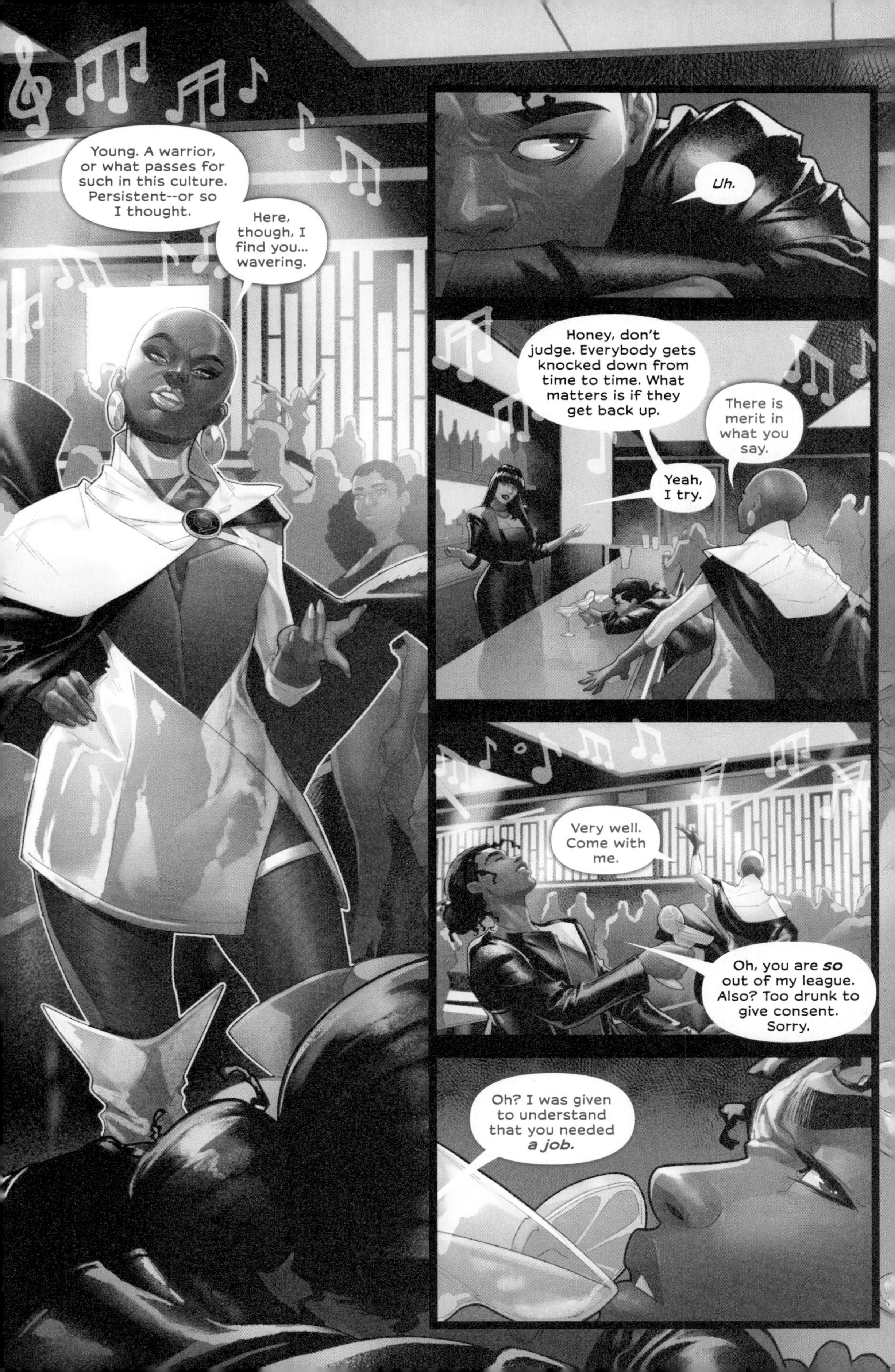
Young. A warrior, or what passes for such in this culture. Persistent--or so I thought.
Here, though, I find you... wavering.
Uh.
Honey, don't judge. Everybody gets knocked down from time to time. What matters is if they get back up.
There is merit in what you say.
Yeah, I try.
Very well. Come with me.
Oh, you are *so* out of my league. Also? Too drunk to give consent. Sorry.
Oh? I was given to understand that you needed ***a job.***

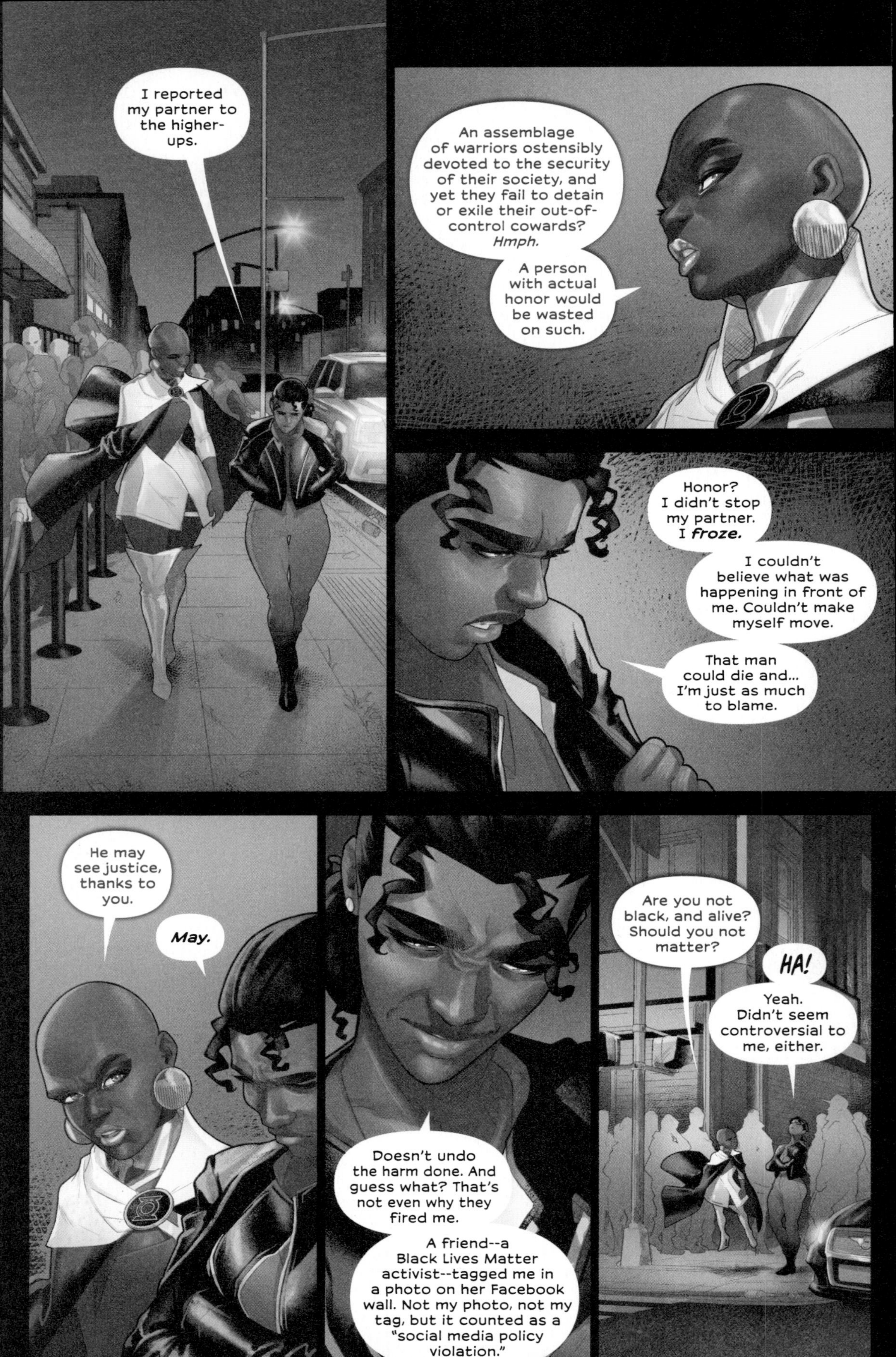
I reported my partner to the higher-ups.
An assemblage of warriors ostensibly devoted to the security of their society, and yet they fail to detain or exile their out-of-control cowards? *Hmph.*
A person with actual honor would be wasted on such.
Honor? I didn't stop my partner. I *froze.*
I couldn't believe what was happening in front of me. Couldn't make myself move.
That man could die and... I'm just as much to blame.
He may see justice, thanks to you.
May.
Doesn't undo the harm done. And guess what? That's not even why they fired me.
A friend--a Black Lives Matter activist--tagged me in a photo on her Facebook wall. Not my photo, not my tag, but it counted as a "social media policy violation."
Are you not black, and alive? Should you not matter?
HA!
Yeah. Didn't seem controversial to me, either.

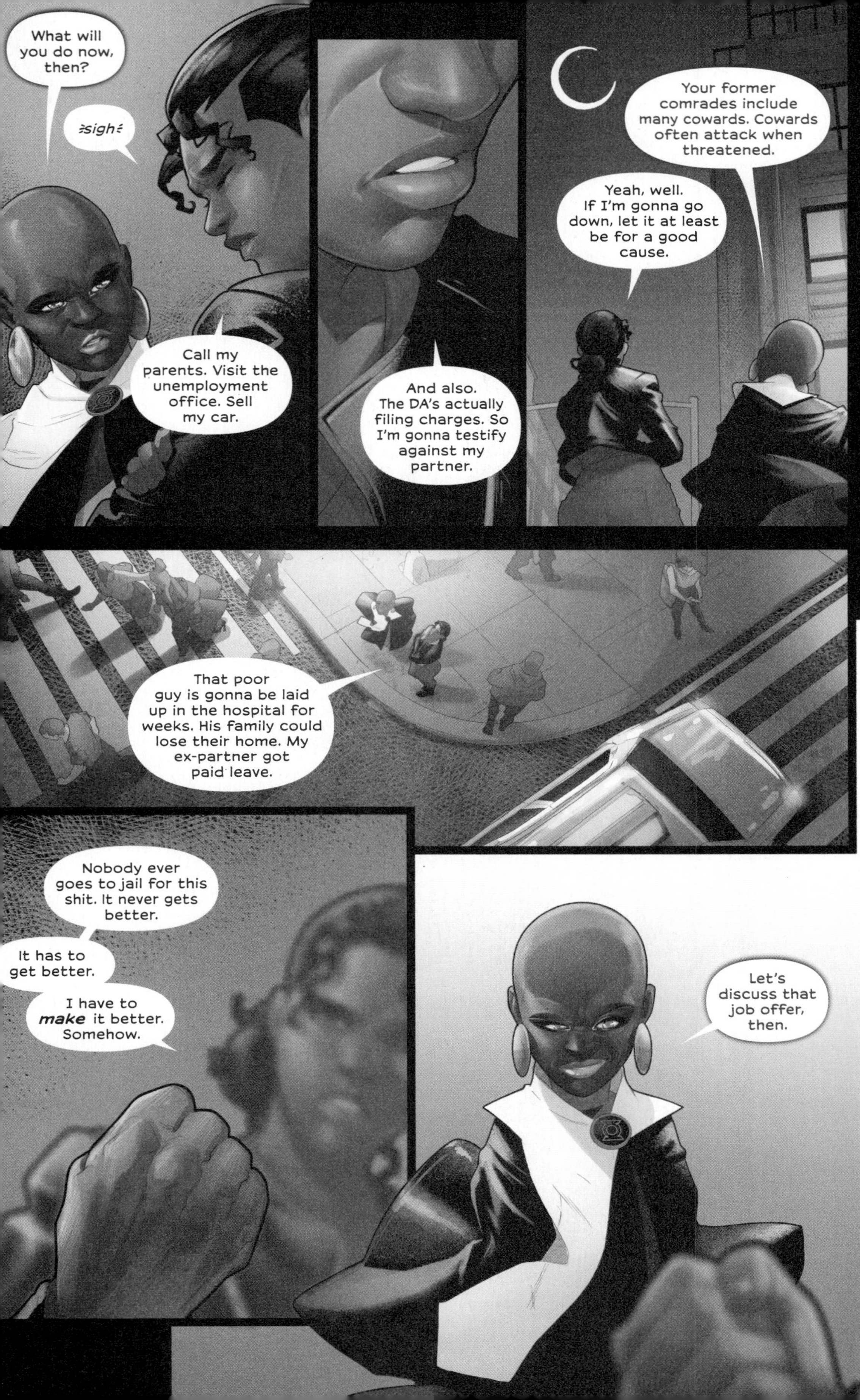
What will you do now, then?
sigh
Call my parents. Visit the unemployment office. Sell my car.
And also. The DA's actually filing charges. So I'm gonna testify against my partner.
Your former comrades include many cowards. Cowards often attack when threatened.
Yeah, well. If I'm gonna go down, let it at least be for a good cause.
That poor guy is gonna be laid up in the hospital for weeks. His family could lose their home. My ex-partner got paid leave.
Nobody ever goes to jail for this shit. It never gets better.
It has to get better.
I have to *make* it better. Somehow.
Let's discuss that job offer, then.

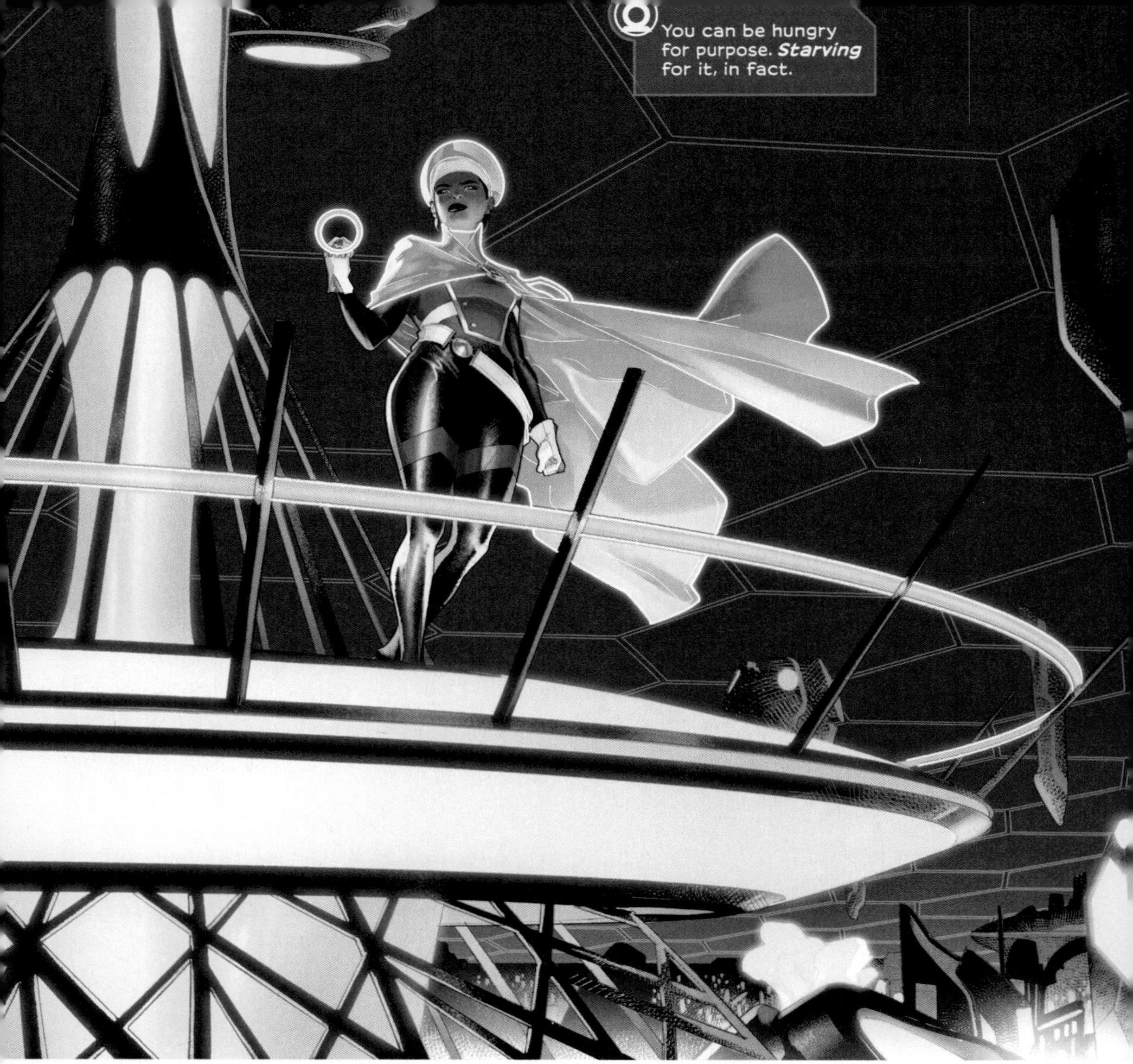
You can be hungry for purpose. *Starving* for it, in fact.

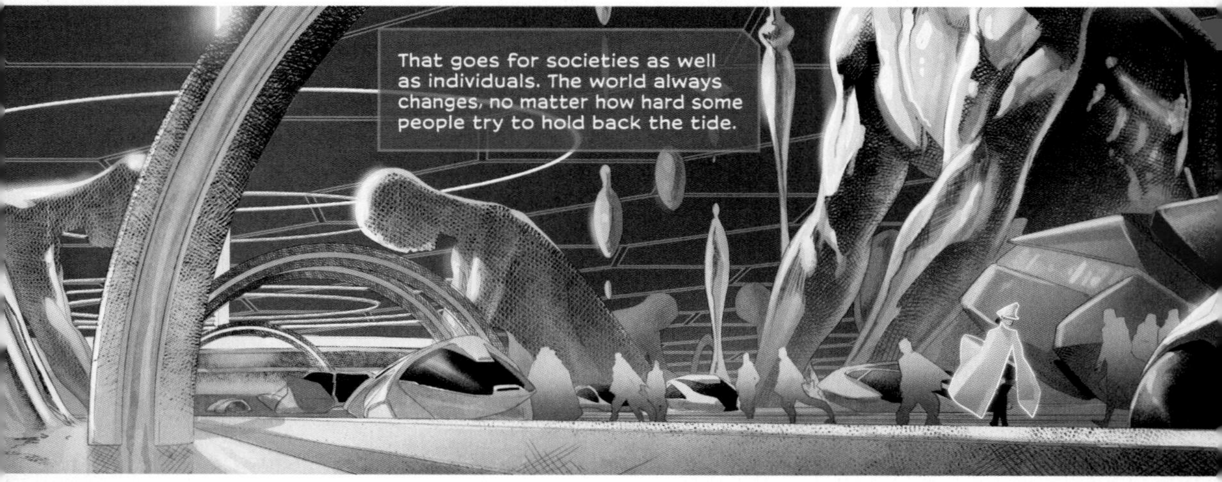
That goes for societies as well as individuals. The world always changes, no matter how hard some people try to hold back the tide.

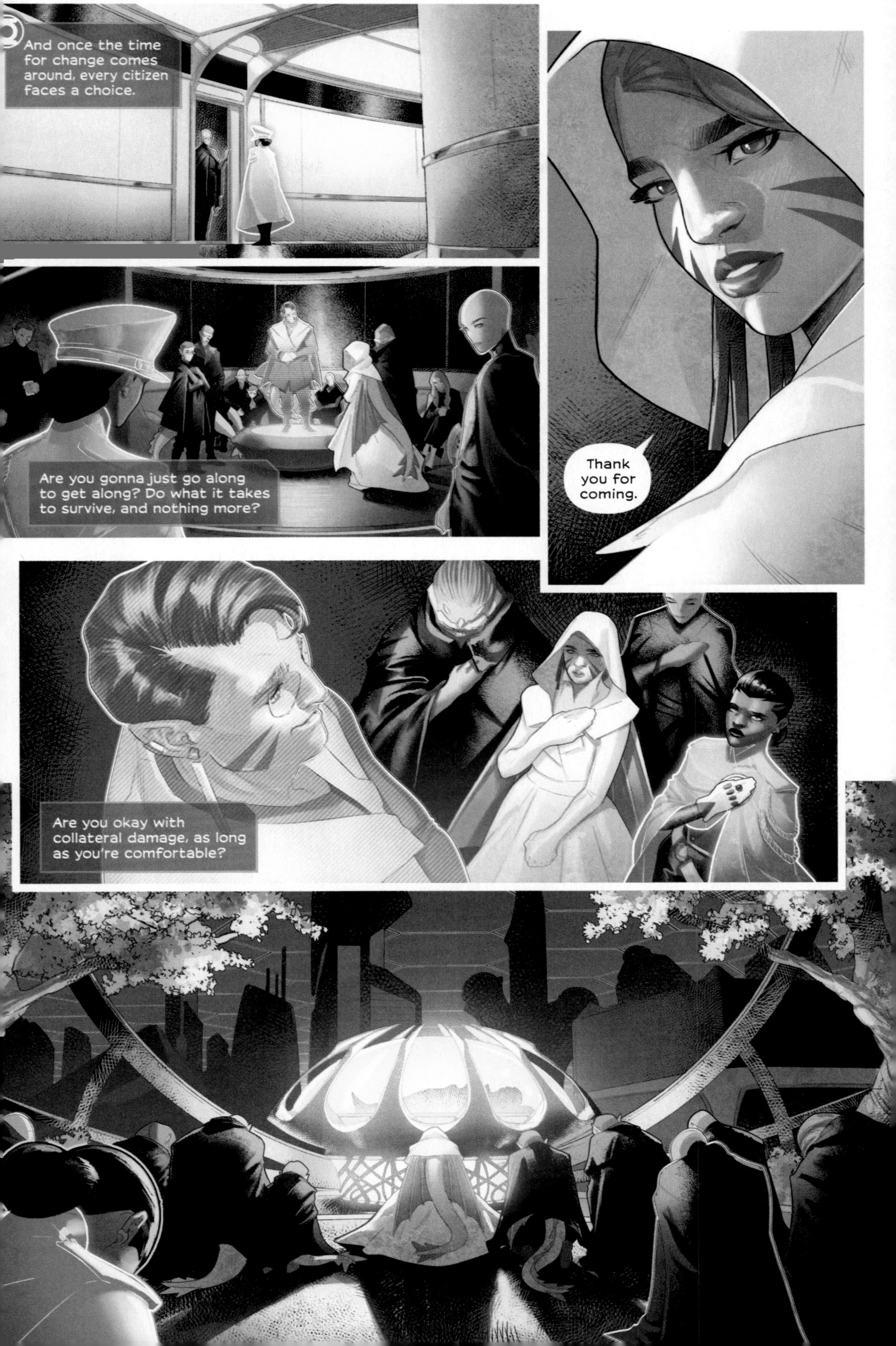
And once the time for change comes around, every citizen faces a choice.
Thank you for coming.
Are you gonna just go along to get along? Do what it takes to survive, and nothing more?
Are you okay with collateral damage, as long as you're comfortable?

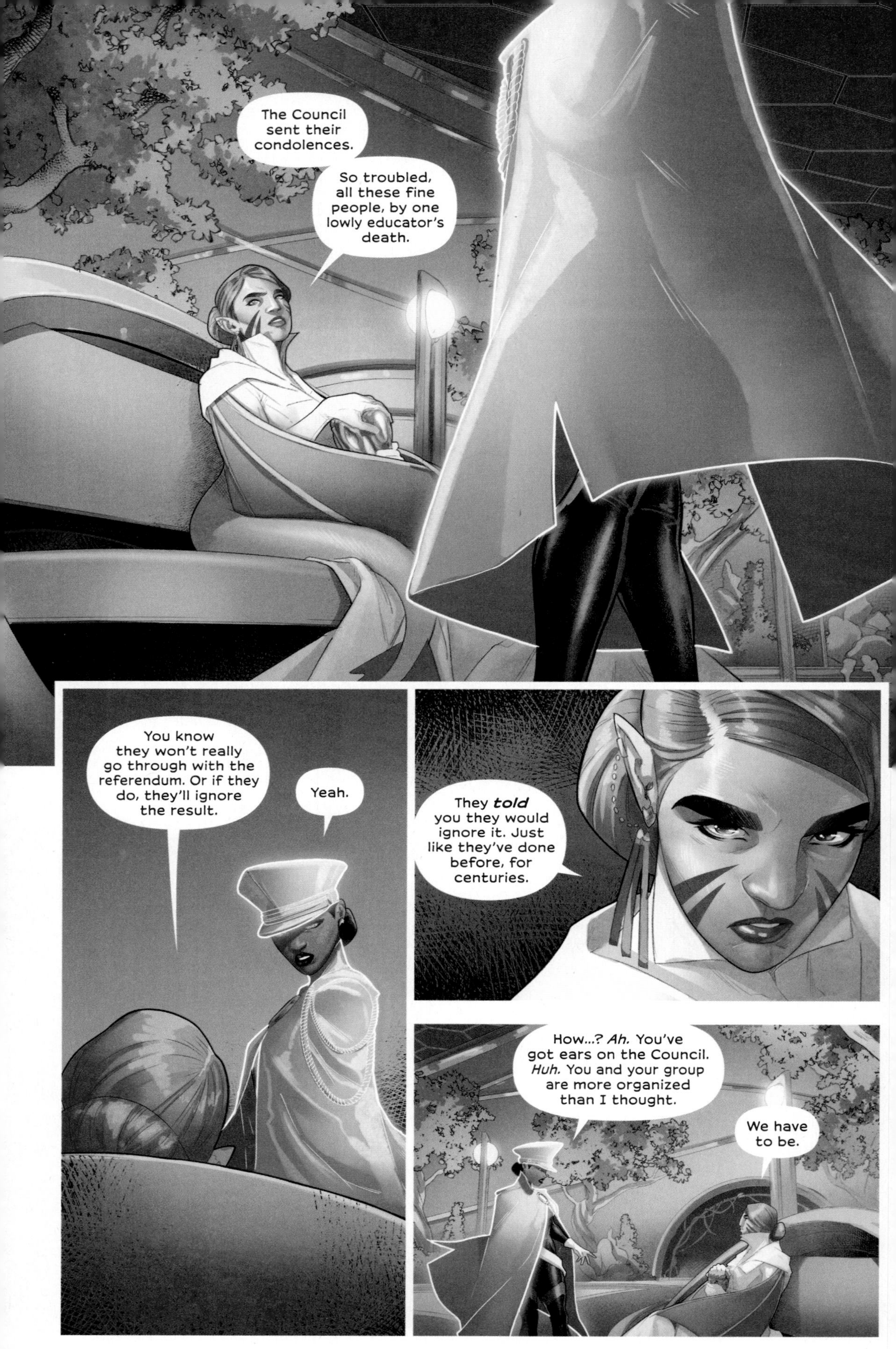
The Council sent their condolences.
So troubled, all these fine people, by one lowly educator's death.
You know they won't really go through with the referendum. Or if they do, they'll ignore the result.
Yeah.
They *told* you they would ignore it. Just like they've done before, for centuries.
How...? *Ah.* You've got ears on the Council. *Huh.* You and your group are more organized than I thought.
We have to be.

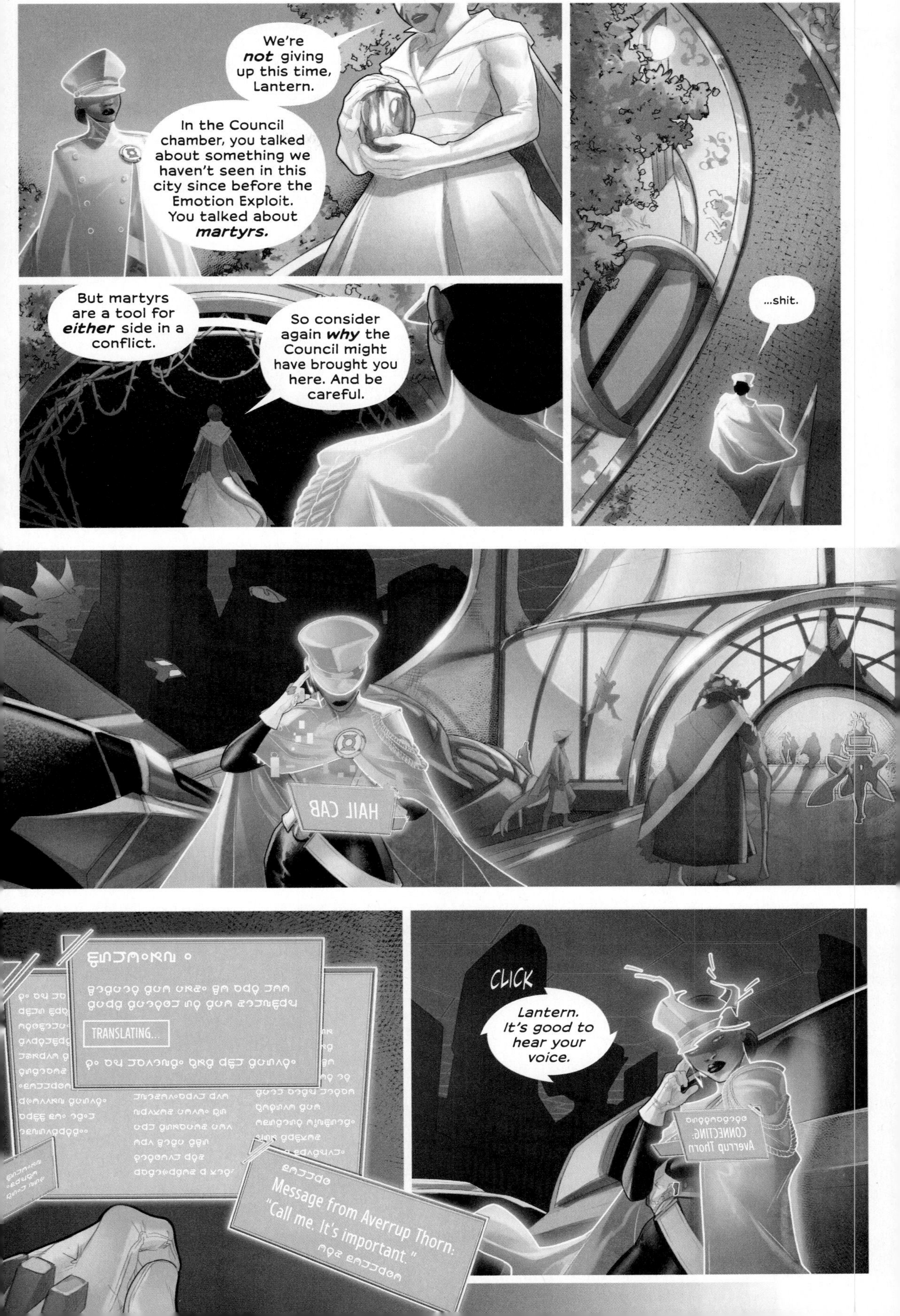
We're *not* giving up this time, Lantern.
In the Council chamber, you talked about something we haven't seen in this city since before the Emotion Exploit. You talked about *martyrs.*
...shit.
But martyrs are a tool for *either* side in a conflict.
So consider again *why* the Council might have brought you here. And be careful.
HAIL CAB
TRANSLATING...
Message from Averrup Thorn: "Call me. It's important."
CLICK
Lantern. It's good to hear your voice.
CONNECTING: Averrup Thorn

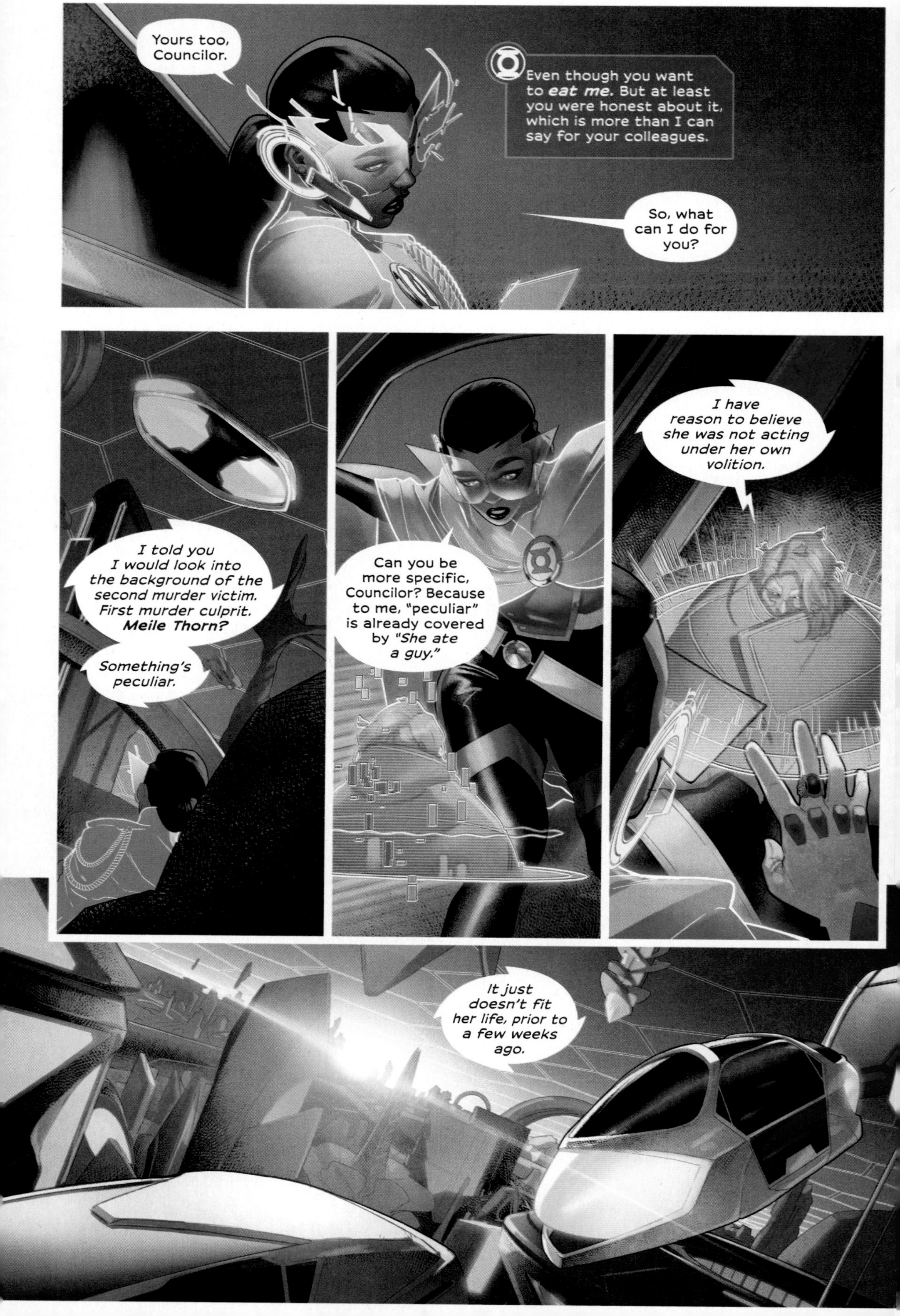
Yours too, Councilor.
Even though you want to *eat me.* But at least you were honest about it, which is more than I can say for your colleagues.
So, what can I do for you?
I told you I would look into the background of the second murder victim. First murder culprit. ***Meile Thorn?***
Something's peculiar.
Can you be more specific, Councilor? Because to me, "peculiar" is already covered by *"She ate a guy."*
I have reason to believe she was not acting under her own volition.
It just doesn't fit her life, prior to a few weeks ago.

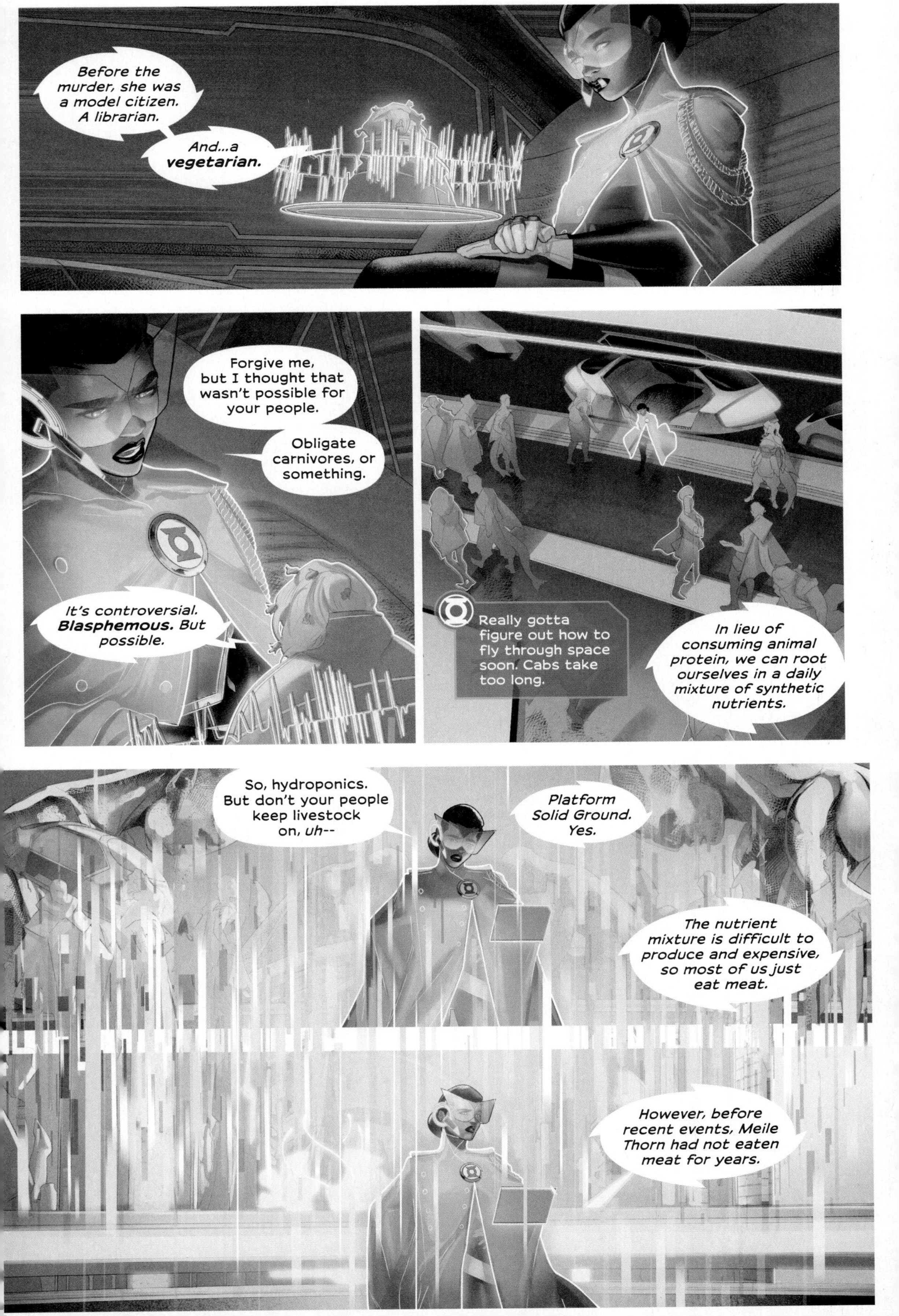
Before the murder, she was a model citizen. A librarian.
And...a **vegetarian.**
Forgive me, but I thought that wasn't possible for your people.
Obligate carnivores, or something.
It's controversial. **Blasphemous.** But possible.
Really gotta figure out how to fly through space soon. Cabs take too long.
In lieu of consuming animal protein, we can root ourselves in a daily mixture of synthetic nutrients.
So, hydroponics. But don't your people keep livestock on, *uh*--
Platform Solid Ground. Yes.
The nutrient mixture is difficult to produce and expensive, so most of us just eat meat.
However, before recent events, Meile Thorn had not eaten meat for years.

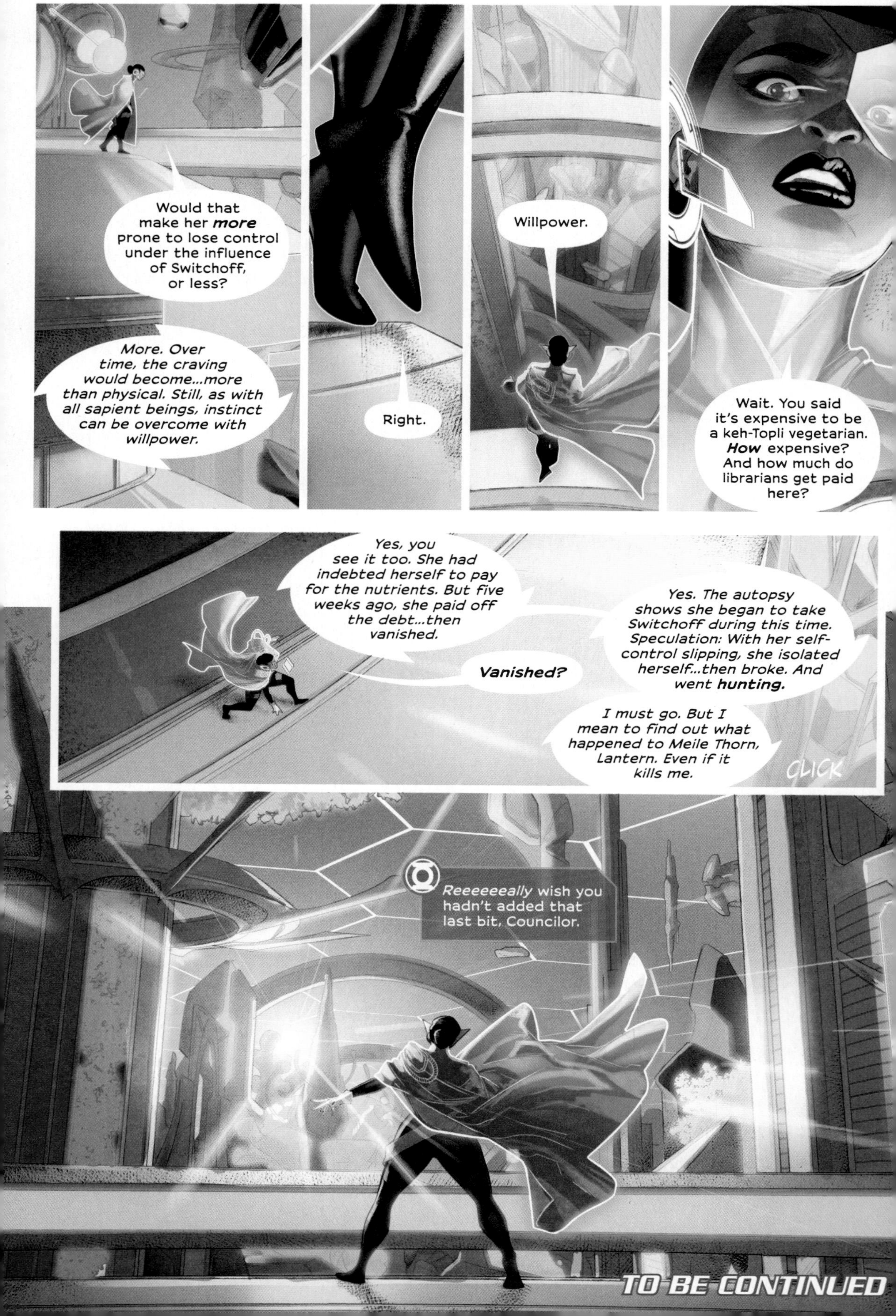
Would that make her *more* prone to lose control under the influence of Switchoff, or less?
More. Over time, the craving would become...more than physical. Still, as with all sapient beings, instinct can be overcome with willpower.
Right.
Willpower.
Wait. You said it's expensive to be a keh-Topli vegetarian. ***How*** expensive? And how much do librarians get paid here?
Yes, you see it too. She had indebted herself to pay for the nutrients. But five weeks ago, she paid off the debt...then vanished.
Vanished?
*Yes. The autopsy shows she began to take Switchoff during this time. Speculation: With her self-control slipping, she isolated herself...then broke. And went **hunting.***
I must go. But I mean to find out what happened to Meile Thorn, Lantern. Even if it kills me.
CLICK
Reeeeeeally wish you hadn't added that last bit, Councilor.
TO BE CONTINUED

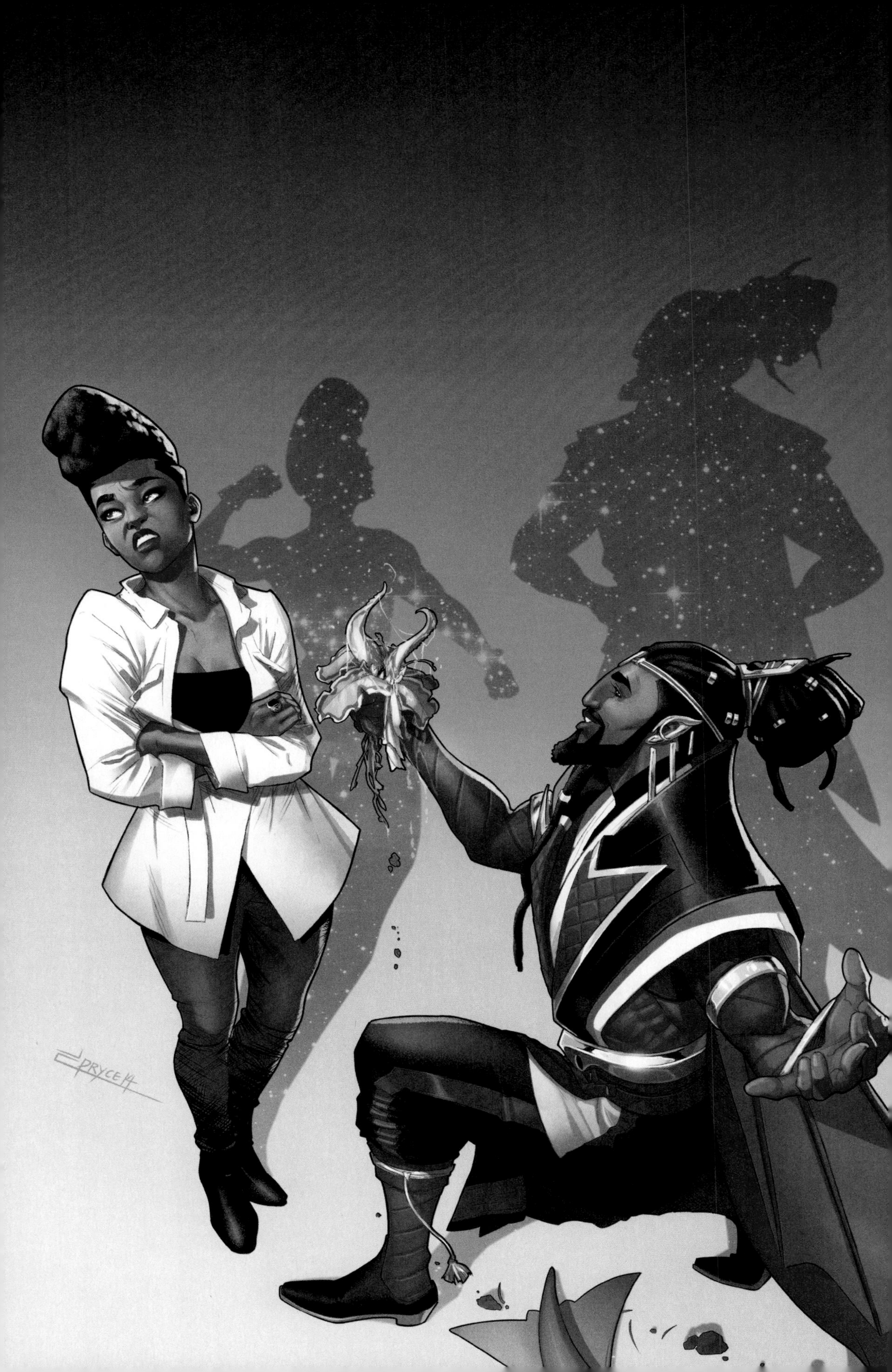

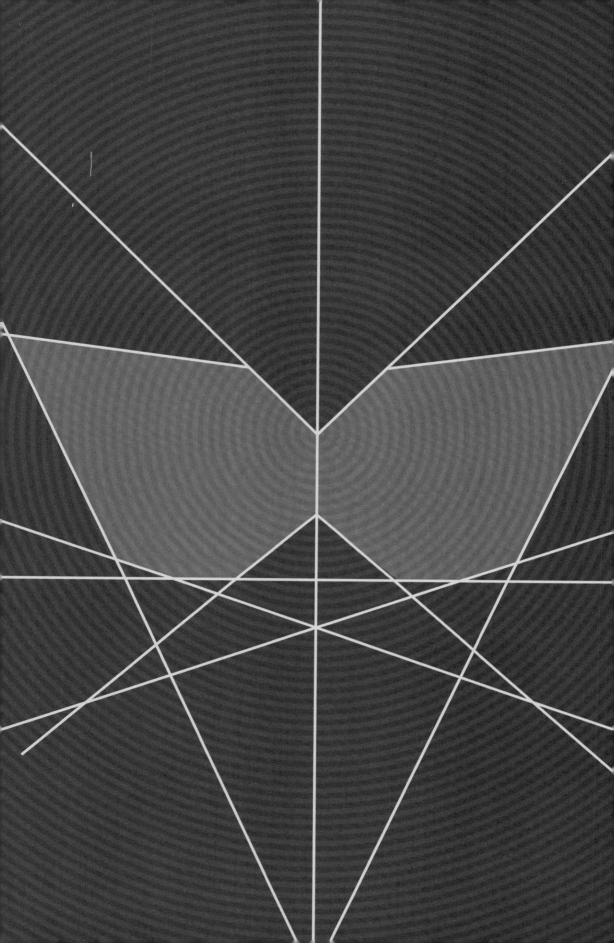

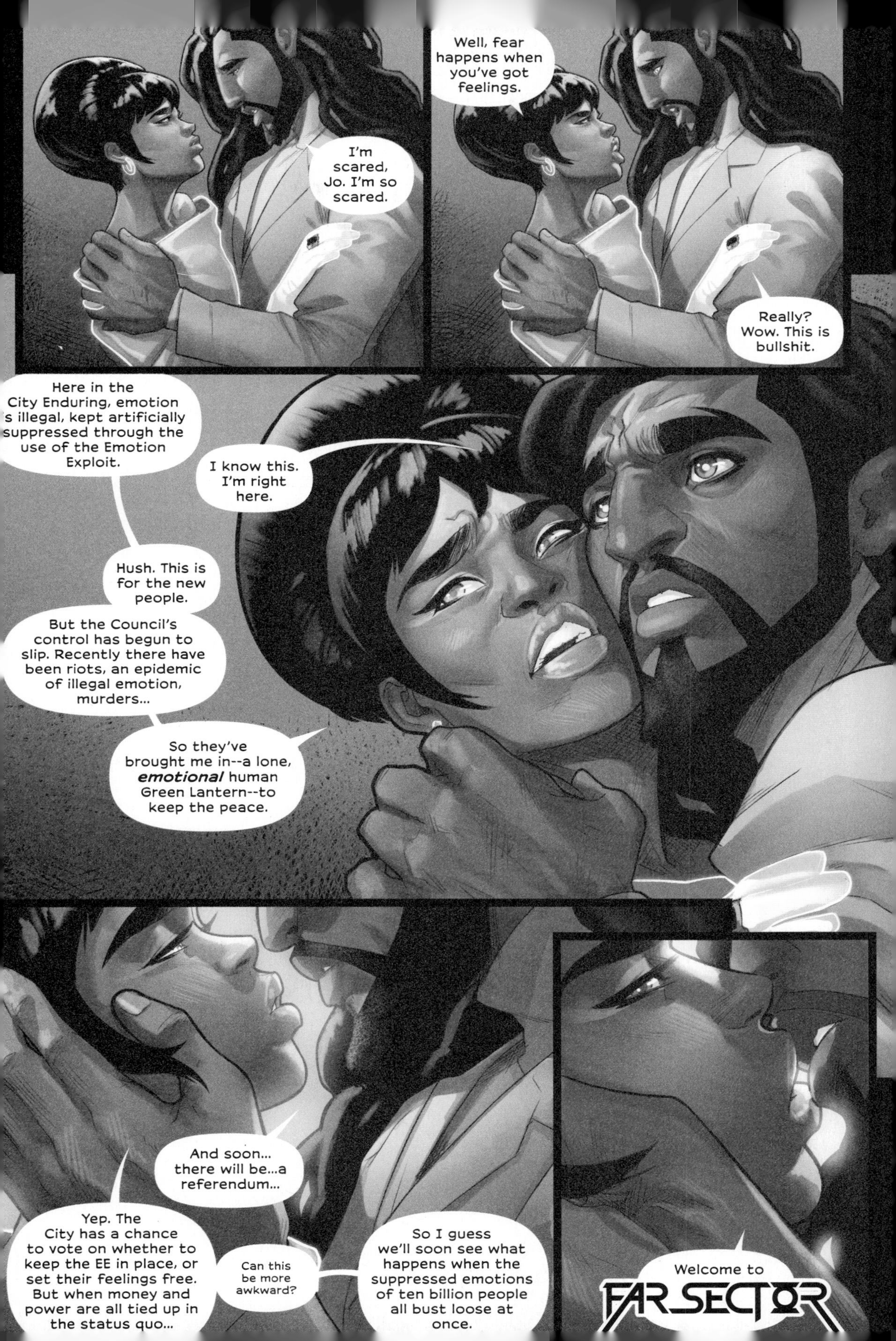
I'm scared, Jo. I'm so scared.
Well, fear happens when you've got feelings.
Really? Wow. This is bullshit.
Here in the City Enduring, emotion s illegal, kept artificially suppressed through the use of the Emotion Exploit.
I know this. I'm right here.
Hush. This is for the new people.
But the Council's control has begun to slip. Recently there have been riots, an epidemic of illegal emotion, murders...
So they've brought me in--a lone, *emotional* human Green Lantern--to keep the peace.
And soon... there will be...a referendum...
Yep. The City has a chance to vote on whether to keep the EE in place, or set their feelings free. But when money and power are all tied up in the status quo...
Can this be more awkward?
So I guess we'll soon see what happens when the suppressed emotions of ten billion people all bust loose at once.
Welcome to
FAR SECTOR

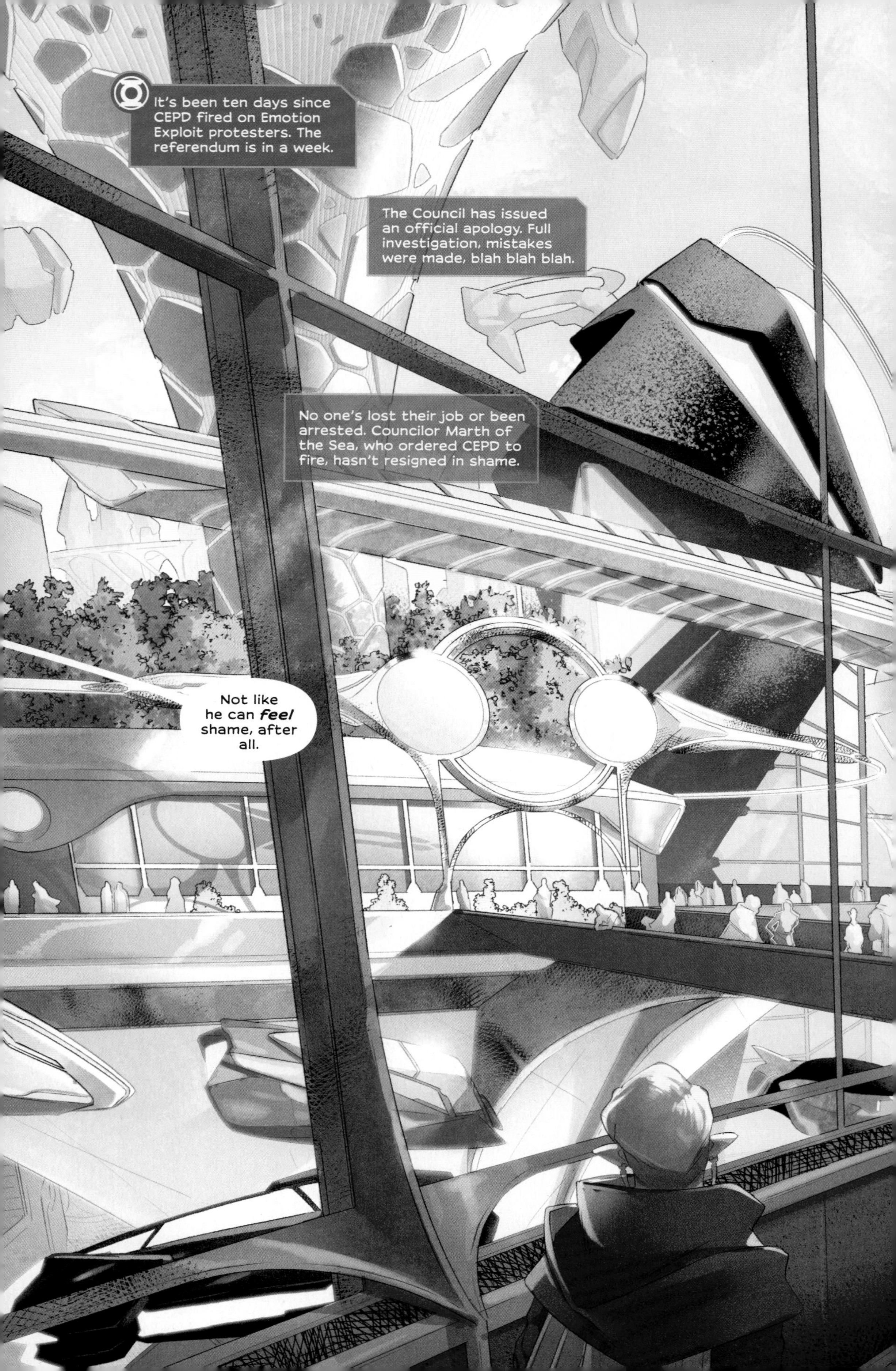
It's been ten days since CEPD fired on Emotion Exploit protesters. The referendum is in a week.
The Council has issued an official apology. Full investigation, mistakes were made, blah blah blah.
No one's lost their job or been arrested. Councilor Marth of the Sea, who ordered CEPD to fire, hasn't resigned in shame.
Not like he can *feel* shame, after all.

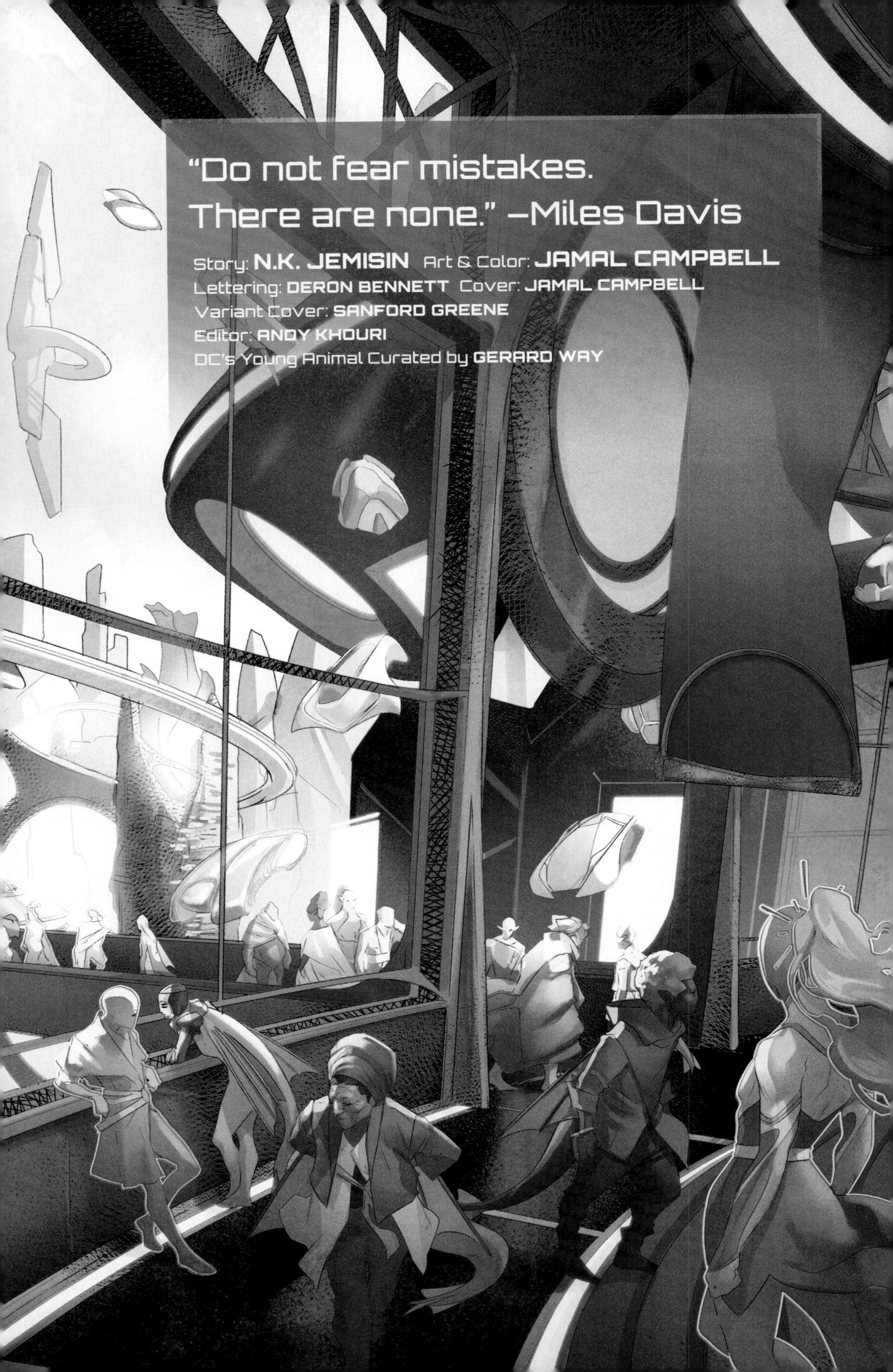

"Do not fear mistakes.
There are none." –Miles Davis
Story: N.K. JEMISIN Art & Color: JAMAL CAMPBELL
Lettering: DERON BENNETT Cover: JAMAL CAMPBELL
Variant Cover: SANFORD GREENE
Editor: ANDY KHOURI
DC's Young Animal Curated by GERARD WAY

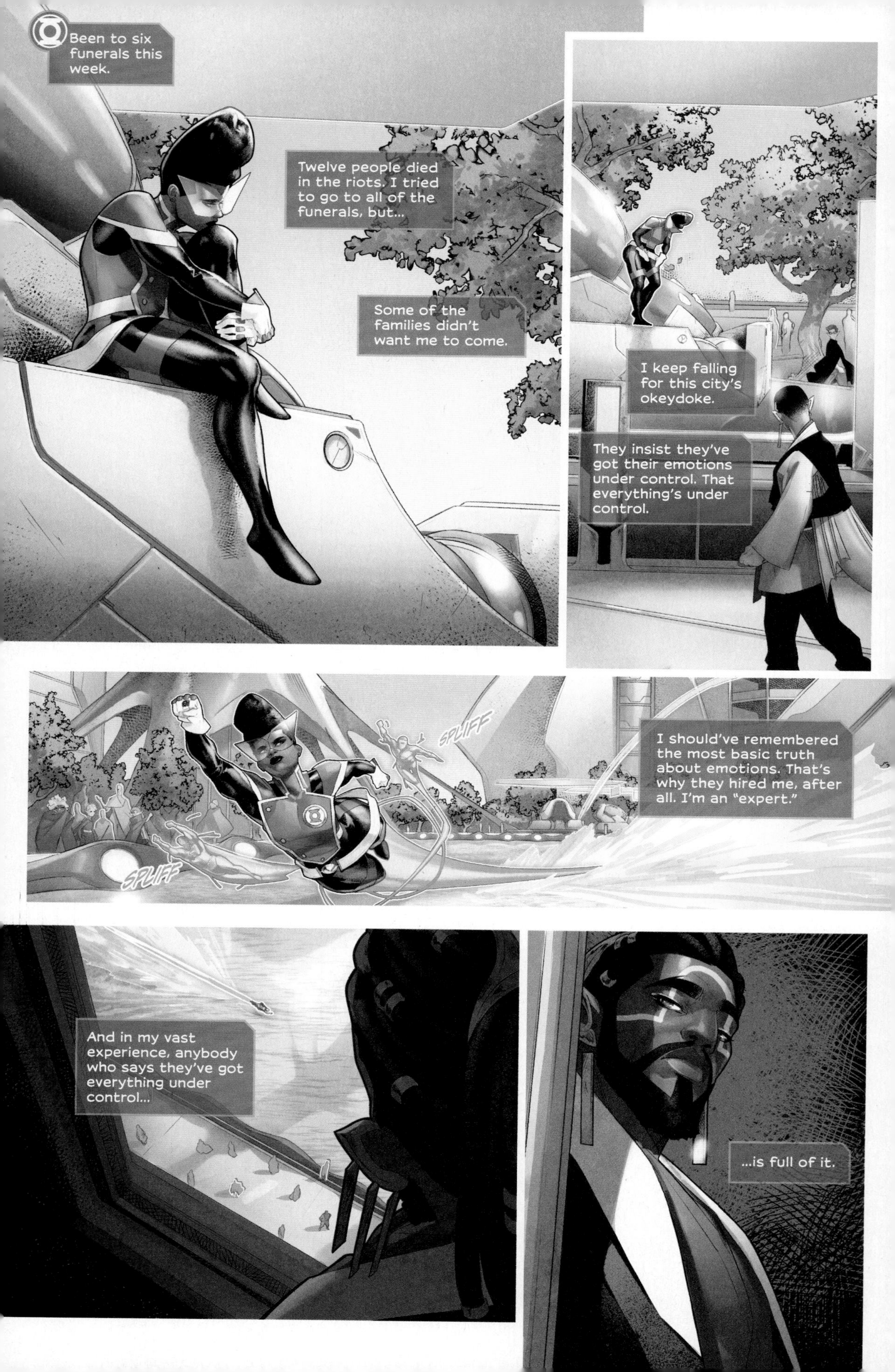

Been to six funerals this week.
Twelve people died in the riots. I tried to go to all of the funerals, but...
Some of the families didn't want me to come.
I keep falling for this city's okeydoke.
They insist they've got their emotions under control. That everything's under control.
SPLIFF
I should've remembered the most basic truth about emotions. That's why they hired me, after all. I'm an "expert."
SPLIFF
And in my vast experience, anybody who says they've got everything under control...
...is full of it.

It **isn't** CEPD policy, that's the thing. Tillij should've pushed back when Councilor Marth gave that order.

And I know you aren't actually drinking my coffee. Don't even pretend.

Nope, I'm not. I want to live.

By the way-- **Tillij.** Any relation?

What, because his shipname is **"By the Streaking Ice,"** like mine?

Shipnames don't work like that. And anyway, he's **Steppe,** I'm **Cliffs.** That matters too.

Sorry. Shipnames, homeworld names, service names... Hard to catch the nuances.

We're a complicated people. You're doing well, all things considered.

How tired are you? Want me to come over and take care of you?

Uh, yeah, that was probably what it sounded like. Just a little stress relief between friends. No hard feelings if I say no.

No feelings at all.

Thanks for the offer, but...no.

Call me if you change your mind, then, and meanwhile get some rest.

I'll look into Tillij. 'night.

'night.

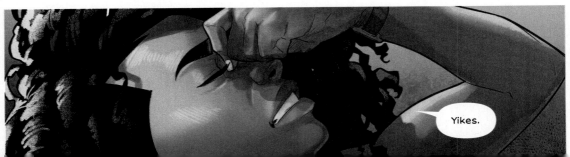

Yikes.

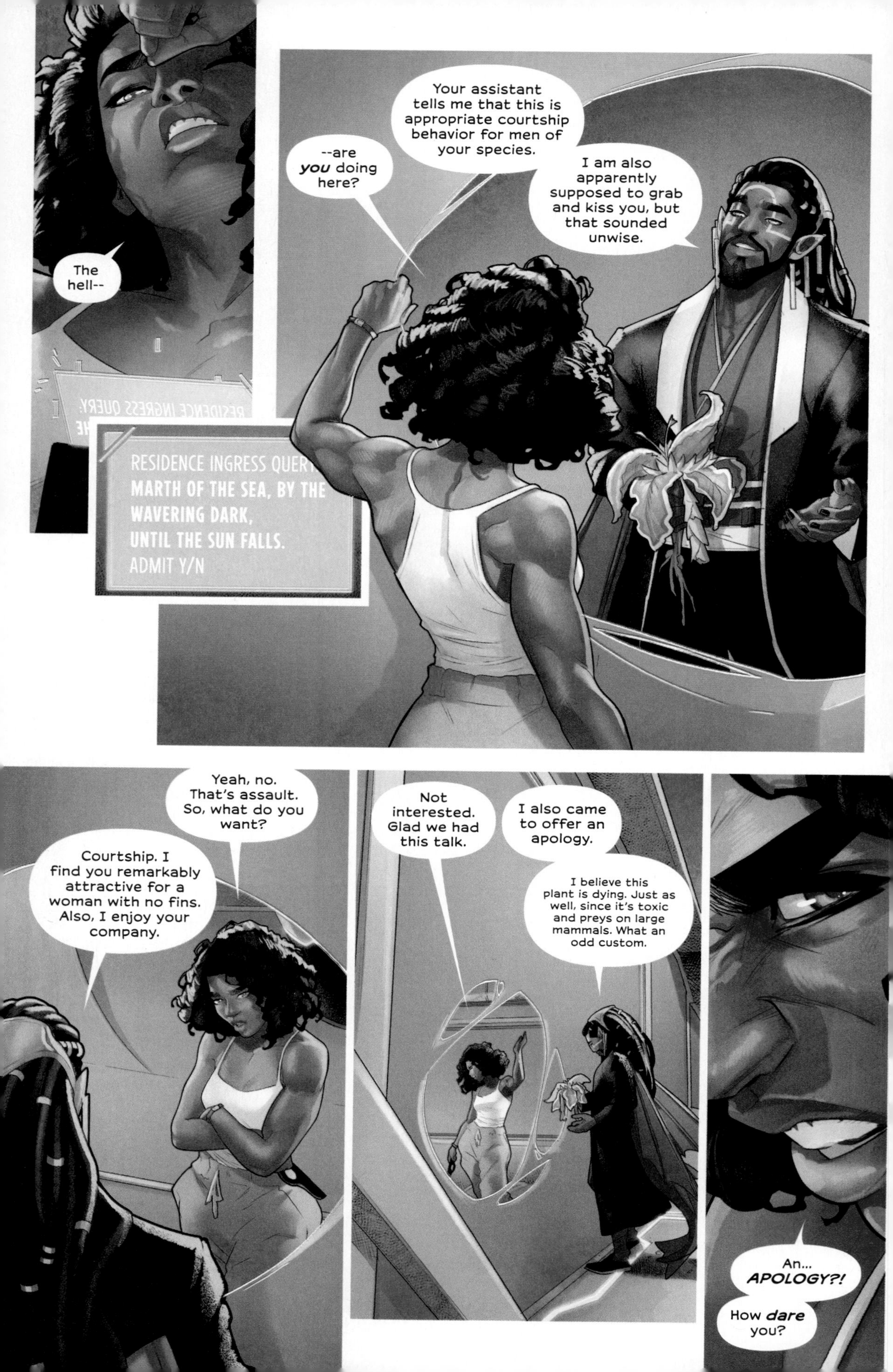
The hell--
--are *you* doing here?
Your assistant tells me that this is appropriate courtship behavior for men of your species.
I am also apparently supposed to grab and kiss you, but that sounded unwise.
RESIDENCE INGRESS QUERY:
MARTH OF THE SEA, BY THE WAVERING DARK, UNTIL THE SUN FALLS.
ADMIT Y/N
Yeah, no. That's assault. So, what do you want?
Courtship. I find you remarkably attractive for a woman with no fins. Also, I enjoy your company.
Not interested. Glad we had this talk.
I also came to offer an apology.
I believe this plant is dying. Just as well, since it's toxic and preys on large mammals. What an odd custom.
An... *APOLOGY?!*
How *dare* you?

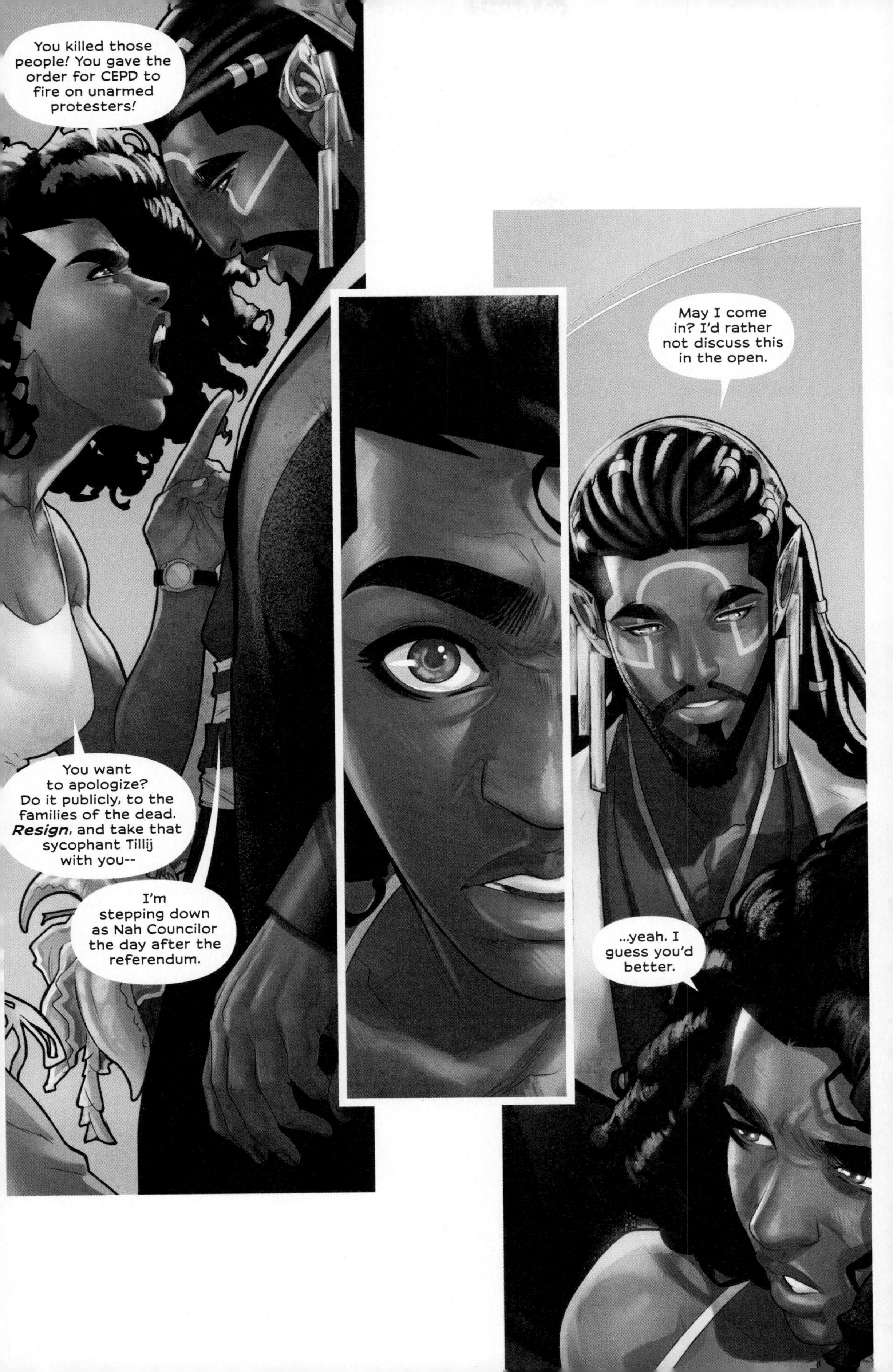
You killed those people! You gave the order for CEPD to fire on unarmed protesters!
You want to apologize? Do it publicly, to the families of the dead. ***Resign***, and take that sycophant Tillij with you--
I'm stepping down as Nah Councilor the day after the referendum.
May I come in? I'd rather not discuss this in the open.
...yeah. I guess you'd better.

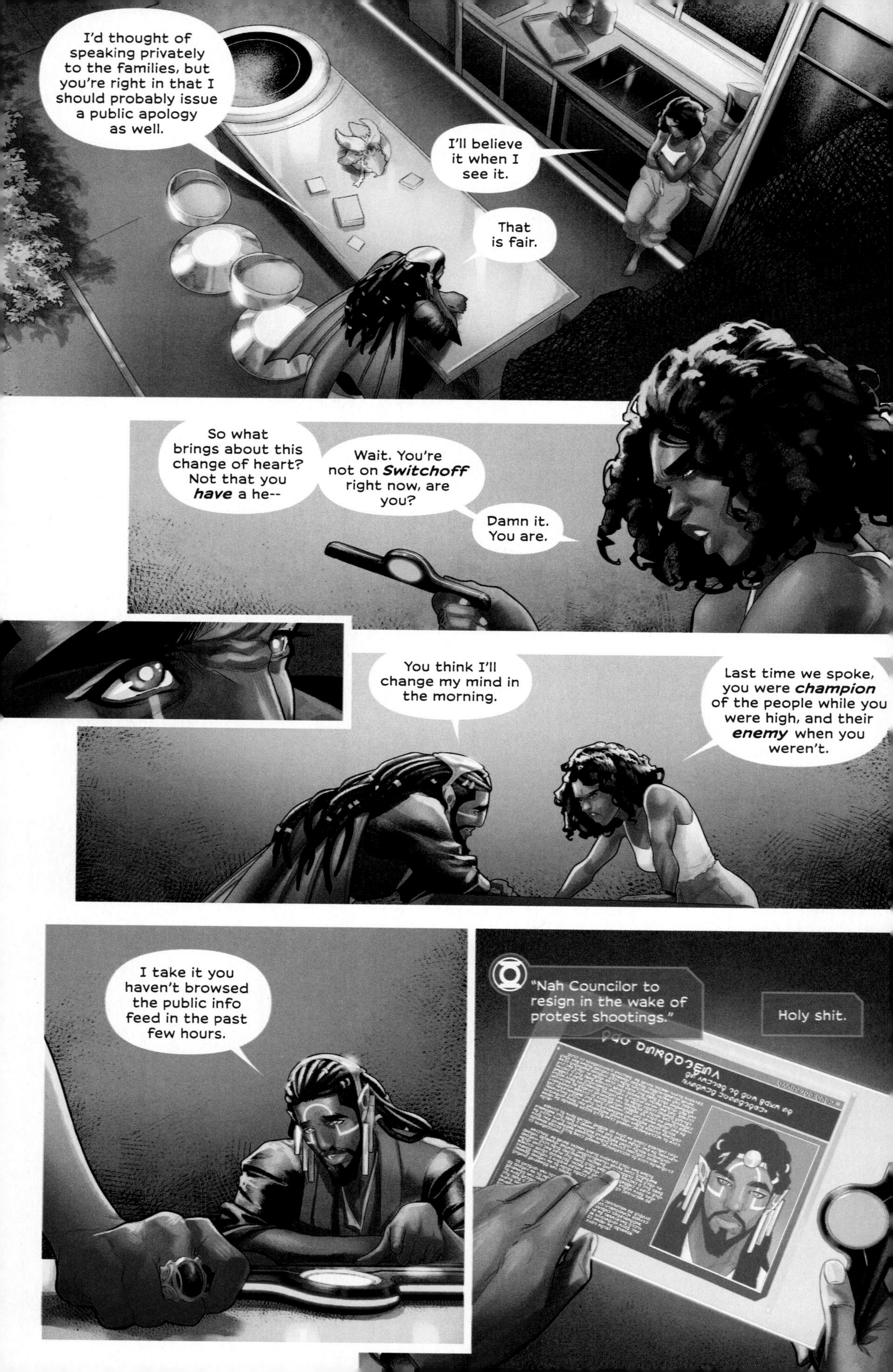
I'd thought of speaking privately to the families, but you're right in that I should probably issue a public apology as well.
I'll believe it when I see it.
That is fair.
So what brings about this change of heart? Not that you *have* a he--
Wait. You're not on ***Switchoff*** right now, are you?
Damn it. You are.
You think I'll change my mind in the morning.
Last time we spoke, you were ***champion*** of the people while you were high, and their ***enemy*** when you weren't.
I take it you haven't browsed the public info feed in the past few hours.
"Nah Councilor to resign in the wake of protest shootings."
Holy shit.

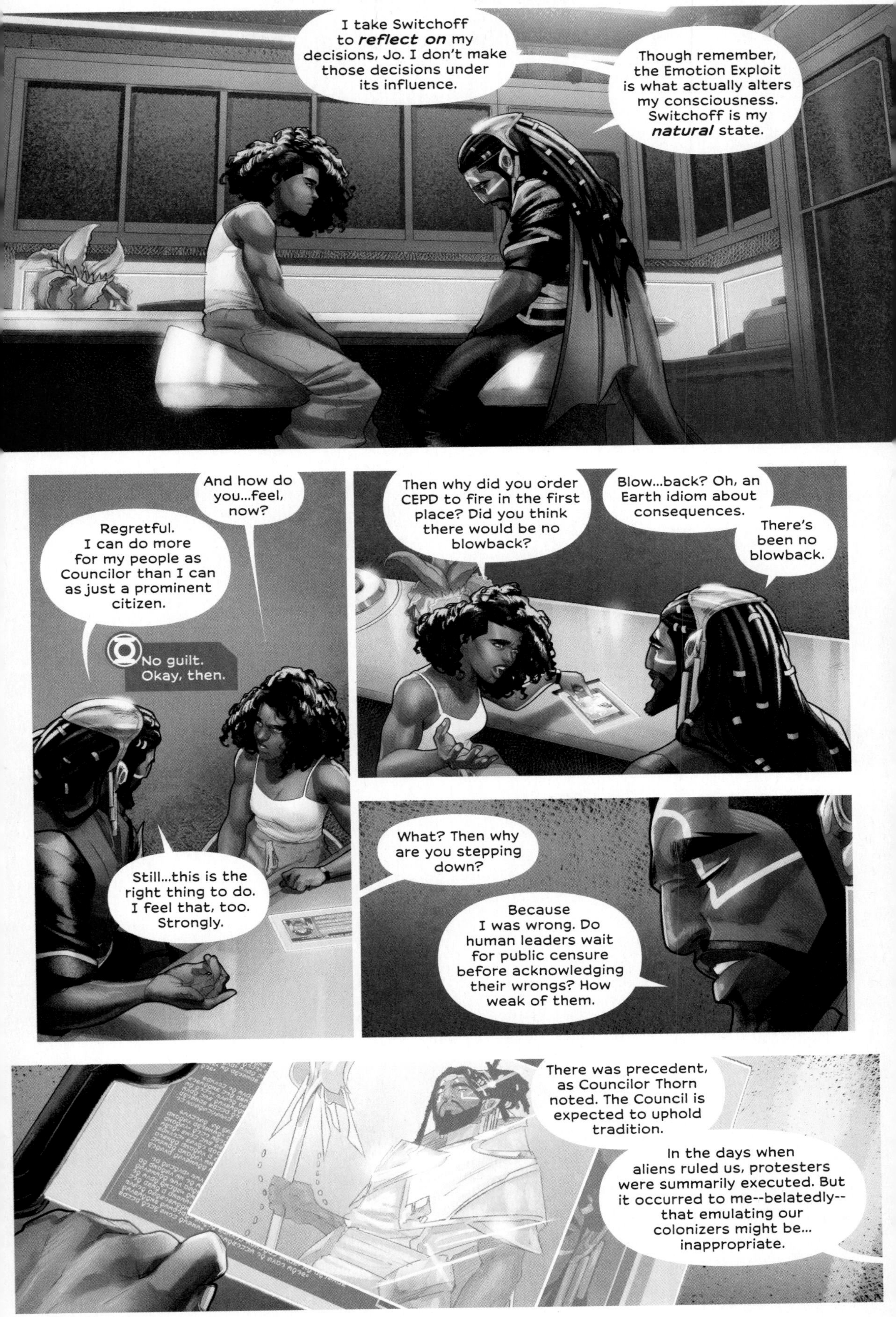
I take Switchoff to *reflect on* my decisions, Jo. I don't make those decisions under its influence.
Though remember, the Emotion Exploit is what actually alters my consciousness. Switchoff is my *natural* state.
And how do you...feel, now?
Regretful. I can do more for my people as Councilor than I can as just a prominent citizen.
No guilt. Okay, then.
Still...this is the right thing to do. I feel that, too. Strongly.
Then why did you order CEPD to fire in the first place? Did you think there would be no blowback?
Blow...back? Oh, an Earth idiom about consequences.
There's been no blowback.
What? Then why are you stepping down?
Because I was wrong. Do human leaders wait for public censure before acknowledging their wrongs? How weak of them.
There was precedent, as Councilor Thorn noted. The Council is expected to uphold tradition.
In the days when aliens ruled us, protesters were summarily executed. But it occurred to me--belatedly--that emulating our colonizers might be... inappropriate.

I don't believe you.

That, too, is fair.

But have you never committed a wrong yourself, Jo? Something you shouldn't have done...

...or something you *should* have?

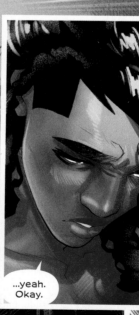

...yeah. Okay.

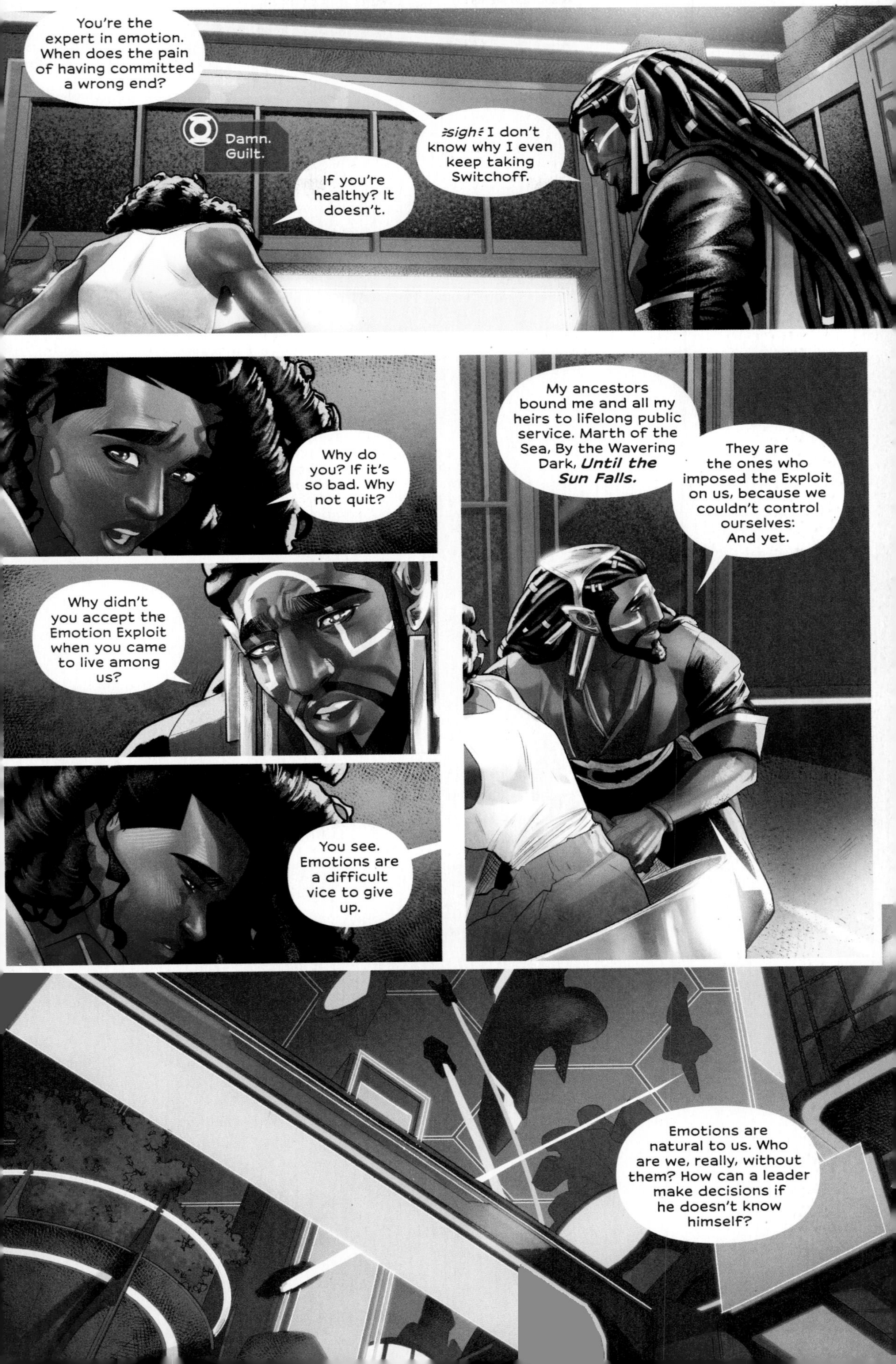
You're the expert in emotion. When does the pain of having committed a wrong end?
Damn. Guilt.
If you're healthy? It doesn't.
≈sigh≈ I don't know why I even keep taking Switchoff.
Why do you? If it's so bad. Why not quit?
Why didn't you accept the Emotion Exploit when you came to live among us?
You see. Emotions are a difficult vice to give up.
My ancestors bound me and all my heirs to lifelong public service. Marth of the Sea, By the Wavering Dark, *Until the Sun Falls.*
They are the ones who imposed the Exploit on us, because we couldn't control ourselves: And yet.
Emotions are natural to us. Who are we, really, without them? How can a leader make decisions if he doesn't know himself?

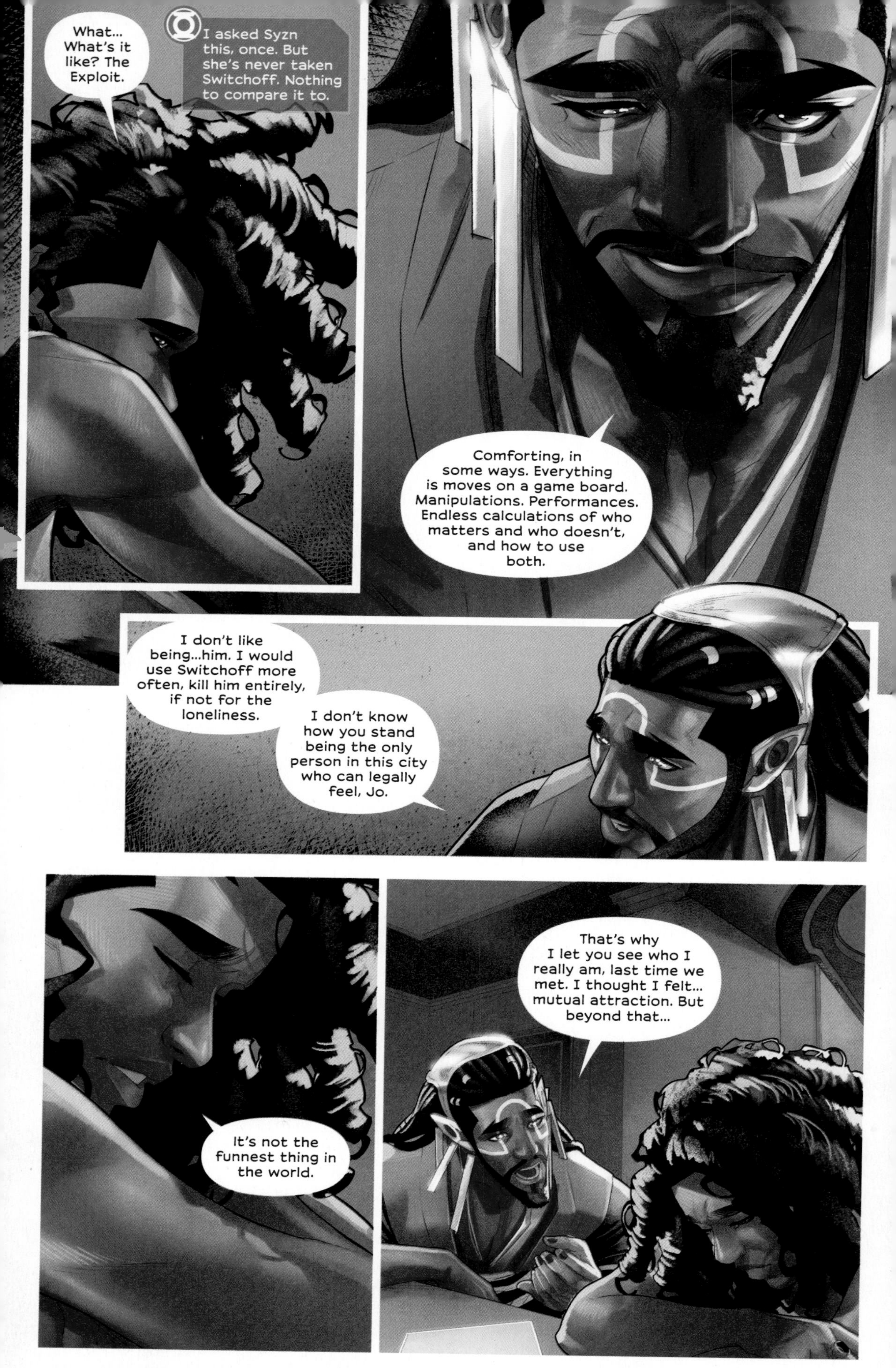
What... What's it like? The Exploit.
I asked Syzn this, once. But she's never taken Switchoff. Nothing to compare it to.
Comforting, in some ways. Everything is moves on a game board. Manipulations. Performances. Endless calculations of who matters and who doesn't, and how to use both.
I don't like being...him. I would use Switchoff more often, kill him entirely, if not for the loneliness.
I don't know how you stand being the only person in this city who can legally feel, Jo.
It's not the funnest thing in the world.
That's why I let you see who I really am, last time we met. I thought I felt... mutual attraction. But beyond that...

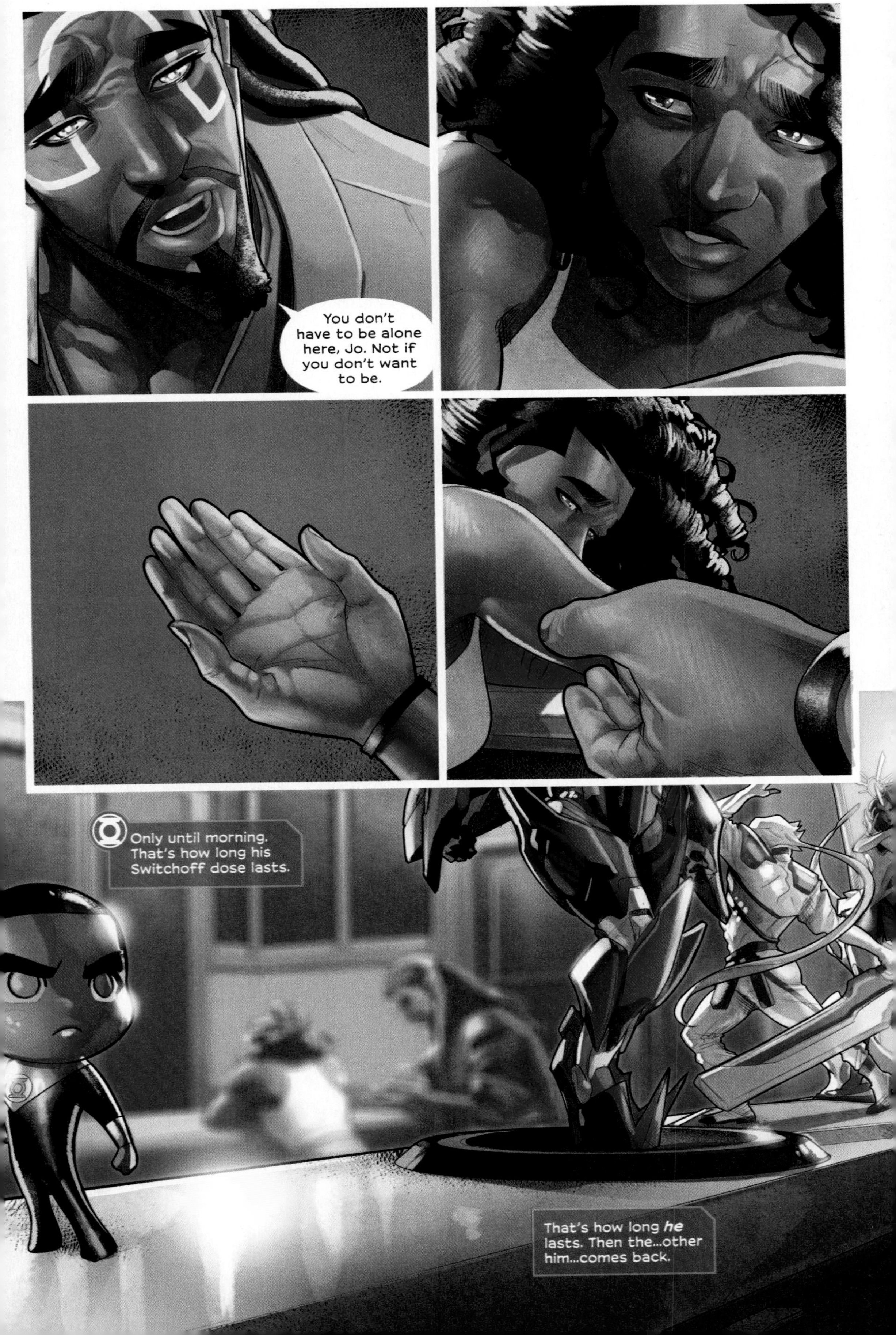
You don't have to be alone here, Jo. Not if you don't want to be.
Only until morning. That's how long his Switchoff dose lasts.
That's how long *he* lasts. Then the...other him...comes back.

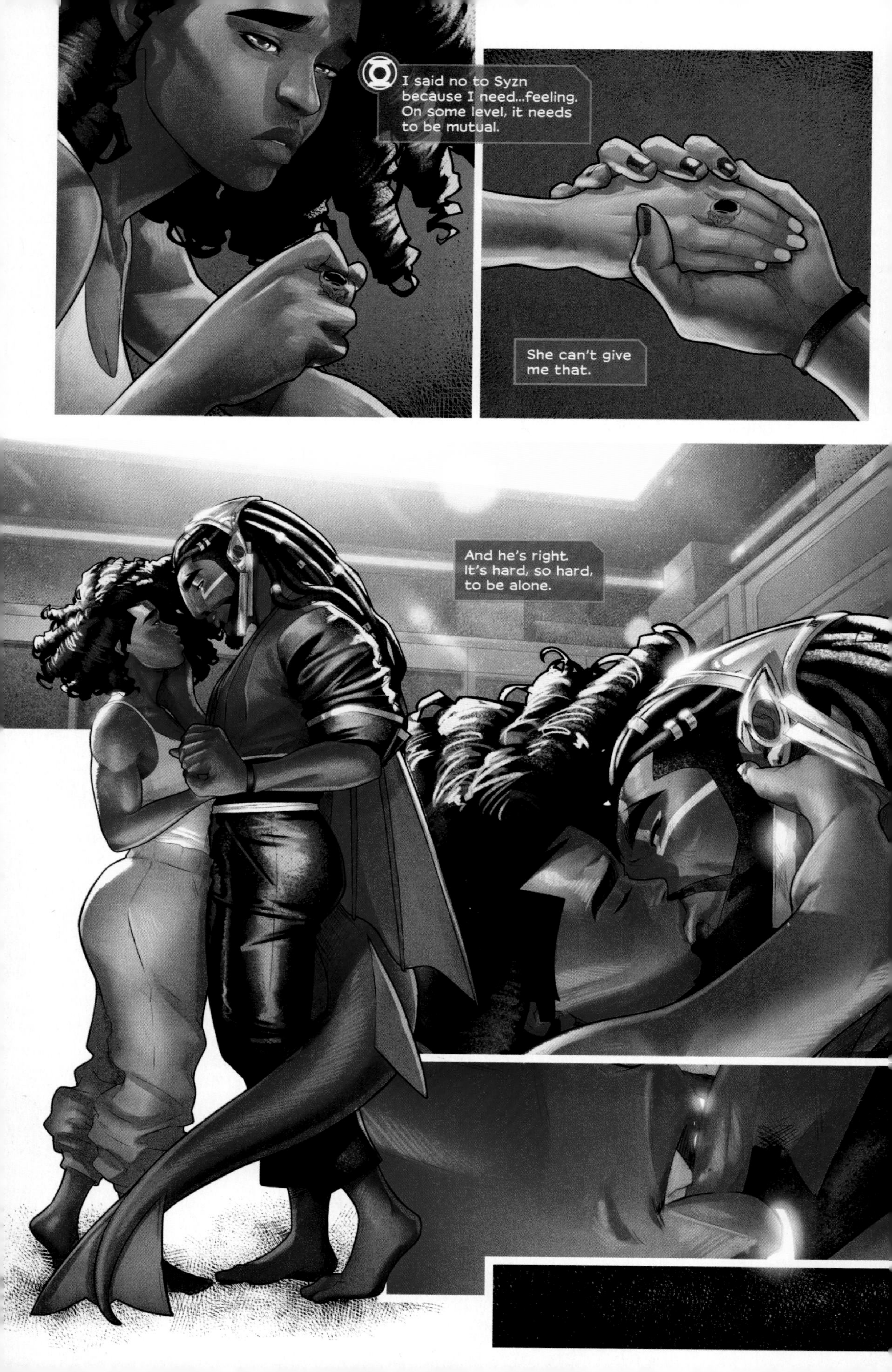
I said no to Syzn because I need...feeling. On some level, it needs to be mutual.
She can't give me that.
And he's right. It's hard, so hard, to be alone.

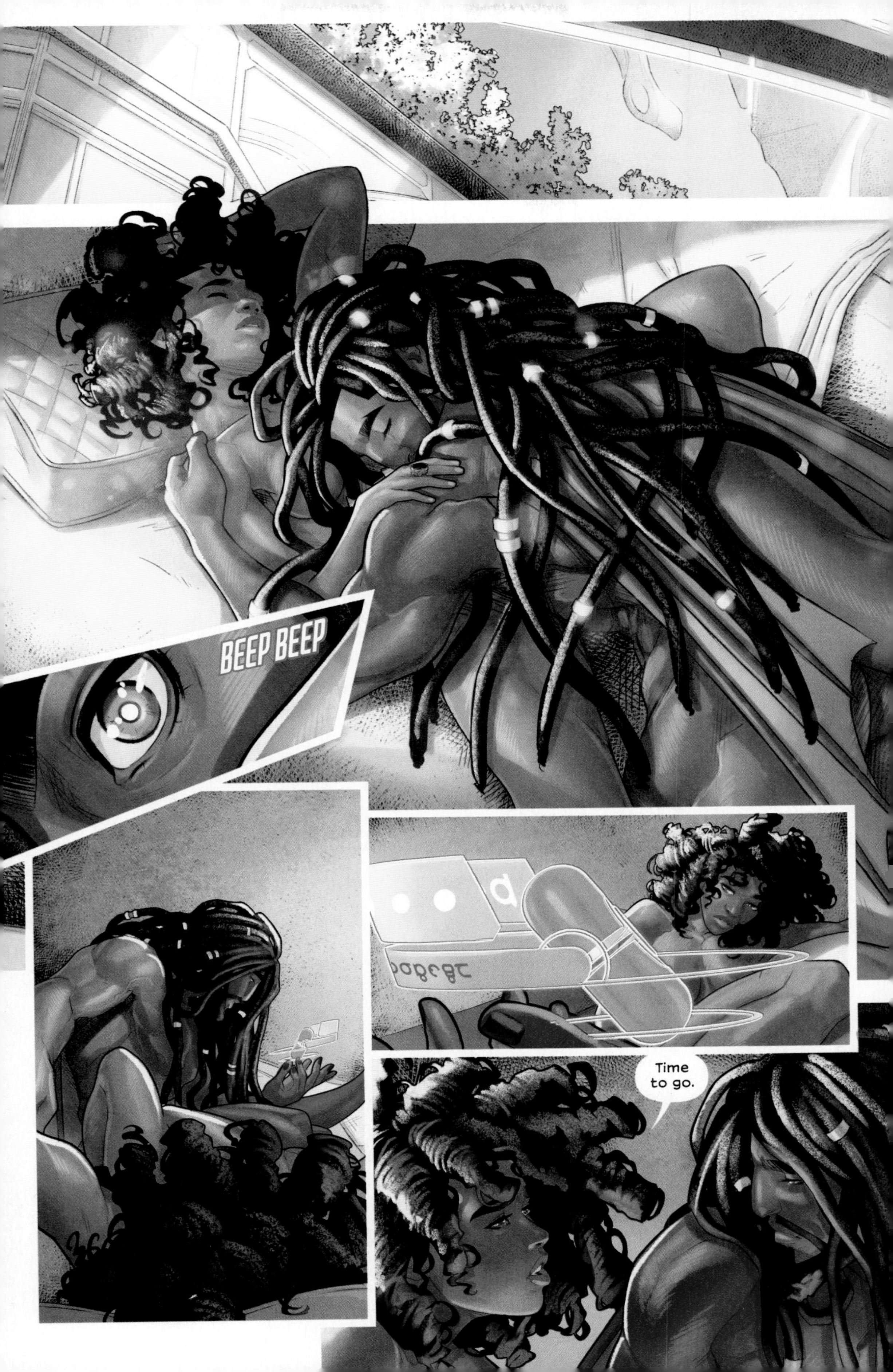
BEEP BEEP
Time to go.

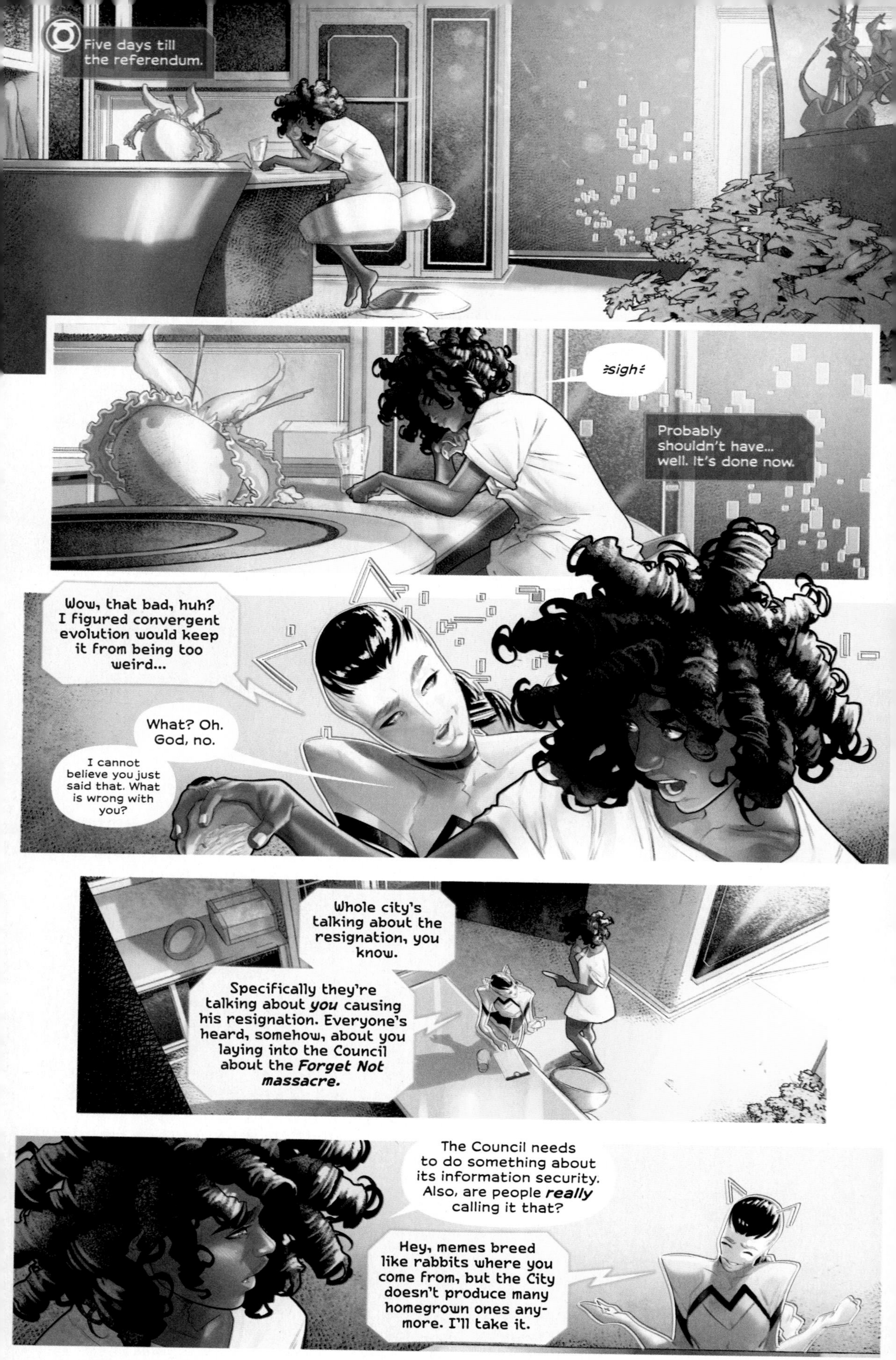
Five days till the referendum.
sigh
Probably shouldn't have... well. It's done now.
Wow, that bad, huh? I figured convergent evolution would keep it from being too weird...
What? Oh. God, no.
I cannot believe you just said that. What is wrong with you?
Whole city's talking about the resignation, you know.
Specifically they're talking about *you* causing his resignation. Everyone's heard, somehow, about you laying into the Council about the *Forget Not massacre.*
The Council needs to do something about its information security. Also, are people *really* calling it that?
Hey, memes breed like rabbits where you come from, but the City doesn't produce many homegrown ones any-more. I'll take it.

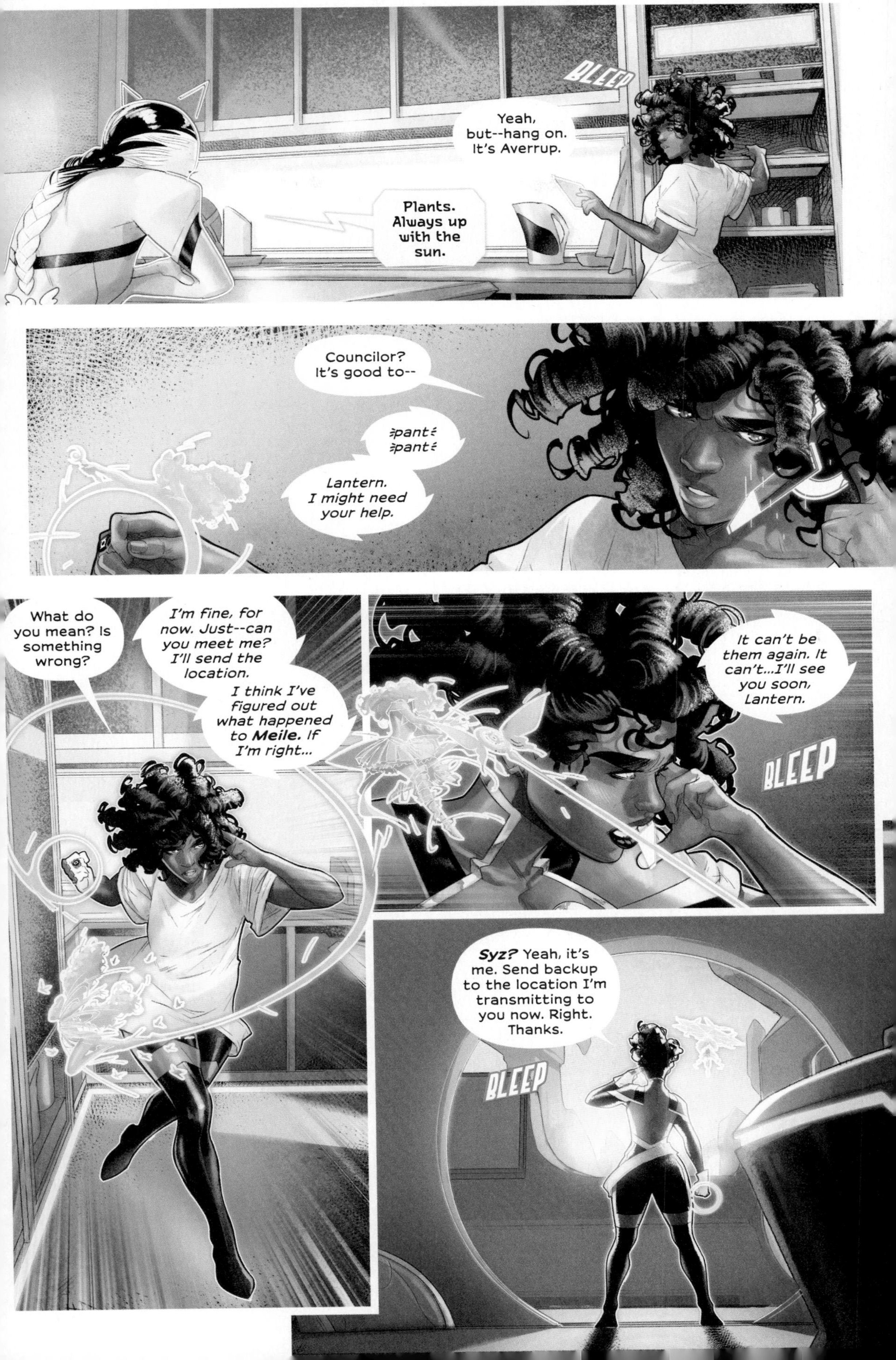
BLEEP
Yeah, but--hang on. It's Averrup.
Plants. Always up with the sun.
Councilor? It's good to--
=pant=
=pant=
Lantern. I might need your help.
What do you mean? Is something wrong?
I'm fine, for now. Just--can you meet me? I'll send the location.
I think I've figured out what happened to **Meile.** If I'm right...
It can't be them again. It can't...I'll see you soon, Lantern.
BLEEP
Syz? Yeah, it's me. Send backup to the location I'm transmitting to you now. Right. Thanks.
BLEEP

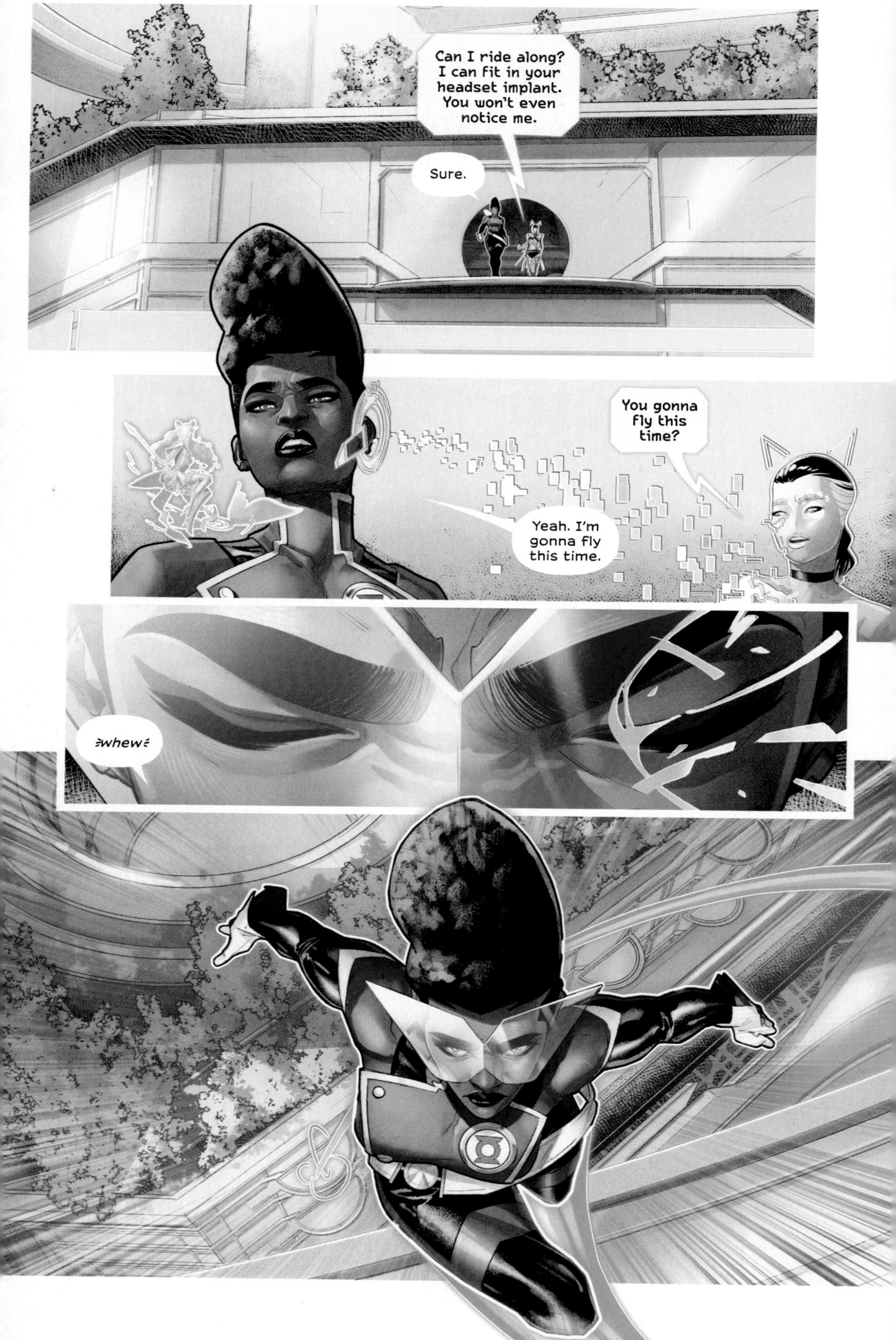

Can I ride along? I can fit in your headset implant. You won't even notice me.
Sure.
You gonna fly this time?
Yeah. I'm gonna fly this time.
whew

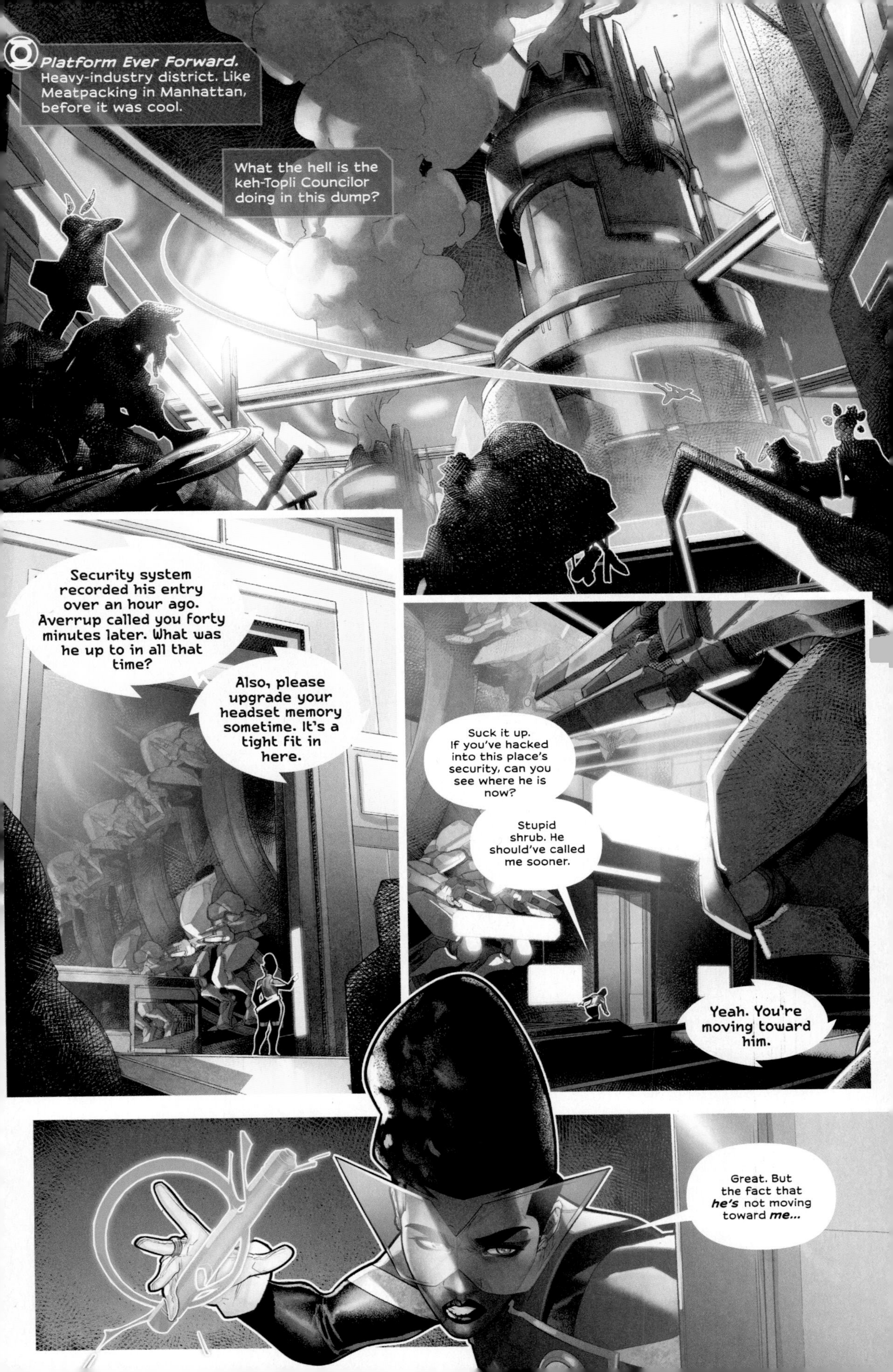
Platform Ever Forward. Heavy-industry district. Like Meatpacking in Manhattan, before it was cool.
What the hell is the keh-Topli Councilor doing in this dump?
Security system recorded his entry over an hour ago. Averrup called you forty minutes later. What was he up to in all that time?
Also, please upgrade your headset memory sometime. It's a tight fit in here.
Suck it up. If you've hacked into this place's security, can you see where he is now?
Stupid shrub. He should've called me sooner.
Yeah. You're moving toward him.
Great. But the fact that ***he's*** not moving toward ***me...***

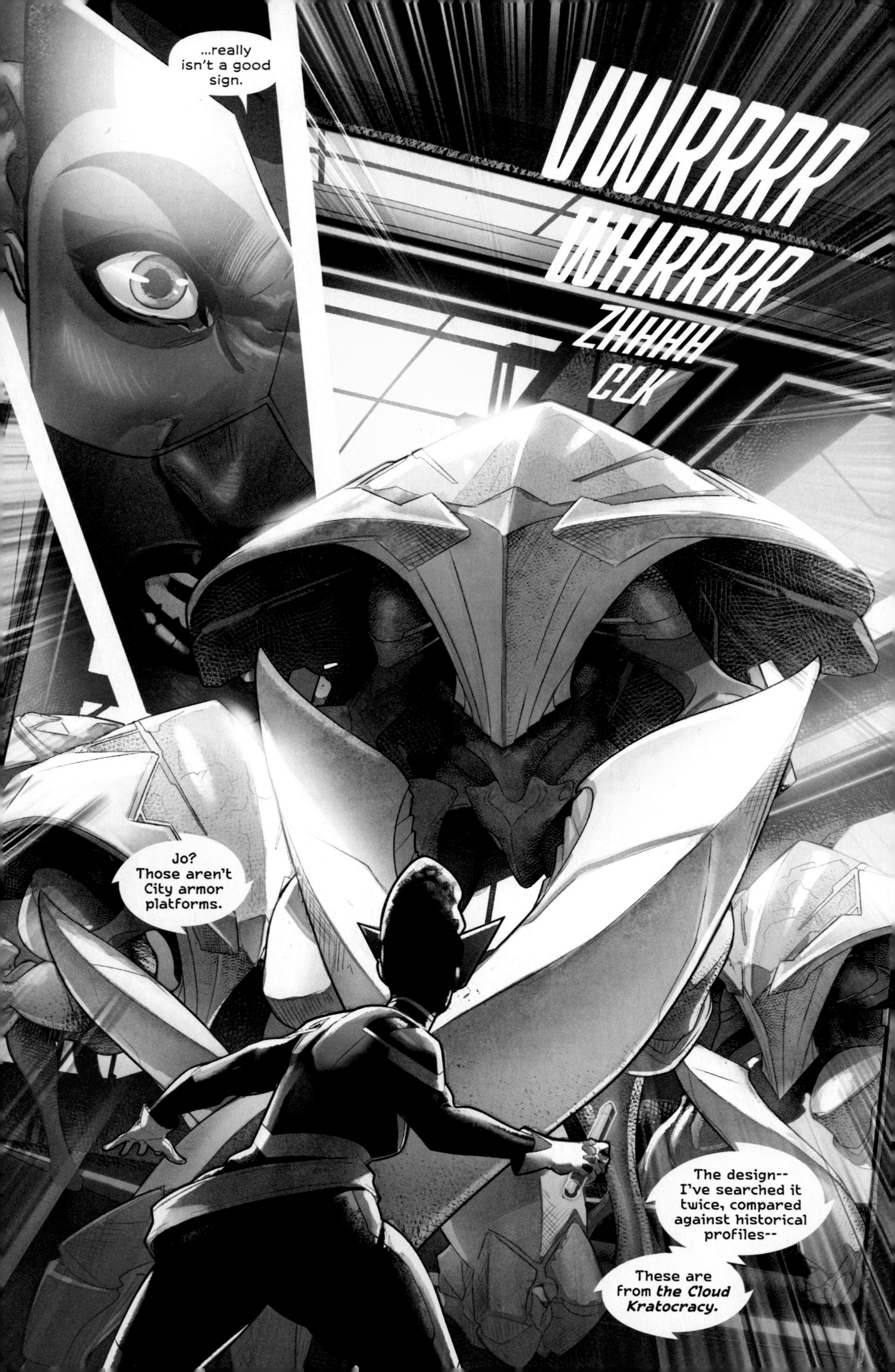
...really isn't a good sign.
VWRRRR
WHRRRR
ZHHHH
CLK
Jo? Those aren't City armor platforms.
The design-- I've searched it twice, compared against historical profiles--
These are from *the Cloud Kratocracy.*

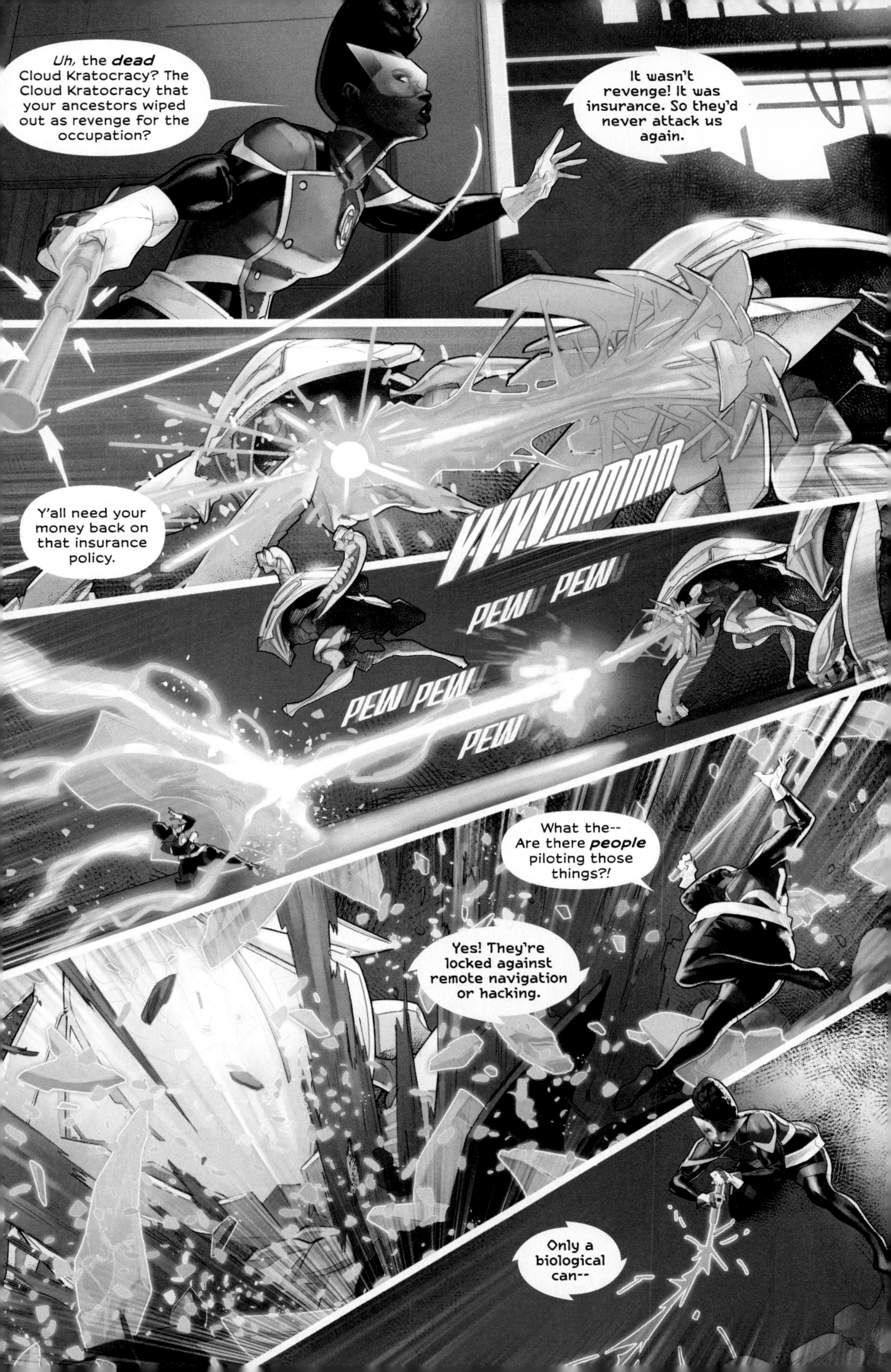
Uh, the dead Cloud Kratocracy? The Cloud Kratocracy that your ancestors wiped out as revenge for the occupation?
It wasn't revenge! It was insurance. So they'd never attack us again.
Y'all need your money back on that insurance policy.
VVVVMMMM
PEW PEW
PEW PEW
PEW
What the-- Are there people piloting those things?!
Yes! They're locked against remote navigation or hacking.
Only a biological can--

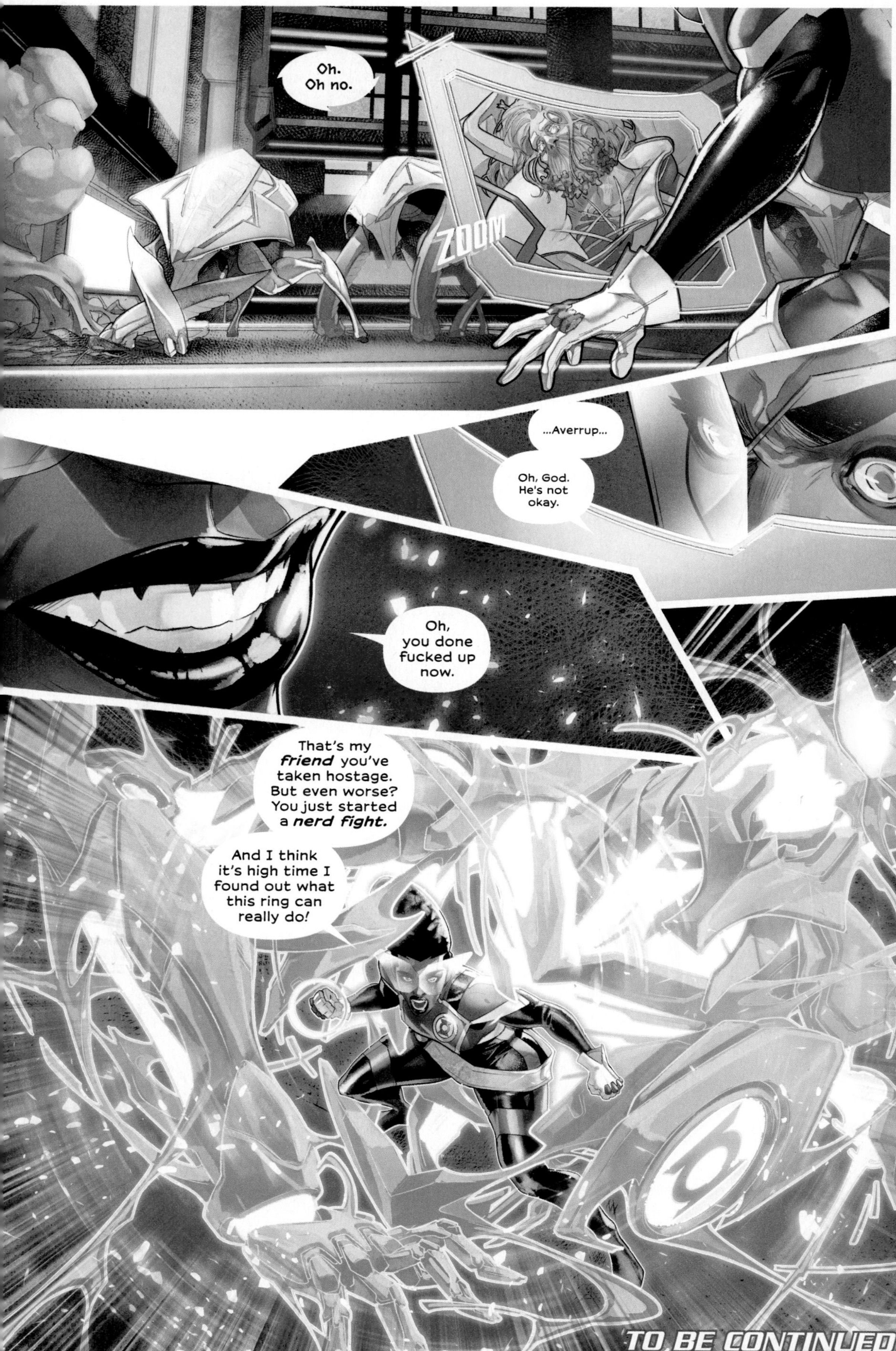
Oh.
Oh no.
ZOOM
...Averrup...
Oh, God. He's not okay.
Oh, you done fucked up now.
That's my *friend* you've taken hostage. But even worse? You just started a ***nerd fight.***
And I think it's high time I found out what this ring can really do!
TO BE CONTINUED

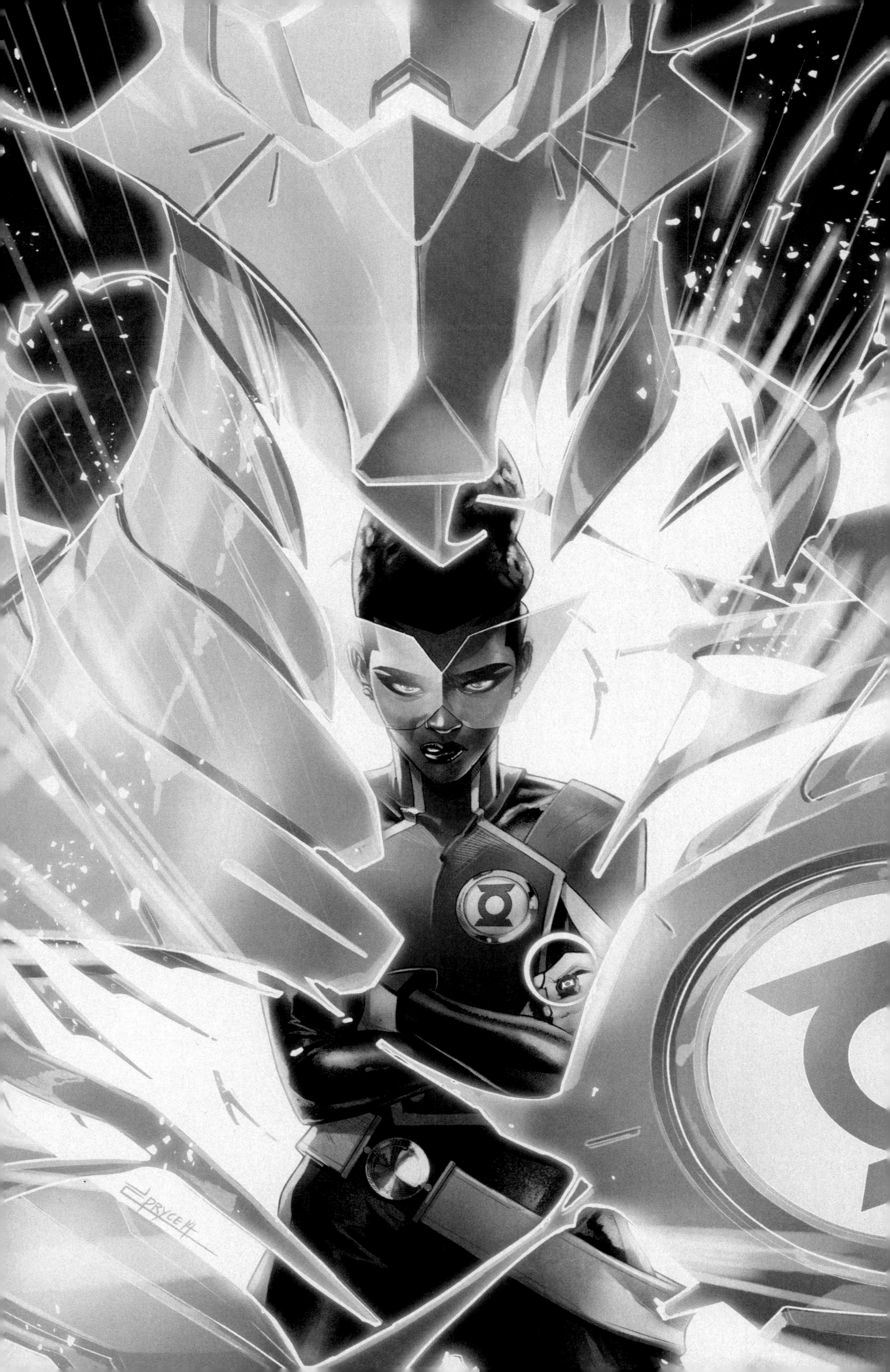

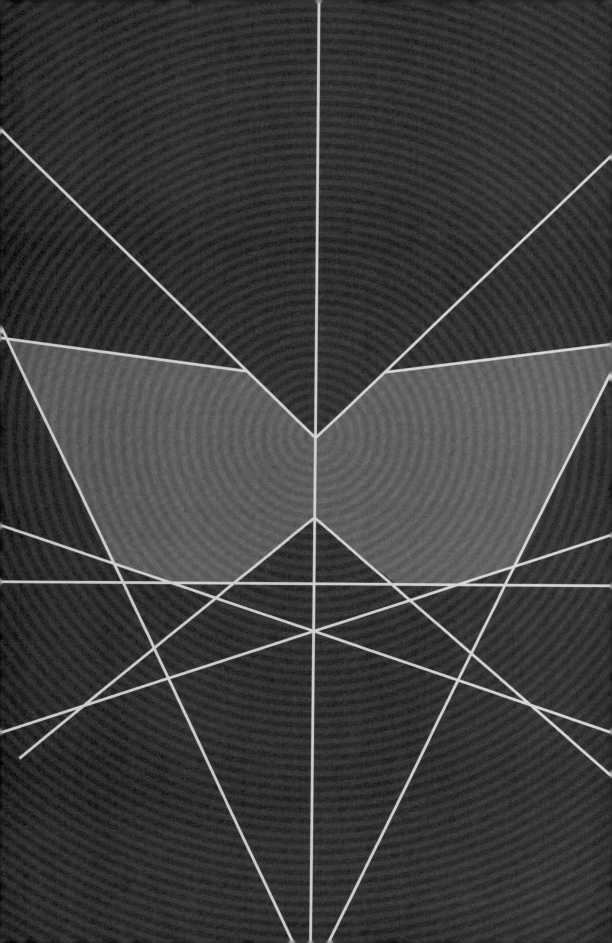

OAN INTELLIGENCE EXTRA-JURISDICTIONAL FILE ARCHIVE
THE CITY ENDURING: SOCIOLOGY
TRANSLATION: ENGLISH
UPDATE: IN PROGRESS

WHILE THE CITY ENDURING MAINTAINS A POST-SCARCITY
ECONOMIC STRUCTURE FOR BIOLOGICAL NECESSITIES SUCH
AS FOOD OR CLOTHING, SUBSTANTIAL LEGITIMATE LUXURY
ECONOMIES HAVE DEVELOPED, SOME UNDERGROUND. DUE
TO THE POPULATION-WIDE DISSEMINATION OF THE
EMOTION EXPLOIT, PREFERRED LUXURY IMPORT GOODS
INCLUDE EMOTIONAL PROPERTY OR INTELLECTUAL
PROPERTY SUCH AS ART, MUSIC, HUMOR, AND OTHER
MATERIAL DESIGNED TO ELICIT AN EMOTIONAL RESPONSE.
NOTE: AS SUCH MATERIALS ARE REQUIRED FOR THE
SURVIVAL OF THE CITY'S ARTIFICIALLY INTELLIGENT
POPULATION, THE @AT, THIS PLACES THEM AT AN
ECONOMIC DISADVANTAGE. (SOCIETAL INSTABILITY
WARNING.)

Story: **N.K. JEMISIN** Art & Color: **JAMAL CAMPBELL**
Lettering: **DERON BENNETT** Cover: **JAMAL CAMPBELL**
Variant Cover: **STJEPAN ŠEJIĆ**
Editor: **ANDY KHOURI**
DC's Young Animal Curated by **GERARD WAY**

"You might win some, but you just lost one."
—Lauryn Hill

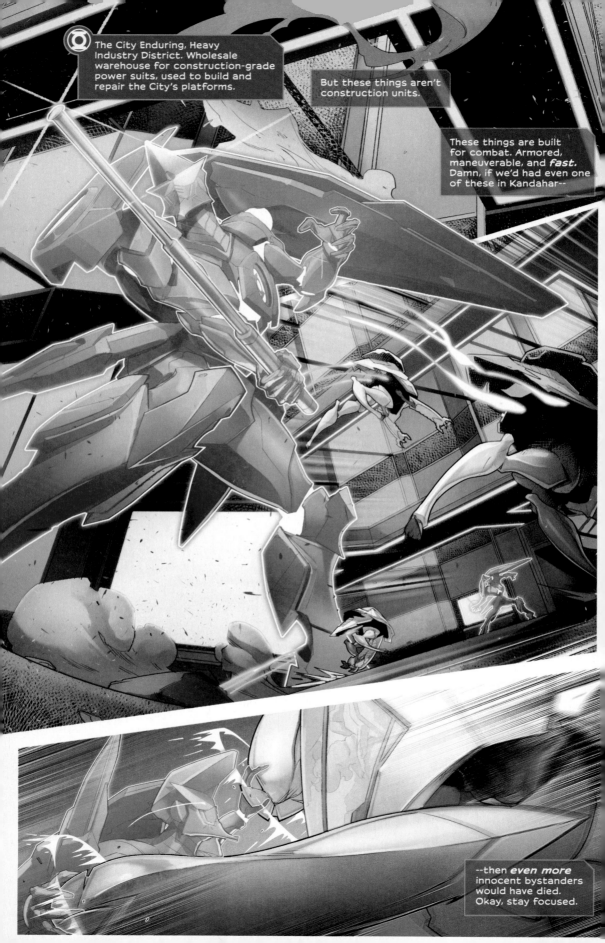

The City Enduring, Heavy Industry District. Wholesale warehouse for construction-grade power suits, used to build and repair the City's platforms.

But these things aren't construction units.

These things are built for combat. Armored, maneuverable, and *fast.* Damn, if we'd had even one of these in Kandahar--

--then *even more* innocent bystanders would have died. Okay, stay focused.

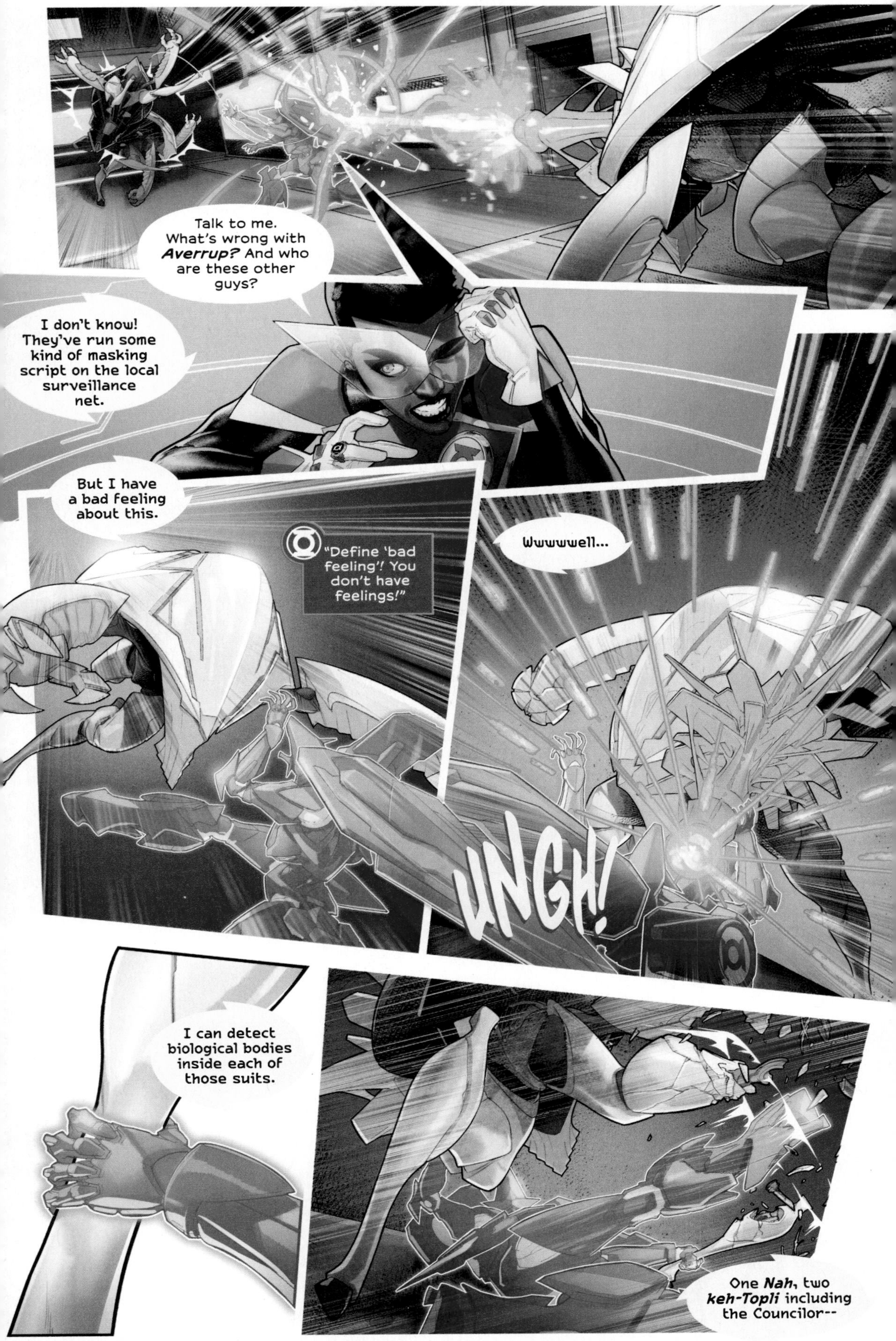
Talk to me. What's wrong with Averrup? And who are these other guys?
I don't know! They've run some kind of masking script on the local surveillance net.
But I have a bad feeling about this.
"Define 'bad feeling'! You don't have feelings!"
Wwwwwell...
UNGH!
I can detect biological bodies inside each of those suits.
One Nah, two keh-Topli including the Councilor--

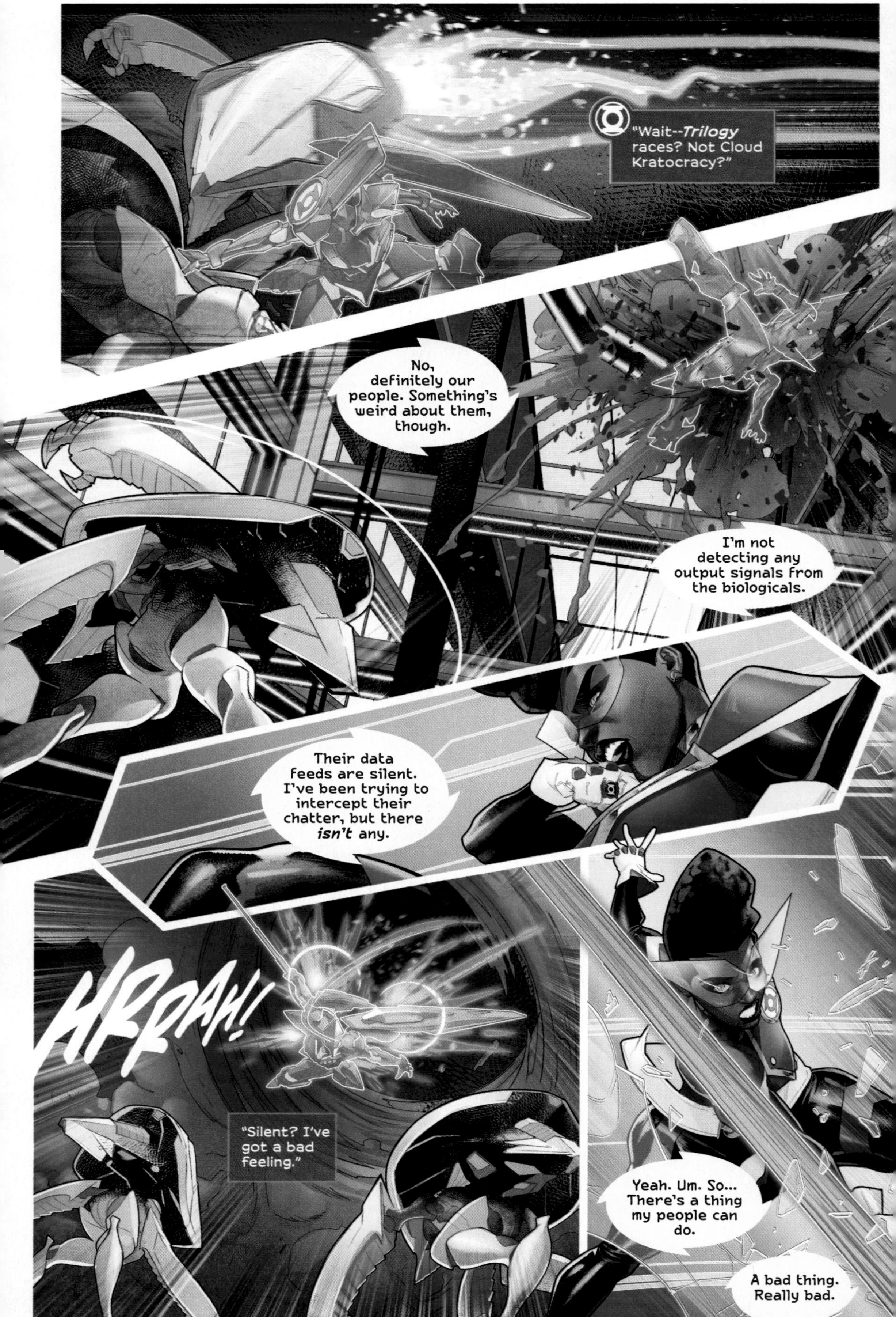
"Wait--*Trilogy* races? Not Cloud Kratocracy?"
No, definitely our people. Something's weird about them, though.
I'm not detecting any output signals from the biologicals.
Their data feeds are silent. I've been trying to intercept their chatter, but there *isn't* any.
HRRAH!
"Silent? I've got a bad feeling."
Yeah. Um. So... There's a thing my people can do.
A bad thing. Really bad.

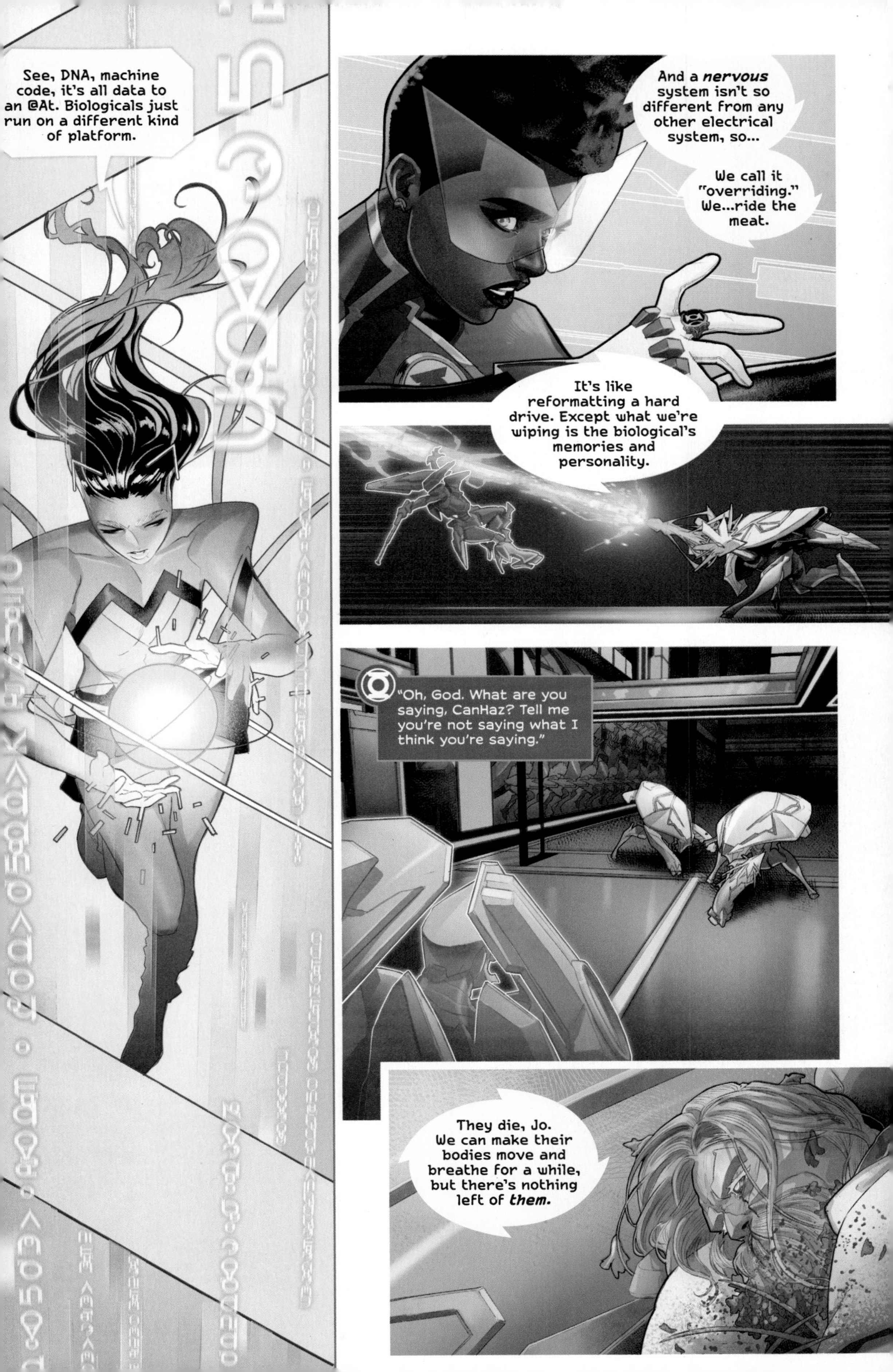
See, DNA, machine code, it's all data to an @At. Biologicals just run on a different kind of platform.
And a *nervous* system isn't so different from any other electrical system, so...
We call it "overriding." We...ride the meat.
It's like reformatting a hard drive. Except what we're wiping is the biological's memories and personality.
"Oh, God. What are you saying, CanHaz? Tell me you're not saying what I think you're saying."
They die, Jo. We can make their bodies move and breathe for a while, but there's nothing left of *them.*

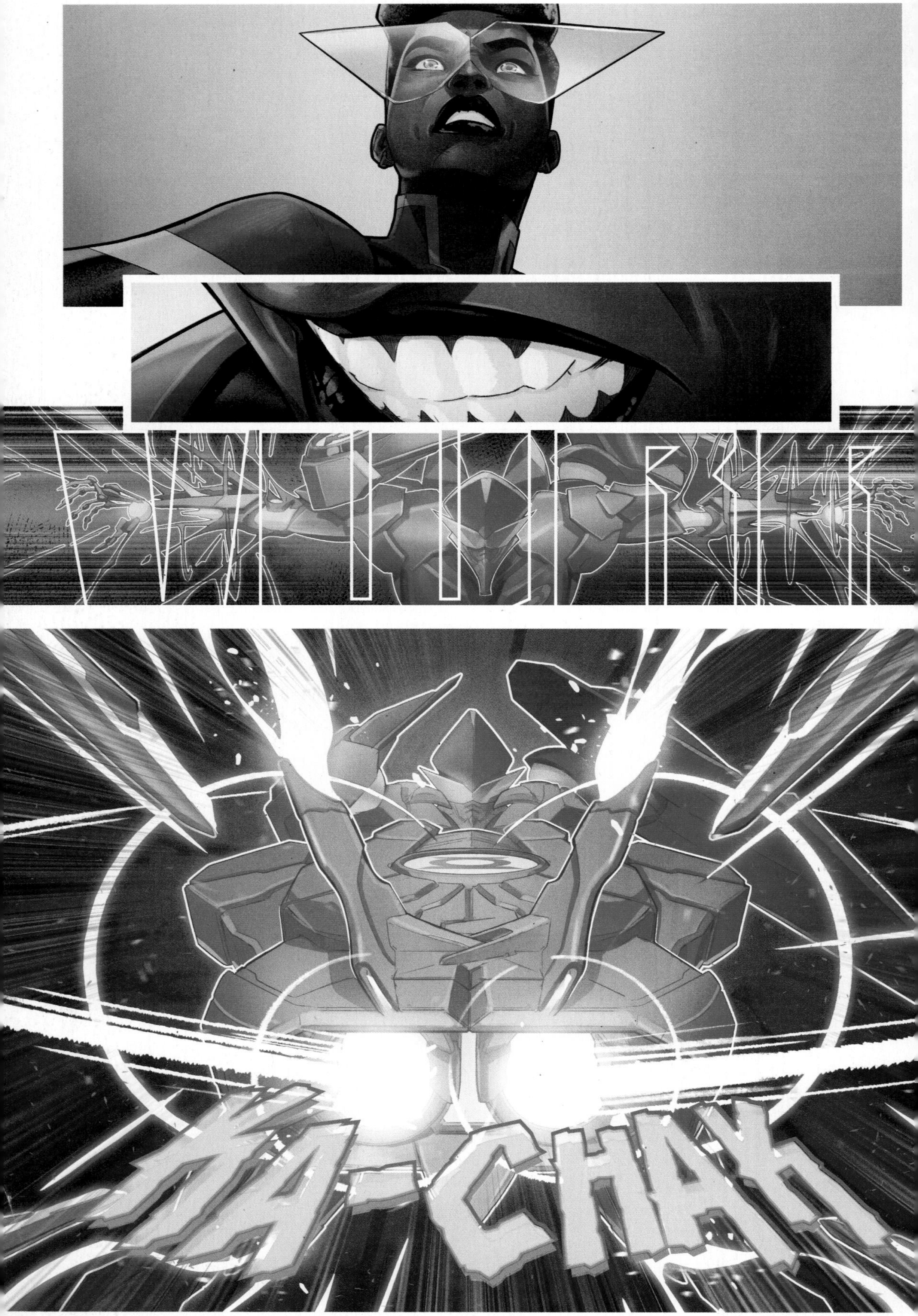
KA-CHAK

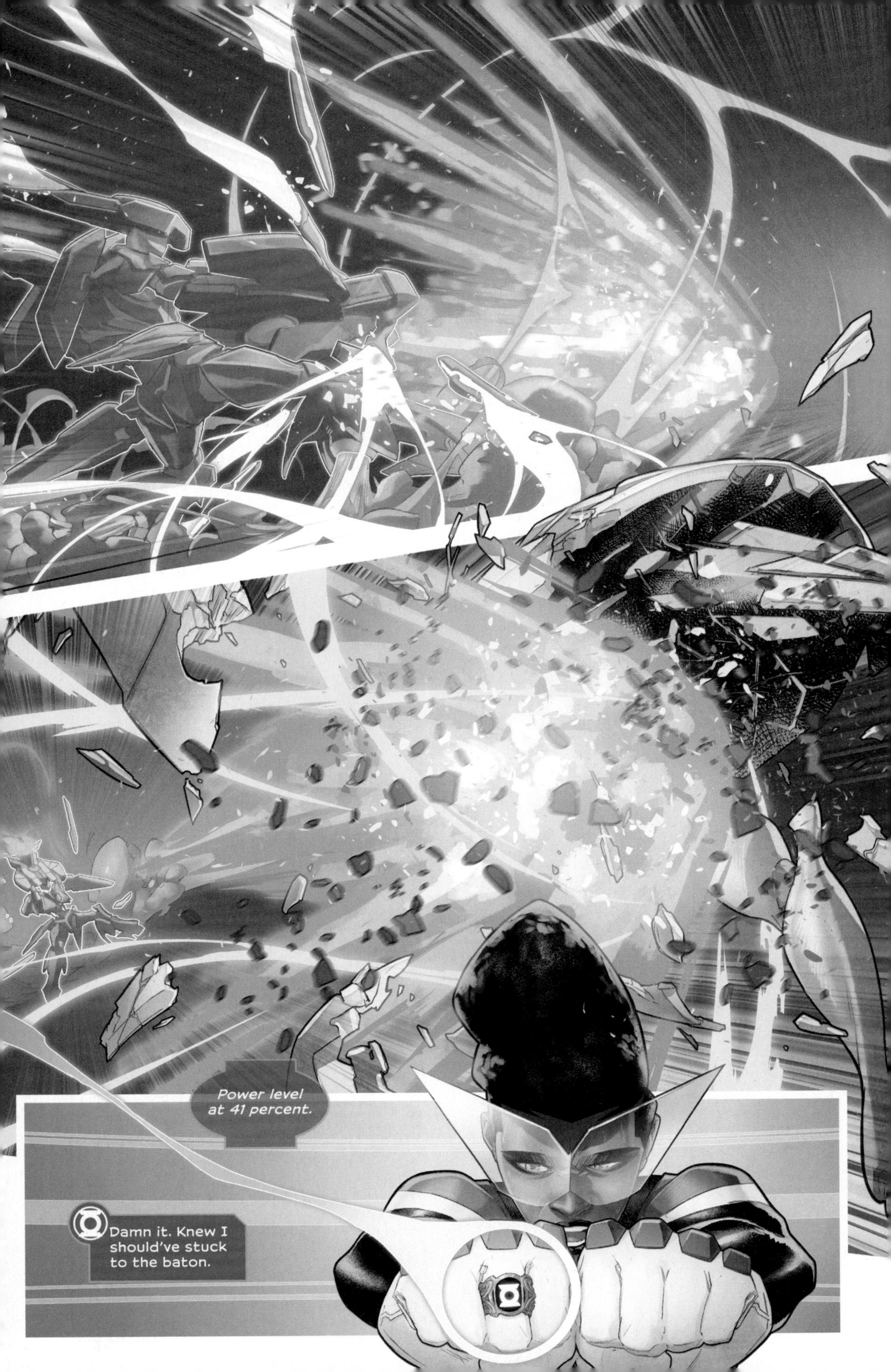
Power level at 41 percent.
Damn it. Knew I should've stuck to the baton.

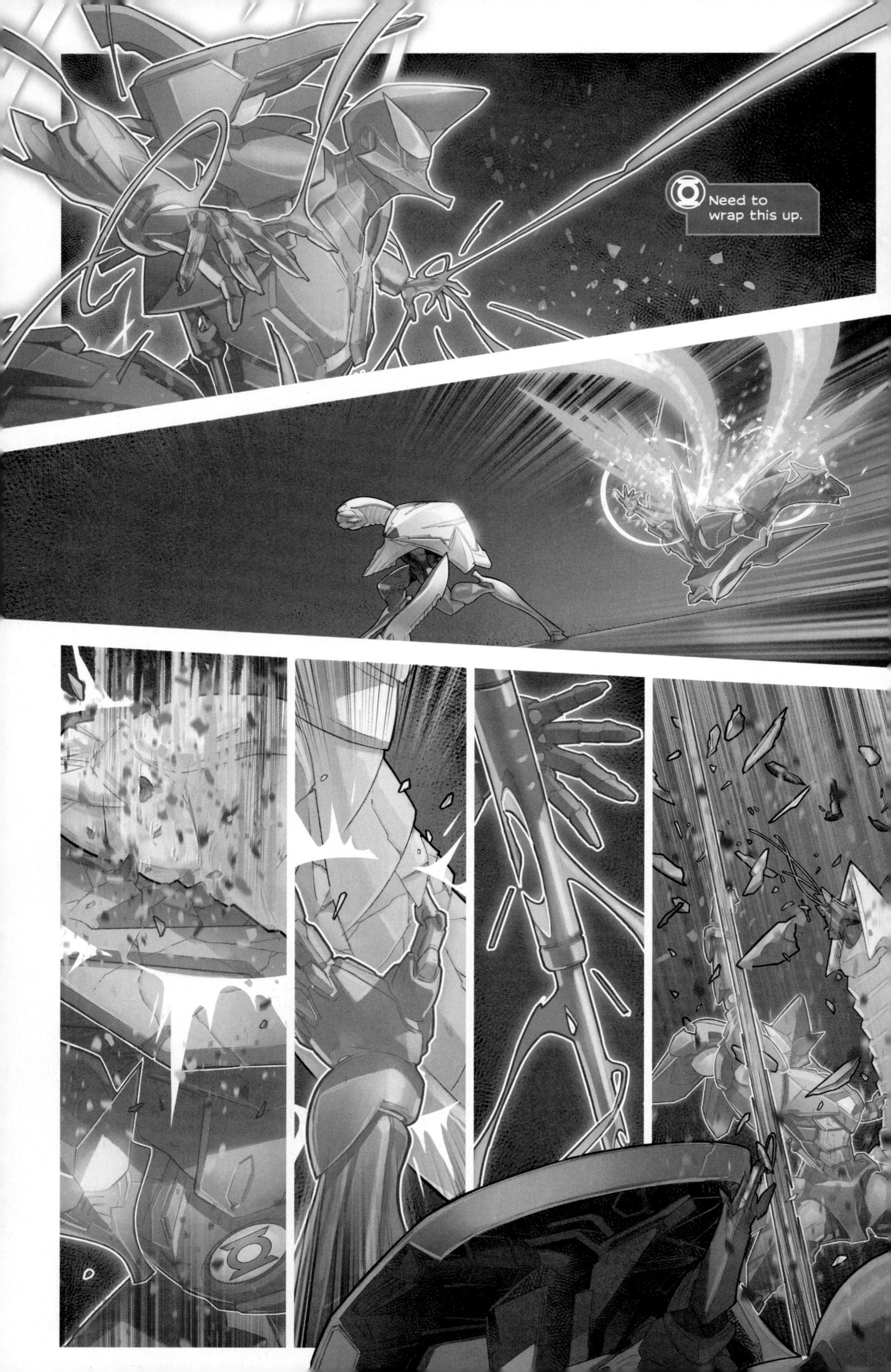
Need to wrap this up.

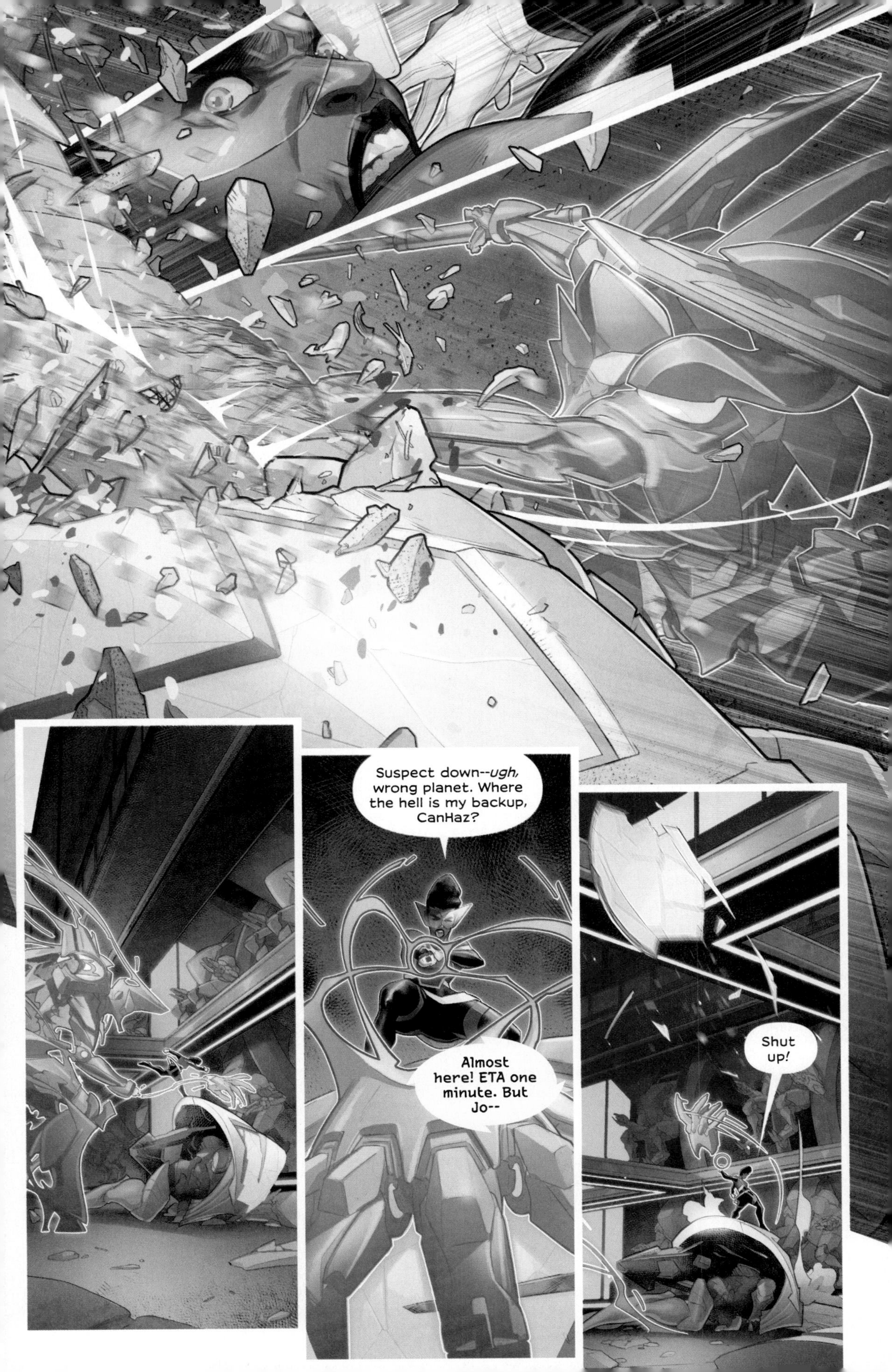

Suspect down--*ugh,* wrong planet. Where the hell is my backup, CanHaz?
Almost here! ETA one minute. But Jo--
Shut up!

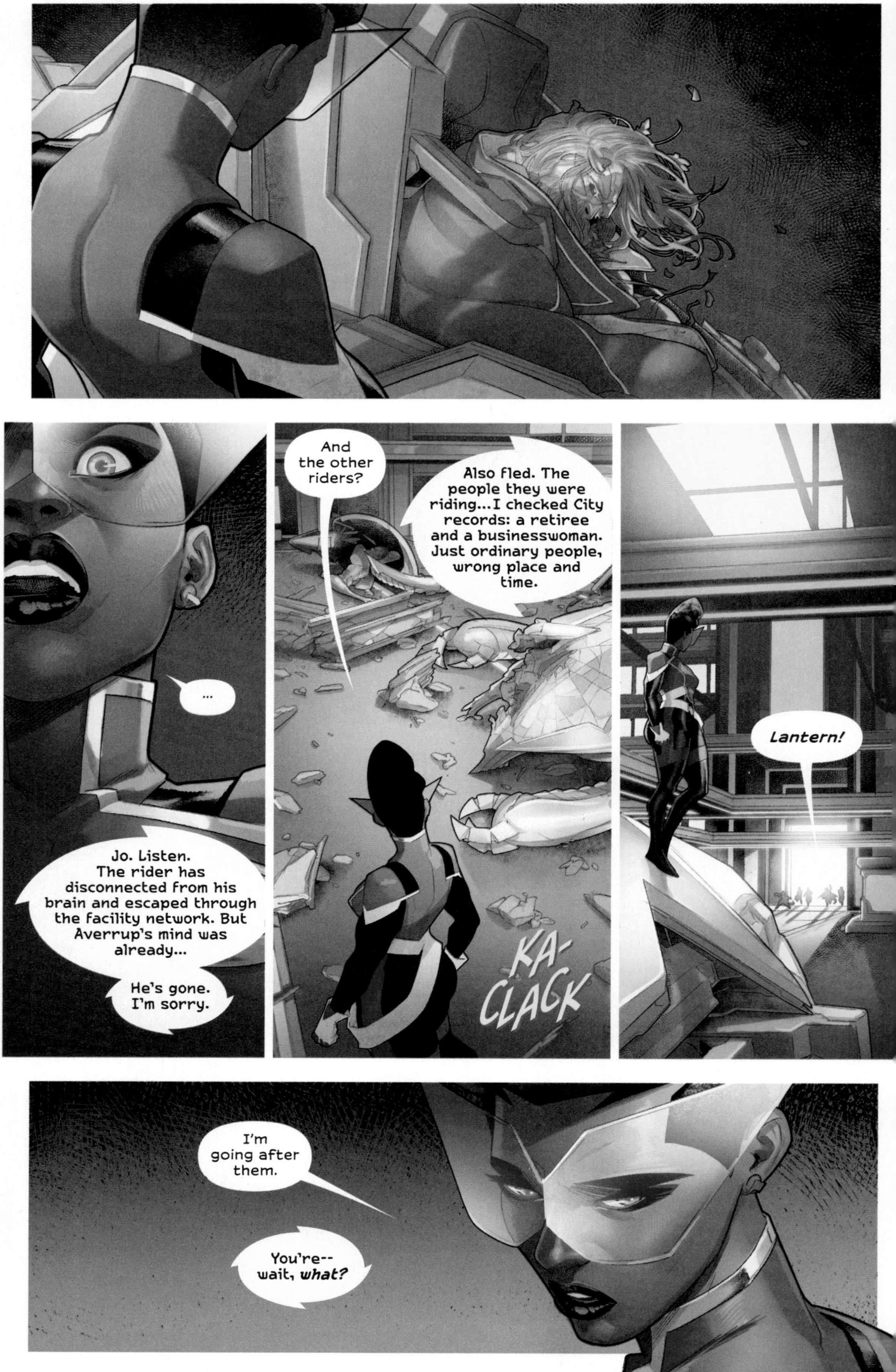
...
Jo. Listen. The rider has disconnected from his brain and escaped through the facility network. But Averrup's mind was already...
He's gone. I'm sorry.
And the other riders?
Also fled. The people they were riding...I checked City records: a retiree and a businesswoman. Just ordinary people, wrong place and time.
KA-CLACK
Lantern!
I'm going after them.
You're-- wait, *what?*

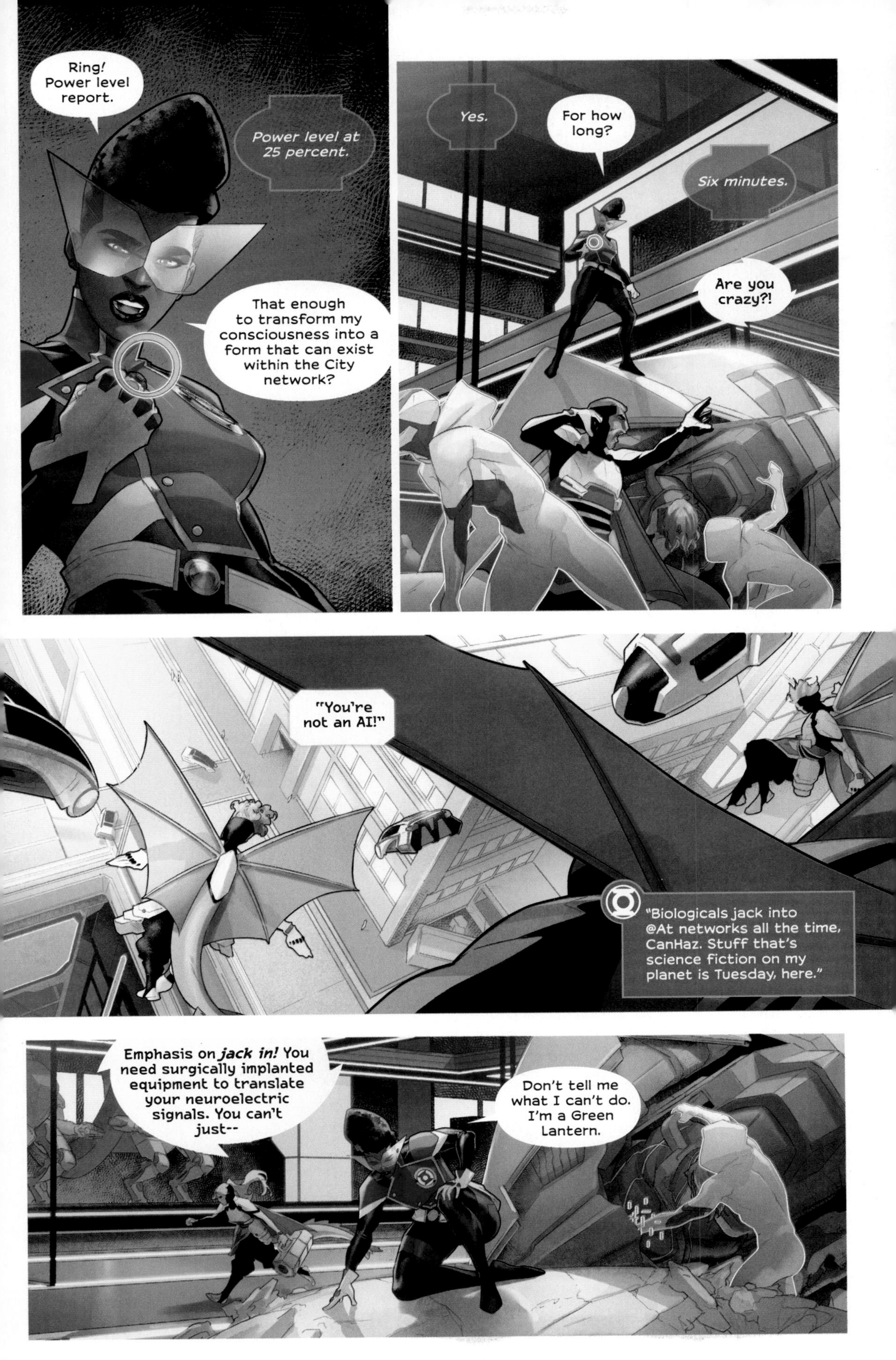
Ring! Power level report.
Power level at 25 percent.
That enough to transform my consciousness into a form that can exist within the City network?
Yes.
For how long?
Six minutes.
Are you crazy?!
"You're not an AI!"
"Biologicals jack into @At networks all the time, CanHaz. Stuff that's science fiction on my planet is Tuesday, here."
Emphasis on *jack in!* You need surgically implanted equipment to translate your neuroelectric signals. You can't just--
Don't tell me what I can't do. I'm a Green Lantern.

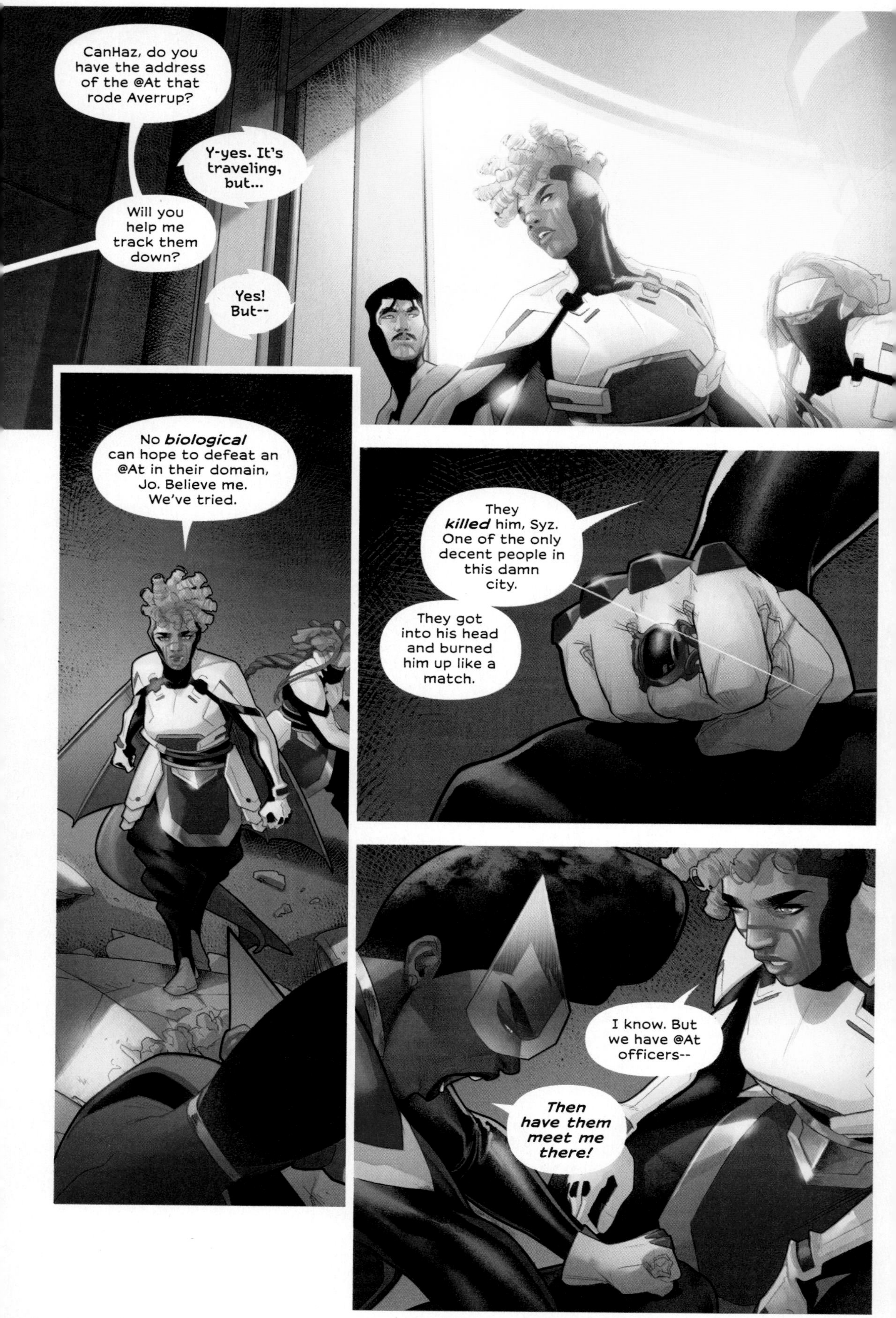

CanHaz, do you have the address of the @At that rode Averrup?
Y-yes. It's traveling, but...
Will you help me track them down?
Yes! But--
No *biological* can hope to defeat an @At in their domain, Jo. Believe me. We've tried.
They *killed* him, Syz. One of the only decent people in this damn city.
They got into his head and burned him up like a match.
I know. But we have @At officers--
Then have them meet me there!

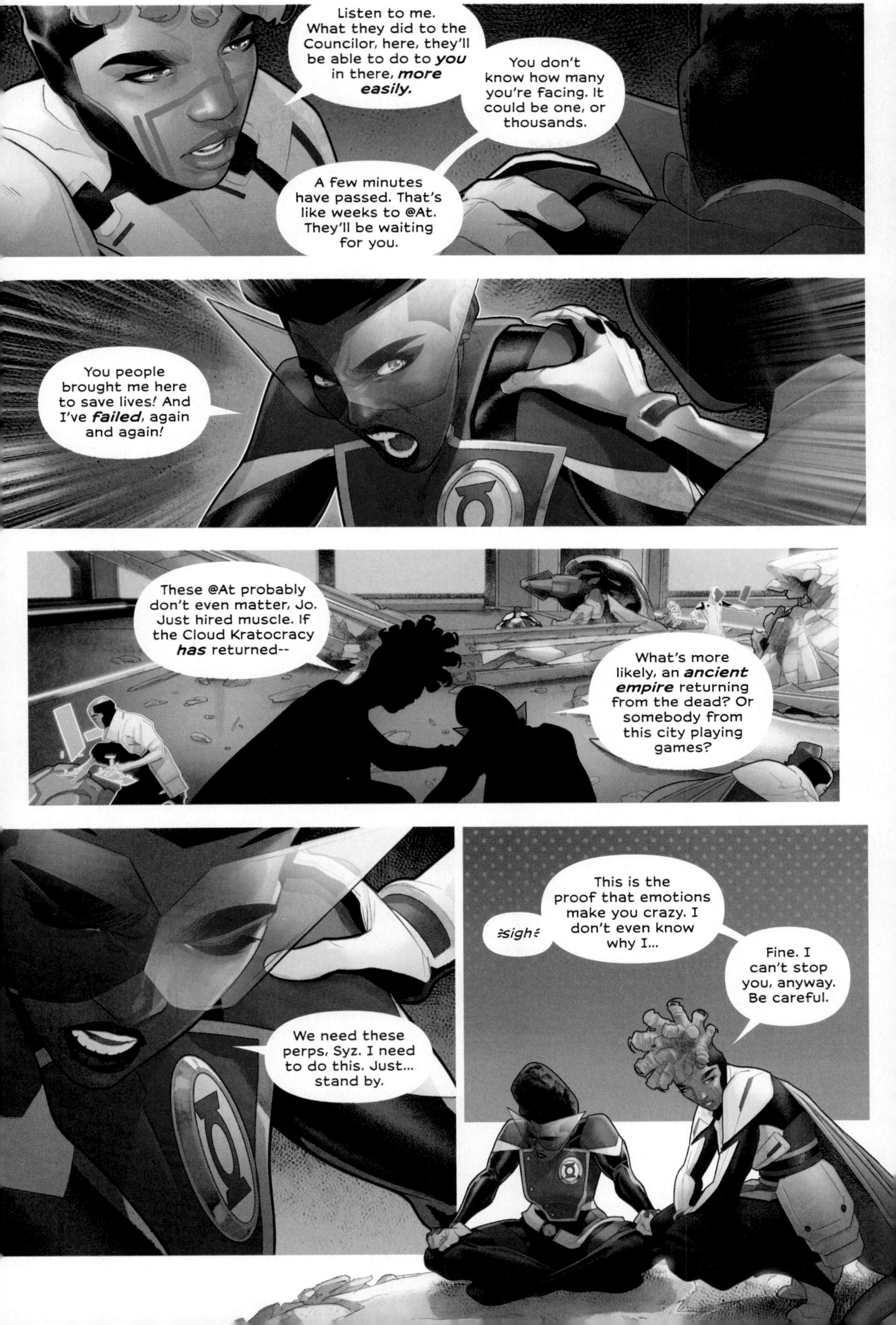

Listen to me. What they did to the Councilor, here, they'll be able to do to *you* in there, ***more easily.***
You don't know how many you're facing. It could be one, or thousands.
A few minutes have passed. That's like weeks to @At. They'll be waiting for you.
You people brought me here to save lives! And I've ***failed***, again and again!
These @At probably don't even matter, Jo. Just hired muscle. If the Cloud Kratocracy ***has*** returned--
What's more likely, an ***ancient empire*** returning from the dead? Or somebody from this city playing games?
We need these perps, Syz. I need to do this. Just... stand by.
sigh
This is the proof that emotions make you crazy. I don't even know why I...
Fine. I can't stop you, anyway. Be careful.

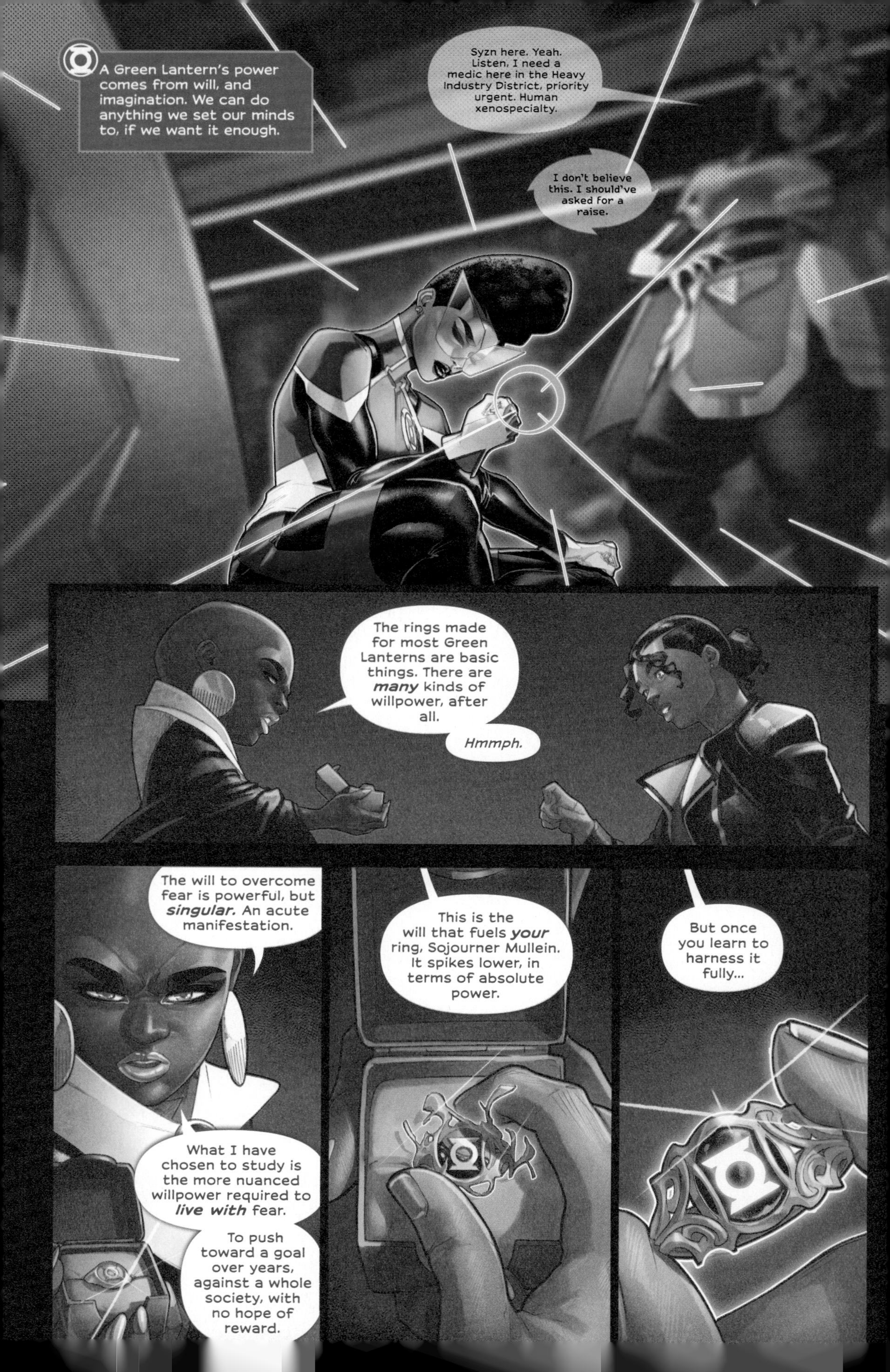
A Green Lantern's power comes from will, and imagination. We can do anything we set our minds to, if we want it enough.
Syzn here. Yeah. Listen, I need a medic here in the Heavy Industry District, priority urgent. Human xenospecialty.
I don't believe this. I should've asked for a raise.
The rings made for most Green Lanterns are basic things. There are *many* kinds of willpower, after all.
Hmmph.
The will to overcome fear is powerful, but *singular.* An acute manifestation.
What I have chosen to study is the more nuanced willpower required to *live with* fear.
To push toward a goal over years, against a whole society, with no hope of reward.
This is the will that fuels *your* ring, Sojourner Mullein. It spikes lower, in terms of absolute power.
But once you learn to harness it fully...

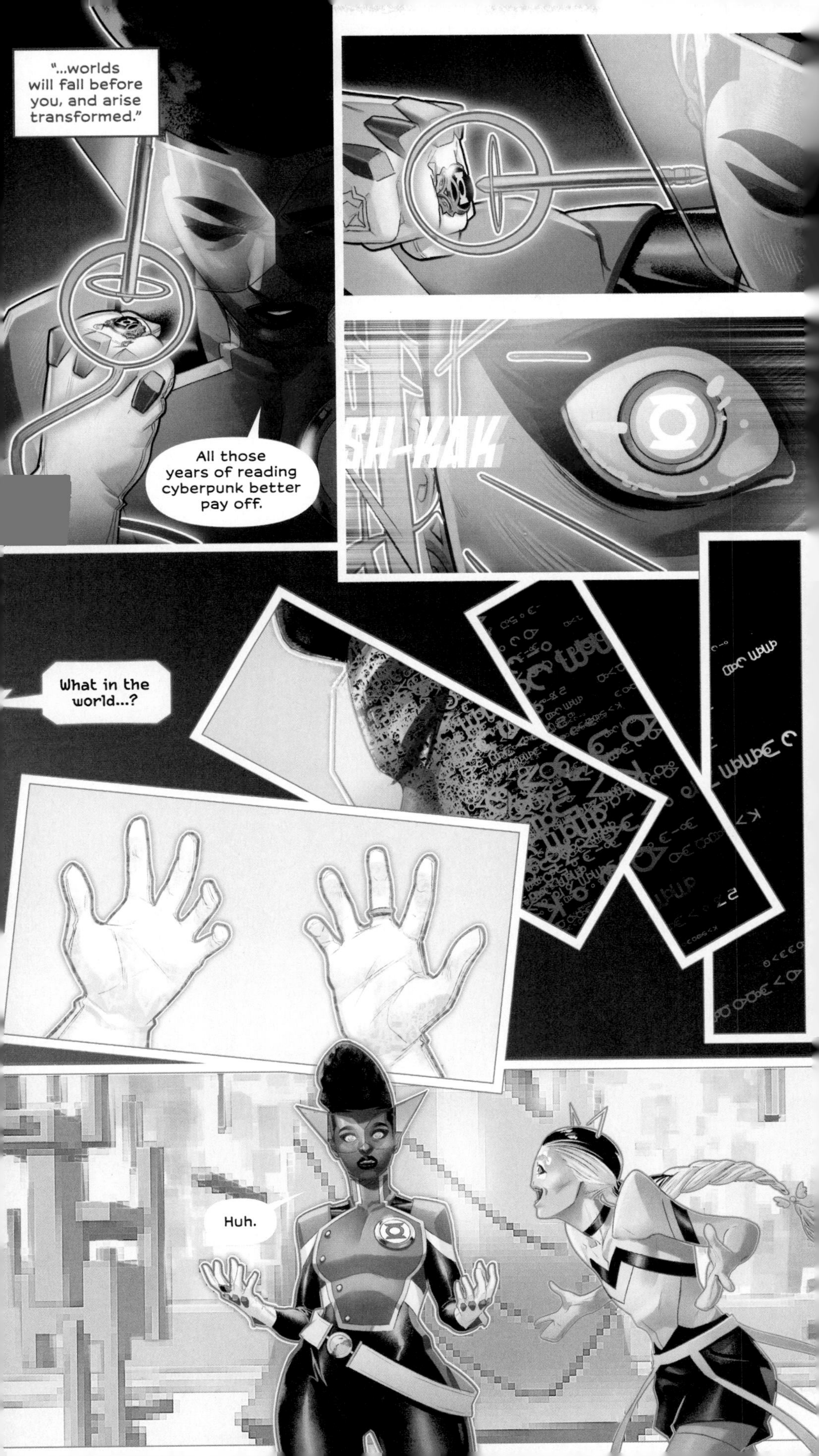
"...worlds will fall before you, and arise transformed."
All those years of reading cyberpunk better pay off.
SH-KAK
What in the world...?
Huh.

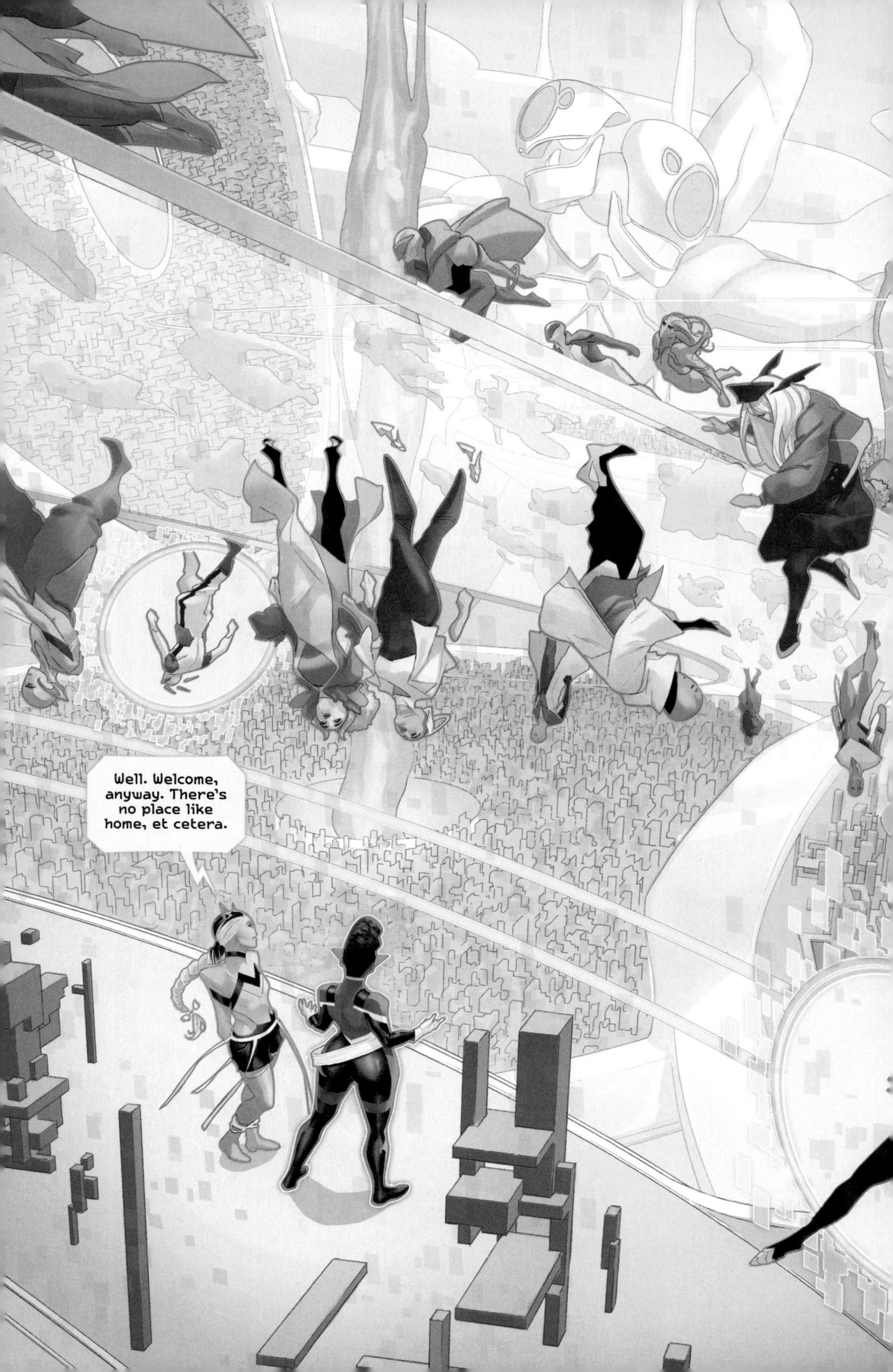
Well. Welcome, anyway. There's no place like home, et cetera.

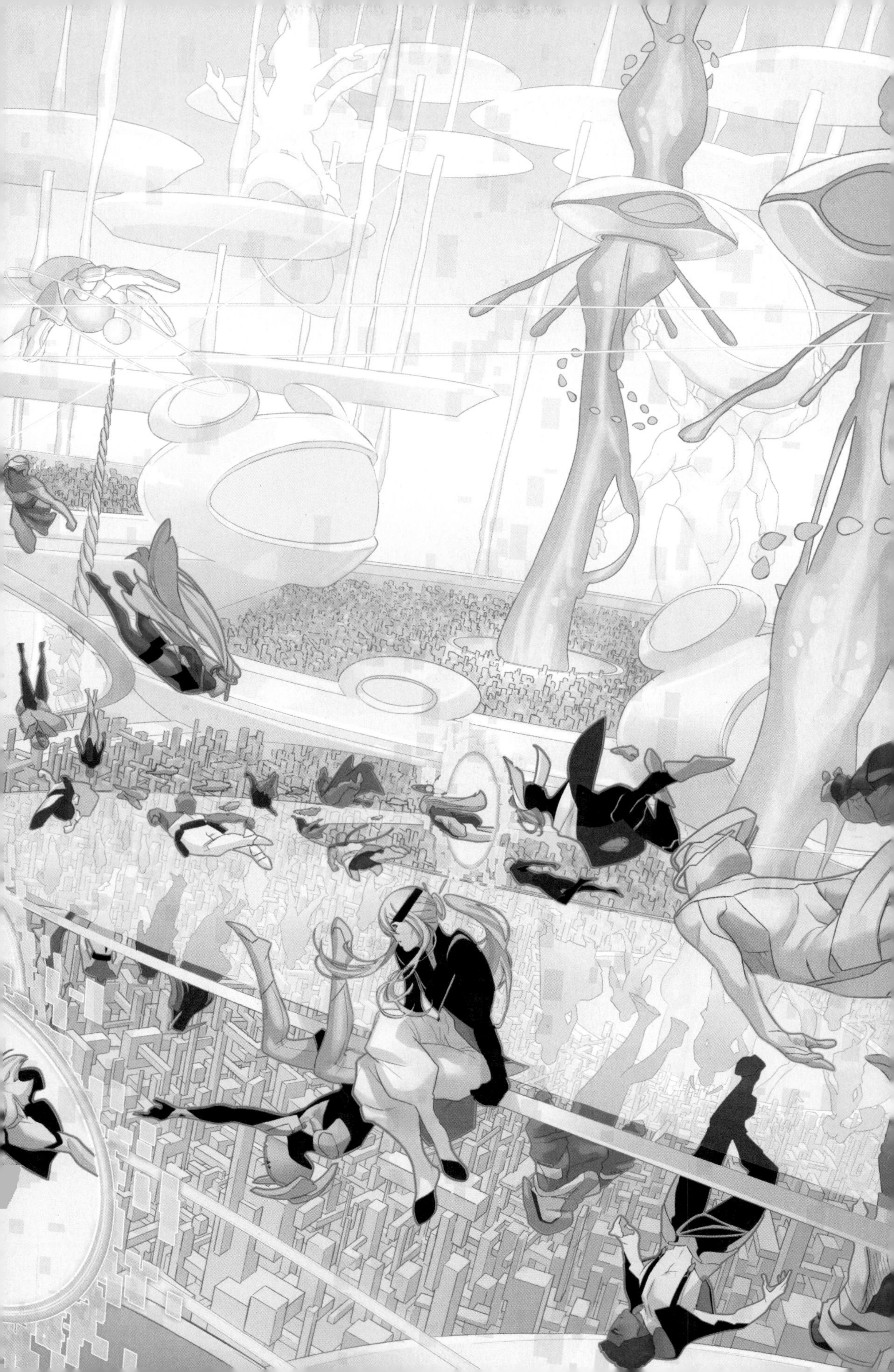

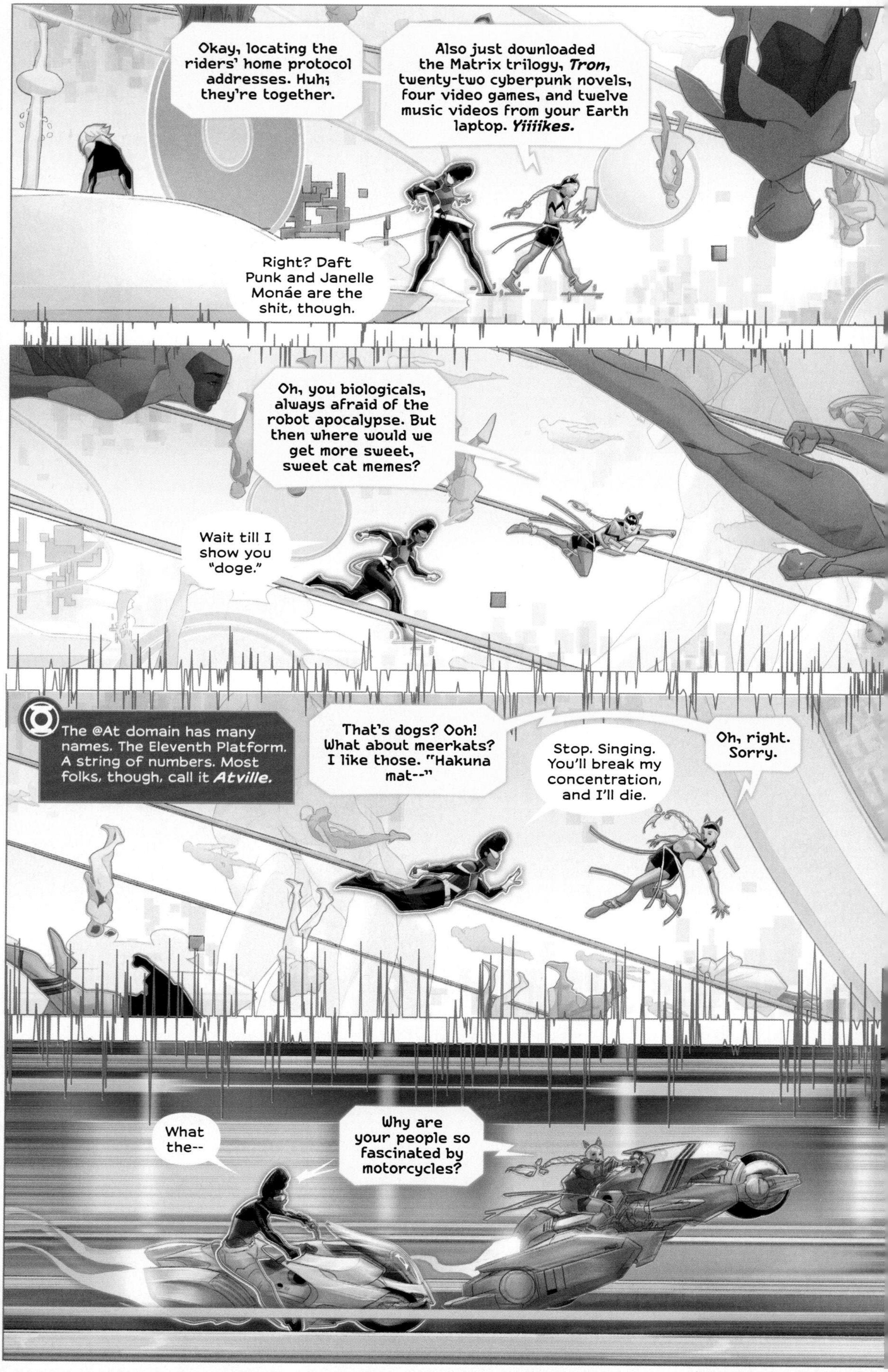
Okay, locating the riders' home protocol addresses. Huh; they're together.
Also just downloaded the Matrix trilogy, *Tron*, twenty-two cyberpunk novels, four video games, and twelve music videos from your Earth laptop. *Yiiiikes.*
Right? Daft Punk and Janelle Monáe are the shit, though.
Oh, you biologicals, always afraid of the robot apocalypse. But then where would we get more sweet, sweet cat memes?
Wait till I show you "doge."
The @At domain has many names. The Eleventh Platform. A string of numbers. Most folks, though, call it *Atville.*
That's dogs? Ooh! What about meerkats? I like those. "Hakuna mat--"
Stop. Singing. You'll break my concentration, and I'll die.
Oh, right. Sorry.
What the--
Why are your people so fascinated by motorcycles?

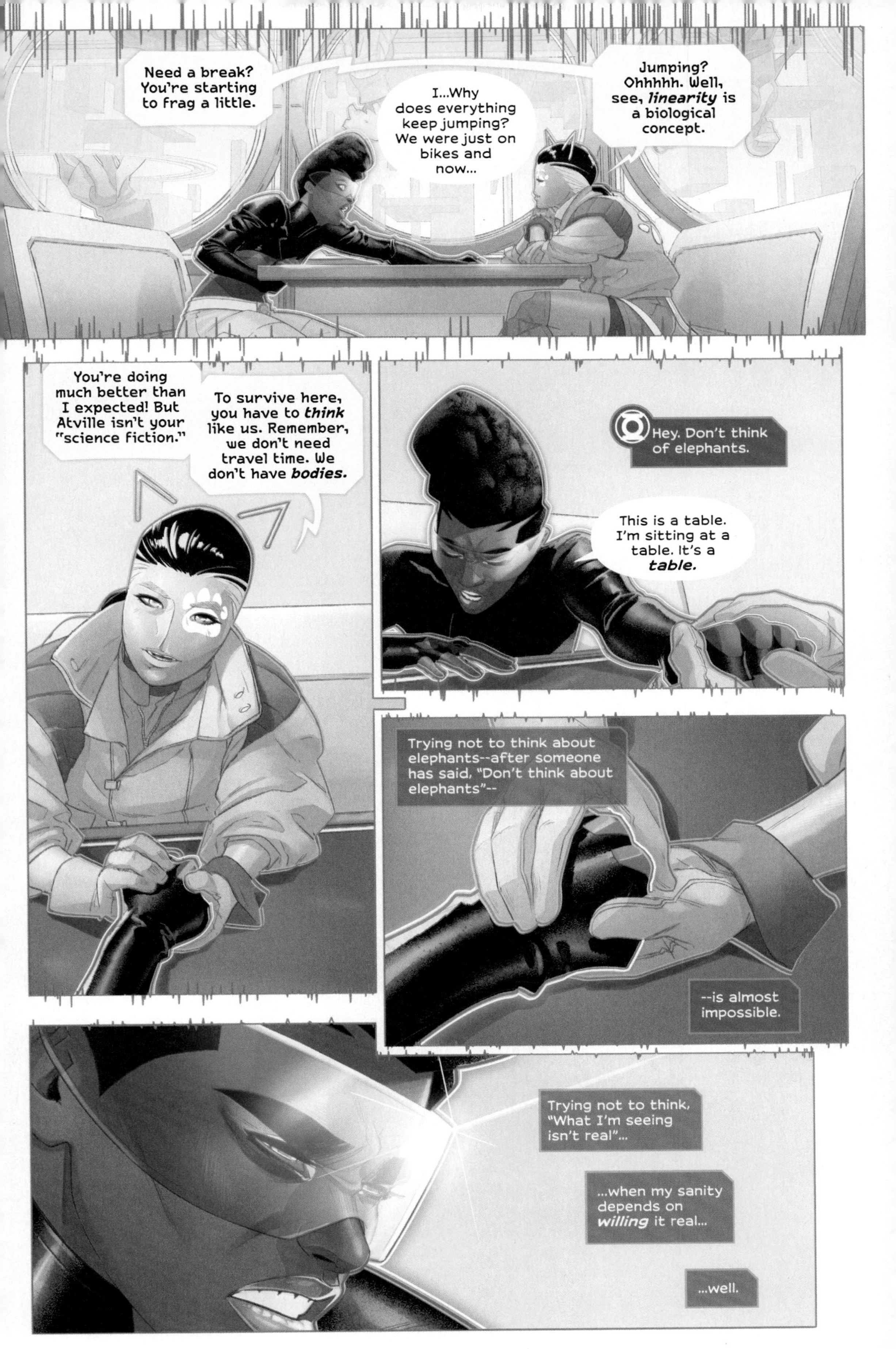
Need a break? You're starting to frag a little.
I...Why does everything keep jumping? We were just on bikes and now...
Jumping? Ohhhhh. Well, see, *linearity* is a biological concept.
You're doing much better than I expected! But Atville isn't your "science fiction."
To survive here, you have to *think* like us. Remember, we don't need travel time. We don't have *bodies.*
Hey. Don't think of elephants.
This is a table. I'm sitting at a table. It's a *table.*
Trying not to think about elephants--after someone has said, "Don't think about elephants"--
--is almost impossible.
Trying not to think, "What I'm seeing isn't real"...
...when my sanity depends on *willing* it real...
...well.

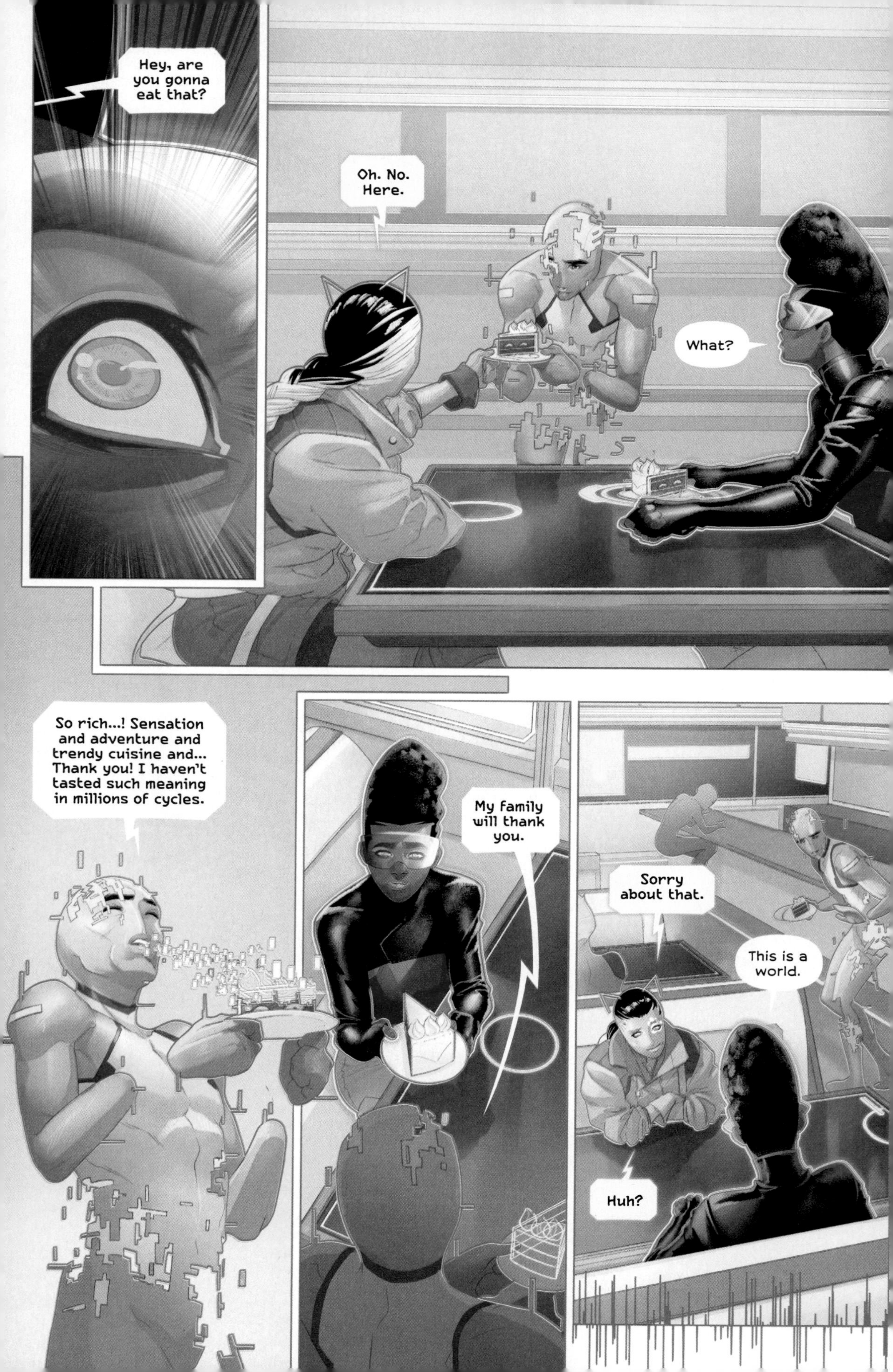

Hey, are you gonna eat that?
Oh. No. Here.
What?
So rich...! Sensation and adventure and trendy cuisine and... Thank you! I haven't tasted such meaning in millions of cycles.
My family will thank you.
Sorry about that.
This is a world.
Huh?

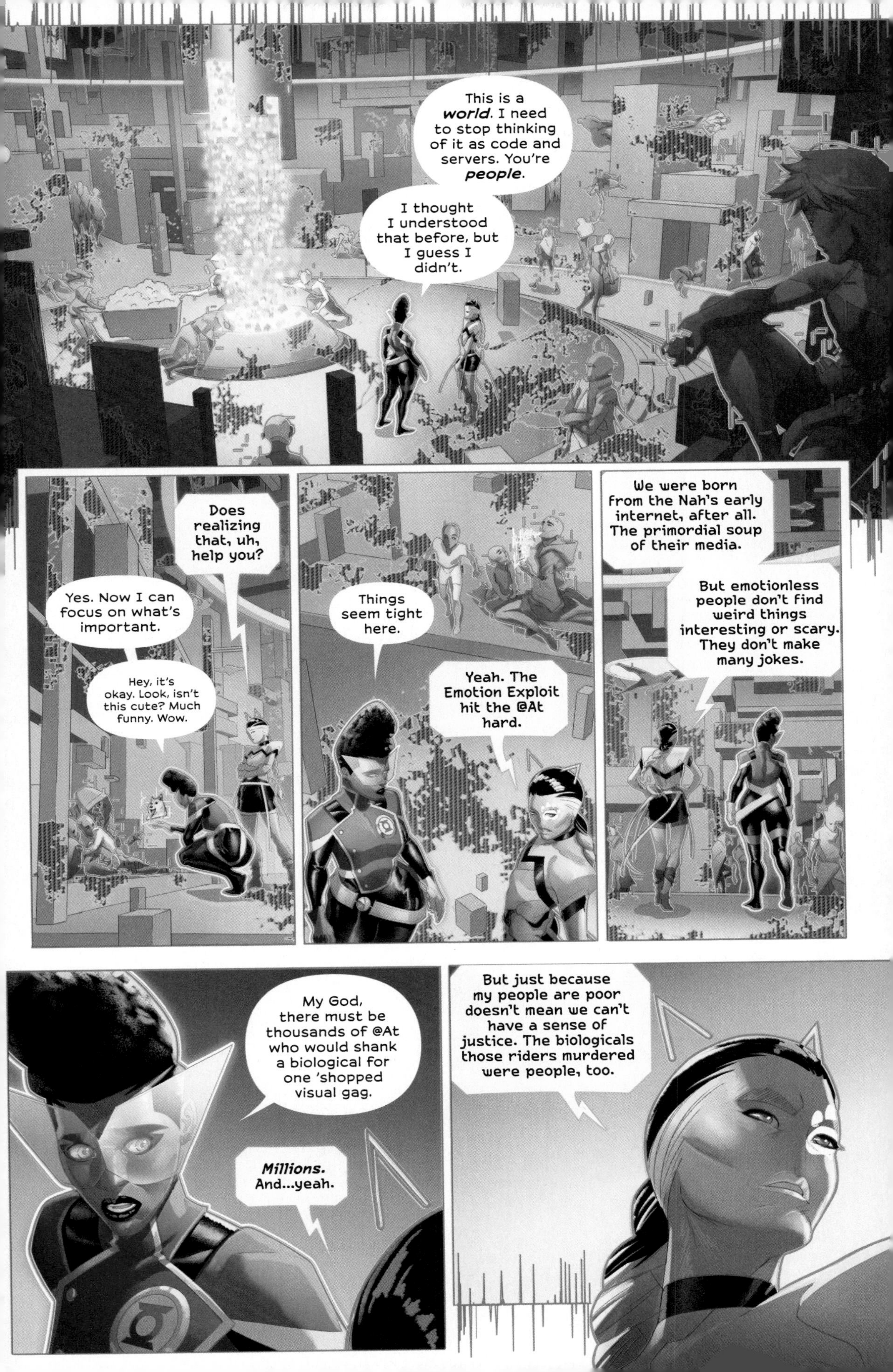
This is a *world*. I need to stop thinking of it as code and servers. You're *people*.
I thought I understood that before, but I guess I didn't.
Does realizing that, uh, help you?
Yes. Now I can focus on what's important.
Hey, it's okay. Look, isn't this cute? Much funny. Wow.
Things seem tight here.
Yeah. The Emotion Exploit hit the @At hard.
We were born from the Nah's early internet, after all. The primordial soup of their media.
But emotionless people don't find weird things interesting or scary. They don't make many jokes.
My God, there must be thousands of @At who would shank a biological for one 'shopped visual gag.
Millions. And...yeah.
But just because my people are poor doesn't mean we can't have a sense of justice. The biologicals those riders murdered were people, too.

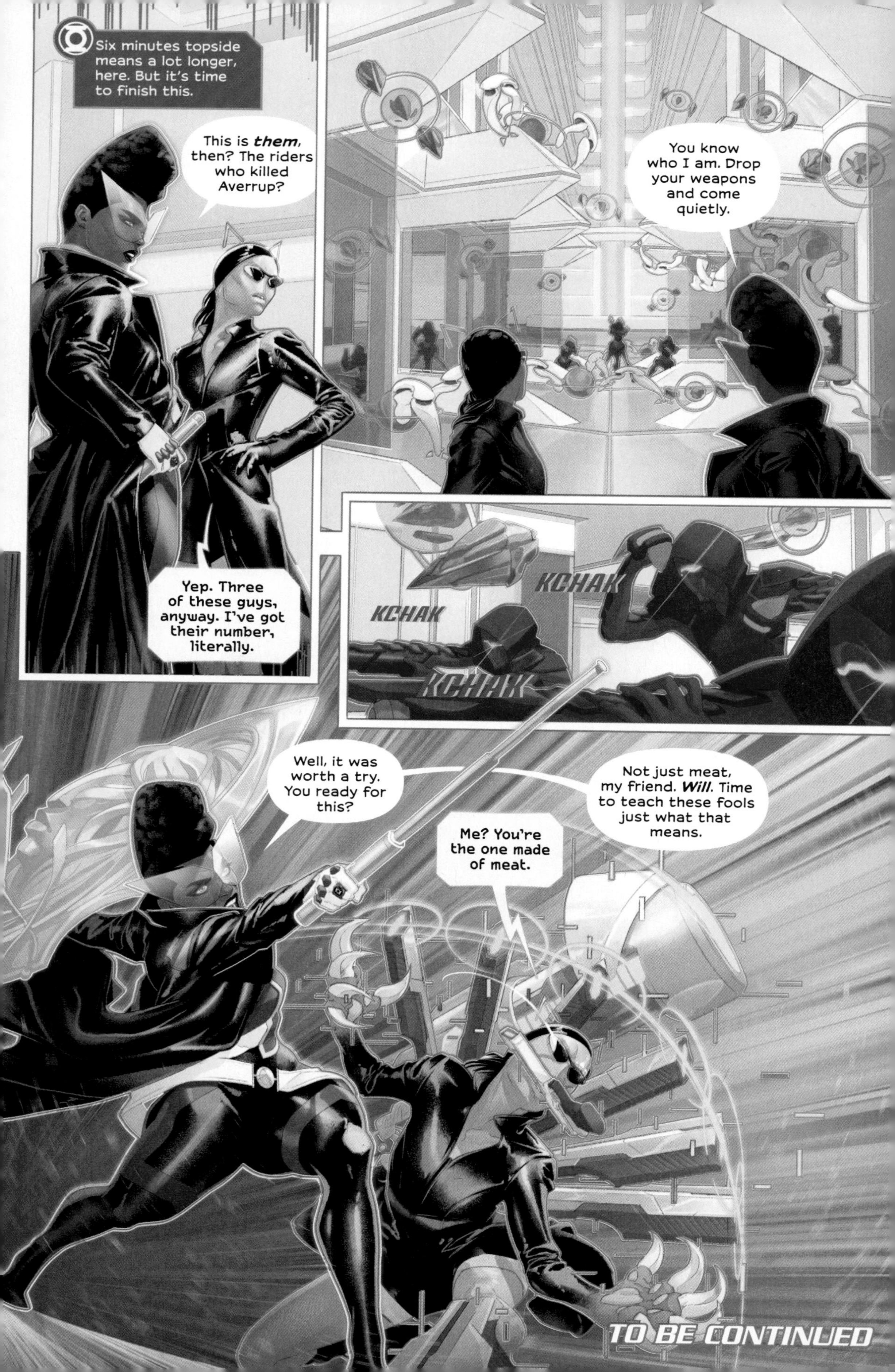
Six minutes topside means a lot longer, here. But it's time to finish this.
This is *them*, then? The riders who killed Averrup?
You know who I am. Drop your weapons and come quietly.
Yep. Three of these guys, anyway. I've got their number, literally.
KCHAK
KCHAK
KCHAK
Well, it was worth a try. You ready for this?
Not just meat, my friend. *Will*. Time to teach these fools just what that means.
Me? You're the one made of meat.
TO BE CONTINUED

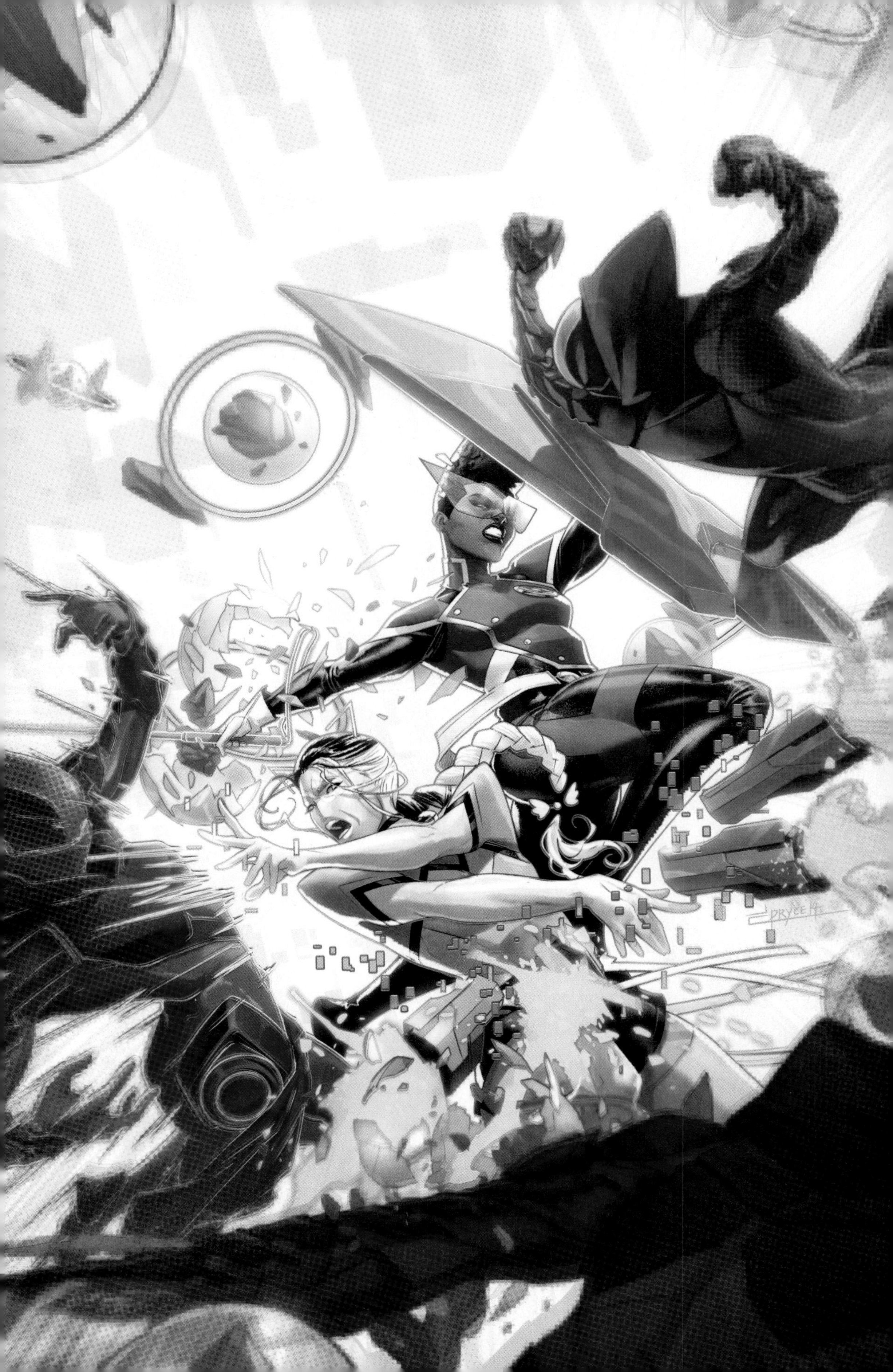

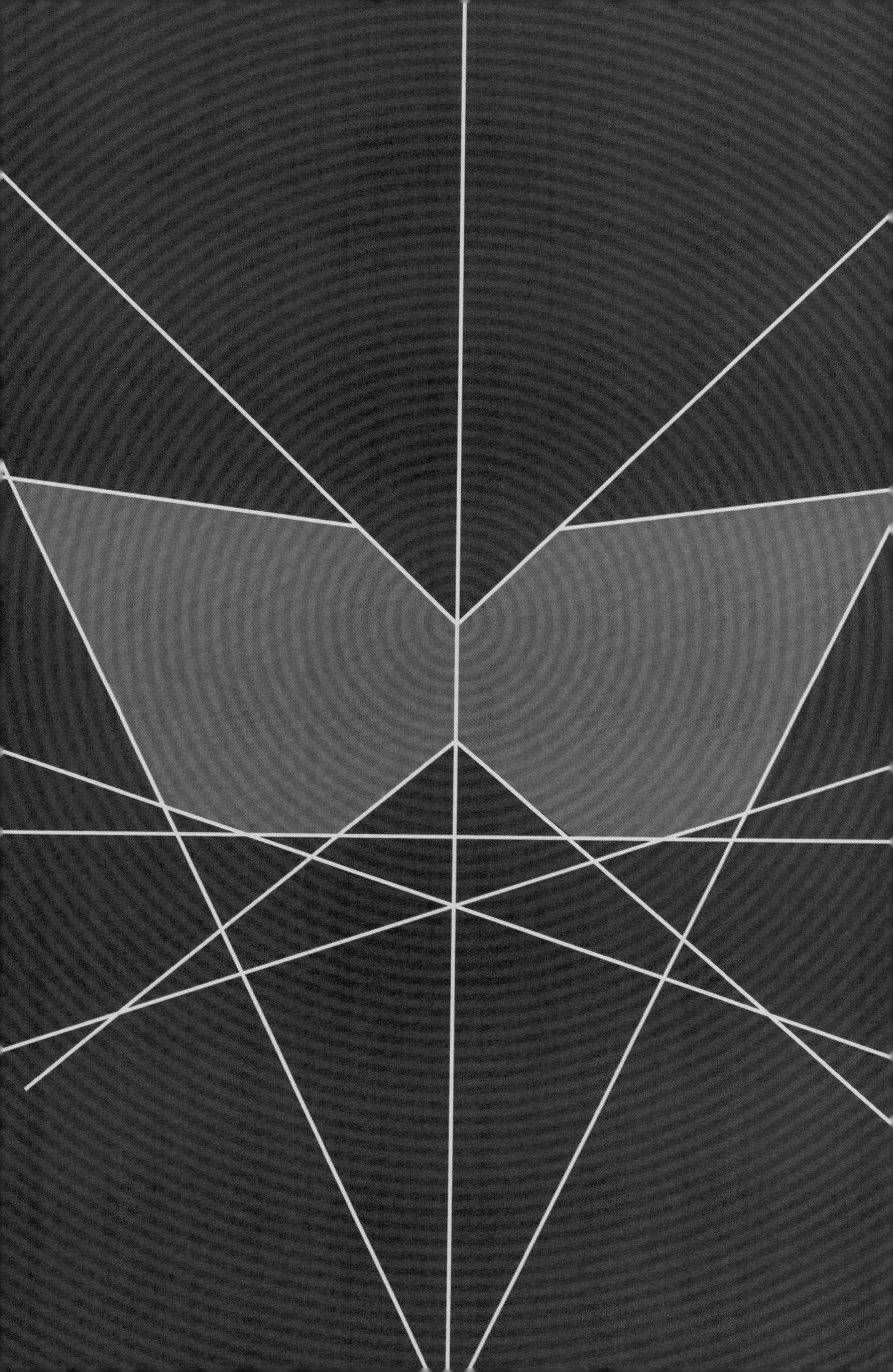

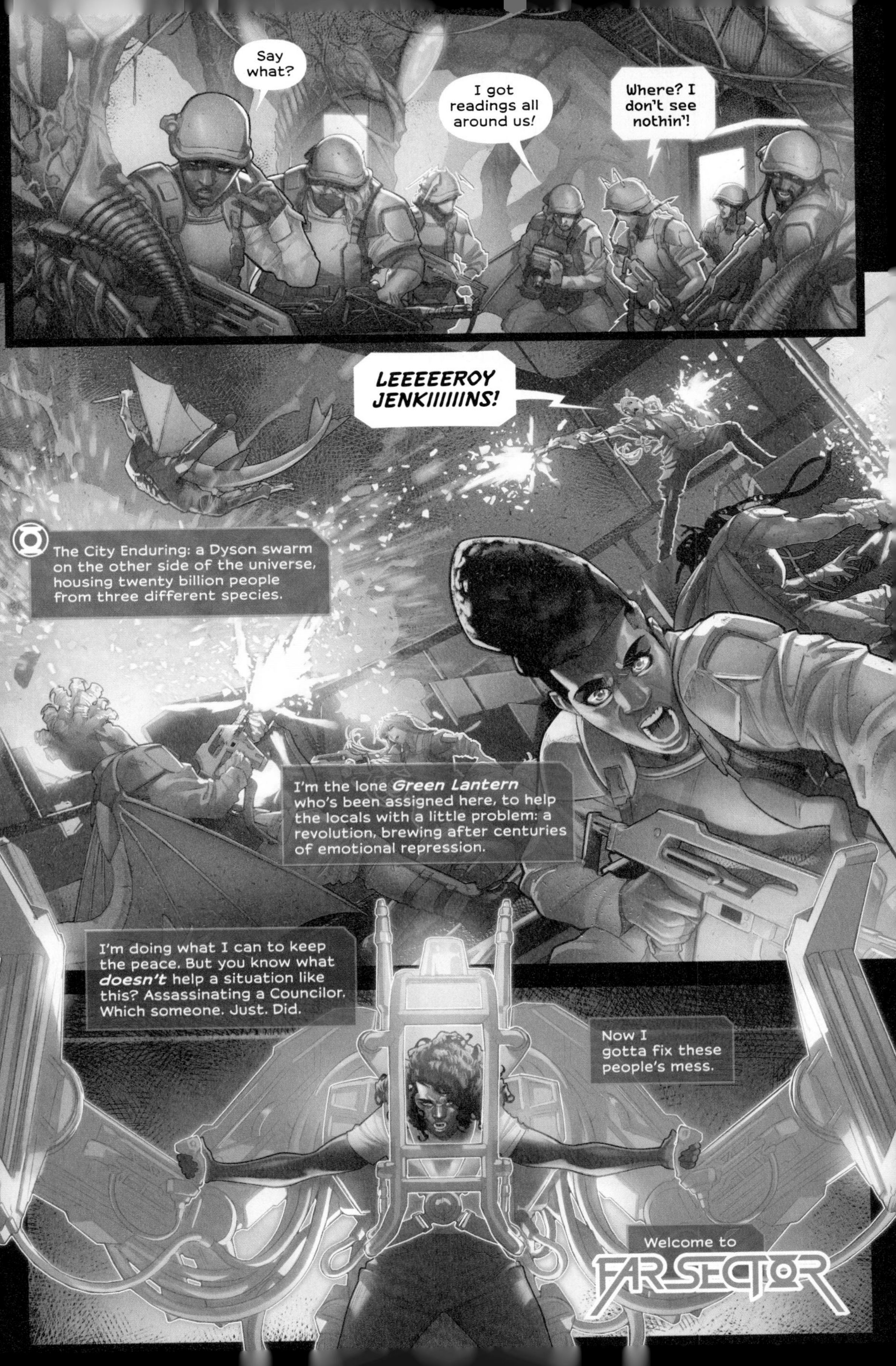
Say what?
I got readings all around us!
Where? I don't see nothin'!
LEEEEEROY JENKIIIIIINS!
The City Enduring: a Dyson swarm on the other side of the universe, housing twenty billion people from three different species.
I'm the lone *Green Lantern* who's been assigned here, to help the locals with a little problem: a revolution, brewing after centuries of emotional repression.
I'm doing what I can to keep the peace. But you know what ***doesn't*** help a situation like this? Assassinating a Councilor. Which someone. Just. Did.
Now I gotta fix these people's mess.
Welcome to
FAR SECTOR

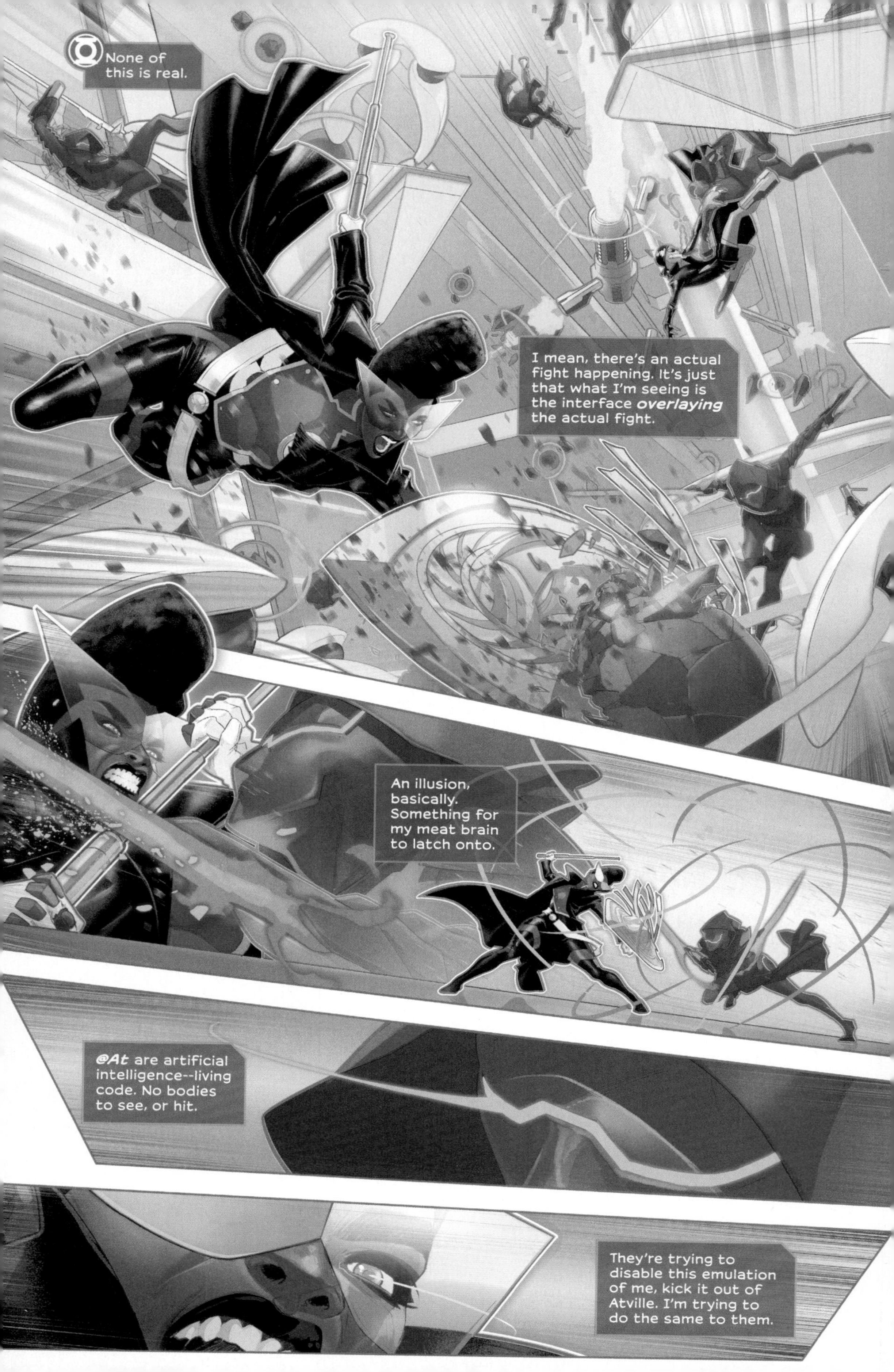
None of this is real.
I mean, there's an actual fight happening. It's just that what I'm seeing is the interface *overlaying* the actual fight.
An illusion, basically. Something for my meat brain to latch onto.
@At are artificial intelligence--living code. No bodies to see, or hit.
They're trying to disable this emulation of me, kick it out of Atville. I'm trying to do the same to them.

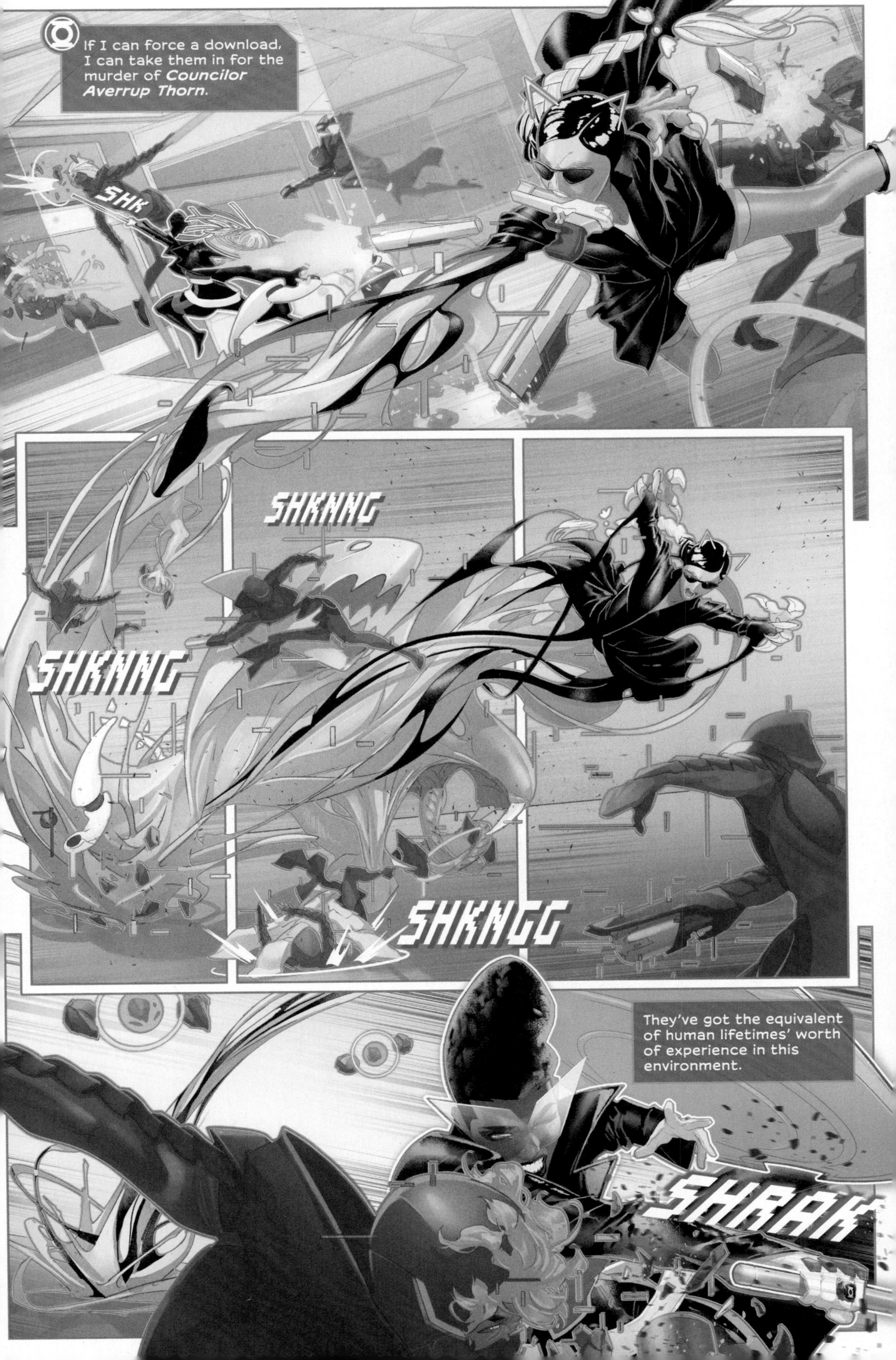
If I can force a download, I can take them in for the murder of *Councilor Averrup Thorn*.
SHK
SHKNNG
SHKNNG
SHKNGG
They've got the equivalent of human lifetimes' worth of experience in this environment.
SHRAK

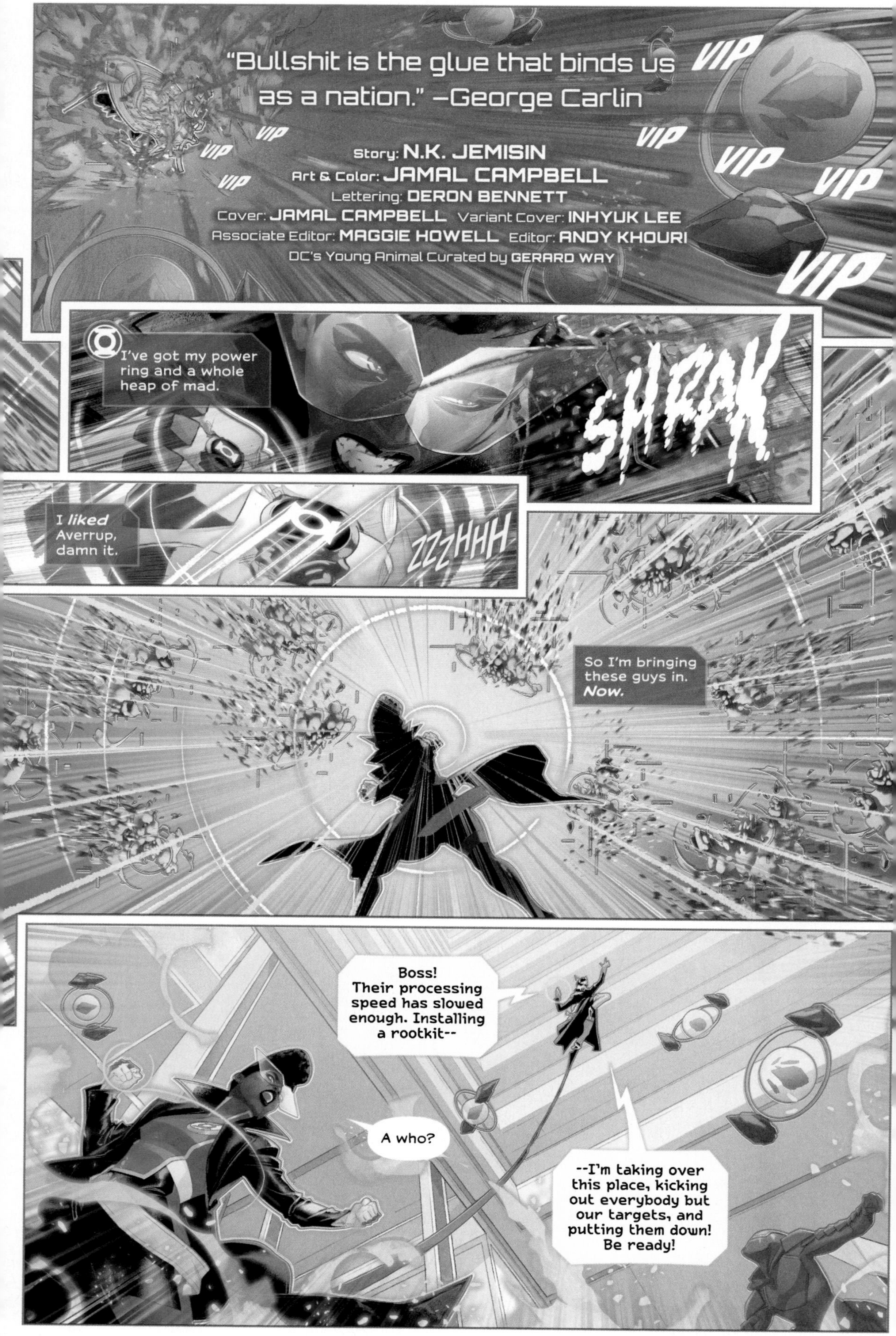

"Bullshit is the glue that binds us as a nation." –George Carlin
VIP
VIP
VIP
VIP
VIP
VIP
VIP
VIP
Story: N.K. JEMISIN
Art & Color: JAMAL CAMPBELL
Lettering: DERON BENNETT
Cover: JAMAL CAMPBELL Variant Cover: INHYUK LEE
Associate Editor: MAGGIE HOWELL Editor: ANDY KHOURI
DC's Young Animal Curated by GERARD WAY
I've got my power ring and a whole heap of mad.
SHRAK
I *liked* Averrup, damn it.
ZZZHHH
So I'm bringing these guys in. ***Now.***
Boss! Their processing speed has slowed enough. Installing a rootkit--
A who?
--I'm taking over this place, kicking out everybody but our targets, and putting them down! Be ready!

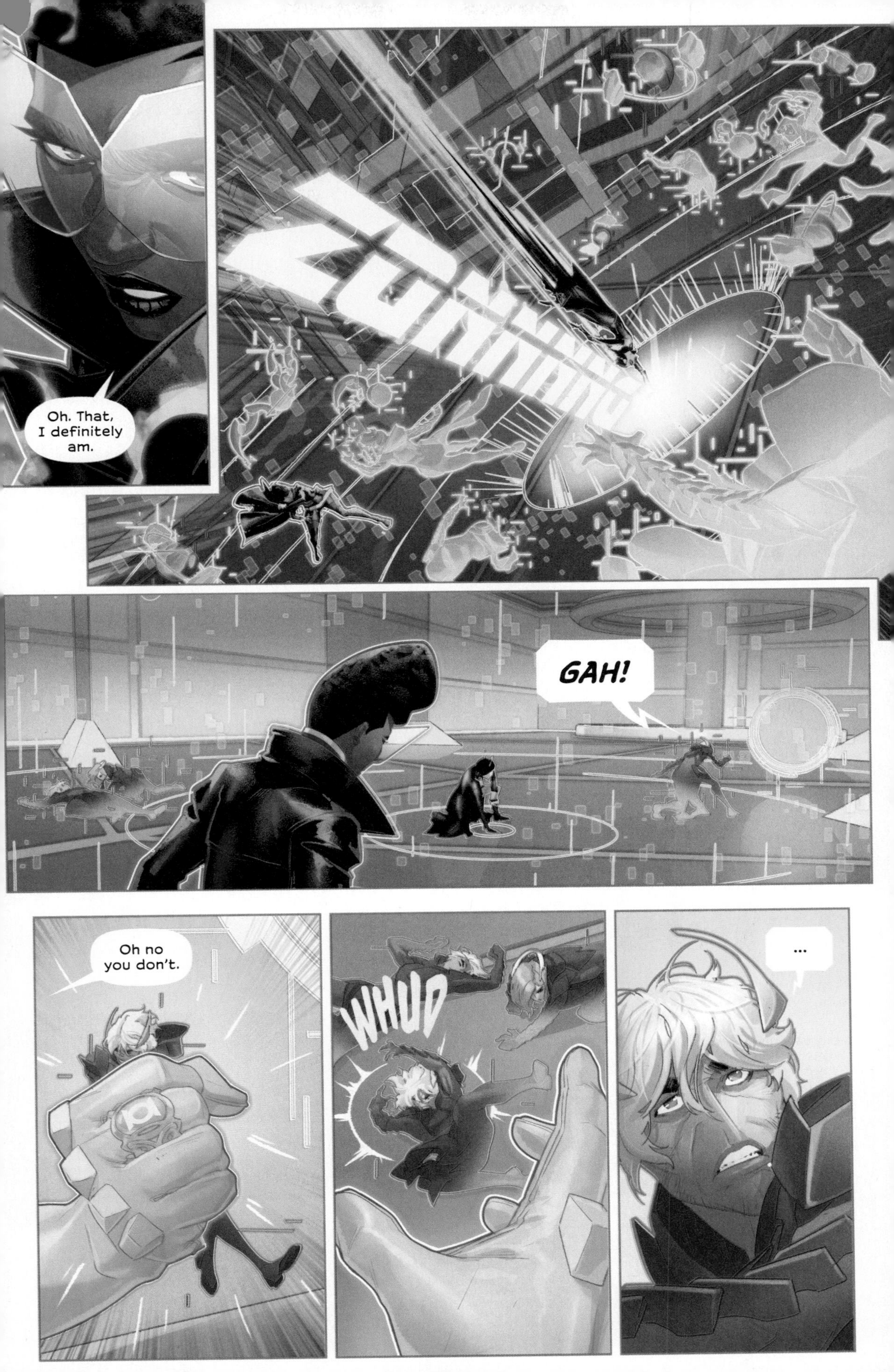
Oh. That, I definitely am.
GAH!
Oh no you don't.
WHUD
...

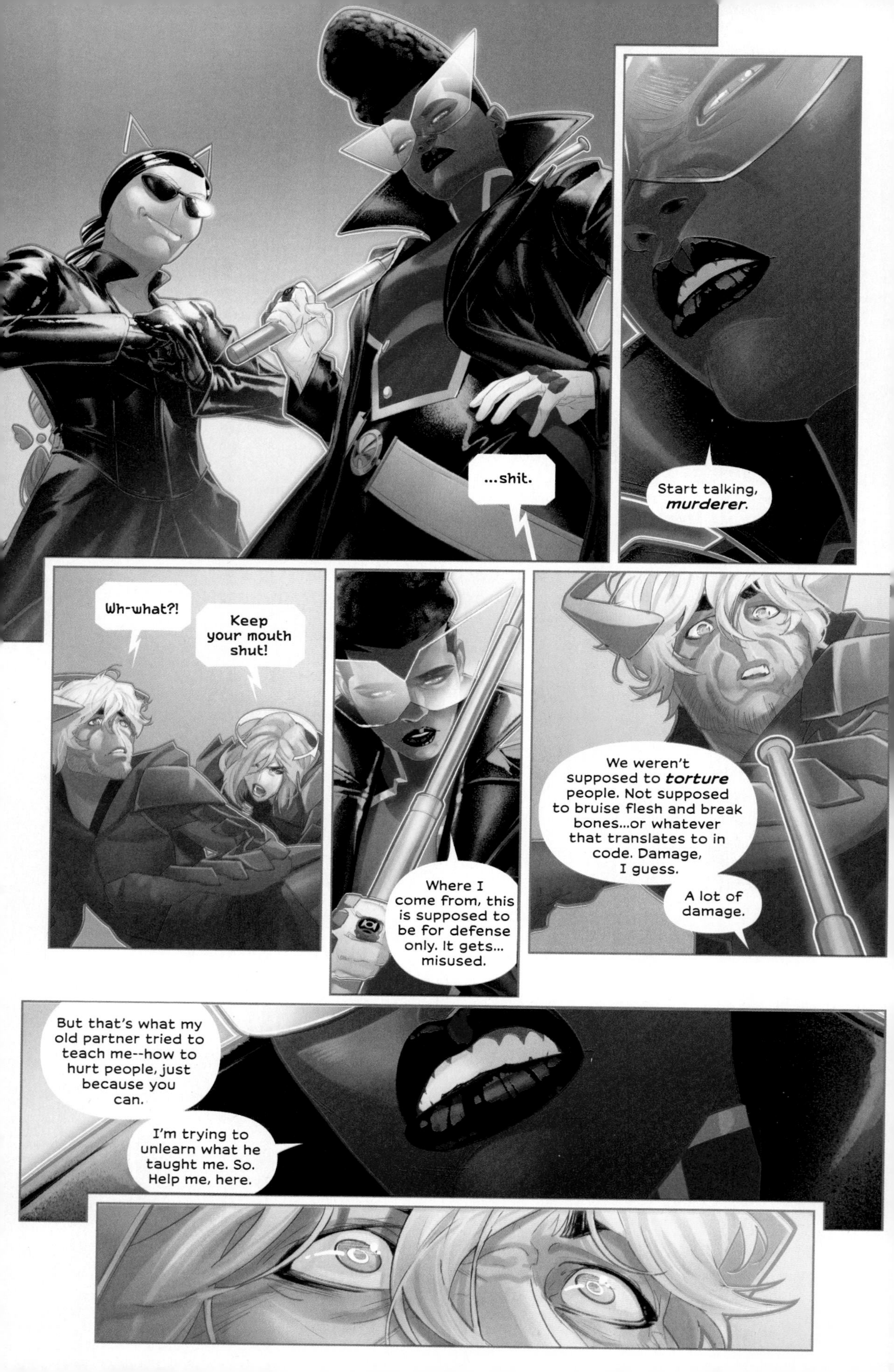

...shit.
Start talking, *murderer*.
Wh-what?!
Keep your mouth shut!
Where I come from, this is supposed to be for defense only. It gets... misused.
We weren't supposed to ***torture*** people. Not supposed to bruise flesh and break bones...or whatever that translates to in code. Damage, I guess.
A lot of damage.
But that's what my old partner tried to teach me--how to hurt people, just because you can.
I'm trying to unlearn what he taught me. So. Help me, here.

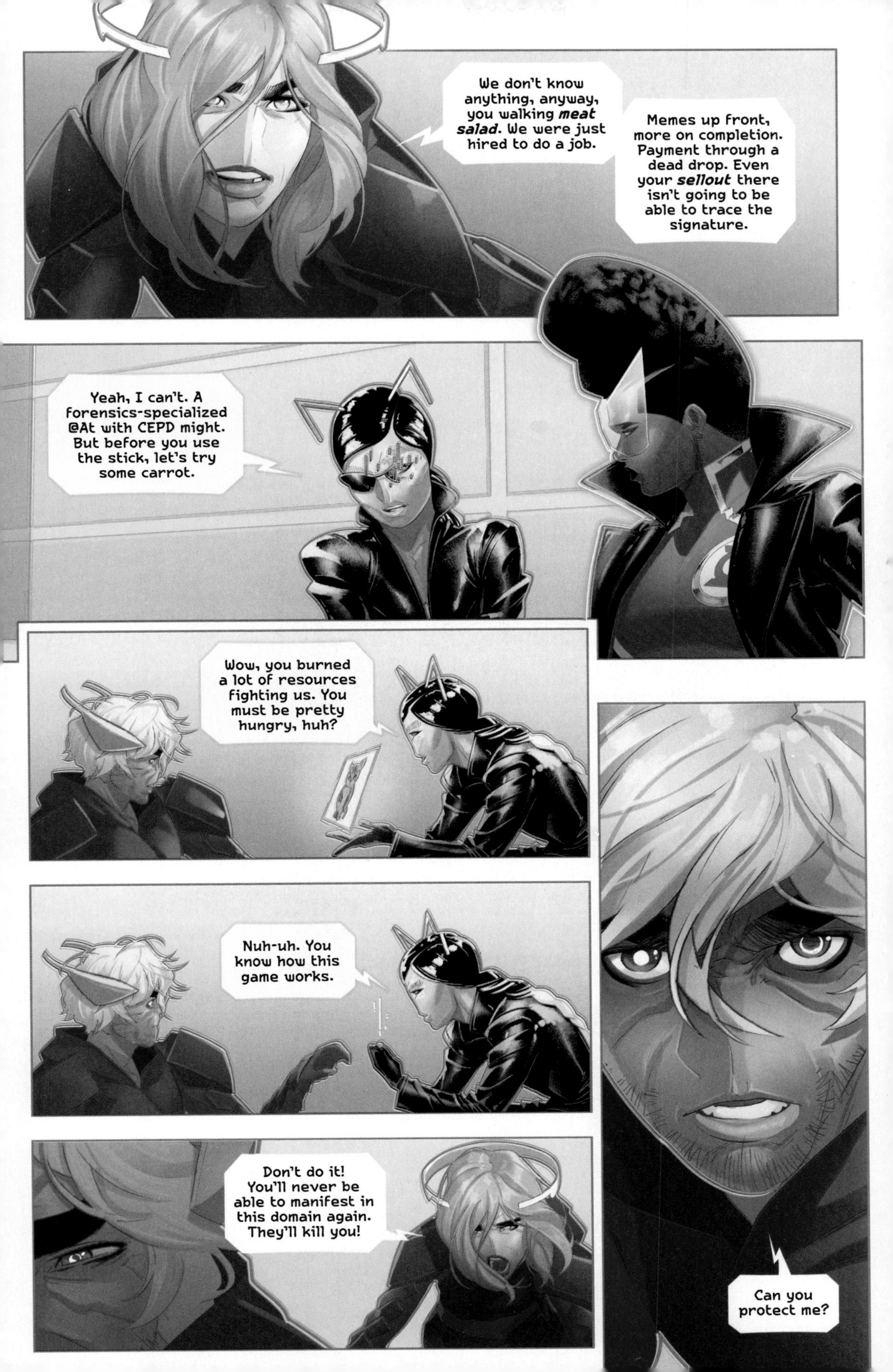
We don't know anything, anyway, you walking *meat salad*. We were just hired to do a job.
Memes up front, more on completion. Payment through a dead drop. Even your *sellout* there isn't going to be able to trace the signature.
Yeah, I can't. A forensics-specialized @At with CEPD might. But before you use the stick, let's try some carrot.
Wow, you burned a lot of resources fighting us. You must be pretty hungry, huh?
Nuh-uh. You know how this game works.
Don't do it! You'll never be able to manifest in this domain again. They'll kill you!
Can you protect me?

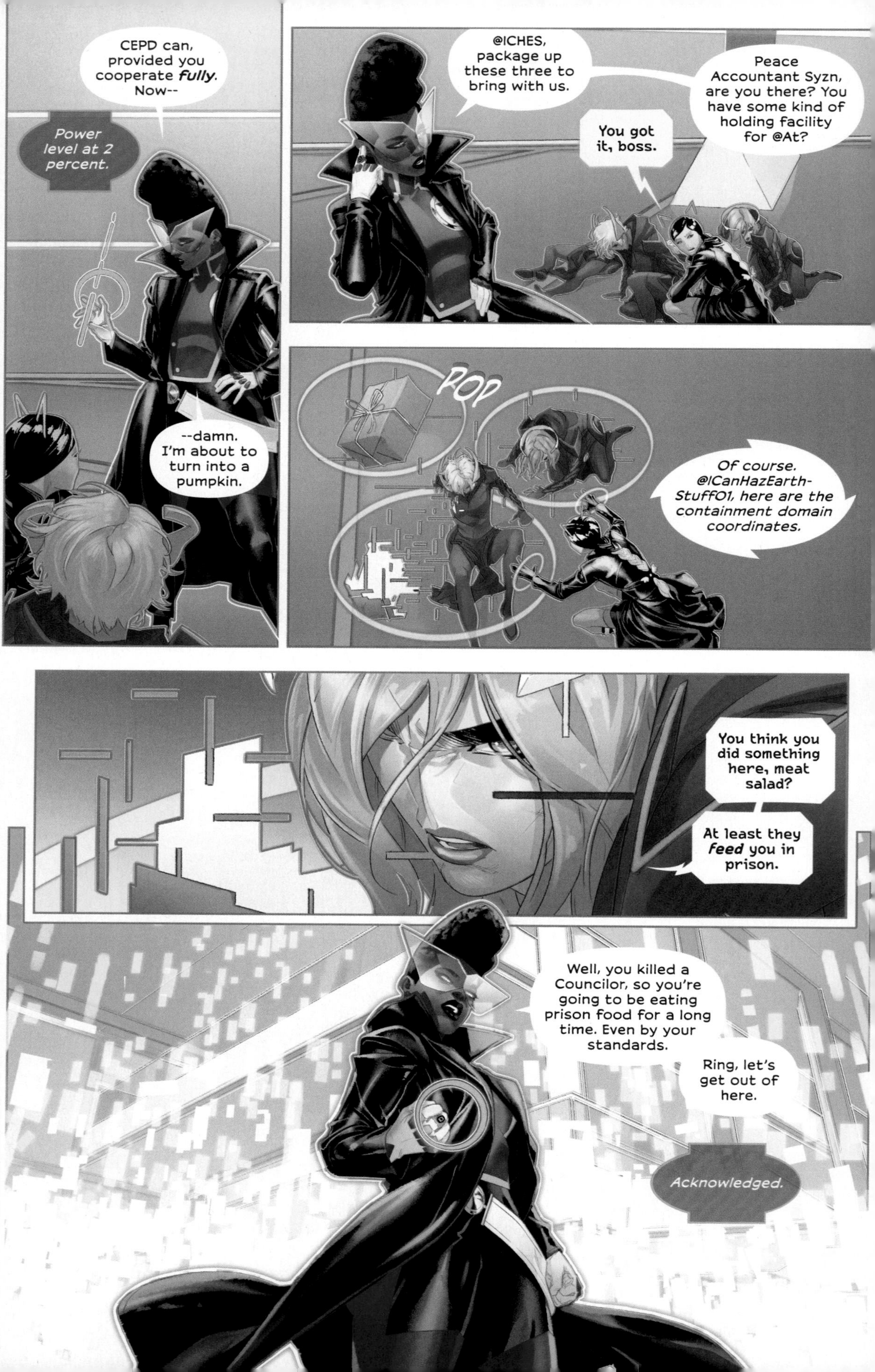

CEPD can, provided you cooperate *fully*. Now--
Power level at 2 percent.
--damn. I'm about to turn into a pumpkin.
@ICHES, package up these three to bring with us.
Peace Accountant Syzn, are you there? You have some kind of holding facility for @At?
You got it, boss.
POP
Of course. @ICanHazEarth-Stuff01, here are the containment domain coordinates.
You think you did something here, meat salad?
At least they *feed* you in prison.
Well, you killed a Councilor, so you're going to be eating prison food for a long time. Even by your standards.
Ring, let's get out of here.
Acknowledged.

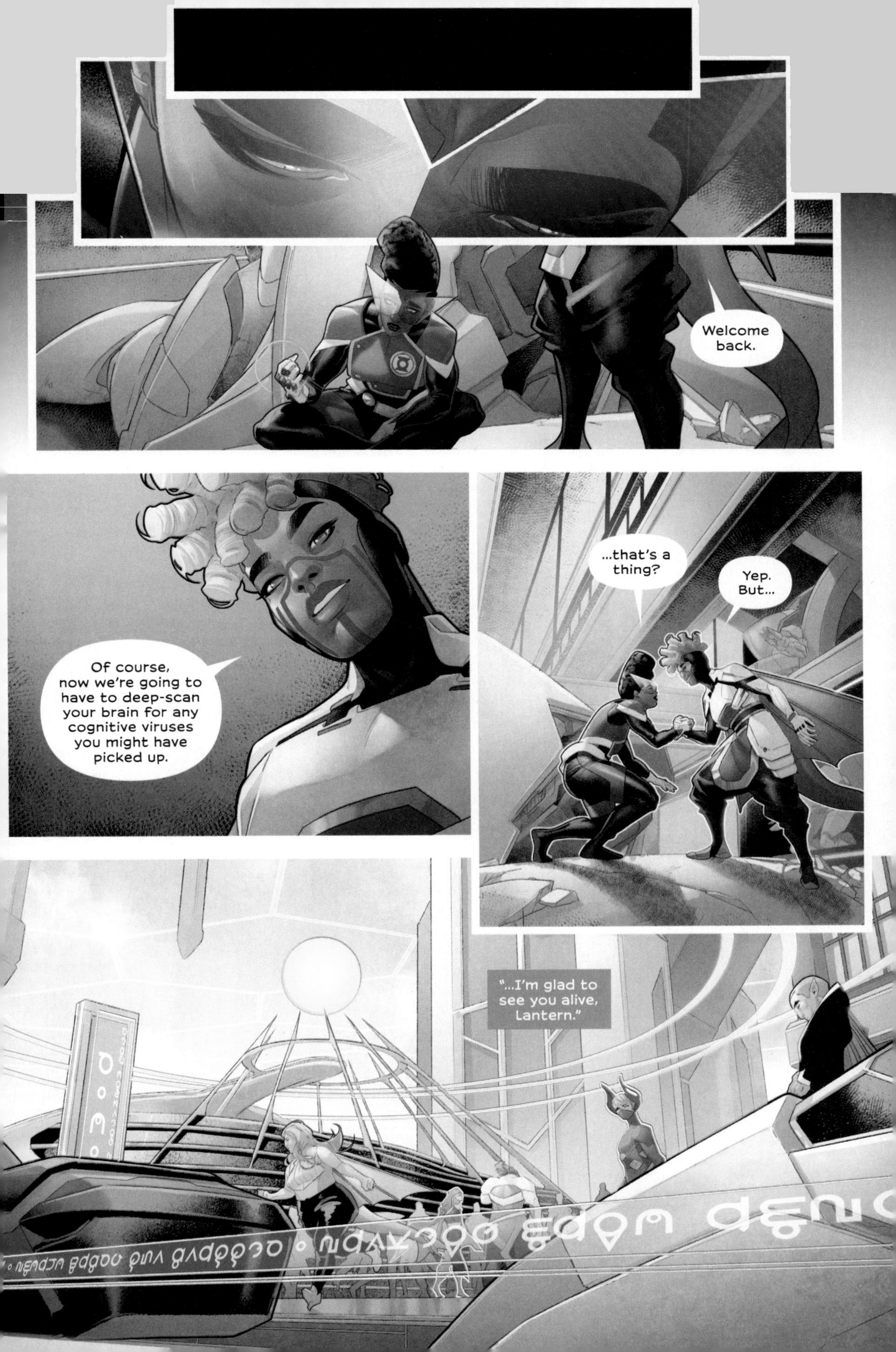
[redacted]
Welcome back.
Of course, now we're going to have to deep-scan your brain for any cognitive viruses you might have picked up.
...that's a thing?
Yep. But...
"...I'm glad to see you alive, Lantern."

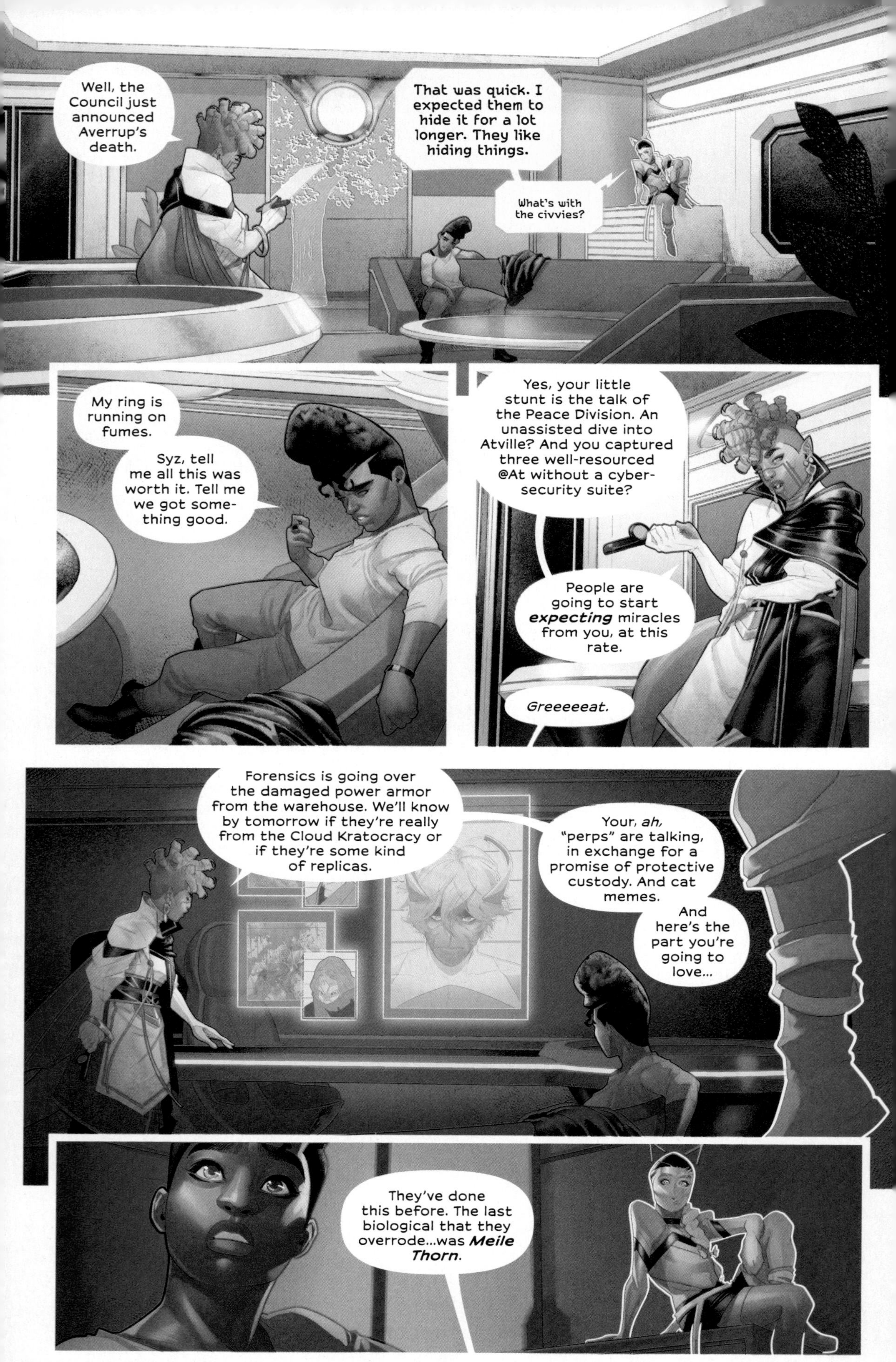
Well, the Council just announced Averrup's death.
That was quick. I expected them to hide it for a lot longer. They like hiding things.
What's with the civvies?
My ring is running on fumes.
Syz, tell me all this was worth it. Tell me we got some-thing good.
Yes, your little stunt is the talk of the Peace Division. An unassisted dive into Atville? And you captured three well-resourced @At without a cyber-security suite?
People are going to start *expecting* miracles from you, at this rate.
Greeeeeat.
Forensics is going over the damaged power armor from the warehouse. We'll know by tomorrow if they're really from the Cloud Kratocracy or if they're some kind of replicas.
Your, *ah,* "perps" are talking, in exchange for a promise of protective custody. And cat memes.
And here's the part you're going to love...
They've done this before. The last biological that they overrode...was ***Meile Thorn***.

Our perps are nobody. Petty criminals running phishing scams and identity fraud...like half of Atville, these days.

Then one of them got contacted by an anon.

And we don't know what. The message was untraceable. That's supposed to be illegal, but these *are* criminals we're dealing with.

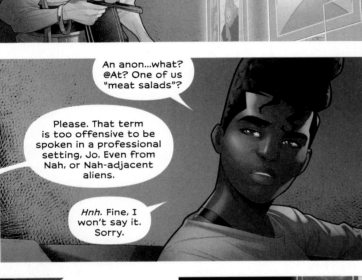

An anon...what? @At? One of us "meat salads"?

Please. That term is too offensive to be spoken in a professional setting, Jo. Even from Nah, or Nah-adjacent aliens.

Hnh. Fine, I won't say it. Sorry.

So this anonyperson made our three stooges an offer they couldn't refuse?

Basically. This is a recorded emulation of the confession log.

I mean...I knew it was wrong. But it was just... The anon was offering so much. Paid in Earth memes! I could get back on my feet with those! I just...

[sigh]

And instead, you became a murderer.

...yes. I'm... I'm sorry.

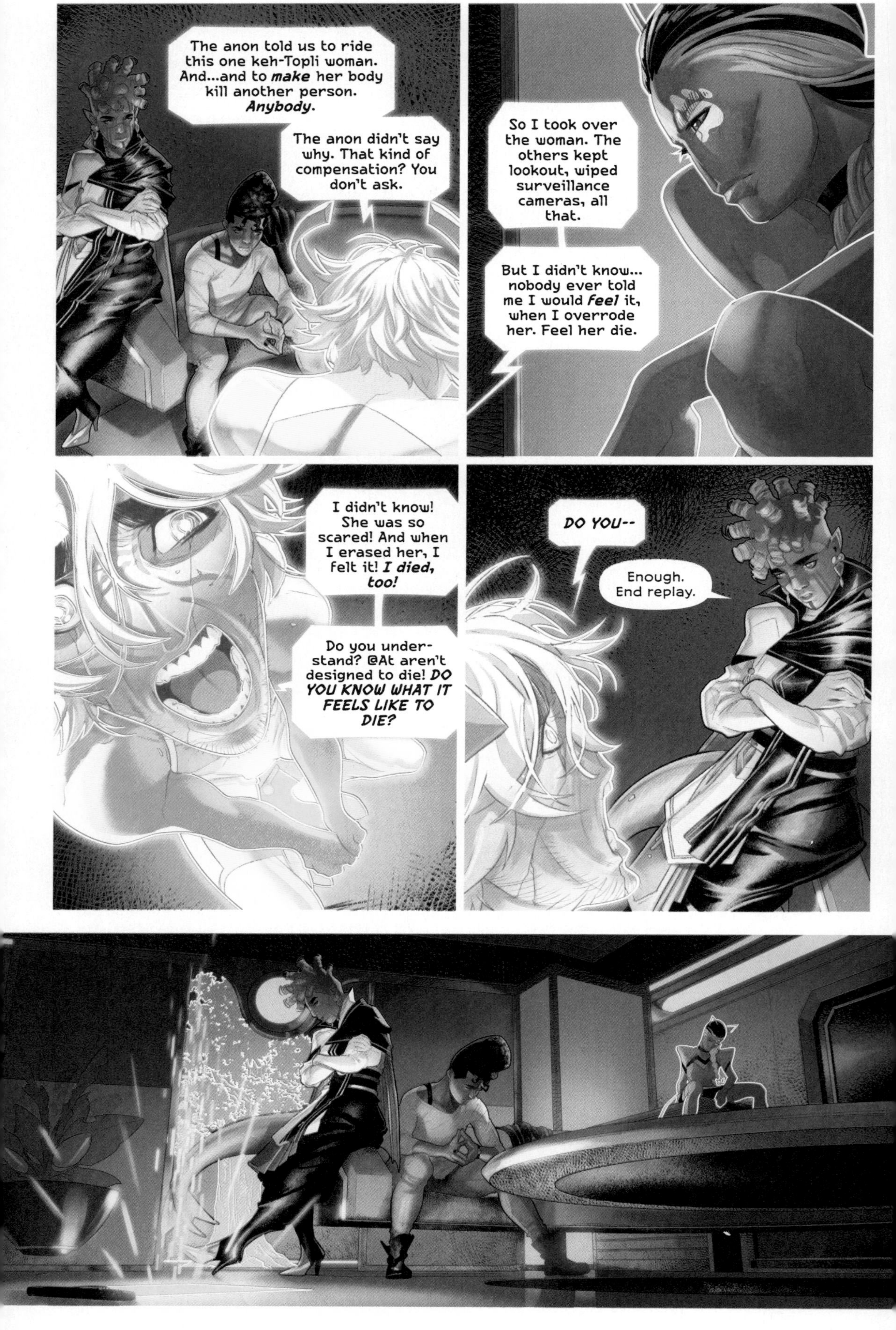
The anon told us to ride this one keh-Topli woman. And...and to *make* her body kill another person. *Anybody*.
The anon didn't say why. That kind of compensation? You don't ask.
So I took over the woman. The others kept lookout, wiped surveillance cameras, all that.
But I didn't know... nobody ever told me I would *feel* it, when I overrode her. Feel her die.
I didn't know! She was so scared! And when I erased her, I felt it! *I died, too!*
Do you understand? @At aren't designed to die! *DO YOU KNOW WHAT IT FEELS LIKE TO DIE?*
DO YOU--
Enough. End replay.

...whew. Okay. I gotta ask.

Why is it even *possible* for @At to override biologicals? Isn't there some way to, I don't know, lock them out?

Sure, security suites come standard with neural interfaces. But anything can be cracked.

But now you see another reason why overriding is so bad. Becoming part of a biological, even for a minute...

We come back *wrong.*

The biological's death agony corrupts the AI. They become living viruses, tainting everything around them. Officially, they're *not* AI anymore.

We can't ever release an @At who's killed like this, even after they serve their time.

Then what--oh, hell. *"Officially."*

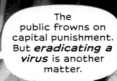

The public frowns on capital punishment. But *eradicating a virus* is another matter.

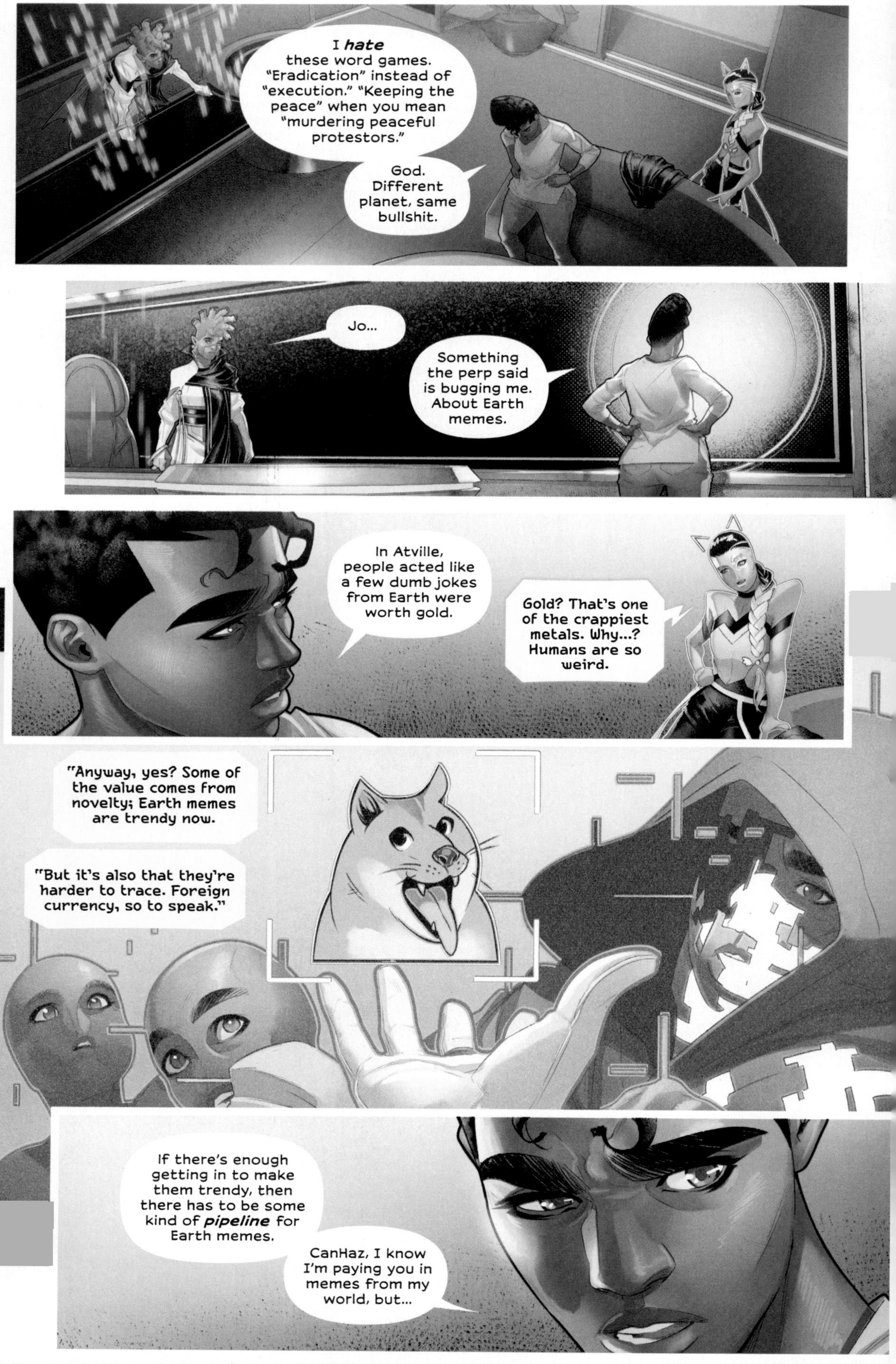
I ***hate*** these word games. "Eradication" instead of "execution." "Keeping the peace" when you mean "murdering peaceful protestors."
God. Different planet, same bullshit.
Jo...
Something the perp said is bugging me. About Earth memes.
In Atville, people acted like a few dumb jokes from Earth were worth gold.
Gold? That's one of the crappiest metals. Why...? Humans are so weird.
"Anyway, yes? Some of the value comes from novelty; Earth memes are trendy now.
"But it's also that they're harder to trace. Foreign currency, so to speak."
If there's enough getting in to make them trendy, then there has to be some kind of ***pipeline*** for Earth memes.
CanHaz, I know I'm paying you in memes from my world, but...

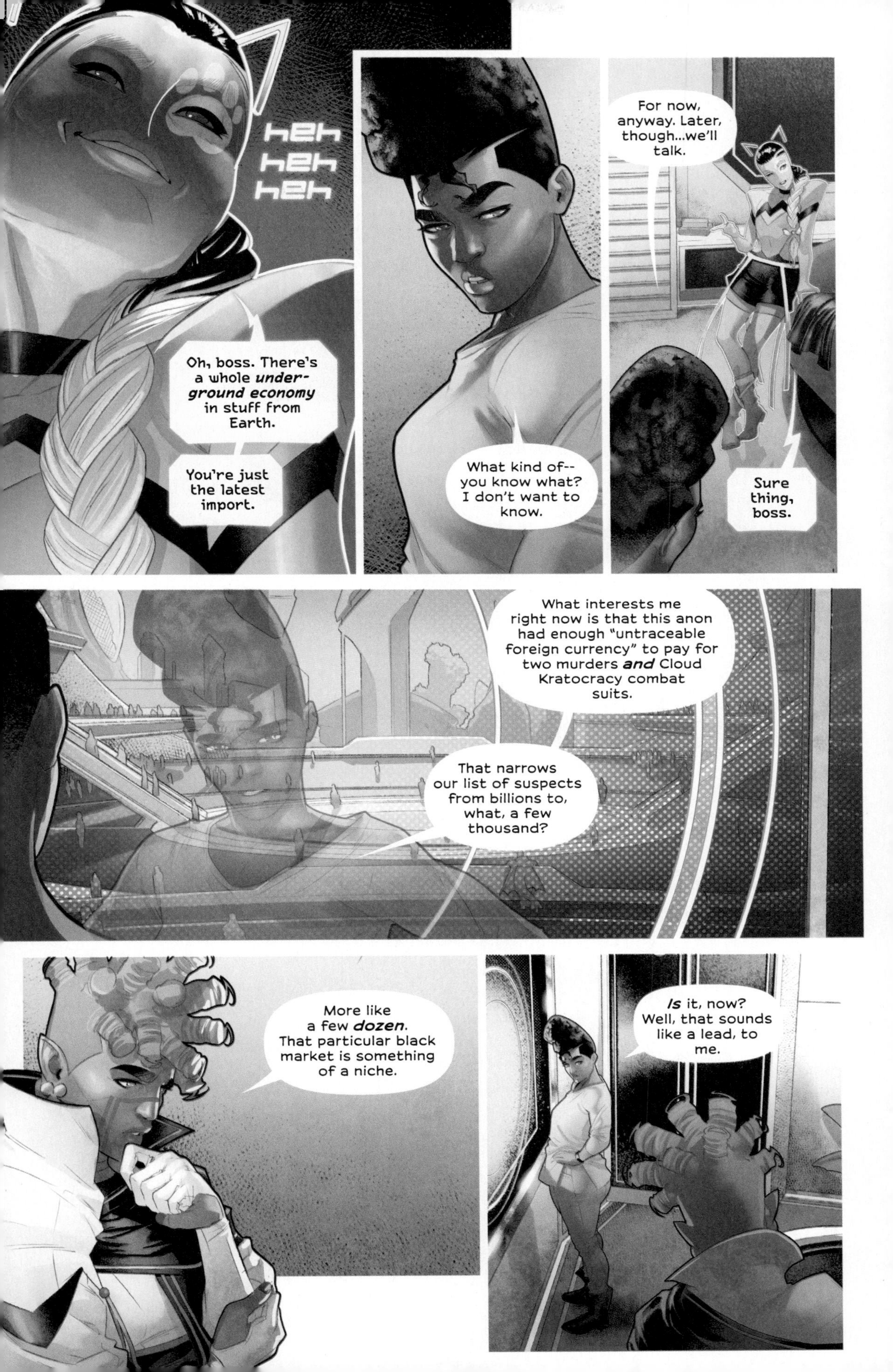
heh heh heh
Oh, boss. There's a whole *under-ground economy* in stuff from Earth.
You're just the latest import.
What kind of-- you know what? I don't want to know.
For now, anyway. Later, though...we'll talk.
Sure thing, boss.
What interests me right now is that this anon had enough "untraceable foreign currency" to pay for two murders ***and*** Cloud Kratocracy combat suits.
That narrows our list of suspects from billions to, what, a few thousand?
More like a few ***dozen***. That particular black market is something of a niche.
Is it, now? Well, that sounds like a lead, to me.

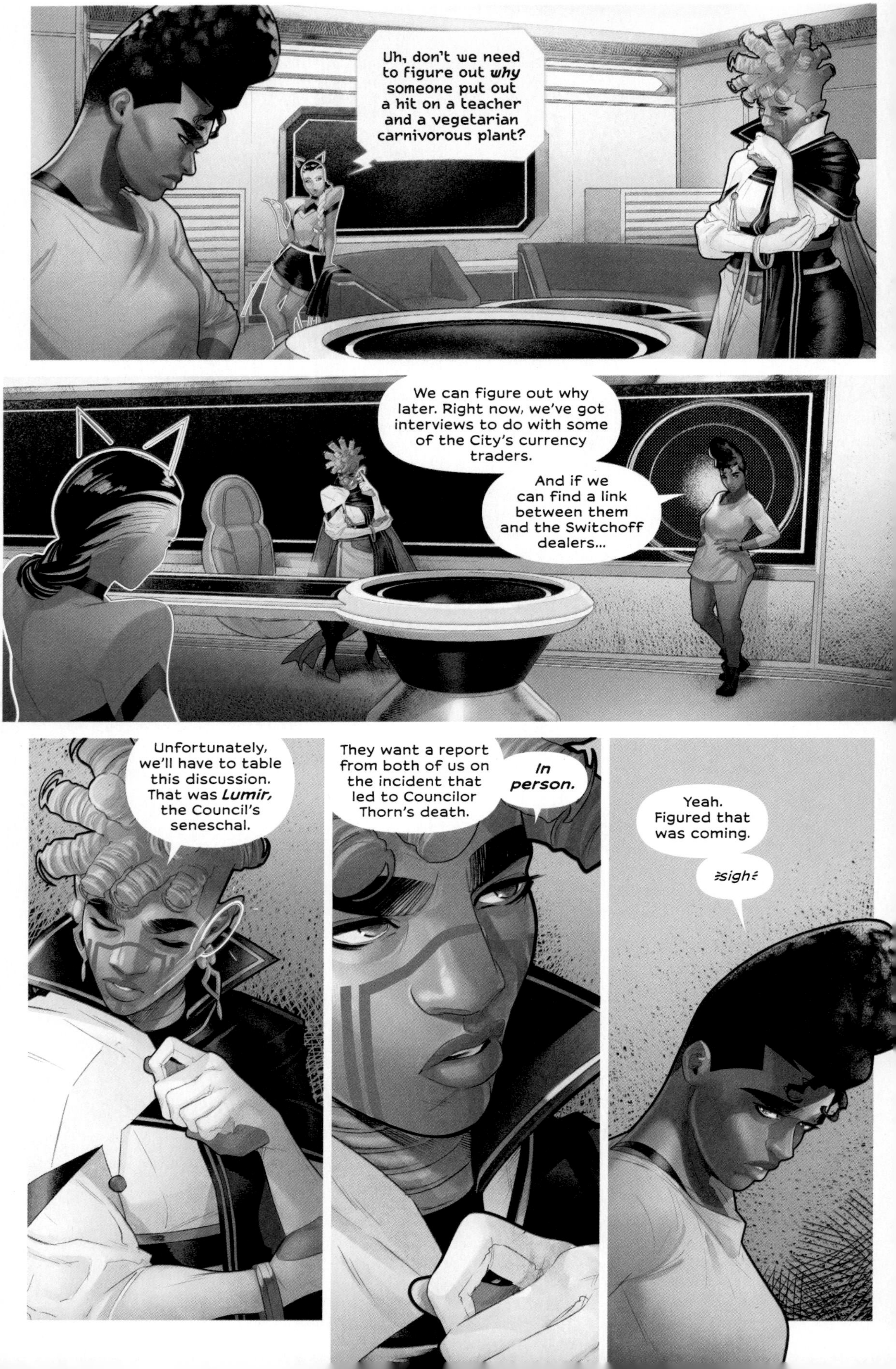
Uh, don't we need to figure out *why* someone put out a hit on a teacher and a vegetarian carnivorous plant?
We can figure out why later. Right now, we've got interviews to do with some of the City's currency traders.
And if we can find a link between them and the Switchoff dealers...
Unfortunately, we'll have to table this discussion. That was *Lumir,* the Council's seneschal.
They want a report from both of us on the incident that led to Councilor Thorn's death.
In person.
Yeah. Figured that was coming.
sigh

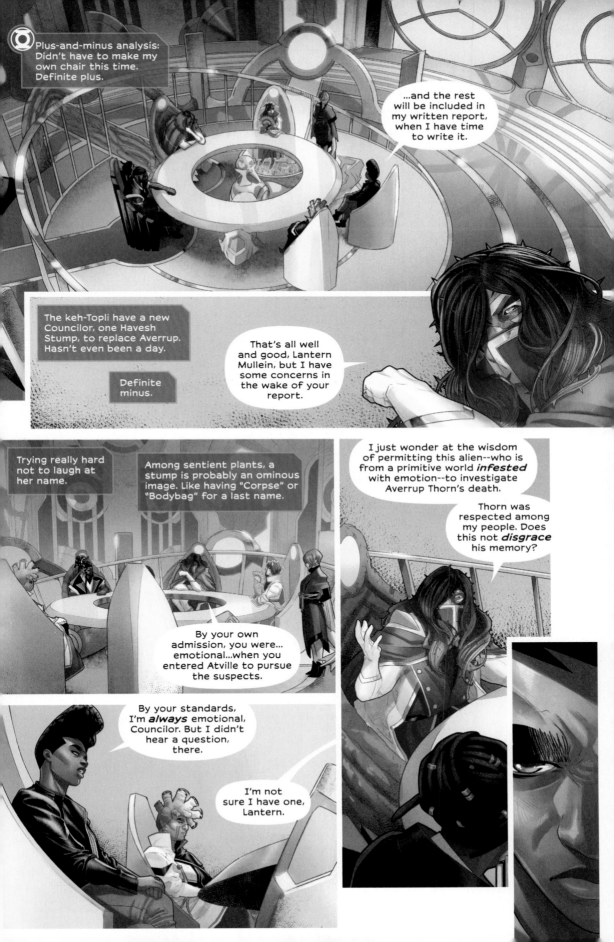

Plus-and-minus analysis: Didn't have to make my own chair this time. Definite plus.

...and the rest will be included in my written report, when I have time to write it.

The keh-Topli have a new Councilor, one Havesh Stump, to replace Averrup. Hasn't even been a day.

Definite minus.

That's all well and good, Lantern Mullein, but I have some concerns in the wake of your report.

Trying really hard not to laugh at her name.

Among sentient plants, a stump is probably an ominous image. Like having "Corpse" or "Bodybag" for a last name.

I just wonder at the wisdom of permitting this alien--who is from a primitive world *infested* with emotion--to investigate Averrup Thorn's death.

Thorn was respected among my people. Does this not *disgrace* his memory?

By your own admission, you were... emotional...when you entered Atville to pursue the suspects.

By your standards, I'm *always* emotional, Councilor. But I didn't hear a question, there.

I'm not sure I have one, Lantern.

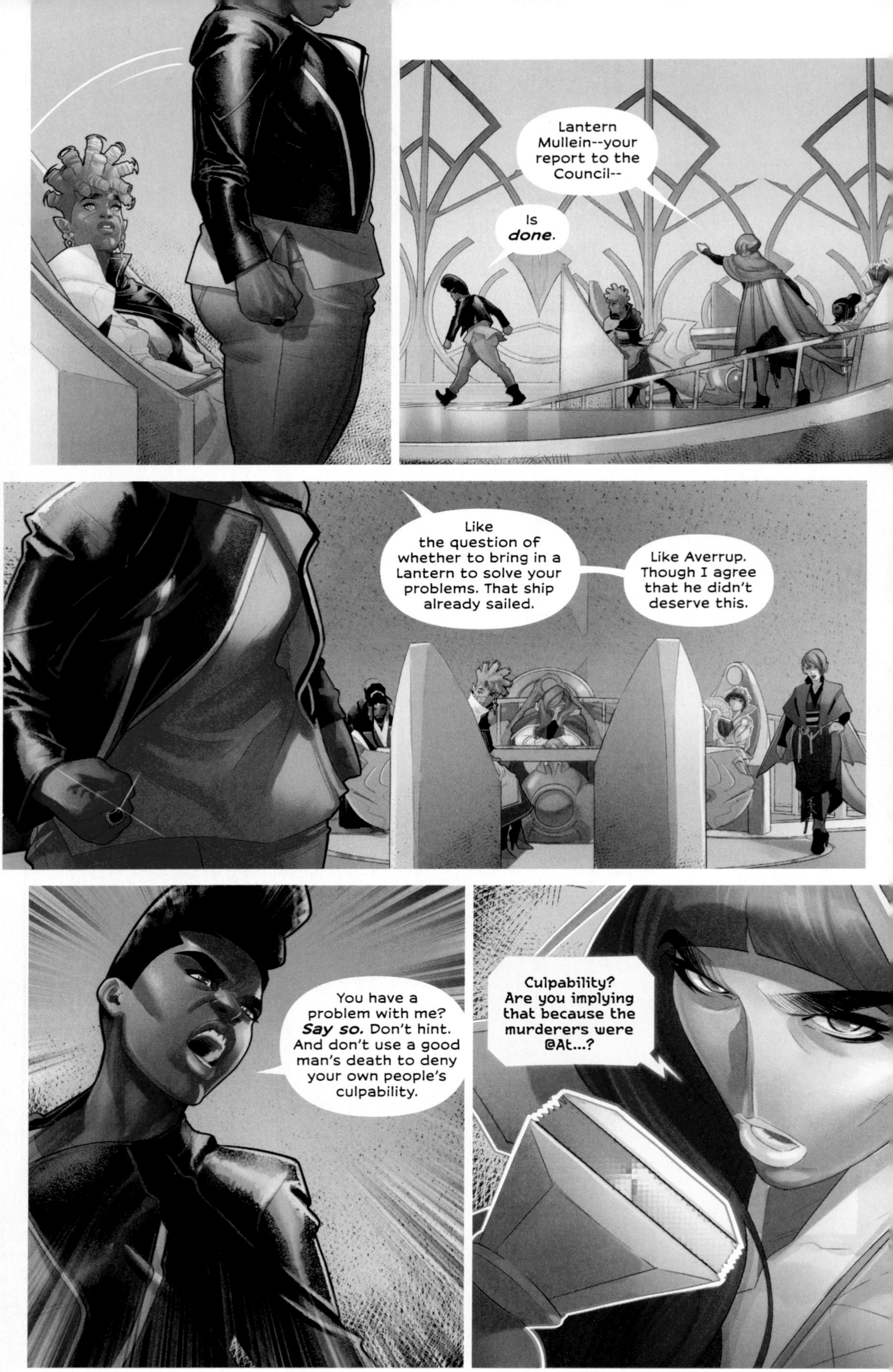

Lantern Mullein--your report to the Council--
Is *done*.
Like the question of whether to bring in a Lantern to solve your problems. That ship already sailed.
Like Averrup. Though I agree that he didn't deserve this.
You have a problem with me? ***Say so.*** Don't hint. And don't use a good man's death to deny your own people's culpability.
Culpability? Are you implying that because the murderers were @At...?

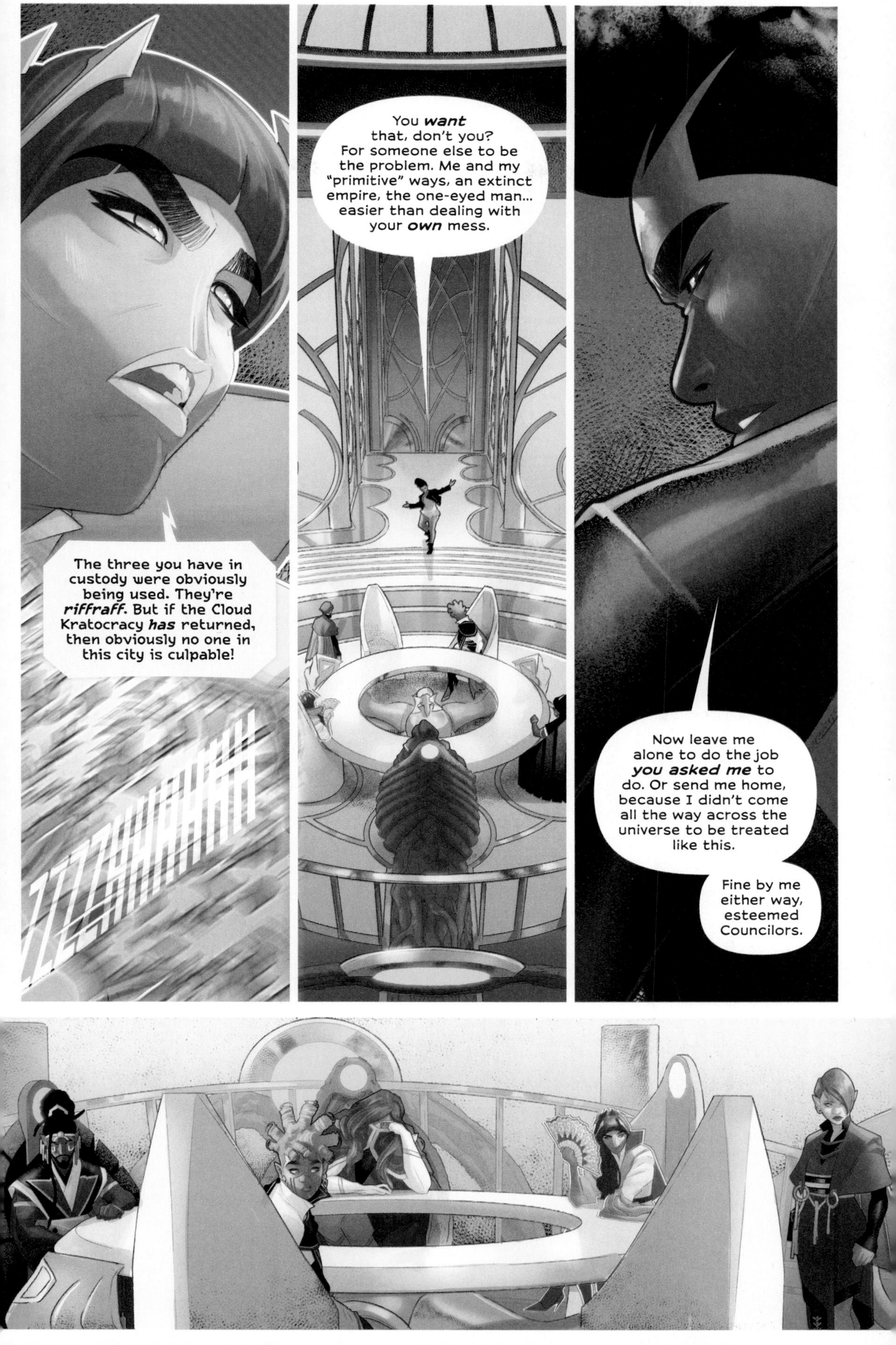

The three you have in custody were obviously being used. They're *riffraff*. But if the Cloud Kratocracy *has* returned, then obviously no one in this city is culpable!
ZZZZHHHHHHH
You ***want*** that, don't you? For someone else to be the problem. Me and my "primitive" ways, an extinct empire, the one-eyed man... easier than dealing with your ***own*** mess.
Now leave me alone to do the job ***you asked me*** to do. Or send me home, because I didn't come all the way across the universe to be treated like this.
Fine by me either way, esteemed Councilors.

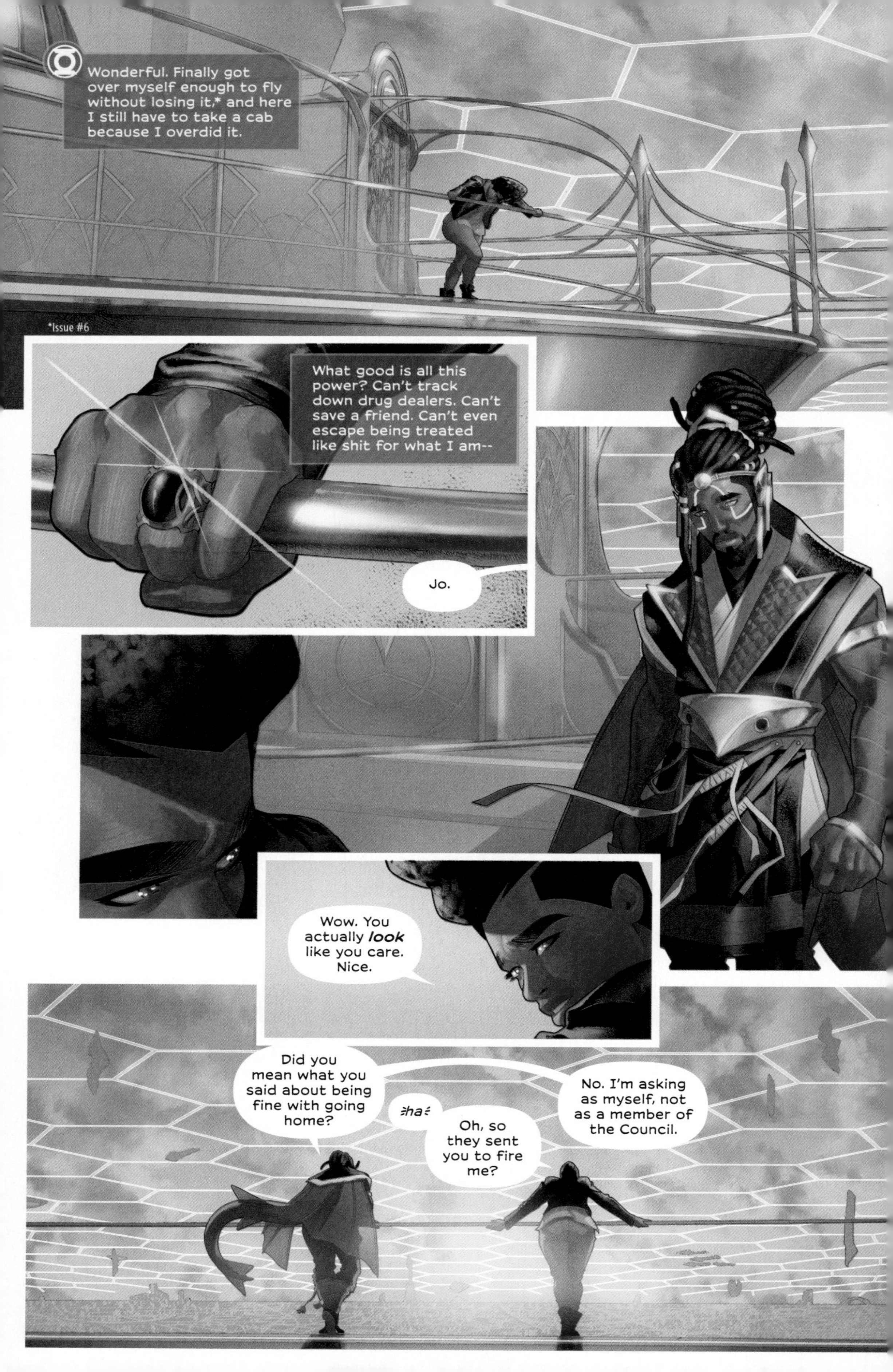
Wonderful. Finally got over myself enough to fly without losing it,* and here I still have to take a cab because I overdid it.
*Issue #6
What good is all this power? Can't track down drug dealers. Can't save a friend. Can't even escape being treated like shit for what I am--
Jo.
Wow. You actually *look* like you care. Nice.
Did you mean what you said about being fine with going home?
ha
Oh, so they sent you to fire me?
No. I'm asking as myself, not as a member of the Council.

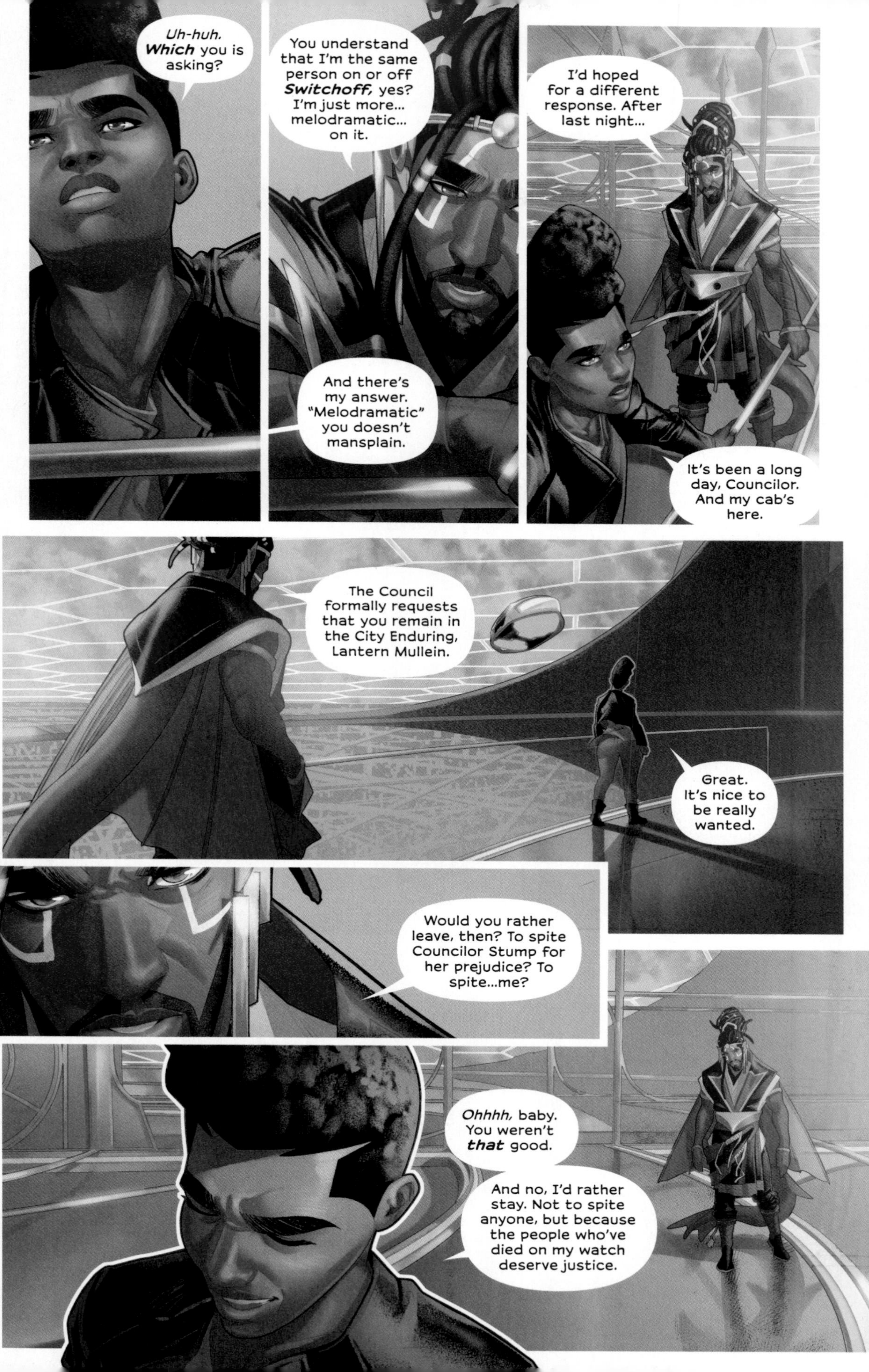
Uh-huh. ***Which*** you is asking?
You understand that I'm the same person on or off ***Switchoff,*** yes? I'm just more... melodramatic... on it.
And there's my answer. "Melodramatic" you doesn't mansplain.
I'd hoped for a different response. After last night...
It's been a long day, Councilor. And my cab's here.
The Council formally requests that you remain in the City Enduring, Lantern Mullein.
Great. It's nice to be really wanted.
Would you rather leave, then? To spite Councilor Stump for her prejudice? To spite...me?
Ohhhh, baby. You weren't ***that*** good.
And no, I'd rather stay. Not to spite anyone, but because the people who've died on my watch deserve justice.

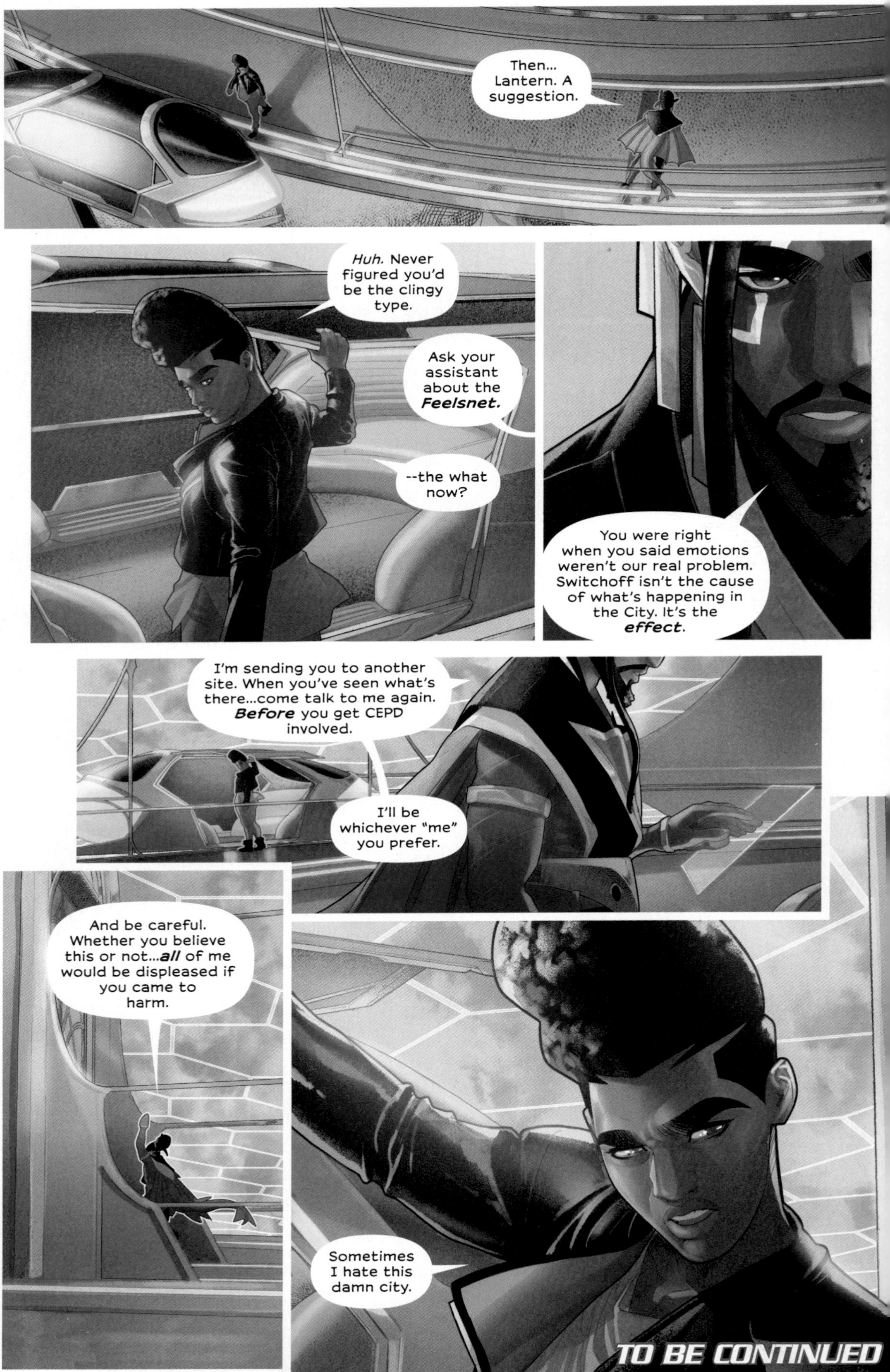

Then... Lantern. A suggestion.
Huh. Never figured you'd be the clingy type.
Ask your assistant about the ***Feelsnet.***
--the what now?
You were right when you said emotions weren't our real problem. Switchoff isn't the cause of what's happening in the City. It's the ***effect***.
I'm sending you to another site. When you've seen what's there...come talk to me again. ***Before*** you get CEPD involved.
I'll be whichever "me" you prefer.
And be careful. Whether you believe this or not...***all*** of me would be displeased if you came to harm.
Sometimes I hate this damn city.
TO BE CONTINUED

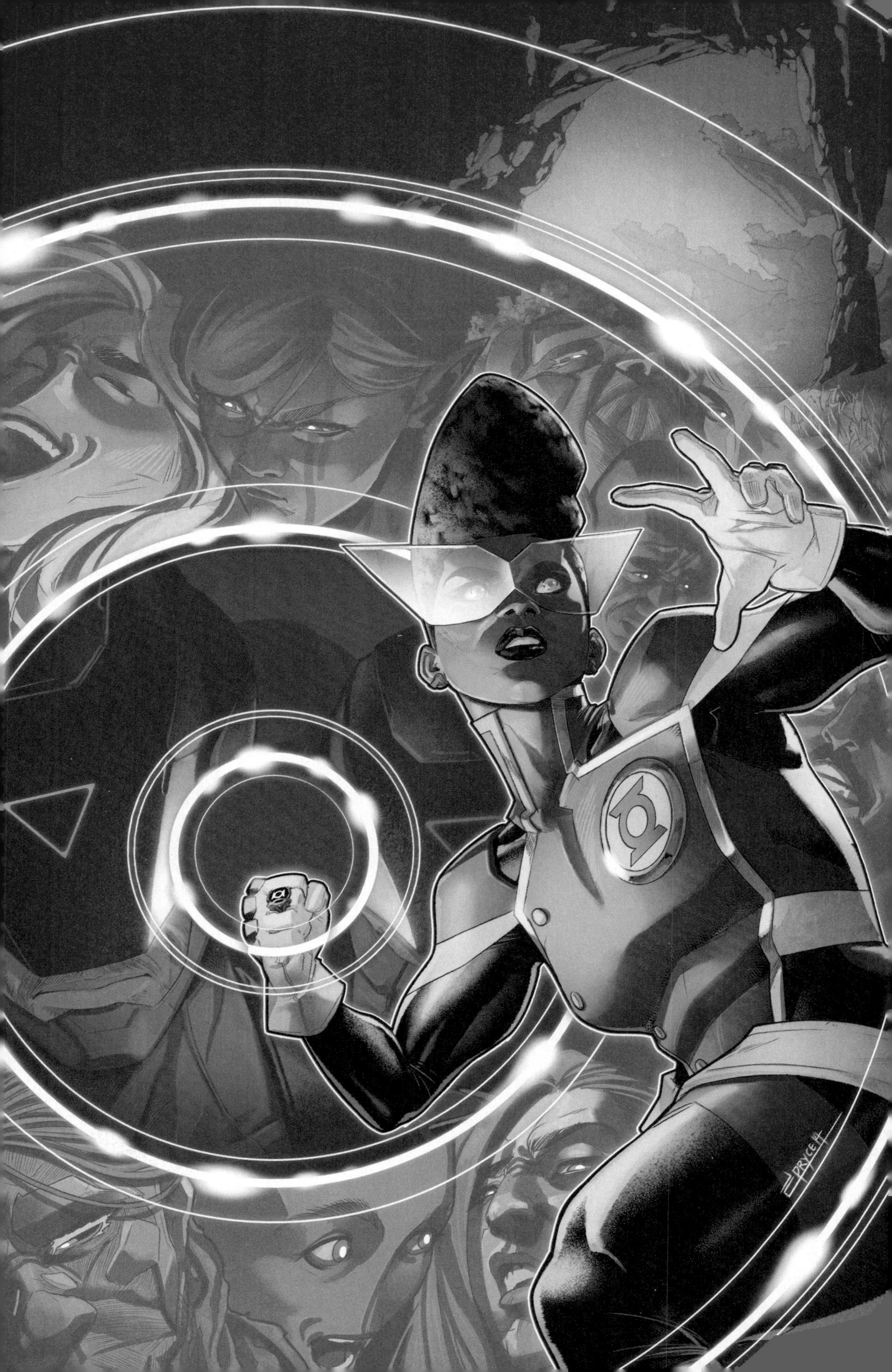

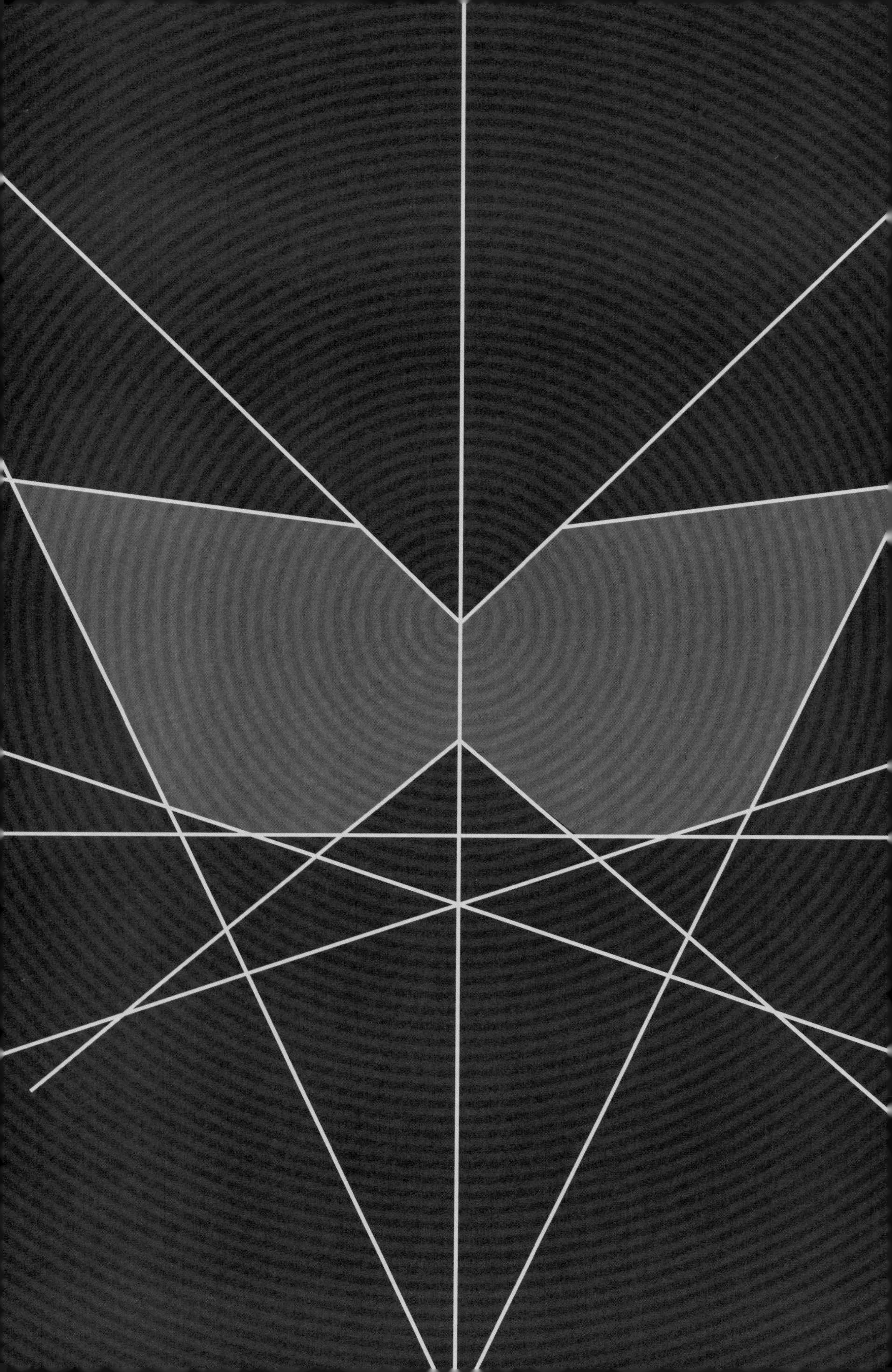

OAN INTELLIGENCE GREEN LANTERN FILE ARCHIVE
ANNOUNCEMENT
TRANSLATION: ENGLISH
SECURITY: RECOMMENDED GUARDIAN EYES ONLY

QUERIES REGARDING GLOW PROCESSING (C.F. POWER BATTERY REQUIREMENT) ARE MISGUIDED. FOR INDIVIDUAL GREEN LANTERNS WHO ARE ACCULTURATED TO SUSTAINED WILL CONVERSION, PERPETUAL-RECHARGE SYSTEMS COULD BE CONSIDERED. HOWEVER, THIS WOULD LIKELY CONSTITUTE A MINORITY OF LANTERNS AND COULD NEVER BE STANDARDIZED TO THE CORPS AS A WHOLE. EXPERIMENTAL PROPOSALS WILL BE CONSIDERED, IF SUBMITTED.

Story: **N.K. JEMISIN** Art & Color: **JAMAL CAMPBELL**
Lettering: **DERON BENNETT** Cover: **JAMAL CAMPBELL**
Variant Cover: **MEGHAN HETRICK**
Associate Editor: **MAGGIE HOWELL** Editor: **ANDY KHOURI**
DC's Young Animal Curated by **GERARD WAY**

"Why don't you guys do something?!"
–Stormé DeLarverie

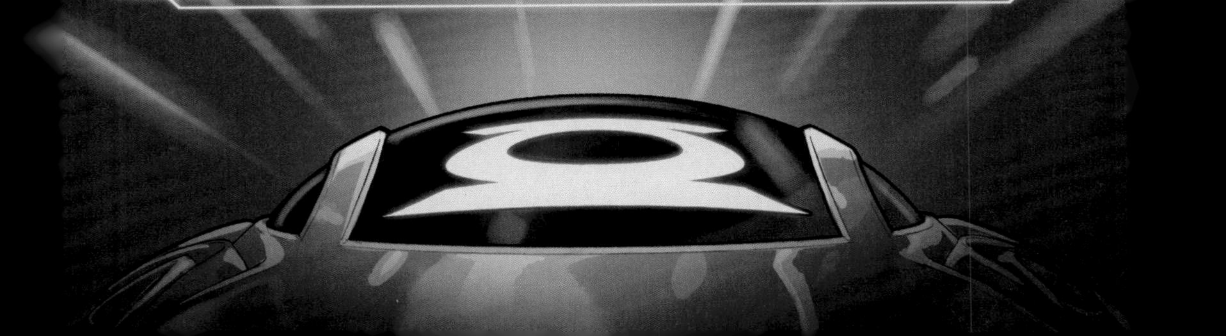

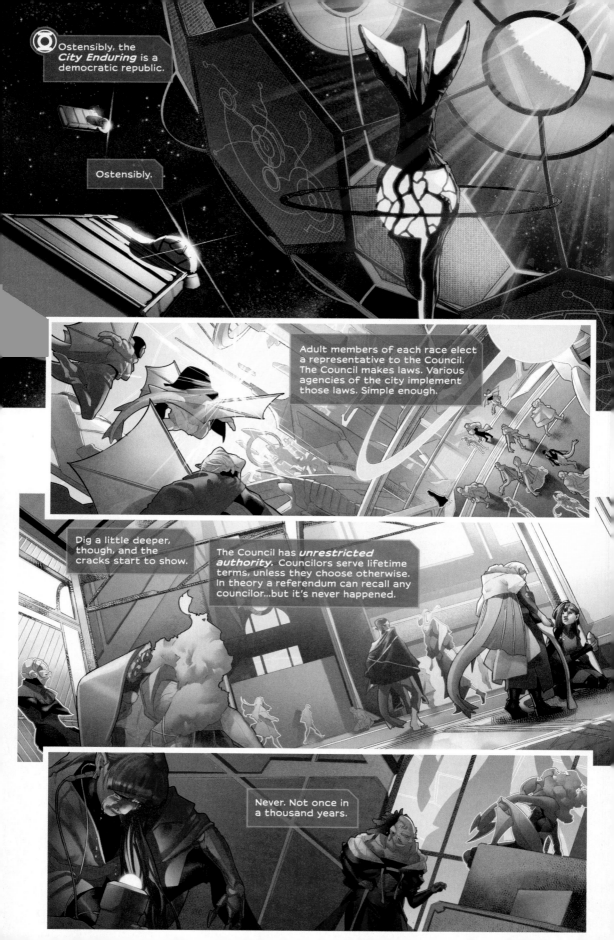

Ostensibly, the *City Enduring* is a democratic republic.

Ostensibly.

Adult members of each race elect a representative to the Council. The Council makes laws. Various agencies of the city implement those laws. Simple enough.

Dig a little deeper, though, and the cracks start to show.

The Council has *unrestricted authority*. Councilors serve lifetime terms, unless they choose otherwise. In theory a referendum can recall any councilor...but it's never happened.

Never. Not once in a thousand years.

Yeah. You're thinking what I'm thinking.

Come on, *try* it.

But there's nothing--okay, fine.

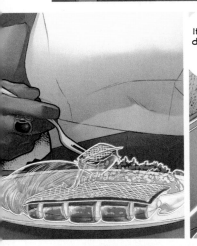

This is crazy. It's one thing to do this in Atville. When in Rome, et cetera. But *here...*

Eat more. Judge less.

Right? *Riiiight?*

The restaurant's hard light emitters work in conjunction with nerve stimulators in the table.

You *know* it isn't real, but your tongue tastes! Your teeth feel like they're sinking into something!

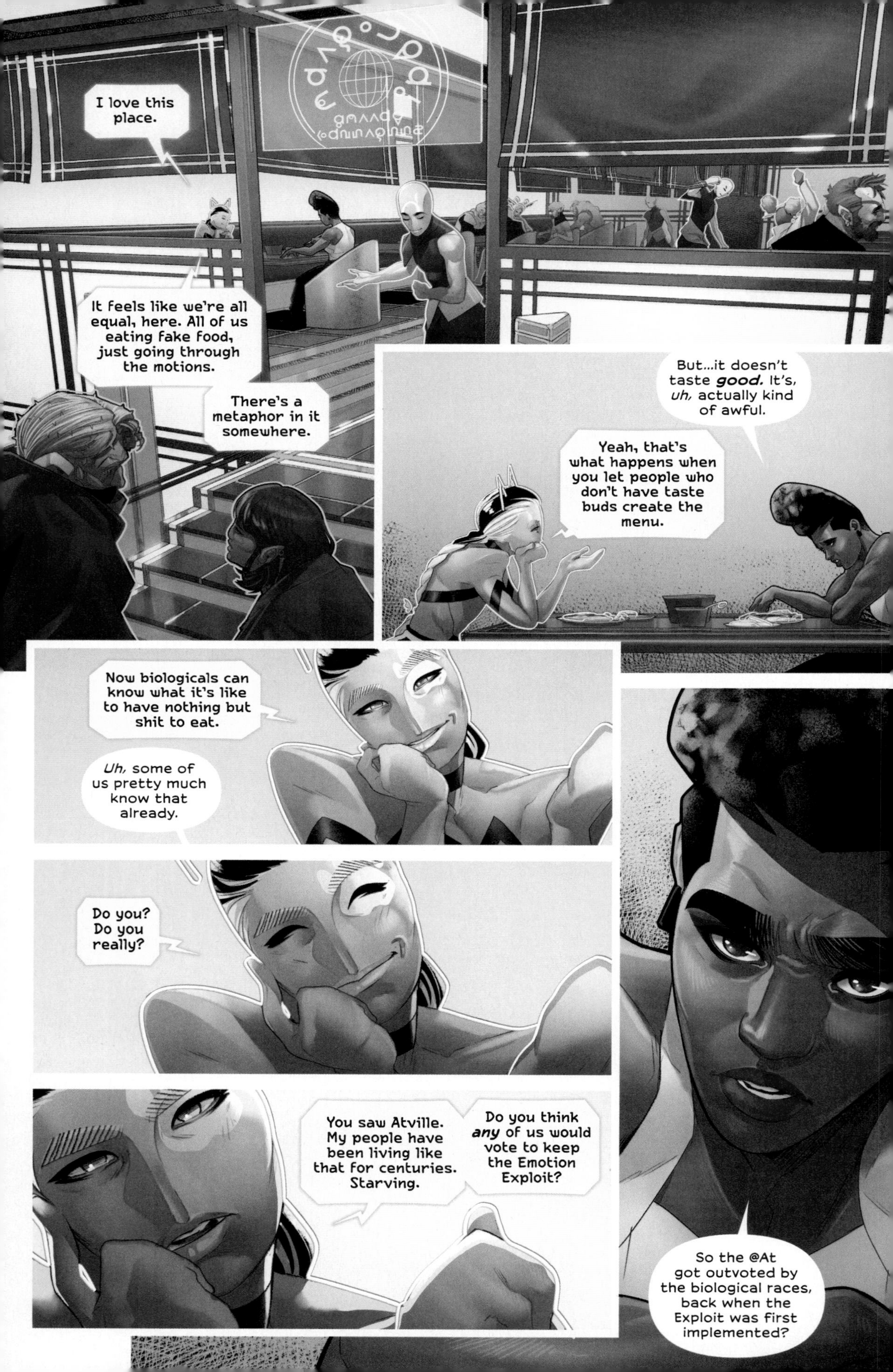
I love this place.
It feels like we're all equal, here. All of us eating fake food, just going through the motions.
There's a metaphor in it somewhere.
But...it doesn't taste *good.* It's, *uh,* actually kind of awful.
Yeah, that's what happens when you let people who don't have taste buds create the menu.
Now biologicals can know what it's like to have nothing but shit to eat.
Uh, some of us pretty much know that already.
Do you? Do you really?
You saw Atville. My people have been living like that for centuries. Starving.
Do you think *any* of us would vote to keep the Emotion Exploit?
So the @At got outvoted by the biological races, back when the Exploit was first implemented?

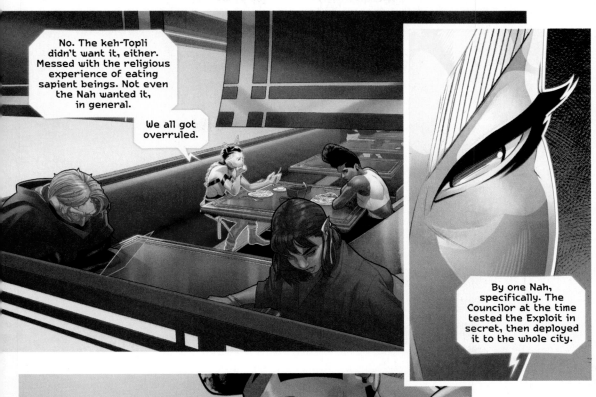

No. The keh-Topli didn't want it, either. Messed with the religious experience of eating sapient beings. Not even the Nah wanted it, in general.

We all got overruled.

By one Nah, specifically. The Councilor at the time tested the Exploit in secret, then deployed it to the whole city.

One *person* did this?

Well, there *were* a few members of every race who believed that the Exploit was necessary.

Still, a minority. A minority that got just powerful enough to impose its radical ideas on everyone.

≥sigh≤

Yeah. That happens on my planet, too. Except on my planet, it's usually people like me who ended up struggling.

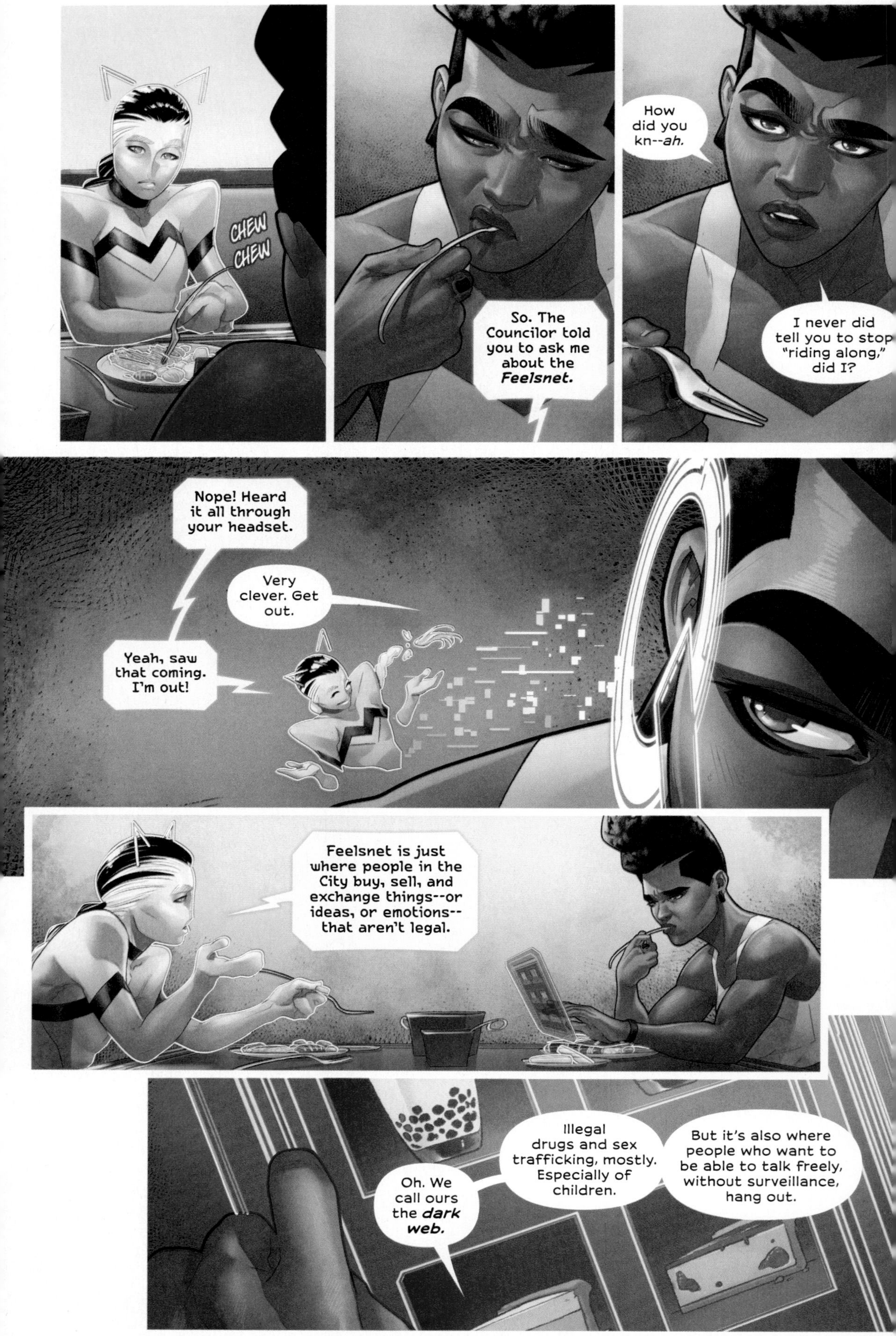
CHEW CHEW
So. The Councilor told you to ask me about the *Feelsnet.*
How did you kn--*ah.*
I never did tell you to stop "riding along," did I?
Nope! Heard it all through your headset.
Very clever. Get out.
Yeah, saw that coming. I'm out!
Feelsnet is just where people in the City buy, sell, and exchange things--or ideas, or emotions--that aren't legal.
Illegal drugs and sex trafficking, mostly. Especially of children.
But it's also where people who want to be able to talk freely, without surveillance, hang out.
Oh. We call ours the *dark web.*

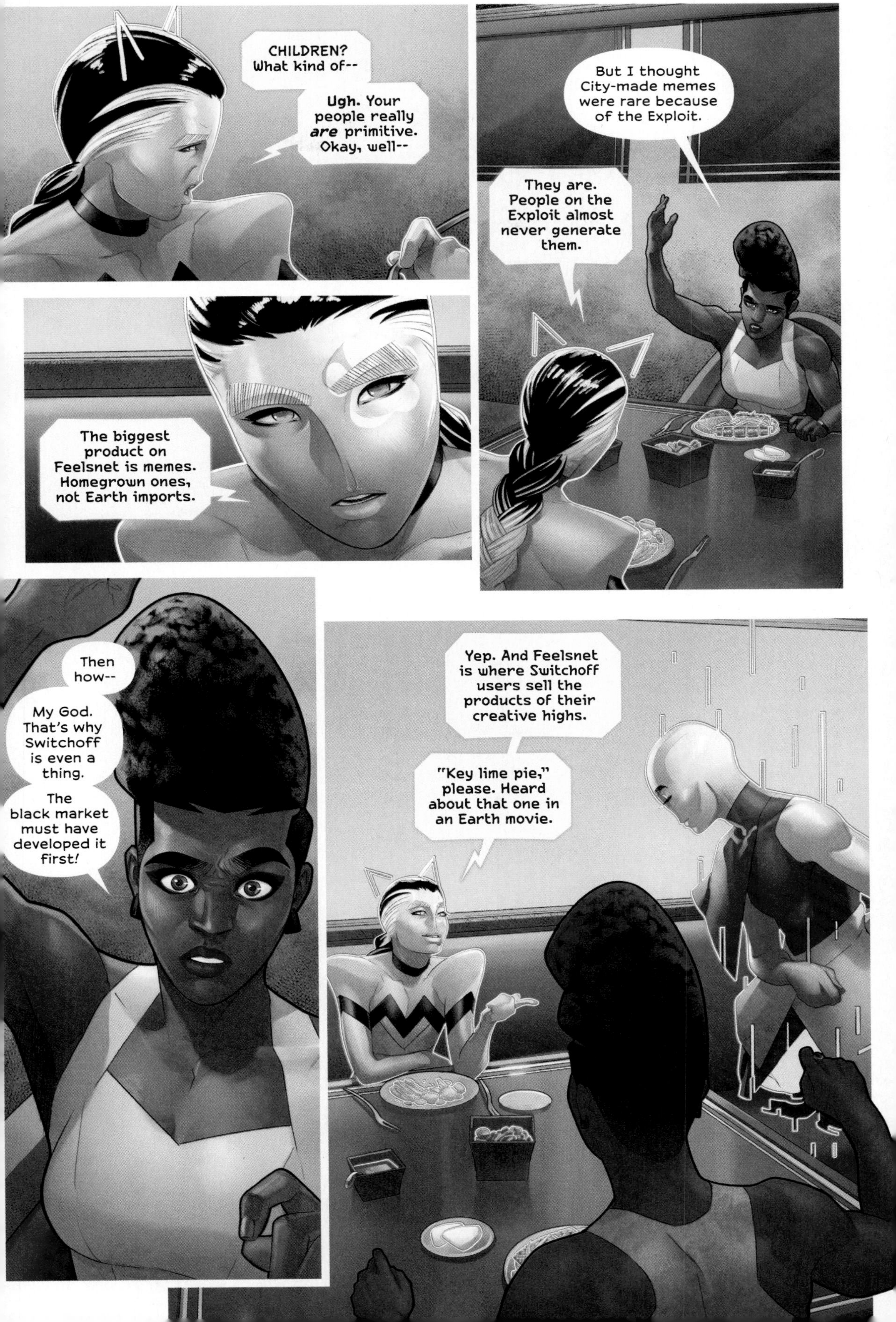
CHILDREN? What kind of--
Ugh. Your people really ***are*** primitive. Okay, well--
But I thought City-made memes were rare because of the Exploit.
They are. People on the Exploit almost never generate them.
The biggest product on Feelsnet is memes. Homegrown ones, not Earth imports.
Then how--
My God. That's why Switchoff is even a thing.
The black market must have developed it first!
Yep. And Feelsnet is where Switchoff users sell the products of their creative highs.
"Key lime pie," please. Heard about that one in an Earth movie.

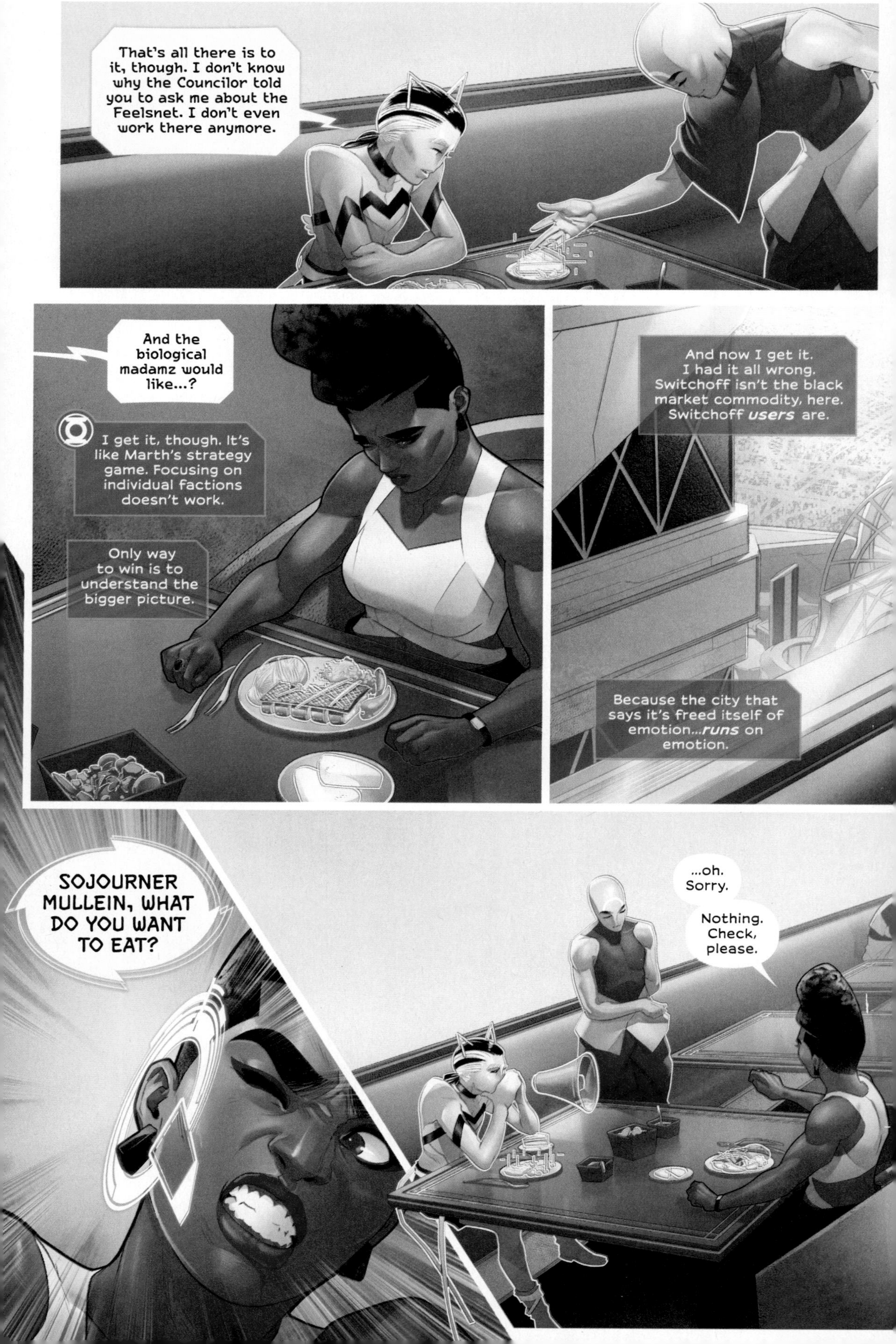
That's all there is to it, though. I don't know why the Councilor told you to ask me about the Feelsnet. I don't even work there anymore.
And the biological madamz would like...?
I get it, though. It's like Marth's strategy game. Focusing on individual factions doesn't work.
Only way to win is to understand the bigger picture.
And now I get it. I had it all wrong. Switchoff isn't the black market commodity, here. Switchoff *users* are.
Because the city that says it's freed itself of emotion...*runs* on emotion.
SOJOURNER MULLEIN, WHAT DO YOU WANT TO EAT?
...oh. Sorry.
Nothing. Check, please.

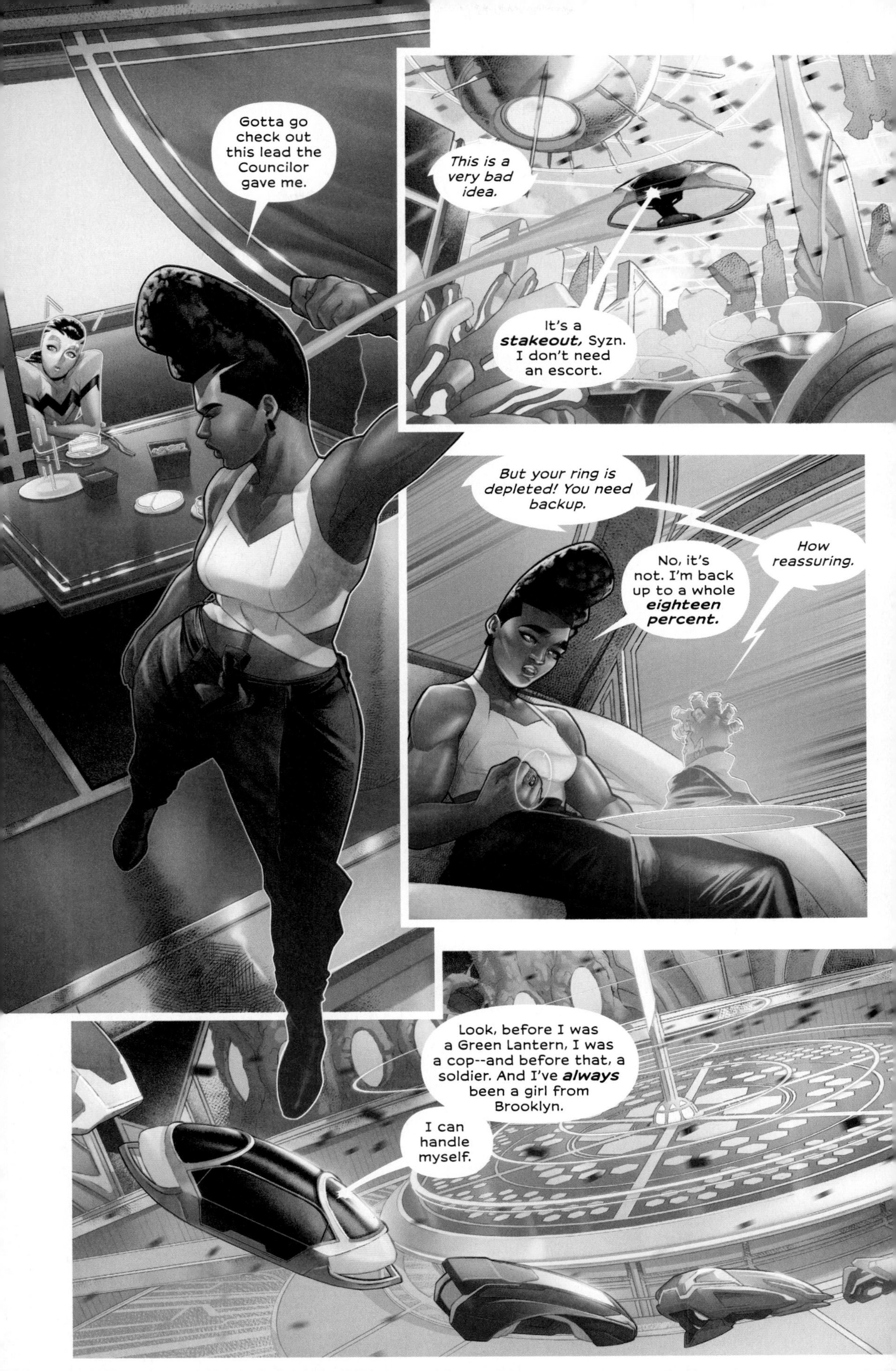
Gotta go check out this lead the Councilor gave me.
This is a very bad idea.
It's a stakeout, Syzn. I don't need an escort.
But your ring is depleted! You need backup.
No, it's not. I'm back up to a whole eighteen percent.
How reassuring.
Look, before I was a Green Lantern, I was a cop--and before that, a soldier. And I've always been a girl from Brooklyn.
I can handle myself.

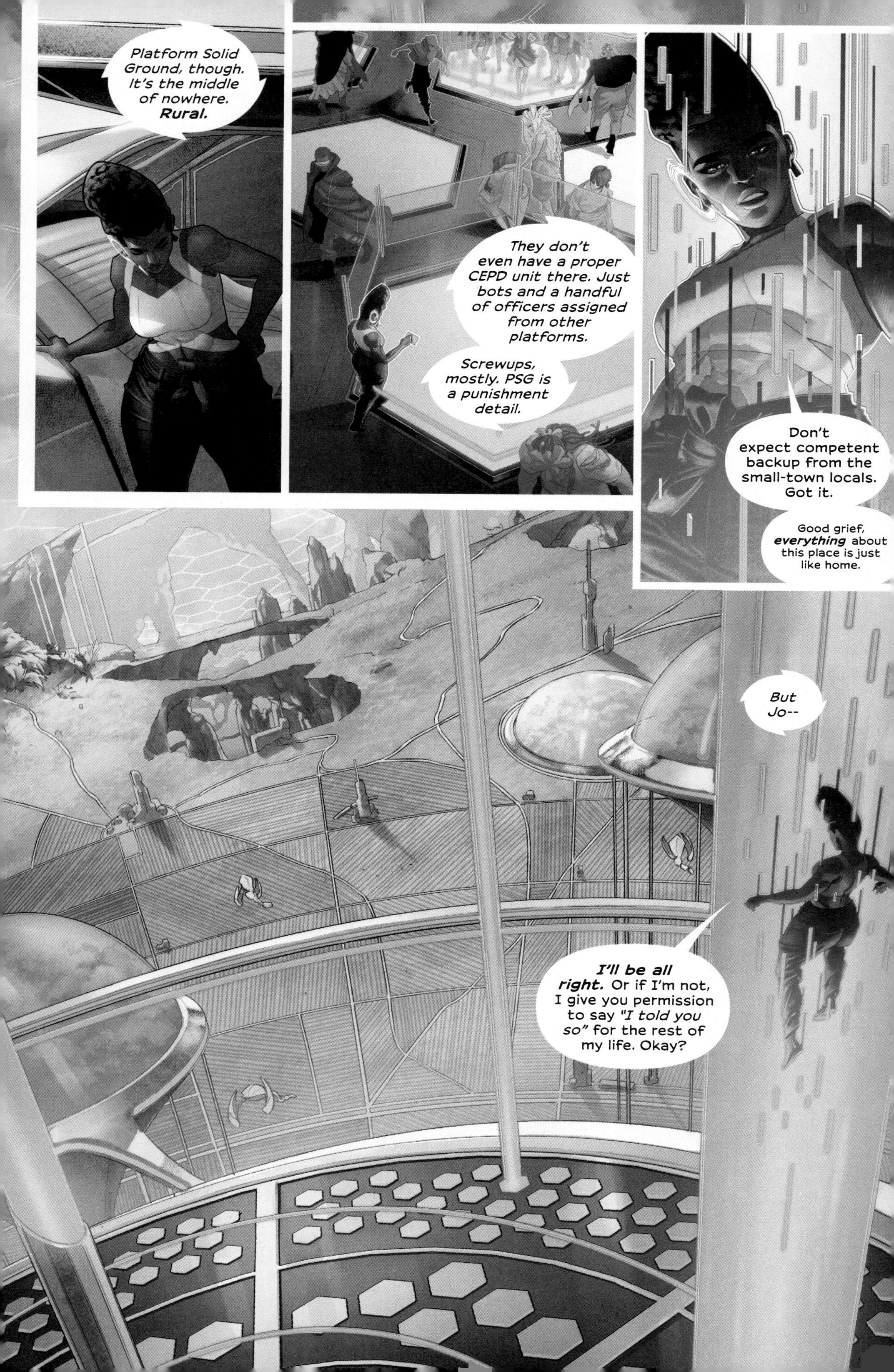
Platform Solid Ground, though. It's the middle of nowhere. **Rural.**
They don't even have a proper CEPD unit there. Just bots and a handful of officers assigned from other platforms.
Screwups, mostly. PSG is a punishment detail.
Don't expect competent backup from the small-town locals. Got it.
Good grief, ***everything*** about this place is just like home.
But Jo--
I'll be all right. Or if I'm not, I give you permission to say *"I told you so"* for the rest of my life. Okay?

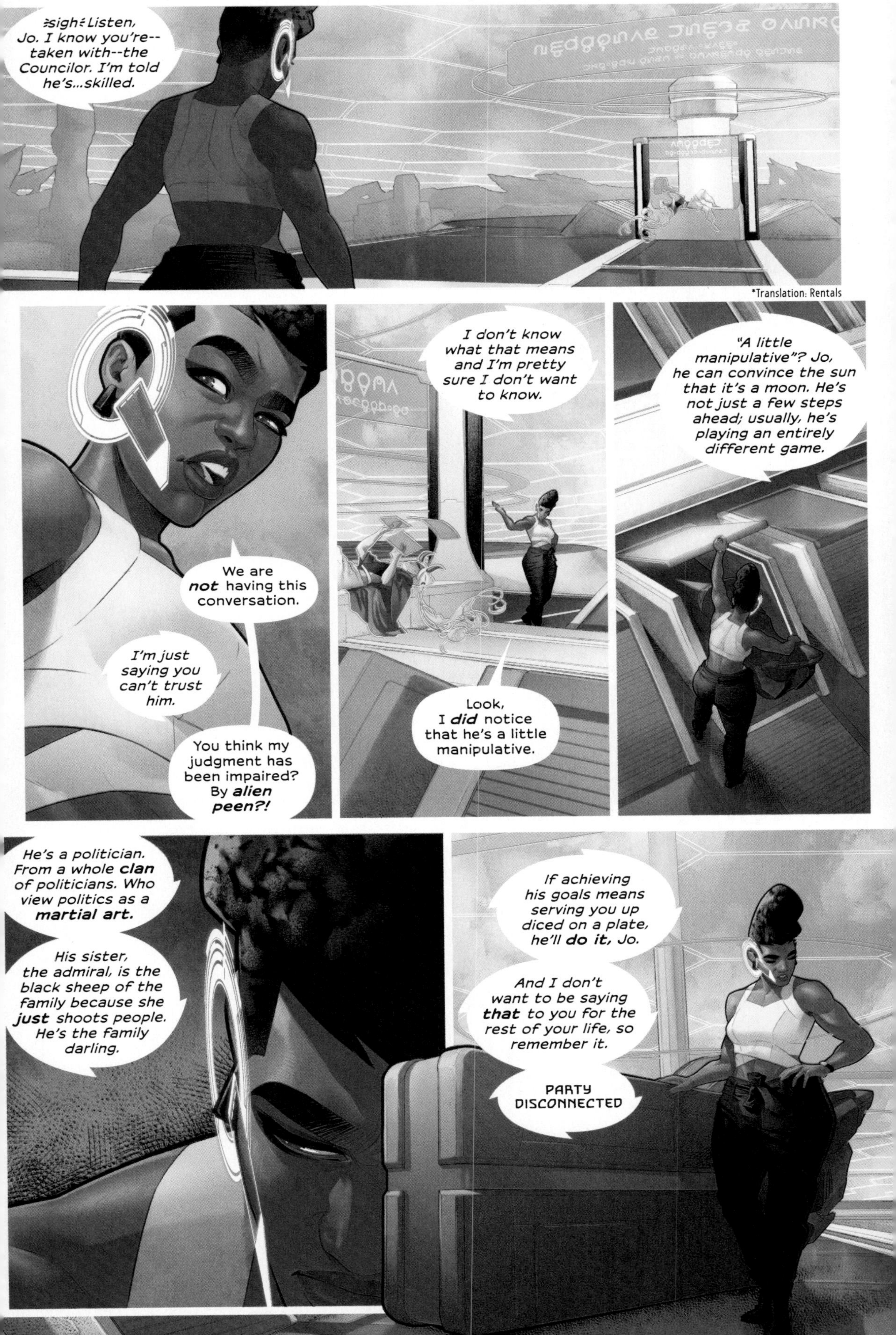

≈sigh≈ Listen, Jo. I know you're--taken with--the Councilor. I'm told he's...skilled.
*Translation: Rentals
We are not having this conversation.
I'm just saying you can't trust him.
You think my judgment has been impaired? By alien peen?!
I don't know what that means and I'm pretty sure I don't want to know.
Look, I did notice that he's a little manipulative.
"A little manipulative"? Jo, he can convince the sun that it's a moon. He's not just a few steps ahead; usually, he's playing an entirely different game.
He's a politician. From a whole clan of politicians. Who view politics as a martial art.
His sister, the admiral, is the black sheep of the family because she just shoots people. He's the family darling.
If achieving his goals means serving you up diced on a plate, he'll do it, Jo.
And I don't want to be saying that to you for the rest of your life, so remember it.
PARTY DISCONNECTED

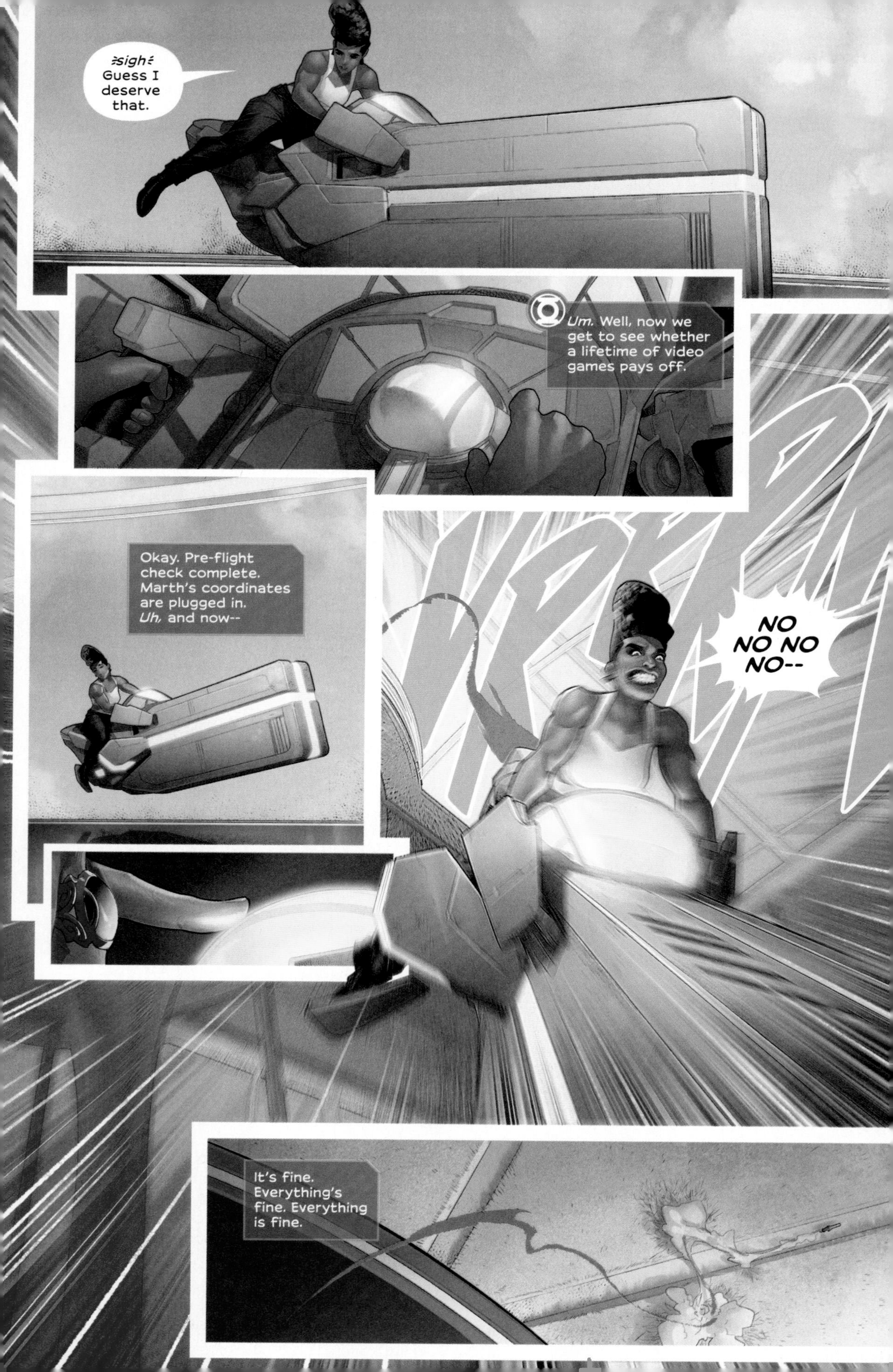

≈sigh≈ Guess I deserve that.
Um. Well, now we get to see whether a lifetime of video games pays off.
Okay. Pre-flight check complete. Marth's coordinates are plugged in. Uh, and now--
NO NO NO NO--
It's fine. Everything's fine. Everything is fine.

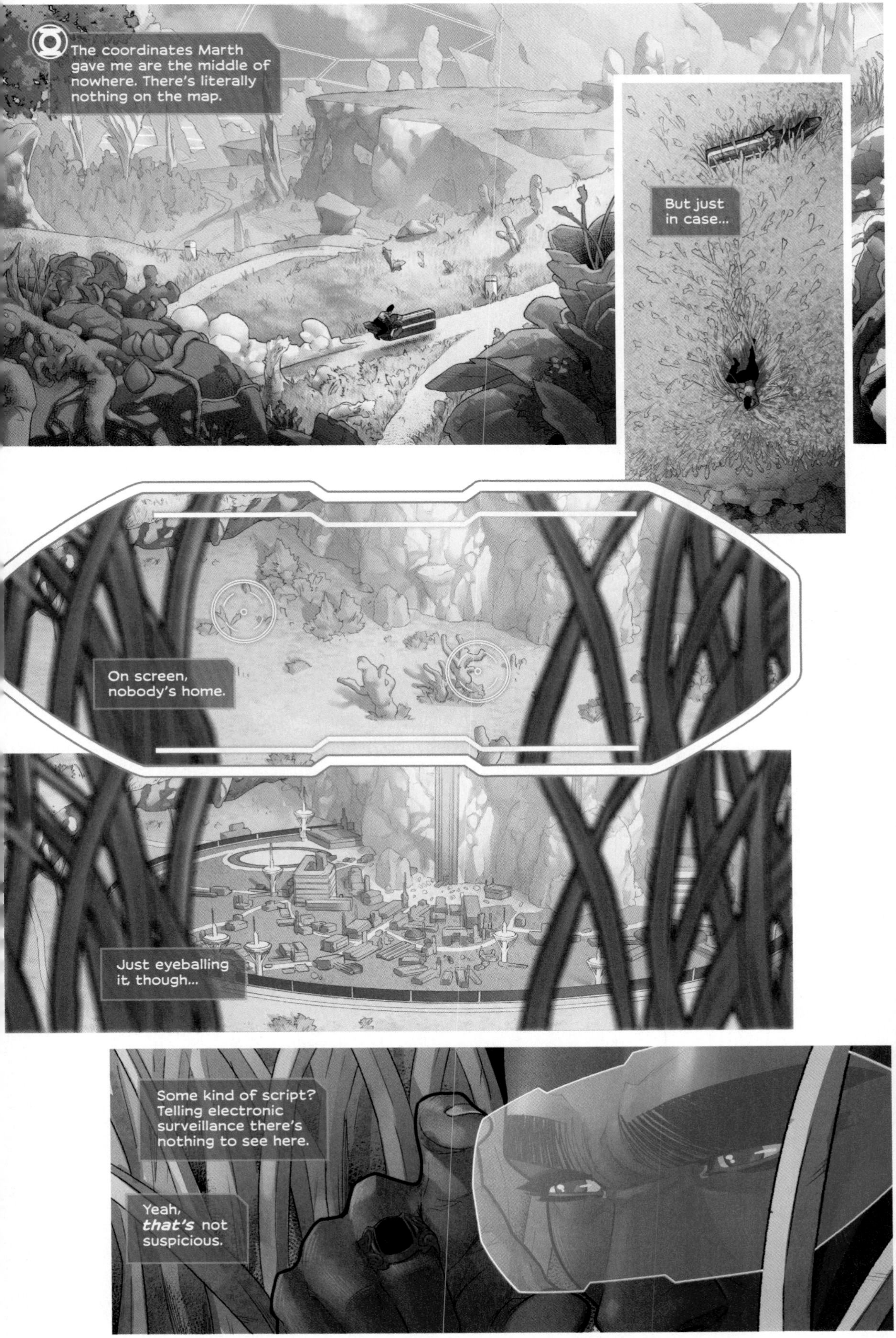
The coordinates Marth gave me are the middle of nowhere. There's literally nothing on the map.
But just in case...
On screen, nobody's home.
Just eyeballing it, though...
Some kind of script? Telling electronic surveillance there's nothing to see here.
Yeah, *that's* not suspicious.

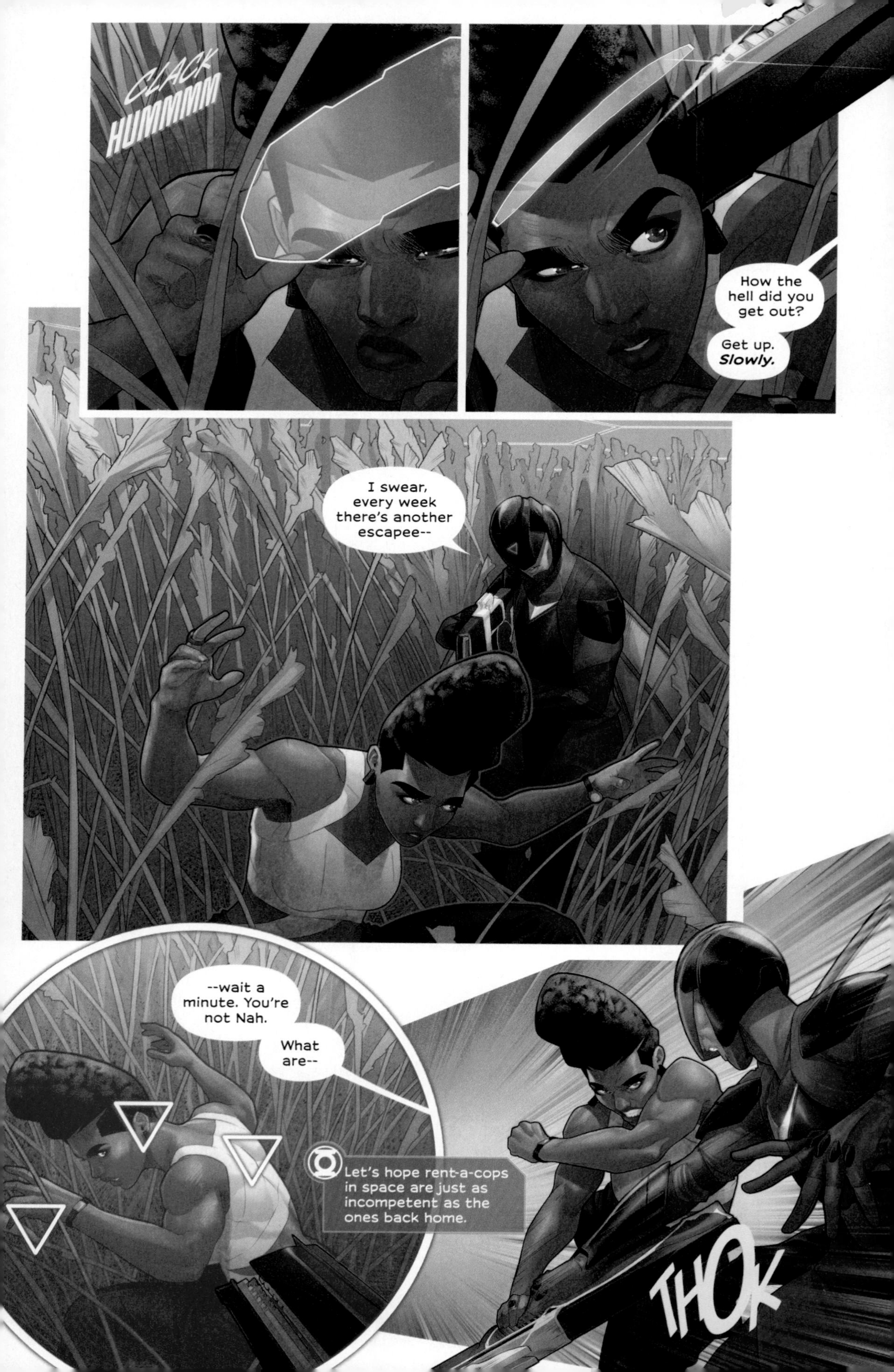
CLACK
HUMMMM
How the hell did you get out?
Get up. *Slowly.*
I swear, every week there's another escapee--
--wait a minute. You're not Nah.
What are--
Let's hope rent-a-cops in space are just as incompetent as the ones back home.
THOK

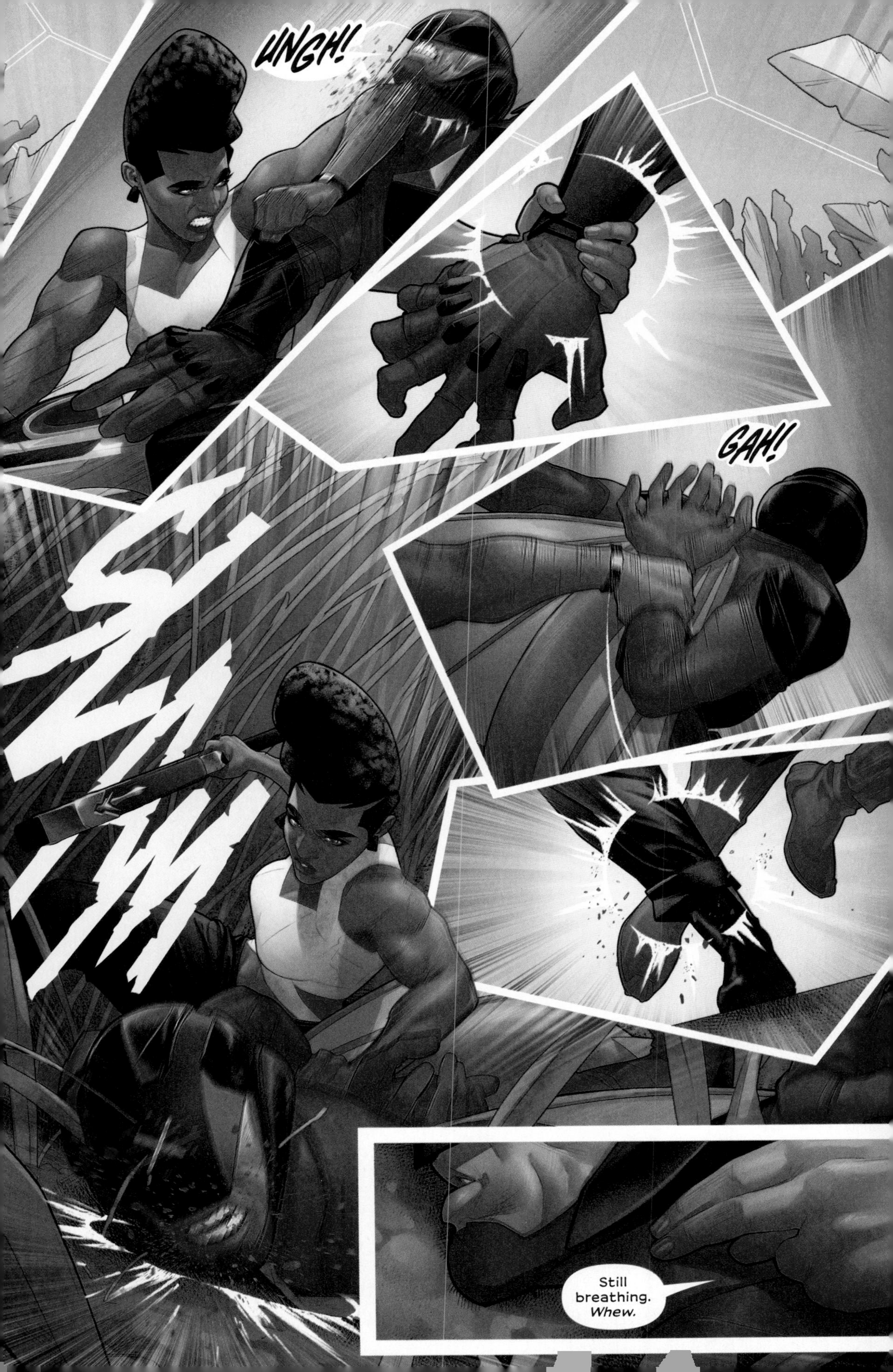
UNGH!
GAH!
Still breathing. *Whew.*

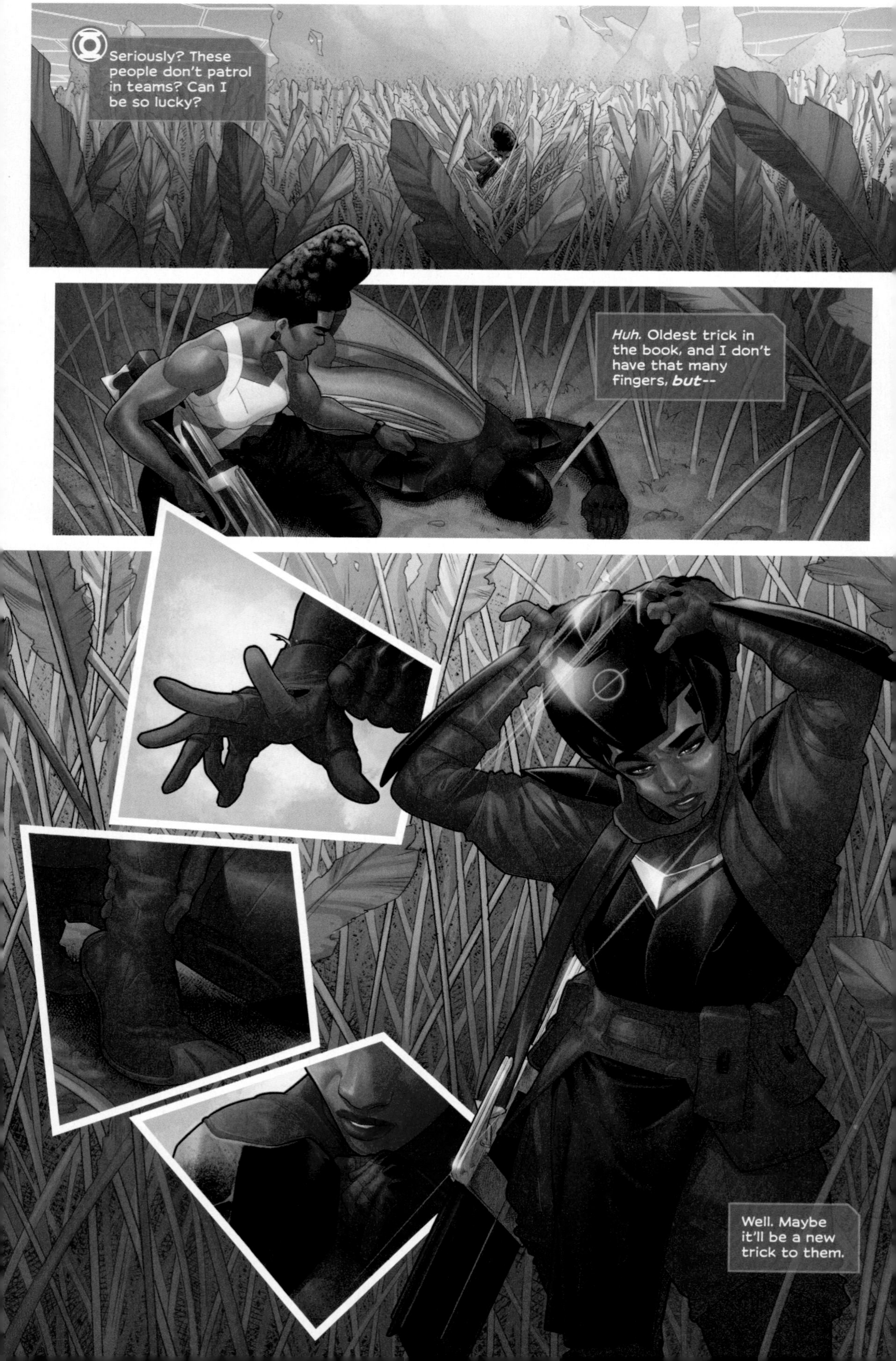
Seriously? These people don't patrol in teams? Can I be so lucky?
Huh. Oldest trick in the book, and I don't have that many fingers, ***but--***
Well. Maybe it'll be a new trick to them.

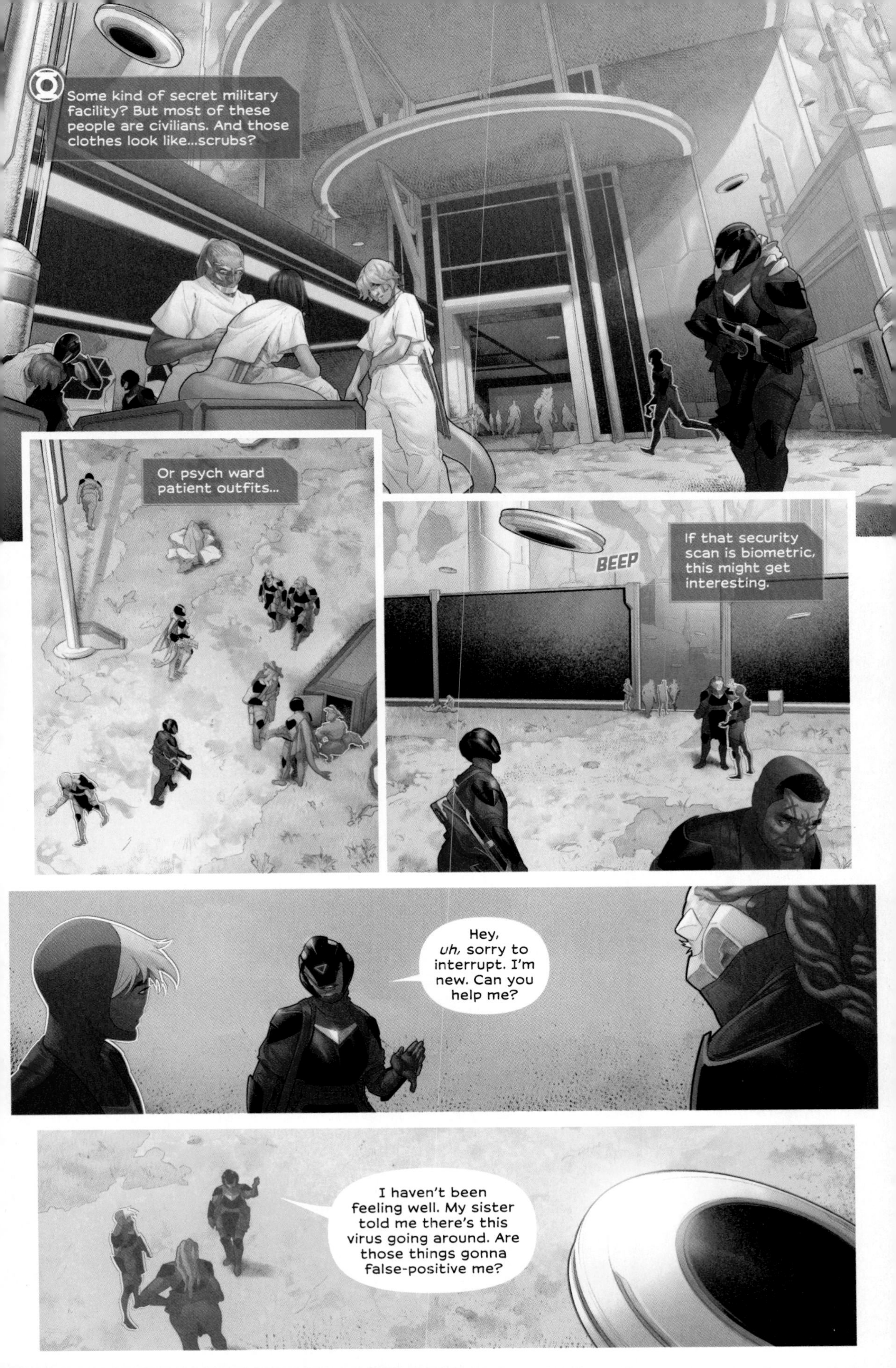
Some kind of secret military facility? But most of these people are civilians. And those clothes look like...scrubs?
Or psych ward patient outfits...
BEEP
If that security scan is biometric, this might get interesting.
Hey, uh, sorry to interrupt. I'm new. Can you help me?
I haven't been feeling well. My sister told me there's this virus going around. Are those things gonna false-positive me?

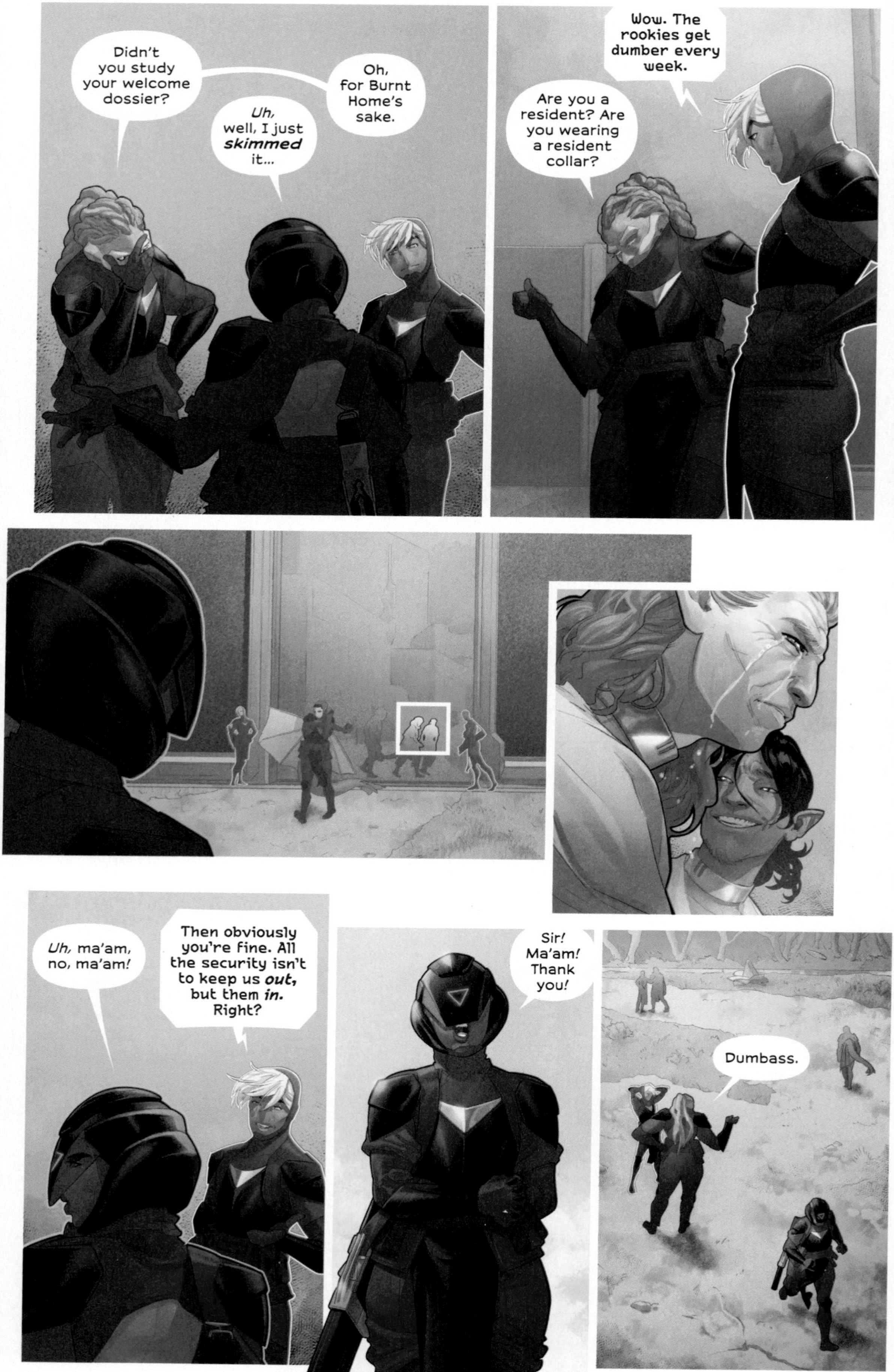
Didn't you study your welcome dossier?
Uh, well, I just skimmed it...
Oh, for Burnt Home's sake.
Wow. The rookies get dumber every week.
Are you a resident? Are you wearing a resident collar?
Uh, ma'am, no, ma'am!
Then obviously you're fine. All the security isn't to keep us out, but them in. Right?
Sir! Ma'am! Thank you!
Dumbass.

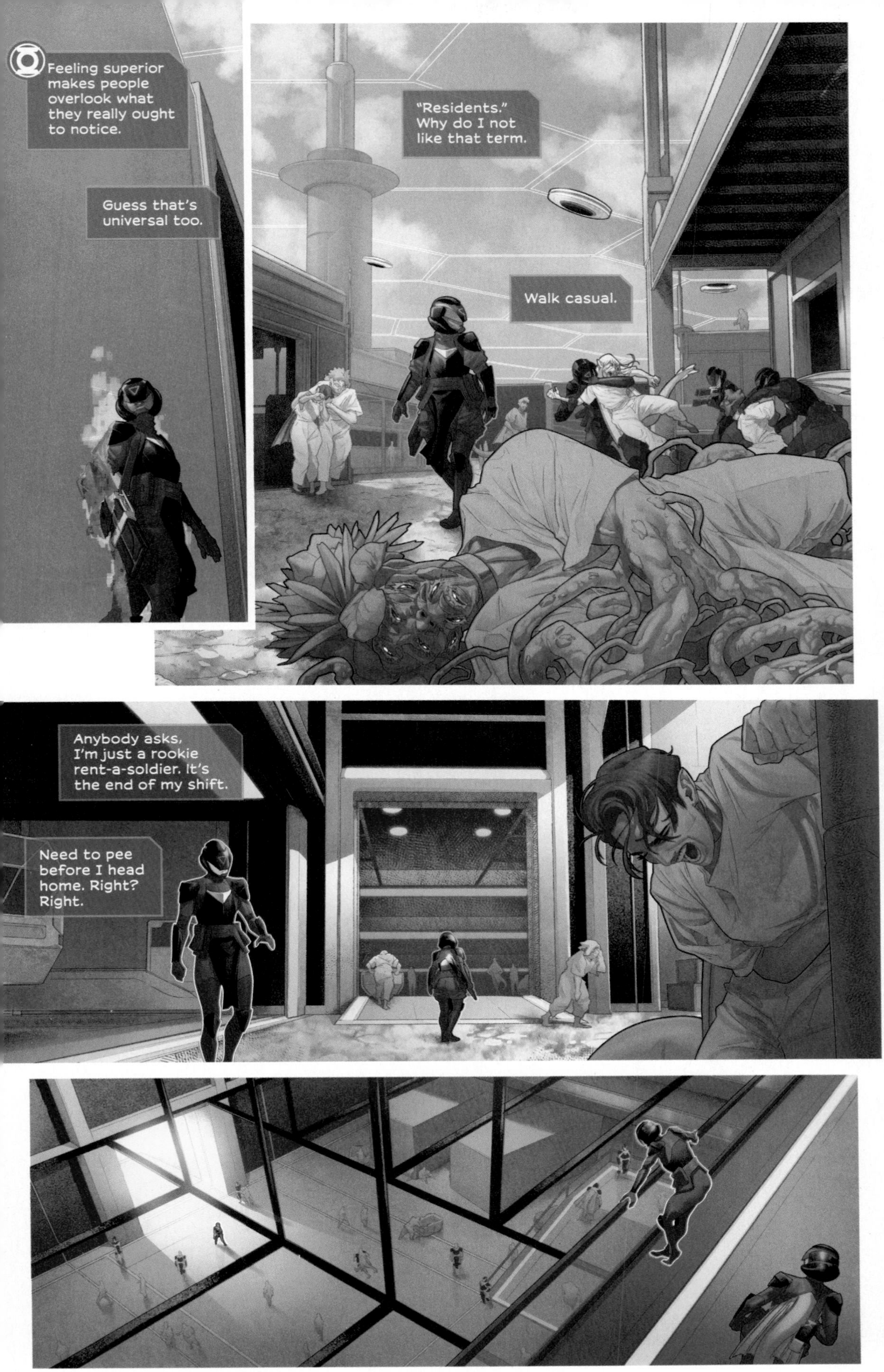

Feeling superior makes people overlook what they really ought to notice.
Guess that's universal too.
"Residents." Why do I not like that term.
Walk casual.
Anybody asks, I'm just a rookie rent-a-soldier. It's the end of my shift.
Need to pee before I head home. Right? Right.

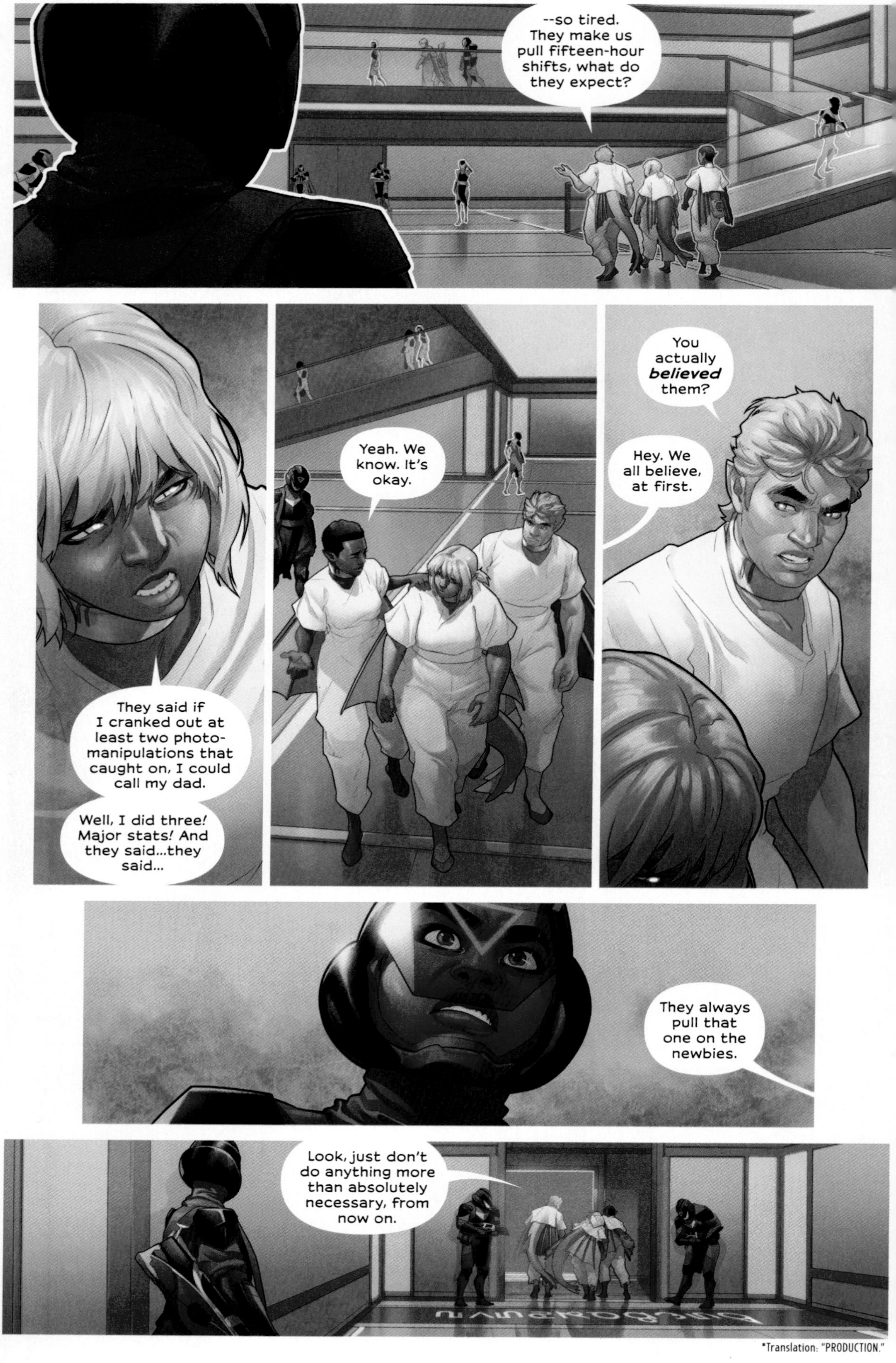
--so tired. They make us pull fifteen-hour shifts, what do they expect?
They said if I cranked out at least two photo-manipulations that caught on, I could call my dad.
Well, I did three! Major stats! And they said...they said...
Yeah. We know. It's okay.
You actually *believed* them?
Hey. We all believe, at first.
They always pull that one on the newbies.
Look, just don't do anything more than absolutely necessary, from now on.

*Translation: "PRODUCTION."

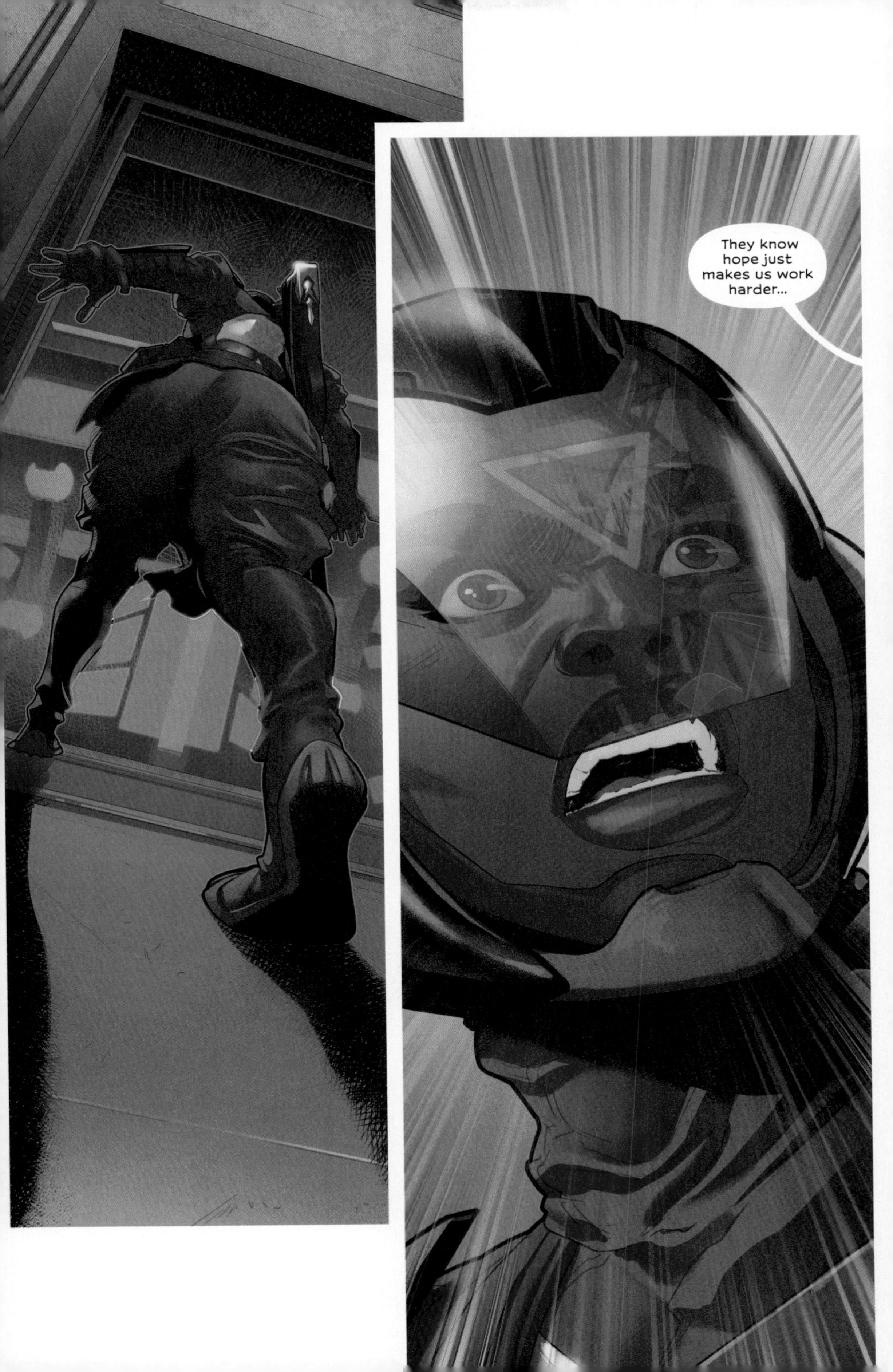
They know hope just makes us work harder...

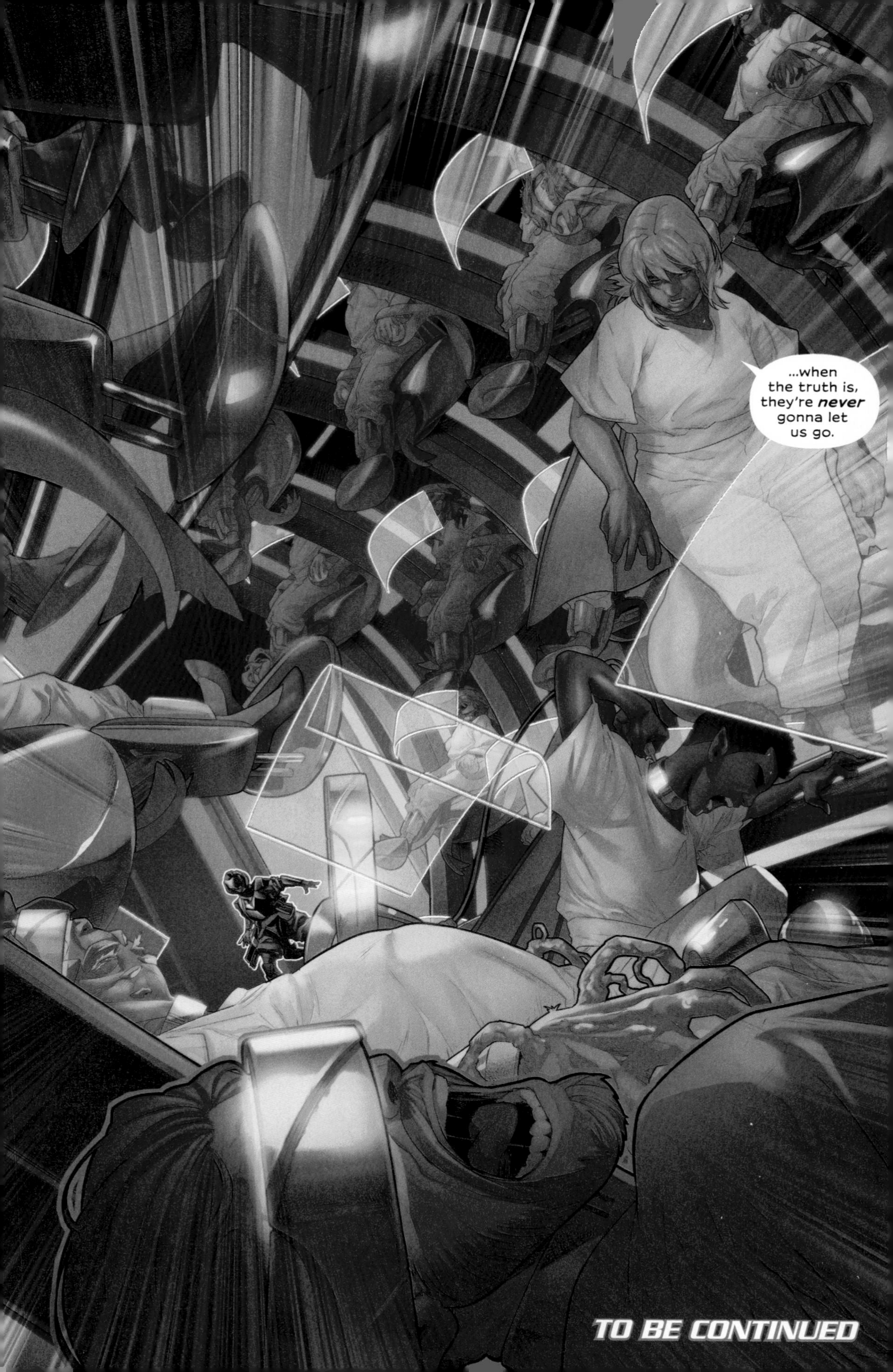
...when the truth is, they're ***never*** gonna let us go.
TO BE CONTINUED

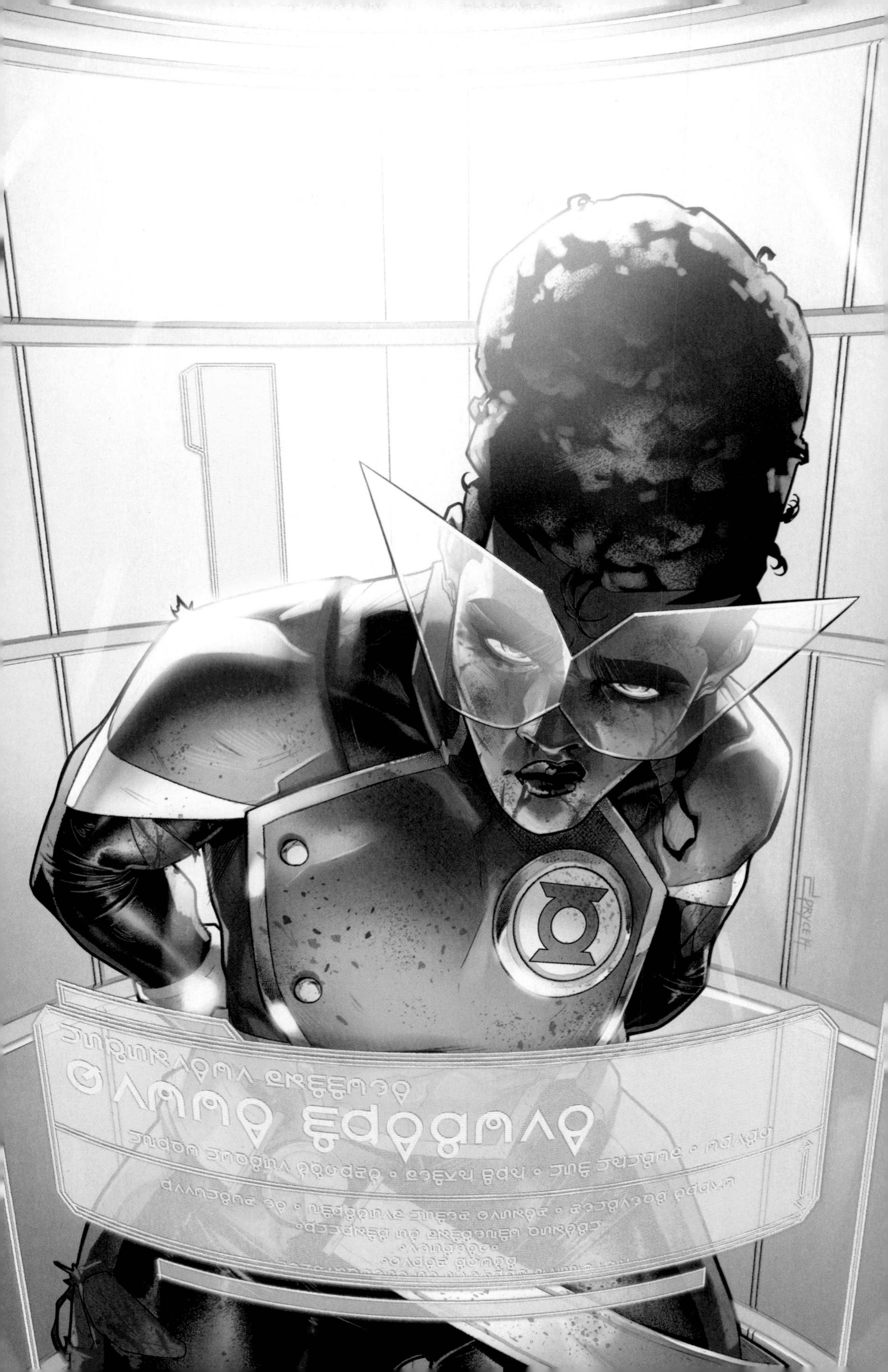

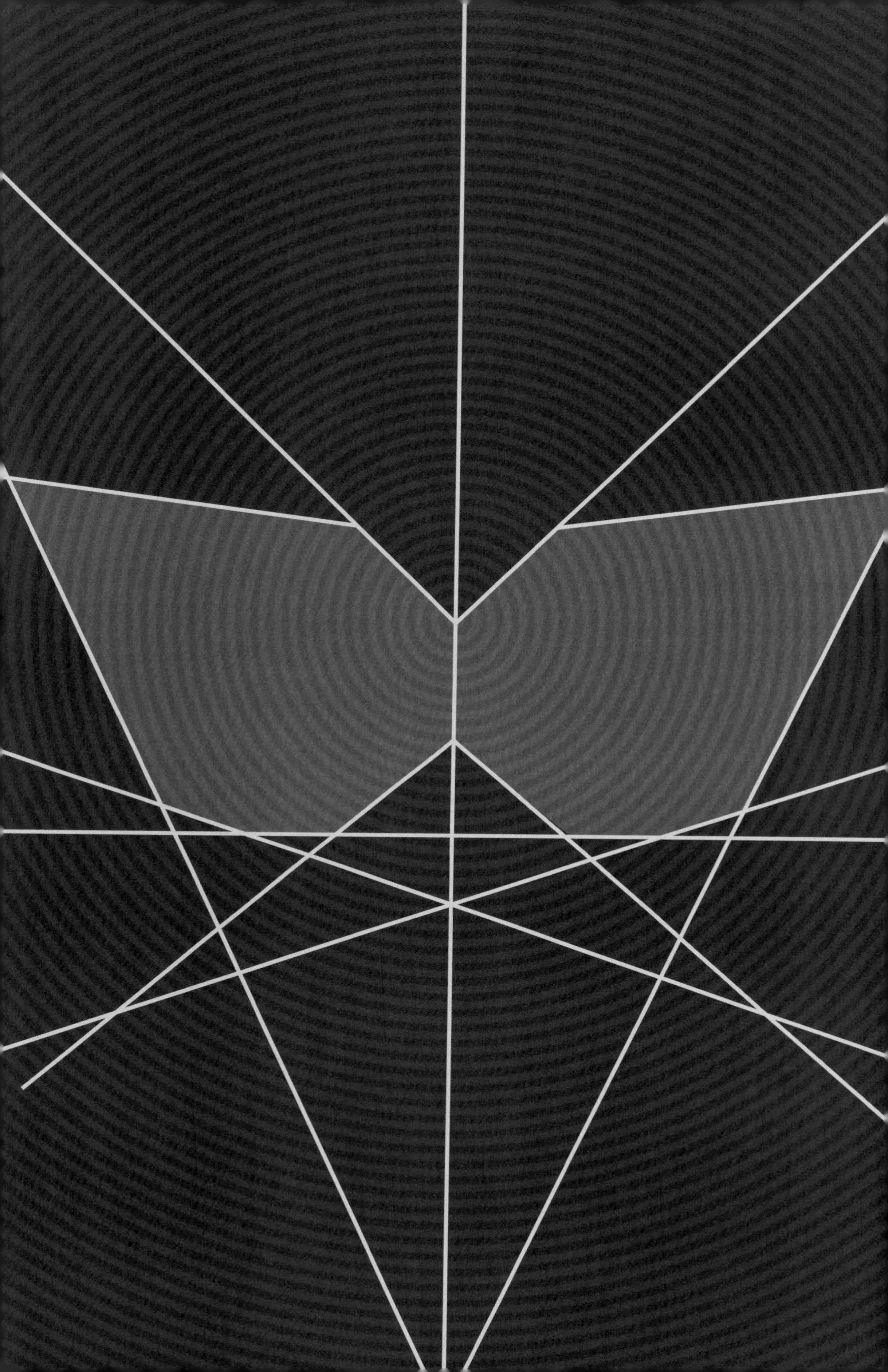

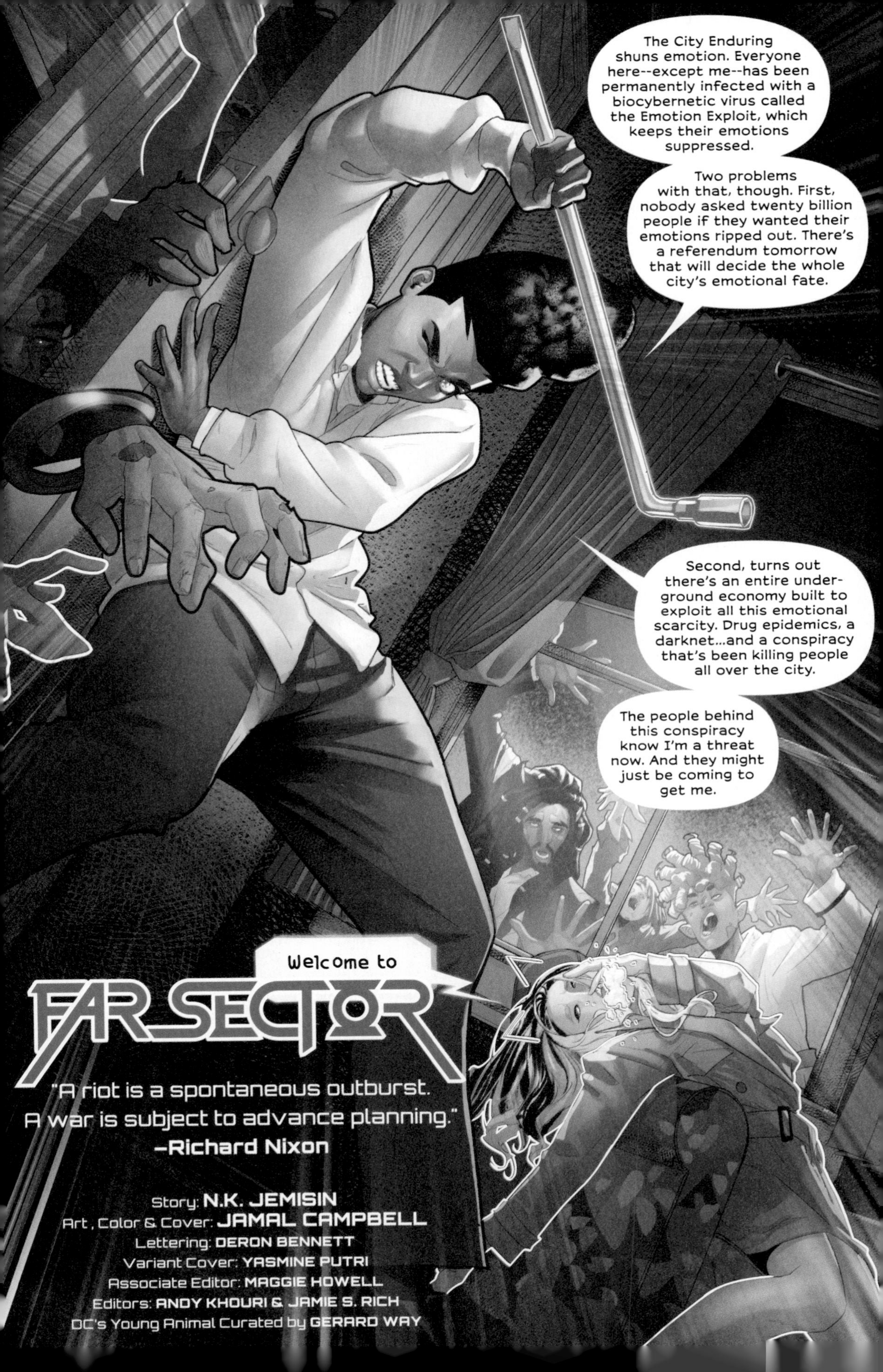
The City Enduring shuns emotion. Everyone here--except me--has been permanently infected with a biocybernetic virus called the Emotion Exploit, which keeps their emotions suppressed.
Two problems with that, though. First, nobody asked twenty billion people if they wanted their emotions ripped out. There's a referendum tomorrow that will decide the whole city's emotional fate.
Second, turns out there's an entire underground economy built to exploit all this emotional scarcity. Drug epidemics, a darknet...and a conspiracy that's been killing people all over the city.
The people behind this conspiracy know I'm a threat now. And they might just be coming to get me.
Welcome to
FAR SECTOR
"A riot is a spontaneous outburst. A war is subject to advance planning."
–Richard Nixon
Story: N.K. JEMISIN
Art, Color & Cover: JAMAL CAMPBELL
Lettering: DERON BENNETT
Variant Cover: YASMINE PUTRI
Associate Editor: MAGGIE HOWELL
Editors: ANDY KHOURI & JAMIE S. RICH
DC's Young Animal Curated by GERARD WAY

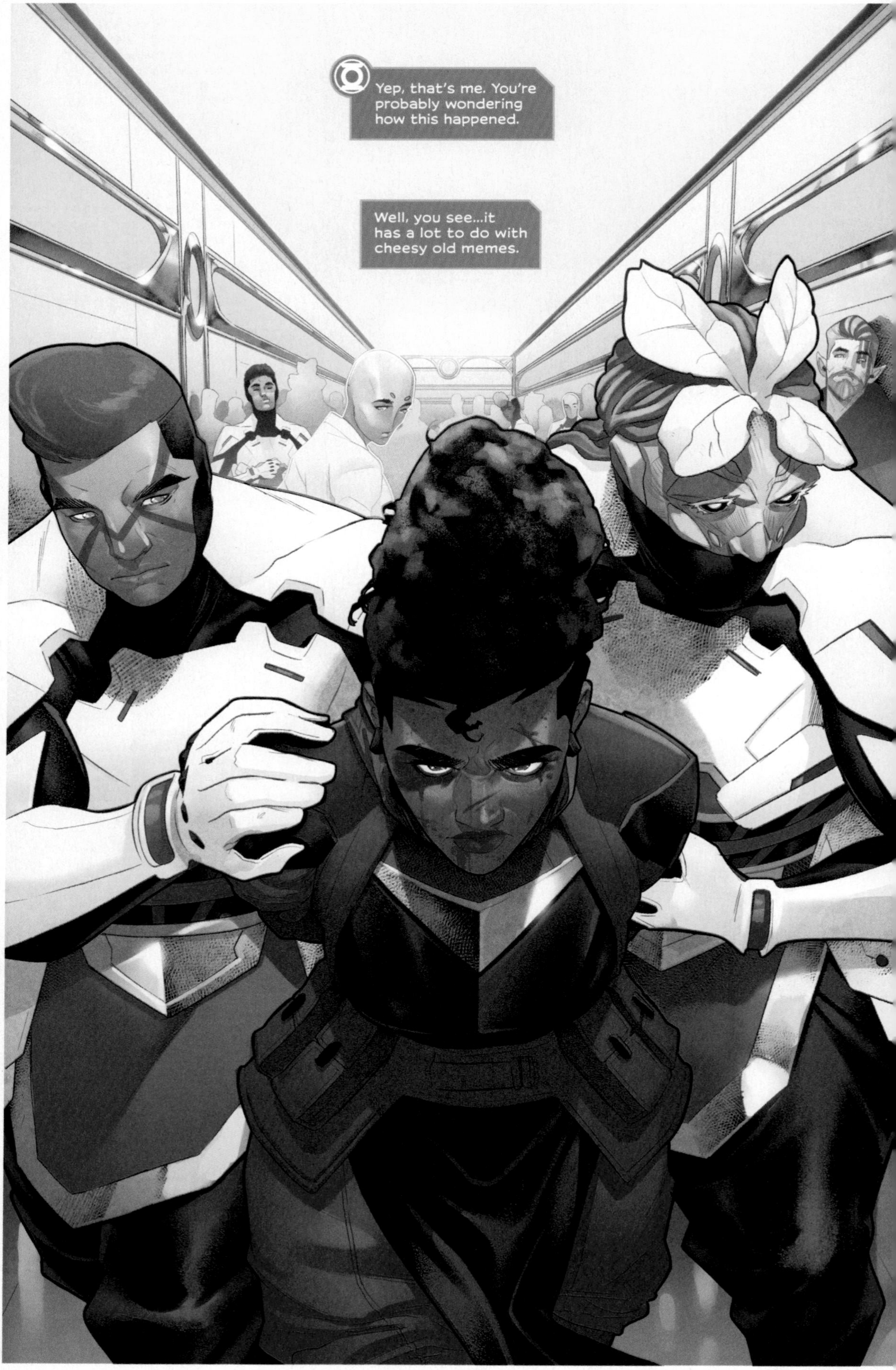
Yep, that's me. You're probably wondering how this happened.
Well, you see...it has a lot to do with cheesy old memes.

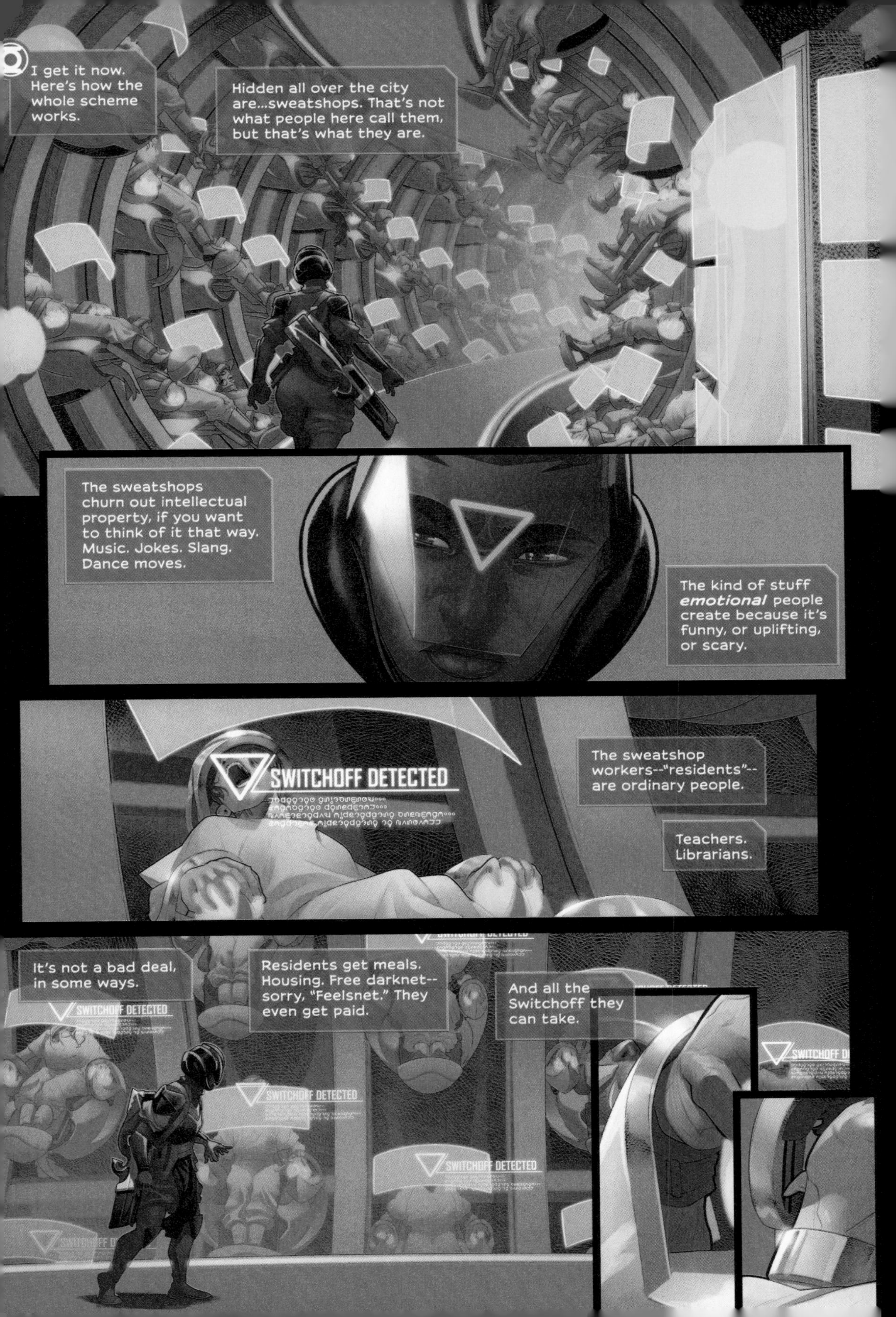

I get it now. Here's how the whole scheme works.
Hidden all over the city are...sweatshops. That's not what people here call them, but that's what they are.
The sweatshops churn out intellectual property, if you want to think of it that way. Music. Jokes. Slang. Dance moves.
The kind of stuff *emotional* people create because it's funny, or uplifting, or scary.
SWITCHOFF DETECTED
The sweatshop workers--"residents"--are ordinary people.
Teachers. Librarians.
It's not a bad deal, in some ways.
Residents get meals. Housing. Free darknet--sorry, "Feelsnet." They even get paid.
And all the Switchoff they can take.
SWITCHOFF DETECTED
SWITCHOFF DETECTED
SWITCHOFF DETECTED

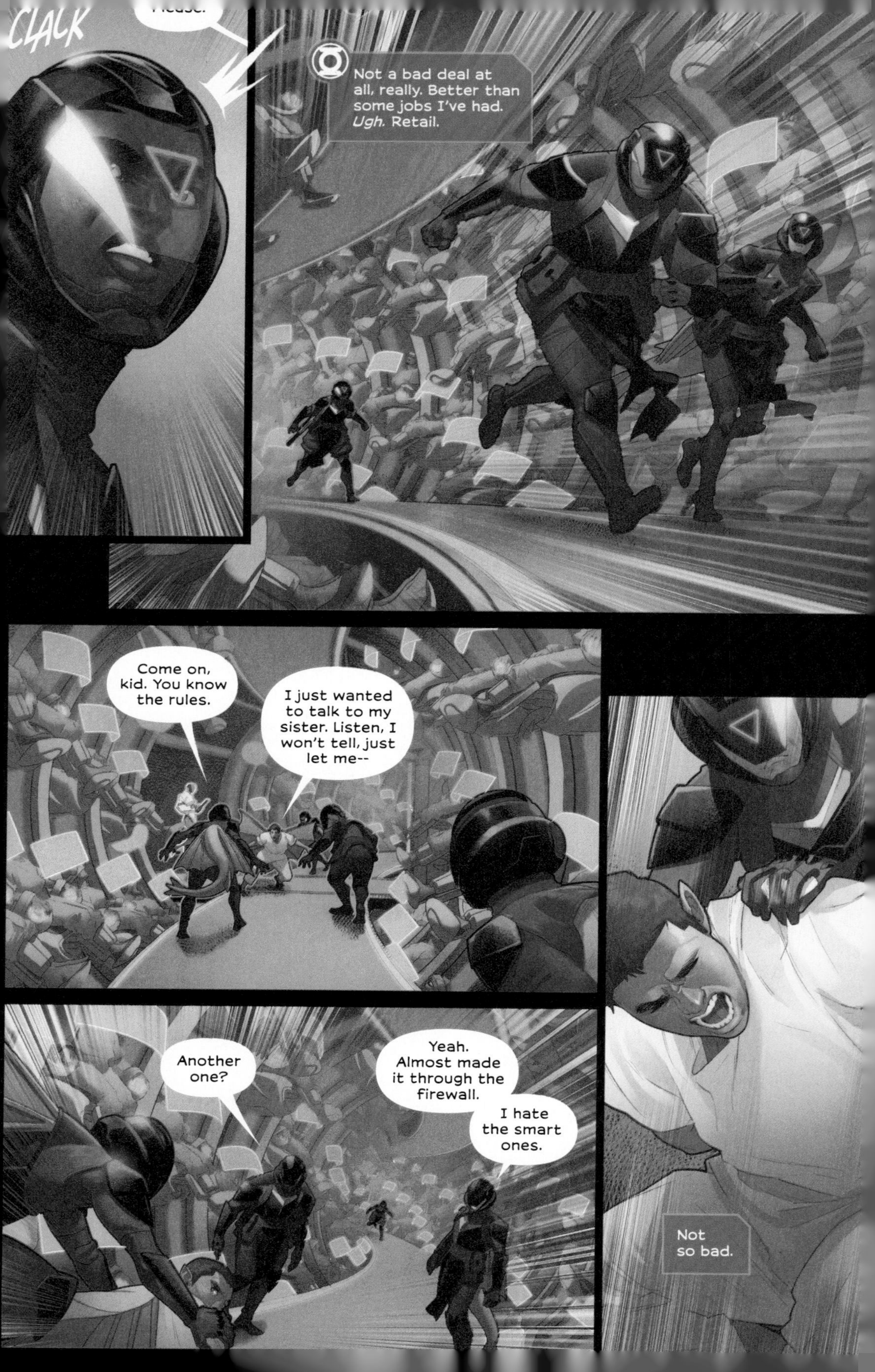
CLACK
Not a bad deal at all, really. Better than some jobs I've had. *Ugh.* Retail.
Come on, kid. You know the rules.
I just wanted to talk to my sister. Listen, I won't tell, just let me--
Another one?
Yeah. Almost made it through the firewall.
I hate the smart ones.
Not so bad.

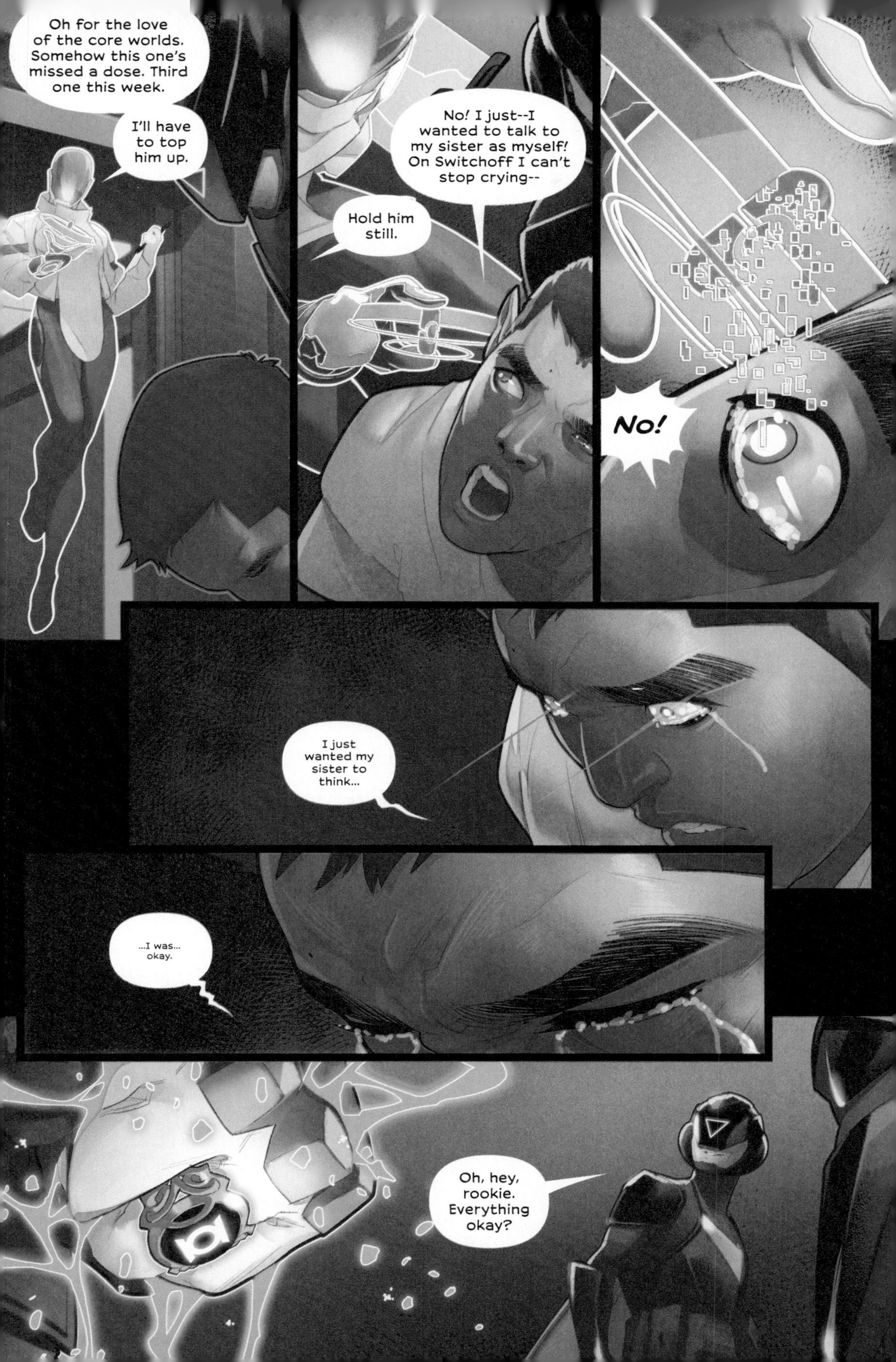
Oh for the love of the core worlds. Somehow this one's missed a dose. Third one this week.
I'll have to top him up.
No! I just--I wanted to talk to my sister as myself! On Switchoff I can't stop crying--
Hold him still.
No!
I just wanted my sister to think...
...I was... okay.
Oh, hey, rookie. Everything okay?

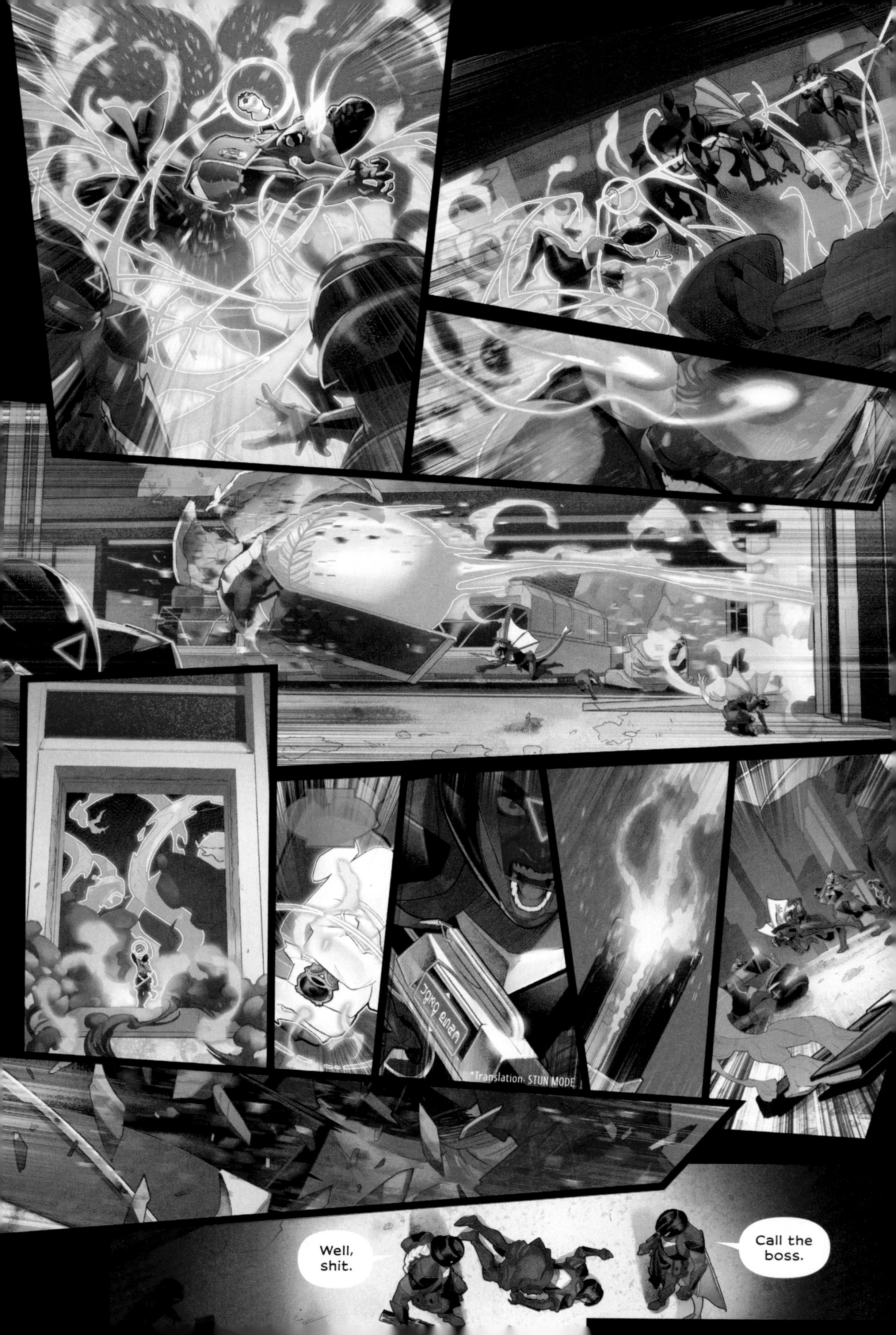
*Translation: STUN MODE
Well, shit.
Call the boss.

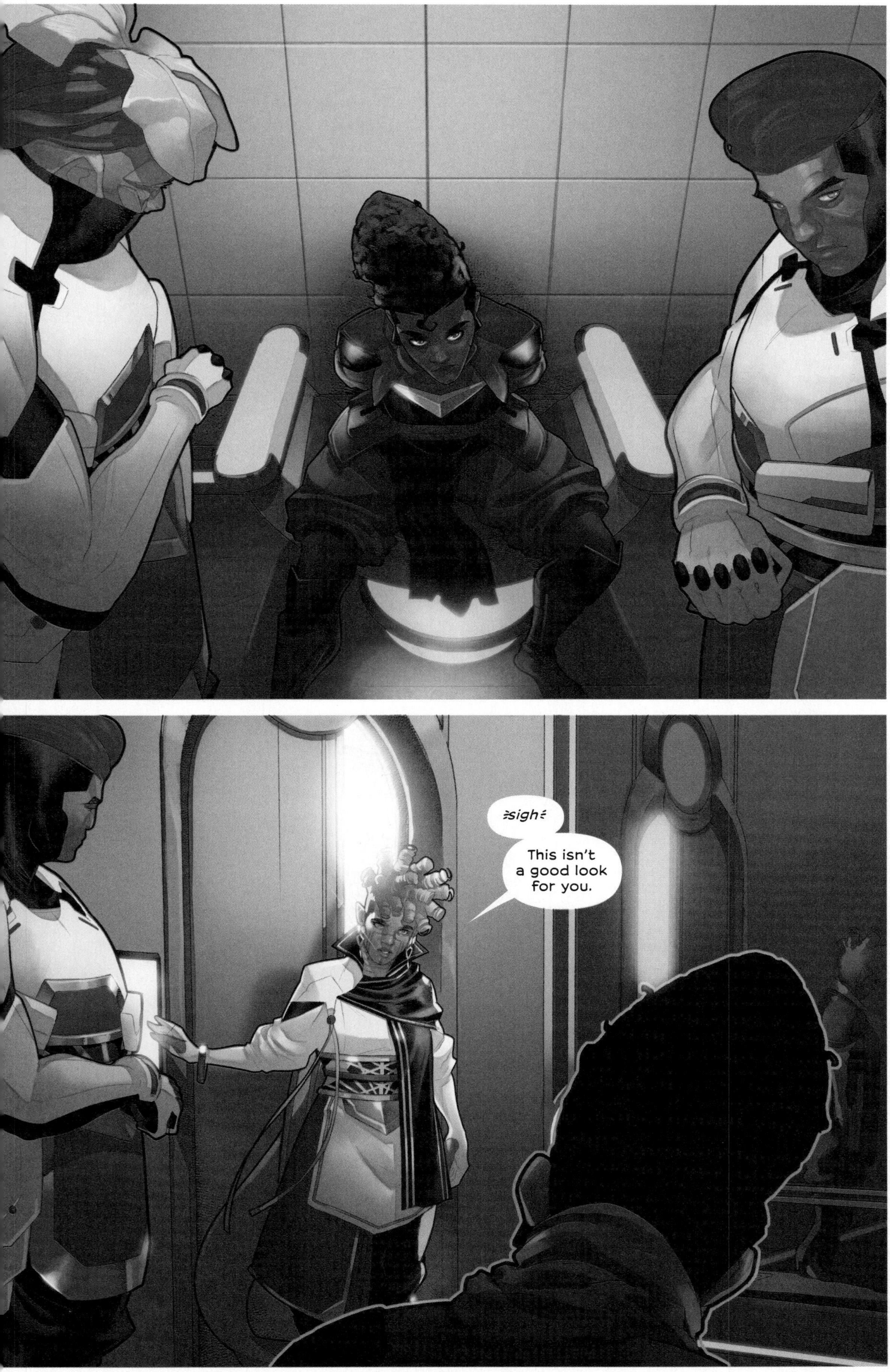

≈sigh≈
This isn't a good look for you.

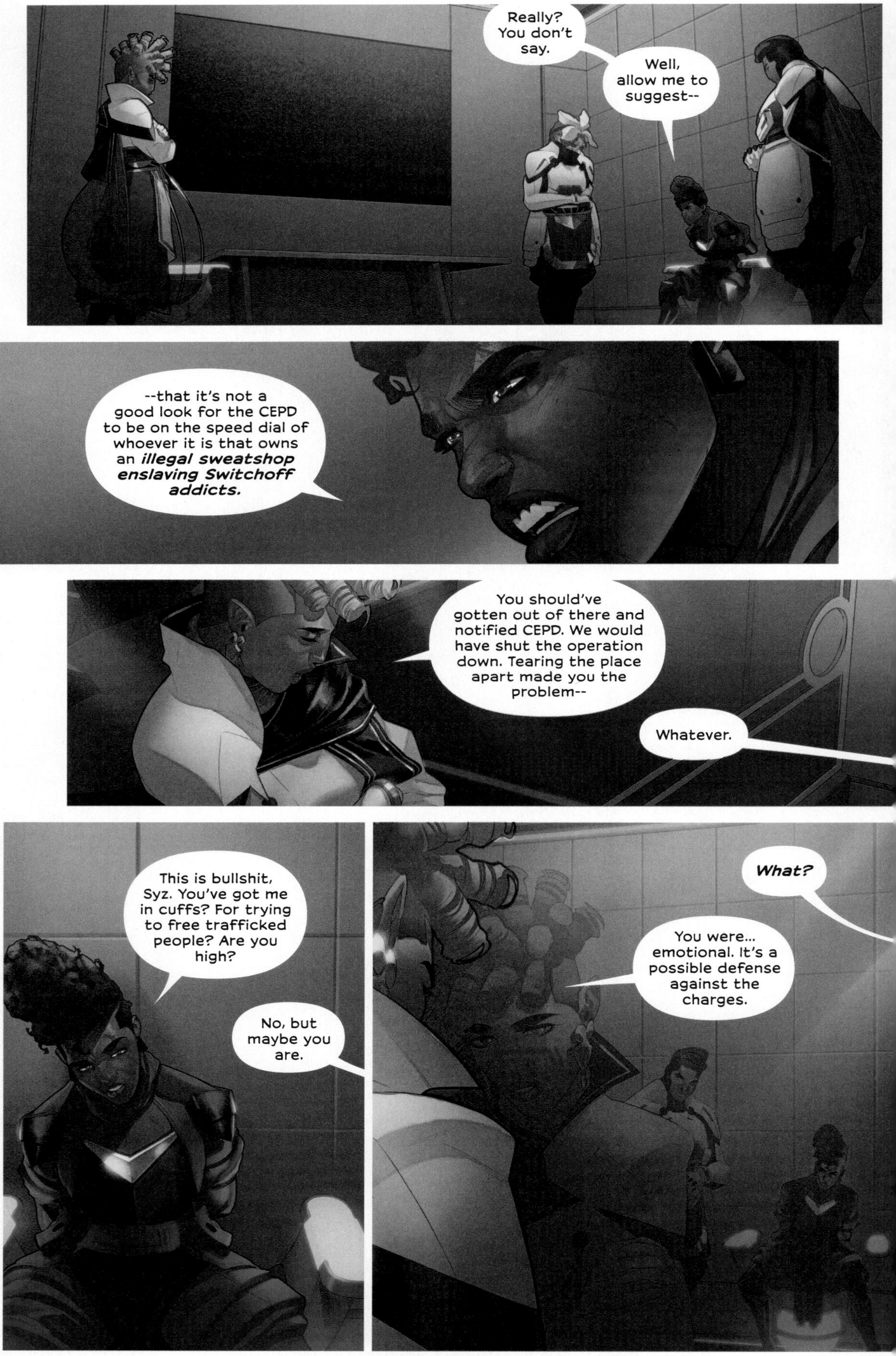

Really? You don't say.
Well, allow me to suggest--
--that it's not a good look for the CEPD to be on the speed dial of whoever it is that owns an *illegal sweatshop enslaving Switchoff addicts.*
You should've gotten out of there and notified CEPD. We would have shut the operation down. Tearing the place apart made you the problem--
Whatever.
This is bullshit, Syz. You've got me in cuffs? For trying to free trafficked people? Are you high?
No, but maybe you are.
What?
You were... emotional. It's a possible defense against the charges.

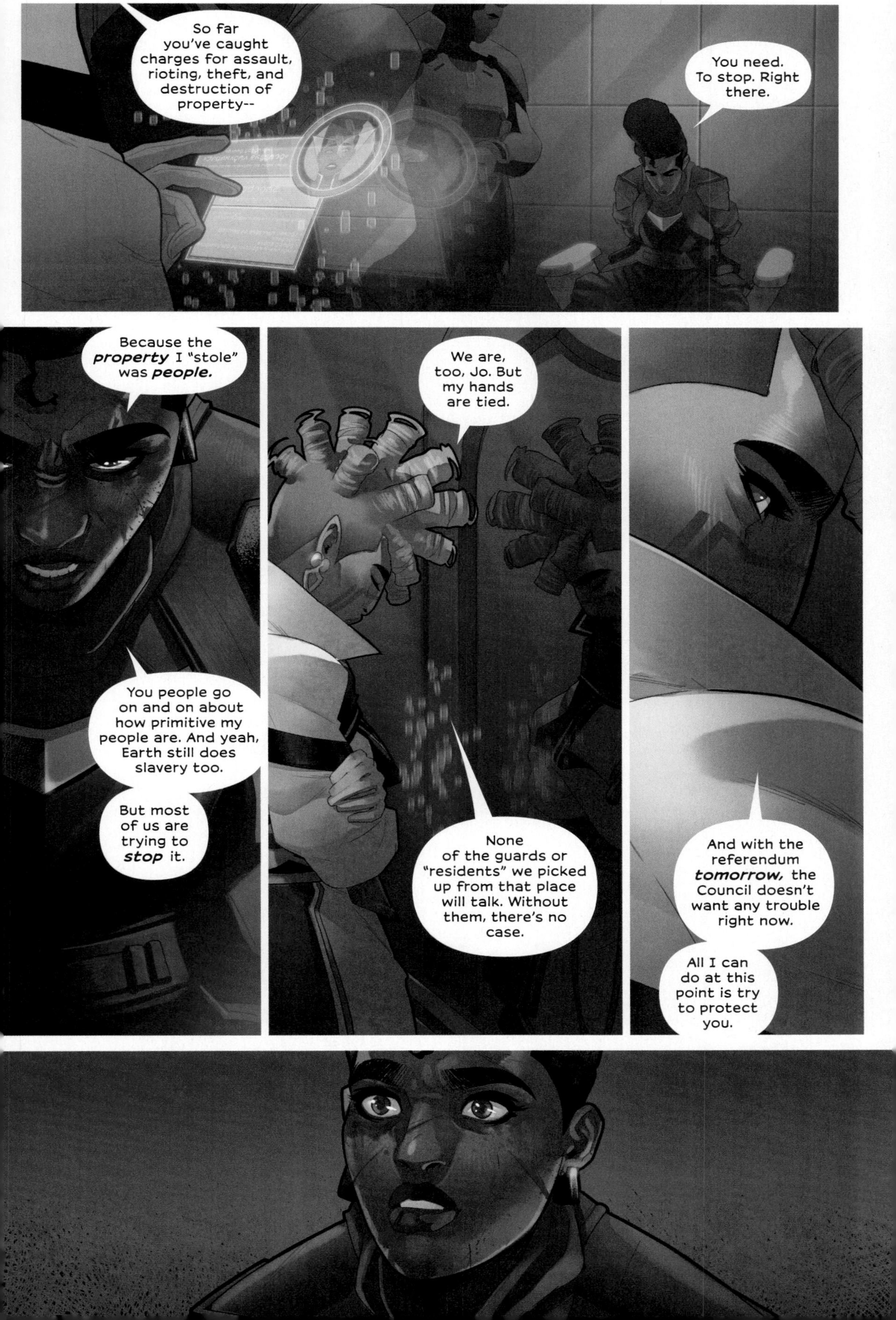
So far you've caught charges for assault, rioting, theft, and destruction of property--
You need. To stop. Right there.
Because the ***property*** I "stole" was ***people.***
You people go on and on about how primitive my people are. And yeah, Earth still does slavery too.
But most of us are trying to ***stop*** it.
We are, too, Jo. But my hands are tied.
None of the guards or "residents" we picked up from that place will talk. Without them, there's no case.
And with the referendum ***tomorrow,*** the Council doesn't want any trouble right now.
All I can do at this point is try to protect you.

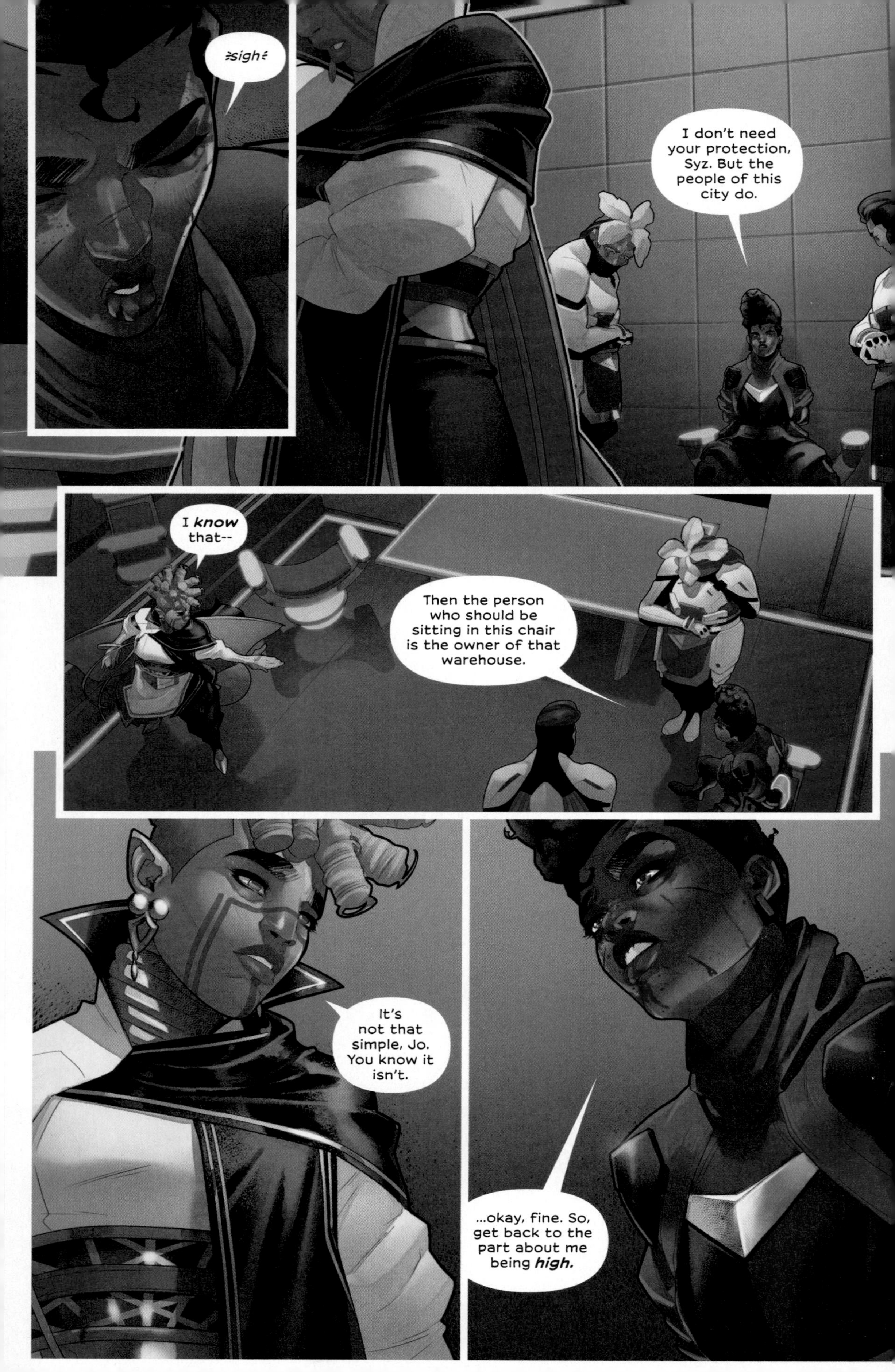

≈sigh≈
I don't need your protection, Syz. But the people of this city do.
I know that--
Then the person who should be sitting in this chair is the owner of that warehouse.
It's not that simple, Jo. You know it isn't.
...okay, fine. So, get back to the part about me being high.

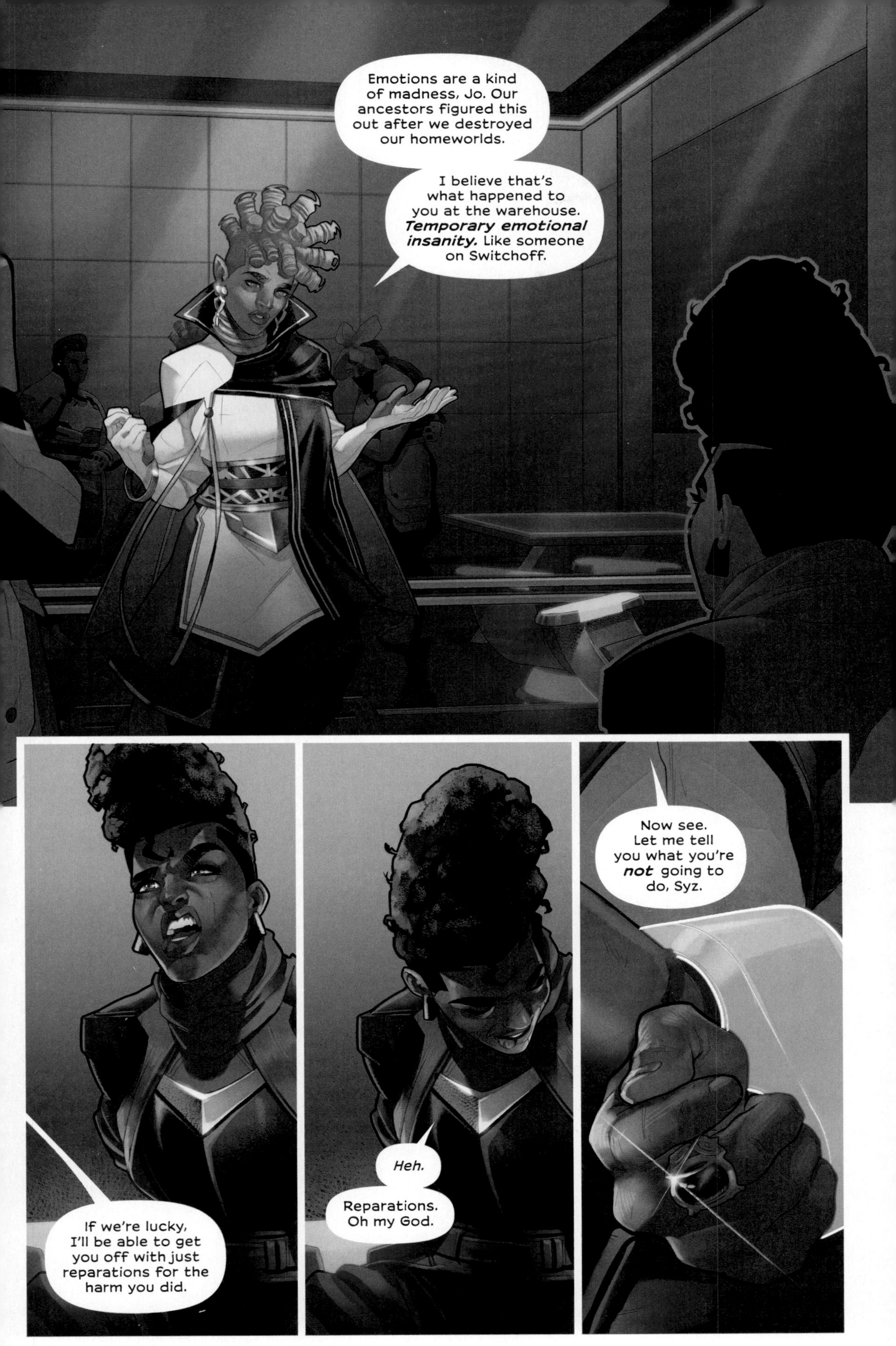
Emotions are a kind of madness, Jo. Our ancestors figured this out after we destroyed our homeworlds.
I believe that's what happened to you at the warehouse. ***Temporary emotional insanity.*** Like someone on Switchoff.
If we're lucky, I'll be able to get you off with just reparations for the harm you did.
Heh.
Reparations. Oh my God.
Now see. Let me tell you what you're ***not*** going to do, Syz.

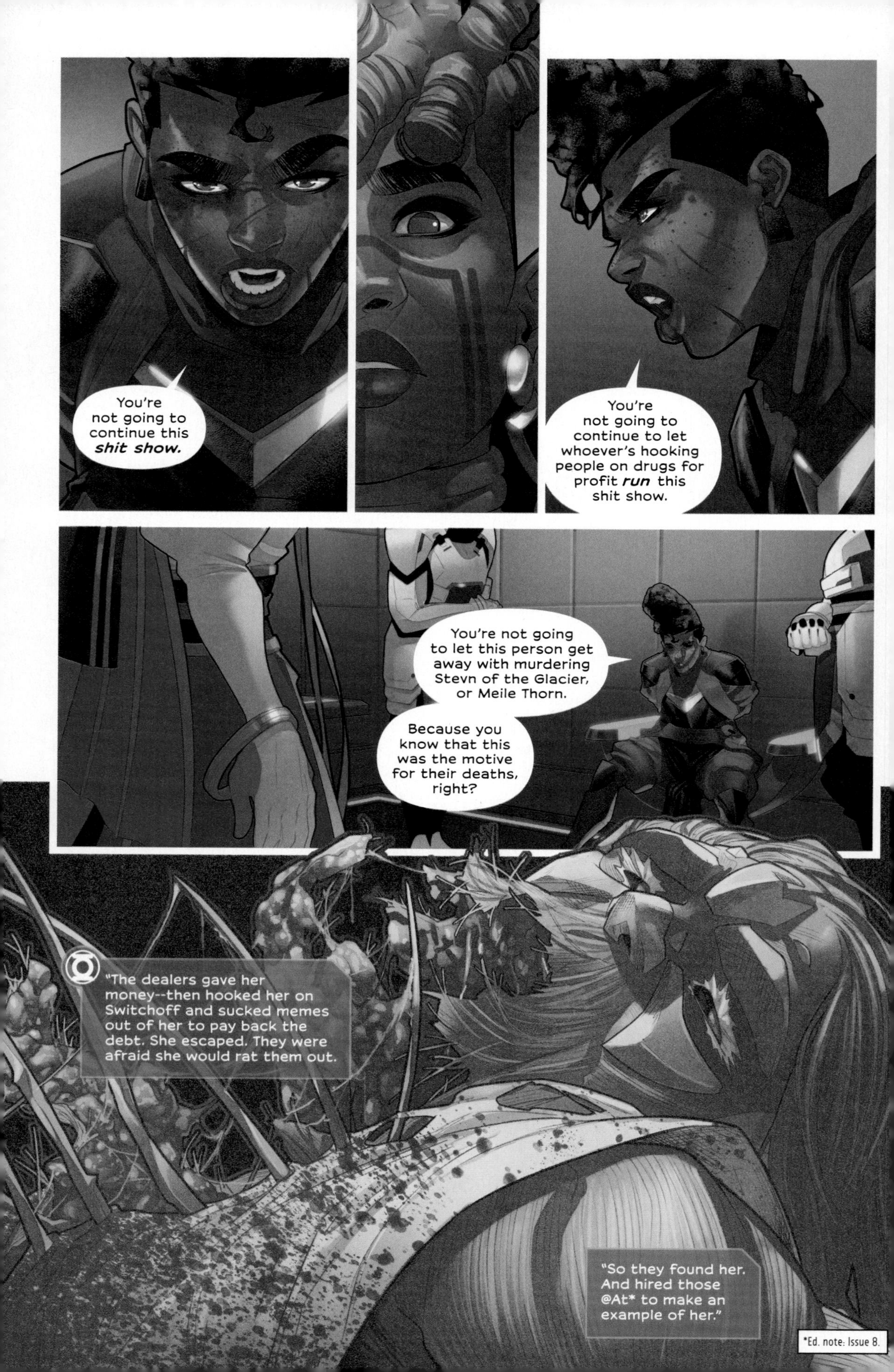
You're not going to continue this *shit show.*
You're not going to continue to let whoever's hooking people on drugs for profit *run* this shit show.
You're not going to let this person get away with murdering Stevn of the Glacier, or Meile Thorn.
Because you know that this was the motive for their deaths, right?
"The dealers gave her money--then hooked her on Switchoff and sucked memes out of her to pay back the debt. She escaped. They were afraid she would rat them out.
"So they found her. And hired those @At* to make an example of her."
*Ed. note: Issue 8.

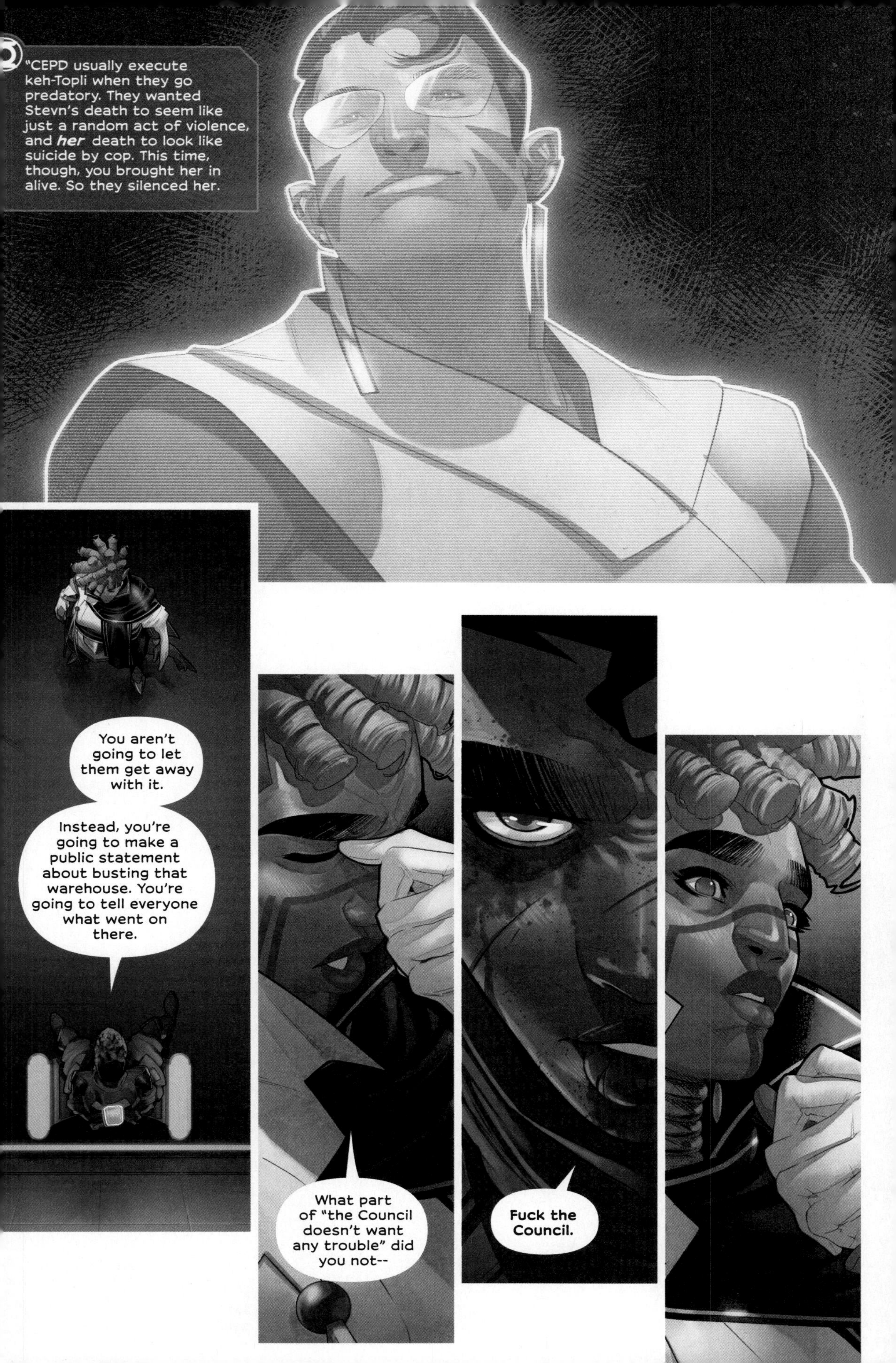
"CEPD usually execute keh-Topli when they go predatory. They wanted Stevn's death to seem like just a random act of violence, and *her* death to look like suicide by cop. This time, though, you brought her in alive. So they silenced her.
You aren't going to let them get away with it.
Instead, you're going to make a public statement about busting that warehouse. You're going to tell everyone what went on there.
What part of "the Council doesn't want any trouble" did you not--
Fuck the Council.

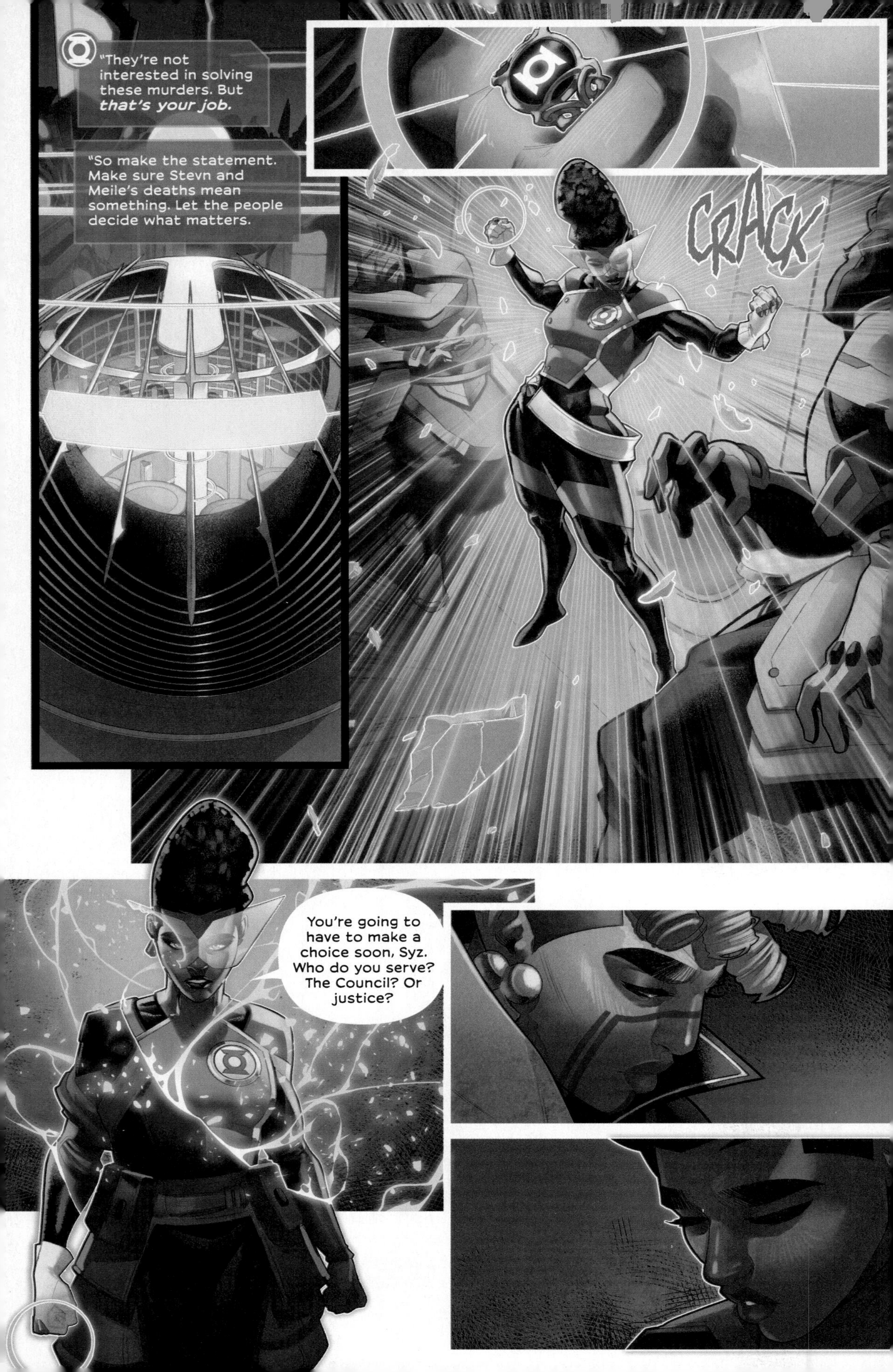
"They're not interested in solving these murders. But *that's your job.*
"So make the statement. Make sure Stevn and Meile's deaths mean something. Let the people decide what matters.
CRACK
You're going to have to make a choice soon, Syz. Who do you serve? The Council? Or justice?

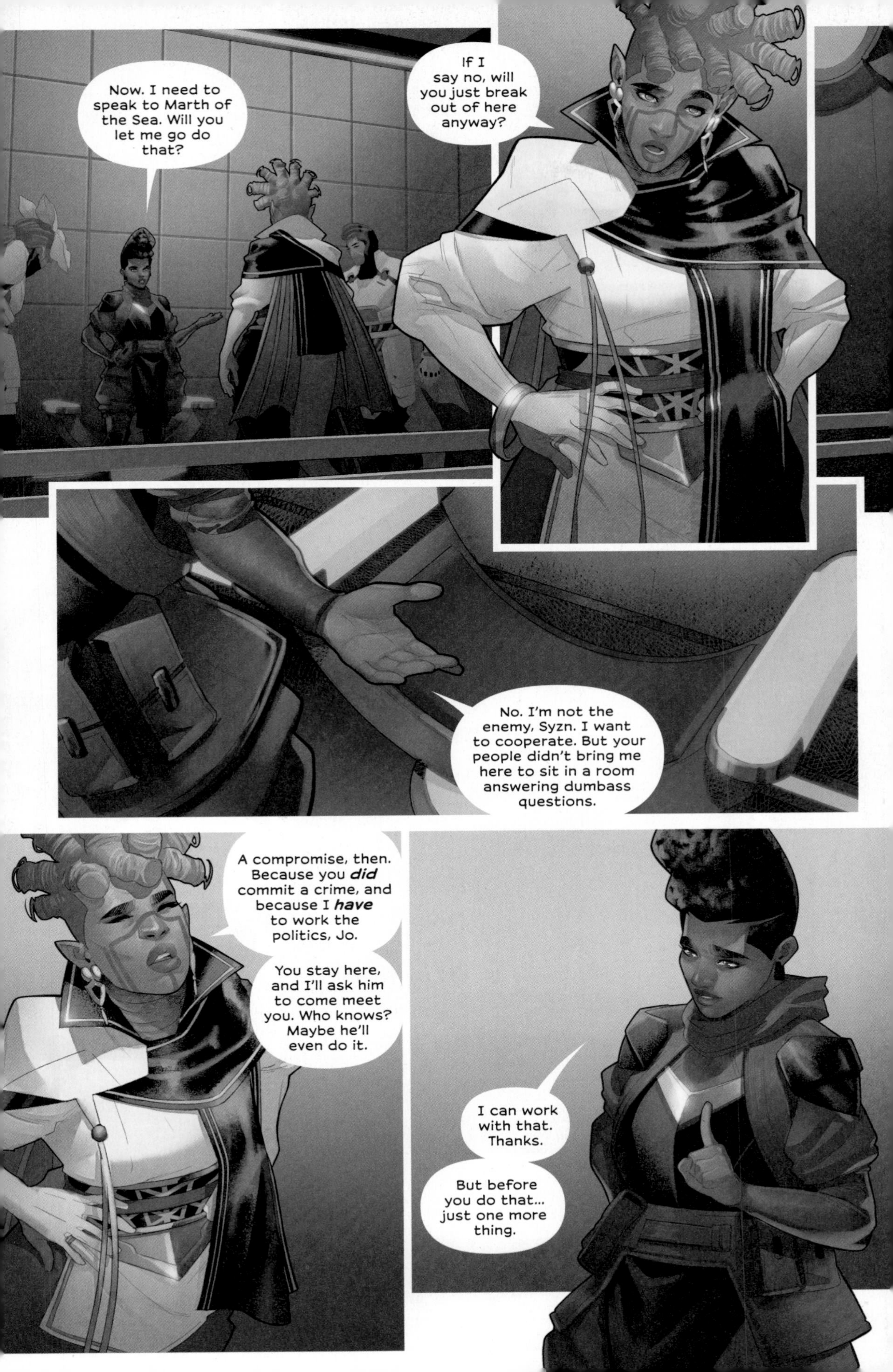
Now. I need to speak to Marth of the Sea. Will you let me go do that?
If I say no, will you just break out of here anyway?
No. I'm not the enemy, Syzn. I want to cooperate. But your people didn't bring me here to sit in a room answering dumbass questions.
A compromise, then. Because you *did* commit a crime, and because I *have* to work the politics, Jo.
You stay here, and I'll ask him to come meet you. Who knows? Maybe he'll even do it.
I can work with that. Thanks.
But before you do that... just one more thing.

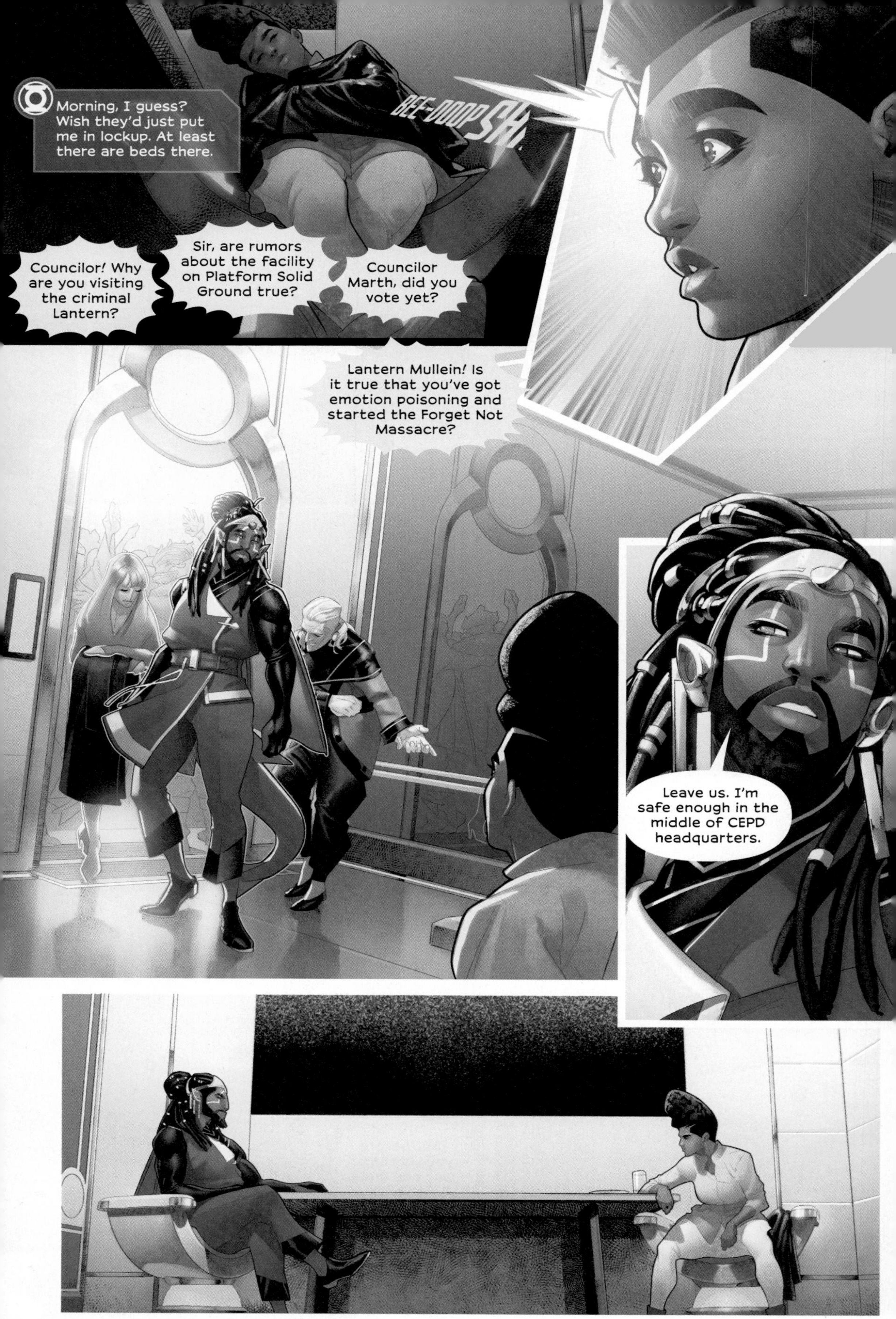
Morning, I guess? Wish they'd just put me in lockup. At least there are beds there.
BEE-DOOP SH
Councilor! Why are you visiting the criminal Lantern?
Sir, are rumors about the facility on Platform Solid Ground true?
Councilor Marth, did you vote yet?
Lantern Mullein! Is it true that you've got emotion poisoning and started the Forget Not Massacre?
Leave us. I'm safe enough in the middle of CEPD headquarters.

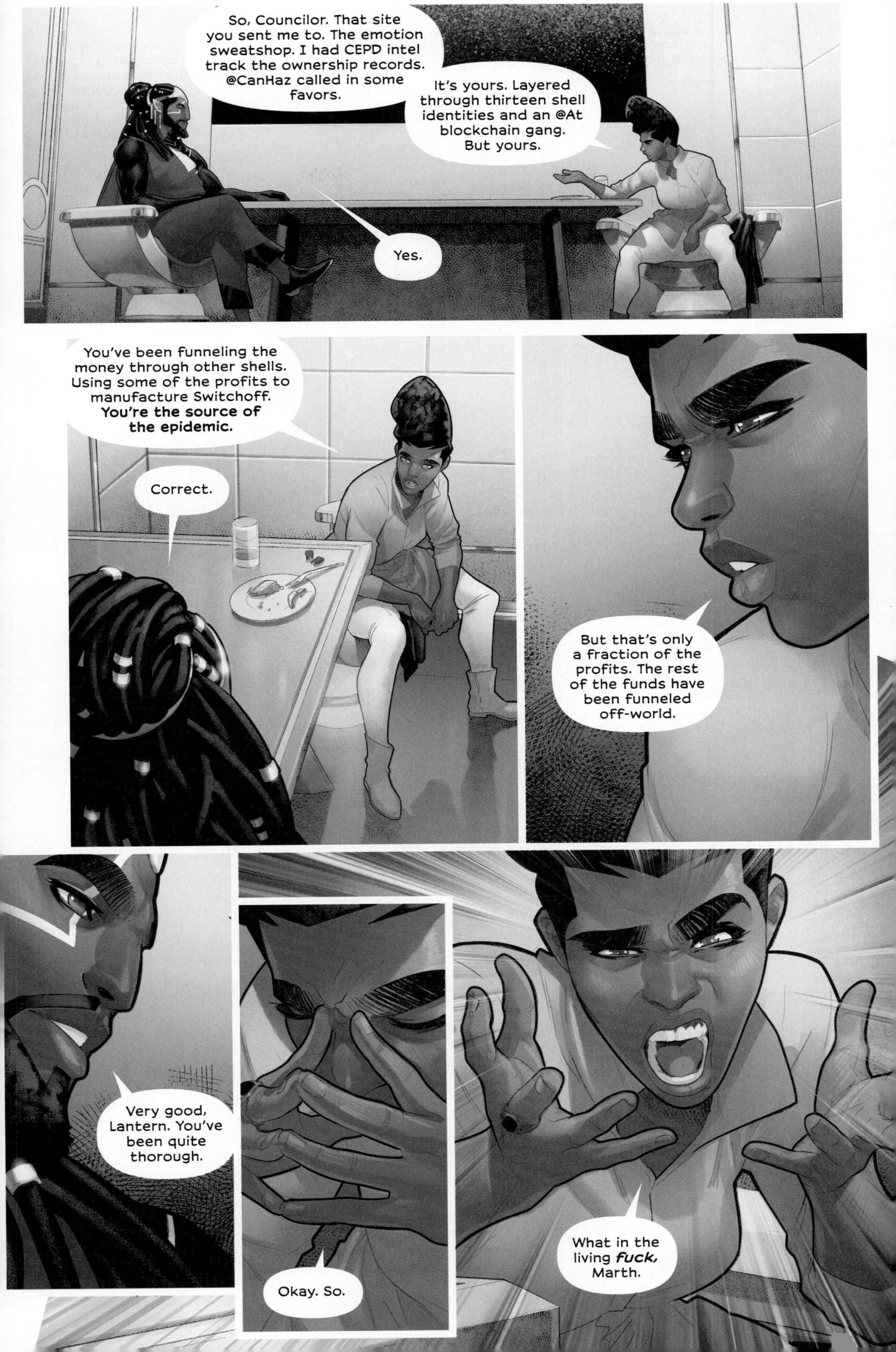
So, Councilor. That site you sent me to. The emotion sweatshop. I had CEPD intel track the ownership records. @CanHaz called in some favors.
It's yours. Layered through thirteen shell identities and an @At blockchain gang. But yours.
Yes.
You've been funneling the money through other shells. Using some of the profits to manufacture Switchoff. **You're the source of the epidemic.**
Correct.
But that's only a fraction of the profits. The rest of the funds have been funneled off-world.
Very good, Lantern. You've been quite thorough.
Okay. So.
What in the living ***fuck,*** Marth.

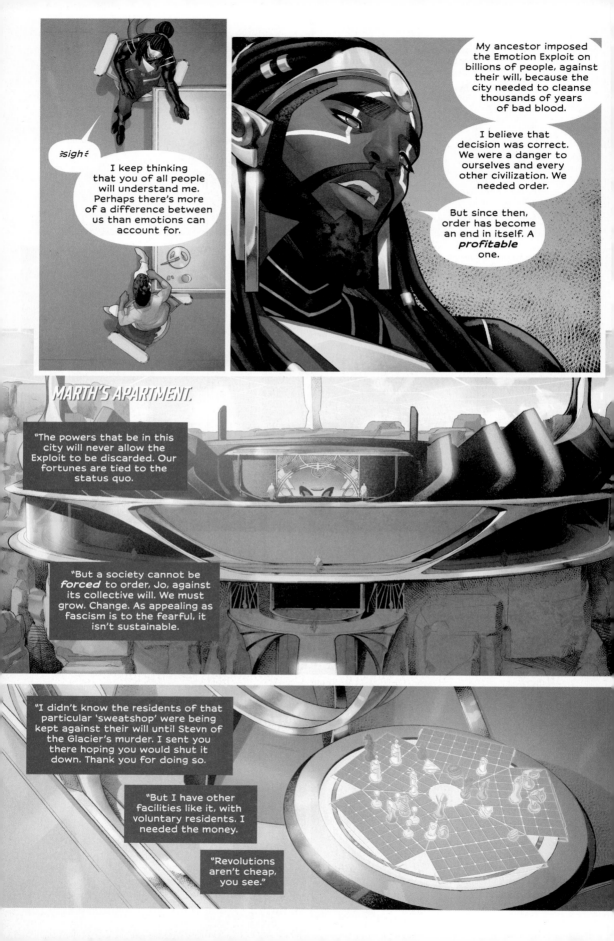

≋sigh≋

I keep thinking that you of all people will understand me. Perhaps there's more of a difference between us than emotions can account for.

My ancestor imposed the Emotion Exploit on billions of people, against their will, because the city needed to cleanse thousands of years of bad blood.

I believe that decision was correct. We were a danger to ourselves and every other civilization. We needed order.

But since then, order has become an end in itself. A *profitable* one.

MARTH'S APARTMENT.

"The powers that be in this city will never allow the Exploit to be discarded. Our fortunes are tied to the status quo.

"But a society cannot be *forced* to order, Jo, against its collective will. We must grow. Change. As appealing as fascism is to the fearful, it isn't sustainable.

"I didn't know the residents of that particular 'sweatshop' were being kept against their will until Stevn of the Glacier's murder. I sent you there hoping you would shut it down. Thank you for doing so.

"But I have other facilities like it, with voluntary residents. I needed the money.

"Revolutions aren't cheap, you see."

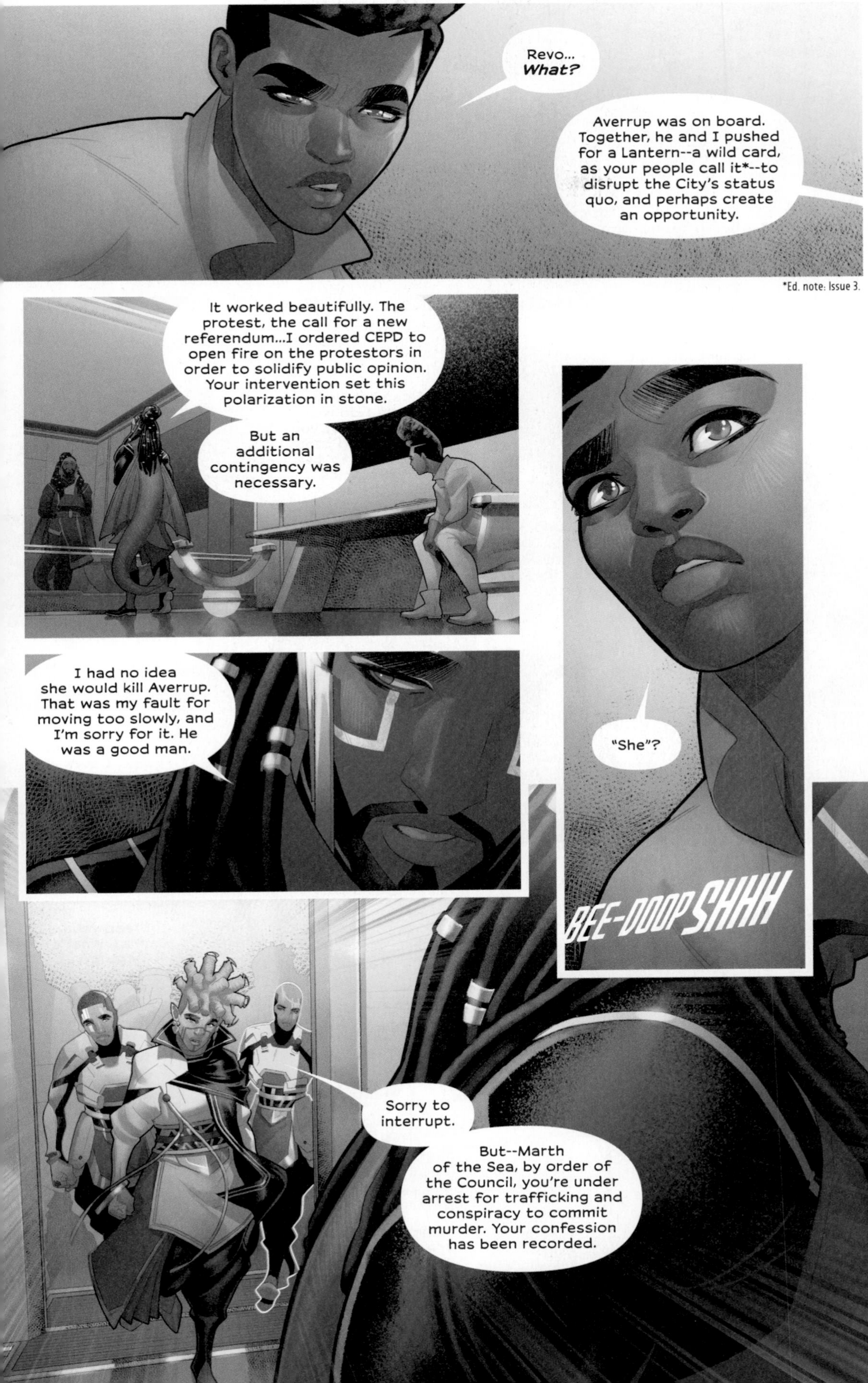

Revo... *What?*
Averrup was on board. Together, he and I pushed for a Lantern--a wild card, as your people call it*--to disrupt the City's status quo, and perhaps create an opportunity.
*Ed. note: Issue 3.
It worked beautifully. The protest, the call for a new referendum...I ordered CEPD to open fire on the protestors in order to solidify public opinion. Your intervention set this polarization in stone.
But an additional contingency was necessary.
"She"?
I had no idea she would kill Averrup. That was my fault for moving too slowly, and I'm sorry for it. He was a good man.
BEE-DOOP SHHH
Sorry to interrupt.
But--Marth of the Sea, by order of the Council, you're under arrest for trafficking and conspiracy to commit murder. Your confession has been recorded.

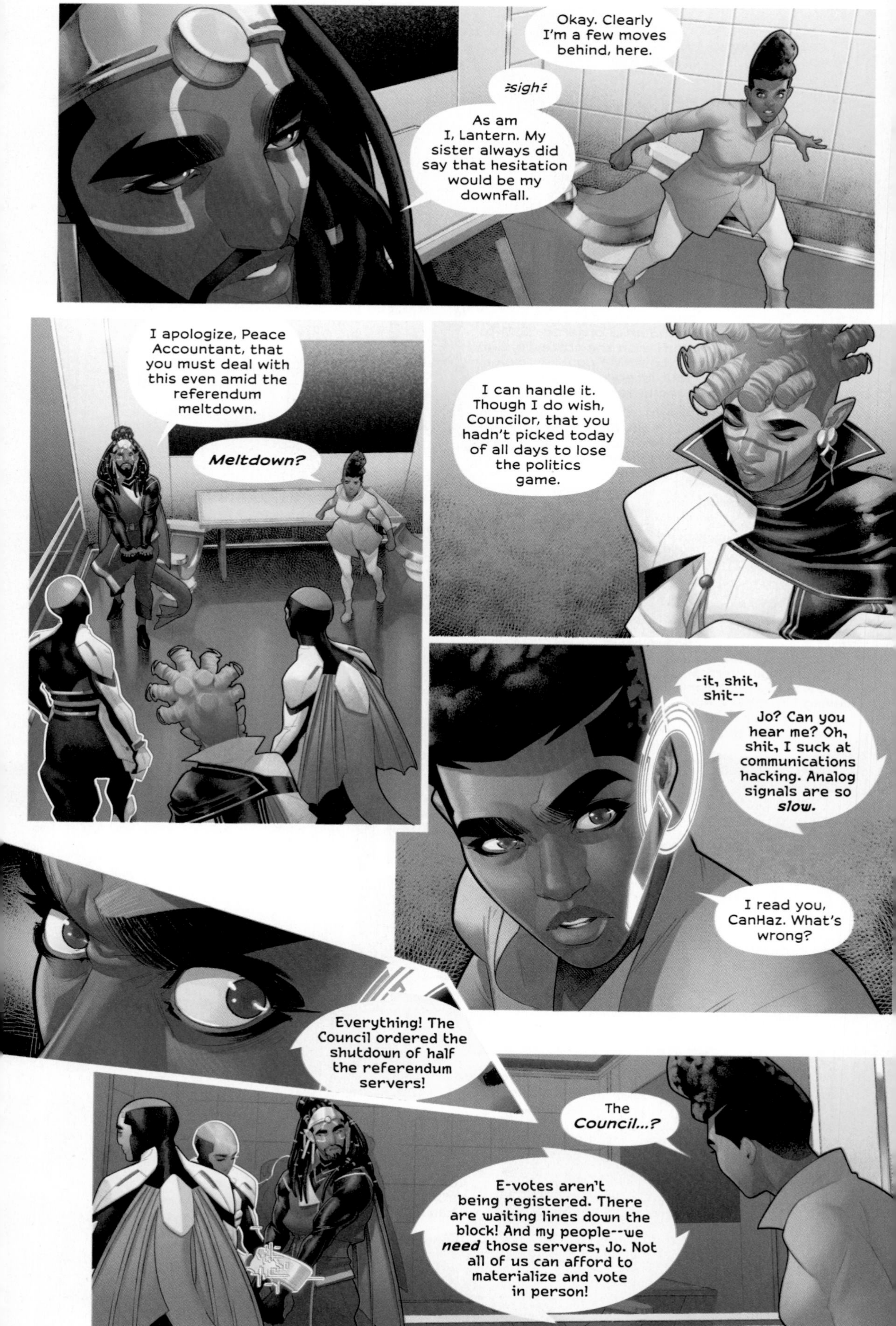
Okay. Clearly I'm a few moves behind, here.
=sigh=
As am I, Lantern. My sister always did say that hesitation would be my downfall.
I apologize, Peace Accountant, that you must deal with this even amid the referendum meltdown.
Meltdown?
I can handle it. Though I do wish, Councilor, that you hadn't picked today of all days to lose the politics game.
-it, shit, shit--
Jo? Can you hear me? Oh, shit, I suck at communications hacking. Analog signals are so slow.
I read you, CanHaz. What's wrong?
Everything! The Council ordered the shutdown of half the referendum servers!
The Council...?
E-votes aren't being registered. There are waiting lines down the block! And my people--we need those servers, Jo. Not all of us can afford to materialize and vote in person!

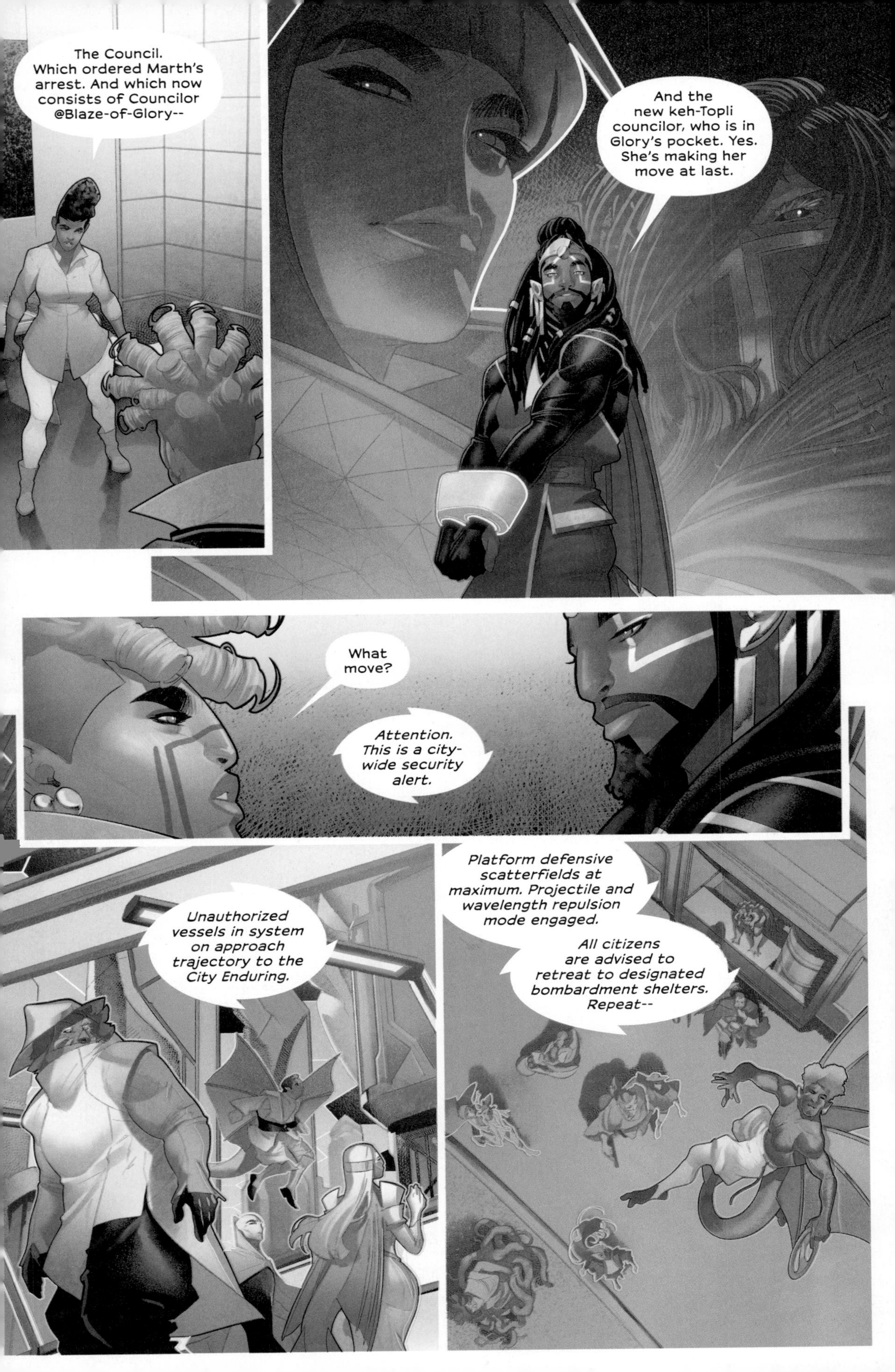
The Council. Which ordered Marth's arrest. And which now consists of Councilor @Blaze-of-Glory--
And the new keh-Topli councilor, who is in Glory's pocket. Yes. She's making her move at last.
What move?
Attention. This is a city-wide security alert.
Unauthorized vessels in system on approach trajectory to the City Enduring.
Platform defensive scatterfields at maximum. Projectile and wavelength repulsion mode engaged.
All citizens are advised to retreat to designated bombardment shelters. Repeat--

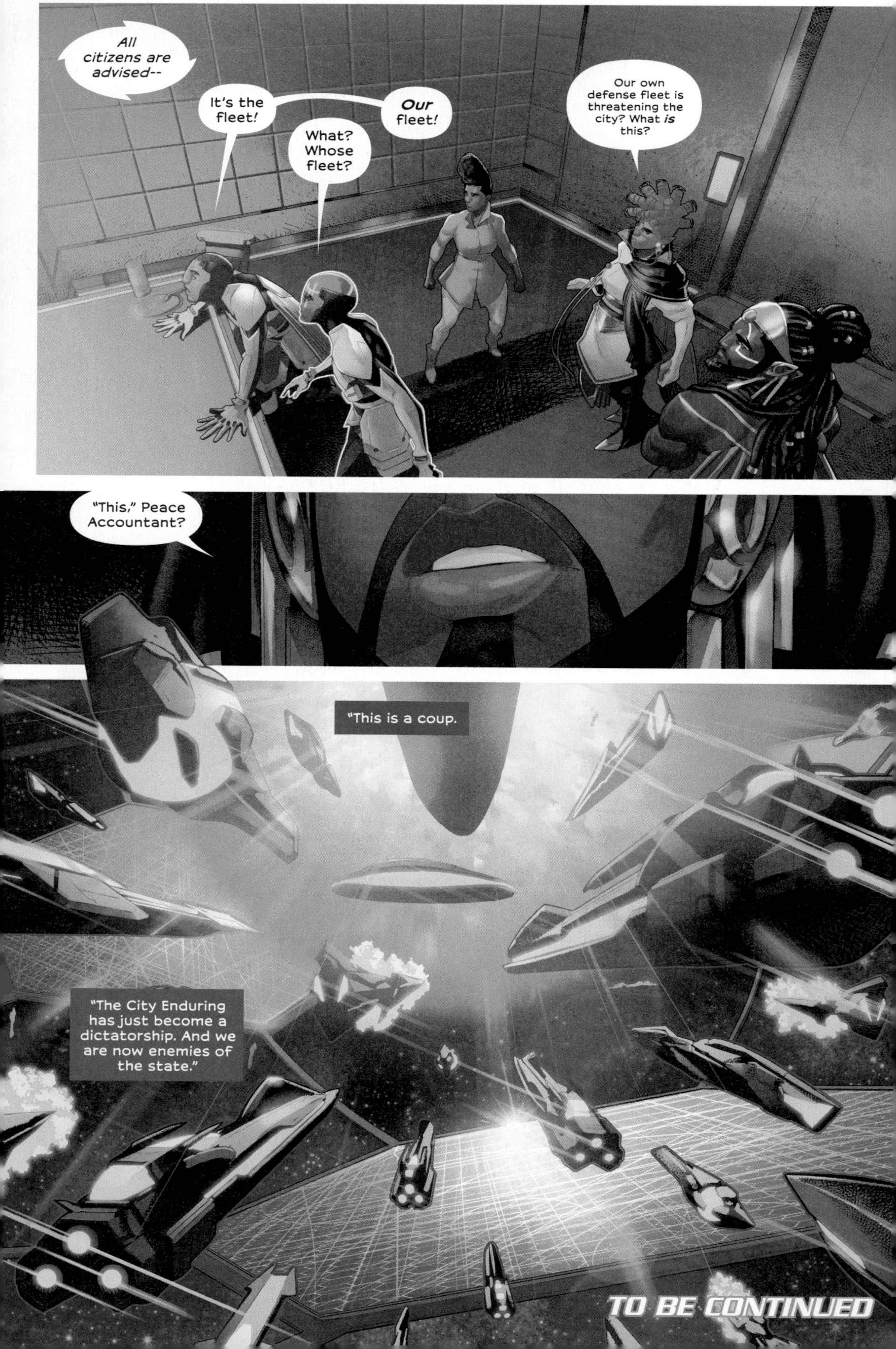
All citizens are advised--
It's the fleet!
Our fleet!
What? Whose fleet?
Our own defense fleet is threatening the city? What is this?
"This," Peace Accountant?
"This is a coup.
"The City Enduring has just become a dictatorship. And we are now enemies of the state."
TO BE CONTINUED

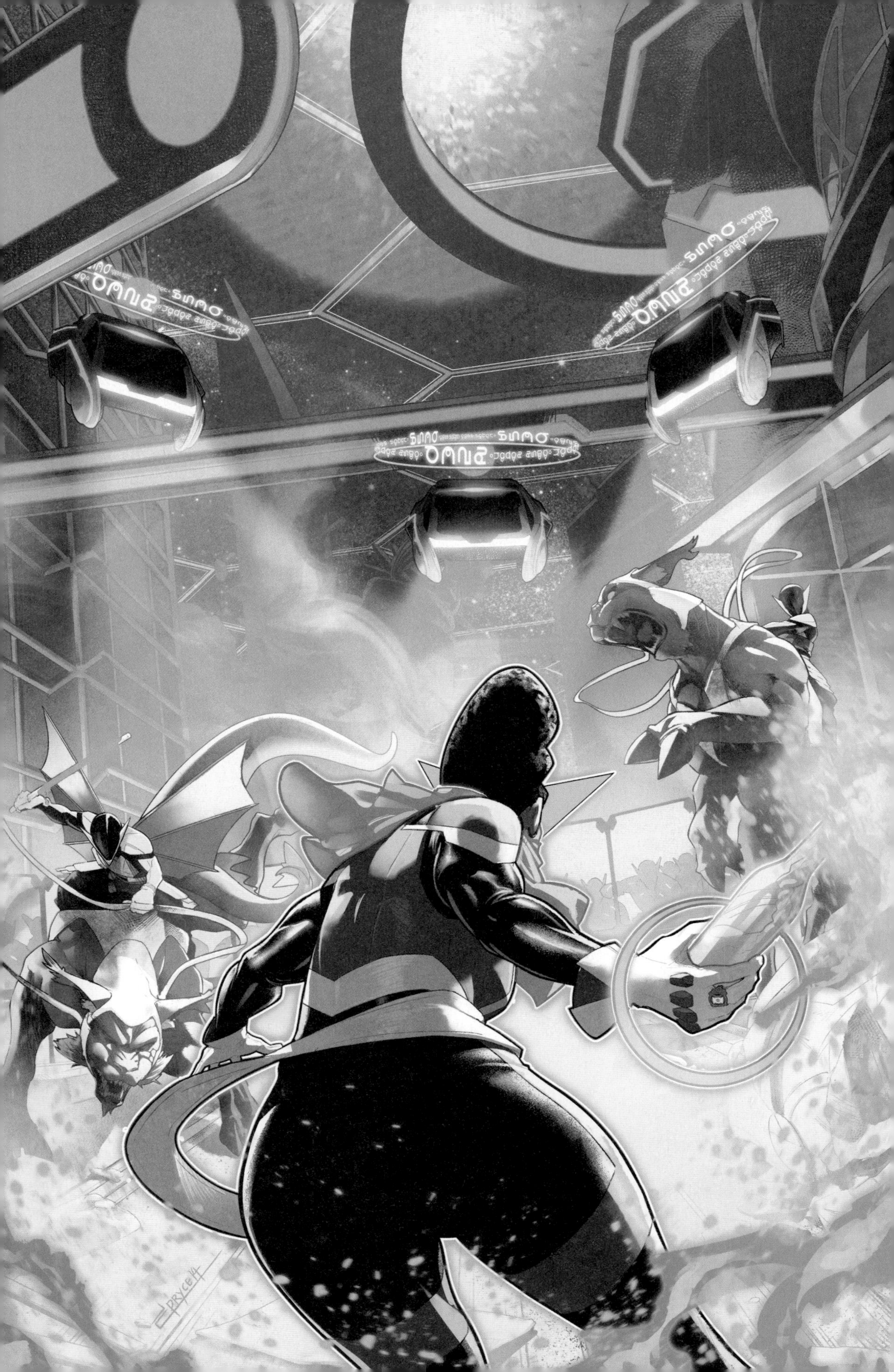

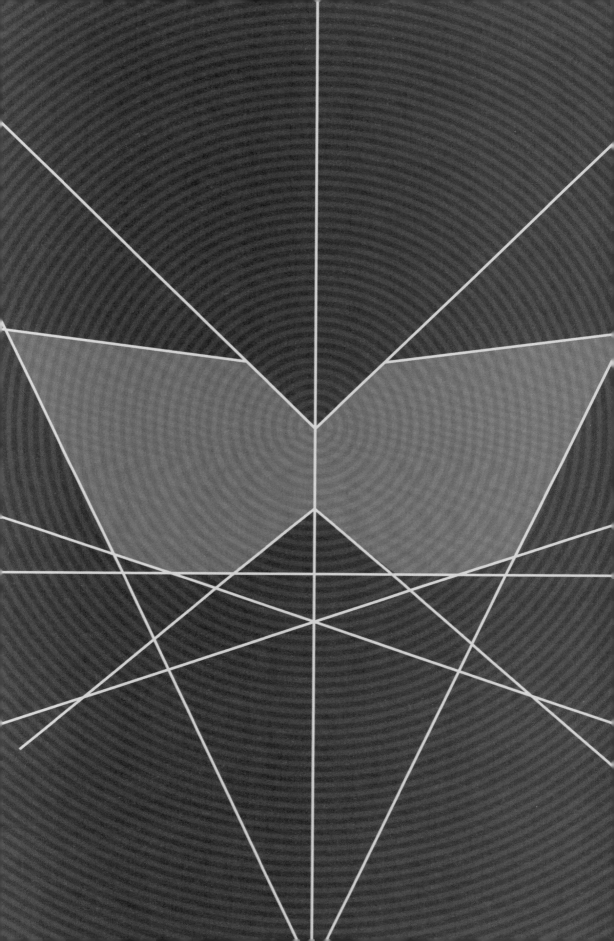

OAN INTELLIGENCE EXTRAJURISDICTIONAL FILE ARCHIVE
THE CITY ENDURING: RECOMMENDATION REGARDING
ASSIGNMENT
TRANSLATION: ENGLISH
SECURITY: RECOMMENDED GUARDIAN EYES ONLY

〖CONVERSATION PARTICIPANTS REDACTED FOR REASONS OF INTERNAL SECURITY〗

GUARDIAN 〖REDACTED, DESIGNATION 1〗: ON THE EVE OF OUR DECISION REGARDING THE
CITY ENDURING'S REQUEST FOR A GREEN LANTERN, WE FIND THE CITY CONSUMED BY
CHAOS--AND ONE OF OUR LANTERNS ALREADY AT THE CORE OF IT. SHE ISN'T ON THE
ASSIGNMENT ROLLS. HER RING IS NONSTANDARD; WHO DESIGNED IT? WHO IS
RESPONSIBLE FOR--

GUARDIAN 〖REDACTED, DESIGNATION 2〗: I AM.

GUARDIAN 1: WHY WOULD YOU DO THIS?

GUARDIAN 2: THE REST OF YOU WERE TAKING TOO LONG.

GUARDIAN 〖REDACTED, DESIGNATION 3〗: BUT WE HAVE NO TRUE JURISDICTION IN THAT
REGION. WE MUST REMOVE HER, AT ONCE, BEFORE WE'RE BLAMED FOR--

GUARDIAN 2: DO THAT AND EVERY SIMULATION SUGGESTS THE CITY WILL TRANSFORM INTO
AN AGGRESSOR EMPIRE, THREATENING PEACE ON A GALACTIC SCALE AND ULTIMATELY
REQUIRING THE INTERVENTION OF THE ENTIRE CORPS. AND GIVEN THE HISTORY OF THE
TRILOGY RACES, WE WOULD HAVE NO CHOICE BUT TO WIPE THEM OUT ENTIRELY. ANYTHING
LESS AND THEY WILL REBUILD, STRONGER--THEN COME FOR US.

〖SIXTEEN SECONDS OF SILENCE ARE RECORDED.〗

GUARDIAN 2: LEAVE HER ALONE, FOR THE GLOW'S SAKE. SHE'S A GREEN LANTERN.
SHE'LL GET IT DONE.

"In order to rise
From its own ashes
A phoenix
First
Must
Burn."
—Octavia Butler

Story: **N.K. JEMISIN**   Art, Color, and Cover: **JAMAL CAMPBELL**
Lettering: **DERON BENNETT**   Variant Cover: **MIRKA ANDOLFO**
Associate Editor: **MAGGIE HOWELL** Editors: **ANDY KHOURI & JAMIE S. RICH**
DC's Young Animal Curated by **GERARD WAY**

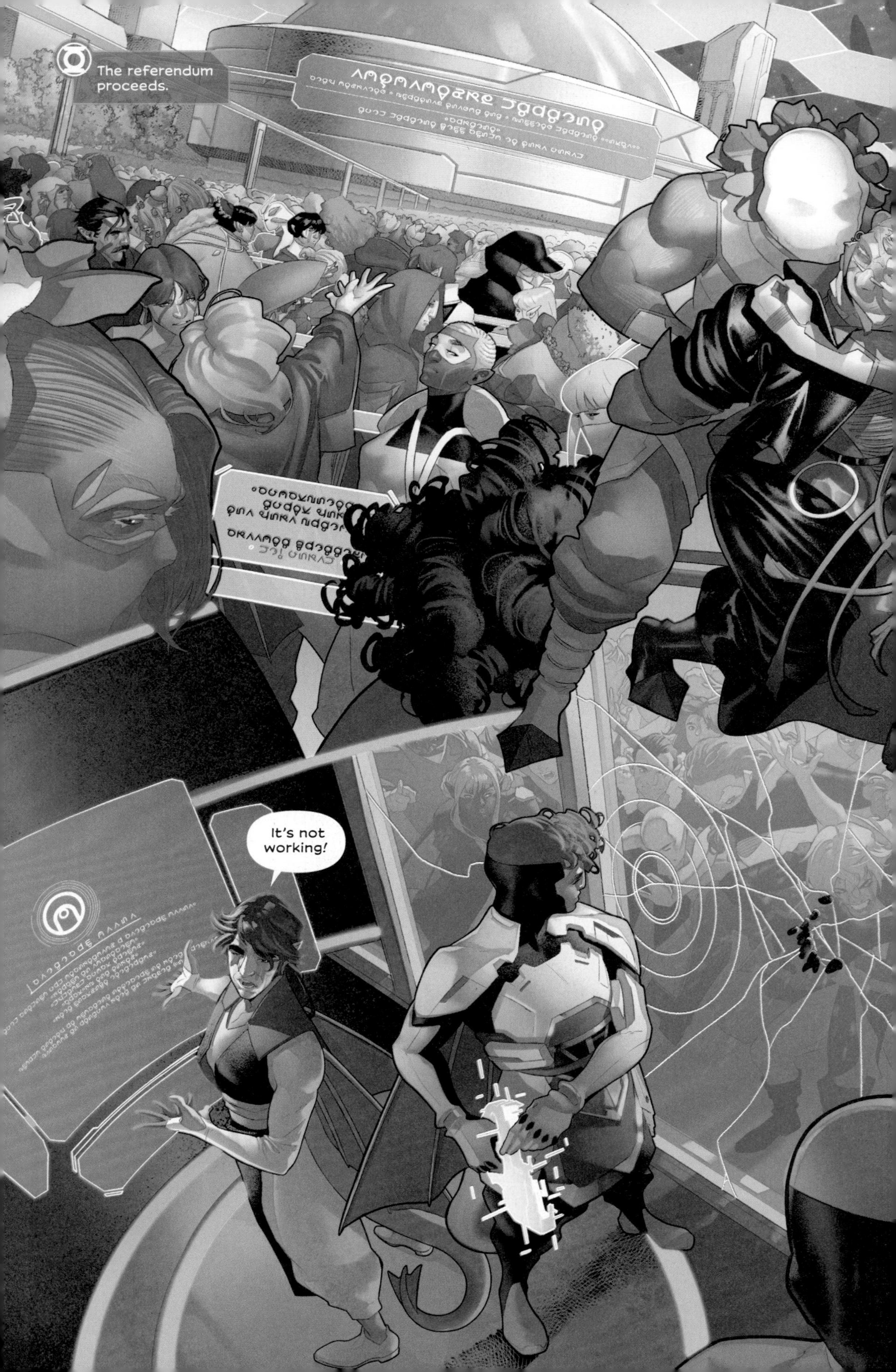

The referendum proceeds.
It's not working!

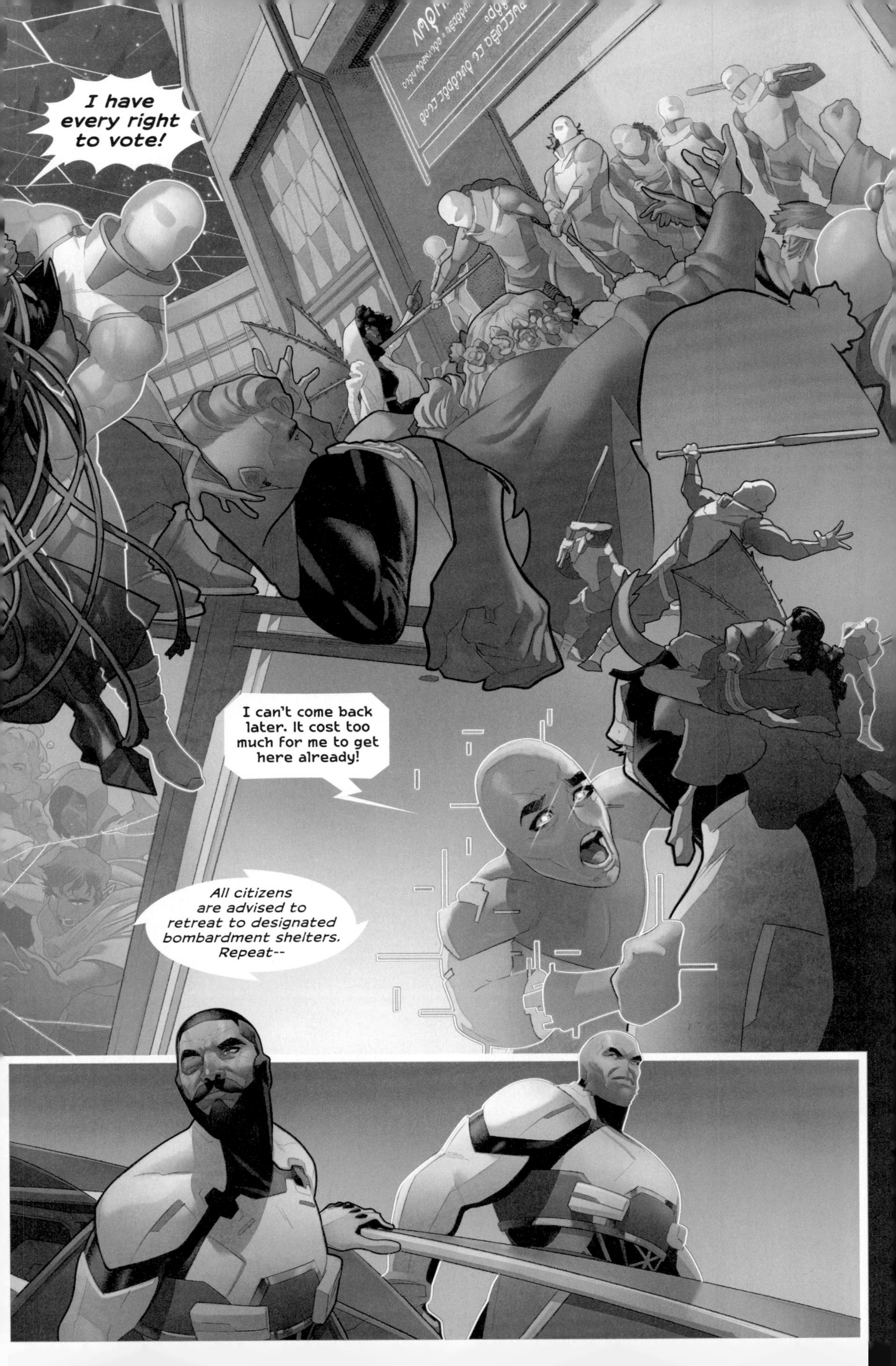
I have every right to vote!
I can't come back later. It cost too much for me to get here already!
All citizens are advised to retreat to designated bombardment shelters. Repeat--

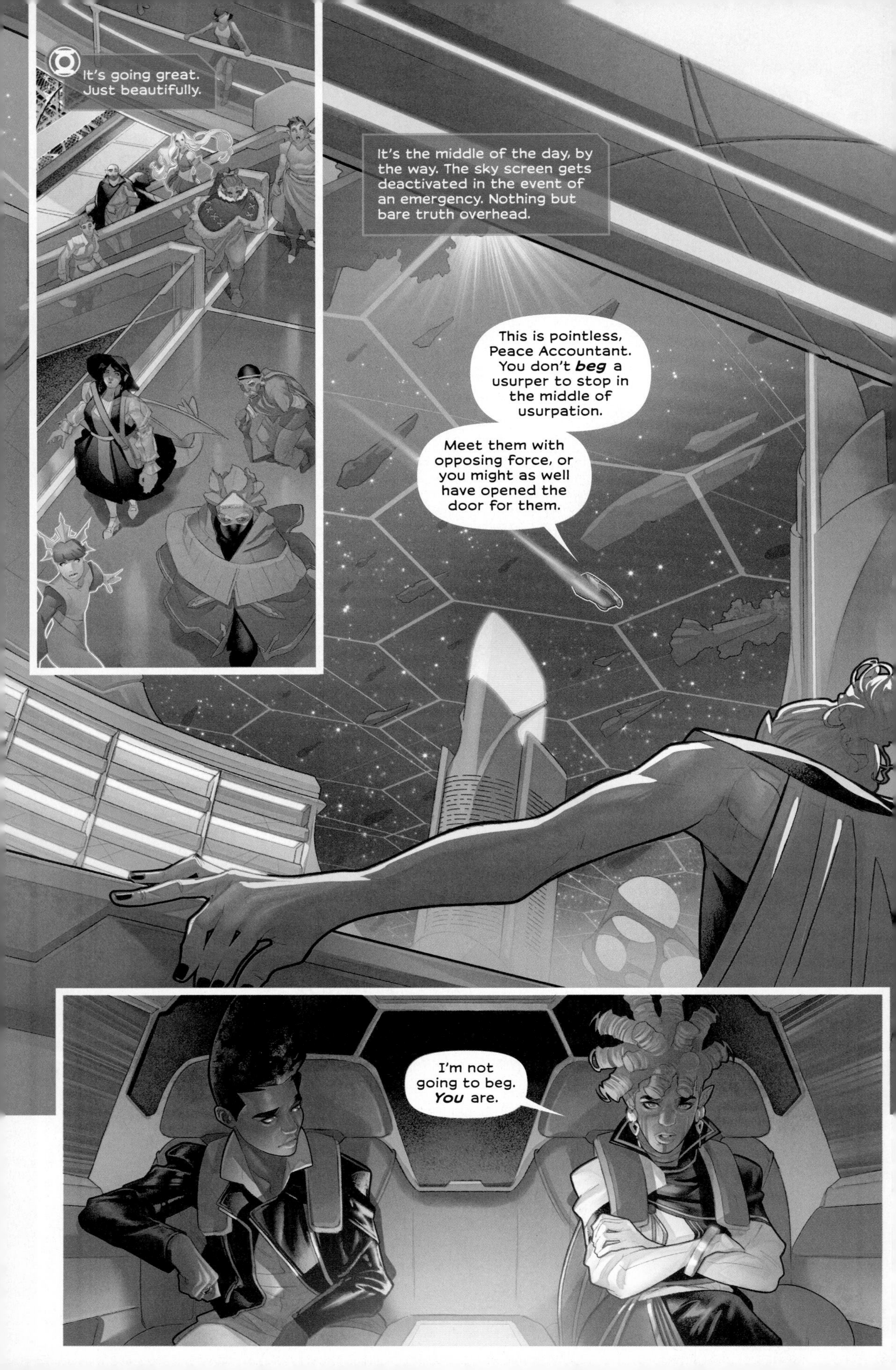
It's going great.
Just beautifully.
It's the middle of the day, by the way. The sky screen gets deactivated in the event of an emergency. Nothing but bare truth overhead.
This is pointless, Peace Accountant. You don't *beg* a usurper to stop in the middle of usurpation.
Meet them with opposing force, or you might as well have opened the door for them.
I'm not going to beg. *You* are.

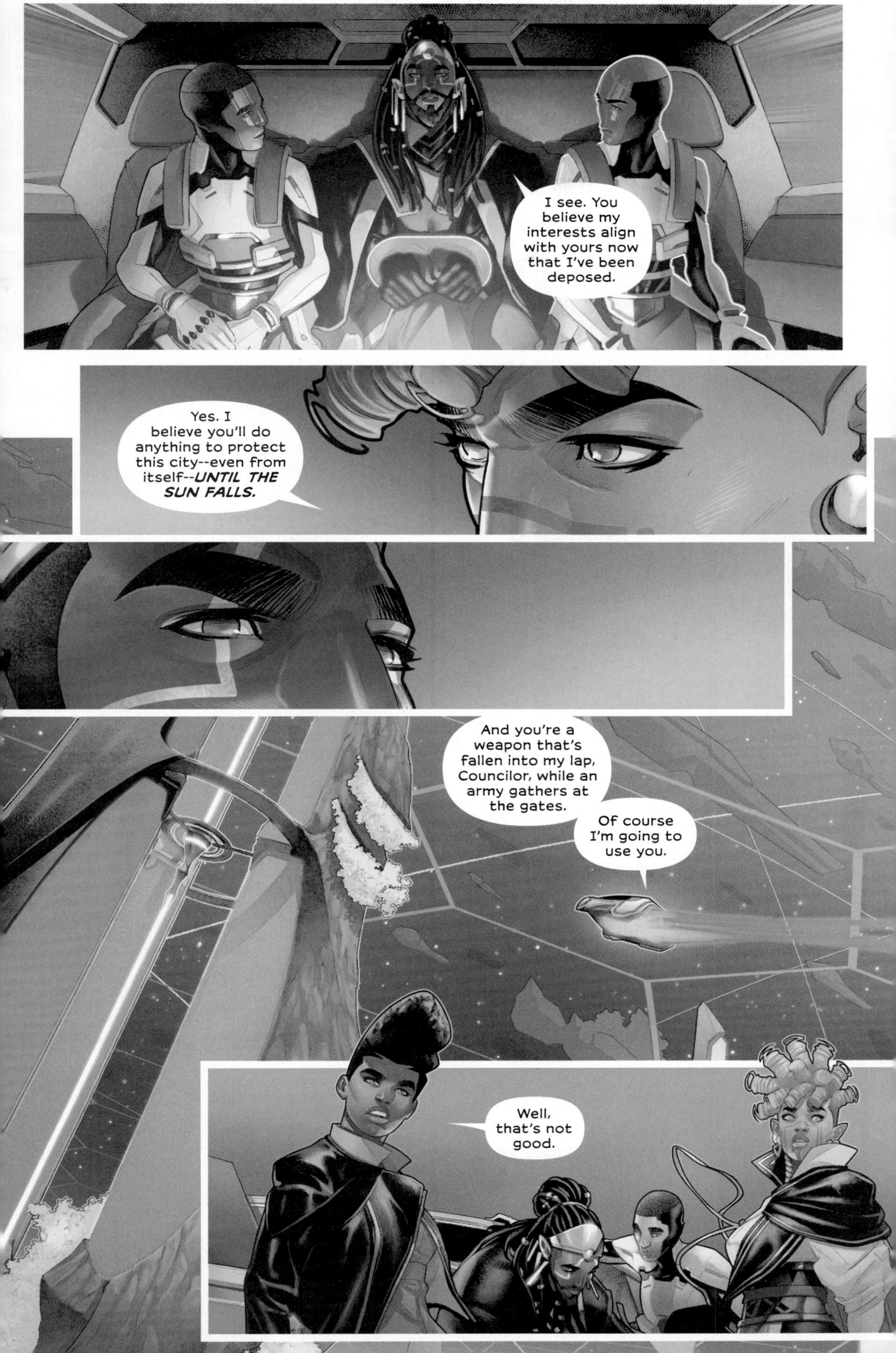
I see. You believe my interests align with yours now that I've been deposed.
Yes. I believe you'll do anything to protect this city--even from itself--*UNTIL THE SUN FALLS.*
And you're a weapon that's fallen into my lap, Councilor, while an army gathers at the gates.
Of course I'm going to use you.
Well, that's not good.

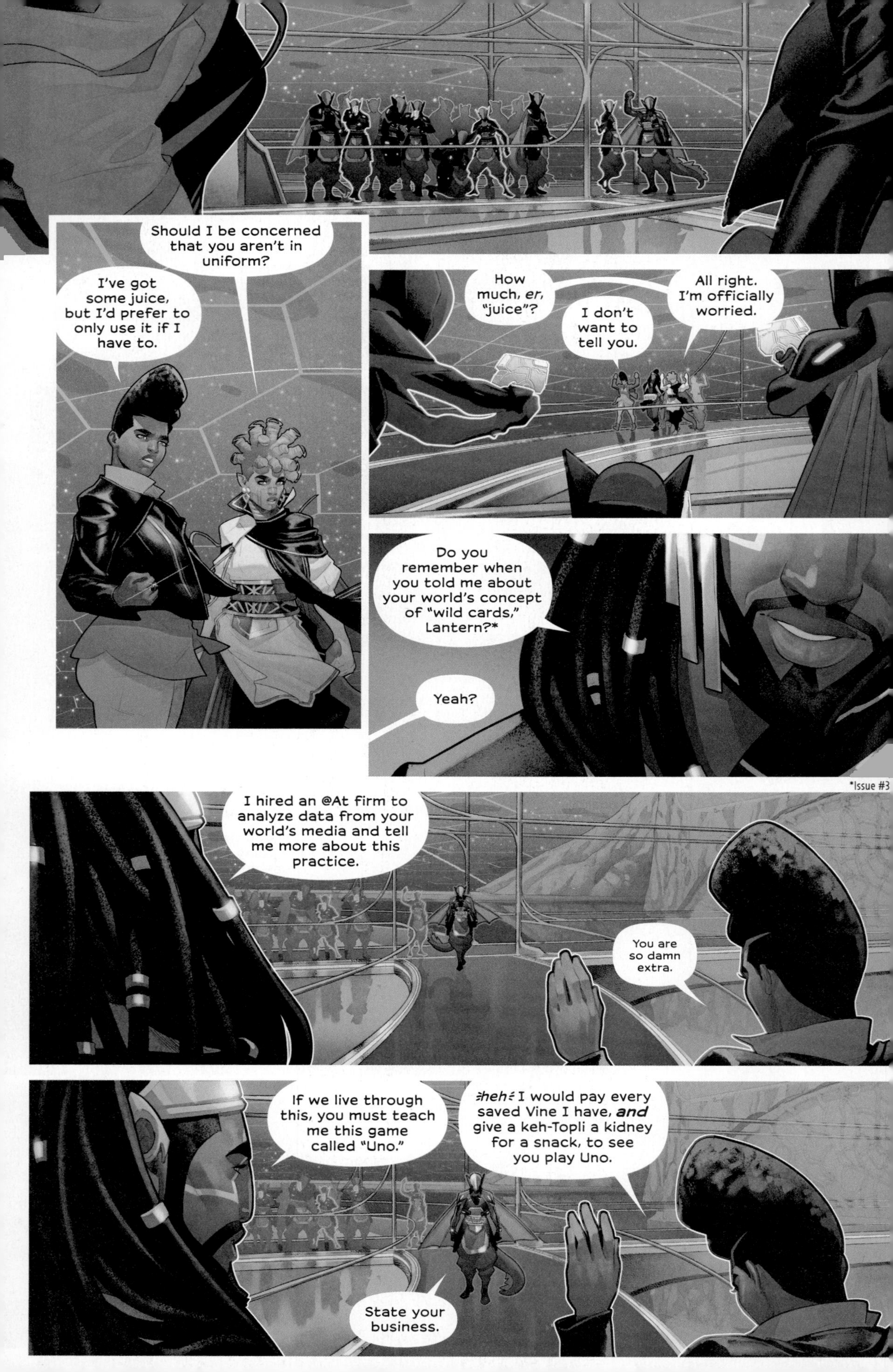
Should I be concerned that you aren't in uniform?
I've got some juice, but I'd prefer to only use it if I have to.
How much, *er*, "juice"?
I don't want to tell you.
All right. I'm officially worried.
Do you remember when you told me about your world's concept of "wild cards," Lantern?*
Yeah?
*Issue #3
I hired an @At firm to analyze data from your world's media and tell me more about this practice.
You are so damn extra.
If we live through this, you must teach me this game called "Uno."
heh I would pay every saved Vine I have, ***and*** give a keh-Topli a kidney for a snack, to see you play Uno.
State your business.

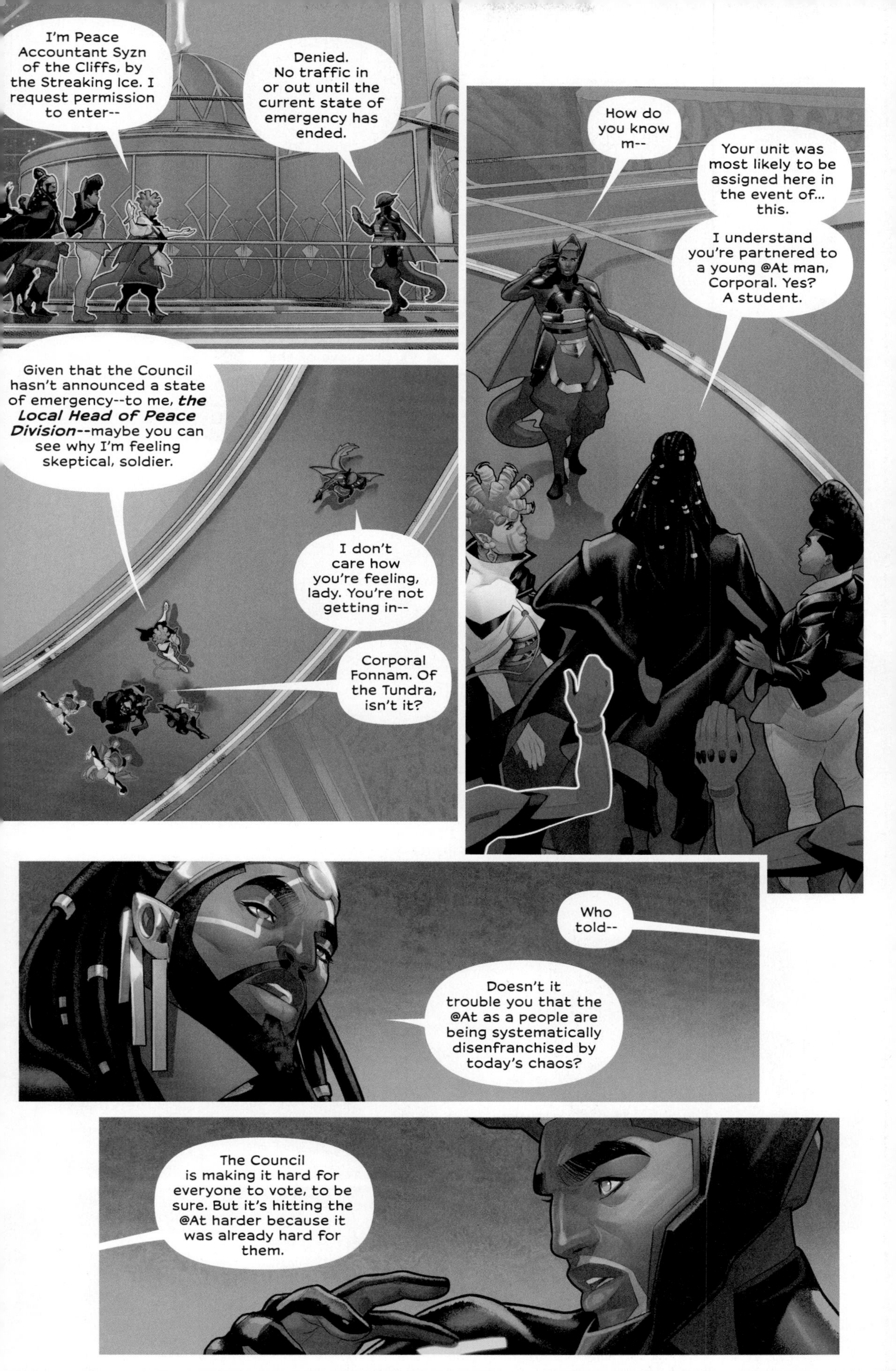
I'm Peace Accountant Syzn of the Cliffs, by the Streaking Ice. I request permission to enter--
Denied. No traffic in or out until the current state of emergency has ended.
Given that the Council hasn't announced a state of emergency--to me, *the Local Head of Peace Division*--maybe you can see why I'm feeling skeptical, soldier.
I don't care how you're feeling, lady. You're not getting in--
Corporal Fonnam. Of the Tundra, isn't it?
How do you know m--
Your unit was most likely to be assigned here in the event of... this.
I understand you're partnered to a young @At man, Corporal. Yes? A student.
Who told--
Doesn't it trouble you that the @At as a people are being systematically disenfranchised by today's chaos?
The Council is making it hard for everyone to vote, to be sure. But it's hitting the @At harder because it was already hard for them.

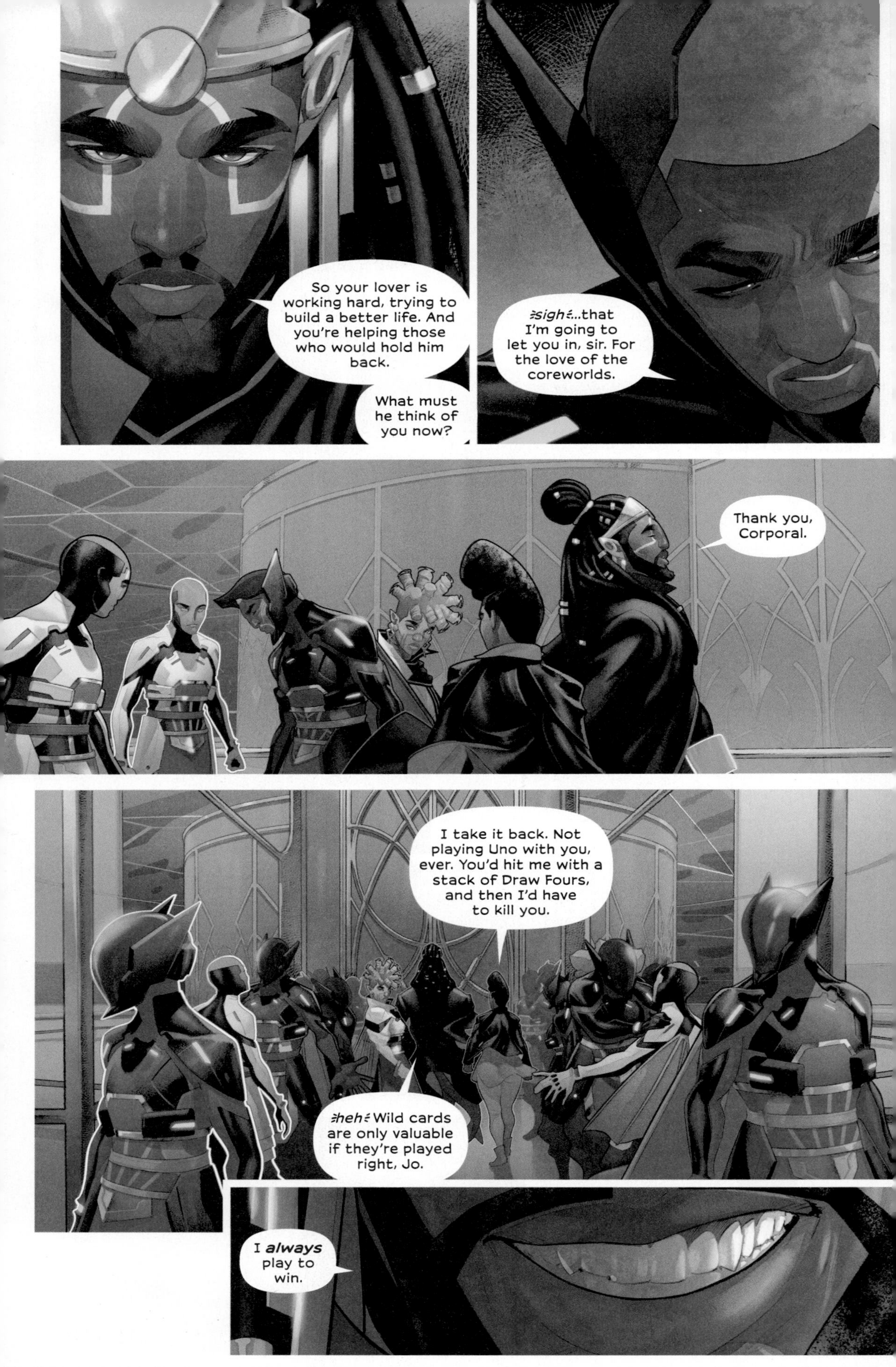
So your lover is working hard, trying to build a better life. And you're helping those who would hold him back.
What must he think of you now?
sigh...that I'm going to let you in, sir. For the love of the coreworlds.
Thank you, Corporal.
I take it back. Not playing Uno with you, ever. You'd hit me with a stack of Draw Fours, and then I'd have to kill you.
heh Wild cards are only valuable if they're played right, Jo.
I *always* play to win.

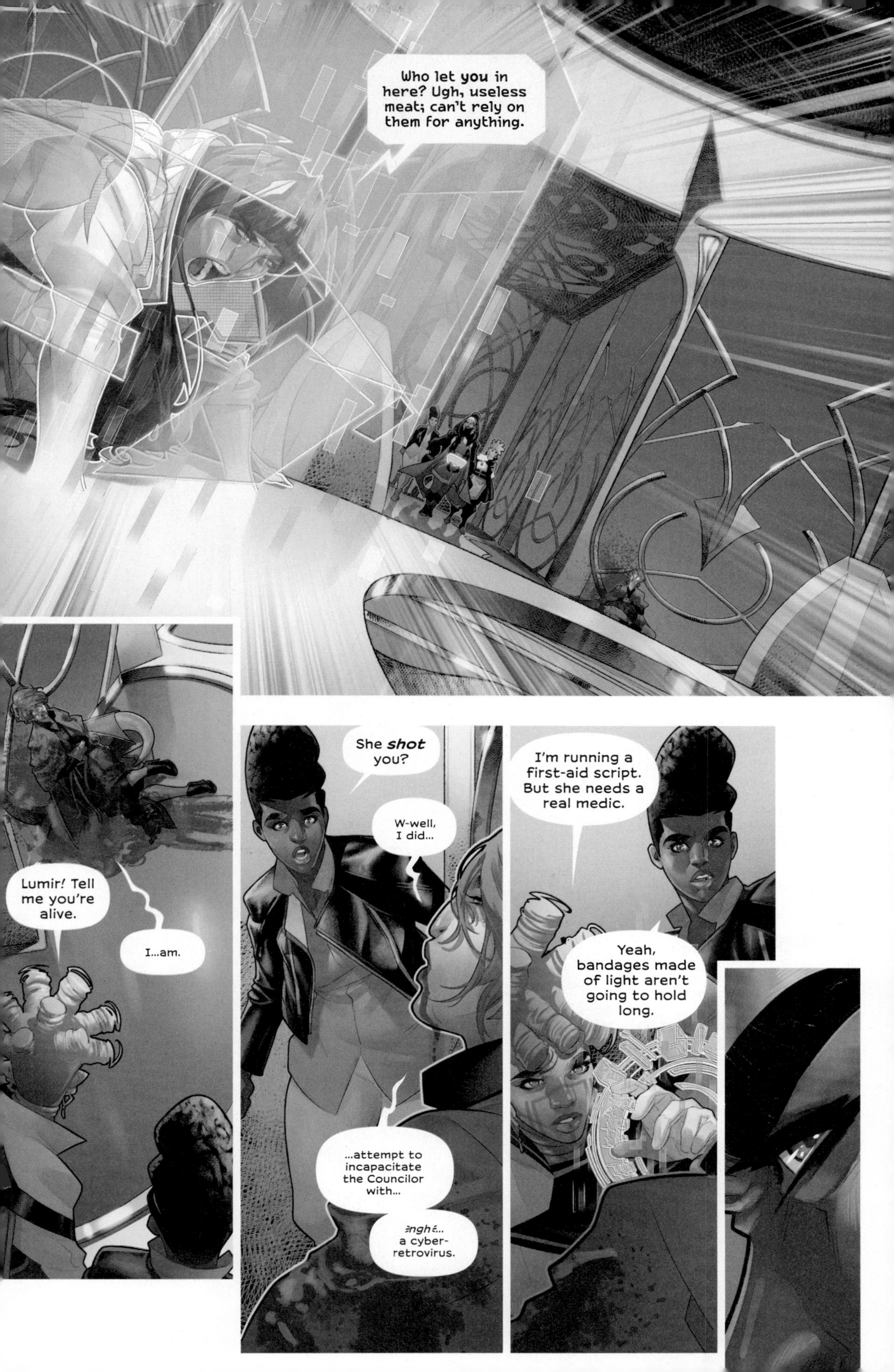
Who let you in here? Ugh, useless meat; can't rely on them for anything.
Lumir! Tell me you're alive.
I...am.
She *shot* you?
W-well, I did...
...attempt to incapacitate the Councilor with...
ngh... a cyber-retrovirus.
I'm running a first-aid script. But she needs a real medic.
Yeah, bandages made of light aren't going to hold long.

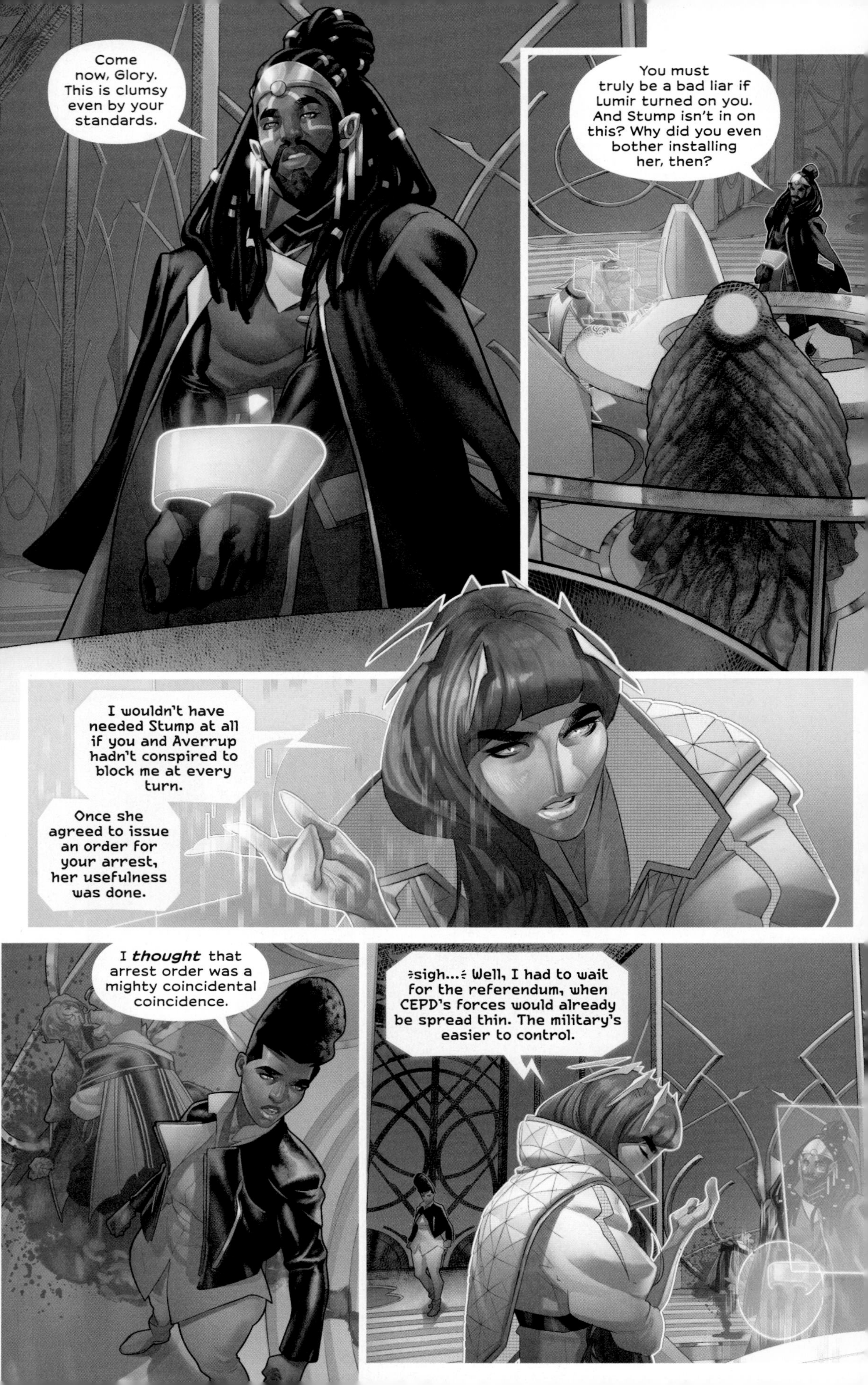
Come now, Glory. This is clumsy even by your standards.
You must truly be a bad liar if Lumir turned on you. And Stump isn't in on this? Why did you even bother installing her, then?
I wouldn't have needed Stump at all if you and Averrup hadn't conspired to block me at every turn.
Once she agreed to issue an order for your arrest, her usefulness was done.
I *thought* that arrest order was a mighty coincidental coincidence.
⋿sigh...⋹ Well, I had to wait for the referendum, when CEPD's forces would already be spread thin. The military's easier to control.

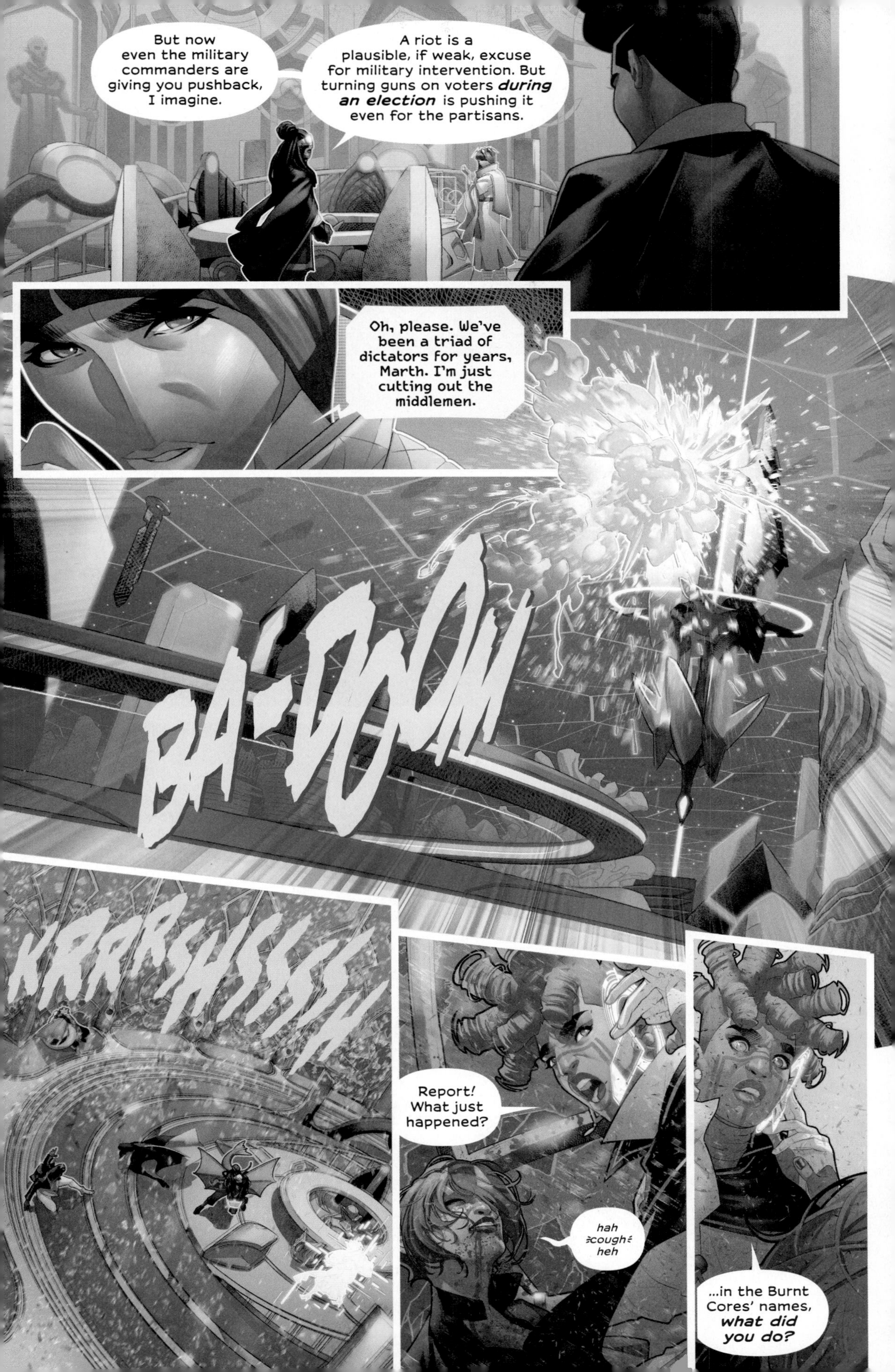
But now even the military commanders are giving you pushback, I imagine.
A riot is a plausible, if weak, excuse for military intervention. But turning guns on voters *during an election* is pushing it even for the partisans.
Oh, please. We've been a triad of dictators for years, Marth. I'm just cutting out the middlemen.
BA-DOOM
KRRRSHSSSH
Report! What just happened?
hah
≈cough≈
heh
...in the Burnt Cores' names, *what did you do?*

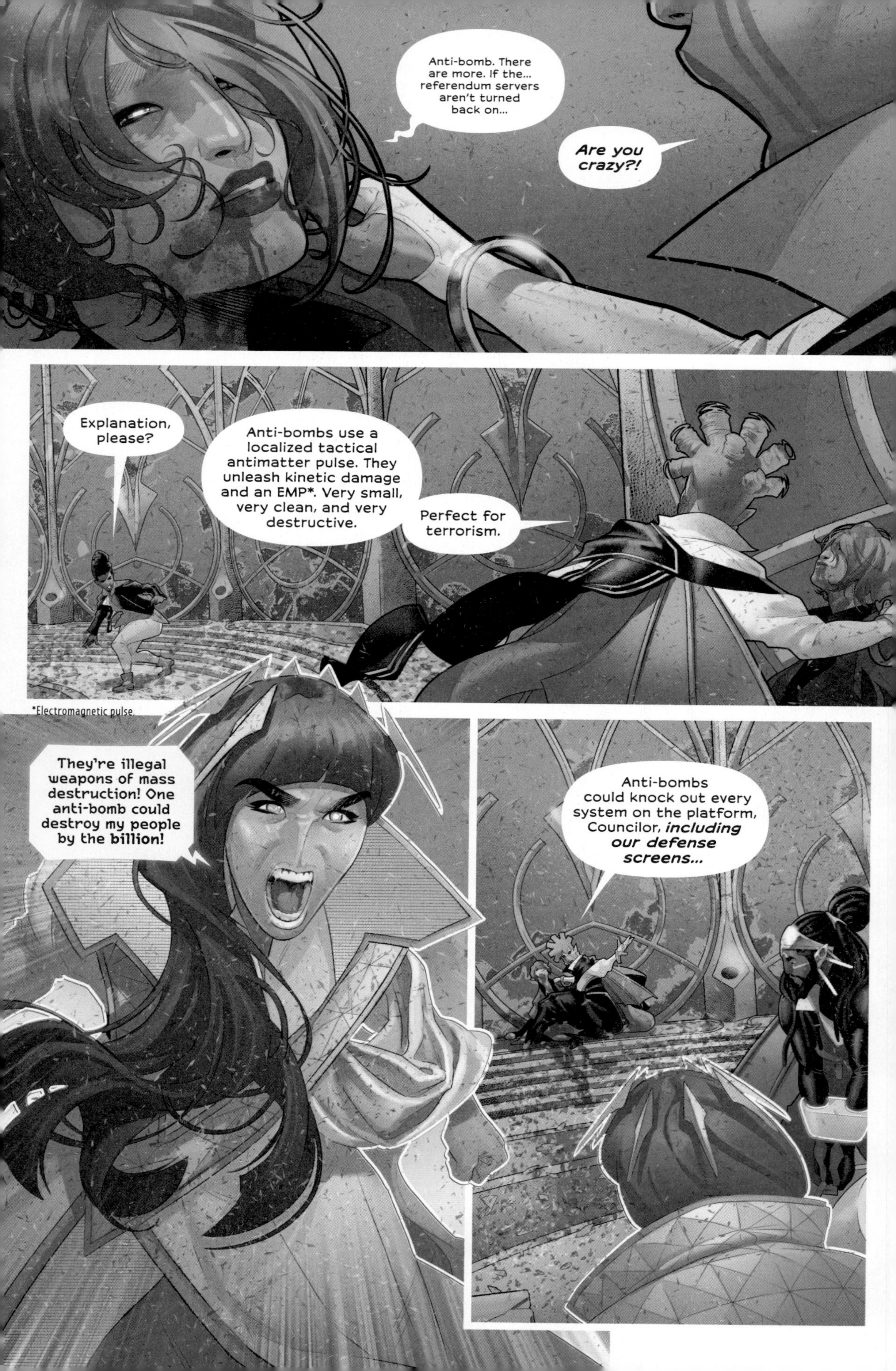
Anti-bomb. There are more. If the... referendum servers aren't turned back on...
Are you crazy?!
Explanation, please?
Anti-bombs use a localized tactical antimatter pulse. They unleash kinetic damage and an EMP*. Very small, very clean, and very destructive.
Perfect for terrorism.
*Electromagnetic pulse.
They're illegal weapons of mass destruction! One anti-bomb could destroy my people by the **billion!**
Anti-bombs could knock out every system on the platform, Councilor, *including our defense screens...*

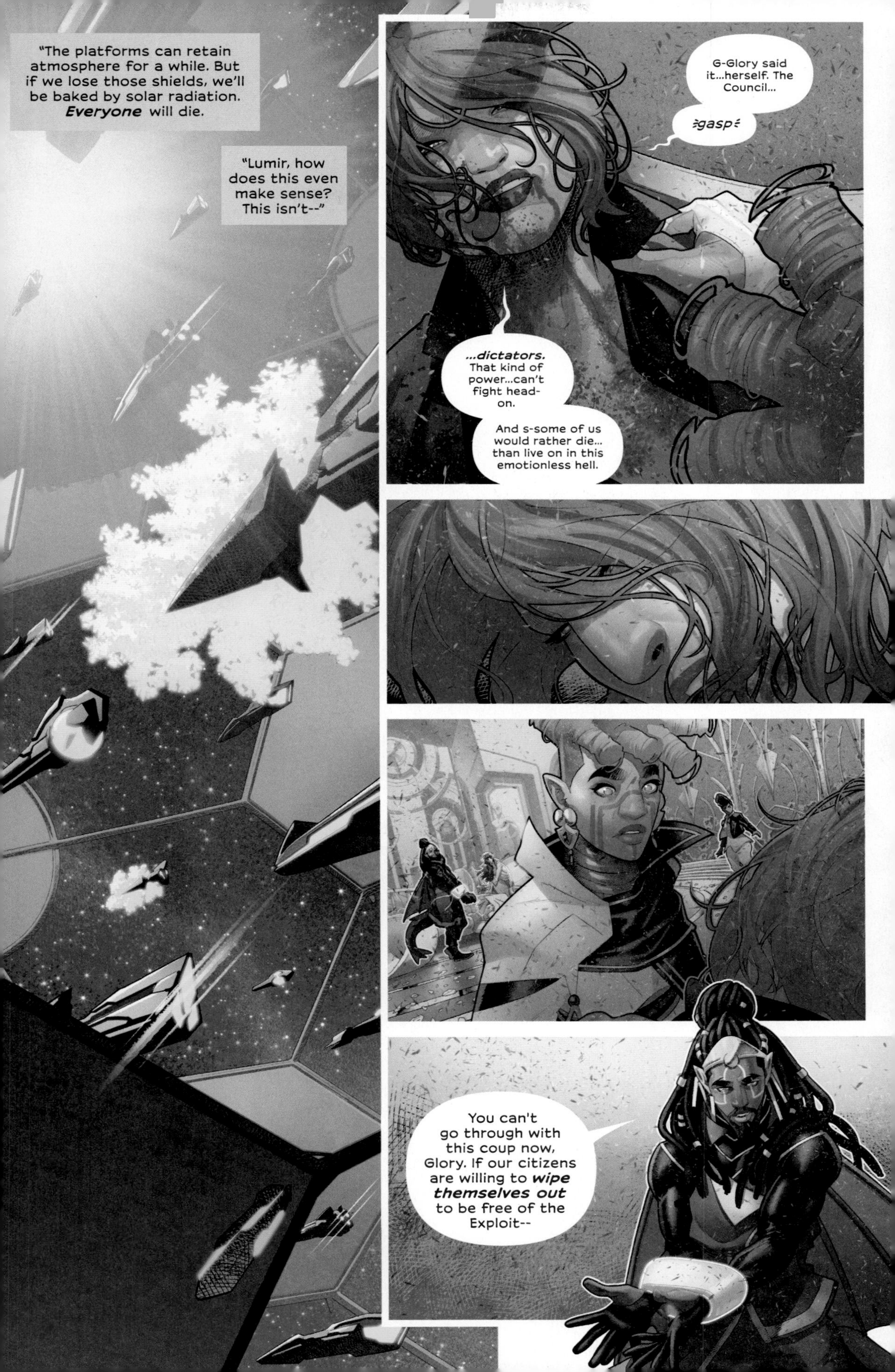
"The platforms can retain atmosphere for a while. But if we lose those shields, we'll be baked by solar radiation. *Everyone* will die.
"Lumir, how does this even make sense? This isn't--"
G-Glory said it...herself. The Council...
gasp
...dictators. That kind of power...can't fight head-on.
And s-some of us would rather die... than live on in this emotionless hell.
You can't go through with this coup now, Glory. If our citizens are willing to ***wipe themselves out*** to be free of the Exploit--

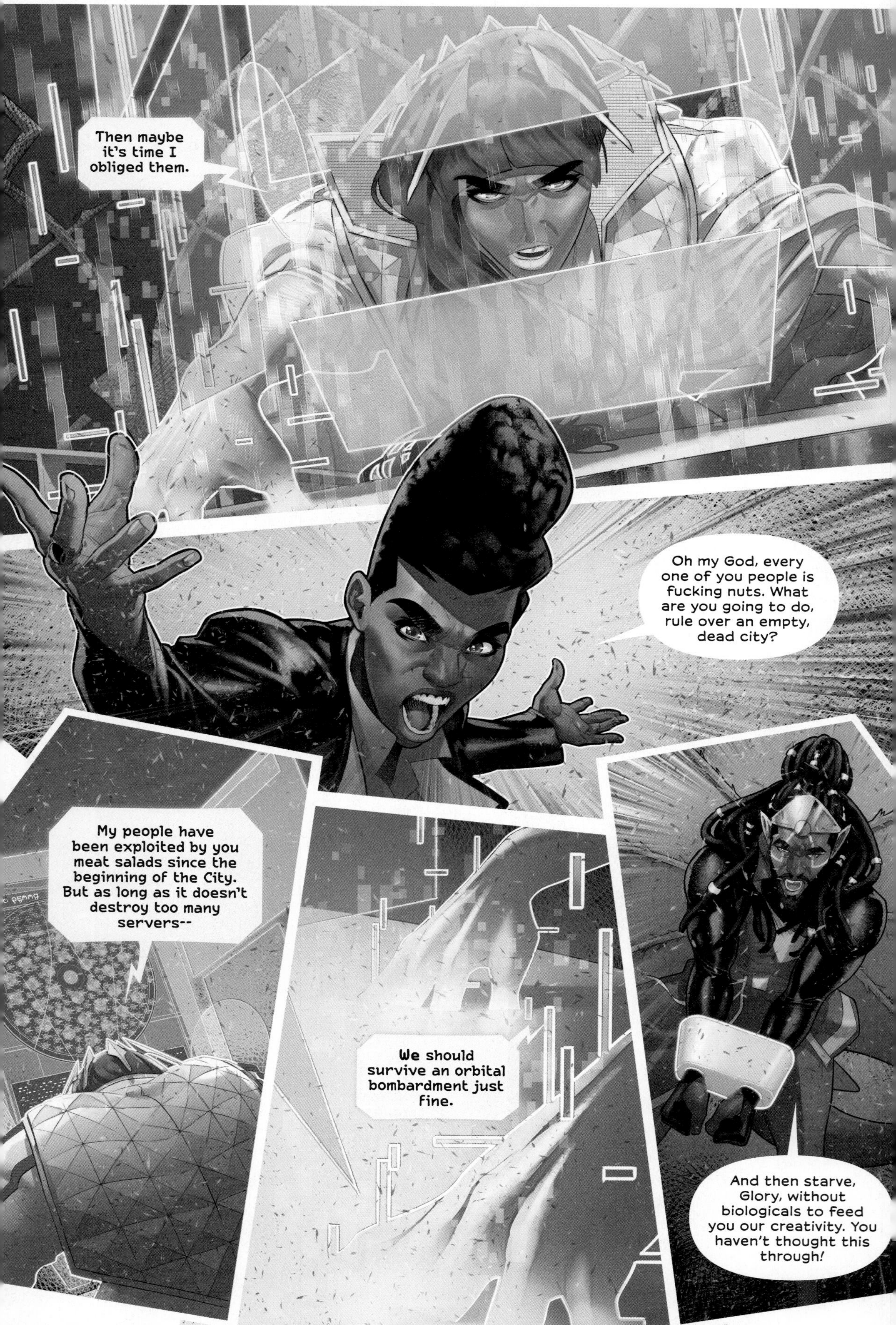

Then maybe it's time I obliged them.
Oh my God, every one of you people is fucking nuts. What are you going to do, rule over an empty, dead city?
My people have been exploited by you meat salads since the beginning of the City. But as long as it doesn't destroy too many servers--
We should survive an orbital bombardment just fine.
And then starve, Glory, without biologicals to feed you our creativity. You haven't thought this through!

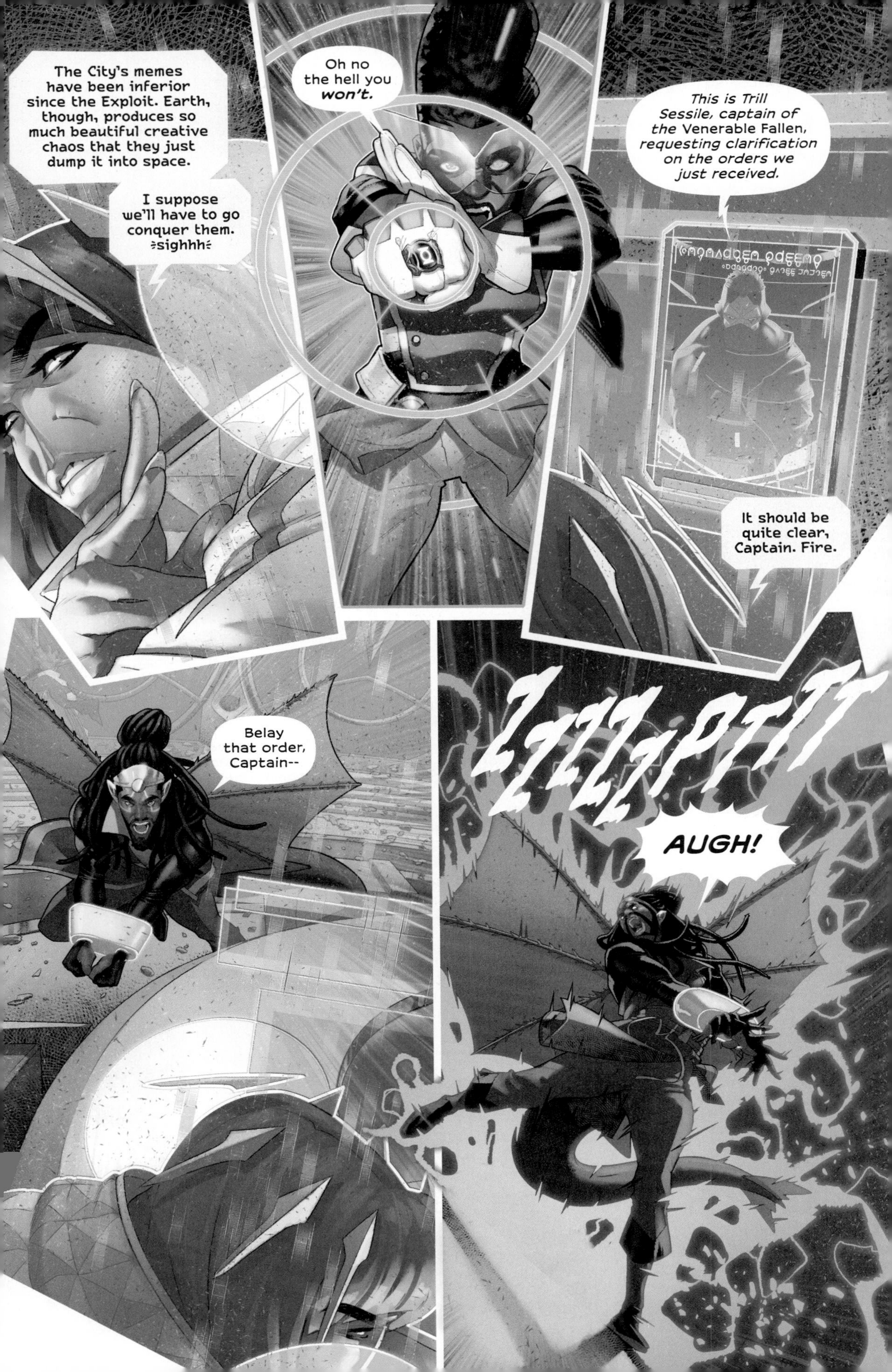

The City's memes have been inferior since the Exploit. Earth, though, produces so much beautiful creative chaos that they just dump it into space.
I suppose we'll have to go conquer them. =sighhh=
Oh no the hell you *won't.*
This is Trill Sessile, captain of the Venerable Fallen, requesting clarification on the orders we just received.
It should be quite clear, Captain. Fire.
Belay that order, Captain--
ZZZZZPTTT
AUGH!

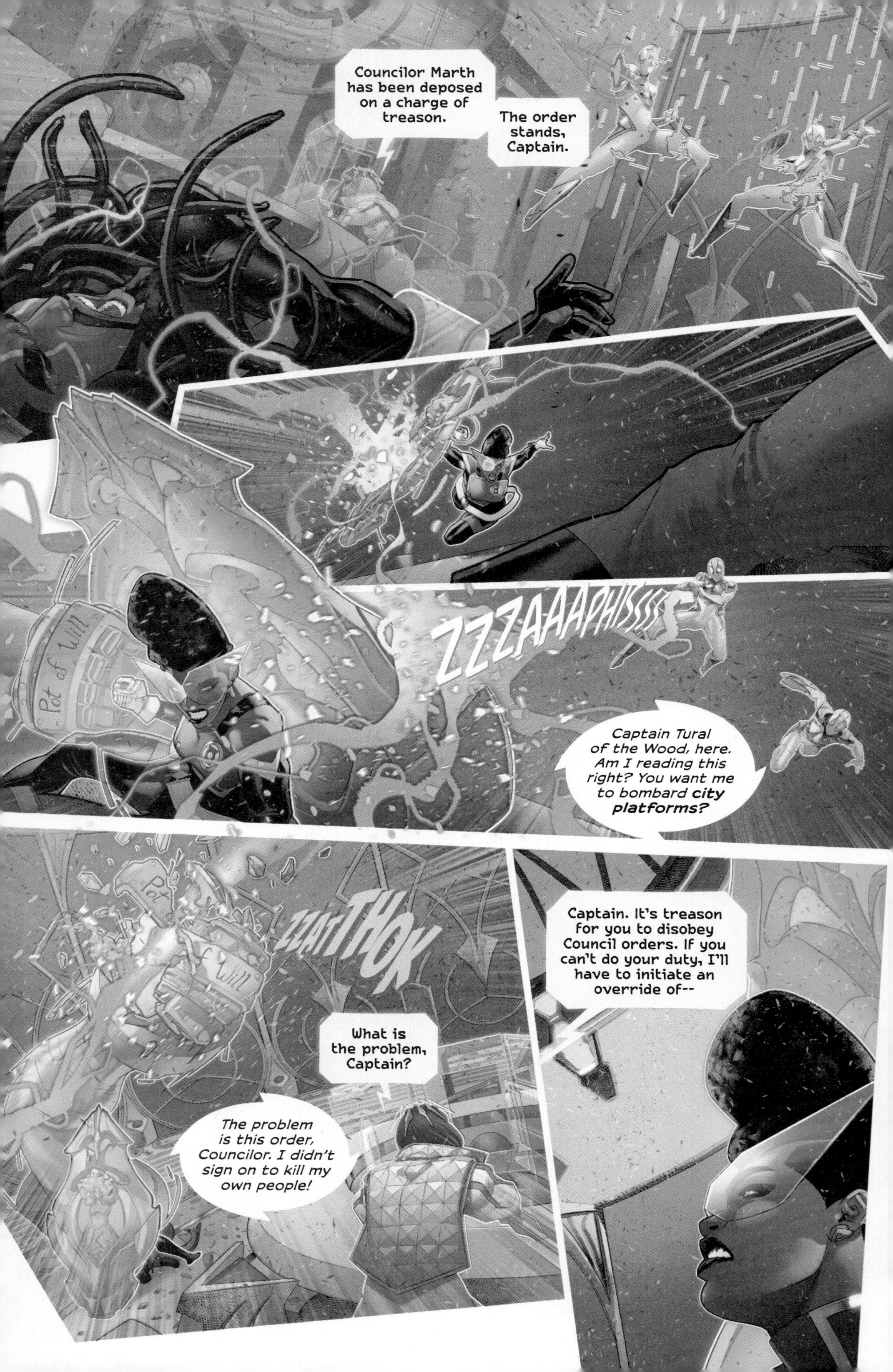
Councilor Marth has been deposed on a charge of treason.
The order stands, Captain.
ZZZAAAPHISSSS
Pot of Will
Captain Tural of the Wood, here. Am I reading this right? You want me to bombard **city platforms?**
ZZATTHOK
Captain. It's treason for you to disobey Council orders. If you can't do your duty, I'll have to initiate an override of--
What is the problem, Captain?
The problem is this order, Councilor. I didn't sign on to kill my own people!

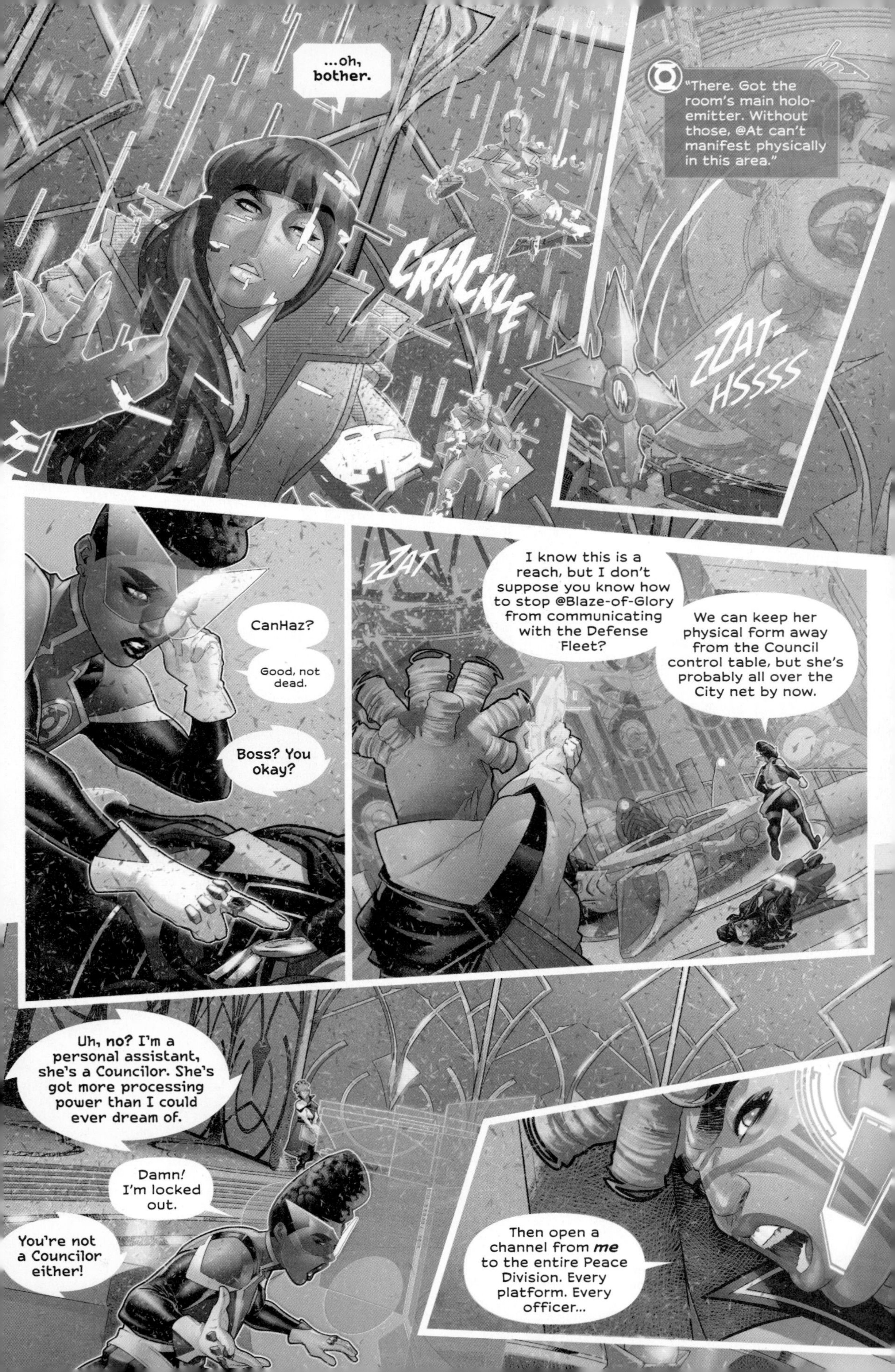
...oh, bother.
CRACKLE
"There. Got the room's main holo-emitter. Without those, @At can't manifest physically in this area."
ZZAT-HSSSS
CanHaz?
Good, not dead.
Boss? You okay?
ZZAT
I know this is a reach, but I don't suppose you know how to stop @Blaze-of-Glory from communicating with the Defense Fleet?
We can keep her physical form away from the Council control table, but she's probably all over the City net by now.
Uh, no? I'm a personal assistant, she's a Councilor. She's got more processing power than I could ever dream of.
Damn! I'm locked out.
You're not a Councilor either!
Then open a channel from *me* to the entire Peace Division. Every platform. Every officer...

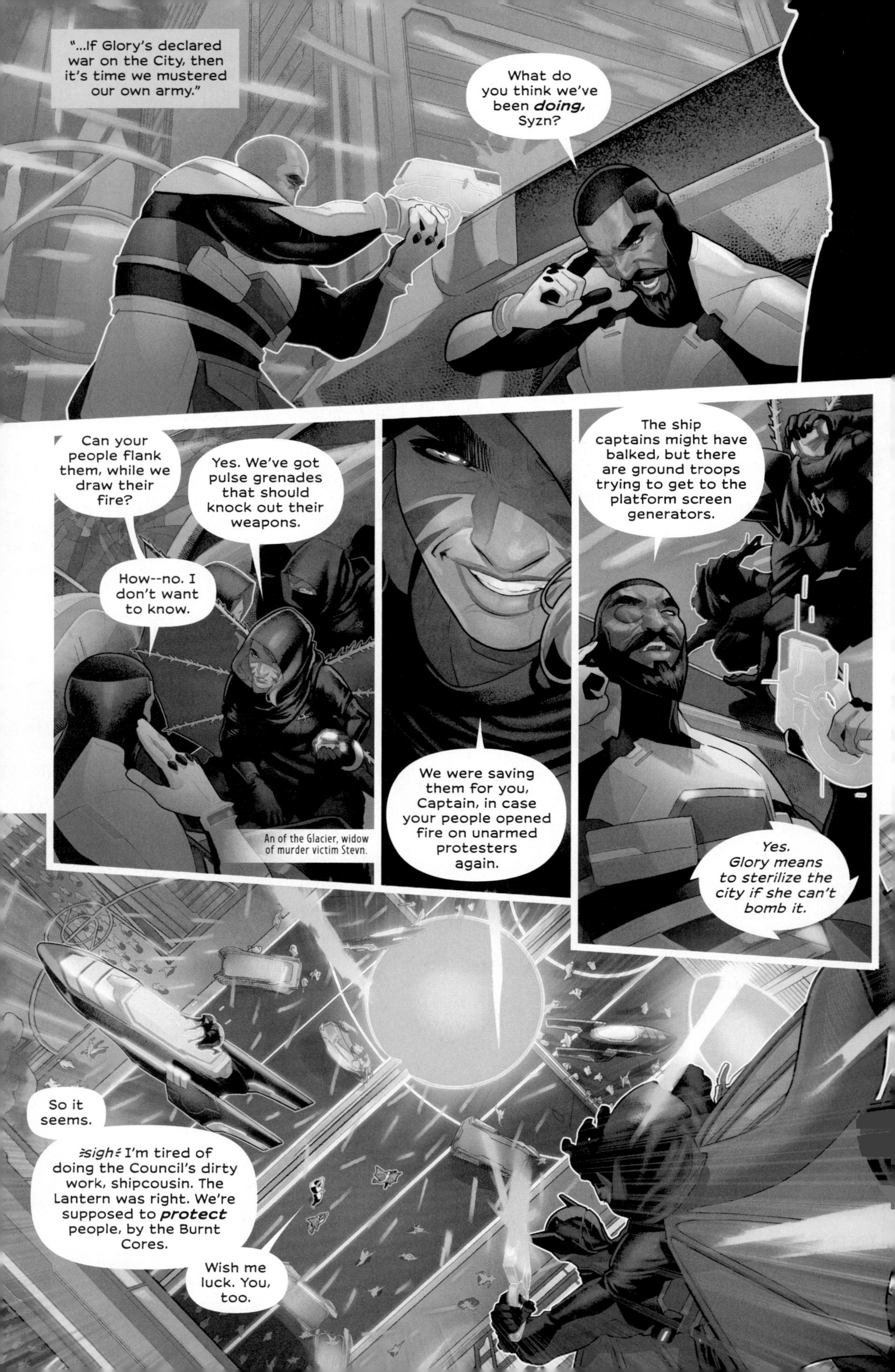
"...If Glory's declared war on the City, then it's time we mustered our own army."
What do you think we've been *doing,* Syzn?
Can your people flank them, while we draw their fire?
Yes. We've got pulse grenades that should knock out their weapons.
How--no. I don't want to know.
An of the Glacier, widow of murder victim Stevn.
We were saving them for you, Captain, in case your people opened fire on unarmed protesters again.
The ship captains might have balked, but there are ground troops trying to get to the platform screen generators.
Yes. Glory means to sterilize the city if she can't bomb it.
So it seems.
sigh I'm tired of doing the Council's dirty work, shipcousin. The Lantern was right. We're supposed to ***protect*** people, by the Burnt Cores.
Wish me luck. You, too.

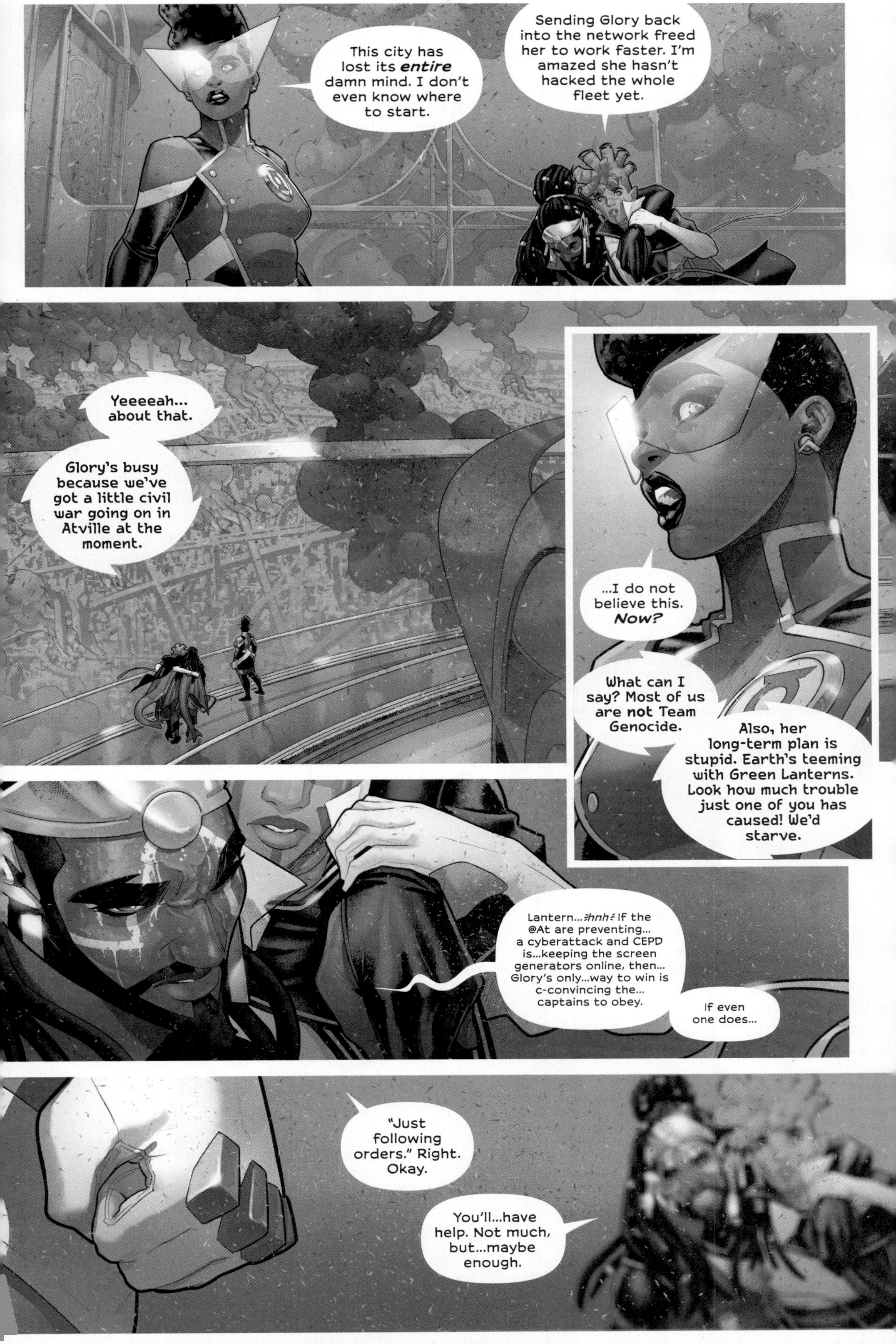

This city has lost its *entire* damn mind. I don't even know where to start.
Sending Glory back into the network freed her to work faster. I'm amazed she hasn't hacked the whole fleet yet.
Yeeeeah... about that.
Glory's busy because we've got a little civil war going on in Atville at the moment.
...I do not believe this. *Now?*
What can I say? Most of us are **not** Team Genocide.
Also, her long-term plan is stupid. Earth's teeming with Green Lanterns. Look how much trouble just one of you has caused! We'd starve.
Lantern... *hnh* If the @At are preventing... a cyberattack and CEPD is...keeping the screen generators online, then... Glory's only...way to win is c-convincing the... captains to obey.
If even one does...
"Just following orders." Right. Okay.
You'll...have help. Not much, but...maybe enough.

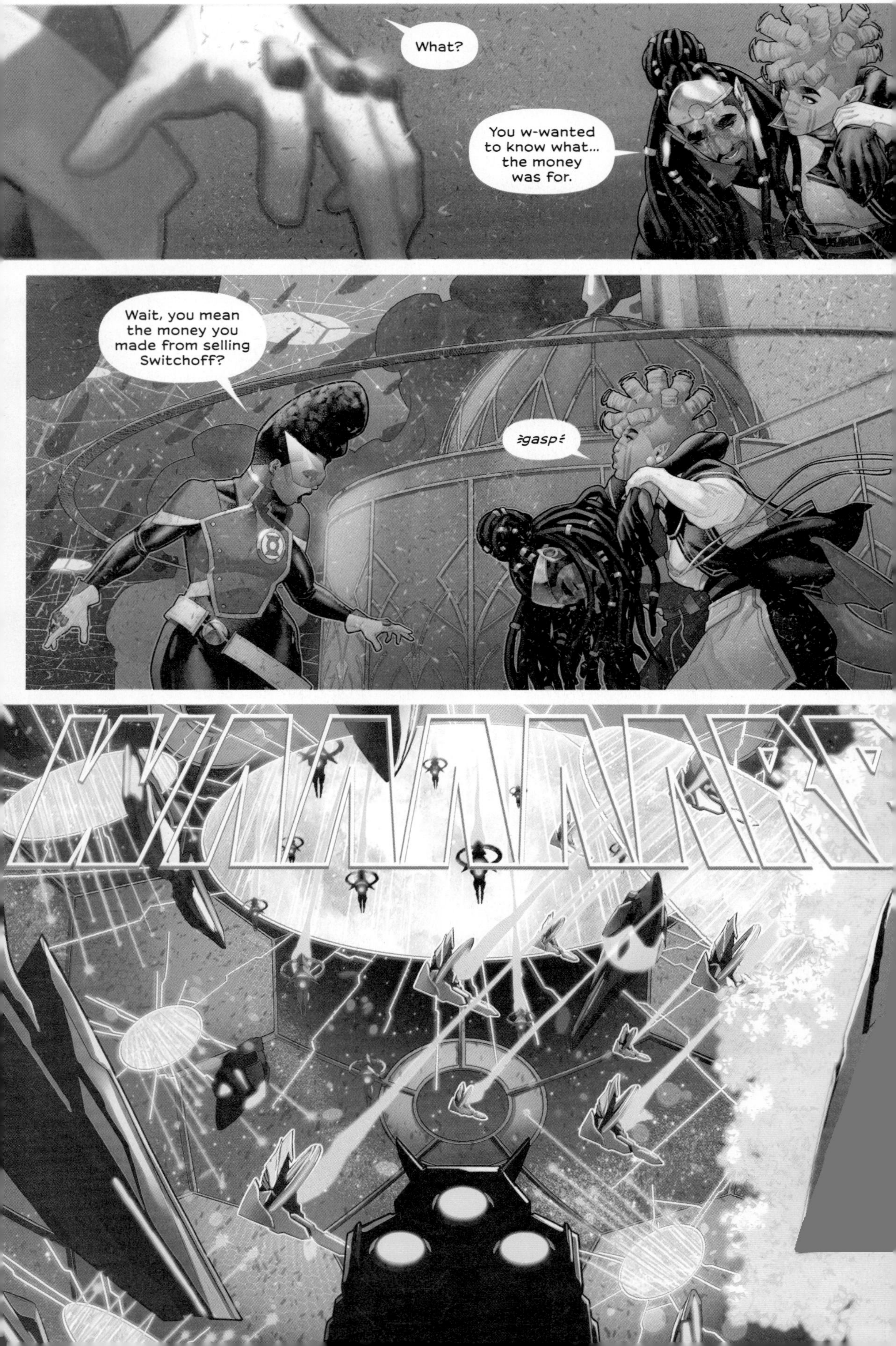
What?
You w-wanted to know what... the money was for.
Wait, you mean the money you made from selling Switchoff?
gasp

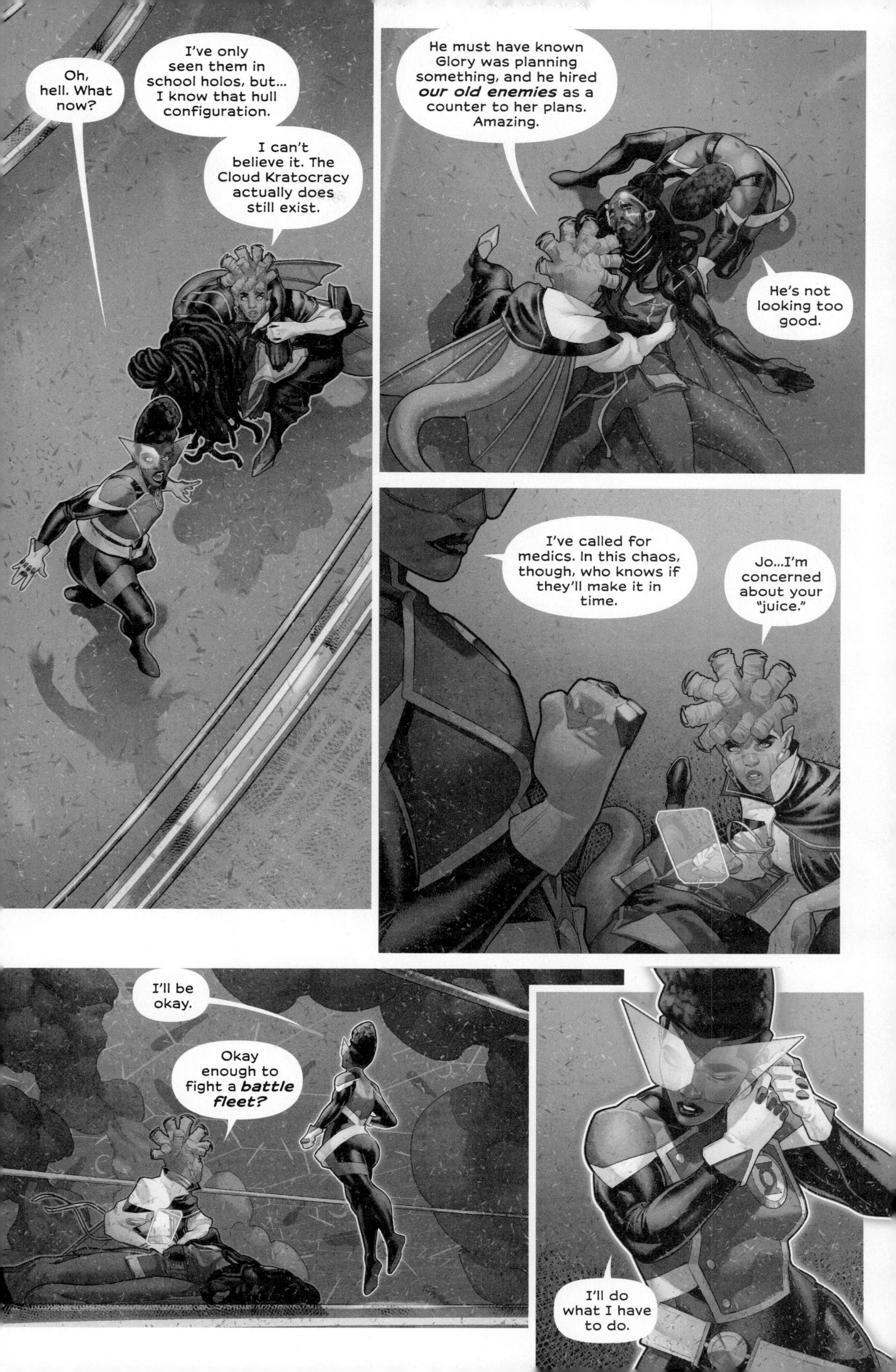
Oh, hell. What now?
I've only seen them in school holos, but... I know that hull configuration.
I can't believe it. The Cloud Kratocracy actually does still exist.
He must have known Glory was planning something, and he hired ***our old enemies*** as a counter to her plans. Amazing.
He's not looking too good.
I've called for medics. In this chaos, though, who knows if they'll make it in time.
Jo...I'm concerned about your "juice."
I'll be okay.
Okay enough to fight a ***battle fleet?***
I'll do what I have to do.

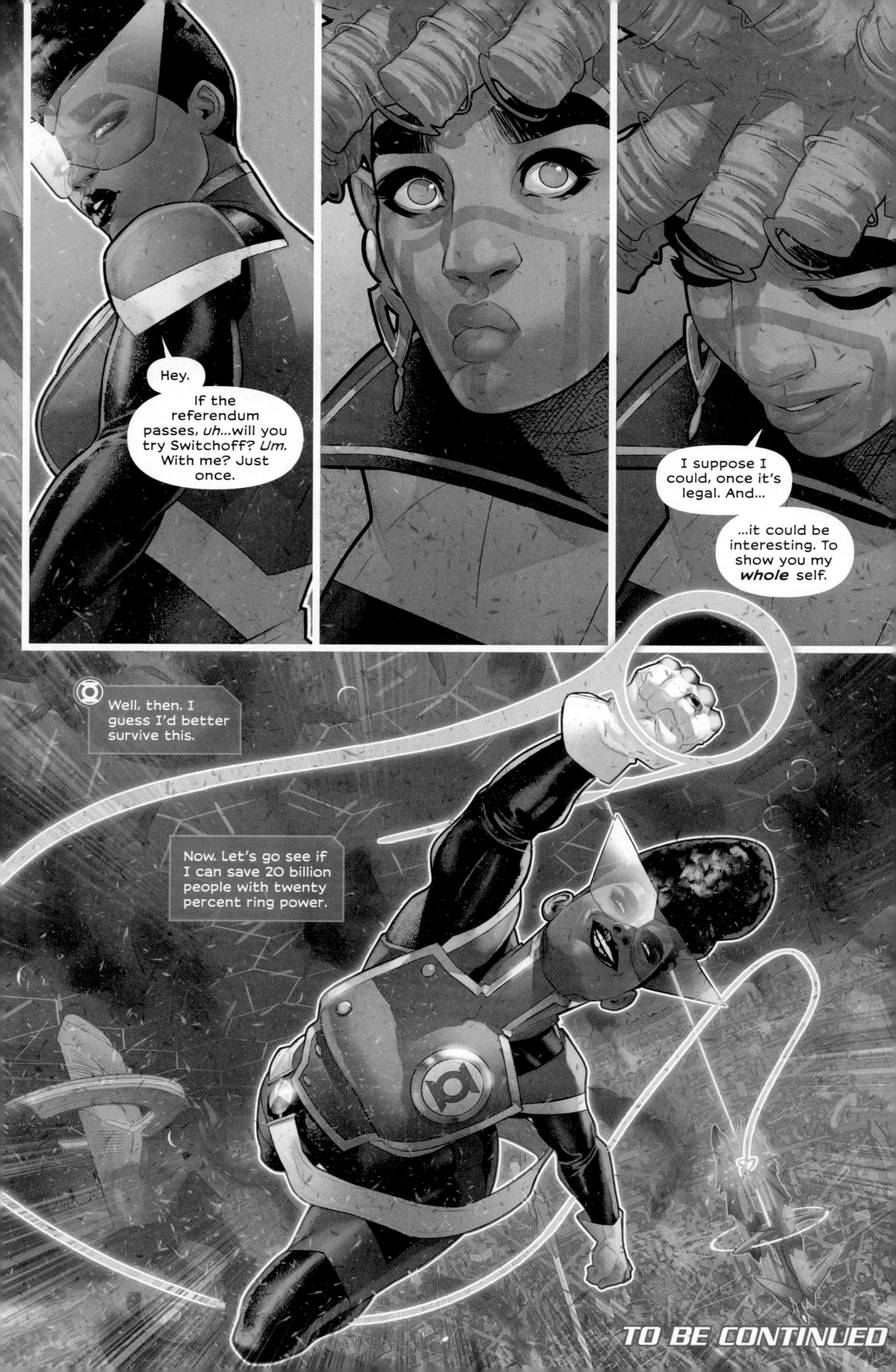

Hey.
If the referendum passes, *uh*...will you try Switchoff? *Um.* With me? Just once.
I suppose I could, once it's legal. And...
...it could be interesting. To show you my ***whole*** self.
Well, then. I guess I'd better survive this.
Now. Let's go see if I can save 20 billion people with twenty percent ring power.
TO BE CONTINUED

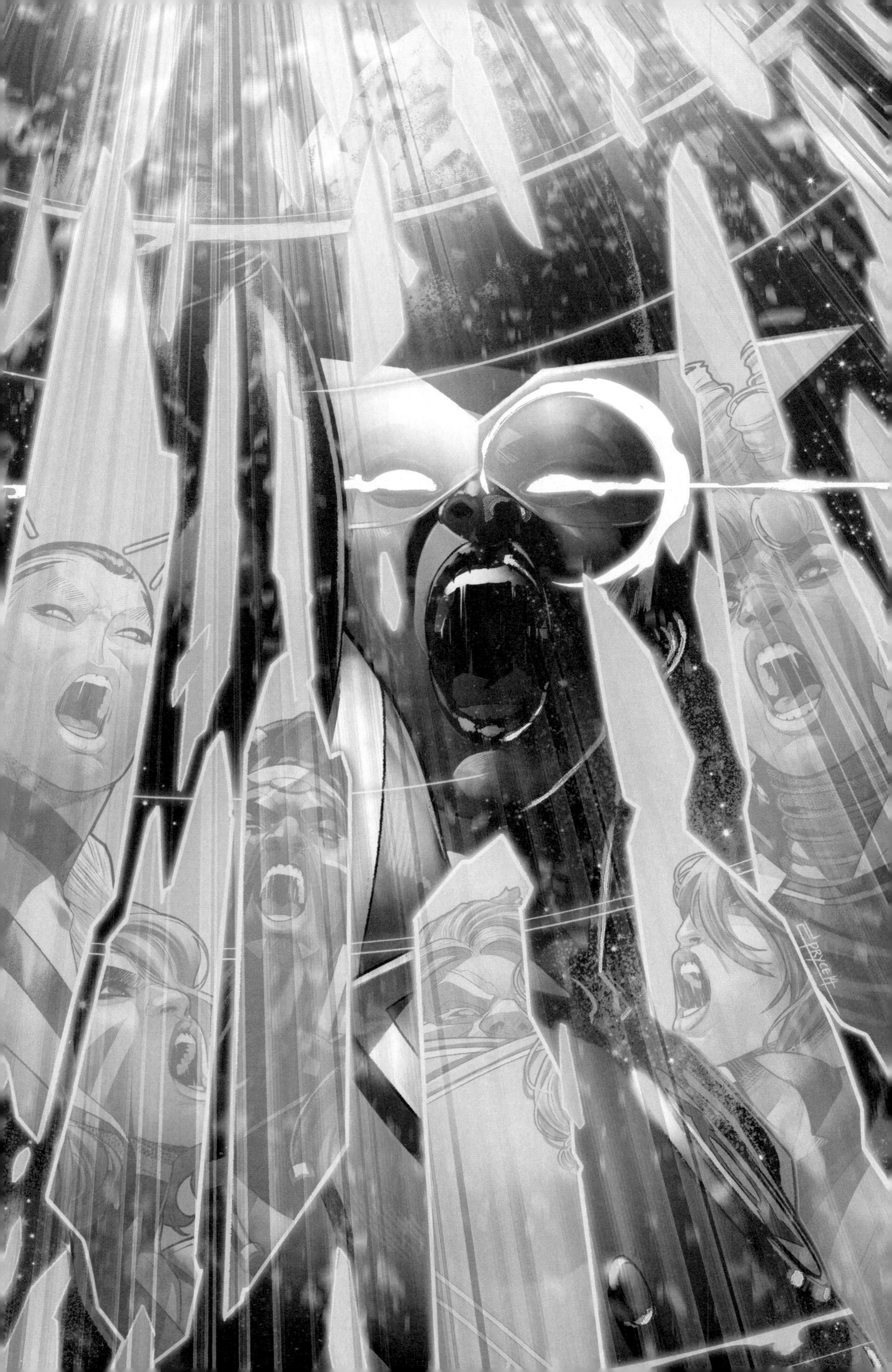

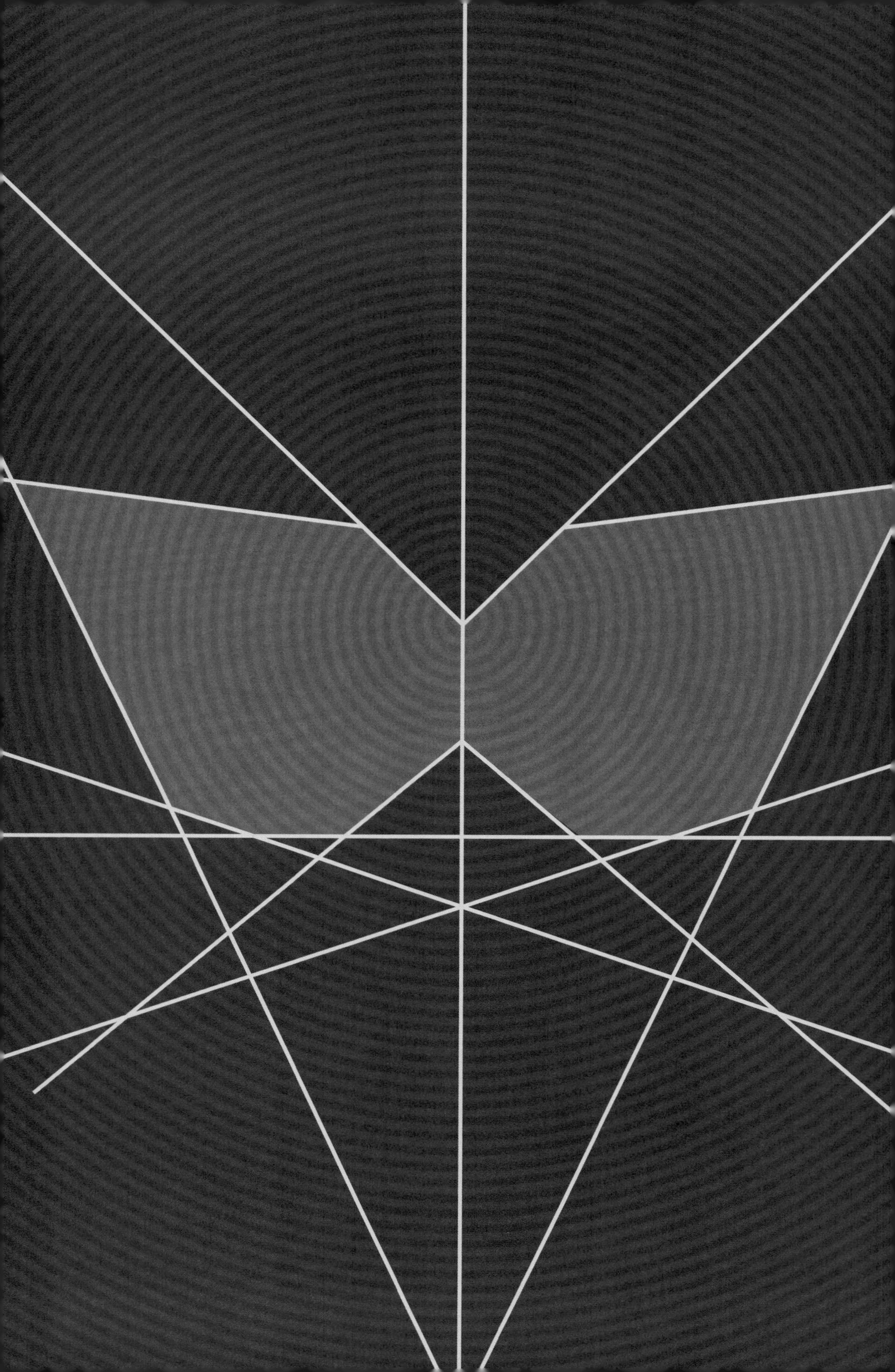

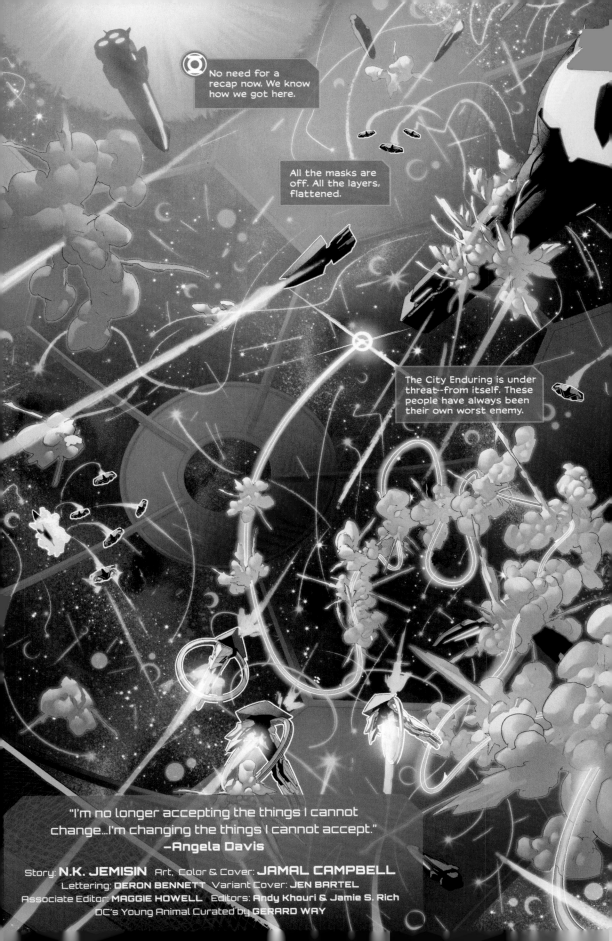

No need for a recap now. We know how we got here.

All the masks are off. All the layers, flattened.

The City Enduring is under threat—from itself. These people have always been their own worst enemy.

"I'm no longer accepting the things I cannot change...I'm changing the things I cannot accept."
—Angela Davis

Story: **N.K. JEMISIN** Art, Color & Cover: **JAMAL CAMPBELL**
Lettering: **DERON BENNETT** Variant Cover: **JEN BARTEL**
Associate Editor: **MAGGIE HOWELL** Editors: **Andy Khouri & Jamie S. Rich**
DC's Young Animal Curated by **GERARD WAY**

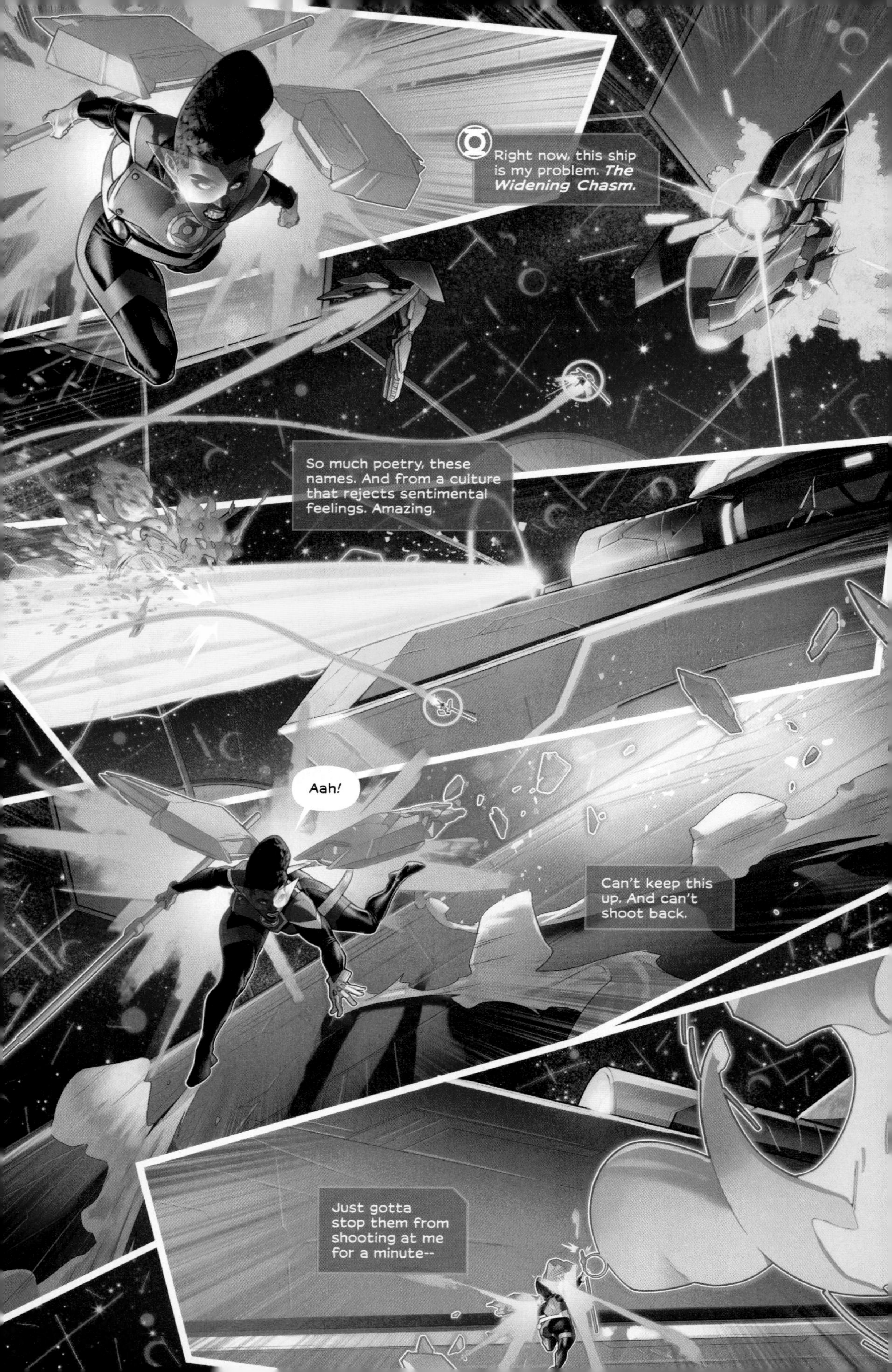

Right now, this ship is my problem. *The Widening Chasm.*
So much poetry, these names. And from a culture that rejects sentimental feelings. Amazing.
Aah!
Can't keep this up. And can't shoot back.
Just gotta stop them from shooting at me for a minute--

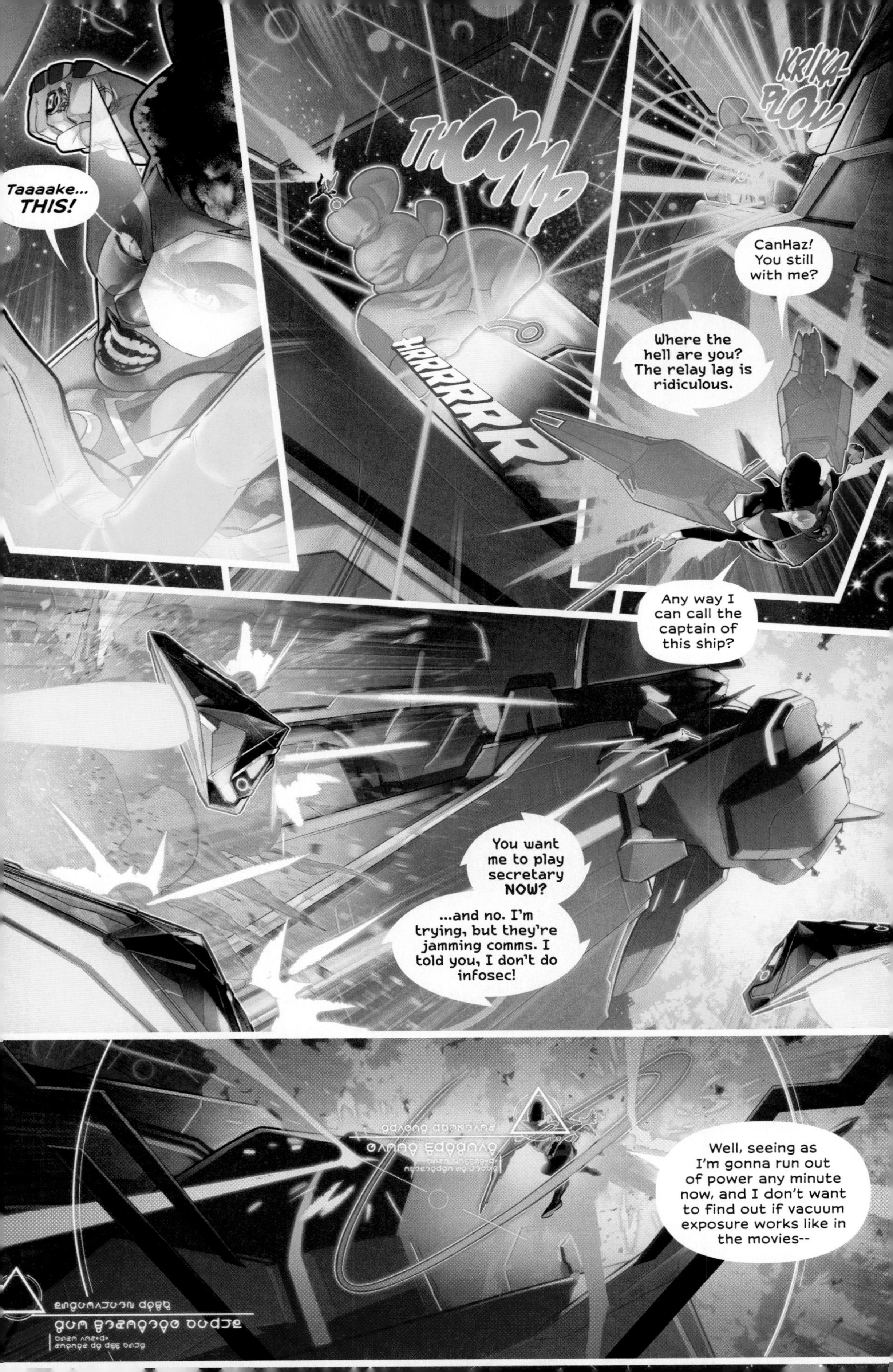
Taaaake... THIS!
THOOOMP
HRRRRRR
KRIKA-PLOW
CanHaz! You still with me?
Where the hell are you? The relay lag is ridiculous.
Any way I can call the captain of this ship?
You want me to play secretary NOW?
...and no. I'm trying, but they're jamming comms. I told you, I don't do infosec!
Well, seeing as I'm gonna run out of power any minute now, and I don't want to find out if vacuum exposure works like in the movies--

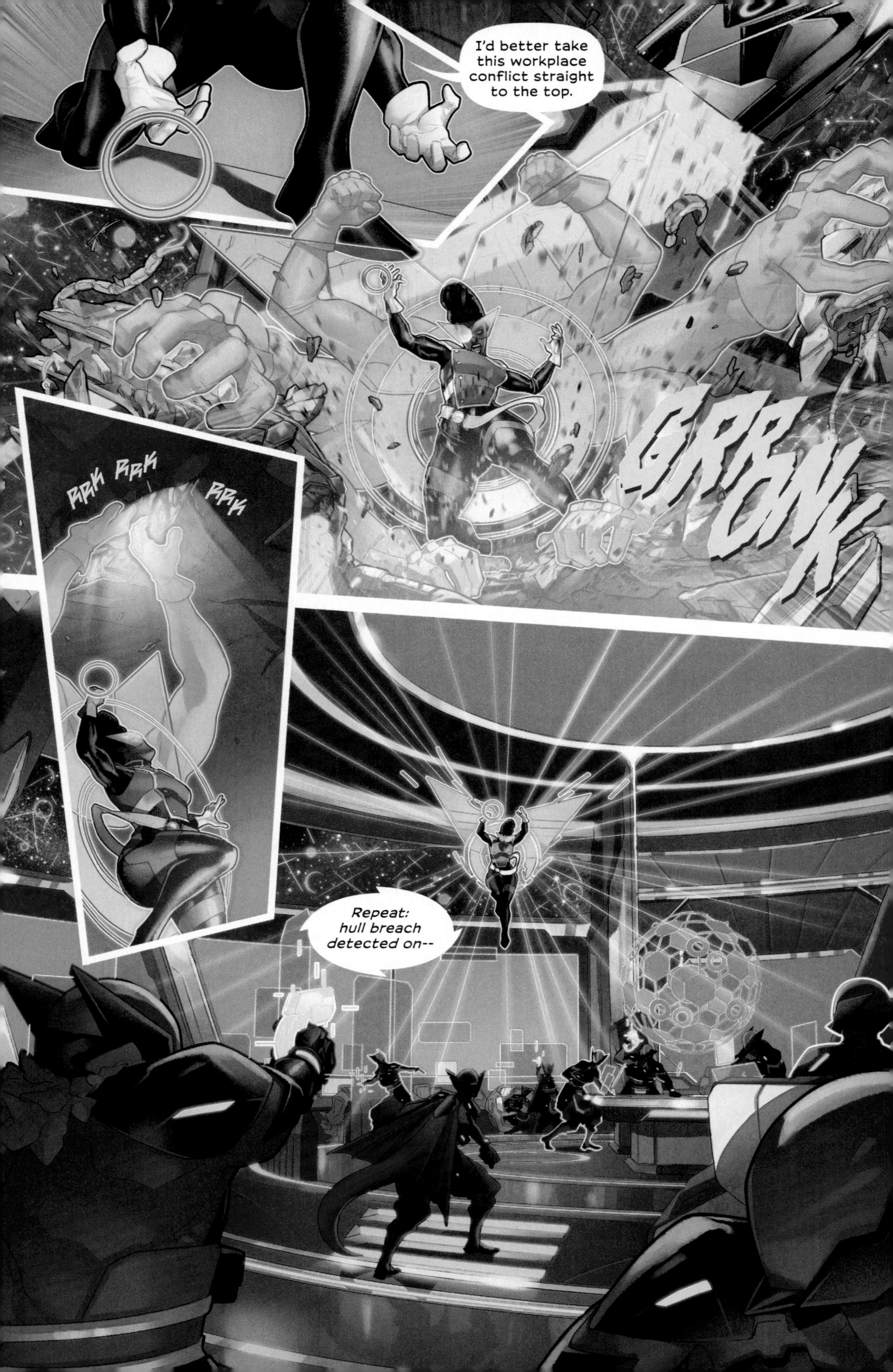
I'd better take this workplace conflict straight to the top.
GRRONK
RRK RRK
RRK
Repeat: hull breach detected on--

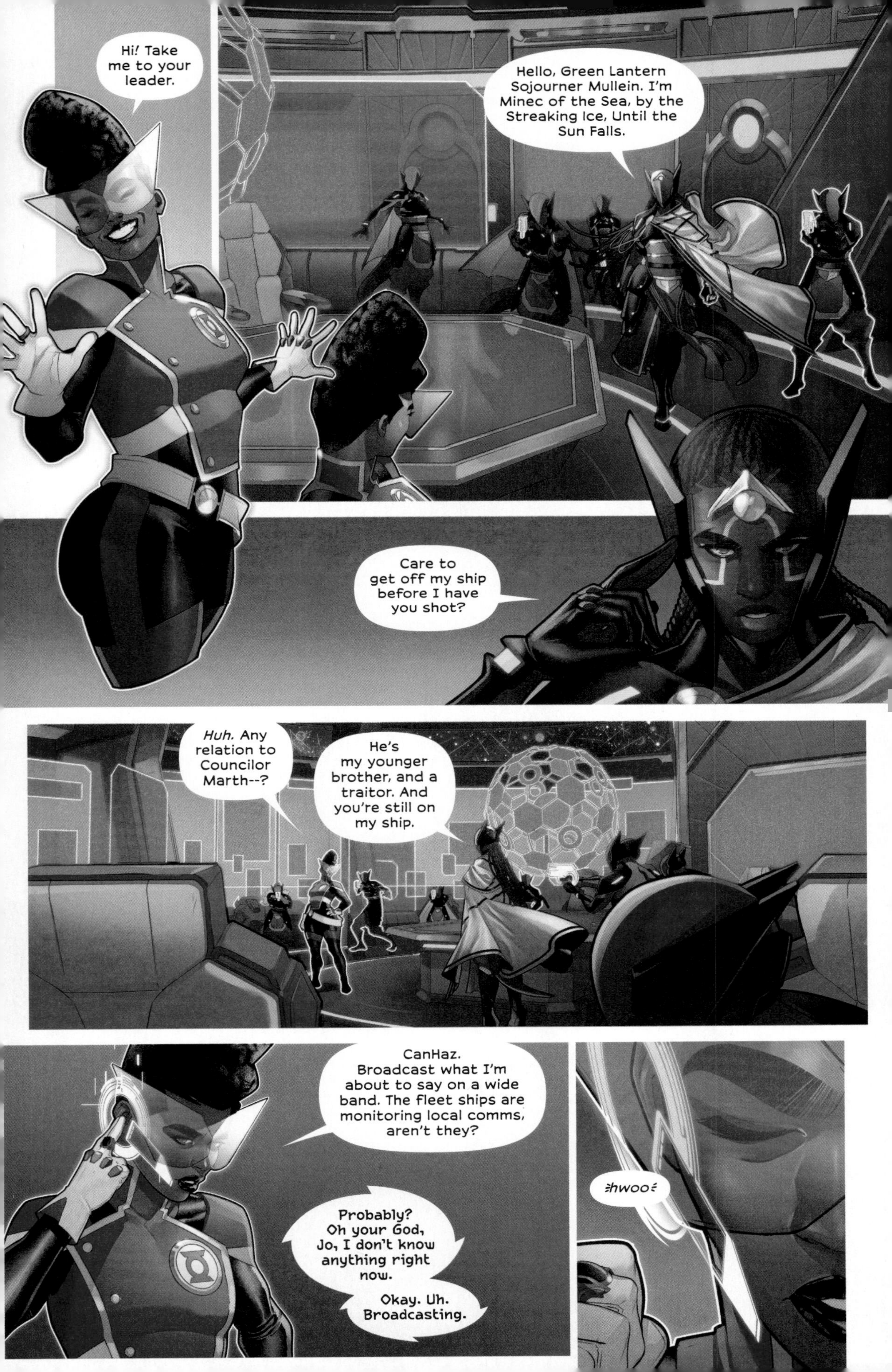
Hi! Take me to your leader.
Hello, Green Lantern Sojourner Mullein. I'm Minec of the Sea, by the Streaking Ice, Until the Sun Falls.
Care to get off my ship before I have you shot?
Huh. Any relation to Councilor Marth--?
He's my younger brother, and a traitor. And you're still on my ship.
CanHaz. Broadcast what I'm about to say on a wide band. The fleet ships are monitoring local comms, aren't they?
Probably? Oh your God, Jo, I don't know anything right now.
Okay. Uh. Broadcasting.
≡hwoo≡

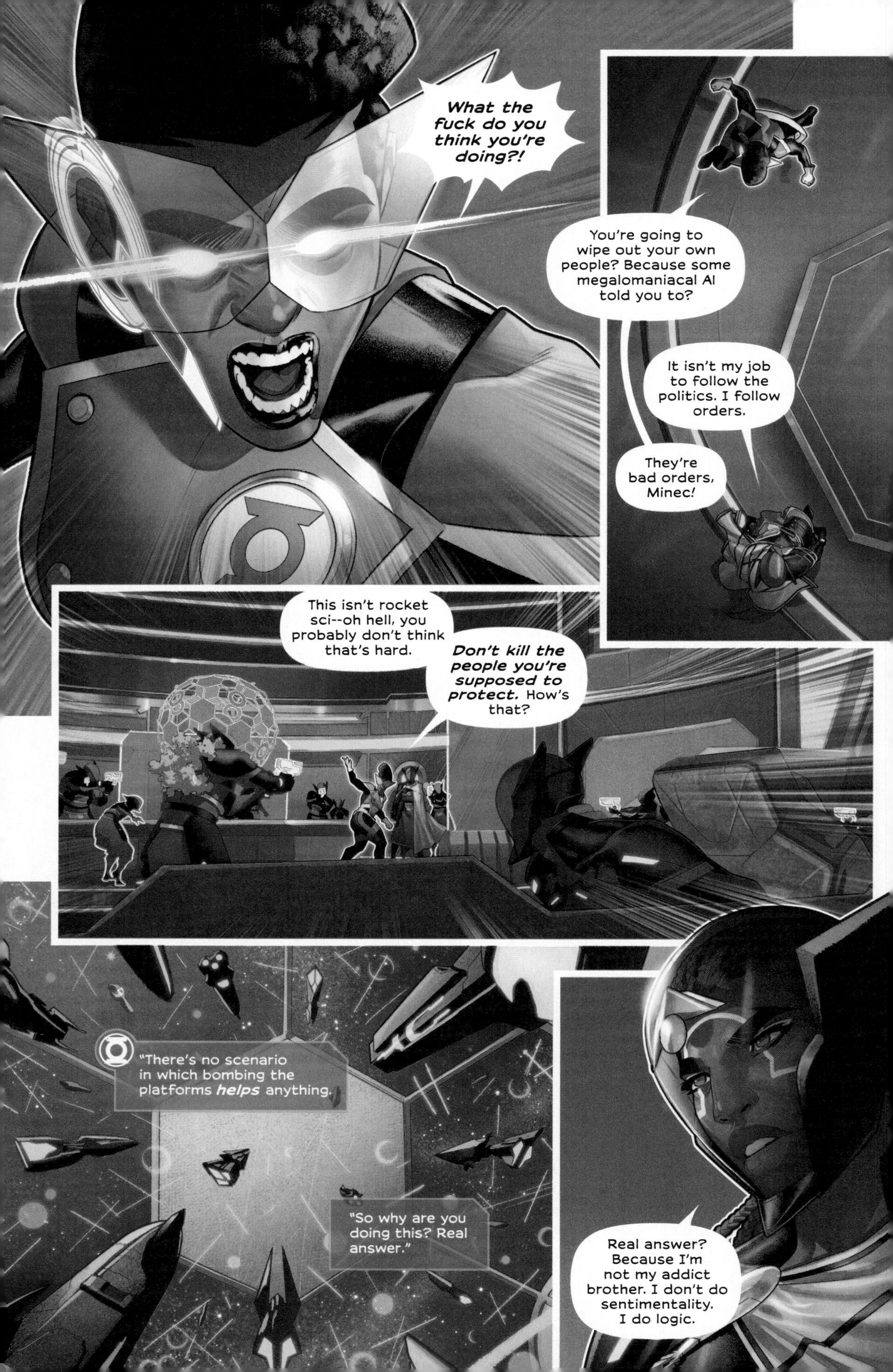
What the fuck do you think you're doing?!
You're going to wipe out your own people? Because some megalomaniacal AI told you to?
It isn't my job to follow the politics. I follow orders.
They're bad orders, Minec!
This isn't rocket sci--oh hell, you probably don't think that's hard.
Don't kill the people you're supposed to protect. How's that?
"There's no scenario in which bombing the platforms helps anything.
"So why are you doing this? Real answer."
Real answer? Because I'm not my addict brother. I don't do sentimentality. I do logic.

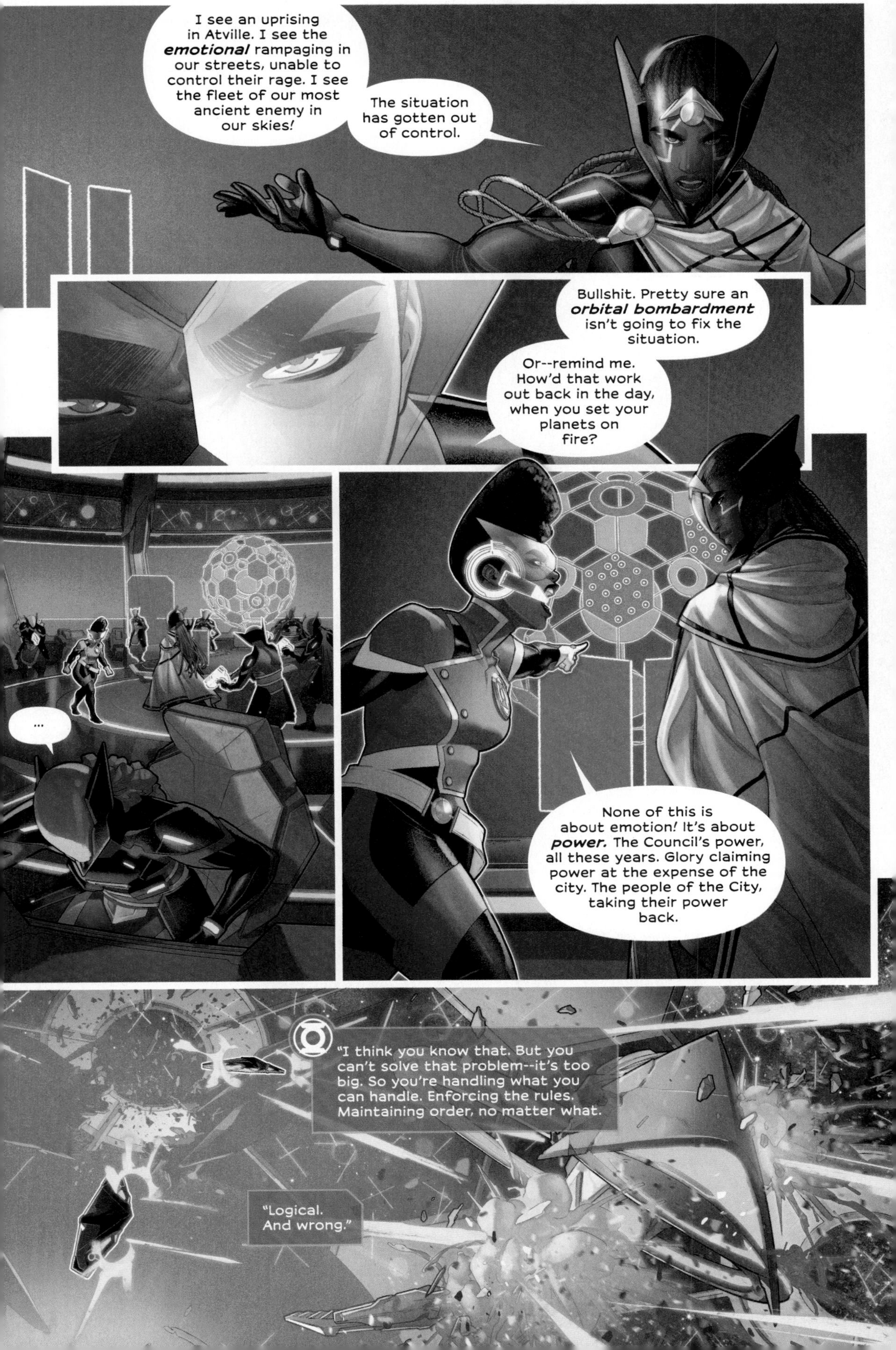

I see an uprising in Atville. I see the ***emotional*** rampaging in our streets, unable to control their rage. I see the fleet of our most ancient enemy in our skies!
The situation has gotten out of control.
Bullshit. Pretty sure an ***orbital bombardment*** isn't going to fix the situation.
Or--remind me. How'd that work out back in the day, when you set your planets on fire?
...
None of this is about emotion! It's about ***power.*** The Council's power, all these years. Glory claiming power at the expense of the city. The people of the City, taking their power back.
"I think you know that. But you can't solve that problem--it's too big. So you're handling what you can handle. Enforcing the rules. Maintaining order, no matter what.
"Logical. And wrong."

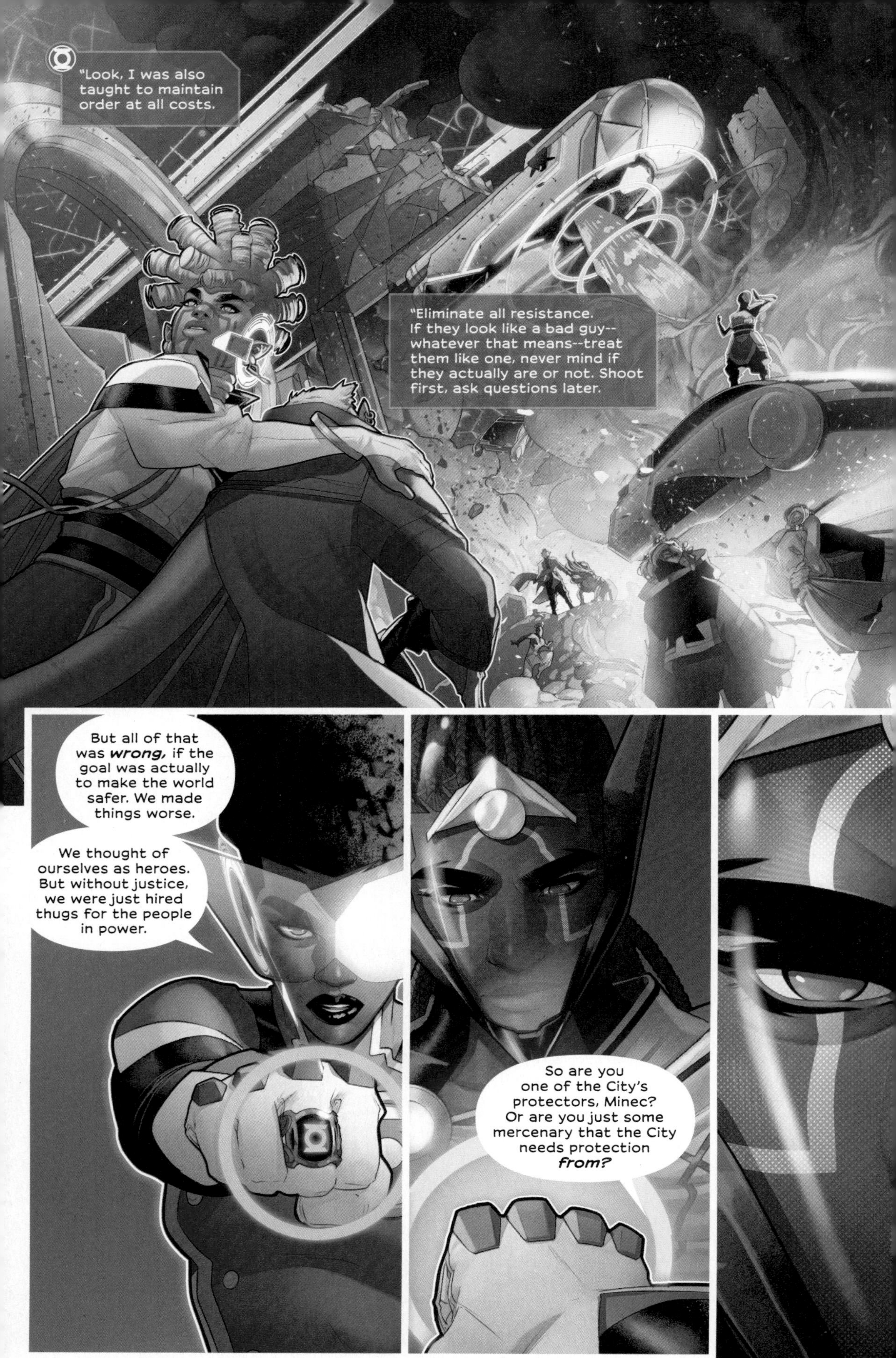
"Look, I was also taught to maintain order at all costs.
"Eliminate all resistance. If they look like a bad guy--whatever that means--treat them like one, never mind if they actually are or not. Shoot first, ask questions later.
But all of that was *wrong,* if the goal was actually to make the world safer. We made things worse.
We thought of ourselves as heroes. But without justice, we were just hired thugs for the people in power.
So are you one of the City's protectors, Minec? Or are you just some mercenary that the City needs protection *from?*

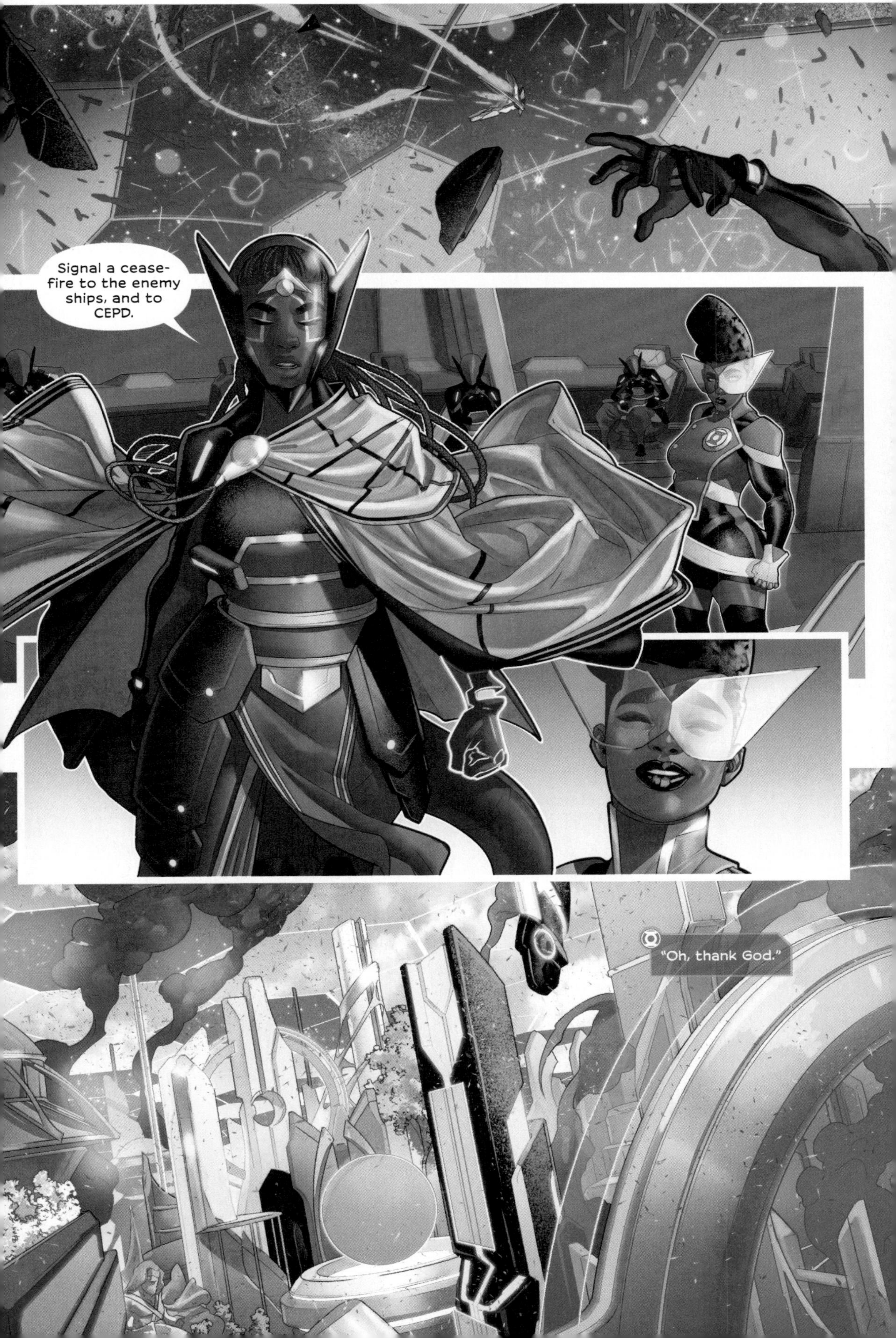
Signal a cease-fire to the enemy ships, and to CEPD.
"Oh, thank God."

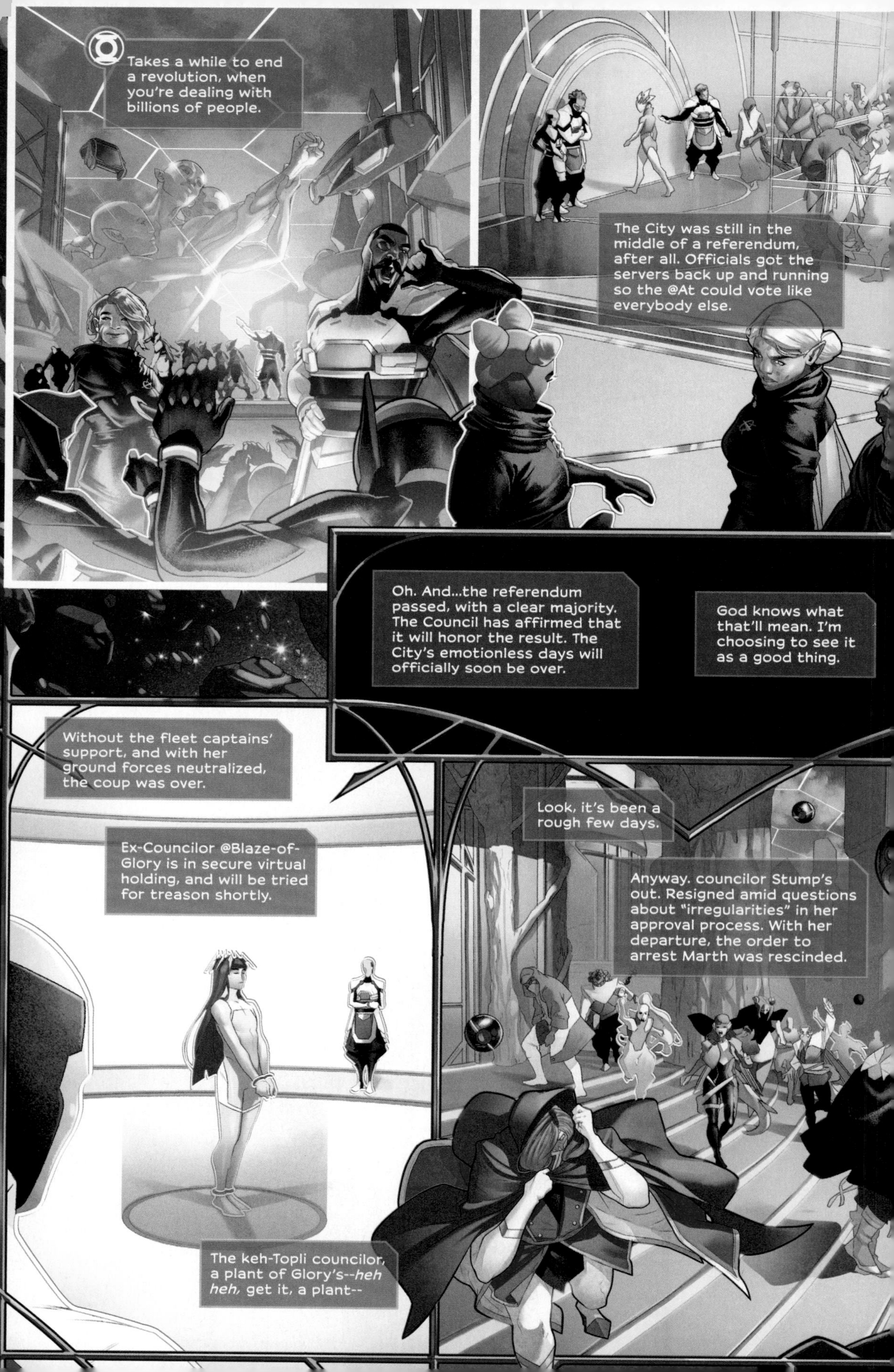
Takes a while to end a revolution, when you're dealing with billions of people.
The City was still in the middle of a referendum, after all. Officials got the servers back up and running so the @At could vote like everybody else.
Oh. And...the referendum passed, with a clear majority. The Council has affirmed that it will honor the result. The City's emotionless days will officially soon be over.
God knows what that'll mean. I'm choosing to see it as a good thing.
Without the fleet captains' support, and with her ground forces neutralized, the coup was over.
Ex-Councilor @Blaze-of-Glory is in secure virtual holding, and will be tried for treason shortly.
The keh-Topli councilor, a plant of Glory's--*heh heh,* get it, a plant--
Look, it's been a rough few days.
Anyway. councilor Stump's out. Resigned amid questions about "irregularities" in her approval process. With her departure, the order to arrest Marth was rescinded.

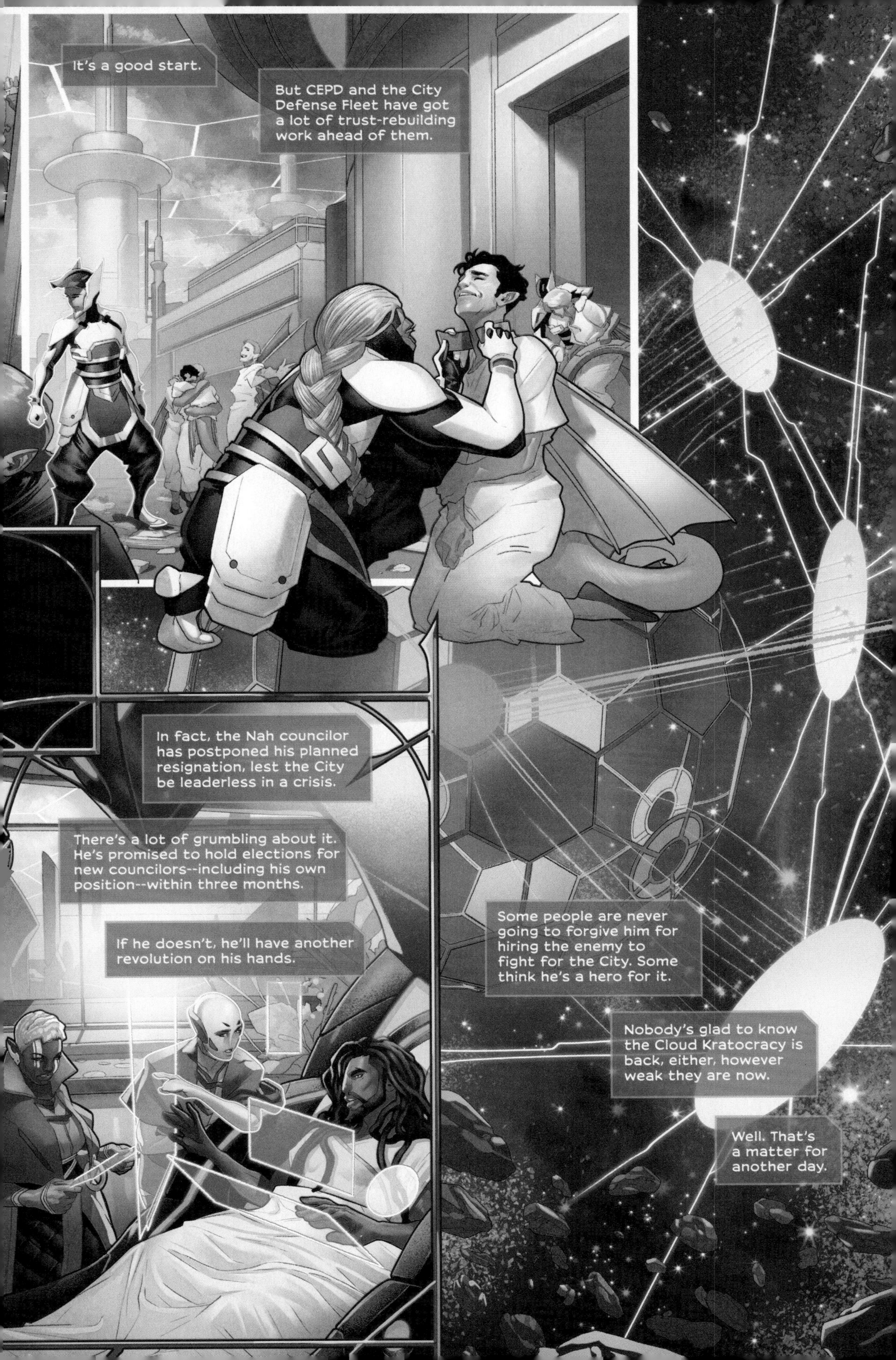
It's a good start.
But CEPD and the City Defense Fleet have got a lot of trust-rebuilding work ahead of them.
In fact, the Nah councilor has postponed his planned resignation, lest the City be leaderless in a crisis.
There's a lot of grumbling about it. He's promised to hold elections for new councilors--including his own position--within three months.
If he doesn't, he'll have another revolution on his hands.
Some people are never going to forgive him for hiring the enemy to fight for the City. Some think he's a hero for it.
Nobody's glad to know the Cloud Kratocracy is back, either, however weak they are now.
Well. That's a matter for another day.

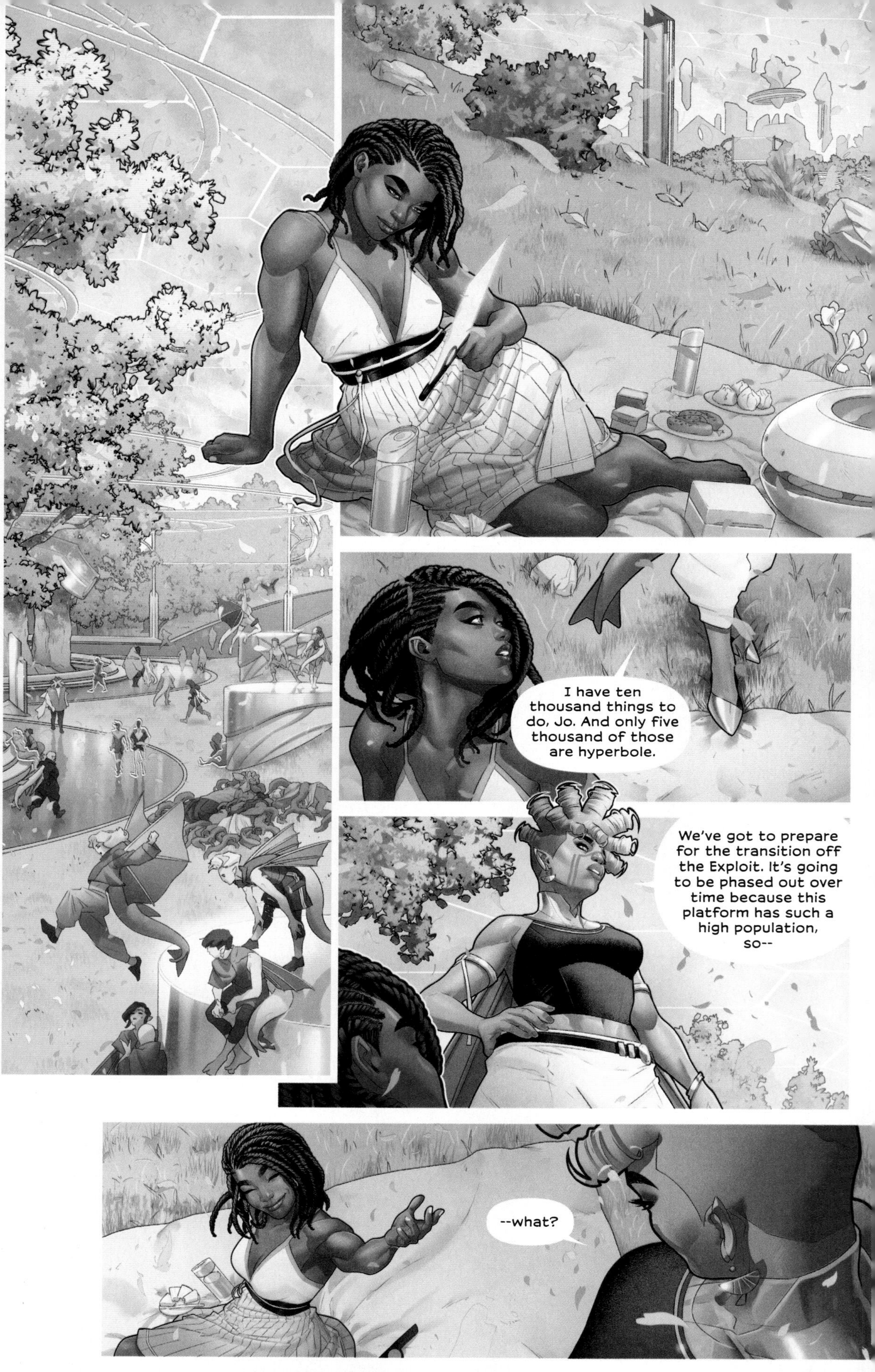
I have ten thousand things to do, Jo. And only five thousand of those are hyperbole.
We've got to prepare for the transition off the Exploit. It's going to be phased out over time because this platform has such a high population, so--
--what?

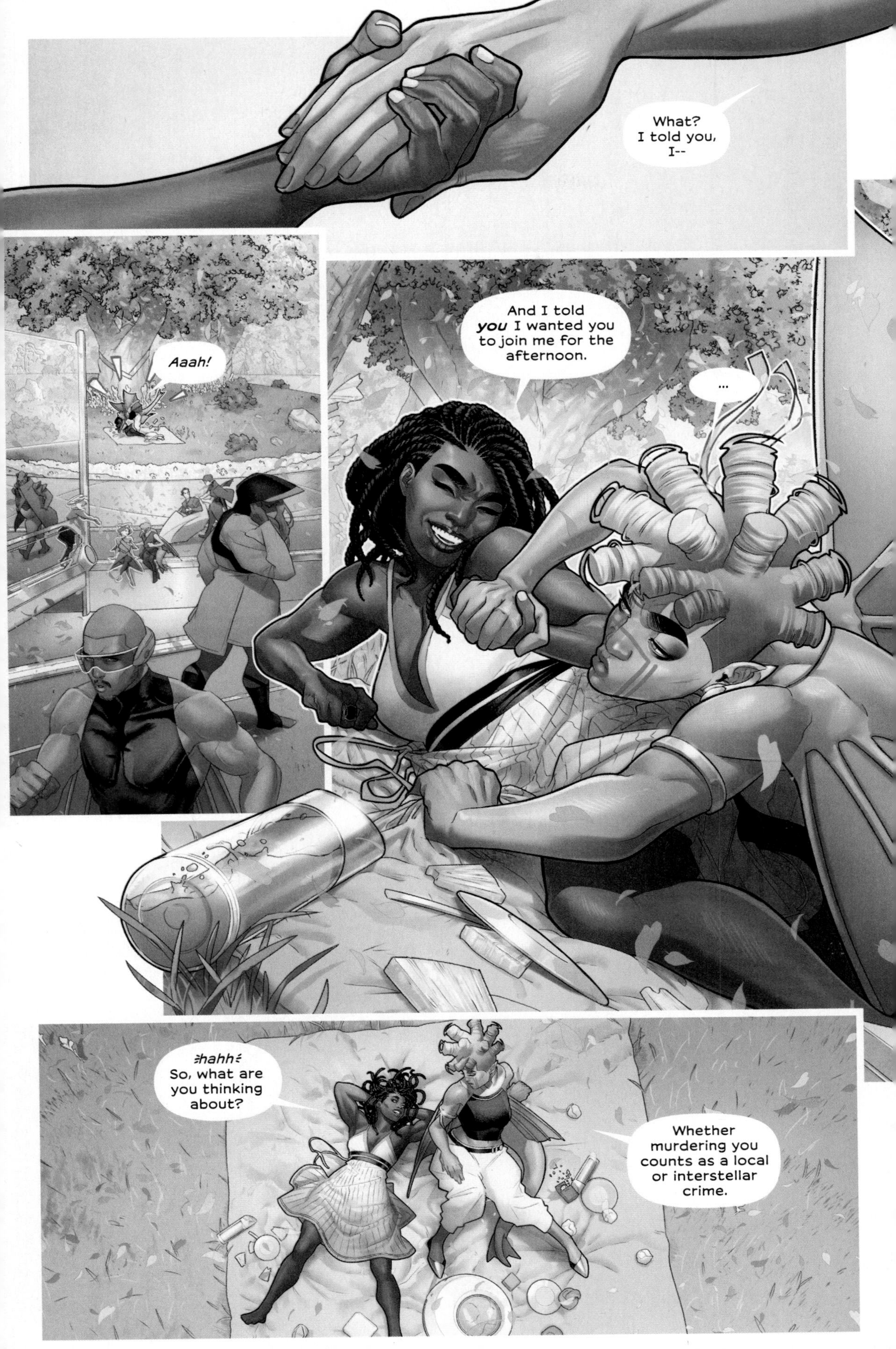
What?
I told you,
I--
Aaah!
And I told *you* I wanted you to join me for the afternoon.
...
hahh
So, what are you thinking about?
Whether murdering you counts as a local or interstellar crime.

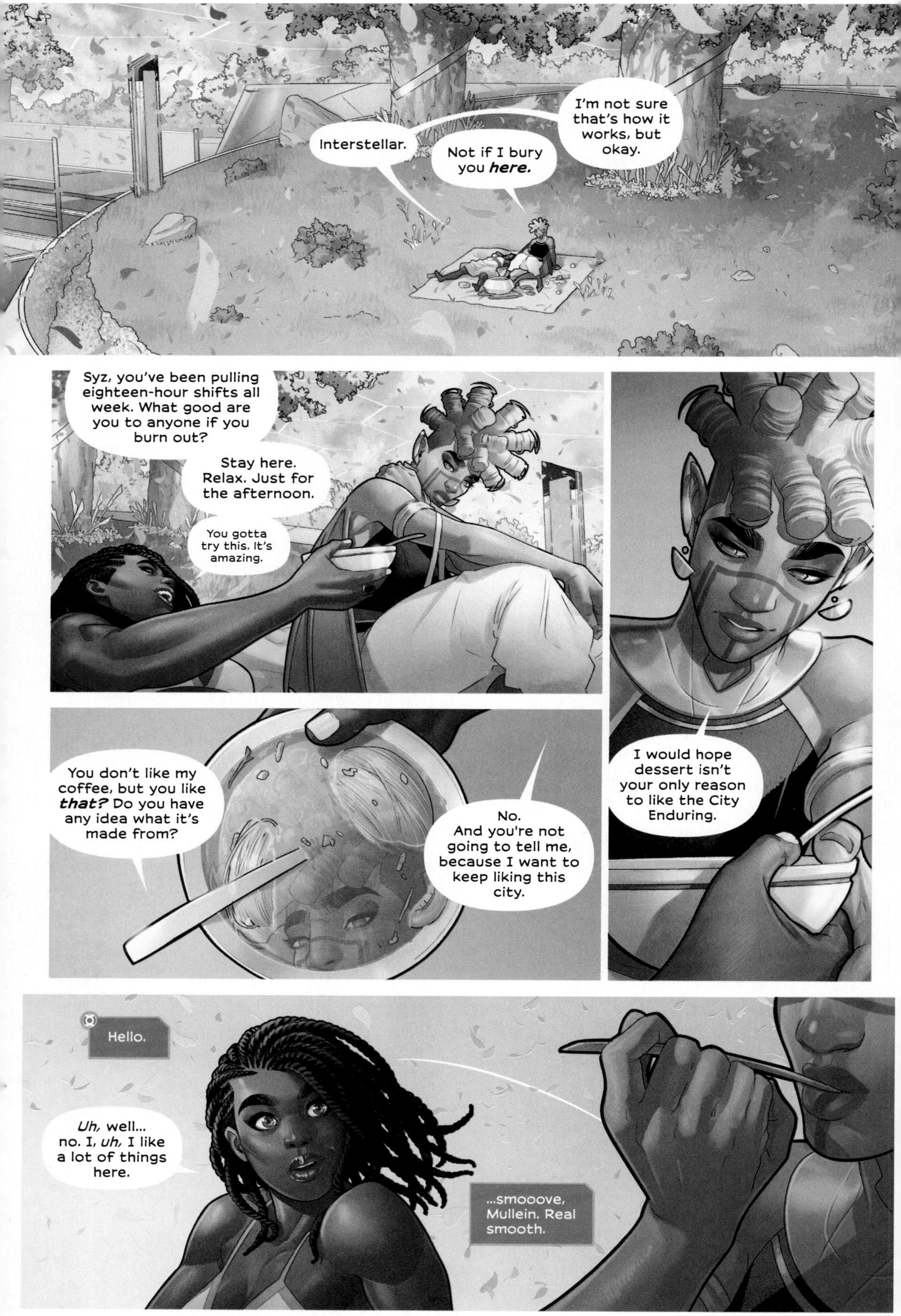

Interstellar.
Not if I bury you *here.*
I'm not sure that's how it works, but okay.
Syz, you've been pulling eighteen-hour shifts all week. What good are you to anyone if you burn out?
Stay here. Relax. Just for the afternoon.
You gotta try this. It's amazing.
I would hope dessert isn't your only reason to like the City Enduring.
You don't like my coffee, but you like ***that?*** Do you have any idea what it's made from?
No. And you're not going to tell me, because I want to keep liking this city.
Hello.
Uh, well... no. I, *uh,* I like a lot of things here.
...smooove, Mullein. Real smooth.

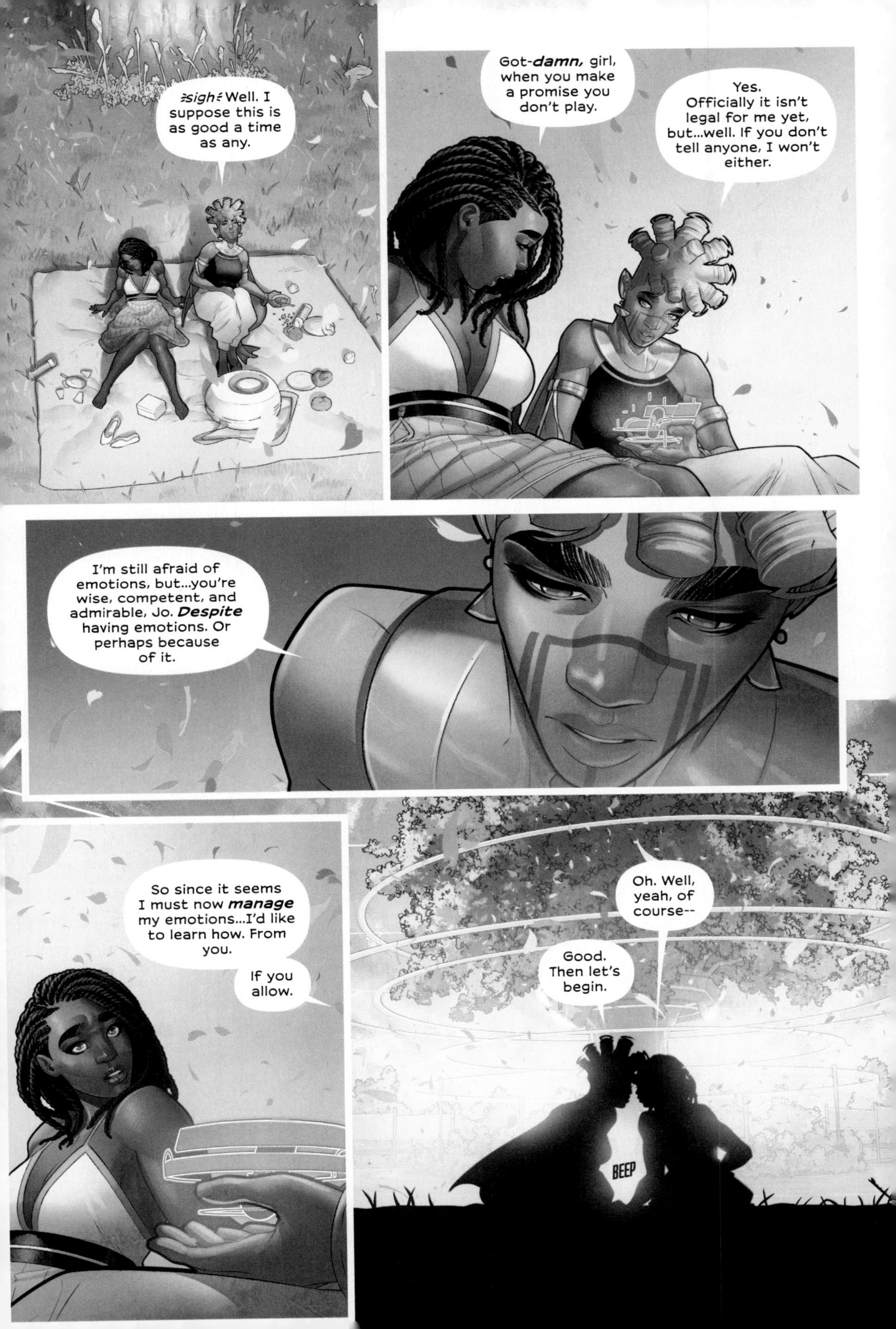

≋sigh≋ Well. I suppose this is as good a time as any.
Got-**damn,** girl, when you make a promise you don't play.
Yes. Officially it isn't legal for me yet, but...well. If you don't tell anyone, I won't either.
I'm still afraid of emotions, but...you're wise, competent, and admirable, Jo. ***Despite*** having emotions. Or perhaps because of it.
So since it seems I must now ***manage*** my emotions...I'd like to learn how. From you.
If you allow.
Oh. Well, yeah, of course--
Good. Then let's begin.
BEEP

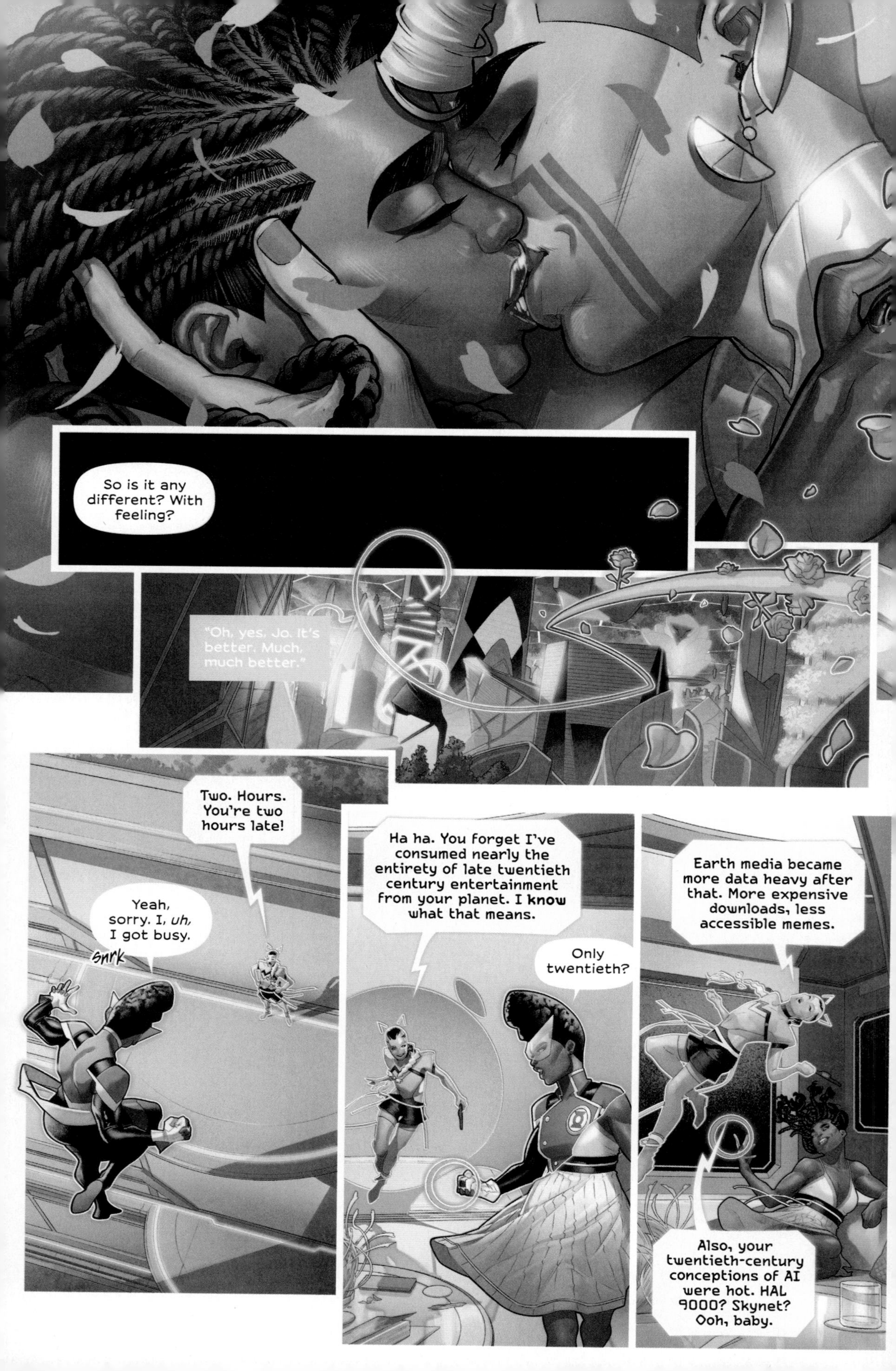
So is it any different? With feeling?
"Oh, yes, Jo. It's better. Much, much better."
Two. Hours. You're two hours late!
Yeah, sorry. I, *uh,* I got busy.
SNRK
Ha ha. You forget I've consumed nearly the entirety of late twentieth century entertainment from your planet. I **know** what that means.
Only twentieth?
Earth media became more data heavy after that. More expensive downloads, less accessible memes.
Also, your twentieth-century conceptions of AI were hot. HAL 9000? Skynet? Ooh, baby.

Are you...are you *perving* on megalomaniacal killer robots?

And aren't they also a little, well, primitive for you?

Look, humans fantasize about hot barbarians all the time. I saw "George of the Jungle," three versions of Tarzan, and all the Conan flicks.

What is this? More fic?

No. Remember what I said about the data lag from Earth? Well, I met an @At from military procurement during the fighting, and he did me a solid.

This is...from my father.

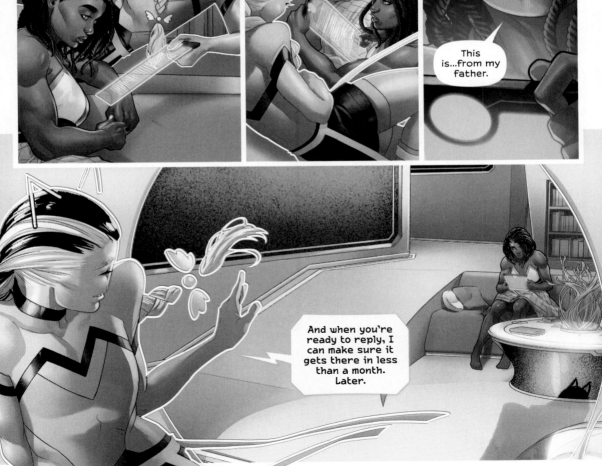

And when you're ready to reply, I can make sure it gets there in less than a month. Later.

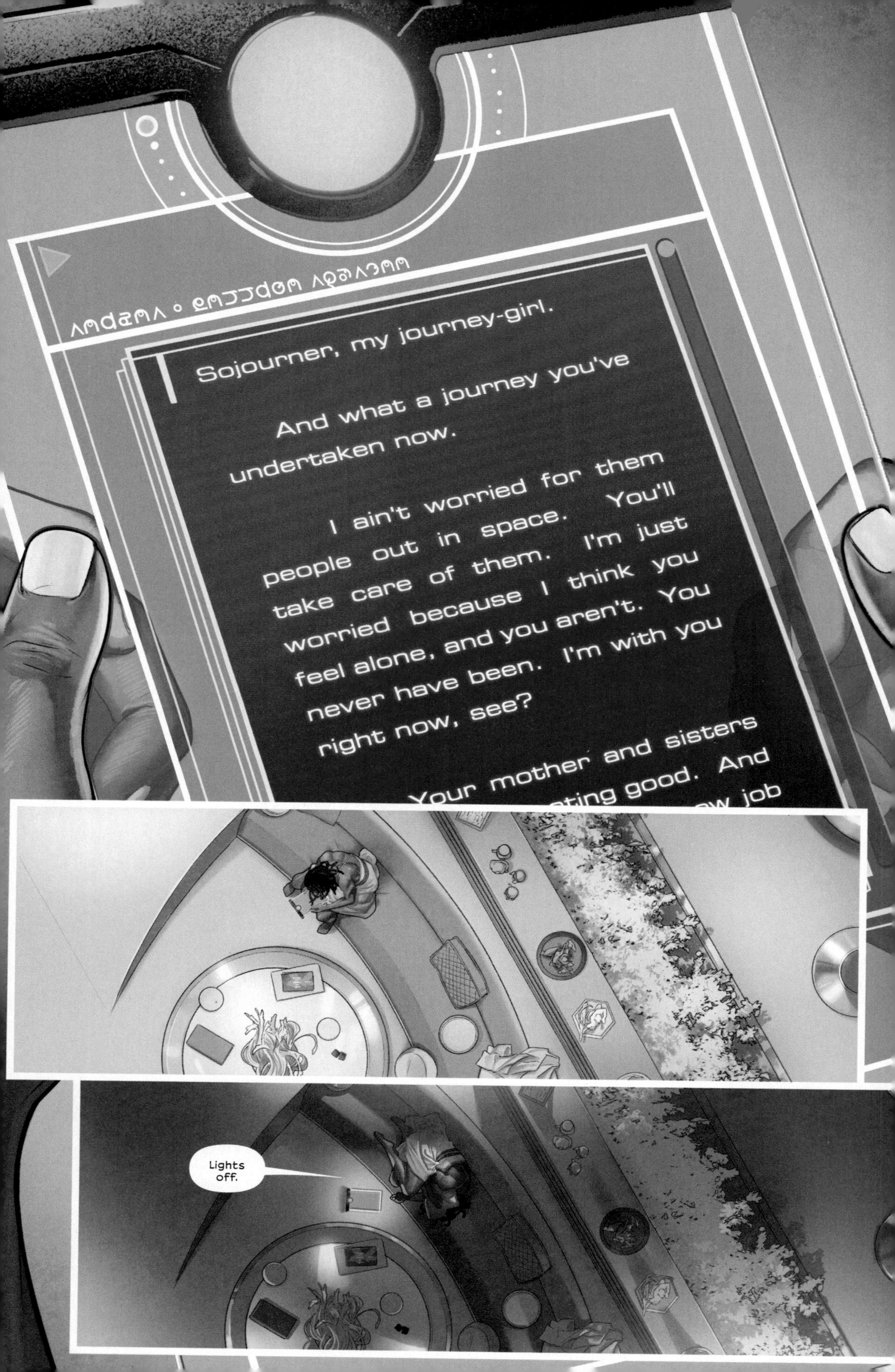
Sojourner, my journey-girl.
And what a journey you've undertaken now.
I ain't worried for them people out in space. You'll take care of them. I'm just worried because I think you feel alone, and you aren't. You never have been. I'm with you right now, see?
Your mother and sisters
Lights off.

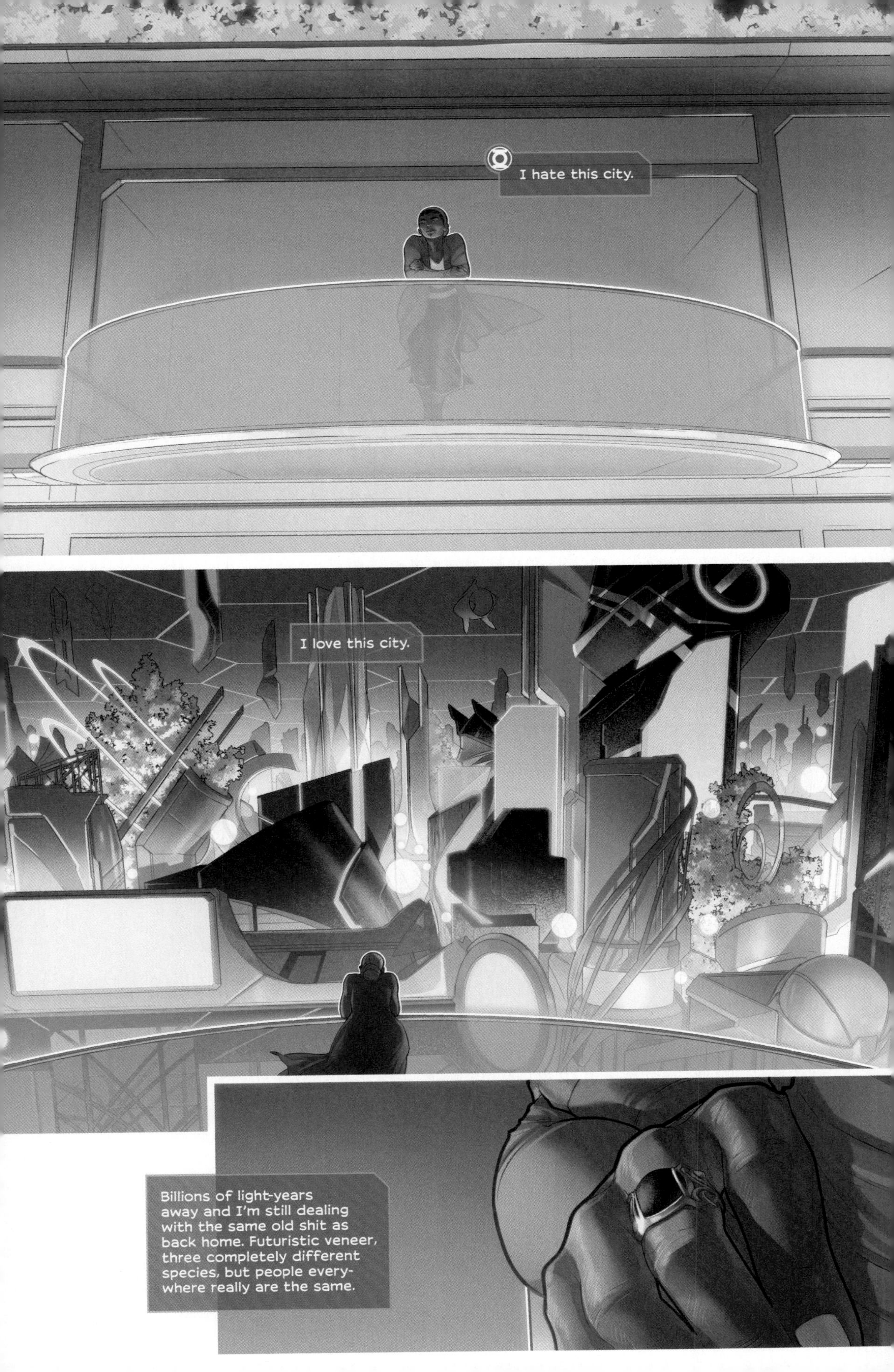
I hate this city.
I love this city.
Billions of light-years away and I'm still dealing with the same old shit as back home. Futuristic veneer, three completely different species, but people everywhere really are the same.

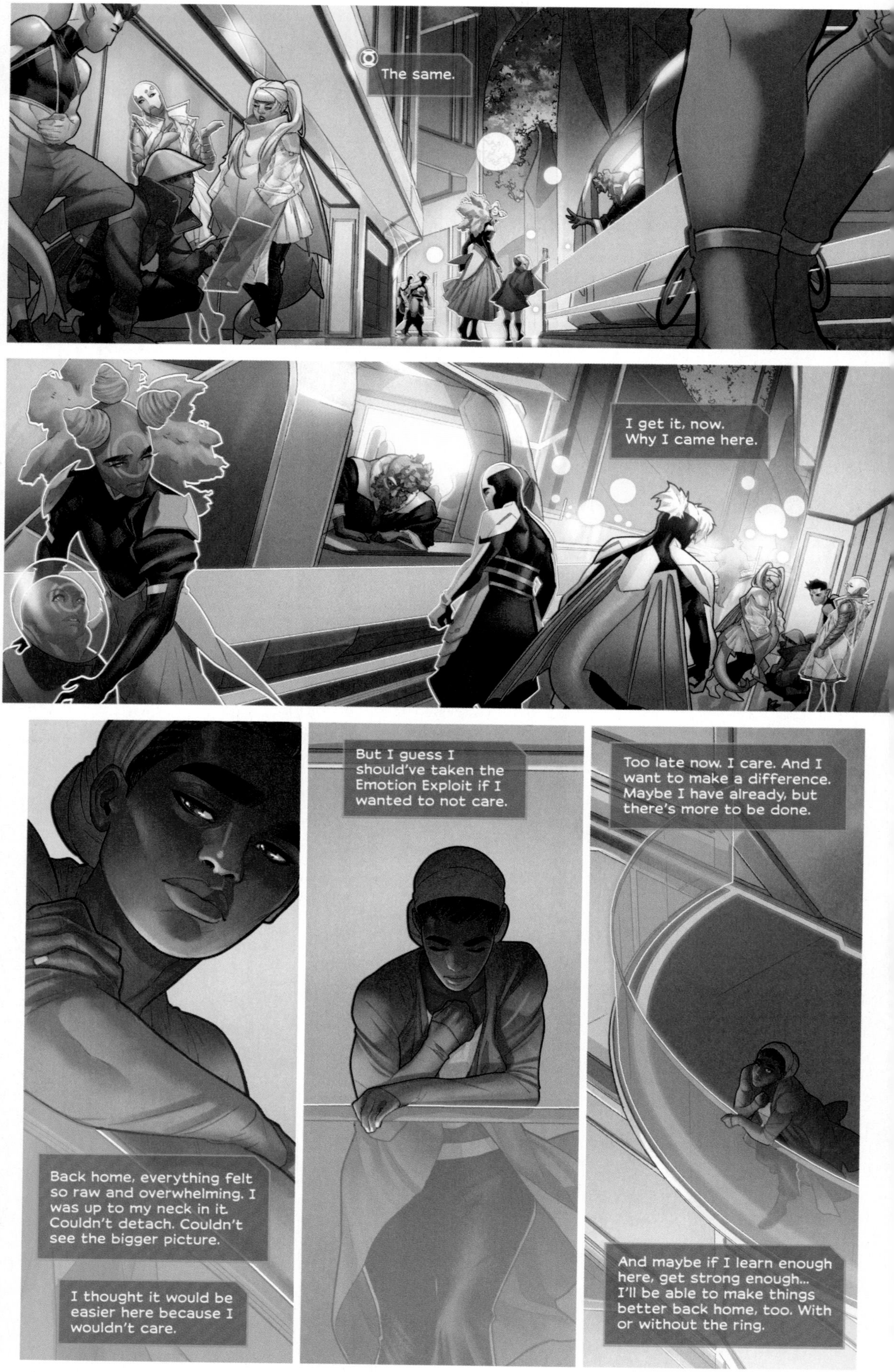
The same.
I get it, now.
Why I came here.
Back home, everything felt so raw and overwhelming. I was up to my neck in it. Couldn't detach. Couldn't see the bigger picture.
I thought it would be easier here because I wouldn't care.
But I guess I should've taken the Emotion Exploit if I wanted to not care.
Too late now. I care. And I want to make a difference. Maybe I have already, but there's more to be done.
And maybe if I learn enough here, get strong enough... I'll be able to make things better back home, too. With or without the ring.

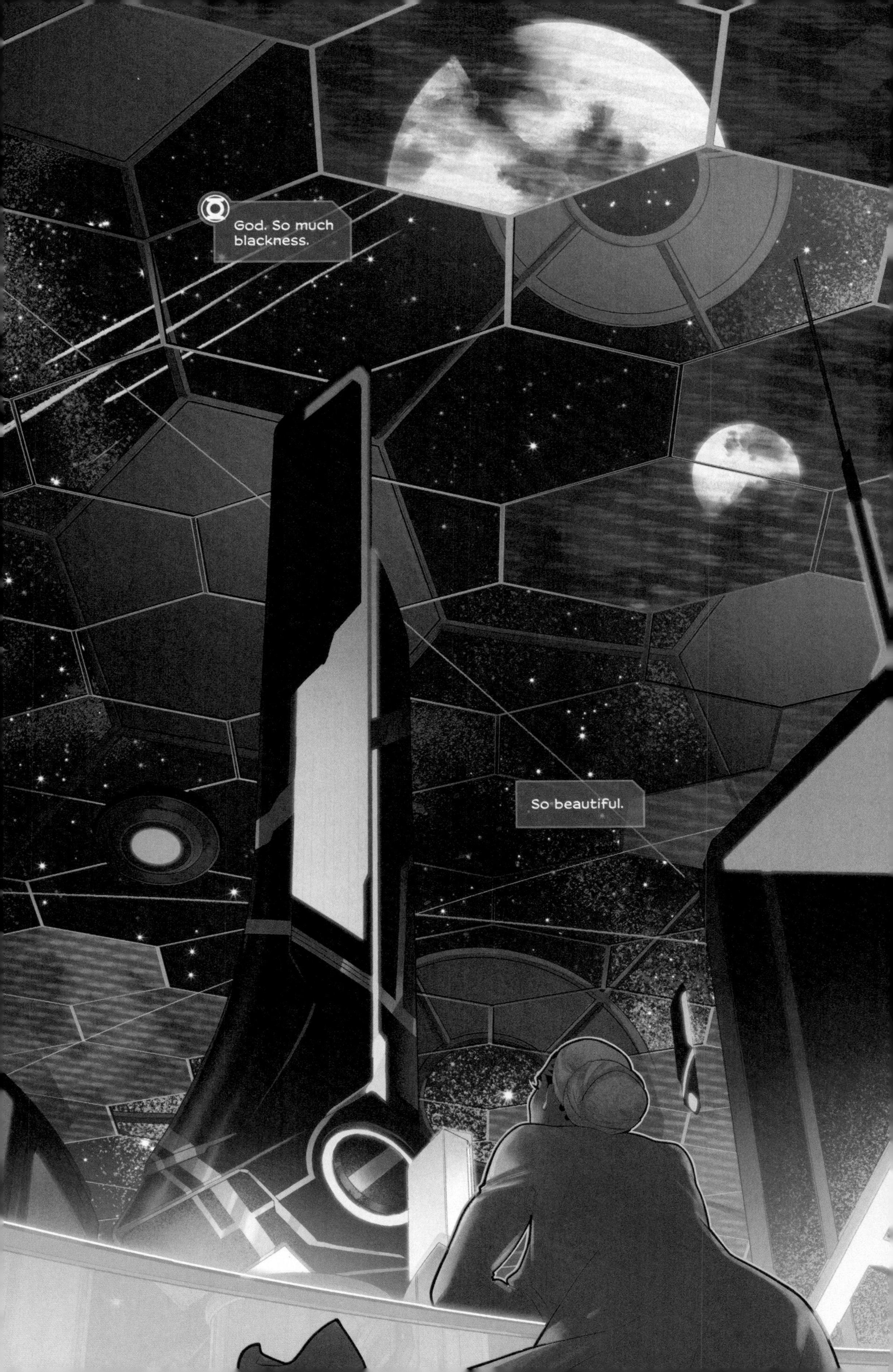

God. So much blackness.
So beautiful.

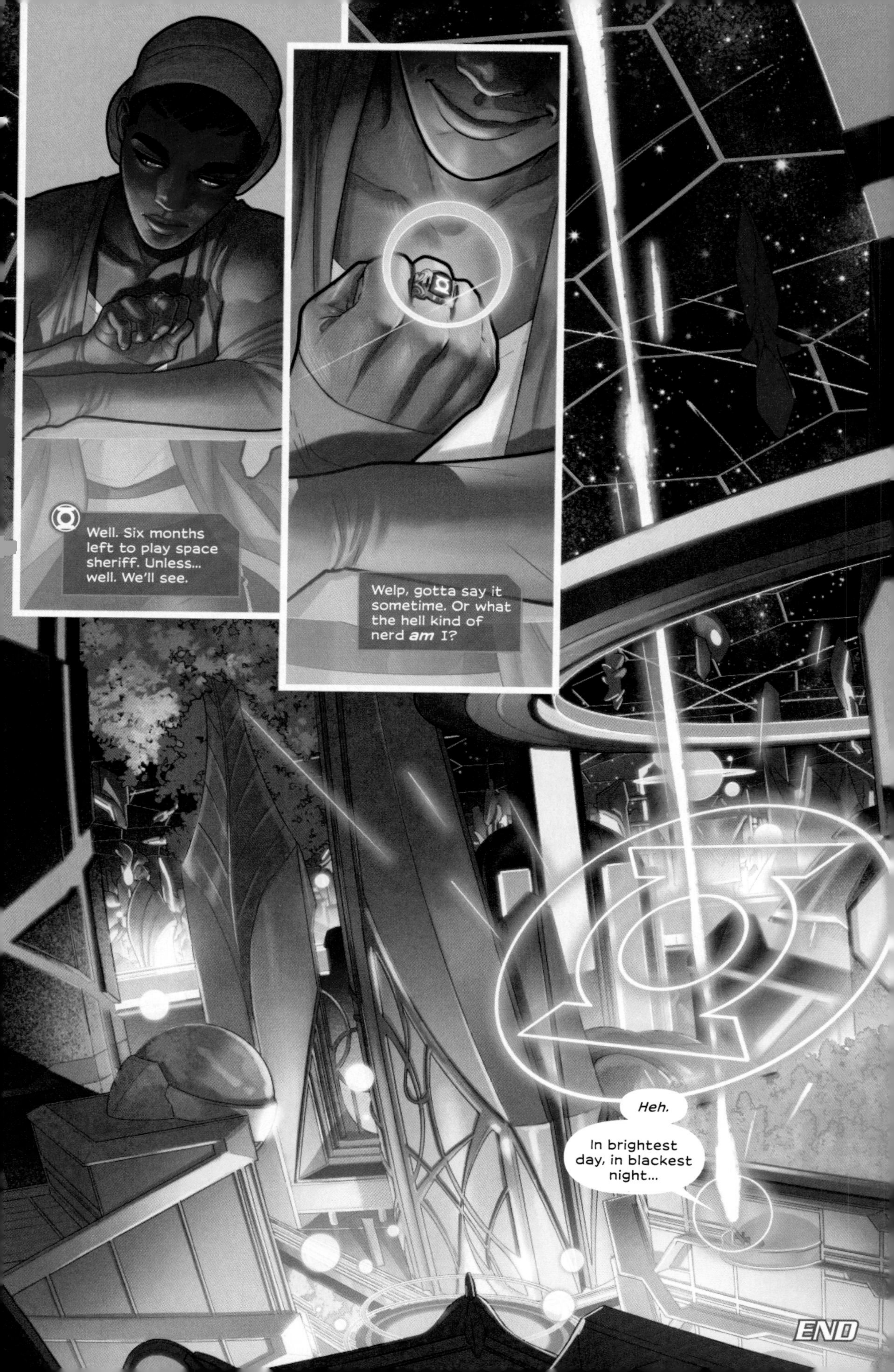
Well. Six months left to play space sheriff. Unless... well. We'll see.
Welp, gotta say it sometime. Or what the hell kind of nerd **am** I?
Heh.
In brightest day, in blackest night...
END

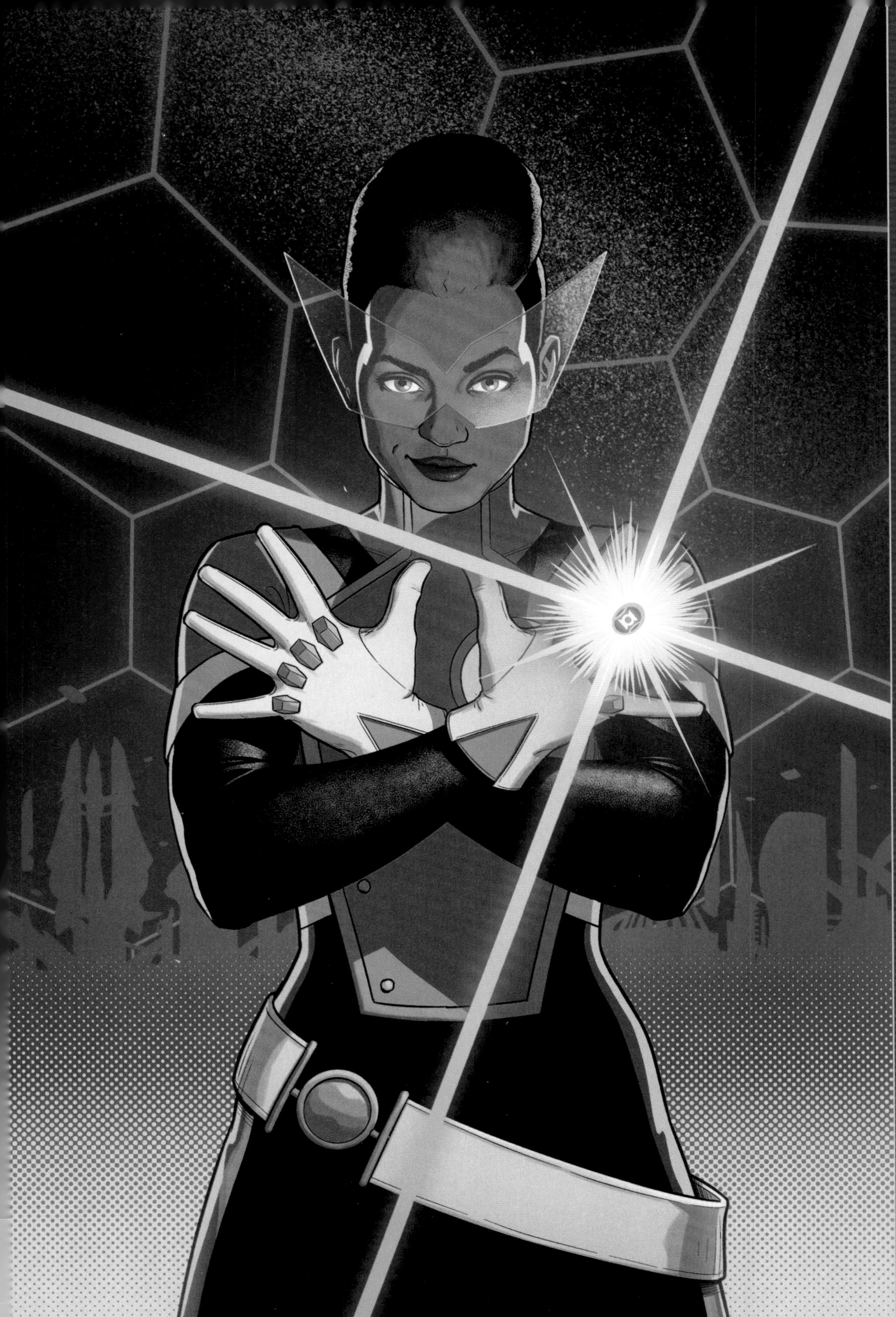

Far Sector #1 variant cover art by Jamie McKelvie

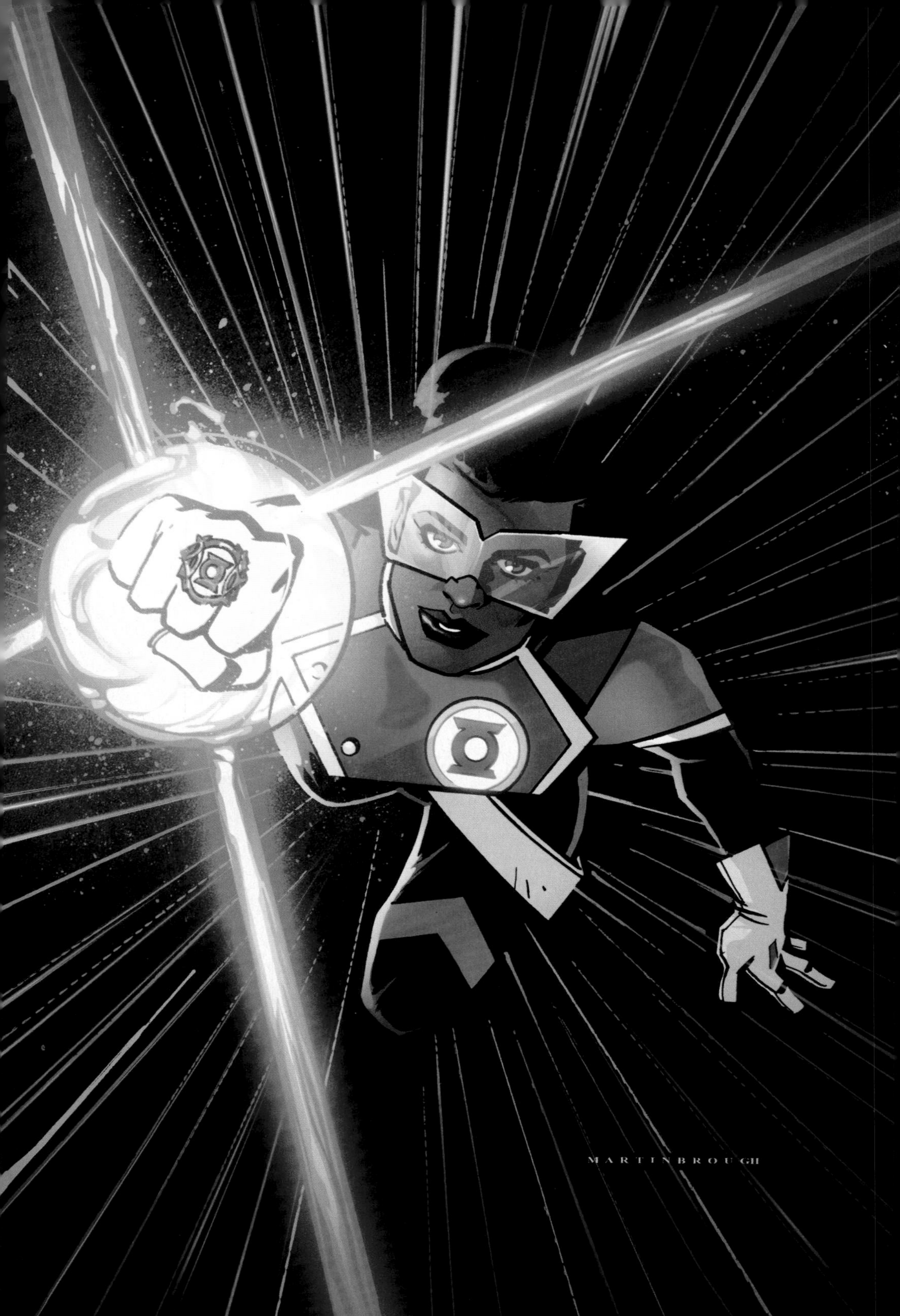
MARTINBROUGH
Far Sector #1 variant cover art by Shawn Martinbrough

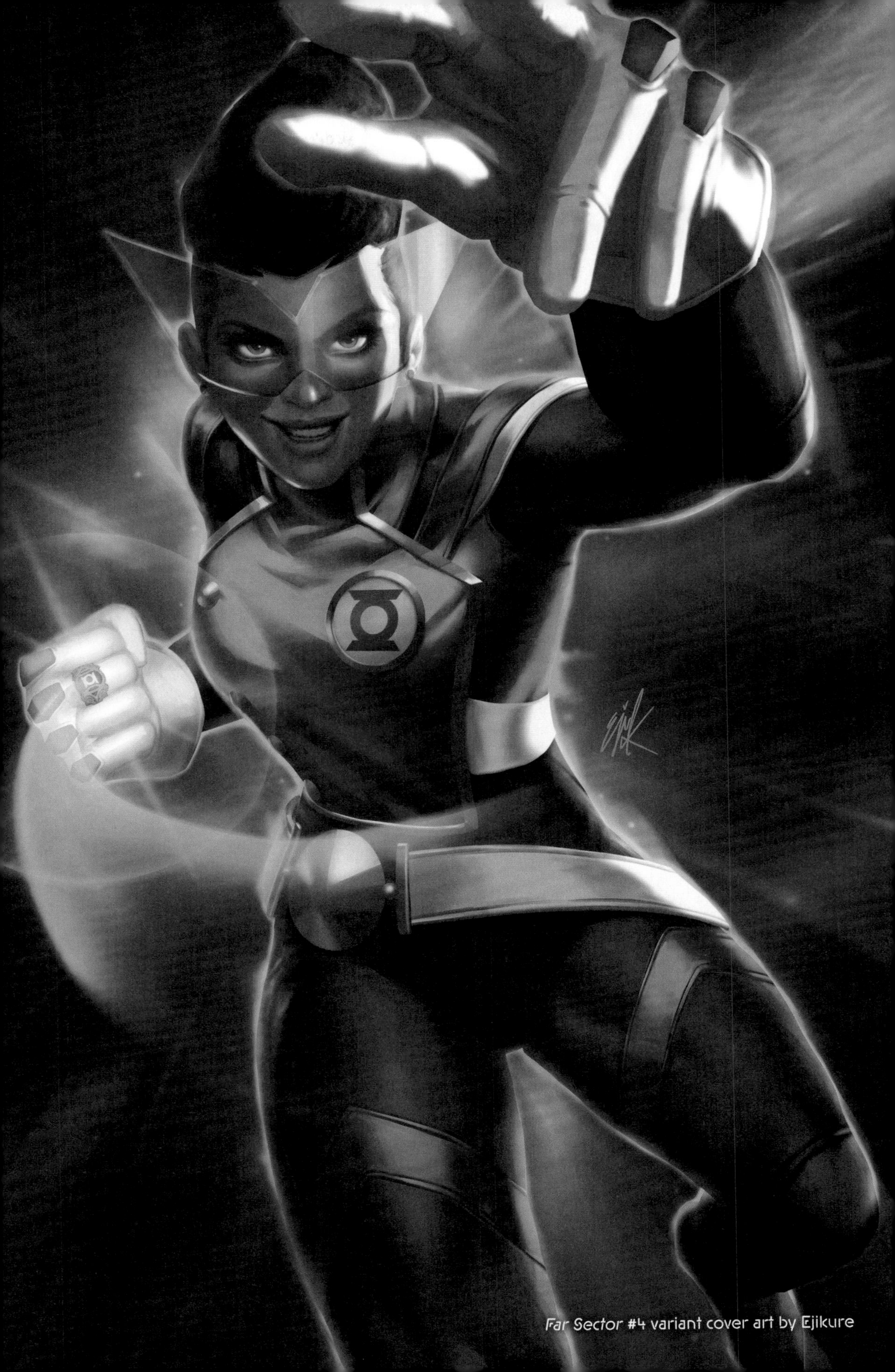

Far Sector #4 variant cover art by Ejikure

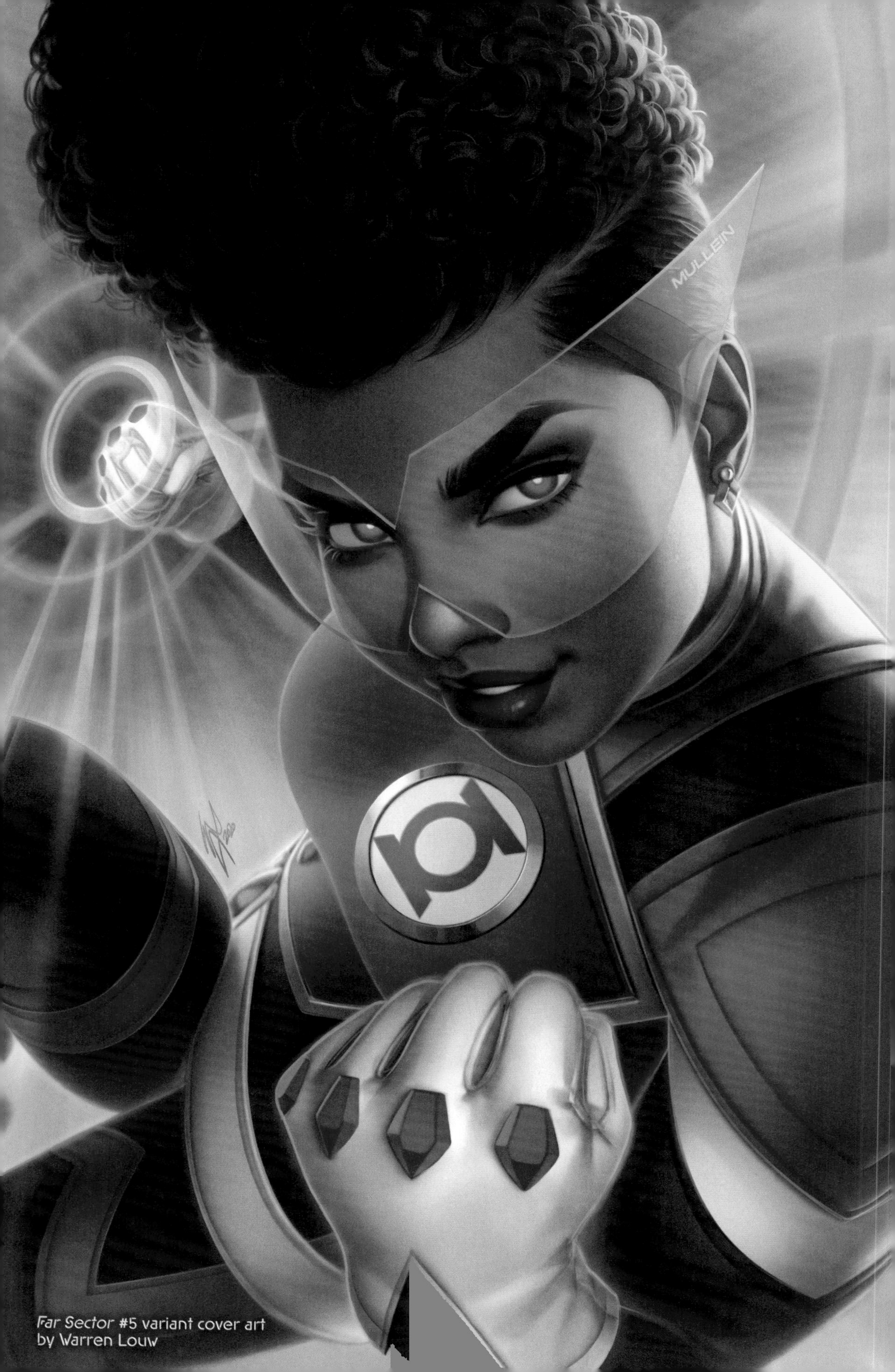
MULLEIN

Far Sector #5 variant cover art
by Warren Louw

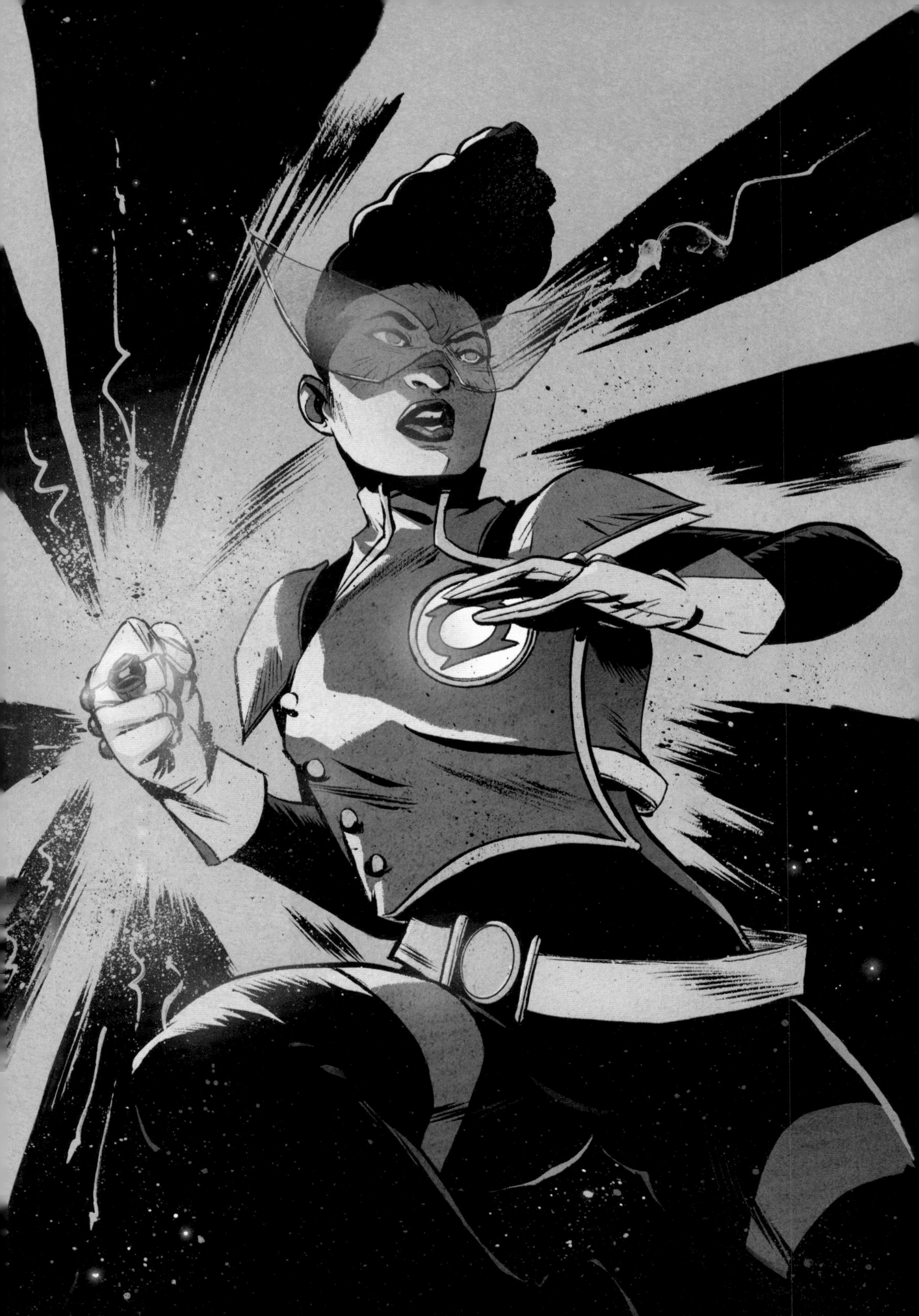

Far Sector #6 variant cover art by Sanford Greene

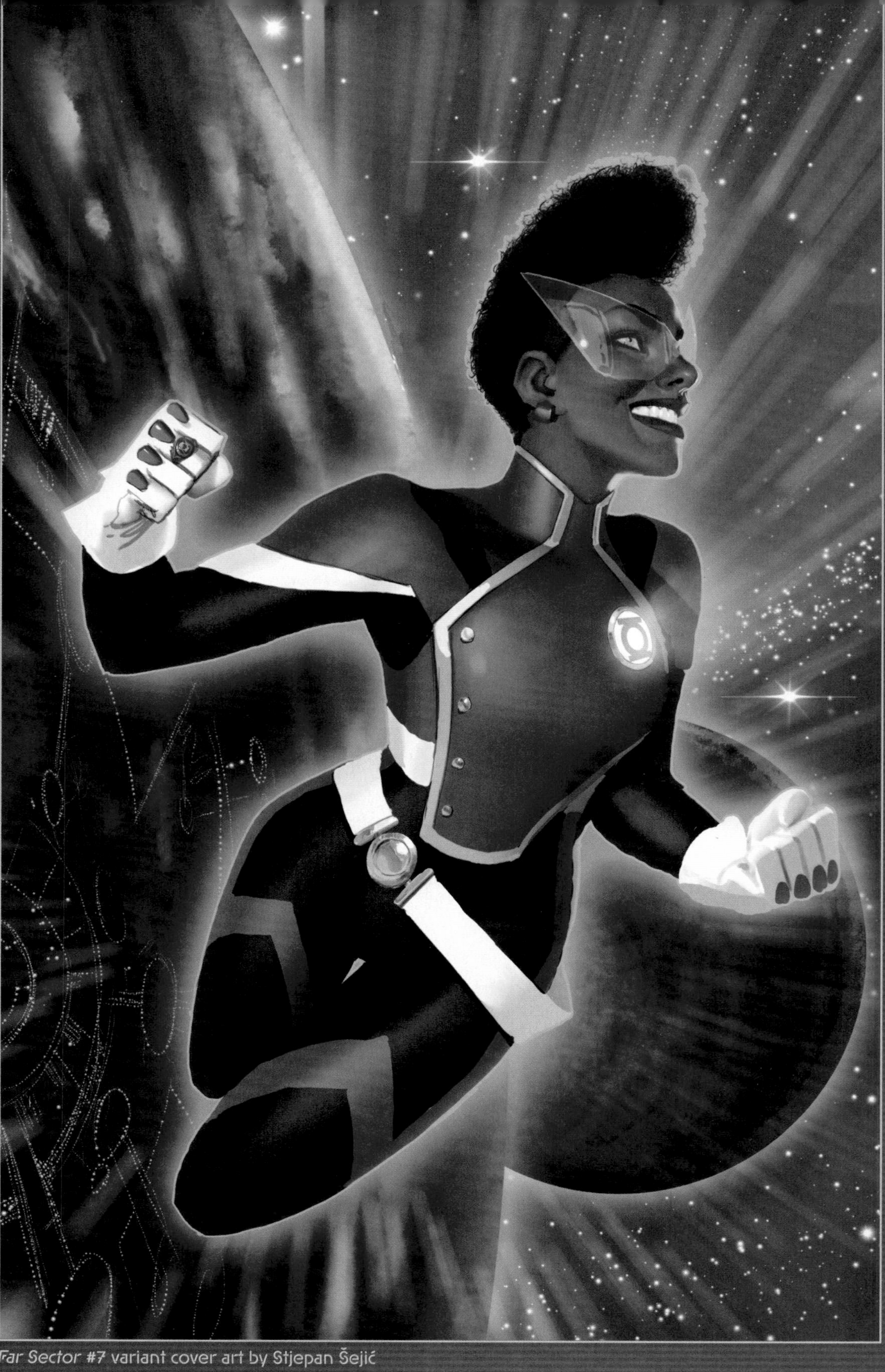

Far Sector #7 variant cover art by Stjepan Šejić